EDUCATIONAL MEDIA AND TECHNOLOGY YEARBOOK

EDUCATIONAL MEDIA AND TECHNOLOGY YEARBOOK

Robert Maribe Branch and Barbara B. Minor, Editors
With Donald P. Ely

1997 VOLUME 22

Published in Cooperation with the
ERIC® Clearinghouse on Information & Technology
and the
Association for Educational Communications
and Technology

1997
Libraries Unlimited, Inc. • Englewood, Colorado

LIBRARIES UNLIMITED, INC.
P.O. Box 6633
Englewood, CO 80155-6633
1-800-237-6124

Library of Congress Cataloging-in-Publication Data

Suggested Cataloging:

Educational media and technology yearbook,
    1997 volume 22 / Robert Maribe Branch and Barbara B. Minor, editors; with Donald P. Ely. -- Englewood, Colo.: Libraries Unlimited, 1997.
    xii, 375 p. 17x25 cm.
    Includes bibliographical references and index.
    ISBN 1-56308-423-6
    ISSN 8755-2094
    Published in cooperation with the ERIC Clearinghouse on Information
& Technology and the Association for Educational Communications and
Technology.
    1. Educational technology--yearbooks. 2. Instructional materials
centers--yearbooks. I. ERIC Clearinghouse on Information & Technology.
II. Association for Educational Communications and Technology.
III. Branch, Robert Maribe. IV. Barbara B. Minor. V. Donald P. Ely.
LB 1028.3.E372   1997   370.778

Contents

Part Three
CURRENT DEVELOPMENTS

Part Four
LEADERSHIP PROFILES

Part Five
THE YEAR IN REVIEW

Part Six
ORGANIZATIONS AND ASSOCIATIONS
IN NORTH AMERICA

Part Seven
GRADUATE PROGRAMS

Part Eight
MEDIAGRAPHY
Print and Nonprint Resources

Preface

Our individual freedoms, societal autonomy, and collective creative potential are influenced by the relationship between knowledge and its applications. Educational Technology is a field that studies those relationships.

The purpose of the 22d volume of *Educational Media and Technology Yearbook* is to present cognitive, factual, and anecdotal perceptions about the trends, issues, and innovations of educational media. This volume of the *Yearbook* extends the ideas expressed by the first editor, James W. Brown, in 1973, who stated that "a publication of this type will provide information to help media professionals 'see themselves' in a changing, expanding field, and to become better informed about the purposes, activities, and accomplishments of the many organizations with activities relative to the utilization of media." This volume also maintains the philosophy of its senior editor for several years, professor emeritus Donald P. Ely, that "the definition of the field of *instructional* technology has evolved over the years and this publication has been the chronicle of its development."

The evolution of educational media and advancements in information delivery technology are requiring educators to reconsider the traditional concept of audiovisual aids and to consider the concept of multimedia applications. Technology is being defined more broadly than in the past, such as being referred to as techniques and procedures derived from scientific research about methods for promoting change in human performance. Technology is *not* restricted to machines and hardware, but is perceived as a way of organizing thought, science, art, and human values. While behaviorist theory still informs many applications of media and technology, cognitivism, constructivism, and postmodernism have emerged as significant complementary approaches to the ways in which technological innovations are used. Such approaches to the use of educational media and technology clearly represent a focus shift. This volume of the *Yearbook* reflects current thinking by including perspectives about the devolution of American educational technology, new paradigms for instructional systems design, and trends in situated learning technologies.

Educational Media and Technology Yearbook has become a standard reference in many libraries and professional collections. This volume of the *Yearbook* contains sections devoted to Trends and Issues, The Profession, Current Developments, Leadership Profiles, The Year in Review, Organizations and Associations in North America, Graduate Programs, and a Mediagraphy (of print and nonprint resources). The topics herein allow this volume to remain consistent with most standard references, where the contents contain elements that readers expect to find in each new edition. The editors, publishers, and professionals dedicated to the field believe it is important to record the events associated with educational technology through reviews of the profession, leaders involved in its evolution, and the influence of culture relative to the use of educational media and technology.

ROBERT MARIBE BRANCH

Contributors to the
Educational Media and Technology Yearbook 1997

Larry S. Anderson
National Center for Technology Planning
P.O. Box 5425
Mississippi State, MS 39762

Dale Avers
P.O. Box 5295
Bloomington, IN 47407

Robert E. Berkowitz
93 S. Ridge Trail
Fairport, NY 14450

Robert Maribe Branch, Assoc. Prof.
Instructional Technology
Department of Education
University of Georgia
607 Aderhold Hall
Athens, GA 30602

William J. Burns, Dir.
Phoenix Learning Group
2349 Chaffee Drive
St. Louis, MO 63146

Michael B. Eisenberg, Dir.
ERIC Clearinghouse on Information &
    Technology
4-194 Center for Science and Technology
Syracuse University
Syracuse, NY 13244-4100

Donald P. Ely
ERIC Clearinghouse on Information &
    Technology
4-194 Center for Science and Technology
Syracuse University
Syracuse, NY 13244-4100

Nancy L. Floyd
National Library of Education
555 New Jersey Avenue NW
Washington, DC 20208-5721

Judith A. Grunert
Center for Instructional Development
111 Waverly Avenue, Suite 220
Syracuse University
Syracuse, NY 13244-2320

Kent L. Gustafson
Instructional Technology
Department of Education
University of Georgia
607 Aderhold Hall
Athens, GA 30602

Steven Hackbarth
400 E. 80th Street, #3B
New York, NY 10021-1000

Norman C. Higgins
Dowling College
School of Education
Oakdale, NY 11769-1999

Glen A. Holmes, Assoc. Prof.
Educational Technology Laboratory
Virginia Tech
Blacksburg, VA 24061-0341

Doug Johnson, District Media Supvr.
I.S.D. 77, Mankato Public Schools
P.O. Box 8713
Mankato, MN 56002-8713

Anna Maria D. Lankes
OCM BOCES
P.O. Box 4754
Syracuse, NY 13221

Timoth C. Lederman, Prof.
Department of Computer Science
Siena College
515 Loudon Road
Loudonville, NY 12211-1462

Edward J. Miech
17B Francis Avenue
Cambridge, MA 02138

Lynn Milet, Dir.
Media Services
Lehigh University
Fairchild-Martindale Library 8-A
Bethlehem, PA 18015

Frederick Mosteller
Harvard University
Science Center
Room 603
1 Oxford Street
Cambridge, MA 02138

Bill Nave
P.O. Box 382355
Cambridge, MA 02138

Laurie Miller Nelson
Instructional Systems Technology
Indiana University
Education 2276
Bloomington, IN 47405

Charles M. Reigeluth, Prof.
Instructional Systems Technology
Indiana University
Education 2276
Bloomington, IN 47405

Deborah Tyksinski, Dir.
Continuing Professional Education and
    Sponsored Research
SUNY Institute of Technology
P.O. Box 3050
Utica, NY 13504

John Wenrich
Educational Technology Laboratory
Virginia Tech
Blacksburg, VA 24061-0341

Andrew R. J. Yeaman, Adj. Prof.
9016 Vance Street, #305
Westminster, CO 80021

Part One
Trends and Issues

Introduction

Technological innovations and applications of educational media are often predicated on previous occurrences: trends. However, trends do not necessarily predict the future, nor is predicting the future the intent of trends. But there is some logic in tracing the trends of educational media and technology to determine *indicators* for the future of the field. Sooth-saying notwithstanding, Don Ely provides a content analysis of current trends in educational technology that gives baseline information about current practice. In addition, Charles Reigeluth and Laurie Miller Nelson suggest that we consider a new paradigm of instructional systems design.

Past editions of *EMTY* have highlighted issues regarding the perceptions that educators hold about the field as well as definitions of the domains of educational technology. Judith Grunert and Andrew Yeaman encourage educational technology professionals to consider the increasing pressures for change and the devolution of American educational technology as we become fully immersed in an Information-Age, holistic, critical-thinking approach to learning technologies.

A review of computer-assisted language learning in U.S. colleges and universities by Edward Miech, Bill Nave, and Frederick Mosteller allows this volume to focus on revisiting the purposes of theories and practice that inform the field. The perspectives offered in the five chapters of this part may challenge our comfort zone of educational media and technology use; however, it is important for a chronicle of this nature to critically view itself as a field of study and practice.

Trends in Educational Technology 1995*

Donald P. Ely
Professor Emeritus of
Instructional Design, Development and Evaluation
Syracuse University

This is the fourth monograph in the Trends in Educational Technology series. It covers the period from October 1, 1994 through September 30, 1995. Previous editions covered the years 1988, 1989, and 1991. This monograph incorporates data and trends from the previous editions and adds current information and analysis. This attempt to identify the trends in educational technology in 1995, and to relate them to earlier trend studies, provides a platform for discussion of the issues facing the field, and a launching pad for future studies.

INTRODUCTION

There are many ways in which trends may be identified: expert opinion, panels of specialists, or informed observation. This study uses content analysis as the primary vehicle for determining trends. It is based on earlier works of Naisbitt (1982) and his inspiration (Janowitz 1976). The basic premise of these works is that current trends can best be determined by analyzing what people are saying publicly, through newspapers and magazines. Naisbitt used actual counts of linear inches in key periodicals to determine trends. This study, and the three that have preceded it, used the same basic procedure: the identification of emerging topics in key publications over a period of one year. It is possible to determine trends by considering what people are saying publicly about matters within the field.

There may be other ways to determine trends, such as counting sales of products or discovering where professionals are being placed and analyzing what they are doing. We have chosen to use the literature of the field as the best comprehensive coverage of current thinking and events in the field. We have carefully reviewed a selected body of literature using a team of educational technology specialists to determine the status of the field as it exists today, and to indicate where it might be headed in the future.

A consistent methodology has been used from year to year. It follows the general principles of content analysis and uses a group of trained coders to make independent judgments about the literature being reviewed. Group discussion about findings has to reach high interrater reliability for each item before it is placed in an agreed-upon category. When items fall into more than one category, the dominant content or emphasis determines placement into the most appropriate category. The recording units have remained constant (for the most part) each year. Additional subcategories are used as needed to reach a higher level of specificity.

When reading this study, one must be careful not to extrapolate the trends too far into the future. It is often tempting to use trends as predictors of future developments. Actually, trends are more like indicators that foreshadow the future. They are statements of current happenings in the field and, as such, must be considered tentative movements that will bear watching as time goes on. They are useful because they represent current public statements that have been systematically analyzed and reported.

---

*Four graduate students in the IDD&E program participated in this study: Paul E. Blair, Paula Lichvar, Deborah Tyksinski, and Melissa Martinez.

Literature Sources

To maintain consistency from year to year, the same sources of information were used in the 1995 study as were used in the 1988, 1989, and 1991 studies, with a few exceptions. To aid in the selection of sources, the Moore and Braden (1988) report was used. This source reported the people, publications, and institutions that were identified by a survey of personnel in the field. The highest-ranking journals and the dissertations produced by the universities that ranked the highest served as two major sources of literature. Additional sources of data were papers given at major national and international conferences, and input to the ERIC database in the field of educational technology. Conference presentations are visible ways to present new ideas and findings to colleagues, and therefore contribute to the trends. The ERIC system solicits unpublished materials such as reports, evaluations, studies, and papers for review, and, following evaluative criteria, selects the best for inclusion in the database. The ERIC Clearinghouse on Information & Technology is responsible for the field of educational technology, and documents selected from that source are likely to represent current developments in the field. The sources are presented in figure 1.

Figure 1. Content sources.

JOURNALS

British Journal of Educational Technology (United Kingdom)

Innovations in Education and Training International (United Kingdom)
(New title replacing *Educational and Training Technology International*)

Educational Technology

Educational Technology Research and Development

TechTrends

DISSERTATION SOURCES

Arizona State University

Florida State University

Indiana University

Syracuse University

University of Southern California

CONFERENCES

Association for Educational Communications and Technology

Educational Technology International Conference (United Kingdom)

International Society for Performance Improvement (formerly National Society for Performance and Instruction)

ERIC INPUT

All documents in the field of educational technology entered into the ERIC system. All journals were published between October 1994 and September 1995. The conferences were held in 1995. The ERIC documents were entered into the system between October 1, 1994, and September 30, 1995.

LEADING TOPICS

Four coders analyzed nearly 1,200 articles, documents, and other sources and produced a list of content analysis categories that were most frequently presented in the literature. That list, together with the 1988, 1989, and 1991 numbers, is presented in table 1, page 4.

Table 1

Rank Order of Content Analysis Categories

	1995	1991	1989	1988
Instructional processes	1	1	1	1
Technological developments	2	3	2	3
Management	3	2	3	4
Research/theory	4	4	8	8
The field	5	5	4	5
Services	6	6	5	6
Personnel	7	8	6	2
Society and culture	8	7	7	7

Each of the above categories has a series of subtopics (or recording units) that were used to identify content more specifically. Themes were identified from the subtopics (recording units). The themes were later translated into trends as additional information sources were consulted. Table 2 shows the top 13 themes for 1988, 1989, 1991, and 1995.

Table 2

Themes of Top 13 Recording Units

	1995	1991	1989	1988
Design and development*	318	203	259	448
Research/theory	118	91	38	51
Evaluation**	103	144	99	97
Computer-related	93	65	90	82
Interactive learning***	68	41	83	29
Distance education	67	88	81	61
Implementation	62	146	98	24
Telecommunications	59	59	71	14
Status	47	80	95	61
Society and culture	37	45	71	72
Curriculum support	17	51	79	25
Artificial intelligence/Expert systems	8	35	46	31
Logistics	4	3	32	43
Others	204	265	387	228
TOTAL	1205	1316	1529	1266

* Includes message design, product development, learner characteristics.

** Includes process evaluation, product evaluation, formative evaluation, cost/effectiveness evaluation.

***Includes multimedia and hypermedia.

The recording units offered a first indication of trends. Further analysis of each category and subcategory revealed sharper distinctions. At that point, the key literature was added to the mix. Key literature included policy papers, reports, and statistical data for each category published during the dates of the study. This literature came from professional associations representing large numbers of people within and outside the field of educational technology, state and national governmental agencies that speak with some authority, organizations of policy-makers, and business/industry sources. This information, together with the content of the literature reviewed, was studied by the author, who, using personal observations (probably with some personal biases), drafted the trends and sent them to the individuals who reviewed and categorized the literature for further discussion. A copy of the final draft was sent for review to recognized professionals in the field and to a reviewer in the Office of Educational Research and Improvement (OERI) of the U.S. Department of Education. Changes were made when compelling arguments to do so were presented.

Concerns About Previous Studies

When past editions of the *Trends and Issues* publications were read and critiqued, four concerns were expressed, and they were addressed before the 1995 version was prepared:

- First, whether content analysis is effective for large bodies of text;
- Second, the validity and reliability of coding;
- Third, the selection of the documents reviewed; and
- Fourth, the translation of quantitative content data into descriptive trends.

Content Analysis of Large Bodies of Data

Conventional content analysis looks at words and phrases in an effort to extract substantive meanings. The approach followed herein uses complete journal articles, doctoral dissertation abstracts, conference program descriptions, and ERIC document input. Weber (1990) says:

> Large portions of text, such as paragraphs and complete texts, usually are more difficult to code as a unit than smaller portions, such as words and phrases, because large units typically contain more information and a greater diversity of topics. Hence they are more likely to present coders with conflicting cues (p. 16).

The findings of this study must be tempered by Weber's caution. He points out that "There is no simple *right* way to do content analysis. Instead, investigators must judge what methods are most appropriate for their substantive problems" (p. 13). Analyzing the periodical and document literature for a specified period of time still seems to be a useful procedure for identifying the general trends or emphases that come from the literature of that period. Much of the value comes from the consistency of recording thematic units that have been used over the past seven years.

The Validity and Reliability of Coding

The concern here is the stability, reproducibility, and accuracy of the coding process (Krippendorff 1980, 130-54). Weber says: "Classification by multiple human coders permits the quantitative assessment of achieved reliability" (Weber 1990, 15). Each year, graduate students in educational technology were trained as coders. Definitions of categories were given, together with practice items from each document type. The author provided consistency in reviewing by serving as an additional coder each year. The criterion level for intercoder reliability in 1995 was .66; that is, two of the three coders had to agree upon a category for placement of each item.

Content Selection

Journals, conference programs, doctoral dissertations, and ERIC documents account for a broad range of literature generated by the field each year. Because the content appearing in the literature during any given year is essentially what professionals in the field are saying, one can argue strongly that the content units counted from that literature provide reasonable representation of the topics or themes that are emerging. One must be careful not to use these topics as *projections*, because they essentially represent what has already happened.

When examining the selection of journals, conferences, and universities used in the study, one may ask, "Why *these* and not others?" The choice was based on the survey by Moore and Braden (1988) that reported the most prestigious journals and university programs. Beyond this criterion was another that eliminated journals or conferences that were devoted to a specific medium (e.g., computers in education). If articles about computing were found in the general literature, they were counted. However, selection of a journal or conference devoted entirely to a subfield within educational technology would skew the findings toward one medium.

Translation of Data into Trends

This is a subjective step and probably the most difficult to defend, as it ultimately relies on the judgment of one person. The number of articles, conference papers, dissertations, or ERIC documents, by category, reports the volumes of information about specific topics. These numbers form the basis for identifying the most frequent topics. The topics are the bases for selecting relevant documents in the policy literature that tend to confirm the topics identified. Policy literature includes statements, reports, papers, and other official publications of professional organizations, government agencies, and influential bodies such as foundations. For each of the leading trends, the policy literature is searched for statements to support the dominant trends. For example, in the past, the study team used publications of the Office of Technology Assessment of the U.S. Congress, the National Governors' Association publications about education, publications of the U.S. Department of Education's Office of Educational Research and Improvement, and publications of the various educational laboratories and research and development centers funded by OERI. Public statements and reports of the National Education Association and the American Federation of Teachers are used along with the publications of the Association for Educational Communications and Technology. Quantitative data from Quality Education Data and Market Data Retrieval provide consistent, reliable trend information on hardware and software. When the dominant themes from the primary literature sources are verified by policy statements from responsible organizations, trends are confirmed and provide a reasonable rationale for reporting.

Context

This publication should answer the question, "Where is educational technology headed?" Technology does not move apart from the society in which it exists. Information and communication technologies are used in the home and in the workplace at all levels—local, state, regional, national, and international. To separate technologies from their context is to highlight products alone, rather than to highlight their uses and impact. Therefore, much of the discussion in this monograph involves the total fabric of technology in society, as opposed to technology as an entity in itself. Technology is often referred to as a "tool" that incorporates the "media" of communication. The hardware and systems that carry information are often the primary focus, and little attention is paid to the audience, purpose, and consequences of their use. Design, development, evaluation, and diffusion are lost to the overpowering influence of hardware and software. As the trends are reviewed, the hardware and software appear to dominate. It should be remembered that quantitative information reveals *extent* of use, but does not reveal *quality* of use and *impact* on learners. Trend statements attempt to blend both quantitative and qualitative information by providing *indicators* of use. It is quite clear that educational technology is used frequently in the school and, increasingly, in the home. In the school, college, or university, the individual teacher or professor is the single most important factor influencing appropriate implementation of media and technology for learning. That key individual is usually part of a system that, in turn, is connected to a larger unit—a state department of education or a university. National programs and initiatives are somewhat remote. International efforts seem even more distant.

Since the last study of trends and issues, there have been major national and international efforts to explore and promote the use of educational technology in schools. One of the major outcomes of those efforts is linkage between schools and other entities. This was not evident in the earlier studies. *Networking* is being used as the codeword for the many connections that are being made—most of them new. Networking by definition is the linkage made between and among people held together by a common theme or connection. Networking uses both new and existing systems (e.g., telephone, fax, E-mail, computers, cable and satellite television) that permit "real time," "live," interaction between individuals and groups, as well as face-to-face and traditional correspondence approaches. Other systems store information for use at a chosen time (e.g., videotape recordings, videodiscs, CD-ROM discs, floppy disks, audiocassettes). It is easy to be enthusiastic about these new media (and they dominate the literature), but voices of concern about cost, equity of access, skills required, and purpose are heard still, and will have to be heeded.

Networks exist within the school, within the school system, within the region, within the state, and among the states. Networks exist between schools and business, schools and government agencies (state and federal), schools and universities, schools and public libraries, schools and professional associations, schools and broadcasting sources, and schools and home. There appears to be a movement to create networks where none exist and to connect networks that already exist. The dramatic increase in the use of the Internet is the best example of global networking.

As all these contexts impinge upon educational technology, one must remember that the trends that follow are more *internal* to the field than external to the settings in which they happen to reside. The literature reviewed is authored by people inside the field, and the intended audience is largely people inside the field. They are often practitioner-advocates who have agendas to promote educational technology and who use publications and conferences to do so.

At the same time, there appear to be strong calls by groups outside education (e.g., state governors, business and industry executives, newspaper education writers) to integrate technology into education. The target of both educational technologists and influential critics seems to be the mainline schools—the "establishment" that tends to perpetuate the status quo. Until there is an openness to use technology among educators in general, calls for technology in the schools will be unheeded, or accepted only in marginal ways.

This study focuses primarily on K-12 schools in the United States. Some information speaks to higher and adult education. Information from other technologically advanced nations is used when appropriate.

It should be noted that many trends in the field of educational technology are found outside the education settings featured in this study. New professionals graduating from the many graduate programs in the field are finding places in business and industrial training environments. There is another body of literature, not covered in this study, that reflects the many new developments in nonschool settings. That fact is, in itself, a trend.

In Summary

Fully developed trends do not flow from the literature. Using a content analysis procedure that goes beyond the conventional word and phrase approach, general themes in the annual literature of educational technology are identified, counted, and then verified by the policy literature. The translation from quantitative summaries to qualitative trend statements is mostly subjective.

TRENDS 1995

Trend 1

Computers are pervasive in schools and higher education institutions. Virtually every student in a formal education setting has access to a computer.

The number of computers in schools has grown over the seven years that the trends have been followed. In 1988-1989, the student/computer ratio was 22:1; in 1995 it was 12:1 (Hayes and Bybee 1995). Quality Education Data (1995a) has monitored the student/computer ratio since 1983, when it was 125:1. While numbers alone cannot determine the nature, extent, and quality of use, they are indicators of availability. Access is the first step to use.

Ninety-nine percent of all the elementary and middle schools in the United States have computers. The brands of computers differ in K-12 schools. In all schools where computers are used for instructional purposes, brand names differ. Eighty-six percent of the schools use Apple (including Apple IIGS), 40 percent use IBM, 37 percent use Macintosh, and 20 percent use other DOS units (Quality Education Data [QED] 1995a). More than a third of all computers used in schools are Apple IIs—a line that was discontinued in 1990. Schools do not tend to upgrade computers. They seem to be treated as textbooks—used until they are worn out. Obsolescence does not seem to penetrate K-12 schools as it does universities. There are no specific figures available for computer availability or use in postsecondary institutions.

In 1994-1995, the total computer use in K-12 schools was divided among four major brands: Apple II (46 percent); IBM (24 percent); Macintosh (15 percent), and other MS-DOS (8 percent). [Note: the numbers in the previous paragraph represent total numbers of computers available; some schools have several brands.] Apple IIs have decreased from 63 percent in 1988-1989, and IBM computers have increased from 12 percent. In 1988-1989, Macintosh represented only 1 percent of the use, and other MS-DOS units 2 percent (QED 1995b). The downward trend of the Apple IIs continues, as does the upward trend of the Macintosh and IBM.

In school districts, personnel most likely to have computers are instructional technology specialists, special education teachers, and curriculum supervisors (QED 1995a). Primary locations for computer use in K-12 schools are in computer laboratories and library media centers, although there are modestly increasing numbers in classrooms. A 1995 survey of technology use in the schools reported that 85 percent of teachers and media coordinators used computers during the 1994-1995 school year (Malarkey-Taylor Associates 1995). None of the figures above include administrative use of computers in schools.

There do not appear to be any current studies about ways in which computers are used for instruction. By inference it appears that computer "literacy" is a major use, closely followed by word processing, spreadsheets, and network communication.

The pervasiveness of computers in schools and the continuing advocacy for their use by many educators, equipment manufacturers, parents, and the community in general create a positive image of the computer's role in schools. However, there is some contrary evidence that brings into question the role and use of computers in schools. The Children's Partnership published *America's Children and the Information Superhighway: Skills for the Future* in 1995. There are some disturbing statistics:

1. Eighty percent of all school computers are considered to be obsolete according to the U.S. Department of Commerce's Information Infrastructure Task Force.

2. The top 20 percent of schools (i.e., those with the highest ratio of computers to students) have nine times as many computers as schools in the bottom 20 percent.

3. Some 27 to 39 percent of all students report that computers are frequently unavailable at school.

4. American students rank behind Austria, Germany, and the Netherlands in practical computer knowledge.

Postsecondary statistics are more difficult to obtain. Since 1989, Kenneth C. Green has conducted an annual survey of computer use based on the responses of about 600 higher education administrators. In the 1995 edition (Green 1995b) he reports that 24 percent of classes were being held in computer-equipped classrooms, up 15.8 percent from 1994. Green's interpretation of the growth is that the use of technology for teaching is spreading beyond the computer enthusiasts to mainstream professors, who are beginning to use computers in their teaching. Green believes that information technology has emerged as a permanent and respected part of the higher education experience.

In a comparison of courses using technology in 1994 and 1995, Green found that E-mail increased from 8 percent to 20 percent; computer simulations from 9 percent to 15 percent; presentation handouts from 15 percent to 25 percent; use of commercial courseware from 12 percent to 18 percent; multimedia from less than 5 percent to 9 percent; and CD-ROM materials from 6 percent to 15.4 percent (Green 1995).

There is a continuing concern about the costs of technology according to Green's report. Most institutions spent one-time budget allocations to purchase hardware and software, and only 22 percent of the institutions have a plan for replacing old computers with new models. About 20 percent of the institutions reported that they were cutting back on technology expenditures, and about the same number said they were cutting back on campus-wide information technology services.

In an attempt to finance new and continuing expenditures, about 33 percent of the institutions are passing on technology costs to academic departments, and more than 50 percent were either charging computing fees to students or contemplating such fees. Some colleges and universities are exploring the acquisition of less expensive equipment (Green 1995).

Trend 2

Networking is one of the fastest growing applications of technology in education.

It is becoming increasingly difficult to separate educational technology from the milieu in which it exists. The rapid development of networked communications in business, government, and the military has spilled over to the home and school markets. The key word associated with much of the networking is "Internet." A 1995 study (Swisher 1995) concludes that about 37 million people in the United States and Canada have access to the Internet—about 11 percent of the total population over the age of 16. Internet availability includes work settings, home, through friends, or via a commercial online service. The report goes on to say that about 31 percent of Internet users sign on every day. More than two-thirds of the users sign on from their office. They spend an average of 5 hours and 28 minutes a week online. Another study estimated that commercial online services jumped from 5 million users to 12 million during the winter of 1994-1995 (Technology in the American household 1995).

The literature reviewed for this monograph reflects the broader society. There were more articles, conference programs, and ERIC papers about networking than in any of the three previous studies. Several journals and newspapers have established regular columns dealing with networking. States seem to be leading the way in establishing networks. Quality Education

Data (1995c) has conducted studies of state networks for education since 1990. Very little activity was reported until 1993, when 29 states provided limited access to the Internet, primarily for E-mail, using a simple text-based menu. In 1995, 37 states offered more elaborate access, and 13 more states reported network planning in process. World Wide Web (WWW) access is available to educators in 33 states. Other Internet features currently available include: E-mail (37 states); ftp (34 states); telnet (34 states); and gopher (34 states).

The largest professional organization of teachers, the National Education Association, recognized the potential of networking in one of their 1995 resolutions:

> The Association supports the development of a user-friendly infrastructure which can accommodate a decentralized approach to program and product development so that the interaction among educators, students, researchers, and those outside the educational community can occur. The infrastructure should be operated under voluntary standards that promote interoperability and that support user collabora-tion. Adequate measures to protect the security of resources on the network should be put in place. Further, comprehensive directories of information resources and navigation systems should be developed and maintained (*NEA Today* 1995, p. 36).

Further evidence of growth in networking is seen in the number of modems acquired by schools. Computers with modems provide access to networks. In the 1994-1995 school year, modems existed in 29 percent of the elementary schools, 39 percent of the middle/junior high schools, and 51 percent of the senior high schools (QED 1995b). This is an increase from 1991-1992, when 11 percent of elementary schools, 20 percent of middle/junior high schools, and 30 percent of high schools had modems.

Even with the dramatic increase in network access, there is a disappointing report about availability in school classrooms. A study commissioned by the U.S. Department of Educa-tion's National Center for Education Statistics (Heaviside et al. 1995) found that Internet connections are present in only 3 percent of public school classrooms, labs, and media centers. Further, 30 percent of public elementary schools have Internet access compared with 49 percent of secondary schools. However, 75 percent of public schools have access to some kind of computer network, e.g., a local area network (LAN) or a wide area network (WAN). After publication of the report, Vice President Gore urged telephone and cable companies to work with states and local communities to connect classrooms to the information highway by the year 2000.

Commercial suppliers of online services have increased their client base. The number of commercial service subscribers has grown to about 12.5 million users over the past decade, doubling in 1995. The number of World Wide Web users has increased eight-fold to 8 million in just the past year, according to the International Data Corporation ("Exodus . . ." 1996, January 18). The number of people subscribing to more than one online service in 1995 has dropped significantly since 1991, when almost a third of the online users were multiple subscribers. *Business Week*'s January 22, 1996 issue reports that today 98 percent of the online users feel that they can do everything they want with just one service ("Exodus . . ." 1996, January 18).

With all of these developments, it comes as no surprise that the American Association of School Librarians (AASL) has established KidsConnect as a specialized service within their ICONnect technology initiative. KidsConnect is an Internet question-answering service for students in K-12 schools. Students' questions are sent through the Internet to a central "switching" station at Syracuse University. Volunteer school library media specialists from all over the United States respond to students' questions, provide help, and send referrals. KidsConnect is modeled after the AskERIC electronic question-answering service sponsored by the Educational Resources Information Center (ERIC). AskERIC answers an average of 800 E-mail questions weekly from teachers and other educators.

In the January 26, 1996 issue of *The Chronicle of Higher Education*, several information technology officers credit the growth of the World Wide Web as stimulus for the growth of interest in using technology for teaching in the postsecondary classroom (DeLoughry 1996). DeLoughry supports his contention with statements from college and university information technology officers. David Smallen, Director of Information Technology Services at Hamilton College, believes the Web has attracted faculty because they can learn to use it without lengthy training and do not have to worry whether students are using an Apple Macintosh or IBM-compatible computer. The level of use may be rudimentary, according to Polley McClure, Vice-President and Chief Information Officer at the University of Virginia. She suggests that only a few professors are using the equipment to its full potential. The World Wide Web sites that they develop are used to distribute course syllabi and other material that would normally be handed out in class. This rather simplistic use may be a necessary precursor to more sophisticated use later on.

As the magnitude of Internet use increases, it is inevitable that there are some skeptics. One Internet pioneer, Clifford Stoll, wrote *Silicon Snake Oil: Second Thoughts on the Information Highway* (1995), in which he publicly worries about the quality of time spent on the Internet. Neil Postman, a New York University professor of "media ecology," believes that computers and networks have not been scrutinized sufficiently (Postman 1992). He notes that the decision to put computers in schools is seldom challenged, even though there is little evidence to show that computers improve children's problem-solving skills. In a provocative paper about unplanned and unquestioning use of technology in education, Ely (1995) raises the question: "Technology Is the Answer! But What Was the Question?"

Trend 3

Access to television resources in the school is almost universal.

Quality Education Data (1995a) reports that all but two public schools in the United States have videotape recorders. About 75 percent of schools have cable service and 17 percent have satellite dishes. Sixty-one percent have videotape collections ranging from 50 to more than 500 titles.

In 1995, Cable in the Classroom, a public service initiative of the cable television industry, commissioned a study for the National Education Association, National Association of Secondary School Principals, National Association of Elementary School Principals, and the American Association of School Administrators (Malarkey-Taylor Associates 1995). The stratified sample of 1,000 educators who had access to cable television programming represented classroom teachers, media coordinators, and principals from elementary and secondary schools. In schools connected to cable, 58 percent of teachers used commercial-free Cable in the Classroom and 19 percent used Channel One, a free educational programming cable service to schools that carries commercials. Both services are free to education and provide the necessary hook-ups and equipment to receive the programs. Cable in the Classroom serves about 70,000 schools, reaching more than 80 percent of all public school students—more than 38 million students.

The study also determined that the most frequently used in-school television programs were supplied by the Public Broadcasting Service (PBS), the Discovery Channel, and the Cable News Network (CNN). Among the teachers and media coordinators who used Cable in the Classroom, 69 percent used PBS programs during the 1994-1995 school year, 58 percent used the Discovery Channel, and 49 percent used CNN.

The growth of cable in schools has enjoyed a dramatic increase from 1989, when 6,165 schools were wired for the use of cable television, to 1995 when 70,754 were wired for cable. The 1995 figure includes both public and private elementary and secondary schools; the 1989 number is only for public secondary schools (Nielsen Media Research 1995).

The extent to which videotape is used is not available, but with 100 percent penetration of videotape recorders in public schools, it seems reasonable to expect that some cable programs are recorded and reused along with prerecorded videotapes included in a local or district collection. Video equipment used for live recording by students and teachers is another dimension of this trend. The number of articles in the literature about the use of television in teaching indicates that it is a frequently used tool. Perhaps the universality of its availability removes video equipment from educational technology status studies, because it has become an institutionalized medium rather than an innovation.

In higher education institutions, satellite uplinks and downlinks are being used more for short-term staff development workshops than for teaching credit courses. One major player is the Institute for Academic Technology at the University of North Carolina at Chapel Hill, whose satellite conferences on applications of information technology are used nationally. Teleconferences may lead to more specific uses of this technology in the teaching and learning process, but have not yet made any major impact except in cases like the National Technological University (NTU), which offers graduate and continuing education credit courses and degrees in engineering. Forty-five universities provide courses that are uplinked to NTU by satellite from the originating university, and then redistributed by the NTU satellite to the more than 100 corporations and government agencies that subscribe to the service (Moore and Kearsley 1996).

The National University Teleconference Network (NUTN) has more than 250 members from colleges, universities, community colleges, and technical institutes. Most of the programming is professional staff development delivered by satellite. One-way video is complemented by two-way audio to ensure interaction. The typical program is a live video presentation to subscribing sites where a fee is paid to receive each program (Moore and Kearsley 1996).

Trend 4

Advocacy for the use of educational technology has increased among policy groups.

Educational technology has not always been a significant player in education circles. There have been periods since the end of World War II when critics were strong in their opposition to "machines" in the classroom. The predecessor of educational technology, audiovisual education, was viewed suspiciously by teachers, school boards, and administrators. But with the passage of the National Defense Education Act in 1958, there were provisions for the acquisition and improved use of new educational media. As educational television began to be used in the late 1950s and early 1960s, new possibilities were envisioned. When PBS came into existence and incorporated educational television, applications such as *Sesame Street* began to take on a newfound respectability. The "third wave" brought about by computers and information technology has attracted additional supporters for technology applications in schools. This unusual support, at least in comparison with past attitudes, is facilitating the acceptance and use of educational technology in contemporary schools.

A survey of school priorities conducted by the Northwest Regional Laboratory for Research and Development discovered that educational technology is one of the six top issues in schools today. The others were school improvement and restructuring, community engagement, the education profession, curriculum and instruction, and student assessment (*Northwest Report* 1995). In the past, there has never been an expressed priority related to educational technology. It appears that a new era has begun in U.S. education.

One "bellwether" organization is the U.S. Department of Education. For the first time in history, there is an Office of Educational Technology in the Department. This Office has prepared a long-range national plan for the use of technology in education (Roberts 1996). The development of this plan included extensive dialogues with educators; experts; representatives of state, local, and other federal government agencies; the private sector; and the public. The four major issues addressed in the plan are infrastructure and financing, professional development, content and software, and access and equity.

The federal government is working closely with state governments to develop and implement state plans for educational technology. Planning the Secretary's conference on educational technology involved a five-person team of educators, policy-makers, and technology experts assembled by state school superintendents. The purpose of the conference was to develop strategies for the implementation of the long-range technology plan. This was the first major effort of its kind, and results should be monitored to measure progress.

Other federal agencies, such as the departments of Commerce, Agriculture, and Health and Human Services, and the National Science Foundation, have all increased their spending on telecommunications programs designed for education and training. The National Telecommunications and Information Administration (NTIA) within the Department of Commerce manages a $26 million fund to assist educational institutions in developing and implementing innovative applications of computers and telecommunications in learning environments (Hezel 1994).

In 1995, the Office of Educational Research and Improvement awarded five grants for Regional Technology Centers that will provide technical assistance to schools in their respective regions. The Centers are located in California, Illinois, Kansas, New York, North Carolina, and Oregon. The Centers are expected to serve multistate regions and build on existing resources and expertise in school districts, universities, research centers, federal laboratories, and the private sector. Centers will assist local efforts in building communication networks, training teachers, and integrating technology into the curriculum.

Grant programs help to support many specific initiatives in technology applications:

1. National challenge grants for technology in education;

2. Star Schools;

3. Ready-to-learn television; and

4. Special education technology media and materials.

Within other programs there are funding opportunities to incorporate educational technology applications into programs such as basic skills, science and mathematics, and vocational education.

At the annual convention of the National Education Association, resolutions are presented, discussed, and voted upon. During 1995, five resolutions focused on educational media and technology:

1. School libraries/media programs;

2. Information literacy;

3. Media;

4. Technology in the classroom; and

5. Telecommunications technology.

Of special note are the statements of belief about technology in the classroom. These statements offer a dramatic reversal in attitudes held over the past 25 years.

The Association believes that:

a. Education employees should have access to necessary technology for managing and advancing instruction. Such technology must be compatible with, and on at least the same level as technology in general use outside education. Further, encouragement, time, and resources should be provided to experiment with and to research applications of technology in order to integrate technology into the curriculum.

b. Education employees, including representatives of the local association, must be involved in all aspects of technology utilization, including planning, materials selection, implementation, and evaluation. Individuals who teach classes over interactive communications networks should be given sufficient time to prepare for their classes. Additional preparation time should be granted to teachers using technology to enrich their regular programs. Further, classroom teachers and library/media specialists must have collaborative planning time to develop programs.

c. Training should be provided for education employees in the use of technologies and applications, the development of effective materials, and appropriate instructional strategies (National Education Association 1995, p. 36).

Further sections in this unique statement of beliefs discuss preparing new teachers to use technology, awareness of the social and economic impact of technology, understanding the copyright law, distance education, and the evaluation of employees using technology.

The National Coalition for Education and Training (NCTET), through its Policy Committee, has focused on developing plans and monitoring activities related to the integration of technology and the information infrastructure into K-12 education at national and state levels. The purpose of this group is to ensure that the information superhighway is easily and inexpensively accessible to schools for the electronic delivery of educational resources. The recommendations of NCTET have been adopted by several states and have become advocacy statements used with legislators and other government leaders (Cradler 1995).

Trend 5

Educational technology is increasingly available in home and community settings.

Studies show an increased use of computers by students at home. In *The Condition of Education 1995* there are comparisons of students who use computers at school and at home, at school but not at home, at home but not at school, and at school or at home. Statistics were recorded for 1984, 1989, and 1993. The home setting is best revealed by those who used computers at school and at home and at school or at home.

	At School and at Home	At School or at Home
1984	5.5%	35.0%
1989	11.6%	53.7%
1993	18.8%	68.1%

Use *only* at home increased from 6.5 percent in 1984 to 9.1 percent in 1993. In all cases, student use of computers was up, with a substantial portion attributed to home use.

A study by the Software Publishers Association reported home sales of education-oriented CD-ROMs increased by 136 percent during the first half of 1995. The increase from the first half of 1994 was from $21.6 to $59.3 million (CD-ROM software sales soar 1996).

A study by EPIC-MRA, based in Lansing, Michigan, reports that nearly one-half of all American households own a computer, and 17 percent of those who do not already own one plan to buy a computer in 1996. About 16 percent of those who own a computer subscribe to an online service. Persons most likely to own computers live in the Northwest, Pacific, and Northeastern parts of the United States. (Survey shows half of American homes . . . 1995). A study by the American Learning Household Survey indicates that more than 80 percent of home computer buyers cited children's education as the primary reason for the purchase. The survey also found that children's use of the computer is shifting away from games and more toward complex uses of the computer as an information access tool (Education is key . . . 1996).

The public library is beginning to offer network access. Many libraries provide computers for personal use, and in some locations software is available for borrowing. A report from the St. Joseph (Missouri) Public Library indicates that there are 278 public library World Wide Web sites listed (St. Joseph's Public Library 1995). The library itself is an active user of computers for management purposes: acquisitions, technical processing, database searching, and circulation. Urban and suburban libraries are beginning to offer network access. The literature indicates many school library/media centers and university libraries already have network access.

The American Library Association (ALA) has announced a partnership with Microsoft Corporation to launch Libraries Online (ALA, Microsoft launch 1996). Nine libraries have been named to participate in a $3 million effort to research and develop innovative approaches to extending information technology to underserved populations. The Seattle Public Library will provide technical assistance to other libraries; the Pend Oreille County (Washington) Library will serve 9,100 people in a rural area that includes the Kalispell Indian Reservation; the Charlotte-Mecklenberg County (North Carolina) Public Library will expand current local networks to rural and disadvantaged urban areas; the Tucson-Pima (Arizona) Public Library will coordinate local school district technology efforts with community services; the Mississippi Library Commission will support recently approved funding to connect every county library to the Internet; the South Dakota State Library will expand the state server network to rural and disadvantaged communities, including Native American reservations; the Baltimore (Maryland) County Public Library will establish a Family Learning Center in a branch that serves a densely populated and disadvantaged community; and the Los Angeles Public Library will create two "virtual electronic libraries" to serve economically disadvantaged communities within the city.

Karen Schneider (1996) sees a trend in the creation and use of library and community networks. In a recent article in *American Libraries*, she provided examples of public library and community networks that are cooperating to provide information and communication opportunities to individuals in their service areas. The locations of these efforts are the Seattle (Washington) Public Library and the Seattle Community Network; the Montgomery-Floyd (Virginia) Regional Library and the Blacksburg Electronic Village; Allen County (Indiana) Public Library and Infonet in Fort Wayne; and the Flint (Michigan) Public Library with the Greater Flint Community Networking Initiative. Schneider says that:

> Increasingly, librarians have been using new technologies to develop or collaborate on community networks—free or low-cost electronic community information systems, usually Internet based, that can provide a variety of services. . . . These community networks are often created in collaboration with other local agencies and advocacy groups, weaving libraries more tightly into the community organism (p. 96).

Trend 6

New delivery systems for educational technology applications have grown in geometric proportions.

Revolutionary developments in technology have replaced the evolutionary pace of previous years. These developments, often referred to as *delivery systems,* are focused on hardware (equipment), software (materials), communications media (transmission), and strategies (techniques for use). The delivery system, as used here, is essentially a combination of all four elements.

The most dramatic and obvious developments are in the area of new hardware. Products are more visible and pervasive than transmission or techniques. Most new delivery systems begin with hardware but do not end there. For example, CD-ROM hardware must be combined with CD-ROM software to have any practical use. CD-ROM is one of the most dramatic of the newer developments. The number of public schools using CD-ROM has increased nearly 250 percent since 1988. In the most recent year for which data are available (1993-1994), the number of schools using CD-ROM increased by 80 percent. CD-ROM drives are used in 37 percent of the public schools, accounting for more than 15 million students in the United States (Hayes 1995).

The growth of CD-ROM is probably influenced by several factors. More personal computers have integrated CD-ROM drives. More multimedia software is delivered on CD-ROM discs. In both community and school settings, CD-ROM software is providing learning resources at a lower cost than printed publications. Encyclopedias and reference books are good examples. Not only are production costs lower (and hence a lower sales price), but it is possible to release up-to-date supplements in a timely fashion at less cost. Public libraries and school library/media centers are especially active in the acquisition and use of CD-ROM software.

A close relative of the CD-ROM in the laser disc family is the videodisc, which requires both hardware and software for delivery of information. With not as dramatic a growth as the CD-ROM, the videodisc reached 28 percent of public schools in 1994-1995 (QED 1995a). This is an increase of 18 percent from 1991-1992. The software associated with videodiscs is usually integrated with computers to allow interactive educational programs with audio and video capabilities. Filmed sequences can be stored less expensively on videodiscs than on computer disks. Since 1991, there has been a growth rate of 160 percent in public schools. More than 20 percent of public schools are using laser disc players with interactive videodisc software for instruction. This percentage represents more than 12 million public school students (Hayes 1995).

One of the newest communication media is the satellite dish. It can be used to receive (download) or send (upload) information. Quality Education Data reports that 10 percent of elementary schools, 22 percent of middle/junior high schools, and 37 percent of high schools had satellite dishes in 1994-1995. This is an increase from 1 percent, 1 percent, and 4 percent respectively since 1991-1992 (QED 1995a).

Another communication medium is the local area network. Local area networks connect computing equipment within one building; wide area networks connect computing equipment from one building to another; and larger networks extend to regional, state, national, and international service areas. Access to networks may be provided through commercial or noncommercial sources. Commercial networks such as America Online, CompuServe, and Prodigy operate as fee-based services. Access can also be obtained through university and governmental networks. The Internet is one of the most frequently used networks. The original noncommercial nature of the Internet seems to be giving way to more commercial applications.

Networks are used for a variety of purposes in education. E-mail, ftp, and listservs constitute much of the use. The World Wide Web has quickly surpassed gopher as an information source. The opportunity to create a personal home page exists for anyone, and the number of web sites has grown dramatically with little formal organization. A few groups have attempted to index some of the web sites as a service to users. Late in 1994, Yahoo was established as one of the first web search engines. Other search engines include Lycos and NetSearch. Several organizations, such as Point Communications, Magellan, and Global Network Navigator, publish critical reviews and rankings of web sites.

The actual number of web sites is unknown. Miller (1995) estimated that there were 10 million electronic web documents. Growth is measured in millions each quarter. In the late 1990s, personal (or institutional) web pages have become a status symbol.

Distance education was a frequent topic in the content analysis of the 1995 literature. While the emphasis is often on the delivery system (i.e., the means of getting instruction to the learner), distance education as described here is a strategy for providing instruction to learners who are geographically separate from their teachers. Much of distance education is delivered by contemporary hardware, software, and transmission systems, but it is the design of the software, the organization of the delivery, and the built-in interaction and feedback that make it a unique application of technology in education.

Most frequently, delivery is by computers, computer networks, or cable and satellite transmissions. Telephone lines, a simpler technology, are often used for "live" audio interactions, and for fax communication between students and teachers. Distance education is active at all levels. On the K-12 level, senior high schools are the most frequent users. At the postsecondary level, adult learners predominate. These adults may be seeking course credit, a college degree, professional updating, or all three.

Some of the most active distance education efforts are at state or regional levels. The client is almost always the individual learner in the local school. From its studios in Texas, the TI-IN service broadcasts courses to high schools in more than 1,000 school districts in 29 states. The Massachusetts Corporation for Educational Telecommunications links 1,300 schools in the state and more than 1,000 schools in surrounding states, as well as 22 colleges in the New England area. Kentucky installed satellite downlinks at every school in the state in 1988 and is fully operational today. Other television-based distance education programs exist in Alaska, Georgia, Indiana, Nebraska, Virginia, and Utah (Moore and Kearsley 1996). The Council for Chief State School Officers (1995) has made a series of recommendations regarding the use of telecommunications in achieving the National Education goals.

Computer networks are also used for distance education. While not as well established as some of the television-based programs, computer networks are often used for E-mail communication between student and teacher and among students. Computer networks are also used as resources, much the same as libraries, where students can find textual material and other resources for learning. Not many complete computer network courses exist as yet for K-12 students, but there are children's network resources such as Kidsnet, Kids Network, NASA Spacelink, and FrEdMail for electronic communication. Higher education is a little further along with the New York Institute of Technology, the University of Phoenix, and the New School for Social Research, which offer complete degree programs via computer conferencing (Moore and Kearsley 1996).

Trend 7

There is a new insistence that teachers must become technologically literate.

One of the early overviews of technology in education, especially oriented toward distance education, was *Linking for Learning* (U.S. Congress, Office of Technology Assessment 1989). It identified the need for teacher training in the use of technology:

> The critical role of teachers in effective learning means that all must have training, preparation, and institutional support to successfully teach with technology.... Few teachers have had either teacher education or field experiences that enable them to be effective distant teachers or successfully use technology in their own classroom (pp. 10-11).

It does not appear from the content analysis of the literature that much progress has been made since that publication was released. An article in *Investor's Business Daily* quotes a *Fortune* magazine article that reports that "last year businesses spent well over $2 billion training their employees on the use of technology, but 90 percent of the teachers in America reported that they were 100 percent self-taught" (p. A8). This statement was backed up by California's Superintendent of Public Instruction, who said that schools are still woefully behind industry in preparing their employees to use technology (Teachers still lag . . . 1995).

The National Education Goals Report (1995) points out that despite the many changes in educational technology and student assessment strategies occurring in 1994, only half of all teachers reported any professional development opportunities in those areas. They were more likely to have participated in in-service courses on methods of teaching a subject matter field than in the use of educational technology.

Teacher education in the application of technology in the classroom is still a high priority need. One sign of increasing interest and action in this area is the publication of a new periodical, *Journal of Technology and Teacher Education*, published by the Association for the Advancement of Computing in Education. The authors are teachers and teacher educators who are actively participating in the movement toward technological literacy for themselves and their students.

Higher education faculty are not immune from updating and upgrading skills in the use of technology in their classrooms. Kenneth C. Green summarizes the current status of technology in many college and universities:

> The presence of technology in the learning environment is increasingly common: an E-mail address on a course syllabus; electronic mail as a supplement to office hours; class sessions held in computer labs; desktop computers in faculty offices; commercial software and simulations as part of the resources provided by textbook publishers; and course assignments that send students to the World Wide Web (WWW) sites in search of information resources (1996, pp. 24-28).

But there are less optimistic viewpoints from some postsecondary faculty. The January 26, 1996 issue of *The Chronicle of Higher Education* reported a new policy paper from the American Federation of Teachers (AFT) calling on its members "to oppose courses taught on the Internet, through videoconferencing, or with other technologies unless they meet faculty members standards of quality." Further, AFT "urged its members to seek restrictions on the number of credits for distance education that students can receive, and to oppose undergraduate programs that are taught entirely with technology." The report raises questions that faculty should pose prior to the adoption of technology, and provides guidelines for using a variety of technological applications in higher education settings (Blumenstyk 1996, A20).

Trend 8

Educational technology is perceived as a major vehicle in the movement toward education reform.

The movement for restructuring education in schools across the United States has generated proposals and plans for reform of the entire educational system. Virtually every proposal or plan includes educational technology as one of the major vehicles for implementing change. One of the key documents published by the Office of Educational Research and Improvement of the U.S. Department of Education is *Using Technology to Support Education Reform* (Means et al. 1993). This publication spells out the roles and functions of technology in the education reform process. The authors cite tutorial presentations, exploratory investigations, tool applications (word processing, spreadsheets, database management, etc.), and communication uses "that allow students and teachers to send and receive messages and information to one another through networks or other technologies" (p. 11). These applications are even more prevalent in 1995, just two years after the publication of this important work. The conclusion by the authors in 1993 was that "support for the use of technology to promote fundamental school reform appears to be reaching a new high" (p. 1). In 1995, the appearance is even more of a reality.

The process for reform and school restructuring is presented by Gillman (1989) in a report based on his doctoral dissertation. Gillman's primary recommendation focuses on the development of an educational technology plan. This plan becomes the framework for strategic planning in which educational technology plays a central role. The recommendations for design and implementation made by Gillman are emerging in state plans for educational technology being created with participation by local school districts. One impetus for developing such plans is the promise of financial support to those schools and districts that have developed and presented plans to state educational agencies for approval. The establishment of the Regional Technology Centers in 1995 by the U.S. Department of Education is a move to assist states with technology planning for purposes of reforming and restructuring schools. State education agencies have been strongly urged to create state plans for educational technology applications in the schools. In 1995, almost every state had completed, or was in the process of completing, an educational technology plan (Hezel 1995). Some plans were part of a larger education reform plan, and others were separate. In either case, the vital role of technology is evident in the plans. These plans are the basis for allocating federal funds for technology in the states.

The Council of Chief State School Officers (CCSSO) published a major report supported by the National Telecommunications and Information Administration (NTIA) that assessed the relationship of distance learning to the nation's educational needs, especially in achieving the National Education Goals (CCSSO 1995). The recommendations made by the combined authority of these two agencies, CCSSO as representative of all state education agencies in the United States and NTIA as lead federal agency in promoting telecommunications, reflect new and powerful support of educational technology at the national and state levels.

In a move to provide technical assistance to the states, six regional educational technology consortia were established in 1995: NetTech at the City University of New York; the North Central Regional Technology Consortium in Oak Brook, Illinois; the Center for Language, Minority Education and Research at California State University, Long Beach; the South Central Regional Technology Consortium at the University of Kansas; SERVE (Southeastern Regional Visions in Education) in Greensboro, North Carolina; and the Regional Technology Consortium at the Northwest Regional Educational Laboratory in Portland, Oregon.

These consortia provide advice to states and local districts concerning technology and training for educators in order to promote the effective implementation of technology. The intent is to build on existing resources and expertise in school districts, universities, research centers, federal education laboratories, and the private sector to help local efforts to build telecommunications networks, train teachers, and integrate technology into the curriculum. The awards for 1995 were approximately $10 million.

In an overview of educational telecommunications development as of 1994, Richard Hezel reports that:

> School "restructuring" and educational reform are influencing the adoption and use of telecommunications. The recognition that the instructional process must evolve from teacher-centered to student-centered learning has evoked imaginative ideas about learning activities and how to construct those activities. Rather than through activities that revolve around teacher-delivery, instruction is increasingly delivered through machines. Under this model, teachers become essential managers and guides for student-centered learning (1994, p. 3).

Hezel has tracked the development of telecommunications in the United States since 1987. This is the fifth edition of this comprehensive study.

While it is clear that technology is at the heart of many reform and restructuring plans, there is a danger that the hardware definition of technology may prevail. The acquisition of computers, videotape recorders, and CD-ROMs may be an observable sign of progress, but it is the creative application and use of such tools that introduce new approaches to learning. A useful definition of instructional technology is:

> The theory and practice of design, development, utilization, management and evaluation of processes and resources for learning (Seels and Richey 1994, p. 1).

With this definition of technology in mind, the probability of school reform and restructuring is enhanced.

ANALYSIS OF TRENDS 1988-1995

Trends are best determined by observing specific actions over time. This monograph, as a continuation of the 1988, 1989, and 1991 analyses, is able to provide a long-range view of trends in educational technology. As a result, a higher confidence level can be established, and the review of trends allows a long-range summary.

The one outstanding finding is that trends have not changed significantly over the seven years. When one reviews the categories of the content analysis, there is very little movement in rank order. Instructional processes have remained in first position over the years (see table 1). Technological developments have been in second or third place since 1988. Services has been in sixth place for three of the four times, and the society and culture category has been in seventh or eighth place during all years of the study. Other categories (management, research and theory, and the field) have changed positions slightly. This consistency contributes to confirmation of the trends.

Trend analysis often uses statistical data to back up the qualitative statements. This study of trends is no different. Most of the trends in the 1995 study use statistical data to justify the statements. By counting the number of computers in schools and looking at the student computer ratio, it is easy to infer the potential impact on K-12 education. What such data do not indicate is a description of the actual use of the computers. What difference are they making in learning? Likewise, the same logic applies to networks, television, and numbers of new delivery systems in schools. It would be easy to say that "educational technology = hardware/software" if only numbers were considered. When one reads about dramatic increases in the number of computers in the home and CD-ROMs in school media centers, it is easy to conclude that availability is equal to creative and appropriate use by students for the purpose of learning in subject matter fields. Actual observations in the schools might diminish the effect of this extrapolation.

There is an undercurrent in the literature that appears to equate educational technology with information technology. As the use of computers, networks, and telecommunications increases dramatically, new advocates are created and replace, to some extent, professionals who have been prepared to serve the field from a broader perspective—that is, from the design and development point of view. Most educational technologists insist that their work emphasizes the design and development of instruction for the improvement of learning, and *not* the application of hardware and software. However, *the trends seem to reflect a hardware emphasis.* When the two top-ranking categories in the content analysis process reflect both design (instructional processes) and hardware/software (technological developments) it should become obvious that *both* are important, and *both* are related, and often necessary, to the process called instructional design and development.

The emergence of a new definition for "educational technologist" is worrisome to some of the more established professionals. This potential conflict is not evident in the current analysis of trends, but it is an undercurrent that may emerge in the future. The better long-range solution would be for professional educational technologists to become more adept with the newer technologies, and for the latter-day practitioners to gain new skills in design, development, and evaluation. There seems to be room for both "camps," but adjustments must be made on both sides.

Some of the "soft" trends are not as quantitative but nonetheless important. The increase of advocacy voices, evident in the 1995 trends, was not as visible in the earlier studies. Educational technology is becoming an acceptable term in the higher echelons of education hierarchy. Public statements offer evidence of this fact. Likewise, the role of educational technology in education reform and restructuring is an integral part of the plan for each. On the cynical side, one might say that hardware and software offer visible evidence that something is happening in a school. There is not much hard evidence that there is an improvement in learning in settings where such equipment has been added. However, optimism prevails, and schools continue to purchase hardware and software as symbols of progress and change.

More obvious is the increasing use of distance education to provide resources that are not available in a local school. Distance education requires a means or medium to make it work. Satellite and cable television, along with computers and networks, provide the means. It is difficult to offer distance education without the hardware and software. Such installations are increasing, and seem to make more sense than simply adding equipment to the school's computer laboratory. The impact on learning is still unclear.

Inherent in many of the emerging trends in educational technology is the increasing wish for teacher education and staff development programs that will help teachers and other educators become more proficient with today's technology. School administrators, boards of education, and teachers themselves realize that the development of educational technology competencies are absolutely essential for survival as the twenty-first century approaches. Professional education organizations that were silent about the use of technology, or even opposed to its use, are now speaking out in its favor, but with carefully phrased statements that protect their constituents. These statements do not reach the educational technology literature as much as the publications of the teachers' associations and other policy groups. Therefore, the content analysis of educational technology trends has to extend its reach to related literature, not just the publications directly related to the field.

Trends can be used to determine future directions if carefully applied. An organization that does not have its mission, goals, and objectives clearly stated will not find that local adoption of trends will advance the organization. When trends fit the purpose and desired outcomes of an organization, they can be applied and adapted to fit local circumstances. The guideline should be: "Apply with care."

REFERENCES

ALA, Microsoft launch "Libraries Online!" (1996, January). *American Libraries 27*(1), 7.

American Federation of Teachers. (1996). *Teaming up with technology: How unions can harness the technology revolution on campus.* Washington, DC: Author.

Blumenstyk, G. (1996, January 26). Faculty group calls for caution and curbs on distance education. *The Chronicle of Higher Education,* p. A20.

CD-ROM software sales soar. (1996, January 4). *Edupage.* Internet WWW page at URL: http://www.utopia.com/mailings/edupage/Edupage.4.January.1996.html.

The Children's Partnership. (1995). *America's children and the information superhighway: Skills for the future.* Santa Monica, CA: Author.

The condition of education 1995. (1995). Washington, DC: U.S. Department of Education, National Center for Education Statistics, pp. 183-85.

Council of Chief State School Officers. (1995). *United States education and instruction through telecommunications: Distance learning for all learners.* Washington, DC: Author.

Cradler, J. (1995). *The national and state-by-state "Education Technology Annual Report."* San Francisco: Far West Laboratory for Educational Research and Development.

DeLoughry, T. J. (1996, January 26). Reaching a "critical mass": Survey shows record number of professors use computer in the classroom. *The Chronicle of Higher Education,* pp. A17, A20.

Education is key to home PC market. (1996, February 18). *Edupage,* Internet WWW page at URL: http://www.utopia.com/mailings/edupage.

Ely, D. P. (1995). *Technology is the answer! But what was the question?* Paper presented at the James P. Curtis Distinguished Lecture. Capstone College of Education Society, University of Alabama. (ED 381 152)

Exodus from commercial services? One is enough. (1996, January 18). *Edupage,* Internet WWW page at URL: http://www.utopia.com/mailings/edupage.

Gillman, T.V. (1989). *Change in public education: A technological perspective.* Eugene, OR: ERIC Clearinghouse on Educational Management. (ED 302 940)

Green, K. C. (1996, March-April). The coming ubiquity of information technology. *Change 28*(2), 24-28.

Green, K. C. (1996). *Campus computing 1995.* Encino, CA: Campus Computing.

Hayes, J. (1995). Multimedia in schools. *Educational IRM Quarterly 3*(3-4), 46-48.

Hayes, J., and Bybee, D. L. (1995, October). Defining the greatest need for educational technology. *Learning and Leading with Technology 23*(2), 48-53.

Heaviside, S., Farris, E., Malitz, G., and Carpenter, J. (1995). *Advanced telecommunications in U.S. public schools, K-12.* (Report No. NCES95-731). Washington, DC: National Center for Education Statistics. (ED 378 959)

Hezel Associates. (1994). *Educational telecommunications: The state-by-state analysis 1994.* Syracuse, NY: Author.

Janowitz, M. (1976). Content analysis and the study of sociopolitical change. *Journal of Communication 26*(4), 20-21.

Krippendorff, J. (1980). *Content analysis: An introduction to its methodology,* Vol. 5. Beverly Hills, CA: Sage Publications.

Malarkey-Taylor Associates, Inc. (1995). *1995 Education technology survey.* Washington, DC: Author.

Means, B., et al. (1993). *Using technology to support educational reform.* Washington, DC: Government Printing Office. (ED 364 220)

Miller, T. (1995, December 10). Getting to know all about you. *The New York Times,* p. F14.

Moore, D. M., and Braden, R. (1988). Prestige and influence in the field of educational technology. *Performance and Instruction 21*(2), 15-23.

Moore, M. G., and Kearsley, G. (1996). *Distance education: A systems view.* Belmont, CA: Wadsworth Publishing.

Naisbitt, J. (1988). *Megatrends.* New York: Warner Books.

National Education Association. (1995). Resolutions. *NEA Today 14*(36), 36.

The National Education Goals Report. (1995). Washington, DC: Government Printing Office.

Northwest Regional Educational Laboratory. (1995, Summer). *Northwest report.* Portland, OR: Author.

Piele, P. K. (1989). *The politics of technology utilization: From microcomputers to distance learning.* Eugene, OR: ERIC Clearinghouse on Educational Management. (ED 318 132)

Postman, N. (1993). *Technopoly: The surrender of culture to technology.* New York: Random House.

Quality Education Data. (1995a). *Technology trends in U.S. public schools.* Internet WWW page at URL: http://www.edshow.com/QED (version current as of April 5, 1996).

Quality Education Data. (1995b). *Education market guide and mailing list catalog 1995-1996.* Denver, CO: Author.

Quality Education Data. (1995c). *Networks now, 1995.* Denver, CO: Author.

Roberts, Linda. (1996). A transformation of learning: Use of the national information infrastructure for education and lifelong learning. In *Educational Media and Technology Yearbook 1995-96,* ed. Donald P. Ely and Barbara B. Minor. Englewood, CO: Libraries Unlimited, 50-66.

St. Joseph Public Library. (1995). Internet WWW page at URL http://sjcpl.lib.in.us/homepage/Public Libraries/ PubLibSrvsGpherWWW.html/#wwwsrv.

Schneider, K. G. (1996). Community networks: New frontier, old values. *American Libraries 27*(1), 96.

Seels, B. B., and Richey, R. C. (1994). *Instructional technology: The definition and domains of the field.* Washington, DC: Association for Educational Communications and Technology.

Stoll, C. (1995). *Silicon snake oil: Second thoughts on the information highway.* New York: Doubleday.

Survey shows half of American homes have computers or will buy one soon. (1995, August 1). *Education Technology News 12*(16), 126. (Sample issue.)

Swisher, K. (1995, October 31). Internet's reach in society grows, survey finds. *The Washington Post*, pp. 1, 6.

Teachers still lag on technology training. (1995, September 28). *Edupage,* Internet WWW page at URL: http://www.elk-grove.k12.il.us/archives/edupage/0082.html.

Technology in the American household: Americans going online. . . . Explosive growth, uncertain destinations. (1995). *Times Mirror Center for The People and The Press.* Internet WWW page at URL http://soundprint.org/???~democracy/polls2.html.

U.S. Congress, Office of Technology Assessment. (1989, November). *Linking for learning: A new course for education.* Washington, DC: Government Printing Office. (ED 310 767)

Weber, R. P. (1990). *Basic content analysis*, 2d ed. Beverly Hills, CA: Sage Publications.

Withrow, F. B. (1995). *USE IT (United States education and instruction through telecommunications).* Washington, DC: Council of Chief State School Officers.

A New Paradigm of ISD?*

Charles M. Reigeluth
Laurie Miller Nelson
Instructional Systems Technology
Indiana University

DO WE NEED A NEW PARADIGM OF ISD?

There is a lot of talk lately about new paradigms. The word "paradigm" is rapidly becoming one of the most used (if least understood) words in the current vocabulary. And now they want to apply it to Instructional Systems Design (ISD)? What in the world for? Many would argue that ISD has been very successful the way it is—both parts of it: ISD process models (see Gustafson 1991) and ISD product models, better known as instructional-design strategies and theories (see Reigeluth 1983).

But ISD's middle name is "systems." We know that every system is a subsystem in a larger system. And we know that when the larger (super) system changes in significant ways, the system itself must change in equally significant ways for it to survive, because it must meet the needs of its supersystem in order for the supersystem to continue to support it (Hutchins 1996). So if ISD's supersystem were undergoing a paradigm shift, then (and only then) would ISD need to search for a new paradigm shift or else risk becoming obsolete.

ISD'S SUPERSYSTEM

So, is ISD's supersystem changing dramatically? What is its supersystem, anyway? To oversimplify a bit, it is all those systems that we serve—every context for application of ISD, including K-12 schools, higher education, corporations, health agencies, the armed forces, museums, and other institutions in the private, public, and "third" (not-for-profit) sector. So let's take a look at some of the ones to which we contribute (and on which we depend) the most.

Corporations are undergoing massive restructuring (Hammer and Champy 1993) that certainly fits the definition of a paradigm shift. In the Agrarian Age, businesses were organized around the *family*: the family farm, the family bakery, and so forth. In the Industrial Age, the family was replaced by the *bureaucracy* as the predominant form of business organization. Now, as we evolve deeper into the Information Age, corporations are doing away with many of the middle levels of the bureaucracy and are reorganizing based on holistic processes rather than fragmented departments (Hammer and Champy 1993). Hence, they are organizing as teams that are being given considerable autonomy to manage themselves within the purview of the corporate vision, rather than being directed from above.

Increasingly, other organizations in all three sectors (private, public, and nonprofit) are undergoing similar transformations (see, for example, Osborne and Gaebler 1992). Table 1 shows some of the "key markers" that characterize the differences between Industrial Age organizations and Information Age organizations.

---

*This chapter is an elaboration of an article of the same title in *Educational Technology*. It is included here with permission of Educational Technology Publications.

Table 1

Key Markers That Distinguish Industrial-Age and Information-Age Organizations

Industrial Age	Information Age
Standardization	Customization
Bureaucratic organization	Team-based organization
Centralized control	Autonomy with accountability
Adversarial relationships	Cooperative relationships
Autocratic decision making	Shared decision making
Compliance	Initiative
Conformity	Diversity
One-way communications	Networking
Compartmentalization	Holism
Parts-oriented	Process-oriented
Planned obsolescence	Total quality
CEO as "king"	Customer as "king"

These fundamental changes in the supersystems we serve have important implications for ISD. Employees need to be able to think and solve problems, work in teams, communicate, take initiative, and bring diverse perspectives to their work. Also, "people need to learn more, yet they have less time available in which to learn it" (Lee and Zemke 1995, 30), and they need to demonstrate impact on the organization's strategic objectives (Hequet 1995). Can our systems of education and training meet those needs by merely changing the content—what we teach—or do we need to make more fundamental changes? To answer this question, we must take a closer look at our current paradigm of training and education.

THE CURRENT PARADIGM
OF EDUCATION AND TRAINING

Table 1 indicates that our current paradigm in education and training is based on *standardization*, much like the mass-production of Industrial Age manufacturing, which is now giving way to customized production in the Information Age economy. We know that different learners learn at different rates and have different learning needs. Yet our current paradigm of education and training entails teaching a large group of learners the same content in the same amount of time. Why? Because this allows valid comparisons of students with each other, which met an important need of the Industrial Age: *sorting students*, separating the laborers from the managers. After all, you couldn't afford to—and didn't want to—educate the common laborers too much, or they wouldn't be content to do boring, repetitive tasks, nor to do what they were told to do without questions. When you really think about it, our current paradigm of training and education is not designed for learning; it is designed for sorting (Reigeluth 1994).

Yet, all educators can agree that different people learn at different rates. So, when an educational or training system holds time constant, achievement must vary, as has been the case in our Industrial Age educational system, ever since it replaced the one-room schoolhouse. The alternative is to allow learners as much time as they need to reach attainments. That would be a learning-focused system, which we show signs of moving toward. One could argue that we have held time constant because group-based learning represented economic efficiencies, which is certainly true. But when you consider that student assessment has typically been norm-based, and when you consider that teachers sometimes have an attitude of withholding some information from students to see who the really bright ones are, then it becomes clear that at least part of the reason has been to sort learners—in K-12 schooling, higher education, and corporate training.

But assembly-line workers acting as automatons are becoming an endangered species in the United States. The current corporate restructuring movement with its emphasis on quality requires ever-increasing numbers of employees who can take initiative, think critically, and solve problems independently. To meet this need in industry and the call in education for lifelong learners, we now need a *focus on learning* instead of sorting. This means we need a focus on *customization*, not standardization. This is true in all contexts for ISD: corporations and other organizations, as well as K-12 schools and higher education. Merely changing the content will not meet this new need of ISD's supersystems.

Table 1 indicates that our current paradigm of training and education is also based on *conformity* and *compliance*. Trainees and students alike are usually expected to sit down, be quiet, and do what they are told to do. Their learning is directed by the trainer or teacher. But employers now want people who will take the *initiative* to solve problems and will bring *diversity*—especially diverse perspectives—to the workplace. Both of these enhance the ability of a team to solve problems and keep ahead of the competition. Communities and families also need people who will take the initiative and honor diversity. Changing the content is not sufficient to meet these new needs of the supersystems, for the very structure of our systems of training and education discourages initiative and diversity.

We could continue this process of analyzing how each of the key markers of our current paradigm of training and education (see table 1) are counterproductive for meeting the emerging needs of the Information Age, but the message is already clear: *the paradigm itself needs to be changed*. This is the focus of the emerging field called Educational Systems Design (ESD) (see Banathy 1991; Reigeluth 1995), which is concerned both with what kinds of changes are needed in education and training systems to better meet the needs of their supersystems and their learners (a product issue), and with how to go about making those changes (a process issue). So the next question is, does that mean ISD has to change?

To answer this question, it is helpful to distinguish between process and product, or means and ends, in ISD. The "product" issue is concerned with what the learning experiences should be like (after they have been designed and developed). *Instructional methods and theories* are the knowledge base that addresses this issue (see Reigeluth 1983). Instructional methods are the tools that teachers and designers use to facilitate learning, including both soft (e.g., strategies) and hard (e.g., media) tools. Instructional theories provide guidelines as to when and when not to use the various methods. The "process" issue is concerned with how we go about designing and developing those learning experiences. *ISD process models* are the knowledge base that addresses this issue (see Gustafson 1991). They are the methods that instructional designers use to create instruction, such as the activities represented in the ADDIE (analysis, design, development, implementation, and evaluation) model, including needs analysis, task/content analysis, and formative evaluation. Because changes in the desired product will require changes in the process to create it, let's start by addressing the question as to whether the paradigm of instructional theory needs to change.

IMPLICATIONS FOR INSTRUCTIONAL THEORY

From the above discussion, we have seen that the current paradigm of education and training needs to change from one that is focused on sorting to one focused on learning—from the Darwinian notion of "advancement of the fittest" to the more spiritually and humanistically defensible one of "advancement of all." This means that the paradigm of *instruction* has to change from standardization to customization, from a focus on presenting material to a focus on making sure that learners' needs are met—a "Learning-Focused" paradigm. This, in turn, requires a shift from passive to active learning. It requires a shift from decontextualized learning to authentic tasks. And, most important, it requires a shift from holding time constant and allowing achievement to vary, to allowing each learner the time needed to reach the desired attainments.

But to do this, the teacher can't teach the same thing to a whole "class" at the same time. This means the teacher has to be more of a "guide on the side" rather than a "sage on the stage." So, if the teacher is the facilitator rather than the agent of most of the learning, what other agents are there? Well-designed resources are one, which is where instructional theory and instructional technology can play particularly large roles. But others include fellow learners (e.g., students or trainees), local real-world resources (e.g., practitioners), and remote resources (e.g., through the Internet). Instructional theories are needed to offer guidelines for the use of all these kinds of resources for the Learning-Focused paradigm of instruction. Furthermore, this paradigm requires that our definition of instruction include what many cognitive theorists refer to as "construction" (see Ferguson 1992)—a process of helping learners to build their own knowledge, as opposed to a process of merely conveying information to the learner. Instruction must be defined more broadly as anything that is done to facilitate purposeful learning.

Clearly, this represents a new paradigm of instruction that requires a new paradigm of instructional theory. But does this mean we should discard current instructional theories? To answer this question, let's consider some of the major contributions of current theories. If someone wants to learn a skill, then demonstrations of the skill, generalities about how to do it, and practice doing it, with feedback, will definitely make learning easier and more successful. Behaviorists recognized this and called them examples, rules, and practice with feedback. Cognitivists also recognized this, but naturally had to give them different names, such as cognitive apprenticeship and scaffolding. And, yes, constructivists also recognize this, and even radical constructivists walk the walk, even though they refuse to talk the talk. An analysis of instruction designed by some radical constructivists reveals a plentiful use of these very instructional strategies. Should we seriously consider discarding this knowledge? We don't think so, but is this knowledge sufficient to design high-quality instruction? We don't think that, either.

The important point here is that instructional designers and other educators should recognize that there are two major kinds of instructional methods: *basic methods*, which have been scientifically proven to consistently increase the probability of learning under given conditions (e.g., for given types of learning and learners), such as the use of generalities, examples, and practice with feedback for teaching a skill, and *variable methods*, which represent alternatives from which you can choose, as vehicles for the basic methods (e.g., it doesn't matter very much whether you use print, computer, or audiotape, as long as you use one of them). Although this greatly oversimplifies the relationships that exist between methods of instruction and the various conditions under which they should and should not be used, it is nonetheless an important distinction for designers to be aware of. And instructional theories are needed that provide guidance as to when to use these variable methods.

To provide this kind of guidance, we need a truly new paradigm of *instructional theory* that subsumes current theory—a paradigm through which flexible guidelines are offered about when and how learners:

- should be given initiative,
- should work in teams on authentic, real-world tasks,
- should be allowed to choose from a diversity of sound methods,
- should best use the powerful features of advanced technologies, and
- should be allowed to persevere until they reach appropriate standards.

The Learning-Focused instructional theory must offer guidelines for the design of learning environments that provide appropriate combinations of challenge and guidance, empowerment and support, self-direction and structure. And the Learning-Focused theory must include guidelines for an area that has been largely overlooked in instructional design: deciding among such variable methods of instruction as problem-based learning, project-based learning, simulations, tutorials, and team-based learning. Tables 2 and 3 show some of these kinds of approaches that Learning-Focused theory might encompass. And we need flexible guidelines for the design of each of those approaches to instruction.

Table 2

Mid-Level Strategies

Apprenticeship: an experiential learning strategy in which the learner acquires knowledge and skills through direct participation in learning under immediate personal supervision in a situation that approximates the conditions under which the knowledge will be used.

Debate: a formally structured discussion with two teams arguing opposing sides of a topic.

Demonstration: a carefully prepared presentation that shows how to perform an act or use a procedure; accompanied by appropriate oral and visual explanations and illustrations; frequently accompanied by questions.

Field trip: a carefully planned educational tour in which a group visits an object or place of interest for first-hand observation or study.

Game: an instructional activity in which participants follow prescribed rules that differ from those of reality as they strive to attain a challenging goal; is usually competitive.

Group discussion, guided: a purposeful conversation and deliberation about a topic of mutual interest among 6-20 participants under the guidance of a leader.

Group discussion, free/open: a free group discussion of a topic selected by the teacher, who acts only as chairman; learning occurs only through the interchange among group members.

Ancient symposium: a group of 5-29 persons who meet in the home or private room to enjoy good food, entertainment, fellowship, and with the desire to discuss informally a topic of mutual interest.

Interview: a 5- to 30-minute presentation conducted before an audience in which a resource person(s) responds to systematic questioning by the audience about a previously determined topic.

Laboratory: a learning experience in which students interact with raw materials.

Guided laboratory: an instructor-guided learning experience in which students interact with raw materials.

Lecture/Speech: a carefully prepared oral presentation of a subject by a qualified person.

Lecture, guided discovery: a group learning strategy in which the audience responds to questions posed by the instructor selected to guide them toward discovery (also called recitation class).

Panel discussion: a group of 3-6 persons having a purposeful conversation on an assigned topic before an audience of learners; members are selected on the basis of previously demonstrated interests and competency in the subject to be discussed and their ability to verbalize.

Project: an organized task performance or problem solving activity.

Team project: a small group of learners working cooperatively to perform a task or solve a problem.

Seminar: a strategy in which one or several group members carry out a study/project on a topic (usually selected by the teacher) and present their findings to the rest of the group, followed by discussion (usually teacher-led) of the findings to reach a general conclusion.

Quiet meeting: a 15- to 60-minute period of meditation and limited verbal expression by a group of five or more persons; requires a group of people who are not strangers to each other; is used at a point when the leaders or members feel that reflection and contemplation are desirable.

Simulation: an abstraction or simplification of some specific real-life situation, process, or task.

Case study: a type of simulation aimed at giving learners experience in the sort of decision making required later.

Role play: a dramatized case study; a spontaneous portrayal (acting out) of a situation, condition, or circumstance by elected members of a learning group.

Think Tank/Brainstorm: a group effort to generate new ideas for creative problem solving; thoughts of one participant stimulate new direction and thoughts in another.

Tutorial, programmed: one-to-one method of instruction in which decisions to be made by the tutor (live, text, computer, or expert system) are programmed in advance by means of carefully selected, structured instructions; is individually paced, requires active learner response, and provides immediate feedback.

Tutorial, conversational: one-to-one method of instruction in which the tutor presents instruction in an adaptive mode; is individually paced, requires active learner response, and feedback is provided.

Socratic dialogue: a type of conversational tutorial in which the tutor guides the learner to discovery through a series of questions.

Note: There are many variations of these approaches, and different approaches are often used in combination.

Source: From Dorsey, Olson, & Reigeluth 1988.

Table 3

Alternative Methods for Instruction

Methods:		Strengths:
Lecture/Presentation	(telling)	Efficient Standardized Structured
Demonstration/Modeling	(Realistic Showing)	Eases Application
Tutorial		Customized Learner Responsible
Drill & Practice		Automatized Mastery
Independent/Learner Control		Flexible implementation
Discussion, Seminar		Meaningful, realism, owned, customized to learner
Cooperative Group Learning	a) artificial conditions b) real-world practice (OJT)	Ownership Team-building
Games (artificial rules)	Artificial rules	
Simulations	Realistic Structure Context	High Transfer High Motivation
Discovery • Individual		
• Group		
Problem Solving/Lab		High Level Thinking in ill-structured problems

(T) = Teacher (Live or Automated)   (L) = Learner   (Ri) = Resource (Instructional)   - - - = Indirect Involvement

(P) = Problem   (LA) = Learning Activity   (Rr) = Resource (raw)   ❯ = Direction of Control

Source: From Molenda 1995.

Furthermore, as the world becomes more complex, learners need more skills for complex cognitive tasks, such as solving problems in ill-structured domains. Instructional theories to date have focused largely on simpler procedural tasks in well-structured domains. Only recently have researchers begun exploring instruction for complex cognitive tasks (see Spiro, Feltovich, Jacobson, and Coulson 1992; Leshin, Pollock, and Reigeluth 1994, 82-100, 230-44), and much work remains to develop powerful guidelines for designing instruction for this important type of learning.

For ISD to remain a vibrant and growing field that will help meet the changing needs of our systems of education and training, we desperately need more theorists and researchers working collaboratively to develop and refine this new paradigm of instructional theories. Formative research (Roma and Reigeluth 1995) represents one possible methodology for developing such theories, because it focuses on how to improve existing theories, rather than on comparing one theory with another (as experimental research does) or on describing what happens when a theory is used (as naturalistic qualitative research does).

Clearly we do need fundamental changes in instructional theory. But does this mean we also need fundamental changes in the ISD process?

IMPLICATIONS FOR THE ISD PROCESS

The ISD process is currently conceived in many different ways by different people and organizations (Gustafson 1991). Most large companies have their own ISD process model. But the predominant characterization of the ISD process is as a series of steps within the basic framework of the ADDIE phases: analysis, design, development, implementation, and evaluation. But do these models reflect how ISD is actually done by experts? More important, do they reflect how it should be done? And most important, are they appropriate for designing the new paradigm of instruction? We believe "No!" becomes progressively louder for each of these questions. But does this mean we should discard the current knowledge about the ISD process? We don't believe that, either. We believe many of the same activities are required, but that they must be combined with other activities and reconfigured into a new kind of process model.

First of all, the current paradigm of ISD models conceives of a single dimension of activities over time, as reflected by the ADDIE phases. The first significant change, in our view, is that the ISD process should be viewed as (and is, in fact, even now intuitively performed by ISD experts as) two dimensions of activities, one of which is nested within the other. The broader dimension is a *series of decisions* about what the instruction should be like, such as deciding what to teach, what sequence to teach it in, what media to use, and so forth. Each of these decisions should be preceded by its own appropriate types of analysis. It is not useful to think in terms of completing all the analysis activities before doing any design activities. We like to think of this change as "just-in-time analysis." Much of the rationale for this is that each decision you make is likely to change the nature of subsequent options, such that it is often impossible to know ahead of time what type of analysis to do (what types of information to collect) for making all your later decisions.

For example, there are many different ways to sequence instruction: historical sequence, procedural sequence, hierarchical sequence, and so forth. Each type of sequence is based on a different type of relationship within the content. Therefore, each requires a different type of content/task analysis to design the sequence, such as chronological analysis for the historical sequence, a procedural-prerequisite analysis for the procedural sequence, and a learning-prerequisite analysis for the hierarchical sequence. Until you have made the decision as to what kind of sequence to use, it is senseless to conduct a content/task analysis.

Furthermore, each decision can and should be evaluated as soon as possible after it is made ("zero-delay evaluation"), to find weaknesses in it and ways of improving it. And organizational change concerns (including implementation, organizational change, and management) should be anticipated and dealt with throughout your analysis, synthesis, and evaluation activities ("ongoing change"), because performance problems almost always require organizational changes as well as changes in the knowledge and skills of individuals. Your evaluation should also look at your process activities (analysis, synthesis, evaluation, and change), as any good reflective practitioner would do.

Consequently, we believe the new paradigm of ISD models will characterize the ISD process as an *iterative series of ASEC cycles* (Analysis-Synthesis-Evaluation-Change) for progressive sets of instructional decisions. Table 4 shows one possible such conception. During a single ASEC temporal progression (left to right in one row of table 4), there is likely to be frequent recycling from synthesis back to analysis, from evaluation back to synthesis or analysis, and from change back to synthesis or analysis. Similarly, during the temporal progression of decisions (the top-to-bottom progression in table 4), there is likely to be frequent revisiting of earlier decisions to adjust them to later decisions and insights. Some ISD experts undoubtedly already perform their work in this manner, but the predominant mindset about ISD entails a one-dimensional rather than two-dimensional temporal progression.

Table 4

A Sample Two-Dimensional Temporal ISD Model

ORGANIZATIONAL CHANGE:	Analysis	Synthesis	Evaluation	Change
1. Intervention Decisions	1.1	1.2	1.3	1.4
INSTRUCTIONAL DESIGN:	Analysis	Synthesis	Evaluation	Change
2. Fuzzy Vision of Ends and Means	2.1	2.2	2.3	2.4
3. Scope and Sequence Decisions	3.1	3.2	3.3	3.4
4. Decisions about what instruction to select and what to produce	4.1	4.2	4.3	4.4
5. Approach Decisions	5.1	5.2	5.3	5.4
6. Tactic Decisions	6.1	6.2	6.3	6.4
7. Media Selection Decisions	7.1	7.2	7.3	7.4
8. Media Utilization Decisions	8.1	8.2	8.3	8.4
DEVELOPMENT AND EVALUATION:	Plan	Do	Check	Change
9. Prototype Development	9.1	9.2	9.3	9.4
10. Mass Production of Instruction	10.1	10.2	10.3	10.4
11. Evaluation of Worth and Value	11.1	11.2	11.3	11.4
ORGANIZATIONAL CHANGE:	Analysis	Description/ Development	Evaluation	Change
12. Implementation, Adoption, Organizational Change	12.1	12.2	12.3	12.4

The numbers represent different activities that compose the ISD model. These activities are not just steps; they are usually also composed of heuristics.

The second significant change we foresee is that the ISD process will be broadened to include greater attention to *impact on the instructional system's supersystems*. In the case of corporate training systems, greater attention will be paid to corporate performance (often called "performance technology") and societal impact (see the "Business Impact ISD Model" proposed by Molenda, Pershing, and Reigeluth in 1996). For K-12 and higher education, greater attention will be paid to the needs of the broader community or society (and its various organizations) that the educational institution serves, as well as to the learners' needs; and greater attention will be paid to organizational changes that will help the institution and its instructional system to meet those needs. Again, the concern for systemic change in education, or Educational Systems Design (ESD), is a reflection of the need for this change in ISD (see Reigeluth 1995).

The third significant change we see flows out of the second: the ISD process should *include all "stakeholder" groups*, so that their interests, values, and perspectives can be accounted for in the instructional design and organizational changes. The stakeholders are all those people who have a stake in the instructional system under design. In a corporation it might include the trainers, trainees, and their managers; higher-level managers; stockholders; and customers. In a school system, it might include the teachers, students, administrators, parents, local businesses, and social service agencies. There are many times and ways the stakeholders should be involved during the process, but the net result should not only be valuable input from these groups, but also the "output" of a sense of *ownership* over the resulting instructional system, which is an important aspect of the implementation/change dimension of ISD.

The fourth significant change we foresee is that the ISD process should have a visioning activity shortly after the needs analysis. This activity should entail having all the stakeholders for the instructional system under design come to consensus on a fuzzy image of what the instruction will be like, both in terms of *ends* (how the learners will be different as a result of it) and *means* (how those changes in the learners will be fostered). This is an opportunity for all the stakeholders to share their values about both ends and means and to reach some consensus, so that there will be no major disappointments, misunderstandings, or resistance when it comes time for implementation. The practice of thinking in the ideal about what the instruction might be like often unleashes creative approaches that are all too often lacking in many ISD products. And this vision should be continually revisited, revised, and elaborated throughout the design process. This kind of visioning activity was advocated by Diamond (1980), whose ID model included the step of "imagining the ideal" immediately after completing the needs analysis. Diamond found a number of practical benefits in this approach, not the least of which is that it gets the design team excited about a solution.

The fifth significant change we foresee is that the ISD process will make much greater use of the notion of "user-designers" (Banathy 1991). This is a natural progression beyond Burkman's (1987) notion of "user-oriented ID" in that it goes beyond measuring and incorporating relevant potential user perceptions—it entails having the users play a major role in designing their instruction. Users are primarily the learners and the facilitators of learning (which would not be confused with the current concepts of students/trainees and teachers/ trainers). Rather than viewing this role through the lens of the current paradigm, as students and teachers working on our current design teams, we could imagine several scenarios.

In one scenario, design teams (including all stakeholders) create flexible, computer-based learning tools, like intelligent tutoring systems, that learners can use—while they are learning—to create or modify their own instruction. This concept is like adaptive instruction, except that the learners have the capability to request the computer system to use some instructional strategies, as well as the computer deciding on some strategies based on learner input. As Winn put it:

> This means that the role of instructional designers will involve less direct instruc-
> tional decision-making and more concentration on the mechanisms by means of
> which decisions are made (Winn 1987). . . . It follows that the only viable way to

make decisions about instructional strategies that meshes with cognitive theory is to do so during instruction using a system that is in constant dialogue with the student and is capable of continuously updating information about the student's progress, attitude, expectations, and so on (Winn 1989, 39-41).

Learners are able to make decisions (with varying degrees of guidance) about both content (what to learn) and strategy (how to learn it) while the instruction is in progress. The work of Dave Merrill and associates on "transaction shells" (Li and Merrill 1990; Merrill, Li, and Jones 1992) could well lead to this type of tool and has shown that such a tool is feasible to create.

A major shift in the paradigm of ISD that this scenario of the concept of user-designers represents is the notion that much of the analysis that is now done by a designer for a whole "batch" of learners well ahead of the actual instruction will soon be done during the instruction. The computer system will continuously collect information from an individual learner or a small team of learners and use that information to present an array of sound alternatives to the learners, both about what to learn next and how to learn it. Also, the teacher or trainer will be afforded the opportunity to modify the system. The systems concept of "equifinality" reflects the reality that there are usually several acceptable ways to accomplish the same end. The new paradigm of ISD will, we believe, allow for such diversity of means, as well as a diversity of ends, for learners.

In another scenario of the concept of user-designers, computers play a relatively minor role in some instructional situations, so the users must—ahead of time—design the framework or support system within which the instruction will occur. Rather than this being done by a designer-based team, in which an instructional designer plays the leading role, it is done by a user-based team in which the designer plays a facilitating role and the users—teachers or trainers, along with learners—play the leading role (Nelson 1995). This user-based approach recognizes the need to put better design tools and knowledge into the hands of those who generally create and deliver the instruction anyway. In order for this to occur, we believe a new paradigm of ISD is needed that will empower the users to play a greater role in designing their instruction than our current conception of ISD allows.

This empowerment is particularly critical in the case of teachers. Teachers are a unique type of clientele for instructional designers. They share with us a common knowledge base in educational theory, as well as powerful perspectives in regards to what typifies appropriate instruction. Teachers also have been empowered, both through formal preparation and class-room practice, to feel a great deal of ownership regarding the instruction they create and deliver. Finally, teachers are the ones closest to the learners. Rather than using preconstructed instructional products, teachers use and create a wide variety of materials that support their own instructional activities. Other than perhaps novice teachers, most teachers tend to take preconstructed instructional products, deconstruct them, and then use the resulting resources in unique ways during instruction. This raises the questions, "Why do we continue to make complete instructional products for a clientele that doesn't want them and will not use them the way we, as instructional designers, intend for them to be used? Have we been out of touch with the real needs of our clients?" We propose that in fact we as a field have not fully recognized the need to support trainers, and particularly teachers, in designing their own instruction. And this should expand to include learners. Thus, our responsibility as a field is to conceive of and develop a whole new type of instructional design process—one that assists trainers, teachers, and learners in meeting their own instructional needs.

All of these significant changes in the ISD process add up to more than a bunch of piecemeal changes, because they are systematically interrelated. They reflect a consistent set of values and a fundamentally different view of how instruction should be designed, primarily including the importance of making the design process more inclusive and less rigidly fixed in time. Because of its centrality to those values, we refer to this emerging paradigm of the

ISD process as the "User-Designer Approach." Regarding *inclusivity*, the User-Designer Approach pays greater attention to the instructional system's supersystems, to all its stakeholder groups, and especially to its users. Regarding *time*, the ASEC cycles reflect the value of just-in-time analysis, zero-delay evaluation, and ongoing change, as well as the "yin and yang" of design:

- the contingent relationships among design decisions (one decision can only be made after another), and

- the iterative nature of the design process (similar activities are engaged in repeatedly, and earlier decisions are frequently revisited and revised).

Both inclusivity and time converge in the visioning activity that occurs with all the stakeholders early in the process and is continually revisited, revised, and elaborated as the process proceeds.

CONCLUSION

The first question posed in this article was, "Do we need a new paradigm of ISD?" We have looked at ISD's supersystems and seen some dramatic changes taking place—changes that have profound implications for what systems of training and education must do to meet the needs of their supersystems. Foremost among those implications is the need for a paradigm of training and education based on learning instead of sorting students. Other implications include the need to develop initiative, teamwork, thinking skills, and diversity. To help all learners reach their potential, we need to customize, not standardize, the learning process.

We have also seen that this new paradigm of education and training has important implications for ISD. Indeed, the health of the field (if not its survival) depends on the ability of its theorists and researchers to generate and refine a *new breed of Learning-Focused instructional theories* that help education and training meet those needs (i.e., that focus on learning and foster the development of initiative, teamwork, thinking skills, and diversity). The health of ISD also depends on the ability of its practitioners and researchers to develop a *User-Designer Approach* to the ISD process, which:

- conceives of the ISD process as a *series of design decisions*, each of which requires a cycle of analysis, synthesis, evaluation, and change (ASEC);

- attends more to the needs of, and ISD's impact on, its *supersystems*;

- includes *all stakeholder groups* in the ISD process; and

- envisions a *fuzzy* image of the instruction early in the ISD process.

Perhaps most important of all implications is that much of the designing should be done by the learners (*user-designers*) while they are learning, with help from a computer system that generates options based on information collected from the learners. We also need to better support trainers and teachers in their instructional design activities.

But with all this talk of a new paradigm of ISD, it is important not to completely reject and discard the old paradigm. In fact, the new paradigm needs to incorporate most of the knowledge our field has generated about both instructional theory and the ISD process. That knowledge must be restructured into substantially different configurations to meet the new needs of those whom we serve. Whether or not the field of ISD makes this transformation to a new paradigm will depend in great measure on the willingness of those of us in academe to develop the necessary theories and ISD processes and to provide the required professional development for the next generation of ISDers.

REFERENCES

Banathy, B. H. (1991). *Systems design of education: A journey to create the future.* Englewood Cliffs, NJ: Educational Technology Publications.

Burkman, E. (1987). Factors affecting utilization. In *Instructional technology: Foundations,* ed. R. M. Gagné. Hillsdale, NJ: Lawrence Erlbaum.

Diamond, R. M. (1980). The Syracuse model for course and curriculum design, implementation, and evaluation. *Journal of Instructional Development 4*(2), 19-23.

Ferguson, D. E. (1992). Computers in teaching and learning: An interpretation of current practices and suggestions for future directions. In *New directions in educational technology,* ed. E. Scanlon and T. O'Shea. Berlin: Springer-Verlag.

Gustafson, K. L. (1991). *Survey of instructional development models,* 2d ed. Syracuse, NY: ERIC Clearinghouse on Information Resources, Syracuse University.

Hammer, M., and J. Champy. (1993). *Reengineering the corporation: A manifesto for business revolution.* New York: HarperCollins.

Hequet, M. (1995, November). Not paid enough? You're not alone. *Training 32*(11), 44-55.

Hutchins, C. L. (1998). *Systemic thinking: Solving complex problems.* Aurora, CO: Professional Development Systems.

Lee, C., and Zemke, R. (1995, November). No time to train. *Training 32*(11), 29-37.

Leshin, C. B., Pollock, J., and Reigeluth, C. M. (1994). *Instructional design strategies and tactics.* Englewood, Cliffs, NJ: Educational Technology Publications.

Li, Z., and Merrill, M. D. (1990). Transaction shells: A new approach to courseware authoring. *Journal of Research on Computing in Education 23*(1), 72-86.

Merrill, M. D., Li, Z., and Jones, M. K. (1992). Instructional transaction shells: Responsibilities, methods, and parameters. *Educational Technology 32*(2), 5-26.

Molenda, M. (1995). Personal communication.

Molenda, M., Pershing, J., and Reigeluth, C. M. (1996). Designing instructional systems. In *Training and development handbook*, 4th ed., ed. R. Craig. New York: McGraw-Hill.

Nelson, L. M. (1995). *A user-based approach to instructional design.* Unpublished manuscript.

Olson, J., Dorsey, L., and Reigeluth, C. M. (1988). *Instructional theory for mid-level strategies.* Unpublished manuscript.

Osborne, D., and Gaebler, T. (1992). *Reinventing government: How the entrepreneurial spirit is transforming the public sector.* New York: Penguin Books.

Reigeluth, C. M., ed. (1983). *Instructional-design theories and models: An overview of their current status.* Hillsdale, NJ: Lawrence Erlbaum.

Reigeluth, C. M. (1994). The imperative for systemic change. In *Systemic change in education,* ed. C. M. Reigeluth and R. J. Garfinkle. Englewood Cliffs, NJ: Educational Technology Publications.

Reigeluth, C. M. (1995). Educational systems development and its relationship to ISD. In *Instructional technology: Past, present, and future,* 2d ed., ed. G. Anglin. Englewood, CO: Libraries Unlimited.

Reigeluth, C. M. (in press). *Scope and sequence decisions for quality instruction.* Book manuscript submitted for publication.

Roma, C. M., and Reigeluth, C. M. (1995). *A study of formative research as a methodology to improve prescriptive theory.* Manuscript submitted for publication.

Spiro, R. J., Feltovich, P. J., Jacobson, M. J., and Coulson, R. L. (1992). Cognitive flexibility, constructivism, and hypertext: Random access instruction for advanced knowledge acquisition in ill-structured domains. In *Constructivism and the technology of instruction: A conversation,* ed. T. Duffy and D. Jonassen. Hillsdale, NJ: Lawrence Erlbaum.

Winn, W. (1989). Toward a rational and theoretical basis for educational technology. *Educational Technology Research & Development 37*(1), 35-46.

Educational Technology
Increasing the Pressure for Change

Judith A. Grunert
School of Education, Syracuse University

*Is the search for meaning among the high heaps of the meaningless a fool's
game? Is it art's game? . . . our human endeavor is to extend the boundaries
of sense and meaning; it is to shift phenomena one by one out of the nonsense
heap and arrange them in ordered piles about us.*

Annie Dillard

Often, educational technologists describe themselves as innovators and agents of change. Now pressure for change has shifted direction to bear down on the field of Educational Technology itself, demanding new frameworks for thought and action. Competing attempts to locate the sources of rising pressure and to propose directions for change are generating discussion concerning both fundamentals and ethics of professional practice. Recent issues of *Educational Technology* initiated a compelling discussion among traditional mainstream educational technologists' concerns (*Instructional design fundamentals* 1993) and contrasting critical positions (*The ethical position of educational technology in society* 1994).

Briefly, the mainstream views educational technology as a means-ends orientation, predominantly based in positivistic, rational, and technical ways of knowing, such as scientific empiricism and experimental research. The means-ends model stresses efficiency, effectiveness, and goal orientation (Yeaman, Koetting, and Nichols 1994) in the interest of understanding, predicting, and controlling complex systems.

Based in critical theory, feminism, and postmodernism, another orientation to educational technology has emerged that focuses on underlying root interests, assumptions, and approaches (Hlynka 1994). It asks why things are the way they are and analyzes what beliefs underlie educational technology, what these beliefs mean, why these beliefs are chosen, whose interests are served, and what these choices mean when operationalized as behaviors. The focus is not so much on prediction as it is on understanding with an intent to build more meaningful instructional actions based on that understanding (Yeaman and others 1994).

While the proponents of various views address the issue of pressure on the field for change, each sets the "problem" and proposes a response that reflects their position's values, specific theories, and views of practice. The first section of this paper asks: How has the field of educational technology been defined by those in the mainstream position? How do they set the problem of change? What is their view of how to deal with the problem? The second section will consider these questions as they relate to alternative positions emerging from the field. The third section will extend the discussion of pressure for change on the values, theoretical commitments, and views of practice in educational technology. It will point to opportunities intended to provoke further thought and action. The section will address how we educational technologists might educate *ourselves* to reframe our thinking about what we do, proposing critical examination of existing practices, suggesting tools for considering other perspectives, and inviting the conceptualization of alternate visions.

THE MAINSTREAM VIEW

How have those in the mainstream position defined the field of educational technology? In a special issue of *Educational Technology* (February 1993), the proponents of this position address the state of the field, pressures and trends related to the fundamentals of instructional design theory, research, practice, and curricula. A brief history accounting for how the field has emerged and reached its present state will help to situate their views.

While it would be possible to write many histories of educational technology, Wager (1993) provides a history of the field that helps to clarify the mainstream position. The need for rapid and effective training during World War II drove the visual-instruction movement. Training devices became a major medium of instruction. Arising from audiovisual education and educational technology programs, the systematic application of communications and systems theory and, later, information-processing theory have served the field well.

In the 1950s the focus switched from visual instruction to visual communication. Audiovisual programs previously concentrating on production and administration began adding media research programs. The purpose of this research was to build models of message design that had as a foundation the study of symbols and their effects on cognition (Wager 1993).

During the 1960s behavioral psychology theories were being applied to education in the form of programmed instruction. The programmed instruction movement became an important part of instructional technology research and training programs. Saettler breaks the programmed instruction movement into six areas that markedly influenced educational technology: the behavioral-objectives movement, teaching machines, programmed instruction, individualized instruction, computer-assisted instruction, and the systems approach. These movements formed the foundations for instructional systems technology (Wager 1993).

In 1977, the Association for Educational Communications and Technology developed a lengthy definition:

> Educational Technology is a complex, integrated process involving people, procedures, ideas, devices, and organizations for analyzing problems, and devising, implementing, evaluating, and managing solutions to these problems, involved in all aspects of human learning. In educational technology, the solution to problems takes the form of all "Learning Resources" that are designed or selected as Messages, People, Materials, Devices, Techniques, and Settings. The processes for analyzing problems and devising, implementing, and evaluating solutions are identified by the "Education-Development Functions" of Research-Theory, Design, Production, Evaluation, Selection, Logistics, and Utilization. The process of directing or coordinating one or more of these functions are identified by the "Educational Management Functions" of Organization Management and Personnel Management (AECT 1977).

Now Dick (1993) suggests that, with the wide attention gained by new ideas, it would be valuable to revisit the fundamental concepts and procedures associated with ISD (Instructional Systems Design) to determine their continuing viability, beginning with an agreement about what he puts forward as ISD fundamentals:

> At the most general level, ISD is a process for determining *what* to teach and *how* to teach it. The assumption is made that there is a target population (somewhere) that should learn something. To determine what is to be learned, the designer analyzes a goal statement to identify subordinate skills, and formulates specific objectives and associated criterion-referenced assessments. How the information or skills will be taught is spelled out in an instructional strategy, which is the blueprint for the development of the instruction in a selected medium. The instruction is formatively evaluated with appropriate learners until the desired criterion level of

performance is met. The entire ISD process is systematic in that each step flows from the preceding one, and evaluation and associated revisions are used to determine when the instruction is acceptable to the client (p. 12).

Wager's history, the AECT definition, and Dick's description of Instructional Systems Design fundamentals illuminate the mainstream position. The authors present the problem of pressure for change as arising from outside the field. Problems are perceived as technological problems to be solved by technical means based on specialized scientific knowledge. The responses, while varied, are couched in the language of "Technical Rationality," in which "professional activity consists in instrumental problem solving made rigorous by the application of scientific theory and technique" (Schon 1983, p. 21).

For example, Gustafson (1993) writes that all fundamental areas of instructional design are being influenced by powerful and continuing forces outside the field: rapid changes in world economic conditions causing the enormous pressures on business and industry to become more competitive and help their employees become more productive; the need for faster and less costly practices; the need to contribute to solving the problems of education; the need for new forms of analysis and evaluation and continuous modification of electronic performance support systems (EPSS), artificial intelligence expert systems, and intelligent tutors; and the need to examine and develop instructional models for hypermedia, exploratory environments, virtual reality, and microworlds.

In another example, Dick (1993) argues that it may be necessary to add more items to our list of fundamentals. He lists these items as: identifying real problems through better organizational needs assessment models, differentiating among appropriate processes for designing solutions that affect the organizational bottom line performance, and using electronic performance support systems to aid the designer or actually do the design process.

ALTERNATIVE FRAMEWORKS

A second special issue of *Educational Technology* (February 1994) examines the ethical position of educational technology in society from a critical perspective. The authors address the field's ethical aspects by applying critical theory feminist and postmodern cultural analysis to stimulate questions and dialogue about the ethics of educational technology as social responsibility and to identify and confront hidden agendas. This approach is inherently concerned with the ethics of social responsibility and is rooted in the arts and humanities.

The authors write from theoretical bases that are humanistic, nonpositivistic theories of criticism that include overlapping ideas from the critical theory of the Frankfort School, feminist theory, and postmodern and poststructural theory. Critical theory examines and demystifies significant unequal social relations and dominant structures of a given age in pursuit of greater freedom and equality. Feminist theory aims to bring the views of those in the margins of society to full participation in social and political contexts. Postmodern theory critiques various social relations to expose problems of modern life. Postmodern studies in educational technology explore the way the field is structured and the paradigms that provide power and legitimization within the field (Yeaman and others 1994).

Yeaman (1994) discusses and deconstructs two metanarratives of modern educational technology: the linear transmission of information based on the 1949 Shannon-Weaver component model for telecommunication apparatus (Shannon and Weaver 1949), which became the foundation for information theory; and the systems approach associated with von Bertalanffy (1968) and the biological basis of general systems theory.

The epistemology of educational technology follows the linear transmission of the Shannon-Weaver model based on hardware and data transmission. Basic textbooks in educational technology, says Yeaman (1994), accept the way that the model reduces communication between people to an abstraction. Thinking about the human activity of communication as a pipeline ignores the context in which communication takes place. The pipeline builds a neutral image. In the model's subsequent elaborations, the feedback loops and overlapping fields of experience give a false appearance of consensual communication and conceal the fact that social roles and purposes can be coercive.

Yeaman (1994) writes that systems science is the source of instructional design technique and reflects the top-down management point of view, in which system and subsystem components must be identified and their relationships understood to cause and improve functioning. The result is the development of steps for successfully designing and delivering instruction that ensures successful performance. These procedures are descended from instructional management, an application of systems analysis. They are often known by their military name of Instructional Systems Development (ISD) and are usually referred to as "models." Instructional management and instructional systems are recognized for their business and military values in managing human behavior.

Yeaman contends that the heritage of information theory and the systems approach is problematic to educational technology. He cites Noble (1991):

> The goal of education is neither the engineering of learning as an end in itself nor the production of cognitive components or technical skills for technological infrastructure of the information age; rather it is the cultivation of human beings, through an encouragement of a deep self-understanding along with an understanding of and participation in the world. The best schools are those that are personalized, that are organized as communities of teachers, students and parents who are fully engaged, who understand why they are learning and teaching, and who together construct a rich interdisciplinary curriculum, a nurturing, attentive pedagogy, and a sense of worldly commitment and care (p. 190).

Yeaman concludes that:

> There are severe problems with the univocal meaning of modern educational technology in a democratic society: it casts aside the epistemological dimensions of the social context as power relations; the cultural context of stereotypes; the varying interpretations of readers and viewers; the multiplicity of voices, messages, languages; and the choice of media as ways of representing and shaping thought. . . . By following and perpetuating the grand myth of technological and scientific progress, the modern profession of educational technology will neglect its ethical obligation to every human being (1994, p. 22).

Communicating the gap between positivist educational technology tradition and emancipatory pedagogy, Anderson (1994, p. 30) looks to Foucault's notions of the "microphysics of power," "docile bodies," and "the instruments of training." The microphysics of power pays great attention to how things should be done. Rather than letting workers do activities in their own way, power holders devise procedures for doing specific activities. These procedures set standards and become part of what a worker must know, eventually shaping most people into obedient workers or docile bodies. For Foucault, docile bodies cannot be ethical because they have lost the will to make informed decisions. Anderson (1994) notes that training people to perform tasks effectively and efficiently is a product of the Enlightenment, the Age of Reason. She points out that three instruments of training evolved from the eighteenth-century European legal, military, and religious cultures: hierarchical observation, normalizing judgment, and the examination.

In emancipatory pedagogy, Anderson notes the use of Paulo Freire's work advocating critical literacy projects, in which "people learn how to describe the conditions they experience, how to represent these conditions to others, and how to actively participate in redescribing their condition. . . . Rather than learning by acquiring facts, they learn by constructing their situation in dialogue with others" (1994, p. 31). People are encouraged to create descriptive and explanatory texts that acknowledge their individual and community interest to arrive at a greater understanding of their own agency. Group action on a specific shared problem builds group solidarity; people gain and lend one another support, and also practice expressing, defending, and exchanging their ideas (1994).

Damarin (1994) expresses concern for equity understood as measurable equal opportunity for all persons (related to gender, class, native language, and learning or other disabilities) to enjoy a full education and its benefits. Today the idea of educational equity is totally confounded with ideas of scientific progress, national economic interest, and technological supremacy. The equity arguments raised by "radical" reformers have been adopted by the most conservative scientific and business communities, who see in the demand for equal educational outcomes an opportunity to capitalize upon "human resources" from a larger pool of individuals. Already powerful institutions will gain access to knowledgeable persons from all societal subgroups, and equity loses its position as the ethical center of feminist and multiculturalist efforts toward educational reform.

The feminist movement, says Damarin, "is deeply ethical in nature; the questions it raises are those of human relation and right action" (1994). Feminist pedagogy honors the knowledge gained through concrete experience and values multiple lines of connectedness among knowledge communities. It acknowledges, values, and nourishes the agency and authority of individuals as freethinkers who are capable of negotiating new relationships with knowledge and with each other. She cites two basic assumptions that are at the foundation of feminist ethics: (1) women and their values are of profound moral significance in and of themselves, and (2) social institutions and practices have encouraged discrimination against women and suppression of their moral views.

Summarizing her views for instructional designers and developers whose ethics are rooted in the return of persons to the educational setting (that is, teachers in caring relationships with students), Damarin (1994) suggests the usefulness of methods models and materials that could serve as resources for teachers to develop strategies for insight and resistance toward the sexist and racist construction of classroom environments.

Responding to the authors in this issue, Jamison (1994) writes that in her scholarly work, teaching, and practice as an educational technologist, critical theory has helped her challenge the mainstream history and foundations of educational communications and technology:

> I have discovered that the field is not merely a product of industrial progress, but also of the technocratic mindset that assists the current of postindustrial society. . . . I have found that the field and its ideology are most likely the result of societies (including governments of other nations who seek Western intervention) forging relationships with institutions, businesses, and industries that promote an overwhelming reliance on technical systems and artifacts (1994, p. 66).

In the last decades, many societies have increased their reliance on Western commercial, industrial, and technical developments. Therefore, Jamison suggests,

> For educational technology to be responsible in assisting societies, they would be wise to (1) examine the sociopolitical beliefs and practices embodied in the philosophies of their instructional plans, systems and products, and (2) develop a responsible stance toward technology (both discourse and artifact). This requires more than just scientific examination of the development and implementation of instructional and technical systems . . . it requires criticism as an alternative mode of inquiry (1994, p. 66).

Further, Jamison (1994) questions whether educational technology can transgress its biases to reframe its theory and practices in ways that are less oppressive, if societies and educational institutions do not also reconceptualize their views of learning and instruction.

REFRAMING THE BOUNDARIES OF DISCUSSION

The discussion among those advocating mainstream and those advocating critical, feminist, and postmodernist positions can be summarized as follows:

Educational technology, as it developed, did so within a system and structure that defined its client as organizational units [military, industrial, institutional] within the larger system. The more recent critical approaches wish to redefine the individual learner as the client and to define the learners' needs in humanistic rather than instrumental terms. The two visions contemplate different worlds both in the present and for the future (Briggs 1991).

The mainstream perspective has established a strong technical framework for the field. However, one author expresses critics' fear that the systems approach will destroy itself by the weight and number of its own component procedures (Richey 1993). Another writes that present skills are inadequate and incomplete for facing the many coming challenges—that the current educational technology paradigm has not achieved, and will not see, widespread application in public education (Gustafson 1993).

Critical theorists and feminist scholars help us to see both the enabling and the constraining aspects of the mainstream perspective. They have begun to establish a framework with which to question the root interests, assumptions, and approaches on which educational technology has been developing. However, the field remains tilted toward a top-down technical perspective. Other perspectives must be considered, and alternative visions must be conceptualized.

The final section of this paper extends the discussion of pressure for change on educational technology framed by concern for its methods and procedures, its range of applicability, and its ability to serve the interests and purposes of individuals (i.e., teachers and students) as well as the organizational clients it now serves. The purpose of the discussion is to point to opportunities intended to provoke further thought and action. The section addresses how we educational technologists might educate *ourselves* to reframe our thinking about what we do, proposing critical examination of existing practices, suggesting tools for considering other perspectives, and inviting the conceptualization of alternate visions.

INCREASING THE PRESSURE FOR CHANGE

Critical Examination

As many, if not most, potential educational technologists learn about the field of Educational Technology through graduate programs in higher education, this is a place to begin. Educational technology might be characterized by its responsiveness to the narrowly functional market demands of industrial and corporate sponsorship for whom knowledge is a commodity (Becher 1989). We should analyze educational technology programs of study to understand how, in descending from systems science, the models and metaphors in use tend to reinforce the top-down management point of view and reflect business and military values in managing human behavior (Yeaman 1994). These values may prevent educational technologists from being responsive to a range of disciplines in which individuals' freedom and ability to question established values and challenge received orthodoxies are developed as an essential ingredient of any society aspiring to virtues of participatory democracy. Instructors of educational technology should examine our courses to analyze whether the convergent instructional design and development models being taught are responsive to the variety and idiosyncrasy of all that count as legitimate forms of intellectual endeavor.

Educational technology affords opportunities to work in many domains, that is, academic disciplines in higher education, K-12 education, health, business, industry, and government.

Each domain orders and interprets the world according to different constructs and systems of relevance. Each educational or training setting provides a host of contributing forces and factors that will affect the development of an educational design. Each client will have unique circumstances, contexts, and potentials. Therefore, it is important that educational technologists be able to go beyond generalized prescriptions to discover and develop the unique potential of particular educational contexts.

Current courses in educational technology that reflect the mainstream practice of the field propose methods and models that reduce complex issues in ways that can be mechanistic and overly simplistic. The approach is often linear, and its application lacks flexibility (Richey 1993). Courses in instructional design and development give much attention to rule-governed processes and fixed-decision procedures as templates for professional practice. Goal orientation, rule, and structure may increase the comfort level of novice educational technologists. But they may also suppress suppleness of thought rather than exercise the use of the insight and imagination required to understand, negotiate, and develop designs for diverse learning contexts. The thoughtful application of a few rudimentary tools will be more effective than the mechanical application of a template or a preconceived plan, as it allows the design/development team to be responsive to the vicissitudes of client and learner/user intentions.

Tools. Preconceived notions of what is important in an educational setting may inhibit careful attention to dynamics of context, alertness to values implicit in language used by clients, or concern for unspoken needs and desires of learner/users. In-depth training in qualitative research methods and ethnography offer flexible possibilities for understanding the constructs and systems of relevance that members of an educational field use to make sense of their world. Asking questions, listening to what is spoken and for what remains unspoken, and observing and learning the language and the culture of the content area are key parts of exploration. Careful observation allows the instructional designer to perceive what makes a situation unique; provides developers with clues to inherent values and concepts that might otherwise be left undisclosed; and illuminates existing and perhaps hidden or undervalued capabilities, resources, and talents. These methods provide an effective means for documenting educational purposes and intentions from the perspectives of both teachers and students.

Other Perspectives

While science currently provides the ground for research and practice in educational technology, science is a special frame of meaning whose language reflects its own internally consistent interpretive practices. It is important to remain aware of the distinctiveness of scientific knowing and the limited character of the conclusions that can issue from that distinctiveness (Smith 1982). Additional perspectives should also be considered.

Educational technology may learn from inquirers in many educational fields who open perspectives on what it is possible to know and how it is possible to know it in other ways from that of science. Jensen (1964) suggests that borrowing and reformulating concepts and processes from other fields and disciplines involves determining which have investigated phenomena inherent to our problems of practice. What do a field's practitioners investigate? How do they approach their problems of practice? What phenomena are inherent in this kind of problem of practice? By examining their concepts, methods, and presentation of research findings, we can translate them in ways useful to our purposes.

We should look to other fields of education where iterative design is very much the norm, such as landscape architecture, urban planning, and architecture. In these fields, concern for various stakeholders and social, political, aesthetic, kinesthetic, economic, and environmental contexts are inseparable from the design process (Alexander 1977, 1979; Halprin 1969; Lynch and Hack 1988; Spirn 1984).

We may learn from disciplines in the arts and humanities (where personal connection to the object of study is valued) to develop instructional materials that allow for prior knowledge and intentions of both students and teachers, and that stimulate ingenuity and create opportunities for connected learning. We can consider and develop learning outcomes that go beyond compliance with pre-ordinate objectives to foster the idiosyncratic response.

For example, we may learn from Susan Stewart's (1979) exploration of the "labyrinthian" relationships between common sense and nonsense within a context of the social manufacture of order and disorder, and the uses of incongruity in learning and change. How is it, she asks, that starting from the same place (if we are ever in the same place) and using a few simple tools and operations, we can arrive at radically and idiosyncratically different places? We may also learn from conceptual poet and art critic David Antin (1984), who explores the nature of language, the engagement of the mind, and the ways in which we come to understand things. How is it, Antin asks, that starting from different places and experiences, traveling by different pathways and at different paces, we can come to common knowing?

We may learn how to create new forms from artists who clarify and intensify in their artworks what belongs to everyday experience (Dewey 1934); who explore a variety of media for their form-giving and thought-shaping qualities; who cultivate periods of resistance and tension for their potential to induce reflection; and who work to deliberately and systematically increase art's range of meaning (Eco 1989).

As new educational perspectives and more appropriate procedures to support human agency increase our range of potential applications, evaluation criteria and methods for programs and products should be developed to account for these possibilities. Becher's (1989) study of academic disciplines suggests that it is inappropriate to lump together, for purposes of efficiency and accountability, methods developed for use by historical purposes of the field, and to suppose that they can be applied with impartiality across the whole range of academic endeavor. Becher (1989) cautions against using evaluation criteria that favor simple and uncontentious measures as against complex and contestable judgment, or those that view disciplines in terms that are too simple to match the realities of attitudes and activities within disciplines. Critical methods can lead to a more complex and particularistic view of an educational situation when aimed at the illumination of complexities rather than their reduction, at the factors and qualities that make situations unique as well as general (Eisner 1985). Rather than measurement against pre-ordinate objectives, criticism can identify the "idea" embodied in the "work" and assess the adequacy of its embodiment (Danto 1990). These views can challenge our thinking about evaluation, and additional perspectives can be sought.

We can seek models for development and change other than industrial and instrumental models. Educationist models, feminism, and transformative and emancipatory learning provide language with which to describe alternate ways to think about development and change, to explain our relationship to contemporary society, and to focus and direct our energies (Fay 1977; Bunch 1987; Freire 1992; Mezirow 1991).

Conceptualizing Other Perspectives

If educational technology is going to play a more significant role in public and higher education, Becher's suggestion of a horticultural analogy is more appropriate than an industrial one in the advancement of learning:

> A market garden is successful insofar as it cultivates a variety of produce to meet its clients' disparate needs. To drive a bulldozer through it in the interests of greater efficiency and higher productivity makes sense only if one wishes to produce a cornfield. Corn grows easily, but too assiduous a concentration on producing it will—as we now know to our cost—create a massive and useless surplus of one particular commodity and a corresponding scarcity of those whose cultivation, though beneficial in its own right, happens to be more demanding, more labor intensive, and generally less easy to govern (1989, p. 166).

Our social and political life is taking on new and broader dimensions that involve making choices and choosing directions, not only for oneself but for whole societies. This means taking positions; proposing or supporting particular plans, programs, and perspectives when you believe you are right; and taking sides and conflicting with people over issues that are not purely technical questions but involve actual choices and principled decisions (Boggs and Boggs 1974). In educational technology we take responsibility for those decisions by deciding what should and should not be done, what should not and should be produced, and in whose interests. We can take positions by which we and others establish frameworks and within which we can grapple with fundamental issues.

As educational technologists we may brush off our responsibility with complaints about client demands, the government, or the system, as if the system were somewhere outside ourselves. This is a convenient fiction to help us evade the fact that agents and systems (disciplines, professions, and institutions) are mutually constituted; the system functions through values, structures, and institutions of which everyone is a part and which everyone keeps in operation.

Educational technologists must persist in constructing bold, speculative, and imaginative alternatives to current theory and practice based on different assumptions and values; presenting clear analysis of each issue to show how it connects to other problems; drawing out the consequences of our theories and suggesting general directions for change; and presenting these perspectives in the "public space" of our professional journals and conferences where they can be analyzed and challenged (Bunch 1987). We must seek frameworks that acknowledge, as the technical framework does not, the social, political, emotional, moral, imaginative, and aesthetic complexity of human interaction with the world.

ACKNOWLEDGMENTS

I would like to thank Roger Hiemstra for his thoughtful reading and comments on a recent draft of this paper, and Emily Roberts, John Briggs, and Jane Blinns for their comments on an earlier draft.

REFERENCES

Starred (*) items appeared in the February 1993 and 1994 issues of *Educational Technology*.

Alexander, C. (1977). *A pattern language*. New York: Oxford University Press.

Alexander, C. (1979). *The timeless way of building*. New York: Oxford University Press.

*Anderson, J. (1994). The rite of right or the right of rite: Moving toward an ethics of technological empowerment. *Educational Technology 34*(2), 29-34.

Antin, D. (1984). *Tuning*. New York: New Directions Publishing.

Association for Educational Communications and Technology Task Force on Definition and Terminology. (1977). *Educational technology: Definition and glossary of terms*, Vol. 1. Washington, DC: AECT.

Becher, T. (1989). *Academic tribes and territories: Intellectual enquiry and the cultures of disciplines*. Bristol, PA: Society for Research into Higher Education and Open University Press.

Boggs, J., and Boggs, G. L. (1974). *Revolution and evolution in the twentieth century*. New York: Monthly Review Press.

Briggs, John. (1991, June 16). Personal communication.

Bunch, C. (1987). *Passionate politics: Feminist theory in action*. New York: St. Martin's Press.

Critical theory, cultural analysis . . . (1994). *Educational Technology 33*(2). [Special issue].

*Damarin, S. K. (1994). Equity, caring and beyond: Can feminist ethics inform educational technology? *Educational Technology 34*(2), 34-40.

Danto, A. (1990). *Encounters and reflections*. New York: Farrar, Strauss & Giroux.

Dewey, J. (1980). *Art as experience.* New York: Perigee Books. (Original work published 1934)

*Dick, W. (1993). Enhanced ISD: A response to changing environments for learning and performance. *Educational Technology 33*(2), 12-16.

Dillard, A. (1982). *Living by fiction.* New York: Harper & Row.

Eco, U. (1989). *The open work.* (Anna Cancogni, trans.). Cambridge, MA: Harvard University Press.

Eisner, E. W. (1985). *The educational imagination: On the design and evaluation of school programs.* New York: Macmillan.

The ethical position of educational technology in society. (1994). *Educational Technology 34*(2). [Special issue].

Fay, Brian. (1977). How people change themselves: The relation between critical theory and its audience. In *Political theory and praxis: New perspectives,* ed. Terrance Ball (Minneapolis, MN: University of Minnesota Press), 200-33.

Freire, P. (1992). *Pedagogy of the oppressed.* (Myra Bergman Ramos, trans.). New York: Continuum.

*Gustafson, K. L. (1993). Instructional design fundamentals: Clouds on the horizon. *Educational Technology 32*(2), 27-36.

Halprin, L. (1969). *RSVP cycles: Creative processes in the human environment.* New York: George Braziller.

*Hlynka, D. (1994). Glossary of terms. *Educational Technology 34*(2), 14-15.

*Jamison, P. K. (1994). The struggle for critical discourse: Reflections on the possibilities of critical theory for educational technology. *Educational Technology 34*(2), 66-69.

Jensen, G. (1964). How adult education borrows and reformulates knowledge of other disciplines. In *Adult education: Outlines of an emerging field of university study.* Ed. G. Jensen, A. A. Liveright, and W. Hallenbeck. Washington, DC: Adult Education Association of the U.S.A., pp. 105-11.

Lynch, K., and Hack, G. (1988). *Site planning.* Cambridge, MA: MIT Press.

Mezirow, J. (1991). *Transformative dimensions of adult learning.* San Francisco: Jossey-Bass.

Noble, D. D. (1991). *The classroom arsenal: Military research, information technology, and public education.* Bristol, PA: Falmer Press.

*Richey, R. C. (1993) Instructional design theory and a changing field. *Educational Technology 33*(2), 16-21.

Schon, D. (1983). *The reflective practitioner: How professionals think in action.* New York: Basic Books.

Seels, Barbara. (1994). Instructional design fundamentals: A review and reconsideration. *Educational Technology 33*(2). [Special issue].

Shannon, C. E., and Weaver, W. (1949). *The mathematical theory of communication.* Urbana, IL: University of Illinois Press.

Smith, H. (1982). *Beyond the post-modern mind.* New York: Crossroads Publishing.

Spirn, A. W. (1984). *The granite garden.* New York: Basic Books.

Stewart, S. (1979). *Nonsense: Aspects of intertextuality in folklore and literature.* Baltimore, MD: Johns Hopkins University Press.

von Bertalanffy, L. (1968). *General systems theory: Foundations, development, applications.* New York: George Braziller.

*Wager, W. W. (1993). Instructional systems fundamentals: Pressures to change. *Educational Technology 33*(2), 8-12.

*Yeaman, A. J. (1994). Deconstructing modern educational technology. *Educational Technology 34*(2), 15-24.

*Yeaman, A. J., Koetting, J. R., and Nichols, R. G. (1994). Critical theory, cultural analysis, and the ethics of educational technology as social responsibility. *Educational Technology 34*(2), 5-13.

The Discourse on Technology

Andrew R. J. Yeaman
Consultant, Westminster, Colorado

INTRODUCTION

Technology is being taken for granted. Graduate students are unable to explain their dogmatic computerism. They write sentences like these in their papers:

"Computers are the future of education."

"Students need to be connected with the technological age in order to succeed in our society."

"By 2010, 90 percent of all jobs will be computer dependent."

This chapter looks at technology as a current professional issue and suggests strategies of interpretation from anthropology, history, sociology, and the humanities that will promote understanding.

INCLINATION AND INSTITUTION

> *Here, I would like to recount a little story so beautiful I fear it may well be true. It encompasses all the constraints of discourse: those limiting its powers, those controlling its chance appearances and those which select from among speaking subjects.*
>
> Foucault 1972, p. 225

At the end of spring semester I listened as a capable graduate student gave a final report on a term project. The class was on the Management of Information and Learning Technology Programs. The student explained, like many others in the management class, that at the beginning of the term the project had started out as writing a policies and procedures manual. The work site was a school computer lab. In compiling the background literature it became apparent that computer labs were not the best way of setting up educational computers because they are needed all around the school. The project had taken this turn and become a position paper. I nodded because it was quite a reasonable development. The student concluded, "My big realization was that technology is what can drive educational reform. If we just got the computers in there, it might happen naturally."

There was no explanation beyond Information Age idealism, but as the next student began speaking, I thought to myself about how computerization enabling schools to change might not be quite as naïve as it seems. There is social power in communication technologies, and Innis (1951) shows that new regimes can assert themselves effectively through their communications. Innis's theorizing is substantial, has withstood half a century, and is cited by Postman (1992, pp. 9-20) and Schrage (1990, pp. 18-23).

Politics and new media reweave cultural fabric along the warp of space and the woof of time. An example of social power being legitimated by authorized media is the 1930s efforts to cause Germans to buy radios, which, in part, enabled the Nazis to triumph through their broadcasts (Ellul 1990, p. 277). It is not only language, in a wide sense, that conquerors impose, but also limits on the thoughts that can be expressed and the actions that can be performed. However, in the 1950s radio assisted in the liberation of Algeria from its status as a French colony (Fanon 1965). In spite of technological media being inconsistent in direction, moving either away from freedom or toward freedom, computerization could redefine what messages are permissible in schools. Computerization could regulate behavior appropriate to sustaining a particular reform.

There are already some major changes from technology in education. Through the 1970s teachers and professors were expected to provide their own typewriters. It was the same in earlier decades although there may have been relatively more assistance with typing and duplicating. In the 1990s computers are becoming standard equipment, particularly for word processing. Tasks previously considered as clerical are now delegated to professionals. There is an unwritten expectation that all documents will be word processed. This applies from an instructor's class assignment sheet to a student's term paper to a school librarian's annual report. There may be not so much a shortage of supplies in education as a general abundance, and computerization fits into cultural beliefs about education and training.

DÉJÀ VU

When I began writing this chapter, the first draft title was "Devolution" after the clichéd science fiction plot. It was meant figuratively. As my writing took shape out of the accumulated notes, the instructional systems approach of the 1960s and 1970s first appeared as an achievement that had been allowed to slip away. There was a decade or two of rapid progress, but severe problems were not solved and remain present. These questions came back to me:

Do you have a feeling of déjà vu about the current situation in education? If so, then you were around during the latter part of the 1950s and the decade of the 1960s. Public criticism and Soviet scientific success combined to put pressure on the schools to improve instructional effectiveness and academic standards. We in instructional technology knew we had methods and techniques to do the job. The 1950s saw the teaching of entire courses by television and then by film. The emergence of the programmed instruction movement gave us great confidence in our ability to design effective and replicable instruction—and isn't that what America needed more than a good five-cent cigar? (Heinich 1984, 1995, p. 67).

In matching up what is said with what is done, I was fulfilling Rob Branch's request to be postmodern and poststructural. I repeatedly found myself at the crossroads of culture where people neither say what they mean nor mean what they say. Those are the grounds visited by Derrida's *Of Grammatology* (1967, 1976) and Lyotard's *Postmodern Condition* (1979, 1984). Words and actions disintegrate at that theoretical junction:

- The reflexive poststructural insight is that the meanings that are discovered may be imported with the method of analysis.

- The reflexive postmodern insight is that the most important human problems, such as getting people to treat each other decently, will not be solved by science and technology.

When systems development is applied not only to instruction but also to the reform of whole education institutions, much of the design work is well supported, but the hand-waving about the cultural and social aspects is somewhat uncharacteristic (Yeaman 1995, p. 75). Discussions of technological change are enthusiastic but seldom consider a wide range of what is and what is not possible or what is and what is not desirable. It is ironic that professors have perhaps been unable or unwilling to provide practitioners with *research* skills useful in creating products and services (see also Campbell and Stanley 1963, p. 21; Gibson 1986, pp. 162-65; and Hollingsworth 1994). While the communication problems between academics and the real world are hard to overcome, there is a need for instructors, designers, and managers to be involved in any kind of institutional reconfiguring. There is insufficient attention to action research or participatory research, and that neglect hints at the academy seeing itself as the ultimate source of knowledge.

Despite concern for people, and especially in regard to cognition and achievement, there is almost no contact by technologists with social theories applicable to this field. Meanings are not questioned for being most appropriate to the established point of view. There is a leaning away from artistry and toward bureaucracy. Much of the time the significance of things is accepted as given on the surface. Beyond the Information Age idealism mentioned earlier, a historical and theoretical base is necessary for understanding educational reform and technology.

INTERPRETATION

One qualitative theory available comes from cultural anthropology and requires interpreting the causal web by viewing it as a text:

> To see social institutions, social customs, social changes as in some sense "readable" is to alter our whole sense of what such interpretation is and shift it toward modes of thought rather more familiar to the translator, the exegete, or the iconographer than to the test giver, the factor analyst, or the pollster (Geertz 1983, p. 31).

Geertz demonstrates the validity of the interpretive approach in explaining everyday events (1973, pp. 144-46). Hindu and Islamic religions interacted with the modernization of Java in the early 1950s to create conflict around the funeral of a boy in a village (pp. 146-69). A traditionalist in his 80s complained, "You can't even die any more but what it becomes a political problem" (p. 156). The incident shows how individuals and their personalities operate inside both their culture and their social system:

> On the one level there is the framework of beliefs, expressive symbols, and values in terms of which individuals define their world, express their feelings, and make their judgments; on the other level there is the ongoing process of interactive behavior, whose persistent form we call social structure. Culture is the fabric of meaning in terms of which human beings interpret their experience and guide their action; social structure is the form that action takes, the actually existing network of social relations (Geertz 1973, pp. 144-45).

In the web of significance these three aspects are linked without separation: individuals, cultural meaning, and social function. Making sense of daily experiences is connected with personal values and with the power of social stability (Geertz 1973, p. 169). When there is an incongruous situation, such as that narrated by the student at the start of this chapter or the one described by Heinich (1984, 1995), the call for social change is part of the web. Following Foucault (1972), technology can be identified as a discourse: "The 'self-evident' and 'commonsensical' are what have the privilege of unnoticed power" (Bové 1990, p. 54).

INTERPRETING THE DISCOURSE

A pattern of beliefs emerges from looking at education over the last century. There are repeated promises and hopes about the newest communication media solving the perceived problems. In the early years there was official encouragement (see Sidebar 1).

In 1923 the NEA began its Department of Visual Education due to the interest in slides, films, and visual aids in general:

> Such exotic devices as football games, soap models, slides and films, and teaching machines, however, were only on the outer fringes of what was known as the methods craze. What claimed the attention, if not necessarily the following, of the pedagogical world was a body of approaches often referred to generically as new or modern methods (Krug 1969, p. 164).

The visual educators allied their method with the Progressive Movement. In 1928, Anna Verona Dorris promised that visual instruction will provide natural learning (p. v). The latest followers of this tradition, Roger Schank and Chip Cleary, argue for computer technology because it provides natural learning (1995, p. 72). The visual literacy approach, in contrast, sees little that is natural and much that is cultural in communication and looks for the acquisition of strategies and competencies (Cochran, Younghouse, Sorflaten, and Molek, 1980;[1] Moore and Dwyer 1994).

The audiovisual and information technology industry is always interested in the vast amounts of money spent on education, year after year. From 1913 to 1918 Thomas Edison was one of the first producers of educational films (Carlson 1992). Chris Whittle broadcast news television into schools for no fee and drew revenue from commercials (De Vaney 1994). Whittle subsequently sold Channel One and started Edison Schools (Smith 1994).

There are demands for the improvement of the schools, decade after decade, editor after editor, politician after politician, professor after professor, entrepreneur after entrepreneur. In 1913, George Horace Lorimer used part of his editorial column in *The Saturday Evening Post* to address the possible contribution of Thomas Edison and John Dewey to educational motion pictures:

> How shall a child be educated? No other public question is as important as that. None is more earnestly or extensively debated. That the inherited school system is terribly faulty no one now seriously disputes. The country fairly bubbles with impatience to see it radically improved (p. 26).

The words of Sidebar 2 could come from any time in this century. In the 1990s, Dewey might be replaced by E. D. Hirsch, Jr., and Edison by Bill Gates. Each decade has seen the development of new communication media and advocacy for their use for education and training. The application of these media developments and refinements is not simply from the intent to make money on the educational market. People hope each new medium will answer the latest criticisms of schooling. These beliefs are usually voiced by politicians and appear

---

SIDEBAR 1

Educational Use of Motion Pictures
William H. Dudley
Organization for Visual Education
Department of the Interior: Bureau of Education Bulletin 1921, no. 17, p. 5

The man of vision and mental reach today is thinking of the motion picture in terms of service to education, to commerce and industry, to science and art, to religion and philanthropy; in short of benefit to humanity.

Speaking of the educational value of films, President Emeritus Eliot, of Harvard, says: "The moving picture is a valuable means of instruction, and all our school systems ought to seize upon it."

"The time is at hand when moving pictures will be as much an adjunct of any properly equipped school as textbooks," writes Supt. Hyatt, of California.

"Indeed, the educator must use it," says Henry W. Lanier, "for at the present time film manufacturers are educating about 5,000,000 children a day along more or less undesirable lines."

We may safely assert that we have even now passed beyond the propaganda stage. It is no longer a question of worth while, but rather one of the ways and means to an end now recognized by leading educators as a most worthy and fruitful one. It is not a question of the great possibilities or the practicability of such a service; not a discussion of theories, or of some ultimate ideal for a remote future; we are past that period in thought and largely in action. It is now a question of how to realize in practice, and with the greatest efficiency and economy, the fullness of vision we already behold.

SIDEBAR 2

George Horace Lorimer used part of his editorial column in *The Saturday Evening Post* to address the possible contribution of Thomas Edison and John Dewey to educational motion pictures (October 11, 1913, p. 26):

Poverty-Stricken Schools

How shall a child be educated? No other public question is as important as that. None is more earnestly or extensively debated. That the inherited school system is terribly faulty no one now seriously disputes. The country fairly bubbles with impatience to see it radically improved.

In the United States the public attempts to educate some eighteen million children—with an unhappy consciousness that it is doing the work on the whole very faultily and with a growing anxiety to do it much better; but the public is poverty-stricken.

Broadly speaking; to keep the old system going takes its last dollar. It is like the farmer who sees clearly that he can never make more than a bare living unless he fertilizes, buys efficient machinery and gets better-bred stock: yet he cannot for the life of him scrape up a spare dollar for lime, a sulky plow or a thoroughbred cow.

For example, some distinguished pedagogues recently visited West Orange to see Mr. Edison's exhibition of educational moving pictures. The inventor thinks primary education may be revolutionized by this means. The pedagogues were much impressed, and Professor Dewey remarked regretfully upon "the immense advantage a great commercial enterprise has over the greatest of our educational institutions in the matter of systematic experimenting with a new proposal before putting it into general practice. . . . Where is there a school system having at command a sum of money with which to investigate and perfect a scheme experimentally before putting it into general option?"

The Steel Trust, the oil companies, and a thousand and one business concerns do that very thing day in and day out as a matter of course because they know it pays in the end. But the poor out-at-elbows public has not a dollar for experimental investigation in education.

with the encouragement of newspapers, magazines, radio, and television. News editors see the state of schooling as a sacred cow. It remains a perpetual topic because few citizens positively like school, educators are of somewhat low status, and the universal key to improving the profession is to get rid of the bad teachers.

In 1995, Schank and Cleary want to revolutionize schools with their Institute for Learning Sciences software:

Clearly, the schools are a mess. Today's schools are organized around yesterday's ideas, yesterday's needs, and yesterday's resources (and they were not even doing very well yesterday) (p. ix).

In 1945, Edgar Dale concluded:

The author hopes that as you have read this book, as you have discussed the teaching problems with your colleagues and your instructor, you have not only gained some insight into the use of audiovisual materials in instruction, but you have also acquired a sense of the urgency of improving our schools today (p. 530).

In 1996, AECT describes itself in the call for proposals for the 1997 Convention:

The only national and international professional organization dedicated to the improvement of instruction through the full range of media and instructional technology. Its purpose is to enhance the professional skills of its members and to assist them in dealing effectively with the advances in technology (p. 121).

The pattern detected here shows continual desire for a technological fix in education[2] but no lasting solution. New teaching methods accompany new media as if there were no corresponding need to understand how representation works, as if the same facts were obvious to all viewers. Providing educational supplies from textbooks to online services is business. Complaints about education are heard every day, as often as one hears "Good morning," but demands for improvement offer cultural meaning in providing faith in progress, and a social function in encouraging hard work toward a better life in the future (Lemert 1993, pp. 208-10; Ritzer 1993; Weber 1905, 1993). All of this seems to have been known 100 years ago when the discovery of radium caused physics to be rethought. It was publicly lamented that everyone through the 1890s had been educated with ignorance[3] (Adams 1918, 1995).

DISCONTINUITY AND CONTINUITY

Technology continues into the present from the past, but the way educational technologists think about their professional work has changed. Those developments are reflected by successive formal definitions (Januszewski 1994). Emphasis has shifted from media categories to instructional techniques and theories as domains (Seels and Richey 1994, pp. 8-9). Seels and Richey present the most recent statement from the AECT Committee on Definition and Terminology (p. 10): "Instructional Technology is the theory and practice of design, development, utilization, management and evaluation of processes and resources for learning."

Distinctions made two decades ago between instructional technology and technology in education as subsets of educational technology have faded (Seels and Richey 1994, pp. 4-5). By 1988 the Office of Technology Assessment (OTA) had published this finding: "In the early 1980s only a handful of States were actively involved in educational technology" (p. 25). Despite Seels and Richey's concern for encouraging diversity and creativity (1994, pp. 5-6), without discussion or argument there has been a national redefinition of educational technology, educational media, and educational computers as *technology*. An older idea has returned. Delivering instruction with talk, textbooks, blackboards, and assignment sheets is less desirable at present because technology is considered more effective. Although technology indicates electronic media such as computers and videos, the return to the earlier meaning shows that educational technology is reverting from instructional systems to audiovisual aids. Information technology in learning situations has been redefined as being no different from educational technology. The regression to the long-obsolete concept of audiovisual aids is concealed by the step forward in adopting the rhetorical power of technology as *computers*. By 1995 the rhetoric[4] of "only" was extended in *Teachers & Technology*: "Only 6 percent of elementary and 3 percent of secondary schools have a full-time, school-level computer coordinator for technical support" (OTA 1995, p. 19).

In the 1990s there is rivalry between media specialists, librarians, technology specialists, computer coordinators, computer teachers, math and science teachers, and technicians for control of this general area of work in education. The boundary dispute is enabled by rhetorical strategies surrounding the definition of technology. It became clear when a library-media intern showed me an announcement for a position opening. I realized that any of these professionals can have a line in their job description about managing a Novell local area network, although the meaning of "keeping the LAN running" varies from place to place.

Who does what is a sociological matter. Present-day sociologists look for the interrelatedness of cultural practices and products. This can be understood through Abbott's theorizing on professions (1988). Abbott presents a competition model to account for the struggle between professions to control tasks. The boundaries distinguishing professions will change when different occupational groups claim jurisdiction over diagnosis, inferential interpretation, and treatment of problems. Although conflict over a professional boundary is always settled in a unique way, the struggle takes place in the legal world of legislatures and courts, the public world of media representation and popular opinion, and the actual work site of professional practice. Rather than an empire-building mentality of expansion, boundaries are redefined by culture and social structures.

Gieryn condenses the factors into this list (1995, p. 410):

- Technological changes.
- Changes in organizational settings such as bureaucratization.
- Co-optation of professions by external powers.
- Shifting values that legitimate (or not) jurisdictional claims.

- The growth of modern universities as sites for credentialing and the creation of new knowledge.

Jurisdiction is predicted for the profession with the national association best at reaching the public and its members through public relations and publications (Abbott 1988). The actions of the American Association of School Librarians (AASL), the Association for the Advancement of Computing in Education (AACE), the Association for Educational Communications and Technology (AECT), the International Society for Technology in Education (ISTE), and their affiliates will continue to be significant in publishing monthly magazines for practitioners and research journals for professors; in organizing national conferences; and in advising local, state, and national government agencies about issues of individual certification and institutional accreditation.

INDIVIDUALS AND CONTEXTS

If there is the incompetence of disorganization, there is also the tyranny of planners.

Adams 1988, p. 3

Attending school may be generally unpopular, much like going to the dentist. There is an assumption that one needs to be processed, one needs to be improved, one is deficient, one is unacceptable, one needs to be fixed, and the experience will be intrusive and may be unpleasant. Nevertheless, both schooling and dentistry are socially accepted as being necessary.

As individual personalities, the people who push for major reforms reveal they did not grow up in the conditions they advocate. Creative adults such as Papert (1993) and Schank and Cleary (1995) muse on their unrestrained intellectual powers and forget that they did not willingly learn the basic skills of literacy and numeracy; that their writing, speaking, and thinking are based on internalized discipline. This reflection from the reformers' adult point of view is augmented by political ideals. Consequently, reform movements inspired by visionaries[5] often center on independent study unaware that this is an expression of the cultural myth of individualism. Reformers calling upon the authority of business seek to improve efficiency by increasing the number of students taught by each teacher. The rhetoric of school reform through technology tends to be self-contradictory, with arguments for more individual contact between teachers and children running against arguments for more efficiency due to decreasing the need for teachers. Mass media such as television, radio, electronic mail listservs, and correspondence courses are advocated for distance learning. More tutoring and fewer teachers may be part of the same reform platform, although they tend to cancel out each other.

The profession of education also exerts authority. It is not only the teacher preparation programs of higher education that seek to knock the stars out of the starry-eyed new teachers, but also the teachers and principals in the schools who will not accept the utopianism of "If we all taught the right way (my way) then things would improve." It is relevant to note that the value of the systematic, instructional design approach as a social technology is in the curriculum with instructional procedures being logical, rational, examinable, and modifiable. This approach is not necessarily accompanied by the physical technologies of media delivery hardware. A historical perspective on how projections were made about the present day can be helpful:

Why should the classroom be less automated than the family kitchen? This is the taunt thrown at us by B. F. Skinner of Harvard, a leader in the development of teaching machines. His question is especially relevant in this headlong technological age. By the year 2000 A.D., we are told, our world will be automated beyond the wildest dreams of an H. G. Wells. But by the year 2000 students now in first grade will be no older than the average Phi Delta Kappan is today. Obviously, education must not continue to lag behind by the traditional fifty years (Fry 1964, p. 22).

Thirty years have passed, but there is an ongoing mistaking of educational procedures for physical objects that are merely working as symbolic representations. Barns's 1926 cartoon indicates the beginning of awareness about the interactions[6] between society and technology. The discourse on technology continues like déjà vu:

> By the time the external evidence has been compiled, "proving" that technology integration works and districts are ready to commit to purchases of the appropriate hardware and software, the technology that has been researched may be obsolete and a golden opportunity to use it for current students will have been lost (OTA 1995, p. 15).

Figure 1. Mr. Barns' Own Idea of the Circle [Original caption.]
Illustration credit: Burton A. Barns.

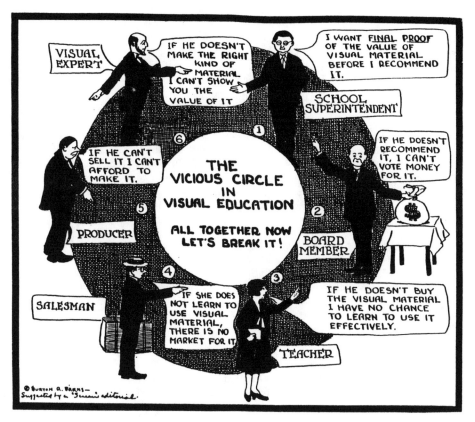

Note. From "United We Stand" by Burton A. Barns, *Educational Screen* 5(5) (September 1926), 396.

Nevertheless, when administrators in the 1990s provide TVs, VCRs, telephone lines, and computer networks they are not always used by teachers and their classes. This is not much different from administrators in the 1920s buying motion picture projectors, stereographs, phonographs, and radios.

A DISCOURSE OF INCONGRUITY?

> *We are all natives now, and everybody else not immediately one of us is an exotic. What looked once to be a matter of finding out whether savages could distinguish fact from fancy now looks to be a matter of finding out how others, across the sea or down the corridor, organize their significative world.*
>
> Geertz 1983, p. 151

A question arises from considering education and technology through the anthropological theory of interpretation: Are there genuine problems or incongruities requiring a technological solution? Schools are not independent but reflect the place and time in which they are situated. Just as school culture is part of local culture, people work in education because they see a role for themselves as part of their society and in assuring cultural continuity. There is a hidden curriculum: "A lesson plan that no one teaches but everyone learns. It consists of the symbolic contours of the social order" (Gerbner 1974, p. 476). Its function is self-contradictory: "The hidden curriculum cultivates the illusion of social reform through education and, at the same time, helps pave the way for the perennial collapse of its achievement" (1974, p. 496).

If there is a dimension of meaningfulness and meaninglessness to continuously improving education, then the uses of technology to instruct may also be ambiguous. There is social power: "Technologically based instruction poses a threat to the base of our present system and the more comprehensive the technological effort, the greater the threat" (Heinich 1970, p. 177). Technology advocates are like Wolcott's principals, who are in a predicament "to present the appearance of change and to provide the stabilizing effects of continuity" (1973, p. 321). Perhaps this evaluation fits many people in education, including the next generation, in being "agents of the rhetoric of change rather than agents of change itself." This empty promise is at the center of the technological fix:

> The tech-fix is the belief that technology can be used to solve all types of problems, even social ones. Belief in progress and the tech-fix has long been used to rationalize inequity: it is only a matter of time until technology extends material benefits to all citizens, regardless of race, sex, class, religion, or nationality (Bush 1983, p. 152).[7]

More questions should be asked: Exactly what is the problem that computers will solve? Why must everyone be trained for an imagined future where they will accept instructions from electronic screens and respond by typing on keyboards? Is this what a historian will write about us one day?

> Somewhere between 1980 and 2030 a point would be reached where computers existed among all classes. It is hardly a coincidence that this diffusion should occur at the exact moment when the developments of the information revolution would demand a greater computerization of labor (Yeaman 1994, p. 71).

Perhaps that historian will conclude that the information revolution was part of the discourse on technology and supported by taken-for-granted computerism.

CONCLUSION

Mr. Dnirgdarg: "Interpretations! You can only form the minds of reasoning animals upon interpretations. What use are facts without interpretations? That's what these boys and girls need. Stick to interpretations!"

Going beyond Dickens's parody of cultural literacy (1854, 1990), we should enjoy the opposite of Mr. Gradgrind's schooling in facts with Mr. Dnirgdarg. I used this to explain interpretation to a class on Research in Information and Learning Technologies. After I went through Mailloux's parable of the Strategic Defense Initiative (1990), a student who had worked for NASA on SDI insisted I had got the facts wrong. I listened and then responded, "You understand my point, exactly. Issues of interpretation may be so severe that sometimes we cannot even agree on what are the facts."

Wired, for example, is a factual magazine that asks experts for interpretations: "Today, educational technology means much more than dim overhead projectors or crackly filmstrips synched with audiotapes" (Pescovitz 1996). Readers of the bottom line learn there will be Mandatory Tech Studies for Teachers by the year 2000 and that the Death of the U.S. Public School System is unlikely, although not everyone agrees.

Maybe I should challenge readers with criticism and resistance through interpretation. "If the information you need is available on the Web and the Net, why are you reading this book?" I had better provide some answers: "The publisher has an established reputation and maintains it by keeping to high standards regarding accuracy, currency, and distinctions between facts and opinions. There is a responsibility to provide reasonable texts from knowledgeable authors. In comparison, there is no social structure upholding the reliability of information on the Web and the Net."

Going beyond the facts, it is possible to develop our own interpretations:

As long as we continue to treat the imaginative as a negative force, we imprison ourselves in a disciplinary construction of the actual. The imaginative, on the other hand, is a precondition of making the impossible possible. It is the source of the impossible whose possibility we are prohibited from addressing (Sosnoski 1995, p. 147).

SIDEBAR 3

Stepford Technology[8]

- A faster way to learn . . . it offers a learning curve you can take at your own speed. It's smart, concise, and fast.
- SOMEWHERE ON THE INTERNET IS THE INFORMATION YOU WANT.
- Putting the world at your students' fingertips.
- Hands-on experience makes learning fun.
- It does all the research. You get all the credit.
- This system is an advancement that finally provides real-time on-line access to vital student information.
- While computers have been fixtures in many schools for more than 15 years, they're only part of the solution. . . . The first group works with computers in active, collaborative pairs. The next group works independently with writing journals, books and manipulatives designed to improve mathematical, language and critical thinking skills. The teacher becomes a **mentor** to the remaining group, working directly with the students.
- Knowing Internet terminology is not vital, but it may save you from an embarrassing moment or help dazzle one of your colleagues.
- EASY. All you have to know is how to read and use a mouse.
- Register students without lines. Fundraising without fumbling through files. Add new classes without adding new instructors.
- Until Now, Surfing the Internet Was No Day at the Beach.
- Teachers can send and retrieve documents, launch and quit applications, view student screens, and "freeze" workstations to grab students' attention. All from the teachers' workstation. . . . You can shutdown and restart computers, lock and unlock applications, and generate student statistics. All with the click of a mouse.
- Teach your students information literacy skills for college, while they're still in grade school. . . . Your students will have a world of resources at their fingertips—from CD-ROMs to on-line access to public libraries and the Internet.
- It Turns Your Classroom Into a Theater for Young Minds.

Consider the contribution of advertising to the discourse on technology. Ellul writes: "Its messages are meant to model life-styles and attitudes, to adapt them to their setting, which is made up of objects like that which is being sold" (1990, p. 351). Think about resisting the puffed up, sugary, meringue words by pulling them out of advertisements and creating a found poem.[9]

NOTES

1.   This foundational review article was also the first to mention deconstruction in the field of educational communications and technology (Cochran and others 1980, p. 261).

2.   An excellent book on this topic in the United Kingdom is *The Technical Fix: Education, Computers and Industry* (Robins and Webster 1989).

3.   "The date was convenient and convenience was truth." Henry Adams wrote his point of view in the third person, and with irony he continued: "He could not deny that the law of the new multiverse explained much that had been most obscure, especially the persistently fiendish treatment of man by man; the perpetual effort of society to establish law, and the perpetual revolt of society against the law it had established" (1918, 1995, p. 433).

4.   The rhetoric is also visual. On the same page is a picture of a computer box with a video display screen. Next to it is a steno book and a pencil mounted on the wall like a fire alarm. There is an accompanying instruction: "In Case of Emergency Break Glass." Possibly these images are digitized clip art. An identical steno book and pencil appears with the same "emergency" joke in a back page advertisement for Action Computers, Inc., published in *ComputorEdge [sic]: Colorado's Free Weekly Computer Magazine* on October 16, 1995. It is worth commenting on a government agency and a business using the same humorous graphic because of the shared assumptions. They reverse the rhetoric of workers in an automated factory contemptuously labeling an axe in a control room with "IN CASE OF COMPUTER FAILURE USE FIRE AXE" (Zuboff 1988, p. 269).

5.   "Followers do not usually have the complete resynthesis produced by the leader. A social movement (a revitalization or reactive movement) results and is aimed at creating a more satisfying culture. Movements vary in degree of success based on the amount of rationality and reality-based planning done by their leaders" (Spindler 1977, p. 87). For further analysis of ideology, see Eagleton (1991) and Geertz (1973, pp. 193-233).

6.   Current theorizing models a network of social actors and artifacts propelled towards finding solutions for problems until the technological frame freezes (Bijker 1995).

7.   Bush gives a graphic example of the tech-fix fallacy: "Jobs, which have always provided men with access to material goods, do not get women out of poverty" (1983, p. 153).

8.   This text is selected from advertisements in *T.H.E. Journal: Technological Horizons in Education* 23(7) (February 1996). As social commentary it is meant neither to diminish the magazine's contribution as a valuable resource nor to mean that readers are unable to read critically for themselves. It is meant to encourage critical reading of the discourse on technology.

9.   This literary technique was used to create the narration for the title track on *Jeff Beck's Guitar Shop* (Beck, Bozzio, and Hymas 1989).

RECOMMENDED READING
ON THE DISCOURSE OF TECHNOLOGY

Belland, J. C., Duncan, J. K., and Deckman, M. (1991). Criticism as a methodology for research in educational technology. In *Paradigms regained: The uses of illuminative, semiotic and post-modern criticism as modes of inquiry in educational technology: A book of readings*, ed. D. Hlynka and J. C. Belland (Englewood Cliffs, NJ: Educational Technology Publications), 151-64.
This chapter describes how the literary and artistic judgments of criticism can be applied to guide inquiry and practice. Six methodical considerations are given:

- Criticism could help explain a technological object or process in terms of the quality of the relationship between its content and its form.

- Criticism could help explain a technological object or process in terms of the relationship among the constituent parts and the whole.

- Criticism may provide insight into the unifying theme(s) and design(s) that help to hold the technological object or process together in all its richness and complexity.

- Criticism may reveal the nature of the intimate experience that a well-informed, sensitive, and reflective individual has with the process or product of educational technology.

- Criticism may reveal the grounds upon which interpretations and judgments of the processes and objects of educational technology may rest as well as the consequences the object or process may entail in human experiences.

- Criticism may serve to synthesize the knowledge derived from disparate research processes into more comprehensive theory.

Damarin, S. K. (1993). Technologies of the individual: Women and subjectivity in the age of information. *Research in Philosophy and Technology 13*, 183-98.
Suzanne Damarin's article is published in a prestigious journal and thoughtfully examines how the technologization of the West is affecting women in particular. It argues that the distinctions between people and machines are becoming blurred not only by computer-mind metaphors but also in the everyday reality of social control. It concludes that without developing a postmodern subjectivity of self-awareness in relation to technology, there is a serious threat that women may cease to exist.

De Vaney, A. (1994). Ethical considerations of visuals in the classroom: African-Americans and Hollywood film. In *Visual literacy: A spectrum of visual learning*, ed. D. M. Moore and F. M. Dwyer (Englewood Cliffs, NJ: Educational Technology Publications), 355-68.
Ann De Vaney relates the production and consumption of mass media images to the presentation of educational visuals. A qualitative analysis of eight films by African American directors reveals insights about how African Americans are portrayed. Another chapter by De Vaney on cultural representation appears in Muffoletto and Knupfer's *Computers in Education* and looks at the best-selling, award-winning educational computer program *Where in the world is Carmen Sandiego?*

Erdman, B. (1990). The closely guided viewer: Form, style, and teaching in the educational film. In *The ideology of images in educational media: Hidden curriculums in the classroom*, ed. E. Ellsworth and M. H. Whatley (New York: Teachers College Press), 27-42.
Fifteen educational films produced between 1930 and 1960 were selected from the American Archives of the Factual Film at Iowa State University. These film lessons were analyzed with formalist methodology and compared with the traditional classroom lesson. As in later work on *Channel One*, published in De Vaney's *Watching Channel One*, Erdman perceives that there is a strong tendency for these productions to be teacher-proof viewing experiences. The current trend in format, illustrated by *CNN Newsroom*, is to enable teachers to choose segments for their instructional purposes.

Hlynka, D. (1991). Applying semiotic theory to educational technology. In *Paradigms regained: The uses of illuminative, semiotic and post-modern criticism as modes of inquiry in educational technology: A book of readings,* ed. D. Hlynka and J. C. Belland (Englewood Cliffs, NJ: Educational Technology Publications), 37-50.
Denis Hlynka's chapter explores how educational technology can be read as a system of signs. This work is founded in literary theory and has colorful examples, such as the Canadian preference for soggy french fries despite modern management studies on the importance of training employees to cook french fries so they are crispy.

Robinson, R. S. (1994). Investigating Channel One: A case study report. In *Watching Channel One: The convergence of students, technology, and private business*, ed. A. De Vaney (Albany, NY: State University of New York Press), 21-41.
Rhonda Robinson reports how she conducted an observation in a junior high school to study how *Channel One* viewing was being implemented. The description is highly effective in giving readers the feeling of actually being there in the school.

Yeaman, A. R. J. (1993). The mythical anxieties of computerization: A Barthesian analysis of a technological myth. In *Computers in education: Social, political, historical perspectives*, ed. R. Muffoletto and N. N. Knupfer (Cresskill, NJ: Hampton Press), 105-28.
This chapter reconsiders the assumption that people are computer-anxious and need to be educated out of computer anxiety. The work was originally reported in *Tech Trends*, expanded into a chapter for Muffoletto and Knupfer's *Computers in Education*, and reprinted in *Education Digest*.

SUGGESTIONS FOR FURTHER READING

Anglin, G. J., ed. (1995). *Instructional technology: Past, present, and future*, 2d ed. Englewood, CO: Libraries Unlimited.

Bowers, C. A. (1988). *The cultural dimensions of educational computing: Understanding the non-neutrality of technology.* New York: Teachers College Press.

De Vaney, A., ed. (1994). *Watching Channel One: The convergence of students, technology, and private business.* Albany, NY: State University of New York Press.

Ellsworth, E., and Whatley, M. H., eds. (1990). *The ideology of images in educational media: Hidden curriculums in the classroom.* New York: Teachers College Press.

Hlynka, D., and Belland, J. C., eds. (1991). *Paradigms regained: The uses of illuminative, semiotic and post-modern criticism as modes of inquiry in educational technology: A book of readings.* Englewood Cliffs, NJ: Educational Technology Publications.

Hlynka, D., and Yeaman, A. R. J. (1992). *Postmodern educational technology* (ERIC Digest No. EDO-IR-92-5; ED 348 042).

Jamison, P. K. (1995). Postmodern possibilities of instructional development. In *Instructional design: The state of the art,* Vol. 3, ed. C. Dills and A. Romiszowski (Englewood Cliffs, NJ: Educational Technology Publications).

Kerr, S., and Taylor, W. D., eds. (1985). *Educational Communications and Technology Journal 33*(1). [Special issue].

Koetting, J. R., ed. (1989). *Research and Theory: AECT-RTD Newsletter 13*(3). [Special issue].

Koetting, J. R., and Januszewski, A. (1991). The notion of theory and educational technology: Foundations for understanding. *Educational and Training International 28*, 96-101.

Lanham, R. A. (1993). *The electronic word: Democracy, technology, and the arts.* Chicago: University of Chicago Press.

Moore, D. M., and Dwyer, F. M. (1994). *Visual literacy: A spectrum of visual learning.* Englewood Cliffs, NJ: Educational Technology Publications.

Muffoletto, R., and Knupfer, N. N. (1993). *Computers in education: Social, political, and historical perspectives.* Cresskill, NJ: Hampton Press.

Nichols, R. G. (1994). An incomplete caution: "Beware the computer technocrats." In *Educational media and technology yearbook: Vol. 20,* ed. D. P. Ely and B. B. Minor (Englewood, CO: Libraries Unlimited), 66-69.

Noble, D. D. (1991). *The classroom arsenal: Military research, information technology, and public education.* London: Falmer Press.

Robinson, R. S., ed. (1990). *Journal of Thought 25*(1/2). [Special issue].

Ulmer, G. L. (1994). *Heuretics: The logic of invention.* Baltimore, MD: Johns Hopkins University Press.

Yeaman, A. R. J. (1994a). Cyborgs are us [1,409 lines]. *Electronic Journal on Virtual Culture* [Online serial], 2(1). Available E-mail: listserv@kentvm.kent.edu. Message: get yeaman v2n1.

Yeaman, A. R. J., ed. (1994b). The ethical position of educational technology in society. *Educational Technology 34*(2). [Special issue].

REFERENCES

Abbott, A. (1988). *The system of professions: An essay on the division of expert labor.* Chicago: University of Chicago Press.

Adams, H. (1988). *The academic tribes,* 2d ed. Urbana, IL: University of Illinois Press.

Adams, H. (1995). *The education of Henry Adams.* London: Penguin. (Original work published 1918)

Association for Educational Communications and Technology. (1996). *1996 AECT national convention program and InCITE '96 exhibit guide.* Washington, DC: Author.

Barns, B. A. (1926, September). United we stand. *Educational Screen 5*(5), 395-96.

Beck, J., Bozzio, T., and Hymas, T. (1989). Guitar shop. On *Jeff Beck's Guitar Shop* [CD]. Los Angeles: CBS Records.

Bijker, W. E. (1995). *Of bicycles, bakelites, and bulbs: Toward a theory of sociotechnical change.* Cambridge, MA: MIT Press.

Bové, P. A. (1990). Discourse. In *Critical terms for literary study,* ed. F. Lentricchia and T. McLaughlin (Chicago: University of Chicago Press), 50-65.

Bush, C. G. (1983). Women and the assessment of technology: To think, to be; to unthink, to be free. In *Machina ex dea,* ed. J. Rothschild (New York: Pergamon Press), 151-70.

Campbell, D. T., and Stanley, J. C. (1963). *Experimental and quasi-experimental designs for research.* Boston: Houghton Mifflin.

Carlson, W. B. (1992). Artifacts and frames of meaning: Thomas A. Edison, his managers, and the cultural construction of motion pictures. In *Shaping technology/building society: Studies in sociotechnical change,* ed. W. E. Bijker and J. Law (Cambridge, MA: MIT Press), 75-198.

Cochran, L. M., Younghouse, P. C., Sorflaten, J. W., and Molek, R. A. (1980). Exploring approaches to researching visual literacy. *Educational Communications and Technology Journal* 28(4), 243-66.

Dale, E. (1945). *Audio-visual methods in teaching.* New York: Dryden Press.

Derrida, J. (1976). *Of grammatology* (G. C. Spivak, trans.). Baltimore, MD: Johns Hopkins University Press. (Original work published 1967)

De Vaney, A., ed. (1994). *Watching Channel One: The convergence of students, technology, and private business.* Albany, NY: State University of New York Press.

Dickens, C. (1990). *Hard times: An authoritative text: Backgrounds, sources, and contemporary reactions: Criticism,* 2d ed., ed. G. Ford and S. Monod. New York: W. W. Norton. (Original work published 1854)

Dorris, A. V. (1928). *Visual instruction in the public schools.* Boston: Ginn.

Eagleton, T. (1991). *Ideology: An introduction.* London: Verso.

Ellul, J. (1990). *The technological bluff.* Grand Rapids, MI: William B. Eerdmans.

Fanon, F. (1965). *Studies in a dying colonialism.* New York: Monthly Review Press.

Foucault, M. (1972). *The archaeology of knowledge and the discourse on language* (A. M. Sheridan Smith, trans.). New York: Pantheon Books. (Original work published 1970)

Fry, E. B. (1964). Teaching machines: The coming automation. In *Educational technology: Reading in programmed instruction,* ed. J. P. DeCecco (New York: Holt, Rinehart & Winston), 21-27.

Geertz, C. (1973). *The interpretation of cultures: Selected essays.* New York: Basic Books.

Geertz, C. (1983). *Local knowledge: Further essays in interpretive anthropology.* New York: Basic Books.

Gerbner, G. (1974). Teacher image in mass culture: Symbolic functions of the "hidden curriculum." In *Media and symbols: The forms of expression, communication, and education: The seventy-third yearbook of the National Society for the Study of Education: Part 1,* ed. D. R. Olson (Chicago: University of Chicago Press), 470-97.

Gibson, R. (1986). *Critical theory and education.* London: Hodder & Stoughton.

Gieryn, T. F. (1995). Boundaries of science. In *Handbook of science and technology studies,* ed. S. Jasanoff, G. E. Markle, J. C. Petersen, and T. Pinch (Thousand Oaks, CA: Sage), 393-443.

Heinich, R. (1970). *Technology and the management of instruction.* Washington, DC: Association for Educational Communications and Technology.

Heinich, R. (1995). The proper study of instructional technology. In *Instructional technology: Past, present, and future,* 2d ed., ed. G. J. Anglin (Englewood, CO: Libraries Unlimited), 61-83. (Original work published 1984)

Hollingsworth, S., ed. (1994). *Teacher research and urban literacy education.* New York: Teachers College Press.

Innis, H. A. (1951). *The bias of communication.* Toronto: University of Toronto Press.

Januszewski, A. (1994). *The definition of educational technology: An intellectual and historical account.* Unpublished doctoral dissertation. Syracuse, NY: Syracuse University.

Krug, E. A. (1969). *The shaping of the American high school. Vol. 2: 1920-1941.* Madison, WI: University of Wisconsin Press.

Lemert, C., ed. (1993). *Social theory: The multicultural and classic readings.* Boulder, CO: Westview Press.

Lorimer, G. H. (1913, October 11). Poverty-stricken schools. *The Saturday Evening Post 186*(15), 26.

Lyotard, J. (1984). *The postmodern condition: A report on knowledge.* Minneapolis, MN: University of Minnesota Press. (Original work published 1979)

Mailloux, S. (1990). Interpretation. In *Critical terms for literary study,* ed. F. Lentricchia and T. McLaughlin (Chicago: University of Chicago Press), 121-34.

Moore, D. M., and Dwyer, F. M. (1994). *Visual literacy: A spectrum of visual learning.* Englewood Cliffs, NJ: Educational Technology Publications.

Office of Technology Assessment. (1988). *Power on! New tools for teaching and learning.* (OTA-SET-379). Washington, DC: Government Printing Office.

Office of Technology Assessment. (1995). *Teachers and technology making the connection.* (OTA-EHR-616). Washington, DC: Government Printing Office.

Papert, S. (1993). *The children's machine: Rethinking school in the age of the computer.* New York: Basic Books.

Pescovitz, D. (1996, June). The future of schools. *Wired,* 82.

Postman, N. (1992). *Technopoly: The surrender of culture to technology.* New York: Alfred A. Knopf.

Ritzer, G. (1993). *The McDonaldization of society: An investigation into the changing character of contemporary social life.* Newbury Park, CA: Pine Forge Press/Sage.

Robins, K., and Webster, F. (1989). *The technical fix: Education, computers and industry.* New York: St. Martin's Press.

Schank, R. C., and Cleary, C. (1995). *Engines for education.* Hillsdale, NJ: Lawrence Erlbaum.

Schrage, M. (1990). *Shared minds: The new technologies of collaboration.* New York: Random House.

Seels, B. B., and Richey, R. C. (1994). *Instructional technology: The definition and domains of the field.* Washington, DC: Association for Educational Communications and Technology.

Smith, D. (December, 1994). An acerbic encounter with Chris Whittle. *GQ 64*(12), 238-41, 271.

Sosnoski, J. J. (1995). *Modern skeletons in postmodern closets: A cultural studies alternative.* Charlottesville, VA: University Press of Virginia.

Spindler, L. S. (1977). *Culture change and modernization: Mini-models and case studies.* Prospect Heights, IL: Waveland Press.

Weber, M. (1993). The spirit of capitalism and the iron cage. In *Social theory: The multicultural and classic readings*, ed. C. Lemert (Boulder, CO: Westview Press), 110-14. (Original work published 1905)

Wolcott, H. F. (1973). *The man in the principal's office: An ethnography.* Prospect Heights, IL: Waveland Press.

Yeaman, A. R. J. (1994). Analysis of computers in education as a cultural field. In *Educational media and technology yearbook: Vol. 20,* ed. D. P. Ely and B. B. Minor (Englewood, CO: Libraries Unlimited), 70-72.

Yeaman, A. R. J. (1995). [Review of the book *Instructional technology: Past, present, and future,* 2d ed.]. *Educational Technology Research & Development 43*(4), 73-76.

Zuboff, S. (1988). *In the age of the smart machine: The future of work and power.* New York: Basic Books.

On CALL
A Review of Computer-Assisted Language Learning in U.S. Colleges and Universities*

Edward J. Miech
Bill Nave
Graduate School of Education, Harvard University

Frederick Mosteller
Professor Emeritus, Department of Statistics, Harvard University

INTRODUCTION

Computers have now become part of the U.S. instructional landscape in formal educational settings from kindergarten through graduate school. The commercial growth of microcomputers over the past decade, with computers becoming more powerful, more compact, and less expensive with each passing year, has been remarkable. The number of microcomputers in U.S. elementary and secondary schools jumped from 630,000 in 1985 to nearly 4 million in 1993, while the median number of K-12 students per computer plummeted from 42 to 14 during the same time period (*Statistical Abstract of the United States* 1994, tables 252 and 253). The number of undergraduates and graduate students who reported using computers at school rose from 30 percent in 1984 to 40 percent in 1989 according to Current Population Surveys conducted by the U.S. Bureau of the Census (*Digest of Educational Statistics* 1993, table 412), and one author writing on the subject has suggested that "it is not overly optimistic to estimate that virtually every institution of higher education in the United States has computers that are available to students, faculty, and administrators" (Ely 1993, p. 53). Although nationwide statistics about computers in higher education are sketchier and less up-to-date than in elementary and secondary education, a 1994 survey of 435 U.S. colleges and universities indicated that 86 percent of these institutions had Internet network affiliations (up from 68 percent reported in the 1993 survey), 93 percent used CD-ROM technology, 19 percent had satellite uplink and downlink capabilities, and 10 percent had speech recognition technology. Furthermore, about 30 percent reported that 100 percent of their students had access to electronic mail, and 37 percent provided student access to computer networks in dorm rooms (Munson, Richter, and Zastrocky 1994, pp. 31, 44, 68-73, 121).

As computer technology in education continues to proliferate, a three-decade-old question remains pertinent: how to translate computer technology into improved teaching and learning. This question applies to the myriad subjects and contexts in which computer-assisted instruction (CAI) has been implemented, including foreign-language teaching and learning in U.S. colleges and universities, the focus of this report. Advocates of computer-assisted language learning (CALL) in particular, and CAI in general, have long made many enthusiastic claims about the instructional power of computer technology in higher education. Empirical evidence, however, has rarely supported these assertions. Furthermore, the experiences of educators with previous technological innovations in education—CALL, for example, inherited the mixed legacy of the audiocassette language lab, which largely did not meet the expectations of practitioners—inform a healthy skepticism on the part of many towards computers. In light of the distinction between theory and practice concerning the use of computers to improve

---

*Study commissioned by the Center for Evaluation of the Program on Initiatives for Children of the American Academy of Arts and Sciences, Cambridge, MA. The complete report of this study with five appendices is available in ERIC as ED 394 525.

teaching and learning, our review of research on CALL provides useful information and insights that educators in colleges and universities may wish to consider when thinking about making a substantial investment of time, energy, and resources into computer-assisted language learning.

The CALL literature addresses a broad array of topics, including descriptions and reviews of software programs, accounts of innovative hardware configurations, theoretical considerations of the relationship between language acquisition processes and software design, discussions of teacher and student attitudes towards computers, reports on pilot CALL projects, and overviews of emergent computer technologies. The complete span of this literature is beyond the scope of this paper. Our review focuses on a subset: empirical studies and reviews that evaluated various aspects of CALL through analyzing the differential learning outcomes of groups of students.

More specifically, we consider 22 empirical CALL studies published between 1989 and 1994, and 13 reviews and syntheses published between 1987 and 1992, that pertain to computer-assisted language learning in higher education in the United States. The cutoff date of 1989 for the 22 empirical studies was selected because of technological advances in CALL hardware and software in recent years, the relative paucity of empirical CALL studies in higher education in the United States published before 1989, and the discovery that several authors had already written a comprehensive summary of CALL research up to 1989 (e.g., Dunkel 1991). The explicit set of inclusion criteria for the 22 empirical studies in this retrospective analysis, then, consisted of works: (1) on CALL, (2) in higher education, (3) in the United States, (4) published since 1989, (5) that considered the differential achievement of at least one group, (6) by analyzing at least one quantitative measure of student performance.

The 13 reviews in this retrospective analysis primarily focused on empirical studies that met the above criteria, with the exception that the studies considered in these reviews could have been published before 1989.

One general finding soon became apparent: CALL has no agreed-upon research agenda. Consequently, CALL researchers examine a wide variety of topics, only rarely giving in-depth consideration of any particular subject. The diverse nature of this literature makes it hard to conduct comparisons across studies, difficult to support generalizations with empirical data, and impossible to carry out a meta-analysis. As a result, available evidence leads to few definitive statements about the efficacy of CALL in institutions of higher learning in the United States.

However, the 22 empirical studies and 13 reviews of CALL offer compelling insights into the conditions under which computer-assisted foreign-language learning can work to improve student achievement. Our retrospective analysis provides an interpretive summary of these findings. Although these findings provide only partial answers to questions about the effective use of CALL in colleges and universities, this synthesis reaps some salient data-based conclusions from an extensive literature.

PART 1: FRAMEWORK OF THREE STREAMS

To avoid conveying an oversimplistic picture of CALL as merely a series of innovations in computer technology, CALL needs to be placed here into a larger context. A "three streams" framework helps to illustrate the different dimensions of CALL. Any specific CALL program involves decisions in relation to developments in at least three fields: (1) educational psychology, (2) linguistics, and (3) computer technology. These three fields may be conceptualized as three streams, where each stream flows independently of the other two, but where the practice of CALL at any given time requires making a passage across all three. A capsule description of each "stream" follows. (For a more exhaustive treatment of educational psychology, linguistics, or computer technology, see the comprehensive literature reviews in Avent 1993; Fox 1991; and Nieves 1994.)

The stream of educational psychology includes three major schools of thought: behaviorism, cognitive psychology, and humanistic psychology. Behaviorism, inspired by the work of B. F. Skinner in operant conditioning, emphasizes reinforcement of observable behavior through feedback and rewards (or punishment) and manifests itself in teaching and learning through, among other methods, a stress on repeated drill and practice. Cognitive psychology, in direct contrast to behaviorism, concerns itself with the inner workings of the mind and emphasizes the importance of meaning-making in learning. Humanistic psychology, associated with Abraham Maslow, emphasizes the subjective world of the individual and emerges in education through areas such as concern for the attitudes, feelings, and learning styles of students. When different people design a CALL lesson on the same language concept using the same computer, they may come up with radically different CALL programs, depending on their preferred theories of learning and educational psychology. Computers themselves do not possess theories of learning; computer programmers and educators, consciously or unconsciously, bring those theories to the task.

The stream of linguistics includes structuralism, transformational grammar, and the "Natural Approach." Structuralism focuses on the form and grammar of language and appears in language learning through the direct translation method. Transformational grammar, which originated with Noam Chomsky, posits that humans have innate capacities for learning languages and considers language learning to be a creative process assisted by intrinsic, universal discovery principles. The Natural Approach, popularized by Stephen Krashen, emphasizes the informal acquisition of language and features key concepts such as the affective filter (the state of relative anxiety experienced by the language learner) and comprehensible input (the messages in the target language that are understandable to the language learner). As in the stream of educational psychology, computers do not subscribe to a theory of linguistics, and the learning experience associated with a particular CALL program relates to the linguistic hypotheses, as well as the preferred theories of learning, of the people who designed and implemented the program.

Finally, the stream of computer technology involves mainframe computers with "dumb" terminals, personal computers with autonomous capabilities, decentralized networks of personal computers and servers linked through cables and modems (e.g., local area networks, online services and databases, the Internet), and personal computers with enhanced capacities (e.g., increased random-access memory and hard drive space, sound and video cards, CD-ROM drives). Throughout the 1960s and 1970s, the large, centralized mainframe computer was prominent, with primarily large organizations able to afford the high cost of developing software. Technology limitations translated into computer activities basically confined to reading and writing on a terminal. The explosive growth of personal computers during the 1980s contributed to the creation of computer labs in many schools and universities and permitted educators to design their own CALL programs with user-friendly authoring systems. The emergence of decentralized networks of personal computers and servers has allowed easy access to vast libraries of information distributed across large geographical areas as well as to authentic communication with other people not in the classroom or language lab. The rise of personal computers with enhanced capacities has facilitated high-quality audio and video interfaces that make it possible for language learners not only to read and write on the computer but also to watch, listen, and speak in response to realistic situations. Again, as with the streams of educational psychology and linguistics, the place at which a CALL designer steps into the stream of computer technology has a strong bearing on the ultimate CALL teaching and learning experience.

Developments in the fields of educational psychology, linguistics, and computer technology proceed more or less independently of one another, but the three streams converge in one way or another in every CALL program. Furthermore, the large number of possible combinations from these three streams harks back to our earlier observation about the diverse nature of CALL research. Although researchers in education can usually agree upon the definition of a variable like class size or college grade point average, and thus conduct logical cross-comparisons of studies on such subjects, various CALL programs may employ completely different uses of learning theory, linguistic approach, and computer technology, sharing little other than the general CALL designation.

PART 2: MAJOR FINDINGS FROM THE 22 EMPIRICAL STUDIES

With this larger framework in mind, then, this retrospective analysis offers an interpretive summary of five major findings from a review of 22 empirical CALL studies published since 1989.

1. *Captioning video segments by including on-screen subtitles in the target language can dramatically boost student comprehension.*

Captioning video segments used in foreign-language instruction may be the most cost-effective measure a college or university can take to improve student learning. In captioning, lines of text appearing on the bottom of the screen provide a written account of the spoken dialogue in a video segment. One way to understand captioning is to imagine watching a foreign-language movie in French with subtitles, except that the subtitles are also in French and correspond exactly to what the characters say in the film.

The simultaneous presentation of language in spoken and written forms through captioning combines a branch of cognitive psychology called information-processing theory with the Natural Approach. Captioning provides more comprehensible input in the target language by engaging both the aural and visual sensory receptors of students. Pertinent computer technology ranges from simple videocassette recorders (VCRs) linked to computers or television sets to sophisticated multimedia workstations.

Available software now makes the captioning process relatively affordable and straightforward to accomplish on a personal computer. For example, with two VCRs, one personal computer, a video monitor, and a decoder, an individual can add captions in Spanish to a Spanish-language video segment by playing the original video on the first VCR, entering one block of text at a time (one to four lines of script prepared ahead of time using a standard word processing program) by pressing <Enter> on the computer keyboard at the appropriate moment, and recording the captioned video on the second VCR.

In a 1991 article, Garza investigated the effect captions in the target language had on 70 students enrolled in intermediate/advanced English as a Second Language (ESL) and 40 students enrolled in an advanced Russian course. Students were randomly assigned into two groups—with captions and without captions—and students in both groups attended one-hour testing sessions where they viewed five "authentic" video segments in the target language. Students in the experimental group watched the video segments with captions, while students in the control group watched the same video segments without captions. For each segment, students were asked to answer 10 multiple-choice questions written in the target language. Students were instructed to mark only answers for which they had a high degree of certainty, and to leave others blank. At the end of each testing session, five students were randomly selected to remain for a five-minute individual interview. In this interview, students were asked to retell one video segment of their choosing, keeping as close as possible to the original language of the segment. These interviews were tape-recorded, and their purpose was to determine if captions affect the way advanced students assimilate the inherent language of a video segment.

Students who watched the segments with captions had a mean gain of 75 percent in correct answers, a mean decrease of 61 percent in incorrect answers, and a mean decrease of 84 percent in unanswered questions over students who watched without captions. Average gains in correct responses were higher for Russian students (90 percent) than for ESL students (60 percent). Interviewed students who saw captioned segments consistently demonstrated greater ability to recall language of the video than students who did not see captions. Garza hypothesizes that "by adding the textual modeling of the captions, the essential language of the segment is made more accessible and, thus (at least potentially) comprehensible to the learner" and concludes that "the most significant conclusion suggested by this study is that captioning may help teachers and students of a foreign language bridge the often sizable gap between the development of skills in reading comprehension and listening comprehension, the latter usually lagging significantly behind the former" (1991, pp. 244, 246).

In her 1993 article, Borras studied the effects of captioning on the oral communicative performance of 44 students of intermediate French, where captioning was part of a multimedia CALL program. Students were randomly assigned to treatment groups with and without captions. As part of a multimedia program called *Practicing Spoken French,* students watched a video segment with or without captions, depending on their treatment group, and then answered comprehension questions about the video. Next, students wrote a draft about events they had seen in the video, and then recorded in French an oral statement up to three minutes in length based on their draft.

Oral statements were scored using an assessment instrument developed by Borras that considers effectiveness, accuracy, organization, and fluency. Students in the groups with captions scored significantly higher than students in groups without captions on overall oral performance.

The Borras study suggests how multimedia computer technology has created a software bridge between captioning and CALL. Borras authored *Practicing Spoken French* using HyperCard and video editing software, which allowed her to integrate computers, video, and captions. As video segments become increasingly frequent components of multimedia CALL, captioning appears to be a worthwhile investment of resources.

Another inexpensive source of video with captions, particularly for educators involved with ESL, is closed-captioned television in the United States. Since July 1993, all new televisions sold in the United States come with built-in chips for decoding closed captions. With the press of a button, captions in English appear at the bottom of the screen for all closed-captioned programs at no cost to the viewer. Current closed-captioned television programming generally includes news programs, prime-time shows, major sporting events, children's shows, and Public Broadcasting System productions. Taping a television show with on-screen captions using a VCR captures the captions along with the image and sound. In addition, the same button on the TV set activates captions for more than 10,000 captioned movies on videotape, which include most new releases. Although this service was primarily designed for hearing-impaired individuals, ESL educators may find closed-captioned television to be a convenient source of captioned video for foreign-language instruction (although proprietary interests dictate that formal permission may be necessary to use this video in a CALL program). Furthermore, the United States and Canada share the same captioning format—called line-21 captioning—and French teachers with access to captioned television programming in French-speaking regions of Canada may want to consider this option. European countries use a captioning system called teletext that, due to its very fast transmission speed, cannot be recorded on a home VCR, and captioned programming is sparse in most other areas around the world (Caption Center 1995).

Whichever method educators use to add captions to foreign-language video—and computer applications have simplified the process considerably—evidence from these studies indicates that captioning can substantially improve student comprehension.

2. *CALL can connect students with other people inside and outside of the classroom, promoting authentic communication in the target language.*

Educators in colleges and universities now use CALL to engage students in conversations in the target language with other people both inside and outside of the classroom through local area networks and wider systems of networks such as the Internet. In a sense, this represents a logical progression in conceptualizing CALL. Early manifestations of CALL usually involved a closed relationship between the student and the terminal of a mainframe computer.

This type of programmed, drill-and-practice instruction placed teachers in a largely peripheral role, as students interacted with the machine and could progress through the sequence of lessons alone. In the 1980s and 1990s, a new generation of CALL programs converted this "line" between the endpoints of student and computer into a triangle, where the third point was a person—a teacher, a tutor, or a fellow student—actively involved in working with the student in the classroom or computer laboratory on the CALL lesson. In the 1990s, this triangle has been reconfigured into multidimensional networks where teachers use CALL to promote person-to-person interactions in the target language, often with "distant others" beyond the walls of the classroom, that transcend obstacles of distance and time.

This use of CALL as a vehicle for interpersonal communication in the target language relates most closely to the humanistic and cognitive currents in the stream of educational psychology and to the Natural Approach in the stream of linguistics. Interactions between people via computer tend to elicit individual, subjective perspectives on topics of mutual interest, and participants in these conversations usually focus on the content, or meaning, of language rather than its form. The Natural Approach advocates this type of communication in the target language on the grounds that second language learning occurs most effectively when people feel more invested in what they want to say than anxious over how correctly they say it.

In a 1994 article, Dorothy Chun describes a two-semester study in which 15 students enrolled in her beginning German course engaged in up to 14 real-time class discussions on a local area network, with each discussion lasting about 20-25 minutes. Chun's entire section traveled to the computer laboratory to conduct these online discussions in German on topics Chun had announced earlier. During these discussions, participants typed comments and read what others wrote. Chun hypothesized that the different format for class discussions "would provide students with the opportunity to generate and initiate different kinds of discourse structures or speech acts" (p. 20).

Chun found that students averaged 8.4 entries per session, and that the ratio of simple sentences to complex sentences improved from 3 to 1 during the fall semester to 4 to 3 during the spring semester. Virtually every question posed by a student or by Chun during an online discussion received an answer, with the total number of replies (229) to Chun's questions numbering about twice as many as the total number of replies (126) to students' questions. The total number of student statements addressed to other students (198), added to the total number of questions asked by students (256), was greater than the total number of replies to questions (454), indicating to Chun that students interacted "directly with each other, as opposed to interacting mainly with the teacher" (p. 28). Chun concludes that the online class discussions helped the section move away from the traditional dynamic of teacher-centered interaction in the target language, as students were "definitely taking the initiative, constructing and expanding on topics, and taking a more active role in discourse management than is typically found in classroom discussion" (p. 28).

In their 1993 article, Terri Cononelos and Maurizio Oliva describe how students in an intermediate/advanced Italian class used Internet-based newsgroups and electronic mail (E-mail) to communicate with native speakers around the country and the world. Students selected a topic of personal interest pertaining to modern Italian culture, such as opera or women's rights, and investigated the subject through independent study. By the third week of the course, students had posted three messages each week on newsgroups located on the Internet, and had to respond to every reply they received at least once. The teacher checked students' contributions to the newsgroups for the quantity and quality of their writing. Students also responded to messages sent to them through E-mail, but the instructor did not monitor these responses. At the end of the semester, students turned in a summary and analysis of their postings and the responses elicited by these postings. Cononelos and Oliva report that students received an average of three replies for each newsgroup posting they wrote, and that the participating students thought that both their confidence in using Italian and the quality of their writing in Italian improved as a result of the experience (pp. 530-31).

In a 1992 monograph, Françoise Hermann investigated a classroom where students had access to each other's written work through CALL. Hermann compared the performance of a section of students (n = 11) enrolled in beginning French that used "agentive" CALL with another section of students (n = 13) enrolled in the same course that used "instrumental" CALL. (In Hermann's study, "instrumental" refers to "using language for action" in socially meaningful tasks; "agentive" refers to "manipulating language," as in drill and practice.) Students were not randomly assigned to these two sections; instead, they enrolled in the different classes on a voluntary and informed basis. Hermann did not teach either section. Students in the agentive group used CALL to complete a series of nine fill-in-the-missing-word (cloze) sets of exercises in French based on the last eight chapters of the class workbook, whereas students in the instrumental group used CALL to create a classroom newspaper in French. The different versions of newspaper articles written by students in the instrumental group were stored on a shared computer directory that allowed students and the teacher to access all student work on the newspaper in various drafts, and students in this instrumental group also used E-mail to send messages to each other, to their teacher, or to Hermann.

Because of the small sample size and nonequivalence between the instrumental and agentive groups in Hermann's study, significance tests comparing the performance of the students in the two groups are inappropriate. Hermann's analysis of student mean scores on a battery of four pre- and posttests during the first and last weeks of the two sections do suggest, however, that students in the instrumental CALL section did as well on these measures as students in the agentive CALL section. Hermann concludes, "The findings of this study indicate that an instrumental approach to the use of the computer in a first year, third quarter French as a foreign language class, and the changes it carries with it, is both an effective and workable alternative approach. . . . Classes in foreign language education could consider using instrumental computer technology in contrast to the prevalent agentive modes of computer use" (p. 159).

The empirical studies of Chun, Cononelos and Oliva, and Hermann feature relatively small sample sizes, but their findings suggest the instructional merits of using computer networks imaginatively. Considered together, these studies indicate a promising direction for the future of CALL: educators can use computers as vehicles both to support new and different interaction among students and teachers in the target language and to create opportunities for students to converse with native speakers and others outside of the classroom and the university.

3. *The type of CALL feedback provided to students can play a central role in student learning.*

The feedback a CALL program gives in response to students' attempts to communicate in the target language, particularly when students make errors, can be of central importance. Types of CALL feedback range from the "wrong, try again" variety to detailed explanations of why the answer was incorrect, complete with examples of model sentences in which the language concepts in question appear in context.

The three streams (educational psychology, linguistics, and computer technology) encompass a wide variety of possible positions with respect to feedback and error correction. Within the stream of educational psychology, for example, behaviorist principles generally follow a "zero tolerance" approach, in which student errors are immediately corrected lest the student mistakenly internalize the wrong ideas and later have to "unlearn" these misconceptions. In contrast, the stream of linguistics includes the Natural Approach, which recommends a more lenient approach towards error correction, as this approach believes that too much emphasis on the formal rules of the target language can interrupt students' tentative attempts to communicate in a new language, raise students' anxiety about language learning (i.e., clog the "affective filter"), and impede the process of second language acquisition. The stream of computer technology can affect the selection of an error-correction strategy in CALL insofar as more sophisticated feedback requires software and hardware configurations capable of supporting artificial intelligence.

In a study published in 1993, Noriko Nagata randomly assigned 34 college students enrolled in an intermediate Japanese course to two groups—a group that used a CALL program that provided conventional feedback on a lesson involving the construction of passive sentences, and another group that used an "intelligent" CALL program on the same subject that gave detailed error analysis—and compared their performance. The CALL program offering "conventional feedback" gave information in English about *what* was wrong with a student's answer in Japanese after comparing the student response with the correct answer stored in the computer, whereas the "intelligent" CALL program explained in English *why* a student response was incorrect through employing artificial intelligence. Nagata demonstrates the difference between the two feedback strategies with an example of the different messages the CALL programs would give to students making the same error in Japanese:

> For this response, T-CALI ["traditional" CALL] provided this feedback: "GA is not expected to be used here. NI is missing. MOMAREMASU is wrong." I-CALI ["intelligent" CALL], however, provided not only these messages but also more detailed grammatical explanations about the errors, e.g., "in your sentence, GAKUSEE is the 'subject' of the passive (the one that is affected by the action), but it should be the 'agent' of the passive (the one who performs the action and affects the subject). Use the particle NI to mark it. The predicate you typed is in the imperfective form. Change it to perfective. Since you are talking with your friend and your friend is using the direct-style (casual style), use the direct-style for your response" (1993, p. 335).

The students participating in the study spent about four hours studying their respective CALL lessons and did not know that a comparison of the two different types of feedback was being conducted. Nagata found that the students in the "intelligent" CALL group significantly outscored the students in the "traditional" CALL group on both a 20-question achievement test on passive sentence construction administered shortly after the last CALL session, and a series of four questions pertaining to passive sentences on the final exam administered three weeks later. Nagata concludes that "the study reveals that the students had difficulty learning Japanese particles, and that the intelligent CALI [CALL] feedback, which explained the functions and semantic relations of nominal phrases in the sentence, was especially helpful to them for understanding the concepts of the particles and passive structures" (1993, p. 337).

In a 1992 article, Bernadin Bationo investigated differences among various types of traditional feedback. Bationo randomly assigned 56 students enrolled in beginning French into four CALL groups receiving either written feedback, spoken feedback, written and spoken feedback combined, or no feedback, where all feedback was given on a Macintosh computer in English. Students in the four groups used the same CALL tutorial to study four lessons on the future indicative mood of regular verbs, receiving the feedback specified for their group.

Bationo found that students receiving written and spoken feedback combined outscored the students in the other three groups on the immediate posttest, with significant differences between the group with written and spoken feedback combined and the groups with written feedback and no feedback (see table 1). The differences among the four groups were not significant for the delayed posttest administered to the students two days later. Bationo notes that the mean score for the no feedback group was surprisingly high on the delayed posttest (14.9), and conjectures that students in the group might have been so frustrated about not receiving any information about their mistakes on the CALL tutorial that they studied the material on their own outside of class (p. 51). Bationo concludes by suggesting that the students in the group with written and spoken feedback combined performed the best because the simultaneous delivery of visual and oral information was most suitable for students with various learning styles and abilities (pp. 47, 51).

Table 1

Comparison of Mean Scores of Students (n = 56) in Four Feedback Groups
on Pre-Test, Immediate Post-Test, and Delayed Post-Test

	Written & Spoken	Spoken	Written	None	F	p
pre-test	0.5	1	0	0.5		
immediate post-test	18.1	14.7	11.5	11.6	4.03	.01
delayed post-test	15.3	12.1	10.6	14.9	2.00	.12

In sum, the findings from these studies demonstrate the importance of paying attention to the type of feedback offered by CALL programs, as different feedback strategies can result in different learning outcomes for students.

4. *No apparent relationship consistently links student attitudes towards CALL with student achievement using CALL.*

The finding that student attitudes towards CALL do not relate consistently to student achievement using CALL surprised the authors of several studies who collected both student test scores and self-reported survey data. These authors posited a hypothesis that sounded reasonable at the outset of their studies: CALL would be more effective with students who reported positive attitudes towards CALL, and less effective with students who reported negative attitudes. This hypothesis, however, was not supported by the evidence.

In a 1989 article on a CALL program for students enrolled in beginning French, Robert Fischer performed correlational analysis of student attitudes towards various components of the CALL program, and posttest achievement scores on those same components: vocabulary, discrete-point grammar, integrated grammar, and irregular verb morphology (see table 2). The only statistically significant correlation between student test scores and student ratings of the usefulness of particular CALL exercises was for vocabulary items ($r = .623$, $p<.001$), and Fischer hypothesizes that this was because this vocabulary was not taught during classroom instruction. Fischer concludes, "The lack of clear relationships between students' perceptions of these CALL lessons and their relevant posttest scores indicates that they did not generally perceive the instructional value of the lessons directly in terms of their end-of-semester achievement" (p. 88).

Table 2

Correlations Between Student Ratings (n = 34) and Post-Test Scores
on Four Components of a CALL Program

	Vocabulary	Discrete-Point Grammar	Integrated Grammar	Irregular Verbs
student ratings	.623	.284	.292	.241

In a 1992 study about the use of CALL to improve the English pronunciation of a group of international teaching assistants, Stenson et al. reported that the 18 participants in the experimental section and their tutors expressed great enthusiasm for the CALL program, but that this enthusiasm did not translate into superior performance: "The fact that the quantitative results do not show more than very minor differences between the experimental and control groups, while the qualitative results suggest that instructors and ITAs [international teaching assistants] alike were enthusiastic about the use of SpeechViewer, is problematic" (p. 14).

In a 1993 article, Jing-Fong Hsu, Carol Chapelle, and Ann Thompson investigated how student exploration within a CALL program correlated with student attitudes for 34 students enrolled in intermediate and advanced ESL courses at Iowa State University who participated in the study. The authors reported that there were no significant correlations between exploration—operationalized as the number of sentences constructed by students during their four hours using the CALL program—and student attitudes towards computers, learning English, and the specific CALL program used in the study, and that the correlation with CALL in general (.25) was significant ($p < .05$) but weak (see table 3).

Table 3

Correlations Between Mean Number of Sentences Constructed by Students (n = 34) and Student Attitudes Towards Computers, Learning English, CALL in General, and the Specific CALL Program Used in the Study

| | **ATTITUDES TOWARDS** | | | |
	Computers	Learning English	CALL	CALL Program
mean number of sentences constructed by students when exploring CALL	.16	-.09	.25	.006

Hsu, Chapelle, and Thompson state in their conclusion that "it was anticipated that students' attitudes would be correlated with their amounts of exploration" (p. 13), but these expected relationships did not surface in the overall correlations.

The overall finding from these studies that student attitudes towards CALL are not consistently linked to student achievement using CALL demonstrates the need for formal measures of learning when assessing the effectiveness of CALL, as students' favorable or unfavorable opinions of CALL do not appear to translate directly into how much they gain from computer-assisted language learning.

5. *CALL can substantially improve student achievement, as compared with traditional instruction.*

Although students using a given CALL program will not always outperform an equivalent group of students in a traditional college foreign-language course, at least one well-designed study has documented a situation in which students in experimental sections of CALL markedly outscored students in control groups on measures of foreign-language achievement (Avent 1993). The evidence from this study establishes that participation in a CALL program has the potential to improve student achievement in a foreign language.

Of the 22 empirical studies we reviewed, only four directly compared CALL instruction with non-CALL instruction; it was much more common for studies to compare one type of CALL program with another type of CALL program. In addition to the Avent study, two other studies (Nieves 1994; Wright 1992) found significant gains for students using CALL as compared with students in traditional classrooms, while a third study that focused on the use of CALL for pronunciation training (Stenson 1992) did not.

In the study reported in his 1993 dissertation, Avent recruited a volunteer pool of 272 students enrolled in beginning German. Students were placed into one of three "achievement level" groups (low, middle, or high) based on their course grades in the previous German course, and then randomly assigned to the CALL or control group.

Instead of going to the language laboratory like the students in the control group, students in the experimental group went to a Macintosh computer lab and worked through the German courseware designed by Avent. Avent reports that the CALL lessons took him approximately

250 to 300 person-hours to develop and test. This CALL courseware covered four units, with each unit including one program focusing on vocabulary and a second program focusing on grammar. Students were required to answer at least 80 percent of items correctly in exercises and achievement checks before proceeding to the next part. Students in the experimental group spent an average of nearly six hours in the computer lab, while students in the control group spent an average of four hours in the language lab. Other than these hours spent in the computer and language labs, students in both groups learned German through traditional classroom instruction during this one-quarter course.

The main evaluation instrument was the final exam, which consisted of a section on listening comprehension and a section on grammar that offered a direct comparison of achievement between students in the CALL groups and those in the control groups. An additional vocabulary test was administered at the end of the quarter that allowed Avent to look at just the experimental group and perform a within-group analysis to compare students' understanding of vocabulary words taught through CALL versus vocabulary words taught by traditional methods over the semester (e.g., oral and written review in the classroom).

The mean score on the final exam among students in the CALL group was higher for grammar (table 4) and vocabulary (table 5) test items than the mean score of those students in the control group who used the traditional language laboratory.

Table 4

Comparison of Mean Scores of CALL (n = 100) and Control (n = 172) Groups on Grammar Test Items on Final Exam

	CALL	Control	F	Level of Significance
mean score	82.2	73.4	49.4	.0001

Table 5

Comparison of Mean Scores of CALL (n = 57) and Control (n = 119) Groups on Vocabulary Test Items on Final Exam

	CALL	Control	F	Level of Significance
mean score	79.7	70.0	16.4	.0001

For the grammar section, the mean score in each achievement group (low, medium, and high) was also higher for the experimental group than for the control group, with significant differences for the "middle group" and the "high group" (table 6).

Table 6

Comparison of Mean Scores of CALL and Control Groups on Grammar Test Items on Final Exam for Low (n = 42), Middle (n = 134), and High (n = 96) Subgroups

Subgroup	CALL	n	Control	n	t	Level of Significance
low	66.6	14	60.6	28	1.67	.10
middle	80.7	50	71.4	84	4.07	.0001
high	90.3	36	82.2	60	3.34	.001

Similarly, the mean score in each achievement group (low, medium, and high) was also higher for the experimental group than for the control group on the vocabulary test items, with significant differences for the "low group" and for the "middle group" (table 7).

Table 7

Comparison of Mean Scores of CALL and Control Groups on Vocabulary Test Items on Final Exam for Low (n = 33), Middle (n = 90), and High (n = 53) Subgroups

Subgroup	CALL	n	Control	n	t	Level of Significance
low	76.3	8	57.2	25	2.35	.026
middle	75.5	28	57.2	62	2.21	.029
high	86.5	21	84.8	32	0.53	.596

On the separate vocabulary test, the overall mean score was higher for those words taught through CALL than through traditional methods (table 8). Mean scores were also significantly higher for all three achievement groups in the experimental group for words taught by CALL than for words taught through traditional methods (table 9). According to Avent, "In this study it is clear that when the students learned vocabulary items by computerized instruction that, without exception, they remembered them better than the words which had been learned using traditional methods" (pp. 82-83).

Table 8

Comparison of Mean Scores of Computer Group on Words Taught Through CALL (number of words = 57) and Traditional Methods (number of words = 57) on Separate Vocabulary Test

	Words via CALL	Words via Traditional	F	Level of Significance
mean score	83.6	74.7	5.48	.0054

Table 9

Comparison of Mean Scores of Low, Middle, and High Subgroups of Experimental Group for Words Taught Through CALL and Words Taught Through Traditional Methods

Subgroup	Words via CALL	Words via Traditional	t	Level of Significance
low	84.1	68.3	5.20	.0013
middle	80.9	71.4	3.34	.0023
high	88.9	82.8	2.26	.037

As stated earlier, students in the experimental group on average spent two hours more in the computer lab than students in the control group spent in the language lab. These disparate times may help explain the differences in achievement scores at the end of the study between students in the two groups, and pose an intriguing question. On the one hand, students using CALL reached higher levels of achievement in German through extended practice in the computer lab. On the other hand, CALL required more time than traditional instruction in this study. Avent himself addresses this issue in his conclusion:

> The information provided by this study does, it seems, indicate that computer-assisted language learning is effective. It works. Whether or not it is efficient is still somewhat open to question. Regardless of the efficiency or lack thereof, if the goal is for the student to learn the material, then the result of this study would indicate that computer-assisted language learning is a viable alternative, and its development should be pursued (pp. 96-97).

In another study, Nieves converted EXITO, a multimedia CALL program in Spanish originally developed by the Central Intelligence Agency (CIA), into a one-semester college course in introductory Spanish, and conducted a formative evaluation of this course under development. Nieves inverted the typical ratio of computer time to classroom time in this experimental course, as students spent four to five hours per week in the computer lab and only one hour per week in class with the instructor. In addition to the largely qualitative formative evaluation of EXITO, Nieves included a modest pilot study in his 1994 dissertation to compare the performance of 19 students in the CALL group with another 18 students in a control group on a Spanish proficiency exam. In comparing the mean scores (out of a possible 160 points) of the students in the CALL and control groups, Nieves found that students in the CALL group scored somewhat higher (CALL mean = 97, control mean = 90) and had a much smaller range between the highest and lowest scores (CALL range = 65, control range = 112). Further, when Nieves broke down these mean scores by "true beginners" and "false beginners," with the former representing students who had never studied Spanish before, the difference between the EXITO and control groups became more pronounced. The mean score on the proficiency exam was substantially higher for "true beginners" in the CALL group (mean = 84) than for "true beginners" in the control group (mean = 60).

Wright's study, a 1992 master's thesis, compared student achievement on three chapter tests in beginning German with an experimental group of 45 students using a computerized workbook and a control group of 62 students using a standard workbook for vocabulary and grammar study. Computerized workbooks and standard workbooks provided similar content and exercises, with computerized workbooks also able to give instant feedback and suggestions for finding correct answers. These computerized workbooks could also help explain to the student why an answer was correct and listed the page number in the textbook where an explanation could be found. By contrast, the standard workbook provided only an answer key to the questions at the back of the book without explanation. Students in both experimental and control groups still used standard workbooks for listening and communication exercises. The mean scores were higher on all three chapter exams for the CALL group (table 10).

Table 10

Comparison of Mean Scores of CALL and Control Groups
on Three Chapter Exams

	CALL	n	Control	n
Chapter 1	84.9	49	79.6	59
Chapter 2	85.3	48	80.4	62
Chapter 3	86.4	49	85.0	42

Wright's findings need to be approached with caution, however. Nonequivalence between experimental and control groups in this study make significance tests inappropriate. Assignment to the experimental and control groups was performed on the level of section, whereas assignment on the level of the individual would have allowed better comparisons between the two groups. In addition, only one experimental section was randomly chosen from a group of seven sections, and the other two experimental sections were taught by Wright himself. Because Wright was involved on such a personal level with the pilot project, he acknowledged that "it was impossible to eliminate teacher/researcher bias completely" (p. 55). The superior performance of students in the experimental group could be plausibly attributed to the personal involvement of Wright as teacher rather than to the efficacy of the CALL workbook program.

Stenson et al.'s 1992 CALL study analyzed the progress in overall English pronunciation—including stress, rhythm, and intonation—of two groups of international teaching assistants enrolled in a quarter-long course to improve their spoken English. One group of 18 students used SpeechViewer, an IBM software program that provides visual representations of speech as part of the class, and a control group of 35 students worked with more traditional methods of pronunciation practice. Stenson and her colleagues make no mention of randomization in the assignment of individuals to experimental or control groups. Students in the CALL and control groups attended one two-hour group session each week, with four students assigned to each group session. Each student also received 50 minutes of one-on-one instruction every week. Students in the CALL group had instructors who regularly used SpeechViewer in the one-on-one tutorials, while students in the control group did not use CALL at all during their 50-minute sessions. For students in the CALL group, the average session on SpeechViewer lasted 15 minutes during a 50-minute tutorial session, and the average total amount of time with SpeechViewer for these students over the quarter was 80 minutes.

Stenson et al. assessed student pronunciation performance using an exam called SPEAK, which is commercially available through the Educational Testing Service, and the "Mimic Test," a test of English language designed for the study by the researchers in which students were asked to listen to a native speaker pronounce words, phrases, and sentences, and then repeat them, mimicking the model as closely as possible. Despite claims of general widespread enthusiasm for SpeechViewer, no substantial differences were found between pre- and posttest scores for the CALL and control groups on both the SPEAK and the Mimic tests. Stenson speculates that the international teaching assistants in the CALL group "simply did not get enough practice with SpeechViewer to show dramatic results" (p. 13).

This last finding based on the empirical CALL studies provides a link to the CALL reviews that also constitute part of this retrospective analysis. Prior to 1990, comparisons of students using CALL with students using traditional methods of language learning appeared more frequently than in recent years. At the time, researchers apparently felt more concern about establishing the efficacy of CALL. The overview of reviews that follows serves as a foundation for the previous analysis of empirical CALL studies by providing a summary of the state of CALL research up to 1990, offering a benchmark against which to assess the direction of current CALL inquiry.

PART 3: REVIEW OF CALL AND CAI REVIEWS

State of CALL Research up to the Early 1990s

Up to the early 1990s, CALL research had yielded no consistent, unambiguous, and definitive findings. Several reviewers concluded that too few studies without obvious validity problems were available for close examination (Niemiec and Walberg 1987; Roblyer et al. 1988; Dunkel 1991; Chapelle and Jamieson 1990; Garrett 1991). Pederson (1987) placed the state of the research enterprise in CALL in the late 1980s into a historical context by comparing it with the experience of language teachers in the early 1960s when the language lab was the emerging technology in language teaching. She asserted that the language lab failed to live up to its high expectations in large part due to the lack of good research on how to use the technology for language learning. In the late 1980s, CALL software designers were similarly handicapped by an inadequate research base.

Smith (1987) offered several observations as explanations for this state of affairs in the CALL research enterprise. First, CALL appeared during the backlash against the behaviorist theoretical underpinnings of the language lab, and, as a result, through the 1980s many second language teachers viewed CALL with a good deal of skepticism. The second language acquisition (SLA) theory current in 1987 rested not on behaviorist theories, but instead viewed language learning as the development of a functional communication ability in the target language rather than as simple acquisition of a vocabulary and the rules of grammar. For example, following the tenets of behavioral theory, the Audio Lingual Method, most common to the language lab, trained students to utter correct sentences in the second language (L2) by memorizing and repeating L2 dialogues from a series of audiotapes. By contrast, the functional communication aspect of SLA theory stresses that one avenue of student language acquisition occurs as a consequence of spontaneous conversation in the L2, the purpose being to communicate with a partner in a conversation. This "functional communication" can occur without formally correct grammar or vocabulary as the partners both modify their L2 utterances in negotiating meaning in the target language. Most CALL programs were not designed to use this "functional communication" paradigm.

Second, because few L2 teachers in the mid-1980s used CALL effectively, few could therefore serve as models or mentors to others. Even if more good examples of the application of CALL had been available, Smith asserted that few teachers in the L2 teaching force of the late 1980s were disposed toward personal computer literacy and toward pedagogical computer literacy using CALL. Furthermore, asserted Smith, many language teachers who did use CALL were not trained to use it effectively.

Third, many CALL programs themselves were flawed. Many L2 teachers who created their own CALL programs generally lacked the technically sophisticated computer programming skills necessary to produce CALL lessons that students would regard as high in quality when compared with other programs in the students' experience (Smith 1987). Conversely, computer program specialists who worked in CALL generally lacked a deep understanding of the theory and pedagogy of SLA. In addition, we found no reports of L2 teachers or CALL programmers working closely with instructional design specialists in the creation of CALL programs.

Several reviews suggested that because CALL had not yet become a mature research field, the validity of a number of primary CALL studies was questionable because of problems in research design and execution (Chapelle and Jamieson 1991; Pederson 1987; Williams and Brown 1991).

The most common objection noted in the reviews in both CAI and CALL research was to the simple research design of computer vs. noncomputer. Many studies thus reported that the differences in experimental outcomes were due to the computer per se rather than to specific features of the CAI or CALL lesson, or possibly to characteristics of the students, or to the nature of the subject matter, or to interactions among these variables (Williams and Brown 1991; Pederson 1987).

In spite of the relative immaturity of research on CAI, investigators could identify some trends by the late 1980s. The most important of these was that CAI seemed to work: students who used CAI in various subject areas achieved more than students who experienced only traditional classroom instruction. An average effect size for CAI of about .36 derived from two extensive CAI meta-analyses (Kulik and Kulik 1991; Niemiec and Walberg 1987) indicated that the median student scoring at the 50th percentile in a traditional classroom would score at the 64th percentile, on average, if he or she used computer-assisted instruction. (See box, page 76, for more thorough explanation of effect size.)

EFFECT SIZES

A common method of reporting results of empirical studies and meta-analyses is to use effect sizes. In brief, an effect size is a simple way to compare the outcomes among studies with differing numbers of participating students by standardizing the results. For example, an effect size of .5 would mean that, on average, students formerly at the 50th percentile would now achieve at the 69th percentile. An effect size of 1.0 would move the median student to the 84th percentile. Educators generally agree that an effect size of around .3 (a move to the 62nd percentile for the median student) or larger represents a substantial education benefit, especially when we consider that these effect sizes represent the average improvement for a *population* of students, not just one student. However, the merit of a given effect size for any education intervention also depends on what other options may be available and on their relative costs.

Sample Effect Sizes and Their Related Percentile Differences

Effect Size	.00	.10	.20	.30	.40	.50	.75	1.0	1.5	2.0
Percentile	50	54	58	62	66	69	77	84	93	98

Not all researchers in the field expressed enthusiasm about the computer vs. noncomputer research designs that produced the average effect sizes reported above, suggesting that it was not the computer itself that was the cause of better student achievement, but the way that the computer lessons were structured that led to increases in student achievement (Dunkel 1991; Pederson 1987; Williams and Brown 1991).

Researchers and reviewers who question the simple computer vs. noncomputer design are, in our judgment, thoughtfully suggesting that the computer is not a magic bullet. Rather, computer lessons contain a number of variables, and each variable needs to be identified, operationalized, and examined in order to determine what it is about CALL lessons that results in improved student achievement and attitudes. Furthermore, different lesson variables affect different students in different ways.

Other Comments on CAI and CALL Research

Williams and Brown (1991) noted that another common problem in CAI research is that many studies did not explicitly base their research design on any particular theory of learning. As a result, the researcher lacked justification for attributing the outcome to any particular aspect of the experimental treatment (Pederson 1987; Chapelle and Jamieson 1989).

In addition, Williams and Brown (1991) expressed disappointment in much of the reporting of CAI studies. Many studies did not describe fully the experimental treatment, the students, or the CALL lessons. Pederson (1987) added that many researchers failed to define adequately and to operationalize the variables the study purported to examine. It is difficult, therefore, to judge the results of such studies.

Williams and Brown (1991) called attention to a subtle interaction among the components of the computer medium, the individual characteristics of the learner, and the specified learning outcomes of the lesson. This interaction precludes treating the instructional medium, be it teacher-lecture, interactive-video, or a computer, as a cohesive whole, and therefore treating experimental outcomes as if they were caused by "the lecture," or by "the video," or by "the computer." In other words, different aspects of lessons on the computer for different subject areas have different effects on different students.

Two reviews provided guidelines for addressing this issue of the quality of research reporting in CAI and CALL. For CAI reporting, Roblyer et al. (1988) suggested that, at a minimum, the researcher provide the reader with an adequate description of the experimental design (including sample sizes of the full sample and any subgroups), information on any testing instrumentation used, more complete statistical data than are sometimes reported, and a description of the experimental treatment so that the reader can understand what was done.

Chapelle and Jamieson (1989) added these suggestions. First, CALL researchers should provide the reader with the SLA theory that informed the study, explain how it applies to the learners in the study, and include a description of the kinds of cognitive processing that this CALL lesson is intended to stimulate. Second, researchers should provide a description of the learners, such as their prior language learning experience and demographic information (e.g., age, gender, ethnicity, grade in schooling). Third, researchers should provide the reader with a description of the CALL lessons used, including at least the following information: type of activity (e.g., drill, game, simulation), planned learning outcomes, learner focus (what the student is actually doing), the linguistic purpose of this lesson, level of the lesson (e.g., beginner, novice, intermediate, advanced), the lesson's degree of tolerance for different levels of performance by different students, and a description of how the teacher integrated the lesson into the course. Fourth, when reporting the outcomes of the lesson, researchers should include a description of the learning strategies that the students appeared to use in response to the lesson.

Attitude. Two of the 13 reviews reported that student attitudes toward computer learning in all subjects are more positive than toward traditional classroom lessons [average effect sizes = .62 (Roblyer et al. 1988) and .28 (Williams and Brown 1991)]. These two reviews also reported that students' attitudes toward school were more positive when CAI was part of their school experience (average effect sizes, .22 and .33, respectively). Roblyer et al. (1988) caution, however, that in their opinion, the positive student attitudes reported may not justify the cost of the hardware, software, and teacher training to establish CAI as an integral part of students' school experience.

Design of CAI and CALL Experiences for Students. The most consistent finding reported in the research on CAI and CALL up to the early 1990s is that, although CAI and CALL are effective in improving student achievement when used as a supplement to traditional classroom instruction, neither is apparently effective as a *replacement* for traditional classroom instruction (Roblyer et al. 1988; Robinson 1991; Williams and Brown 1991).

Language learning is a socially mediated activity, and CALL introduces the computer and other technology as another "player" in the constellation of social interactions in a second language (L2) classroom (Johnson 1991). Citing reports from three investigators, Johnson reported that the group size that promotes the most effective social interactions in the target language when a computer is a member of the group is two or three students, especially if the CALL program assigns specific roles to each of the students. A promising example is collaborative composition among two or three students using a word processing program in the target language.

Use of the computer in the form of local area networks (computers networked within an L2 classroom) and wide area networks (computer access to the Internet) shows promise for extending the kinds of social interactions possible in the target language (Robinson 1991; Scott et al. 1992). For example, students in an American classroom can converse through E-mail with students in a classroom halfway around the world in the language of those other students.

The specific way CALL lessons are put together—what CALL users and programmers refer to as the program's *coding elements*—are important variables in the efficacy of CALL lessons. For example, CALL programs that require students to make extended responses (rather than just type the <**Enter**> key) result in higher student achievement (Chapelle and Jamieson

1990). Similarly, CALL programs that require more interaction between the student and a video with native speakers result in higher student achievement.

Traditional drill and practice CALL programs are more effective if students must understand the meaning of the L2 sentences in which the grammatical corrections are to be made, instead of simply making the corrections mechanically in sentences whose meaning they need not understand in order to complete the exercise (Pederson 1987; Chapelle and Jamieson 1991).

CALL software that leads students to think in new ways, that is, that gives them new patterns of cognition in relation to the target language, are more effective (Pederson 1987). For example, Robinson (1991) asserts that theory suggests that CALL programs that support implicit error correction by students (i.e., leading students to find and correct their own mistakes rather than having mistakes highlighted or otherwise flagged by the computer), will result in higher student achievement.

Finally, programs that lead students to share in the control of the lessons result in higher student achievement. A midway approach with regard to student control of help menus—help functions of the CALL program that are neither totally controlled by the CALL program itself nor completely in the hands of the student—results in better student achievement in the target language (Robinson 1991). For example, an error message that appears on the screen after a student has typed in a sentence in the target language that says simply, "agreement?" could lead the student to examine the sentence for errors in noun-adjective agreement, subject-verb agreement, or noun-pronoun agreement. A student unable to discover the agreement mistake would need to ask for further assistance.

Other Outcomes of CAI and CALL Lessons. Other outcome variables beyond student achievement and student attitude that have been studied include student learning time, course completion rates, retention time, and cost factors for using CALL (Williams and Brown 1991; Niemiec and Walberg 1987).

Scott et al. (1992) reported that the results of the Apple Classroom of Tomorrow study suggest that CAI produces more positive student interactions, such as spontaneous peer tutoring and cooperative learning, and in addition, leads students to become more active learners. Two evaluations of the Apple Classroom of Tomorrow study report that students took more initiative and assumed more responsibility for their own learning when using CAI in the Apple Classroom of Tomorrow.

Teachers and CAI/CALL. Effective integration of CAI or CALL lessons into a curriculum requires that teachers learn a new role, that they learn a new pedagogy that differs from their former teaching methodology. Computers in a classroom can put into the hands of the students more control of their own learning, shifting that control away from the teacher. Scott et al. (1992), reporting again on the Apple Classroom of Tomorrow study, note that new teacher behaviors appeared only after the teachers had solved the new management problems presented by the computer-rich classroom environment. For example, teachers need to discover new ways to keep track of students' learning when each student may be doing different work. Therefore, they conclude, teachers will need much support during the introduction of CAI and CALL lessons into any curriculum.

Pederson (1987) supports this conclusion, noting that the results of teacher surveys on CALL indicate that L2 teachers strongly desire additional and better training in the use of CALL in their classrooms. The same surveys indicate that teachers were not at all satisfied with the CALL software available in the mid-1980s.

Conclusions from the Reviews

In sum, CALL reviewers before the early 1990s had consistently made a handful of recommendations for future CALL researchers. Overwhelmingly, they called for researchers to abandon the simple CALL vs. non-CALL research design and to focus more specifically on finding what components of CALL lessons are effective with what kind of language lessons for what kind of students. That is, what is the nature of the interactions among student characteristics, CALL lesson design, desired learner outcomes, and computer coding capabilities? Two substantial subsets of this general recommendation are specific recommendations (1) to look at components of CALL lesson design (e.g., program branching, error analysis and feedback, screen design) and (2) to examine student characteristics (e.g., learning style, cognitive approach, gender) as they relate to CALL effectiveness.

A number of reviewers suggested that the impact of CALL research would be much enhanced if investigators explicitly designed their studies around theories of linguistics or cognitive development. Several reviewers noted that the power of the computer could be harnessed as a research tool in "observing" student learning behavior by recording all keystrokes made by students during a CALL lesson. Finally, several suggested that researchers examine the cost effectiveness of CALL, especially in comparison with other kinds of language teaching.

Many of the researchers whose studies we reported in Part 2 of this paper have answered these calls of the reviewers. (See table 11.) Twenty-one of the twenty-two studies have in some way examined components of CALL lesson design, linguistic outcomes, or student characteristics, and the interactions among these components. Twenty examined CALL lesson design characteristics in a specific way. Twenty either stated a particular theoretical basis for their study design, or reflected a particular theoretical stance in their design, even though it may not have been specifically identified in the report of the study. Eleven closely examined student characteristics and their influence on CALL outcomes. Ten compared CALL efficacy with other instructional interventions not mediated by a computer. Nine reported using the computer's capabilities to record student keystrokes as the researchers gathered data to explore aspects of various cognitive or linguistic theories.

Table 11

Number of Studies (n = 22) That Addressed Research Issues
Suggested in the 13 Reviews

Suggested Research Issues to Examine	Frequency
Interactions among student, lesson, computer, context	21
Lesson design, computer coding elements	20
Theory	20
Student characteristics	11
Comparison with other instructional interventions	10
Record of student behavior during lessons, e.g., keystrokes	9
Cost compared to other instructional strategies	2

Only two studies addressed the issue of cost, and these did so only in passing. Both studies examined the interactions of CALL and cooperative learning; both found no difference in student achievement between individual student computer use and pairs of students in a cooperative learning situation at the computer. Both suggest that because pairs of students seem to learn no less than do individual students, schools for whom budget constraints are an issue may safely consider purchasing half as many computers for their language classes that use CALL.

As noted earlier, several reviewers noted the questionable validity of many CAI and early CALL studies. These reviewers made a number of suggestions to improve the validity of future studies. We emphasize some of those suggestions here. In doing so, we note the complexity of improving internal and external validity in so complex an endeavor as CALL.

In designing a study, researchers should account for as many variables as possible that may affect student performance on the L2 measure that is being examined. Variables should be carefully defined and operationalized. In addition, variables from all three streams should be included in the study design: desired linguistic learning outcomes (informed by theories of language learning), instructional design of the lesson (informed by theories of cognitive psychology), and the computer coding elements used in the lesson. Finally, variables accounting for student characteristics should be included in the study design.

The 22 empirical studies we examine here exhibited varying degrees of success in addressing these validity issues. We note in particular two studies that did so especially well: Avent's study comparing achievement for students using either the traditional language lab or CALL lessons (1993), and Garza's study of the effect of captioning segments of "authentic" video on students' recall of the dialogue in the video segments (1991).

PART FOUR: RECOMMENDATIONS FOR
THE FUTURE OF CALL

Based on this retrospective analysis of CALL research, we present here three general conclusions, each accompanied by recommendations for future CALL practice and research:

1. *Good CALL programs are hard to find because integrating the three streams of educational psychology, linguistics, and computer technology is difficult to do well.*

    Relatively few individuals have expertise in all three areas of educational psychology, linguistics, and computer technology. Because effective CALL programs seem to require successfully integrating these three streams, we recommend that CALL developers consider working in creative teams and combining different types of expertise when authoring and implementing CALL programs. An example of this kind of model in practice in another technology-conscious field is the children's television show *Sesame Street*, which from its inception developed programming by bringing together a collaboration of television writers and producers, classroom teachers, professors, researchers with expertise in evaluation, songwriters, and animators (Lesser 1974).

    We also recommend that educators in institutions of higher education review CALL programs that have already been developed—especially in federally funded organizations—and investigate the possibility of converting these programs for classroom use. Foreign-language programs in agencies such as the CIA, the Defense Department, the Foreign Service, and the Peace Corps generally represent considerable investments of time and money, and some of these programs may contain CALL or other technological components appropriate for domestic spin-offs in colleges and universities. The Spanish-language program EXITO, originally developed by the CIA, is an example of this conversion of CALL from federal agency to college classroom.

    Representing an investment of millions of dollars and several years of development, EXITO was created by the CIA's Foreign Language Training Laboratory in 1985 as an intensive 10-day course to teach survival Spanish to CIA agents at a proficiency level equivalent to about a year of college Spanish (Speak Spanish like a spy 1994). A multimedia CALL program, EXITO features native speakers in vignettes and lessons that integrate video, audio, graphics, and animation. A workbook and set of six audiotapes supplement the EXITO software. For each of the 10 days in the program, participants are expected, at minimum, to study four hours on the computer, spend one hour in a one-on-one tutorial with an instructor, perform written exercises for one hour in the accompanying workbook, and work one hour with the audiotapes (Nieves 1994). EXITO uses laserdisc technology, and the computer workstations required to support EXITO in its original form cost several thousand dollars each (Forming a more perfect union 1993).

EXITO, however, is now available to universities and schools in a format that requires only a personal computer equipped with a double-speed CD-ROM plus a Motion Picture Experts Group (MPEG) video board, which sold in 1995 for about $400. Several years ago, the CIA entered into an agreement with Analysas, a private company, to develop EXITO for educational and commercial use. According to the agreement, the CIA receives royalties for sales to private organizations but does not profit from sales to schools, which can purchase the EXITO package at discount rates. Kelly Ann Nieves's 1994 dissertation, *The Development of a Technology-Based Class in Beginning Spanish: Experiences with Using EXITO,* chronicles the process of converting this recent version of EXITO into a one-semester Spanish course at George Mason University (Nieves 1994).

2. *New multimedia computer technologies offer ways to develop more CALL programs that emphasize watching, listening, and speaking in addition to the traditional CALL activities of reading and typing, and new networking computer technologies provide opportunities to use CALL to promote person-to-person interaction in the target language that transcend traditional obstacles of distance and time.*

Whereas earlier versions of CALL basically consisted of a closed loop between student and machine and emphasized textbook-style reading and writing activities, educators in colleges and universities can now use CALL both as a vehicle for engaging students in watching, listening, and speaking activities, and for connecting students with other people outside of the classroom for conversations in the target language.

Captioning video segments in the target language represents one way of leveraging new multimedia computer technologies into improved student foreign-language learning, where the simultaneous presentation of language in spoken and written forms provides more comprehensible input in the target language by engaging both the aural and visual sensory receptors of the student. In general, multimedia CALL provides opportunities for students to learn languages in more authentic contexts, as students can observe native speakers in ordinary situations in foreign countries and interact with the CALL program in a variety of manners.

The use of CALL as a vehicle for interpersonal communication in the target language over computer systems such as the Internet allows individual, subjective perspectives on topics of mutual interest to surface. Because participants in these conversations around shared interests usually focus on the content, or meaning, of language rather than its form, this application of CALL corresponds with the humanistic and cognitive currents in the stream of educational psychology. This interaction in the target language via CALL is also consistent with the Natural Approach, a current in the linguistics stream, which posits that second language learning occurs more effectively when people feel more invested in what they want to say than anxious over how correctly they say it.

3. *The field of CALL needs more research, especially formative evaluation, conducted by a larger pool of researchers.*

In the course of conducting our review on CALL in higher education in the United States, we noted that much of the research has been capably conducted by two groups: (1) a relatively small group of researchers whose names appear repeatedly in the literature, and (2) a group of graduate students writing their theses on the subject. Given the potential importance of CALL in colleges or universities, we wonder if the responsibility for CALL research should continue to fall on so few shoulders.

Furthermore, more coordination of CALL research around a better-defined agenda seems highly desirable. If practitioners and researchers in the field of CALL could agree upon a set of key questions for subsequent studies to address, the resulting literature might provide stronger guidance concerning how to use computers to improve teaching and learning in foreign languages in colleges and universities.

Finally, educators might consider the allocation of more resources for formative evaluation in order to investigate the effectiveness of specific CALL programs with particular students at particular sites. Because the "CALL" designation covers a wide variety of programs that can be very dissimilar from one another in their standpoints in relation to educational psychology, linguistics, and computer technology, foreign-language educators may find it helpful to complement the insights offered in the general CALL literature with formative research on programs-in-development.

REFERENCES: GENERAL, EMPIRICAL STUDIES, AND REVIEWS

General

The Caption Center. (1995). *Tech Facts.* Vol. 4. Boston: WGBH Educational Foundation.

Digest of Educational Statistics. (1993). Washington, DC: U.S. Department of Education, National Center for Education Statistics.

Ely, Donald P. (1993). Computers in schools and universities in the United States of America. *Educational Technology 33*(9), 53-57.

Forming a more perfect union. *Computer Reseller News,* September 27, 1993.

Fox, Jeremy. (1991). *Learning languages with computers: A history of computer assisted language learning from 1960 to 1990 in relation to education, linguistics, and applied linguistics.* Doctoral Thesis, University of East Anglia (England).

Lesser, Gerald. (1974). *Children and television: Lessons from Sesame Street.* New York: Random House.

Munson, Janet R., Richter, Randy L., and Zastrocky, Michael. (1994). *CAUSE Institution Database: 1994 Profile.* Boulder, CO: CAUSE.

Speak Spanish like a spy. *Washington Post*, April 3, 1994.

Statistical Abstract of the United States. (1994). Washington, DC: Government Printing Office.

Empirical CALL Studies Published Since 1989

Aspillaga, Macarena. (1991). Screen design: Location of information and its effects on learning. *Journal of Computer-Based Instruction 18*(3), 89-92.

Avent, Joseph. (1993). *A study of language learning achievement differences between students using the traditional language laboratory and students using computer-assisted language learning courseware.* Doctoral Thesis, University of Georgia.

Bationo, Bernadin. (1992). The effects of three feedback forms on learning through a computer-based tutorial. *CALICO Journal 10*(1), 45-52.

Borras, Isabel. (1993). Developing and assessing "Practicing Spoken French." *Educational Technology Research and Development 41*(4), 91-103.

Borras, Isabel, and Lafayette, Robert. (1994). Effects of multi-media courseware subtitling on the speaking performance of college students of French. *The Modern Language Journal 78*(1), 61-75.

Chang, Kuan-Yi, and Smith, Wm. Flint. (1991). Cooperative learning and CALL/IVD in beginning Spanish: An experiment. *The Modern Language Journal 75*(2), 205-11.

Chapelle, Carol, and Mizuno, Suesue. (1989). Students' strategies with learner-controlled CALL. *CALICO Journal*, December, 25-47.

Chun, Dorothy M. (1994). Using computer networking to facilitate the acquisition of interactive competence. *System 22*(1), 17-31.

Cononelos, Terri, and Oliva, Maurizio. (1993). Using computer networks to enhance foreign language/culture education. *Foreign Language Annals, 26*(4), 527-34.

Fischer, Robert. (1989). Instructional computing in French: The student view. *Foreign Language Annals* 26(4), 527-34.

Garza, Thomas. (1991). Evaluating the use of captioned video materials in advanced foreign language learning. *Foreign Language Annals 24*(3), 239-57.

Hermann, Françoise. (1992). *Instrumental and agentive uses of the computer: Their role in learning French as a foreign language*. San Francisco: Mellen Research University Press.

Hsu, Jing-Fong, Chapelle, Carol, and Thompson, Ann. (1993). Exploratory learning environments: What are they and what do students explore? *Journal of Educational Computing Research 9*(1), 1-15.

Jamieson, Joan, Campbell, John, Norfleet, Leslie, and Berbisada, Nora. (1993). Reliability of a computerized scoring routine for an open-ended task. *System 21*(3), 305-22.

Jamieson, Joan, Norfleet, Leslie, and Berbisada, Nora. (1993). *Successes, failures, and dropouts in computer-assisted language learning*. Paper presented at the Annual Convention of the Association for Educational Communications and Technology, New Orleans, LA. (ED 354 786)

Mitchell, Cristi. (1992). *The relationship of computer-assisted language learning environments and cognitive style to achievement in English as a second language*. Doctoral Thesis, University of Miami.

Nagata, Noriko. (1993). Intelligent computer feedback for second language instruction. *The Modern Language Journal 77*(3), 330-39.

Nieves, Kelly. (1994). *The development of a technology-based class in beginning Spanish: Experiences with using EXITO*. Doctoral Thesis, George Mason University.

Raschio, Richard. (1990). The role of cognitive style in improving computer-assisted language learning. *Hispania 73*(May), 535-41.

Shiu, Ka-Fai, and Sharon Smaldino. (1993). *A pilot study: Comparing the use of computer-based instruction materials and audio-tape materials in practicing Chinese*. Unpublished paper, Northern Arizona University. (ED 362 204)

Stenson, Nancy, Downing, Bruce, Smith, Jan, and Smith, Karin. (1992). The effectiveness of computer-assisted pronunciation training. *CALICO Journal* (Summer), 5-19.

Wright, David Allan. (1992). *The reciprocal nature of universal grammar and language learning strategies in computer assisted language learning*. Master's Thesis, University of Arizona.

Reviews of CALL and CAI

Chapelle, Carol, and Jamieson, Joan. (1989). Research trends in computer-assisted language learning. In *Teaching languages with computers: The state of the art*, ed. Martha Pennington (La Jolla, CA: Athelstan), 45-60.

Chapelle, Carol, and Jamieson, Joan. (1991). Internal and external validity issues in research on CALL effectiveness. In *Computer-assisted language learning and testing: Research issues and practice,* ed. Patricia Dunkel (New York: Newbury House), 37-60.

Dunkel, Patricia. (1991). The effectiveness research on computer-assisted instruction and computer-assisted language learning. In *Computer-assisted language learning and testing: Research issues and practice,* ed. Patricia Dunkel (New York: Newbury House), 5-36.

Garrett, Nina. (1991). Technology in the service of learning: Trends and issues. *Modern Language Journal 75*(1), 74-96.

Johnson, Donna M. (1991). Second language and content learning with computers: Research in the role of social factors. In *Computer-assisted language learning and testing: Research issues and practice,* ed. Patricia Dunkel (New York: Newbury House), 61-84.

Kulik, Chen-Lin C., and Kulik, James A. (1991). Effectiveness of computer-based instruction: An updated analysis. *Computers in Human Behavior, 7*(1-2), 75-94.

Niemiec, Richard, and Herbert J. Walberg. (1987). Comparative effects of computer-assisted instruction: A synthesis of reviews. *Journal of Educational Computing Research 3*(1), 19-37.

Pederson, Kathleen M. (1987). Research on CALL. In *Modern media in foreign language education: Theory and implementation,* ed. Wm. Flint Smith (Lincolnwood, IL: National Textbook), 99-131.

Robinson, Gail L. (1991). Effective feedback strategies in CALL: Learning theory and empirical research. In *Computer-assisted language learning and testing: Research issues and practice,* ed. Patricia Dunkel (New York: Newbury House), 155-66.

Roblyer, M. D., Castine, W. H., and King, F. J. (1988). *Assessing the impact of computer-based instruction.* Binghamton, NY: Haworth Press.

Scott, Tony, Cole, Michael, and Engle, Martin. (1992). Computers and education: A cultural constructivist perspective. In *Review of Research in Education - 18,* ed. Gerald Grant (Washington, DC: American Educational Research Association), 191-254.

Smith, Wm. Flint. (1987). Modern media in foreign language education: A synopsis. In *Modern media in foreign language education: Theory and implementation,* ed. Wm. Flint Smith (Lincolnwood, IL: National Textbook), 1-12.

Williams, Carol J., and Brown, Scott W. (1991). A review of the research for use of computer-related technologies for instruction: An agenda for research. In *Educational media and technology yearbook 1991,* ed. Brenda Branyan-Broadbent and R. Kent Wood (Englewood, CO: Libraries Unlimited), 26-46.

Part Two
The Profession

Introduction

   Publishing the text of the keynote address to the annual convention of the Association for Educational Communications and Technology (AECT) by the presiding officer allows us to be informed of the state of the profession. This volume of the *Educational Media and Technology Yearbook* features the 1995 and 1996 keynote addresses. Lynn Milet, the 1995 AECT President, and William Burns, the 1996 AECT President, share their perceptions about action items for the association and alliances the association should consider in the near future.
   The National Library of Education, located in Washington, D.C., and sponsored by the U.S. government, has become the central clearinghouse for education information. Nancy Floyd presents the current status of the National Library of Education and its role in fostering the development of educational media and technology.
   The three chapters that compose this part of the yearbook extend the trends and issues to areas concerned with the professional status of and growth for the field of educational media and technology.

Association for
Educational Communications and Technology
1995 Presidential Address

Lynn Milet
Instructional Technology Services
Lehigh University

A number of years ago, while on a family outing in a state park, we found ourselves in the middle of a clearing with no less than five different paths leading off in all directions. We had no idea which path would lead us to where we wanted to go, and realized we had a dilemma. As you can imagine, each of us felt we should take a different path! Thankfully, while we were debating the pros and cons of each option, a park guide appeared and showed us the correct path to take.

Now, at the end of one century and the beginning of another, the questions "Where do we go from here?" and "Which path should we take?" are operative ones for AECT. It is not that we are lost in the woods . . . we know full well where we are and how far we have come. There are, however, a multitude of pathways before us, and the paths we take will determine where we will be headed as the new century unfolds.

Several weeks ago, I came across a copy of an article about a study that involved 211 professional associations. This study was undertaken to determine what characteristics of an association make it successful and, in the researcher's term, superior. Of the 211 groups involved, the research findings designated 24 as superior. The top five characteristics of these associations were:

- They use and update their strategic plan;
- They are member driven;
- They are politically active on a national, state, and local level;
- They have a positive image; and
- They maintain excellent member services.

If we use these criteria on ourselves, I think we are on the way to becoming one of those superior associations; but we still have a long way to go.

We have, as an Association, taken the first step in determining where and what we want to be, by adopting the Vision 2000 Strategic Plan. This plan will serve as our guide, showing us the different directions we can take to reach our goals.

Will Rogers once wrote, "Even if you're on the right track, you'll get run over if you just sit there."

We now must take the second step, and I think the hardest step: that of implementing the plan. The Board has already begun the process by determining two priority strategies it wanted to implement this past year: electronic services and a process for evaluating and updating the strategic plan to assure that it remains a living document. Many of you have also begun to think about the vision and your participation in implementing specific strategies.

During an interview with three umpires, the same question was put to all of them: "How do you decide which pitches are balls and which are strikes?" The first umpire thought for a while and then answered, "There are balls and there are strikes, and I calls 'em as I sees 'em." The second umpire disagreed. "There are balls and there are strikes, and I calls 'em as they is." The third umpire shook his head. "There are balls and there are strikes, but they ain't nothin' until I calls 'em."

Today, I want to take a few minutes to share with you my vision for AECT, to call the balls and strikes (so to speak), to identify which paths I think we should take during this coming year. These actions will not be easy; but I believe they are necessary for growth.

1. MEMBERSHIP

Membership growth is at a standstill. Even though our staff has and continues to develop new and exciting ways to market our association, we, as AECT members, must take action as well. We need to continue to aggressively fund, promote, and enhance the variety of electronic services we have established this year.

We also need to aggressively market the Annual Convention and InCITE exposition. We are one of the few associations with a large and eclectic technology exposition, and we need to market it, not only to technology-based professionals, but to those professionals involved with making decisions and providing funding.

As members, we must mount an aggressive membership campaign with a significant part of that effort directed at those people. We need to talk about AECT to our administrators and invite them to join the association.

We need to evaluate the membership and activities of our state associations and regions. Some are active and financially healthy, while others are just barely staying alive. Some have active members that include the full spectrum of educational technology environments, while others have become mainly K-12 school media specialist associations. I plan to appoint a task force to work with those groups that need help in providing better services, planning successful conferences, and becoming more active in the AECT.

2. LEADERSHIP DEVELOPMENT

Each year it becomes increasingly more difficult to convince our best and brightest members to take leadership roles and to keep more experienced leaders involved. If we cannot find a way to nurture and mentor new and rising leaders, we will not survive. The Board has already taken action concerning the Summer Leadership Development Conference by giving the planning committee more focused and defined objectives. This summer we will focus on leadership development skills, at every level, that will not only help you within AECT but also in your jobs.

I also want to encourage current leadership to stop looking at the small, short-term picture and to look to the future at how their respective groups can take an active role in implementing the vision. I will ask each division, state affiliate, affiliated organization, and chapter to develop strategic plans of their own and define how they fit into the Vision 2000 plan. I will also ask them to find ways to include proposals for cooperative services and activities that go beyond cosponsoring concurrent sessions or receptions at the annual convention.

One of the greatest wastes of talent we have in our association is the past presidents. I will make every effort to find ways to actively involve them in helping us become more proactive.

3. ORGANIZATIONAL STRUCTURE

Although the Vision 2000 plan makes no specific recommendations concerning organizational structure, we must examine the goals, directions, and activities of each part of our association and begin to streamline our governance structure, which is, I feel, ineffective and inefficient. Two areas I want to focus on this year will be committees and Assembly. I will be asking each committee to present a plan, by the summer conference, describing what and how they can implement portions of the Vision 2000 plan. This is a question of not only should we exist, but if we should, what should we look like and what should we do? I am not looking to do away with committees if they are viable within the context of the strategic plan, but we can no longer use committees as an excuse for people to attend the convention.

As a past Assembly chair no one knows better than I do how cumbersome the assembly process is. I do not want to do away with Assembly. I believe strongly that we need to have a mechanism for input to the Board by the membership. I also believe that Assembly should be used in more productive ways. I will therefore charge a task force to analyze the assembly process and come up with an alternative structure that will be more effective and efficient. Hopefully, we can implement this new structure on a one-year trial basis in 1996; but if not in 1996, then definitely for 1997.

To demonstrate how important I think this issue of restructuring governance is, I will ask the Board to restructure the way it does business, beginning with changing how we conduct meetings. Along with looking at long-term solutions, I will ask the Board to do more business electronically and by telephone so that next summer, while in Arizona, we can devote at least half a day, if not a whole day, to strategic planning rather than business as usual. This will mean more work for each Board member during the year; but it will, I feel, result in a more productive board, able to be proactive rather than reactive. I encourage divisions, state affiliates, chapters, and affiliated organizations to do the same.

4. STRATEGIC ALLIANCES

Continuing the efforts underway to establish strategic alliances with other technology-based professional associations is important, but we cannot stop there. We also need to develop alliances with associations whose members are not technologists but are involved in technology decisions and funding: school principals, school board presidents, higher education administrators, and others. Only if we can join forces will we be able to have an impact on political and legislative issues.

Finally, we need to challenge ourselves and broaden our perspective. An example of broadening perspective is found in the following letter from a college student to her parents.

Dear Mom and Dad,

You've probably been wondering why I haven't written lately. I didn't want you to worry, so I hope that someone else didn't tell you about my dormitory burning down.

I was in the hospital for only a few days, and as soon as all the bandages come off, the doctors assure me that my eyesight will return to almost normal.

Luckily, I found another place to stay right away. The nicest guy from a motorcycle gang let me stay with him and his friends.

I know how you've always wanted to be grandparents, so you'll be happy to hear that the baby is due in about seven months. Since I'm flunking out of school anyway, I should be home with you by then.

Your loving daughter,

Lori

P.S. None of the above is true. The dorm is fine, my eyesight is perfect, and I'm not pregnant. In fact, I don't even have a boyfriend yet. I'm not flunking out of school, but I did get a "D" on my last French test, I'm not doing well in my statistics class, and I could use another $200. I just wanted to make sure that when you got this news, you'd receive it with the proper perspective.

The task is enormous, but the process is exciting.

In a few years, we as an association will celebrate our 75th anniversary. It will occur as one century ends and another begins. I am confident that the anniversary will be a cause for celebration and not regret because we will have successfully met the challenges of change.

As you can see, there is much to be done, and the staff, officers, and Board cannot do it alone. Each of you must be committed to actively take part in creating a new and exciting AECT. I invite you to join me this year in this exciting venture and help us move toward our 75th anniversary in a position of strength and vitality.

Thank you.

Association for
Educational Communications and Technology
1996 Presidential Address

William J. Burns
Phoenix Learning Group
St. Louis, MO

A quick read of Bill Gates's new book, *The Road Ahead,* provides many insights into this entrepreneurial genius. Let me mention a few that struck me. The new house he's building and the technologies he plans for it tell me he does "walk his talk." The electronic pin you'll wear when you're inside will make you feel plugged in. Another impression was Mr. Gates's description of what the computer will give us an opportunity to do in the next 20-30 years. I especially like the one about a body suit that will greatly enhance our ability to feel. But you know, I don't need a body suit to tell you how I feel right now. I am humbled to be standing here this morning and privileged to have this unique opportunity. I also feel honored to have worked with Lynn Milet, and I thank her for her leadership, her generosity of spirit, her senses of seriousness and of humor, and her friendship. AECT is a better association today because of her. Thank you, Lynn.

Now for my task at hand.

For the past few months, I have been conducting surveys, sending out questionnaires, asking for feedback. Nothing very scientific, just Burns scratching where it itches—trying to get information.

Webster tells us that a volunteer is a person who enters or offers to enter into any service of their own free will. So we are a group of volunteers. I think all too often we get caught in the passion of the moment and forget about who we are and what, realistically, AECT can do. We have a large and often unwieldy governance structure. We have created an organizational umbrella that provides a residence for a diverse group of professionals who work in our field, and we will continue to expand that umbrella as others look for a home with us. I don't oppose this design at all, but we must realize that with this kind of structure and with the reality of limited monies and staff, we can't be all things to every group. And we must honor compromise. I haven't been an active member of AECT for over 30 years to worry about convention slots, or honor some call for member exclusivity, or be confronted by one of my cynical friends who rails against AECT and its survival. I listen, yes, and I try to communicate my commitment with realism and sensibility, and, hopefully, with not too much defensiveness.

What is my vision for AECT and for what priorities do I want AECT to stand?

1. A continuous examination and discussion of pedagogy. We are about teaching and about instruction in teaching methods. Whatever your professional role, you are about teaching and learning. Yes, the tools and the technologies are always changing, but the science is a constant. We look to AECT as one vehicle to improve the instruction we provide and the media and technologies we utilize.

2. A requirement for the highest level of research methodology, both qualitative and quantitative. The challenge is to move this research from the perception of isolation to its practical implementation in the classrooms and boardrooms of our society. If a teaching method or instructional product will enhance the student's learning and understanding beyond the excitable moment, how can we ensure that the teacher,

the administrator, the sales professional will incorporate such into their instructional repertoire? What I'm asking is, "Does technology make a difference? Can its use show increases in student achievement?" Read about, for example, the Peakview Elementary School Study in Aurora, Colorado. Don Ely, with the ERIC Clearinghouse at Syracuse University and a longtime AECT leader, says this is one of the finest examples of technology assisting to bring about educational reform. I want our research efforts to answer the commentators who ask, "Can technology enhance the academic standards in our classrooms, or is technology too often used in the 'dumbing down' of American education?" We need to understand that the central mission of AECT is to promote the effective application of technology in the teaching/learning process. Yes, we want to be recognized as a leader in the field of instructional technology. The research area is an arena where we shine. I encourage those divisions and individuals who conduct research to assertively disseminate that expertise into the broader educational community.

3. A commitment to professional ethics and personal integrity. I have no patience with those who pride themselves in the ways they violate copyright, for example, and then rationalize their behavior with excuses that times are different and require compromise. I want the technologies we have at our disposal, all of them, and those we help to develop, to enhance lives and to help eliminate the racism and sexism and intolerance that still haunt our society. I remember as a graduate student in 1963 listening to the ordeal of James Meredith trying to enroll in the University of Mississippi. I still hear today from a stream of radio and television talk show hosts the vitriolic and divisive dialogue that does not hide the vestiges of the thinking that Meredith had to endure. Don't misunderstand my words. My commitment to academic freedom and to First Amendment rights does not preclude me from speaking, and I encourage us to do the same.

4. A real, and realistic, electronic presence. Such a presence must expand on the work that has been accomplished this past year. The Electronic Services Task Force is now a standing committee. Their charge will be to take our electronic developments, our gopher, our listservs, and our home page, and define what the next steps should be. Some tell me we should be doing more. Rather than just expressing your concerns, give us your professional suggestions and expertise and offer to help with this important focus. On a personal level, I think of the words of John Perry Barlow, who suggested that "If you're heading somewhere where everything is new, the best tactic is to enjoy the ride." We all can't just enjoy the ride. Some of us have to help create the vehicle that will make the AECT ride meaningful for our own travelers, and for the many others who will take a short trip with us to check out our scenery. The competition for this piece of our time has become overwhelming. Think of how our conversation has changed in a few short years. I barely know what VRML means, and then there's the pressure to get my company's home page developed. Heck, I had to be dragged to the E-mail altar last year. And now, it's become a major time management challenge. And I'm supposed to be researching electronic commerce and EDI, or electronic data interchange. It was so much simpler in the early 1960s when, as an elementary school librarian, my young students knew that the only important web belonged to Charlotte. And maybe there's a lesson for us now. Charlotte's web was stronger than it looked, and although it was made of thin, delicate strands, it was not easily broken. Let's make certain that the web we are developing, and the links we will be creating, truly help us to communicate more effectively with each other and with the larger community.

5. An openness to working with others, a collaborative posture. The possibilities are endless, be they with existing associations and professional groups, or with those we could be romancing. The work of the AECT/AASL (American Association of School Librarians) Vision and Standards Writing teams is a positive example of a joint effort to generate a proactive document for library media specialists and for all educators well into the twenty-first century. There is the work of NARMC (National Association of Regional Media Centers) and CCUMC (Consortium of College and University Media Centers), both of whom are sponsoring and financially supporting Presidential sessions here in Indianapolis. The satellite distance learning networks, who are meeting here this week, are another group that shares much commonality with AECT. I mention their interactive satellite Presidential session cosponsored with the AECT Division of Telecommunications. Also here are representatives from the Council of the Great City Schools and their Urban Education Technology Forum, an organization that represents our 40 largest public school districts with over a quarter of all K-12 school children in this country. There are other affiliated organizations, like health educators in HeSCA (Health Science Communications Association), the National ITFS (Instructional Television Fixed Service) Association, IVLA (International Visual Literacy Association), FETA (Federal Educational Technology Association), AIME (Association for Indiana Media Educators), CCAIT (Community College Association for Instruction and Technology), and SRMLC (Southeastern Regional Media Leadership Council), also meeting here in Indianapolis. They are among others that are naturals for collaborative programs, projects, and products. And no, I haven't forgotten about ISTE, the International Society for Technology in Education. I have been communicating with their leadership about collaborative possibilities. We also have provided a technology strand for school administrators in cooperation with the Indiana Association of School Principals. And, most importantly, I want to thank AIME, our Indiana affiliate, for having the courage to meet with us. Thanks, especially to AIME President, Anne Mallett, for the encouragement she provided to the Convention Program planner and for her many accommodations. I'm also thinking about how we can partner with business and industry and what more we can do together. And, yes, without sounding too self-serving, I encourage all of you to spend time on the exposition floor. The companies represented invest significant dollars to be here. Don't tell me you don't have time to get there. I might take it personally. I will be appointing an action team to identify others with whom we can dialogue about ways we can share our expertise, like conference sessions and programming (i.e., "technology showplaces" for school administrators of all types), online virtual meetings and publishing, and regional workshops.

6. A program of Leadership Development that helps identify, encourage, nurture, and prepare leaders in our field and in the broader community as well. For years we have provided summer leadership opportunities. We have debated leadership development and association management as the appropriate planning focus. Many here have experienced both, as well as some of us older members who are Okoboji graduates. I will be appointing a leadership action team whose charge will be to study, and then recommend, a leadership development activity (i.e., a leadership academy) for Board consideration and hopefully, implementation in the summer of 1998. I will want this action team to identify partnerships with business and will request a plan that speaks to diverse and equitable representation from among the many strands that encompass AECT.

7. An informed, loyal, and growing membership. In a recent issue of the Illinois AECT Newsletter, President Jim Bradford offers that we need to build our membership by getting in touch with more of the people who share our concern for the use of technology in education at all levels. As members, Jim reminds us that getting involved is sometimes the biggest risk, a risk that can lead to new professional contacts, new ways of looking at old problems, and even new solutions. Yes, we need to grow the membership. Memberships generate income to be used for increased or expanded services. The challenge is to (1) find new members and (2) retain those we have, thus growing the bottom line and providing for greater association health and security. I'm convinced the pool is out there. Help us tap the faucet. I have appointed a membership action team to propose new ways of holding membership in AECT, and I will expect nothing less than positive growth this coming year.

8. A growing and diversified InCITE Conference and Exposition. I want to take this opportunity to recognize Stan, Lois, Maurye, and the entire AECT staff for their year-long efforts. I hope you all realize how much work has been done. On behalf of AECT, I thank each of you for the individual responsibilities you had and the collective results of your efforts. This InCITE kaleidoscope has been a shared responsibility. Thanks especially to Kay Bland for her work as Chair of this year's Convention Planning Task Force. You and Wes Miller, this year's Convention Volunteer Chair, helped to flesh out this outstanding program, and you filled the ranks of the committees and the volunteers who made this major event work. And the exhibition, in spite of competing influences like the Florida Technology show, is a growing recognition that AECT is a good place to be. Each of you can partner with us. Begin helping to sell next year's exhibit floor by visiting with the companies with whom you do business. If they are here, thank them. If you think they should be here and they're not, talk to them. They do listen to their customers.

9. An association that recognizes and honors its history and traditions. By this I mean a celebration of the work of the AECT Foundation and their auctions and scholarships; AECT round-up and wrap-up convention activities; university and regional and Okoboji receptions; and recognition of those members who are no longer with us, this year Denny Meyers and Juanita Skelton. This tradition also honors our past Presidents and the contributions they have made and continue to make. And we should be asking for their leadership and their insights on a continuing basis. We will celebrate our 75th anniversary as an active technology association in 1998. Join with Dave Little, the 75th anniversary chair, as he plans to make this a special event.

10. A strong state and regional foundation. I want us to find new ways to build on our state and regional affiliations. They are a source of membership; many have large and dynamic organizations. Too often the state affiliate is an afterthought when we look for answers to pressing problems. Please don't misrepresent my words as a lack of support for our Divisions and other affiliated organizations. Much of the Convention programming, a significant level of our publishing efforts, and the history of AECT is embedded in the work of our Divisions. Without their leadership and, yes, persistence, we would have little foundation upon which to build. What I will be asking for is more attention to our states and the regions they comprise. Some tell me that AASL has them all locked up, or ISTE has their allegiance. So, if we have a message to share and a product to sell, then I want to be in line, even if my place isn't in front. There's an old sales line that says, "To sell John Smith what

John Smith buys, you must see John Smith through John Smith's eyes." I want to check out the successes of the Wisconsin and Indiana and Michigan and Iowa and Georgia and Kansas and other successful state affiliates. We have much to learn from them and much to share with them. Let me be candid. I hear too often that AECT is only for professionals in higher education. I should say that that's not why I'm a member, nor most of you out there. I want to hear that AECT has something to offer for whomever is asking or looking. I will appoint an action team to examine the state affiliate and regional coordinator possibilities and ask them to report to the Board and to you later this year.

In 1994, the AECT Board adopted the work of the Vision Task Force and their Vision 2000 Strategic Plan. This plan has helped us focus our energies and our resources. Nothing I have said this morning conflicts with the words or the intent of this plan. This past summer the Board set as short-term priorities membership growth and development and expanded electronic services. These priorities will continue, as will my commitment to this sense of continuity. I also want to use some of my own colors as we paint together the broader picture this plan hopes to create.

Emerson wrote that "This time, like all times, is a good time, if we but know what to do with it." That elephant we've been nibbling at for these many years is still out there. Maybe it's time to set it free and order pizza. I look forward to working with your Board of Directors, and I invite you to be involved, to volunteer, to work with us, to recruit, and to be AECT's top salespeople. Do enjoy the rest of the conference; shake some hands and meet some new people, have some fun, visit the exhibits, and make plans now for summer leadership and professional development activities and for Albuquerque next February. And I'll order the pizza.

Thank you for being here.

National Library of Education

Nancy L. Floyd
National Library of Education

INTRODUCTION

The U.S. Congress authorized the establishment of the National Library of Education (NLE) within the U.S. Department of Education in March 1994. Thus the Department's Education Research Library became a *national* library. Already the largest federally funded library in the world devoted entirely to education, the National Library is the federal government's principal center for one-stop information and referral on education.

Currently, NLE houses on-site more than 200,000 books and about 750 periodical subscriptions in addition to studies, reports, Educational Resources Information Center (ERIC) microfiche, CD-ROM databases, and archives. Among the Library's services are reference, including legislative reference services; interlibrary loan; Internet (INet); ERIC; and a technology resources center.

NLE holds books on education, management, public policy, and related social sciences; dictionaries, encyclopedias, handbooks, directories, abstracts, indexes, and legal and other research sources in print and on CD-ROM; current and historical journals and newsletters; and more than 450,000 microforms. The Library serves the U.S. Department of Education staff, its contractors and grantees, and other federal employees; the Executive Office of the President of the United States; the U.S. Congress; education and library associations; researchers, students, and teachers from across the United States; and the general public.

The Library's mission is to ensure the improvement of educational achievement at all levels by becoming a principal center for the collection, preservation, and effective use of research and other information related to education. It also works to promote widespread access to its materials, to expand coverage of all education issues and subjects, and to maintain quality control. Finally, it participates with other major libraries, schools, and educational centers across the United States in providing a network of national education resources.

The Library is organized into three divisions: Collection and Technical Services, Reference and Information Services, and Resource Sharing and Cooperation.

COLLECTIONS

Primary collections include:

- **Circulating**—Books in the field of education published since 1965. The broad coverage of the collection includes not only education but also such related areas as law, public policy, economics, urban affairs, sociology, history, philosophy, and library and information science.

- **Reference**—Current dictionaries, general and specialized encyclopedias, handbooks, directories, major abstracting services, newspapers and journals related to education and the social sciences, and indexes.

- **Serials**—More than 750 English-language journals and newsletters. The collection includes nearly all of the primary journals indexed by *Current Index to Journals in Education* (*CIJE*) and *Education Index*. The Library subscribes to eight major national newspapers and maintains back issues of four national newspapers on microform.

- **Microforms**—More than 450,000 items, including newspapers, the *Federal Register*, the *Congressional Record*, *Newsbank*, college catalogs, the William S. Gray Collection on Reading, the Kraus Curriculum Collection, and various education and related journals. This collection also includes the complete microfiche collection of the ERIC system, a program funded by the U.S. Department of Education. NLE's ERIC collection contains complete sets of the ERIC indexes and recent ERIC Clearinghouse publications and products. Research publications are in varied formats— bibliographies, state-of-the-art papers, reviews, and information analyses in the 16 areas of education presently covered by the ERIC system.

Special collections include:

- Materials dating to the fifteenth century, including books about education; rare books published before 1800; historical books from 1800 to 1864; early American textbooks, 1775–1900; modern American textbooks, 1900–1959; and children's classics.
- Material from the former National Institute of Education, the former U.S. Office of Education, and the U.S. Department of Education, including reports, studies, manuals, and other documents.
- Archives of the former U.S. Office of Education and National Institute of Education, including speeches, policy papers, and other documents.

REFERENCE/RESEARCH/STATISTICS

NLE's toll-free number provides the public with low-cost access to statistics and research. Staff respond to questions about Department programs, activities, and publications; materials from other federal agencies; resources available through the ERIC Clearinghouses and the research institutes; statistics from the National Center for Education Statistics; and general reference questions. More than 100 telephone calls, 200 to 300 letters, more than 50 walk-in customers, and about 10 queries (Internet and fax) are answered daily. Specialized subject searches and retrieval of electronic databases are often performed, and documents are delivered by mail, by fax, and electronically. NLE also maintains an inventory of approximately 300 different OERI (Office of Educational Research and Improvement) publications for distribution on request. For new Department employees, NLE staff give monthly orientations.

NLE's Legislative Reference Service provides services to U.S. Department of Education employees as well as congresspeople, students, and the public. It also incorporates and maintains a library of legislative materials. The legislative materials include histories of education legislation of the U.S. Department of Education from 1867 to the present 104th Congress. These permanent records are maintained in FB-10, the U.S. Department of Education's headquarters building. A history contains the bills as introduced, reported, passed, and testified on; comments to Congress; public law version; and related matter. Copies of the legislative histories of pending bills from the current and one previous Congress are also kept. (Note: NLE does not maintain the Department's Law Library.)

Legislative Reference Services include access to the NLE's holdings via an electronic catalog; NLE books, copies of journal articles, and other documents; CD-ROM access to *Education Index, Readers' Guide to Periodical Literature*, and ERIC indexes; distribution of legislative materials to appropriate personnel; referrals to organizations, agencies, libraries, associations, and individuals as additional sources of information; and access to a small collection of current issues of major education journals and newsletters.

INTERLIBRARY LOAN

Approved libraries request materials from the Library at no charge. Materials are requested either by OCLC (Online Computer Library Center), an American Library Association (ALA) form faxed to the Library, or by E-mail with an ALA form following verification of request. The loan period is four weeks, and renewal of materials is for four weeks. NLE loans most material in the general collection; it does not loan material published before 1900; archives of the Office of Education, NIE, or Department of Education; or books recently added to the collection.

INTERNET SERVICES (INet)/WORLD WIDE WEB SITE

The U.S. Department of Education's Internet site, INet, is maintained by NLE. INet debuted in October 1993, offering public access to education research and statistics via gopher and file transfer protocol (ftp). In March 1994 a World Wide Web site was added (address: http://www.ed.gov). INet now hosts the Department's Online Library, which offers access not only to full-text research studies and syntheses on education, improvement information, and statistics, but also to a substantial and steadily growing collection of information about programs and initiatives across the Department.

The Online Library has become an important tool for providing public access to Department information. The collection has nearly doubled in size in the last year and now contains more than 14,000 files. The site receives more than a million hits each month from tens of thousands of Internet users in more than 80 countries worldwide. It is rated among the top 5 percent of Web sites (*Point Communications*, 10/95), listed as one of the top 1,001 Web sites (*PC Computing*, 12/95), and recognized as being "among the classiest—and most useful—of all federal sites" (*Government Executive*, 11/95).

The Online Library also provides a one-stop entry point to information stored at more than 40 other Department of Education-funded Internet sites, including ERIC, the Regional Educational Laboratories, the Institutes and their National Research and Development Centers, the Eisenhower National Clearinghouse for Math/Science Education, Star Schools, the National Clearinghouse for Bilingual Education, the National Rehabilitation Information Center, and the National Center for Research in Vocational Education.

The OERI Toll-Free Bulletin Board System (BBS) provides public access to most of the information in the Online Library for educators who don't yet have access to the Internet. Using a toll-free number to dial into the BBS, educators can discuss education issues and topics with their peers and share educational software, files, and information with each other and the public.

ERIC

ERIC is a public service that uses technology to increase access to education research and practice. At the core of ERIC is the largest education database in the world; it consists of nearly 900,000 records of journal articles, research reports, curriculum and teaching guides, conference papers, and books. The ERIC database can be accessed online via commercial vendors and public networks, on CD-ROM, or through printed abstract journals.

The ERIC system consists of 16 Clearinghouses, 9 adjunct Clearinghouses, and additional support components. ERIC Clearinghouses collect, abstract, and index education materials for the ERIC database; respond to thousands of requests for information; and produce more than 250 special publications each year on current research, programs, and practices.

The support components are the ERIC Processing and Reference Facility, the technical hub of the ERIC system, which produces and maintains the database and system-wide support products; the ERIC Document Reproduction Service (EDRS), which produces and sells microfiche and paper copies of documents announced in the ERIC database; and ACCESS

ERIC, which coordinates ERIC's outreach, dissemination, and marketing activities, develops system-wide ERIC publications, and provides general reference and referral services.

ERIC maintains an extensive Internet presence, including the award-winning AskERIC question answering service and virtual library, the National Parent Information Network, and more than a dozen subject-oriented gopher and World Wide Web sites. ERIC is proud to be a catalyst in fostering communication among virtual communities through the creation and administration of listservs. These electronic discussion groups (maintained by ERIC components) cover topics such as early childhood education, parenting, school library/media services, and K-12 school administration.

ERIC is assisted in its mission by more than 400 partner organizations that work in cooperation with ERIC to promote the use of education information among their constituents, and by nearly 2,000 groups who have signed acquisition arrangements to ensure that their publications are entered into the ERIC database. By continuing to maintain and improve the world's largest and most frequently accessed education database, ERIC provides a well-organized central repository for information used to make education decisions.

TECHNOLOGY RESOURCES

NLE's Technology Resources Center offers an opportunity to explore what is available in technology, to use the equipment, and to look at programs designed for use in classrooms. The Center has computer programs, CD-ROMs, videotapes, and videodisks. It offers a range of hardware and software for all levels of education and training.

The Center is open to visits from all educators, researchers, administrators, curriculum specialists, teachers, librarians, and others interested in the effective use of technology in education and training. Publishers of computer materials have provided more than 400 programs from preschool to graduate levels. The collection of computer programs is strong in science, reading, mathematics, and word processing. Programs on art, music, science, biology, history, mathematics, chemistry, and employment skills are included.

Equipment represents state-of-the art computer technology available for use in schools. Included are Compaq, Gateway, IBM, and Macintosh systems as well as Kodak Photo CD and Philips Full-Motion CDI systems. Several models of CD-ROM units are demonstrated for both MS-DOS and Macintosh. Interactive videodiscs using computers and bar code readers are shown, and videotape, electronic mail, online data services (including Internet), and closed-captioned decoders are all on display.

NLE's Center periodically gives programs on the use of technology in education. Special presentations and demonstrations can be arranged on request. Tours of the facilities and demonstrations of materials are given for visiting educators and the public. Center staff work with school systems, software publishers, and vendors to arrange special demonstrations related to individual school system needs. The Center does not evaluate, recommend, or endorse hardware or software, nor does it lend software or equipment. Equipment is used solely for demonstration.

RESOURCE SHARING AND COOPERATION

NLE is developing a network of national education technology and related resources. The network will promote greater cooperation and resource sharing among education and library professionals, policy-makers, the public, and other providers and repositories of education information in America. It will also apply information science, computer, and telecommunications technologies for the enhancement of education information dissemination.

NLE has begun to build a list of organizations and to identify key advisors, a broader set of groups to consult, and potential cooperating partners. These include the other national libraries, library associations, education associations, university libraries with major education collections, state departments of education and library agencies, federally funded technical assistance centers and information clearinghouses, the Government Printing Office, and the National Archives and Records Administration.

An introductory meeting with the Special Libraries Association in October 1995 indicated that NLE's Internet presence, which includes an NLE home page and pointers to numerous other library resources on the Internet and the Department of Education's main servers, was an excellent start. An "Education Resources Directory" project has been initiated to provide Internet access to a database of national, regional, and state resources, including education clearinghouses, technical assistance centers, state departments of education and library agencies, and specialized services.

Public Relations

NLE publishes a bimonthly newsletter, *New at NLE.* The newsletter is distributed throughout the U.S. Department of Education and to a special NLE mailing list of about 350 librarians and other interested parties. The Library also has a commemorative poster, bookmarks, rolodex cards, and various fact sheets for distribution by fax or mail.

Briefings and Seminars. Throughout the year, NLE offers a variety of customized briefings, seminars, and orientations to both internal and external groups. These briefings can center exclusively on the services of the Library itself or incorporate information and expertise from OERI. Recently, Library staff have designed, organized, and conducted briefings for groups as diverse as the National Education Association, official delegations from Mexico and the Republic of Korea, and a group of doctoral students from Virginia Tech.

Lecture Series. NLE sponsors a quarterly lecture series titled "Libraries, Research, and Technology." The lectures feature nationally known experts who discuss the latest developments in technology, education, and research, and the impact of these developments on teaching, learning, and the transmission of knowledge in the Information Age. All lectures are open to the public, especially teachers, parents, students, librarians, and federal employees.

Collaborative Projects Between NLE and the School District of Philadelphia. Since March 1995, the School District of Philadelphia and NLE have worked together extensively on many projects. During the course of this partnership, staff from both organizations have designed and conducted focus groups on the changing role of school librarians, the importance of technological innovation and training for all members of the school community, and the value of partnerships. In addition, through collaborative efforts with various university consortia in Pennsylvania, NLE and the School District of Philadelphia offered training sessions to more than 200 Philadelphia school librarians and designed two graduate information science classes that can be given via satellite and over the Internet.

One of the outstanding characteristics of the products and ideas designed by this partnership is their applicability and replicability for other school districts. Already, other school districts have expressed interest in developing similar partnerships with NLE.

FOR MORE INFORMATION

Telephone Numbers:

Library Information	(202) 219-1692
Fax	(202) 219-1696
Reference/Research/Statistics	(202) 219-1692
Outside Washington area	(800) 424-1616
Fax	(202) 219-1696
E-mail	library@inet.ed.gov

Circulation/ILL	(202) 219-2238
E-mail	libloans@inet.ed.gov
Collection Development	(202) 219-1883
Legislative Reference Service	(202) 401-1045
Fax	(202) 401-9023
Technology Resources Center	(202) 219-1699
ACCESS ERIC	(800) LET-ERIC

NLE is open 9 AM to 5 PM Monday through Friday except federal holidays. Located at street level, it is easily accessed by the physically disabled. The address is 555 New Jersey Avenue NW, Washington, DC 20208-5721. Direct entry: 80 F Street NW. The U.S. Department of Education's headquarters building is located at 600 Independence Avenue SW, Washington, DC 20024.

Part Three
Current Developments

Introduction

One of the goals of the *Educational Media and Technology Yearbook* is to present up-to-date information on new developments in the field. Part 3 represents the new products for, innovative ideas about, and creative new applications of media and technology to the teaching and learning process. While this section attempts to be comprehensive in its review of current developments, the range of topics is not exhaustive. An illustrative example of current developments in educational media and technology is the propagation of the World Wide Web and the vast amount of information available via the Internet.

Calls for systematic reform, the increasing importance of information technology, the advent of local area networks in K-12 schools, a fundamental desire for computer skills for problem solving, and basic Internet resources are promoted here as chapters or as ERIC Digests from the Clearinghouse on Information and Technology. The authors for the contributions in this part represent teachers, students, professors, network information specialists, virtual librarians, and administrators from all levels of educational institutions. They are as follows:

Donald P. Ely

Steven Hackbarth

Glen Holmes and John Wenrich

Charles Reigeluth and Dale Avers

Larry Anderson

Timoth Lederman

Michael Eisenberg, Doug Johnson, and Robert Berkowitz

Anna Maria Lankes

The topics presented in Part 3 clearly indicate how educational media and technology have come a long way from traditional audiovisual aids and services. Furthermore, instructional technology and educational technology may actually have different connotations. However, educational media and technology remains the field where such issues and innovations are located.

Technology Is the Answer!
But What Was the Question?*

Donald P. Ely
Professor Emeritus, Instructional Design, Development, and Evaluation
Syracuse University

A person does not have to go very far to interact with technology today. On any given day a person is awakened by a digital alarm clock that emanates music, voice, or an insistent alarm. There may be a message waiting on the answering machine from an overnight call. On the way to work, the control panel on the car indicates status of the vehicle through small computer chips that monitor several functions. A stop at the bank means an interface with the ATM to obtain cash for the day. Once in the office, the first activity of the day is to check E-mail that has been sent from many parts of the world. And so it goes from one technological application to another—all aimed toward making life (and work) more efficient, pleasurable, and convenient. And what about school?

Computers are ubiquitous. Almost every school in the United States has computers, and 75 percent of them have network capabilities (Heaviside and Farris 1995). The student/computer ratio (microdensity) has increased from 1/75 in 1984 to 1/12 last year (Quality Education Data 1994). Seventy-four percent of the schools have cable television access (Heaviside and Farris 1995), which translates to more than 35 million students (Kamil 1995). Ninety-eight percent of the schools have videotape recorders. Equipment does not seem to be a major problem despite major financial limitations in many school systems and universities.

Online computer networks are in the spotlight now. The Internet is probably the best known of all networks, with more than 13,500,000 users (as of yesterday afternoon) and growing at a rate of about 2,000 users every day. The potentials for access to all kinds of information are overwhelming, and the opportunities for connecting to individuals all over the world are mind-boggling. We are developing virtual communities through virtual libraries (e.g., information online and stored on CD-ROMs) and virtual classrooms (through the wonders of satellite and cable-delivered distance education), and the end is not in sight. Soon it may not be possible to tell the functional difference between reality and apparent reality in the home, community, and classroom.

What are the common threads running through the fabric of technology in education and society? Interaction, engagement, community communication—all made possible by digital technologies that are widely available, relatively inexpensive, and (for the most part) easy to use.

There is no doubt that we live in an information age and that technology is the symbol of progress. Each day brings new products, new applications, new hardware and software, and new opportunities to connect with information resources and people. There is an inevitability about the growth of information technology. We expect new developments, new products, and new experiences. I have the uncomfortable feeling that we often overlook the reasons for all of the innovations. We do not seem to ask "Why?" We have been swept up by the tide of technology without fully understanding what purpose it serves and the ultimate consequences of our adoption and use. Robert Snider (1972) said that technology often produces confusion over human means and human ends. When technology makes it possible for people to do something, people do it, not always because it is necessary, but because it is possible. In the process, technology sometimes raises new moral issues related to long-held goals that can now be achieved with unimagined effectiveness. For example, how fast do we want to move across the face of the Earth? For how long shall we defer death?

---

*The James P. Curtis Distinguished Lecture, Capstone College of Education Society, College of Education, University of Alabama, April 14, 1995.

TECHNOLOGY

We must be careful about use of the word *technology*. There is much meaning in the word if we want to explore it. Technology is often used as a synonym for *hardware—machines, equipment.* At best, some think of technology as *hardware + software,* but not many people take it further. What we really need to know is *why* technology is in the school (or home, university, workplace), *how* it is being used, and *what results* have occurred because of its use.

Technology, according to *Webster's Third,* is "the application of scientific knowledge to practical purposes in a particular field." Sometimes the process is reversed; that is, technological developments precede scientific work. James Watts's steam engine, for example, was efficiently running the mills of England for 75 years before a scientific explanation of this phenomenon was forthcoming. There is not much "scientific knowledge" in computer hardware, cable connections, or satellite television except in the design of the instruments themselves. These are the *vehicles* that *deliver* the software that can be applied to "practical matters." What is delivered is *not* knowledge, but data and information; there *is* a difference! Even the hardware plus the software does not accomplish much until it is *designed* and *used* to engage individuals—in a game, an accounting problem, or a physics experiment. The systematic design and use of hardware and software to achieve specific objectives is the way I view educational technology.

We complain that "technology" often makes decisions for us. We say that "television" has a negative influence on children. We curse the computer error in our bills from the credit card company. But it is *not* the hardware, the television set, or the computer terminal that creates our concerns; it is the way in which the software has been *designed* and the way it has been *used* (or abused) that brings about these feelings of frustration. Technology is amoral. In itself it is neither good nor bad, humane or inhumane. The morality of any technology is a function of its *use* as it is applied. Technology, in the sense that has been described here, is our friend—a process or tool that can be used to solve problems and make our life more satisfying. Yes, technology is the answer! But what was the question?

DISTURBING INDICATORS

We may feel comforted that there is hardware and software in the schools. *But . . .* the *questions* are:

> *How* is it being used? By *whom*? For what *purpose*? How *often*? and
> With what *results*?

Schools feel that they must have technology to be up-to-date. If technology is equated to hardware, the statistics are proof of the ubiquitous nature of technology in the schools: in 1994, approximately $2.4 billion was spent for educational technology in the K-12 schools (QED 1994). Higher education spent about $6 billion (Geoghagen 1994). A report of the Software Publishers Association says that "more than half the schools in the country now use computers in almost every discipline."

There is a rush to technology unlike any previous time. Historical cycles of technology in Education often mirror cycles in other sectors of society. These cycles often characterize an era. In this century alone, we have seen the rise and fall of such media as lantern slides, sound recordings, silent (and then sound) movies, filmstrips, radio, and teaching machines. Now computers and television can be found in almost every school and college in the land. One common theme that has run through the introduction of each new medium is that each one was an *aid* (an *enhancement, enrichment*) to the teaching/learning process. None of these media became so pervasive that comprehensive instructional programs were designed to make them integral to the syllabus or curriculum. That is, no teacher was ever *required* to use these media;

it has been possible to teach a class, a unit, a course, or a curriculum without using any of them. It is the same today. Computers are *add-ons*. They rarely *supplant* other media and methods. They may *supplement* other resources, but they are seldom integral to the process of teaching/ learning. Carol Twigg, Vice President of EDUCOM and leader of the National Learning Infrastructure Initiative, is quoted as saying that the problem with all the uses of information technology in the last decade—computer-aided instruction, networked information, distance learning—"is that they were bolted onto current instructional methods" (Reinhardt 1995). How, then, are computers used in schools today?

If we look at recent studies, we find the most frequent location of computers is in the administrative office of the school, the second is in the library media center, and the third is in a computer lab (Heaviside and Farris 1995). Computers do not find their way into classrooms as often as to other locations in the school. Analysis of current practices indicates that the most frequent use is for word processing, followed by drill and practice and educational games (Pelgrum and Plomp 1991). Only 3 percent of all instructional spaces in public schools are connected to the Internet (Heaviside and Farris 1995).

An astute analysis of computer use in schools was developed by David Hawkridge (1990). He specifies four rationales for using computers in schools:

- *The social rationale.* Policy-makers want to be sure that all children are "aware and unafraid of how computers work." Because "computers are pervading industrial societies and are likely to be important in all countries," learners should be prepared to understand computers and be aware of their role in society.

- *The vocational rationale.* Learning to operate computers is an important competency. "Teaching children programming gives them some confidence in their ability to control computers, and may be a foundation for a career in computer science." There will be employment opportunities for people who have the proper computer skills.

- *The pedagogic rationale.* Students can learn from computers: "computers can teach." There are advantages over traditional methods when using computers to learn. No specific type or amount of learning is specified.

- *The catalytic rationale.* "Schools can be changed for the better by the introduction of computers." Computers facilitate change. They are symbols of progress. They encourage learning. "Computers are seen as catalysts, enabling desired change in education to occur" (Hawkridge et al. 1990).

In the United States, the *social* and *vocational* rationales seem to dominate. The rapid and extensive adoption of computers in the schools reinforces the notion that computers are symbols of modern schools. It is the *pedagogic* and *catalytic* rationales that seem to be diminished in our schools. The basic reason for this status is that we have not asked the right questions about *why, how,* and *with what results?*

But . . . *what difference do they make?* A recent report of a $24 million investment in educational technology in a Detroit, Michigan, school district indicated that students who used it continued to remain near the bottom of test scores three years later (*The Heller Report* 1995). Henry Becker, a University of California psychologist, said that "In education, our expectations for what can be done with computers are unduly inflated by our persistent tendency to publicize only our successes. . . . Even worse is the widespread attention we give to partial anecdotal evidence that some children have achieved remarkable things using technology." Becker's studies have shown that computer-based programs at the elementary school level really benefit only two groups of students—the initially highest scoring students and students taught by teachers most knowledgeable about the computer system being used (Becker 1990).

The picture is not much brighter in colleges and universities. William Geoghagen, a former university professor and academic administrator and now consultant to IBM for higher education, says that "Recent surveys [show] . . . that no more than about 10 percent of faculty are doing very much with technology in the classroom, despite a national ownership rate for PCs of about 50 percent among college and university faculty" (Geoghagen 1994).

A bold red headline in a current library publication says: "New technology is exciting. It can also be expensive, inefficient, and exactly what you don't need," and goes on to point out the advantages of microfilm and microfiche.

The cover story in a recent issue of *Byte* says that "Computers in the schools have soaked up huge capital expenditures without providing any appreciable return on investment." Further in the article, the author concludes that "Technology alone is not the solution. Reaping the benefits of computers first requires extensive teacher training, new curricular materials, and, most important, changes in educational models" (Reinhardt 1995, p. 52).

The research findings about learning from computers in schools are sparse and unconvincing. We *do* know that computers are motivating, especially with younger learners; they like to use them. We *do* know that appropriate use of technology can boost retention rates, and we *do* know that the use of technology can reduce boredom and misbehavior. The jury is still out on student achievement because most studies have focused on use of the hardware and have not asked the "right" questions about the software and how it has been used, the type of learner who is using it, and the appropriateness for attaining certain curricular objectives. For the most part, teachers are puzzled because: (1) they are unsure *how* to use technology; (2) they question *why* they should use it; and (3) they do not know *where* to place it in the curriculum. When media are used, they appear to be add-ons most of the time with little direct relevance to the curricula being taught.

In a recent issue of *Educational Technology*, there is confirmation of the uncertainty about computer use in schools:

> If we look at how computer technology is actually being used in the service of education, it is not surprising to find that it turns out to play a very traditional role. It is either viewed as a matter of isolated subject mastery, or as a means of augmenting and enhancing the material to be learned—that is, merely as another tool for presenting the same conceptual toolkit of accepted methods and means representing the body of knowledge currently embraced by the educational system (Lazlo and Castro 1995).

It is unfortunate that, with all the excitement and obvious high motivation of students in using technology, schools and universities, by and large, have not made appropriate or optimal use of the technological resources at hand to improve teaching and learning. Perhaps before we decide to purchase any more hardware or software or conduct any more teacher workshops, we should stop and ask: "What was the question?"

In the popular press, Clifford Stoll has strong words about the wisdom of virtual communities and virtual classrooms in his new book, *Silicon Snake Oil*. He is concerned about Internet home pages that offer electronic gateways to any location in the world and are enticing computer users away from nonvirtual pursuits—away from talking with each other, reading books, and looking up at the sky. Stoll goes on to say that "The key ingredient of their silicon snake oil is a technocratic belief that computers and networks will make a better society. Access to information, better communications and electronic programs can cure social problems. I don't believe them." He adds, "There are no simple technological solutions to social problems. . . . The most important interactions in life happen between people, not between computers." He finds the idea that computers are tools disturbing. "A tool for what? A tool for thinking? Is reasoning so painful that we require a labor-saving device?" Strong words; perhaps too strong, but they offer a warning flag to potential problems down the road.

A PLEA FOR SANITY AND PLANNING

The cynical comments about the bleakness of technology's contributions to schools should be tempered by the fact that we live in a technological society and schools are part of that society. We cannot escape the reality of the Information Age in which we live any more than we can avoid the need for a radio or a telephone in our everyday life. We are caught up in the web of technology. It can serve us well; it can help us to solve some of our most pressing problems in education if only we can step back from it as Robert Pirsig did in his classic *Zen and the Art of Motorcycle Maintenance:*

> The way to solve the conflict between human values and technological needs is not to run away from technology. That's impossible. The way to resolve the conflict is to break down the barriers of dualistic thought that prevent a real understanding of what technology is—not an exploitation of nature, but a fusion of nature and the human spirit into a new kind of creation that transcends both. When this transcendence occurs in such events as the first airplane flight across the ocean or the first footstep on the moon, a kind of public recognition of the transcendent nature of technology occurs. But this transcendence should also occur at the individual level, on a personal basis, in one's own life, in a less dramatic way (Pirsig 1974).

In speaking of school reform, the term *transformation* is often used. As we consider major changes in our schools and universities, and the role of technology in those changes, we need to ask some very fundamental questions:

1. What are we trying to accomplish in our schools and universities?

2. What do we know about the learners we are trying to reach?

3. What can best be learned alone or in small groups? In large groups?

4. What specific skills do we want our students to acquire, and how will we know when they have achieved competence?

A recent discussion group on the Internet inaugurated by technology people in the U.S. Department of Education asked interested educators to discuss five questions:

1. What professional development do teachers need in order to use technology in ways that help students learn?

2. How can technology itself be used to help teachers learn?

3. Are there any schools or communities that are currently using technology effectively for professional development?

4. What can be done to strengthen those efforts? What can be done to encourage more efforts?

5. What should be the role of the federal government in promoting the use of technology for the professional development of teachers?

Are these the *right* questions? *Yes*, some of them are, especially those that target the teacher as a key player in the process. Decisions can be made from the "top," but unless the classroom teacher is convinced that change is important and has the knowledge and skills to make it happen, innovations will languish even as equipment gathers dust.

Are these the *right* questions? *No*, because they do not go far enough and deep enough. If only we could ask questions about where students are in the learning curve; if only we could ask questions about what it is that we want learners to accomplish in a given period of time; and if only we could explore the methods that engage learners ("turn them on") and help them to become responsible for their own learning, then we would find the ways in which technology as our tool and ally could be appropriately used to accomplish our educational mission.

We are too eager for instant results in this age of fast foods, drive-in windows, and fax communication. Immediate feedback, instant gratification, and confirmation without delay are the order of the day. North America is one part of the world where technology has contributed to the solution of many problems—e.g., the nature of our galaxy, the causes of diseases, and universal telecommunications. It is natural, therefore, that we should turn to technology to answer the questions and solve the problems of teaching and learning in schools. But the setting, the expectations, the human interactions that make up this milieu are not always susceptible to technological solutions and certainly not to some solutions that must be implemented over time. We have been brought up on the myth that almost any problem can be solved with a technological solution. In Education, this assumption is dangerous, and in terms of technology, it can be disastrous.

USING TECHNOLOGY EFFECTIVELY

One of the U.S. Department of Education questions seems especially worth exploring: "Are there any schools . . . that are currently using technology effectively?" Yes, there are. Where are they? The ERIC Clearinghouse on Information & Technology at Syracuse University has published a comprehensive report on the program of the Peakview Elementary School District in Colorado, which incorporates some sensible and appropriate applications of technology.

Peakview is a new school that is implementing many organizational changes and teaching strategies advocated by the school restructuring movement. Among the strategies is the placement of more than 80 networked computers in classrooms. A study of the Peakview program discovered that technology had a positive effect on student learning and attitudes. Teachers are using technology to adapt to student needs and interests and to increase the amount and quality of cooperative learning activities. Students use the technology extensively for research and writing and for learning support. Technology has changed the way teachers work professionally, resulting in a net increase in hours and greater productivity, effectiveness, and satisfaction.

Many factors contributed to the success of Peakview's use of technology:

1. *Computers are abundantly available in the classroom.* Each classroom has at least four computers and adjoining classrooms share their computers.

2. *Shared commitment and vision of school reform with technology is an essential component.* An environment was cultivated over time that encouraged mutual support and sharing of resources.

3. *A supportive district and principal.* The principal and staff worked with the district administration to develop a set of innovative values; the principal learned to use computers along with the teaching staff.

4. *A strong computer coordinator.* One full-time teacher assigned to provide leadership and support was critical to the success of the program.

5. *Early and thorough teacher training.* Before the school opened, teachers received training and instructional software to be used in classes. Continuing in-service education is available.

6. *Taking computers home.* After training in the school, teachers were given a computer to take home for six weeks. They became comfortable with the computers, and many received help from their children.

7. *User-friendly systems.* Easy-to-use hardware and quality software contributed to successful implementation (Wilson, Teslow, Cyr, and Hamilton 1995).

At the heart of the change process is the belief that we can no longer teach all the knowledge that individual students will need in the future. Because we cannot expect students to learn all the *answers,* we must help them to learn how to raise the right *questions,* and then help then to learn where to go to get the information and how to find it and apply it. This is a big order, but in an era when the amount of information available exceeds that which was available at any time in history, we have to reconceptualize our schools and make a qualitative change in the nature of learning itself. This is the challenge to Education today. If *Technology Is the Answer!* the questions are:

How can we create the conditions for learners to become increasingly responsible for their own learning?

How can we help learners to use the tools that are required for survival in a technological society?

How can we "humanize" technology in the service of all people?

How can we help learners to raise the "right" questions?

The *answers* are *not* in the technology itself but in the *people* who decide about the *purpose* of its use, the *way* in which it is used, and the *manner* in which we evaluate the *consequences* of our decisions.

The most important outcome in education is to help each learner become responsible for his or her own learning. Call it "innovation" . . . call it the "right question" . . . call it "humane technology"; whatever its name, it is the goal of education for the twenty-first century.

BIBLIOGRAPHY

Becker, H. J. (1990). *Computer use in United States schools: 1989. An initial report of U.S. participation in the I.E.A. Computers in Education Survey.* Paper presented at the annual meeting of the American Educational Research Association, Boston.

Geoghagen, W. H. (1995). *What ever happened to instructional technology?* Norwalk, CT: IBM Academic Consulting.

Hawkridge, D. G., Jaworski, J. and McMahon, H. (1990). *Computers in third-world schools: Examples, experiences and issues.* (London: Macmillan), 16-21.

Heaviside, S., and Farris, E. (1995). *Advanced telecommunications in U.S. public schools, K-12.* Washington, DC: U.S. Department of Education.

The Heller Report 6 (March 1995), 3.

Kamil, B. L. (1995) *Delivering the future: Cable and education partnerships for the Information Age.* Alexandria, VA: Cable in the Classroom.

Lazlo, A., and Castro, K. (1995). Technology and values: Interactive learning environments for future generations. *Educational Technology 35*(2), 7-13.

Pelgrum, W. J., and Plomp, Tj. (1991). *The uses of computers in education worldwide: Results from the IEA Computers in Education survey in 19 education systems.* Oxford, UK: Pergamon Press.

Pirsig, R. M. (1974). *Zen and the art of motorcycle maintenance.* (New York: William Morrow), 284-85.

Quality Education Data. (1994). *Education mailing lists market guide.* Denver, CO: Author.

Reinhardt, Andy. (1995, March). New ways to learn. *Byte 20*(3), 50-52, 54-56, 62, 66-67, 70, 72.

Snider, R. (1972, February). Will technology humanize us? *NASSP Bulletin,* 87-97.

Stoll, C. (1995). *Silicon snake oil.* New York: Doubleday.

Wilson, B. G., Teslow, J. L., Cyr, T. A., and Hamilton, R. (1995). *Technology making a difference: The Peakview Elementary School study.* Syracuse, NY: ERIC Clearinghouse on Information and Technology.

Web-Based Learning
in the Context of K-12 Schooling

Steven Hackbarth
Computer Specialist Teacher, P.S. 6 & 116, Manhattan
Consultant, UNICEF

THE SCHOOLING CONTEXT

Imagine a primary or secondary school in which teachers, administrators, librarians, media specialists, parents, students, and local businesses collaborate in setting and achieving ambitious educational aims. Here, math and science are taught hands-on in labs, with a balance of reading texts, conducting research, and producing exhibits. Social studies entail selecting, evaluating, and synthesizing information from diverse sources—human, videos, computer. Ample exposure to biographies and imaginative literature provide models of good character, not just "authentic" vocabulary and *Goosebumps*. Solving problems that arise in the context of students' daily lives, or from their readings, drive the day-to-day curriculum, along with producing reports, plays, poems, posters, works of art, musical and dramatic performances, and multimedia reports. Instruction meets individual needs and draws upon distinctive talents. Teachers engage students in "impassioned scholarly apprenticeships" across the curriculum, modeling the intense labors and foibles of disciplinary and interdisciplinary inquiry. Assessment is ongoing, shared, multidimensional, and aligned with the evolving curriculum.

Here, in a context of safety (where chronically disruptive students have been placed in alternative settings and sexual harassment is not tolerated), students are challenged to expand their horizons, after first washing their hands, cleaning the floor, and putting their desks in order. As students collaborate in completing classroom activities, they discover such traditional values as fairness, honesty, respect, and sharing, and that the only sure joy comes through *mutual* enhancement (not like Shel Silverstein's *The Giving Tree!*). Bonds of friendship are formed across gender, age, race, and religion.

Teachers at this school are respected for what they already do well, from resolving conflicts and appeasing parents to enhancing literacy and forming character. They are involved in decisions that affect their professional practice. When mandates are issued that require them to change that practice, they are given time, incentives, and information to do so. Media specialists keep equipment in order and recommend suitable programs, freeing the teacher to focus on pedagogical soundness, especially with respect to effectiveness and efficiency.

It is within such a context, and surely within some far less favorable, that computer-based learning (CBL) generally, and Web-based learning (WBL) in particular, need to be incorporated (Schofield 1995). Keeping in mind high ideals, ambitious educational aims, strategies that have proven effective, and media that are suitable and available provides what I consider to be a proper perspective for assessing the roles in K-12 schooling of rapidly evolving computer technologies. Others may advocate more revolutionary approaches; mine is an evolutionary, situated one.

EVOLUTION OF THE "WORLD WIDE WEB"

Que's Computer User's Dictionary (Pfaffenberger 1993) defines *network* as "a computer-based communications and data exchange system created by physically connecting two or more computers" (p. 419). The definition of "local area network" (LAN) is given as "the linkage of personal and other computers within a limited area by high-performance cables so that users can exchange information, share expensive peripherals, and draw on the resources of a massive secondary storage unit, called a *file server*" (p. 359). A "wide area network" (WAN) "uses high-speed, long-distance communications networks or satellites to connect computers over distances greater than the distances—one or two miles—traversed by local area networks" (p. 655). So then, what are the Internet and its World Wide Web?

As far as I was able to piece it together, the story goes like this. In 1969, the U.S. Department of Defense Advanced Research Projects Agency (ARPA, later DARPA) initiated an ambitious project to ensure the reliability of computer networks, vital resources during times of war and peace alike. Linking government and university labs, ARPAnet soon evolved into an efficient means of exchanging information, a largely unanticipated bonus. Military agencies split from ARPAnet in 1983 to form MILnet, but the thread of interconnectivity that remained between them became known as DARPA Internet, soon abbreviated to the Internet.

To facilitate academic research, the National Science Foundation in 1986 tied together five supercomputer centers (NSFnet), and then linked with ARPAnet. The key to this harmonious marriage, and to the "extended family" that moved in rapidly, was the UNIX multiuser operating system that had been developed by AT&T Bell Laboratories and distributed gratis to educational institutions. UNIX's Transmission Control Protocol/Internet Protocol (TCP/IP) enabled linking of diverse LANs and WANs across the globe.

Further impetus was provided in 1987 when Merit Network, Inc., joined with IBM and MCI in expanding NSFnet, the successor to the outmoded (8-bit processor-based) ARPAnet. Jumping on the "Netbandwagon" were CSNet (computer science departments), FidoNet (a worldwide network of personal computers), BITnet (Because It's Time Network, primarily educational institutions), and hordes of Ethernet-based (a high-speed network hardware standard) LANs. Commercial enterprises were granted "gateway" access to the Internet in the early 1990s, and today thousands of networks are joined across the globe.

The Internet might have remained largely a techie toy but for the crafting in 1989 of a tool, the World Wide Web software, which permitted "hypertext" linking of files across computer networks. This innovation is credited to physicist Tim Berners-Lee at The European Center for Particle Physics (CERN, Geneva). With it one need only move one's cursor to a highlighted term and press **<Return>** to be quickly and effortlessly connected to another computer having information related to that term. These hypertext links soon evolved into hypermedia as the kinds of files that could be read expanded to include audio, image, and video. And what the Macintosh operating system and Microsoft's Windows did for making computer technology more easily accessible to the masses, the graphical user interface (GUI) Mosaic software (in 1993) and its successors (e.g., NCSA Mosaic, Enhanced Mosaic, Spry Mosaic, Netscape Navigator) have done for the Internet and its World Wide Web. The addition of such Web browsers in 1995 to the major commercial online services, first Prodigy, then America Online and CompuServe, vastly expanded public access, acceptance, and use.

Returning to my ancient source (Pfaffenberger 1993), the Internet is defined as "a system of linked computer networks, worldwide in scope, that facilitates data communication services such as remote login, file transfer, electronic mail, and distributed newsgroups" (p. 330). The World Wide Web is defined as "an experimental hypertext-based document retrieval system" (p. 663). Added was the tip: "Don't expect every resource on Internet to be accessible through the Web. To be accessible, a document must have been coded with links readable by Web servers, and to date, only a very small proportion of the information available on the net is accessible in this way" (p. 663). Since that was written, the number of documents prepared expressly for the Web has been expanding like the universe. The 1996 *Random House Personal Computer Dictionary* (Margolis 1996) defined this dynamically evolving World Wide Web in understated terms that contrast sharply with the media hype as: "A system of Internet servers that support specially formatted documents . . . in a language called *HTML (HyperText Markup Language)* that supports links to other documents, as well as graphics, audio, and video files" (p. 523). So what are the attributes of this new medium that might be contributing to its headline-making popularity and to claims that it can transform schooling?

ATTRIBUTES OF THE WEB

Does the World Wide Web have distinctive (beyond teachers and multimedia CD-ROM, for example) attributes ("affordances") that permit the design of uniquely superior learning activities? In what sense does it "recontextualize" abstractions that characterize traditional subject matter? What sorts of "interactivity" can be incorporated? In this section I briefly examine these issues.

The Web appears to be distinctive in at least five respects.

- It provides economical access to people and multiformat information in ways unmatched by any other combinations of media.

- Much content on the Web cannot be found in any other format, except the authors' originals.

- The Web permits the work of individuals such as teachers and students to be shared with the world.

- It is a powerful, flexible resource, in some ways (e.g., global hypermedia links) unlike any others, that students are likely to encounter and rely on in the workplace.

- Students approach the Web with eager anticipation and awe, knowing that it is at the cutting edge of technology used by their most progressive peers and by successful adults.

Greg Kearsley (1996) elaborated on attributes of the Web as follows:

> The most significant aspect of the web for education at all levels is that it dissolves the artificial wall between the classroom and the "real world." ... With the web ... students can find original materials and collect first-hand information themselves. ... The second powerful aspect ... is that it provides an easy mechanism for students (and teachers) to make their work public. ... Furthermore, students can examine the work of others ... , [which] allows for global comparisons, collaborations and competition. ... A third aspect ... is that it provides an easy way to create and distribute multimedia materials. ... Finally, ... students ... can include links to the source material in their work. ... [And they can] include input fields in a web document [to] collect data or comments from everyone who visits (pp. 28-29).

That the Web has unquestioned, distinctive merits is reflected in district and national *mandates*, not just recommendations, that all schools "get wired." I believe that the above few core attributes alone are sufficient to open up possibilities for the systemic, systematic design, development, and conduct of productive learning activities surely not previously feasible, many perhaps not even possible. But it remains fair to ask: (1) in what senses WBL conceivably might break down the "artificial wall between the classroom and the 'real world,' " and (2) to what extent WBL may be considered "interactive."

I believe that there are senses in which WBL can "break down the classroom walls." For one, as Odvard Egil Dyrli (1995) pointed out, "much of the information has not been filtered through the popular media (although it will reflect the point of view of the person posting). The Net makes it possible for young people to learn about their government [for example] first hand, by tapping directly into documents such as speeches, bills, and voting records" (p. 10). Thus, students have timely, convenient access to vast multimedia resources not available locally. Second, the Web provides synchronous ("Internet relay chat," "*CU-SeeMe*" video-conferencing) and asynchronous print (E-mail), audio, and video (V-mail and multimedia E-mail [MIME]) communications among students, teachers, parents, and other resource persons worldwide, only now for the price of a local telephone call (Fetterman 1996).

Nevertheless, I would temper our claims for WBL bringing the "real world" into the classroom with the observation that the Web is *not* the "real world," although it may represent a bit of its best and worst aspects. Permit me a few lines of hyperbole for consideration:

- As voyeurs on the Web's so-called "real world stage," we may overlook events and opportunities ever present in our "lived worlds" and those of our students.

- WBL activities can only connect with students' own life experiences if they have first undergone, and reflected upon, such experiences.

It appears to me to be as defensible to claim that WBL is as decontextualized, unsituated, and encyclopedic as textbook-based learning, as to claim the opposite. Both need be grounded in students' lived worlds (and I mean at a deeply introspective, primordial level, not just at the unreflective level of everyday occurrences), and integrated into the larger curriculum with all its scholarly, ethical, aesthetic, and performance components. Thus, I join in Dyrli's (1995) enthusiasm for http://thomas.loc.gov, which "includes the full text of House and Senate bills—all searchable by keyword; discussion of 'hot bills' that are receiving heavy 'floor action'; information on how laws are made; lists of Congressional E-mail addresses; and access to both the House and Senate Gophers . . ." (p. 10). But I am faced with K-6 children who have been excluded from meaningful participation in setting classroom rules and have taken no significant roles in selecting class leaders. These students typically follow a gang ethic of knuckling under threats and acting out at every opportunity, including physical assaults. Indeed, pressures to have children perform well on state-mandated academic achievement tests appear often to distract teachers from other core dimensions of the curriculum.

My preferred approach is to spend much time discussing and practicing with students "rules of conduct," first in the domain of human relations, and second in the domain of disciplined (in both senses) scholarly inquiry. Only after they have taken (ongoing and regular) roles in the setting of rules and in electing class leaders (and in enduring, reflecting upon, and reacting to the consequences), for example, do I feel that students have begun to establish the experiential foundations needed to understand and appreciate congressional debates and national elections.

To illustrate how we all must carefully assess our sources of information, I share with my students such mail addressed to me as magazine publishers' bold-lettered claims like: "YOU'RE OUR BIGGEST WINNER OF ALL TIME WITH $11,000,000.00 GUARANTEED!" Rare is the student who identifies the big "IF" (in fine print). After explaining why I never bother to even open such mail, I engage them in discussions of their experiences with media advertising and relate this to information they might encounter on CD-ROMs and the Internet.

Another issue: Much has been made of the "interactive" attributes of WBL. In the context of a classroom, the term implies that teachers and students collaborate in the learning process. They discuss and come to agreements about goals, aspirations, abilities, interests, activities, and evaluation. Teachers may present information from a variety of sources and ask for contributions from students. Questions put to students may be closed, requiring a "correct" answer, or "open," permitting creative expression. Teachers may give several seconds of "wait time" after asking a question to encourage reflection by all rather than quick, impulsive responding by those most outspoken. The teacher may then pause after hearing a student's response before requesting clarification or elaboration. Students who do not volunteer may be called on. Encouragement and guidance are provided. Progress in comprehension is monitored, and adjustments in presentation are made accordingly. Evaluation is based on what has been presented. Other forms of interaction include teachers' modeling of good conduct and scholarly endeavor, and their responding constructively to students' progress in these areas.

In computer-based learning generally, we think of interactivity largely in terms of adjustments in presentation in response to student input. Tutorial CBL, for example, consists of a series of screens that provide information and pose questions. If students take too long, they may be given a hint. If they make mistakes, they may be routed to remedial screens.

Simulation CBL provides students with regular updates on the quality of their performance. Electronic performance support systems help them solve complex problems.

What about the nature of interactivity that may be incorporated into WBL? Most of what we witness today pertains to facilitating the location of information. "Search engines" seek Web pages worldwide that pertain to sets of keywords selected by students. Common to most Web pages are hypermedia links to related sites and E-mail links to resource persons. And not only are text, audio, image, and video files made available for downloading, but the application programs needed to see, hear, and view them are provided as well, usually at no cost. At designated times, students and faculty may log in to "chat rooms" to discuss issues and concerns, or to act out roles. Indeed, they can view animated (or "live") representations of participants on their screens (Descy 1996, in press)!

As WBL advances we may expect to see sites where teachers hold online "live" office hours and provide 3-D, stereo, "face-to-face" (videoconferencing) homework help. The technology has arrived; only teacher incentives and reliable, equitable access lag far behind. Thus, WBL can incorporate the best senses of "interactivity" long associated with good CBL, and may expand to include some of those "real-time," if not "proximal-space," interhuman senses so much a part of quality education, both classroom-based and at a distance. Nevertheless, for the present we have to acknowledge, with PBS executive Hall Davidson (1996), that "If a toy were being sold with the same veracity as the Web is sanguinely portrayed in the media, there would be people in jail by morning" (p. 22). To this he adds wryly: "It will take time for the young millionaires of the Net to bankroll instructional methodology for their new medium. . . . With no cyber version of PBS to balance the merchants, we as Ednetizens will just have to do it ourselves" (p. 22).

VARIETIES OF WEB-BASED LEARNING ACTIVITIES

Jargon and acronyms aside, when we plug our computers into a telephone jack and activate our communications software we immediately gain direct access to thousands of institutional computers and, indirectly, to people similarly connected. Essentially, we then are able to do at least three closely interrelated things: (1) send and receive messages, (2) obtain information, and (3) share information.

Communications

Language arts surely are at the core of the school curriculum. Advocates of "whole language" watch for and cultivate "emergent literacy" while immersing students in the world of print. Others stress acquisition of basic skills, yet still in the context of acquiring and sharing information, or "constructing meaning," if you prefer. Listening, speaking, reading, and writing rightfully dominate classroom life from pre-K through graduate school.

Facility with language enables us to function effectively as social beings and as productive citizens. The quality of thought per se, the efficacy of decision-making, perhaps even the depth of compassion all may be rooted in language. What opportunities for language use, including social interaction, are afforded by telecommunications?

Research findings by Kallen Tsikalas (1995) about youngsters' use of the Internet should come as no surprise. Kids love to chat and send E-mail. And making friends takes precedence over gathering information. The commercial online services, especially, provide niches for unstructured interactions among children that are, I believe, a bit better monitored than those found on the raw Net. America Online has a "Kids Only" area; CompuServe has separate student "forums" for kids, teens, and adults; and Prodigy has its "Kids Zone" and "Teen Turf." Within these carefully constructed and monitored virtual communities, children can express themselves in chat rooms, on bulletin boards, and via E-mail. Adherence to well-publicized and enforced rules of "netiquette," with their admonitions to be considerate of others, serves to shape and reinforce proper conduct generally (Hackbarth 1996c).

But verbal expression without *knowledgeable* guidance and feedback is of limited academic value. Better are the classroom-based Internet projects that engage keypals across the globe in collaborative writing and research (Dyrli and Kinnaman 1996c). Wentworth Worldwide Media's periodical, *Classroom Connect: Your Practical Monthly Guide to Using the Internet and Commercial Online Services*, regularly describes collaborative classroom projects and lists requests for student keypals by grade level. KIDLINK, sponsored by Duquesne University, has facilitated linking about 50,000 youths in 80 different countries. Those having access to America Online can tap the resources of the Electronic School House's "Projects & Adventures" area. Furthermore, teachers can exchange ideas with colleagues and parents.

Teachers and students alike can interact (read, post, chat) with like-minded souls in special interest forums, long used (e.g., CompuServe) as a medium for trade and scholarly communications, collaborative problem solving, and apprenticeship mentoring. Among the Internet-based "virtual communities" that have evolved among educators and students are World Classroom, Pioneering Partners, ReEdMail, and Global Schoolhouse (Kurshan 1996). The Electronic Emissary Project helps teachers and students locate subject matter experts worldwide who are willing to engage in "online mentoring" (Sanchez and Harris 1996).

Information Retrieval

My conception of information retrieval is multifaceted, parts based on firsthand experience, others on the philosophies of Alfred North Whitehead, John Dewey, Jerome Bruner, and others. From Whitehead we were granted an initial romantic stage in our quests for knowledge. Dewey emphasized active hypothesis creation and testing—"trying and undergoing." Bruner formalized the concept of a spiral curriculum, the systematic and cumulative acquisition of knowledge within and across disciplines.

My dissertation (1976) was an attempt to make sense out of what it might mean to "integrate cognitive and affective dimensions of learning." Thus, I derived a tentative conception of what some then called "confluent education" where students are engaged in spirited, creative, *reflective* recapitulations of the social construction of knowledge. This amounts to "impassioned scholarly apprenticeship," contrasted with a merely "cognitive apprenticeship." The nature of this passion is revealed in concerted, goal-oriented action, and the kind of reflection I have in mind reaches into the depths of what Maurice Merleau-Ponty called "primordial perceptions." An update of this analysis appears in a book edited by Joel Brown (Hackbarth 1996a).

My conception of scholarly apprenticeship resonates with current standards for science, mathematics, history, and other fields that call for design of instruction "to ensure that students have a generative understanding and an inclination to progressively refine their own ideas" (Linn and Muilenburg 1996, p. 18). Marcia Linn and Lawrence Muilenburg rightly observed that:

> The road of science history is littered with cast-off theories at every bend. Even modern theories are constantly being tested, revised, re-evaluated, and sometimes discarded. This testing process is the road of science that scientists travel with so much excitement, and that we wish more students would find as stimulating (p. 18).

Thus, they concluded that:

> Perhaps it would be most beneficial to our incipient life-long learners to join in on the excitement of testing, revising, and re-evaluating scientific models. In order to accomplish this, we should introduce models that compare favorably with the models . . . that students find personally relevant and that they can apply successfully (p. 18).

In their own Computer as Learning Partner (CLP) curriculum, for example, they introduce middle school students to "heat-flow" models that relate more directly to observed phenomena than more technically precise, but abstracted, "molecular-kinetic" models. Students can then, "like scientists, broaden their understanding on a need-to-know basis rather than on an assigned-to-learn basis" (p. 22).

In all these aspects of more or less systematic inquiry, Web sources have much to contribute. Web sites, and the Internet generally, provide vast stores of information—news, references, file libraries—as well as access to knowledgeable people engaged in passionate pursuit of solutions to critical problems facing the world today.

However, I echo here the concerns of many about the "mix of gold and litter" on the Web, reminiscent of earlier media that have been held up as panaceas. The fresh layers of rich and original resources available are intermingled with the whimsical postings of "newbies," the "roadkill" (sorry) of vandals, and the opinions of self-proclaimed experts. Imagine what the Library of Congress would look like if everyone over the age of eight published whatever came into their heads! What are the Web authors' credentials? What are the criteria for selecting content and links? Generally we don't know. The more I hear about the blossoming of Web home pages, the more I wonder if we are entering an "Age of Neo-Scholasticism," where encyclopedic rendition passes for the Classics. Nicholas Burbules and Thomas Callister, Jr. (1996) observed rightly that:

> Hypertext, as should be clear, can be an enormously liberating innovation or a powerful system of ideological hegemony. Too many writings on hypertext, as with so many writings on educational technology in the past [N.B.!], adopt an overly celebratory tone, heedless of the potential for manipulation and control built into any powerful technological system (p. 43).

Nevertheless, Jeff Hill and Bob Buerger (1996) drew upon reflections of those cited below to put a much more positive spin on virtues of the Web:

> In essence, hypermedia can assist the learner in seeking out the "big picture" which the information presents, while at the same time allowing him or her to organize the learning environment in a manner which aids in individual assimilation and integration of the information (Eckols and Rossett 1989). In this regard, hypermedia can be seen as a true "constructivist" educational tool; students construct their own knowledge. Nonetheless, hypermedia also allows the learner to explore the knowledge construction which is embodied in the hypermedia system itself. This may be seen to reflect the knowledge construction of the designer of the system and/or subject matter expert whose content is embodied within the system. Students may benefit greatly from experiencing this "more coherent, deliberate and experienced perspective" (Elliot, Jones, Cooke, Baker 1995, p. 208) (p. 22).

Other noted scholars, Michael Peters and Colin Lankshear (1996), have joined with Burbules and Callister in admonishing us to check our unbridled enthusiasm for the electronic age with reference to such dangers as:

> increased state surveillance of its citizens through information sharing among government departments; the vulnerability of the information system as a whole to breakdowns, sabotage, and computer viruses; the risks of cultural imperialism and the capacity for manipulation of desire and opinion . . . ; and the potential polarizing of information-rich and information-poor economies (p. 67).

Thus, teachers and students need to exercise considerable skill in locating information related to their research topics, and good judgment in assessing its validity (Descy in press; Hackbarth 1996b; Harris 1995a, 1995b, 1995-1996; Junion-Metz 1996).

On an even darker side, the Internet abounds with hate-mongering and pornography (Laughon and Hanson 1996). To date, there are no sure ways to block children from being exposed. *Cyber Patrol* and *SurfWatch* programs serve to block access to known offensive sites, but because children cannot be fully protected, they need to be guided in the taking of personal responsibility. Having them and their parents sign an *acceptable use policy* (AUP) agreement as a condition of Internet access gives them much-needed guidance, and, when consequences for violation are included, serves as a form of "assertive discipline." (For examples, see http://www.ties.k12.mn.us/accept, and http://lausd.k12.ca.us/aup.html.) And teachers need to prepare alternative activities for students whose parents do not want their children subjected to the inevitable risks.

Information Sharing

Considerable sharing of information takes place in chat rooms and on bulletin boards. Here questions are posed and everyone can take a shot at providing answers, or more questions. Works in progress can be uploaded into the appropriate forum library for review by peers. My own uploading of the preface to my book about educational technology resulted in scores of requests for prepublication diskettes from members of each of three online services. Several members provided helpful suggestions that I incorporated in the final draft. More recently, I have taken part in the drafting of an edited book and of a special issue of *Educational Technology* magazine, both about educational uses of the Internet. Here authors posted on a Web site drafts of their contributions for critiques and cross-references by the other authors and the editors. Judi Harris (1995a, b) described ways in which teachers and students can share information via the Internet for such purposes as collaboratively producing essays and solving problems.

Once information has been collected systematically and pieced together into illuminating, dynamic mosaics we call "knowledge," teachers and students typically share what they have learned (or constructed). We might produce illustrated written reports, video scripts, or multimedia portfolios. The Web opens up new avenues of sharing among teachers and students worldwide (Dyrli and Kinnaman 1996d; Harris 1995-1996).

Teachers have uploaded into forum libraries everything from lesson plans and exams to instructional programs. The resultant field testing and feedback is an instance of what constitutes the very essence of educational technology as an iterative process. Students, too, are able to exchange samples of their writing, drawings, and photos and to receive comments from peers. Such opportunities for sharing (and yes, showing off) really energize effort and encourage critical self-assessment prior to "publication."

Crafting an attractive, informative, multimedia personal Web page can be an extension of students' putting together their classroom portfolios. These evolving products permit drawing upon diverse resources, selecting what is most expressive of one's self, and sharing that with others (Descy 1995; Lamb 1996; Powell 1996). Also valuable are projects in which students collaborate in constructing Web pages for their school. Wentworth Worldwide Media (connect@wentworth.com) hosts such pages on its server free of charge, as does the Global SchoolNet Foundation (http://www.gsn.org). And, of course, teachers may design course-oriented Web pages with links to pertinent resources for their students (Quinlan 1996, in press; Starr in press).

Summaries of WBL Activities and Benefits

Maria Cornish and Brian Monahan (1996) summed up nicely the range of Internet-based learning activities:

> Educational professionals, elementary students, and parents all have an opportunity to gather information. Teachers can exchange lesson plans and information, partici- pate in educational discussions, and consult researchers. Students can participate in interactive projects and improve their writing skills by communicating with students around the world. Parents are able to keep in close contact with the school and exchange information with one another via E-mail. They could also get assistance from specialists when available (p. 56).

Odvard Egil Dyrli and Daniel Kinnaman (1996a) dilated enthusiastically on advantages of computer-based telecommunications in terms of bringing "immediacy and individualization to the school curriculum." In their own well-chosen words:

> Teachers and students can individualize learning according to their needs and interests by selecting from a host of online educational experiences such as keypals and electronic field trips. Teachers can also find up-to-date materials including articles, reports, surveys, databases, maps, diagrams, photographs, film clips, and sound bites—and bring them to the classroom at the very time they are needed. Users can connect to world-wide events as they are happening, communicate instantane- ously with people on every continent, participate in cooperative online projects, and explore content themes interactively in an infinite variety of sequences (p. 65).

INTEGRATING WBL INTO THE LARGER CURRICULUM

Use of computer technology in schools must be justified in relation to aims of education. Steeped in the history and philosophy of education as I am, my list ranges from "prepare for productive citizenship" to "develop good character." Perhaps others would place "becoming independent learners" at the top of their list, or "empowerment." There are no wrong answers as long as they satisfy the criterion implied in the word "education"—*worthwhile* (e.g., one is not "educated" in the ways of thieves, though one may thus be trained or instructed).

Yes, educational aims are a bit unwieldy. To facilitate communication and planning we tend to speak in terms of goals and objectives. Thus, there are district-wide, year-long goals for each of the subjects taught in schools, and from these, teachers (ideally) collaborate with students in deriving instructional objectives for lesson units. Very broadly speaking, most goals have to do with facility in the acquisition and use of knowledge, what we call "information literacy." Included here are development of skills in problem finding/solving, disciplinary and multidisciplinary modes of inquiry, and, of course, communications, both oral and written. Equally important are the development of positive attitudes and sound values.

Placed in the context of curricular goals, it becomes clear how computer technology generally, and Web-based learning in particular, can contribute. Those of us who see value in a focus upon each student's construction of personally significant meaning within a socially constructed reality can find rich multimedia resources in addition to "quality literature." Those of us who are asking "Who is going to find cures for breast cancer and AIDS, negotiate settlements among warring ethnic factions, and prevent collapse of the biosphere?" find promise in the diverse forms of computer-based learning, especially when efforts are made to ensure quantity and quality of access across race, class, and gender (Milone and Salpeter 1996).

What is the role of *systematic instructional design and development*? How can we ensure that WBL activities, among others, fit nicely into our curriculums? I suggest that as we try new things, we not overlook our solid roots in doing things "the old-fashioned way" (e.g., Dick and Carey 1996; Kemp, Morrison, and Ross 1994; Reiser and Dick 1996), even in the context of open-ended and other such learning environments that are in accord with constructivist thinking. Following is a suggested outline (Hackbarth 1996b, 20).

Phase I. **DIAGNOSE**
    Step 1. Figure out what students need to know.
    Step 2. Assess what they already know.

Phase II. **DESIGN**
    Step 3. Design tests of learning achievement.
    Step 4. Identify effective instructional strategies.
    Step 5. Select suitable media.
    Step 6. Sequence learning activities within the program.
    Step 7. Plan introductory activities.
    Step 8. Plan follow-up activities.

Phase III. **PROCURE**
    Step 9. Secure materials at hand.
    Step 10. Obtain new materials.

Phase IV. **PRODUCE**
    Step 11. Modify existing materials.
    Step 12. Craft new materials.

Phase V. **REFINE**
    Step 13. Conduct small-scale test of program.
    Step 14. Evaluate procedures and achievements.
    Step 15. Revise program accordingly.
    Step 16. Conduct classroom test of program.
    Step 17. Evaluate procedures and achievements.
    Step 18. Revise in anticipation of next school term.

Although the above has a linear structure, one that I believe our esteemed Roberts Braden (1996) would find appealing, later steps surely inform earlier ones. Thus, at any point we may have to take a few steps back to revise our assessments, tests, procedures, materials, and yes, . . . even our objectives. With respect to the process of designing WBL programs, not utterly unlike designing programs that employ other media, the necessities for flexibility, creativity, reflective thinking, and end user (teacher/student) involvement remain essential. I stand by my Alex Romiszowski-inspired conclusions of over a decade ago (1986):

> Instructional systems design does not provide easy answers to complex questions about the value-laden enterprise of education in "developed" nations, nor does it do so in the rural villages of those less fortunate. Its prime virtues are that it makes explicit how to go about identifying genuine problems wherever encountered, and details how to proceed towards their amelioration based on the best information and resources available. Again, it is not a recipe and can never replace critical judgment or creativity. An ISD procedure that incorporates the elements of systematic planning and local self-determination best ensures that the resulting programmes will provide lasting benefits to the people of all nations (p. 37).

Addressing challenges of constructivist thinking, with its calls for a new "hypermedia design model" based on "cognitive flexibility theory," Thomas Fox McManus (1996) concluded that these significant insights deal "mostly with the pursuit of intermediate and expert knowledge in complex and ill-structured learning domains. If your learning domain is simple or well-structured, you might want to consider using a more traditional ISD model." Katherine Cennamo, Sandra Abell, and Mi-Lee Chung (1996) observed that in the design of materials in accord with constructivist thinking generally (whether the knowledge domain is simple or complex):

> Instructional designers should be guided by, but not limited to, the decisions required by traditional instructional design models. With a knowledge of the questions inherent in each stage of traditional instructional design models, designers can examine the data that evolve through the construction of instructional materials, and make decisions in collaboration with the client, based on shared assumptions about the content and teaching/learning process (p. 47).

Nevertheless, with David Merrill (1996), I would caution that clients might well not be the best judges of what they most need to know to get where they think they want to go, much less of suitable strategies and media. Surely this was the case in 1982 at USC when I attended his Apple IIe networked class on the design of computer-based instructional programs. And Richard Clark long ago had discussed with me his observation that even the best of students tend to select highly structured strategies more appropriate for slow learners, the latter preferring discovery approaches better suited to the gifted. But if constructivism has had any beneficial impact on education, it might have been to remind us, once again, to listen more carefully to our students to ascertain (and respect) what they think and why, and that we give them more "freedom to err" (Neil Postman's [1995] version of Carl Rogers's legacy). With the renowned Stanley Pogrow, who has objected strongly to basing school reform movements on such vague, unproven notions as "child-centered learning" and "using the computer as a tool," I would caution further that "mass advocacy should follow, not precede, the careful development and large-scale testing of techniques" (p. 663). With Charles Reigeluth (1996), and legions of ISD pioneers before him, I would add that models of instructional design surely should allow for the possibility that in many cases, the solutions to problems inherent in teaching and learning are not always instructional in nature, Web-based or otherwise. For example, it now is commonly recognized that achievement is best ensured within a climate of high expectations, where rules of conduct are consistently enforced, and where parents are encouraged to take active roles (Shanker 1995).

How might WBL activities best be *conducted*? Again, not unlike most other activities, these may fit into four phases—prepare, perform, follow-up, and evaluate (Hackbarth 1996b, p. 36):

Phase I. **PREPARE**
  Step 1. Review course components.
  Step 2. Practice presentation.
  Step 3. Procure equipment and materials.
  Step 4. Prepare facilities and personnel.

Phase II. **PERFORM**
  Step 5. Provide orientation.
  Step 6. Present lesson.
  Step 7. Elicit responses.
  Step 8. Provide feedback.

Phase III. **FOLLOW-UP**
    Step 9.   Review and refine.
    Step 10.   Expand on achievement.

Phase IV. **EVALUATE**
    Step 11.   Assess achievements.
    Step 12.   Assess program.

Of course, we must adapt such systematic procedures to suit our contexts, which in some respects are unique. For example, K-12 classroom instruction differs in *many* respects from adult distance education. However, the phases outlined above generally hold across students differing widely in age and motivations, and across subjects.

Evaluation of WBL activities has both process and product components. As I have described in more detail elsewhere (1996b), we administer tests primarily to determine how well students achieved the objectives set for and *with* them. We draw also upon conferences, direct observations of behavior, and portfolios. We note if students learned something of value not anticipated in the objectives, if they enjoyed the experience, and if they felt challenged to explore further on their own. We ask them to discuss with us and write in journals about the quality of our teaching and the value they perceive in what they have learned. Portfolios include both drafts and final products. For each piece, students express why they selected it and how they feel about it. Our own criteria for assessing the quality of work is made explicit, both in written form and in our conversations with students and their parents. We appreciate fully the fact that:

> Much of what we hope students will learn, and much of what they actually do learn, cannot . . . easily be anticipated. . . . [And we] don't let the existence of neatly written outcome objectives blind [us] to the importance of what students get out of the *process*, per se. Discovering the values of sharing and working collaboratively or experiencing the benefits of engaging in conflict resolution may well overshadow the significance of absorbing prescribed subject matter (p. 21).

More explicit criteria for evaluating learning outcomes have been provided by David Jonassen (1996). Though he specified that these be applied primarily to products of "using a computer application program ['mindtool'] to engage learners in constructive, higher-order, critical thinking about the subjects they are studying" (p. iv), they may serve just as well in the context of WBL generally.

- **Originality**—Do the products represent the student's original thoughts, or are they copied from sources or other students?

- **Complexity**—How many ideas are represented, and are those ideas richly interconnected? How useful would that knowledge be in solving problems?

- **Coherence**—Are the relationships that are expressed in the product meaningful and appropriate, and are they consistently used?

- **Inference**—Are the students able to make hypotheses and conjectures based on the information in their products?

- **Predictability**—Are the students able to solve the kinds of problems faced by citizens, consumers, and professionals in the field?

- **Contextual relevance**—Do the learners' responses reflect representations of the contexts encountered in a field of study or in the real "tests" of life?

- **Resource/tool use**—Do the students make effective use of the resources and tools that were made available during the activity and those commonly available in the real world?

- **Repertoire of knowledge**—Did the students' responses call on a repertoire of knowledge and judgment in different forms, that is, a mix of declarative, structural, and procedural knowledge? (pp. 282-83).

Jonassen rightly added that: "The purpose of evaluation is to make a value judgment about students' performance, and that is something that can [should] never be completely objectified" (p. 283). The judged quality of that performance reflects as much on the teacher, curriculum, and context as it does on the students.

WBL WITHIN THE LARGER CONTEXT OF EDUCATION

Thomas Duffy and Anne Bednar (1992), among many others of us who long ago cheered Carl Rogers in his debates with Fred Skinner, have rightly challenged us to focus our attention also on the design of more open-ended learning environments, those for which objectives are less readily prespecified and measured. These they eloquently characterized in terms of:

rich contexts, authentic tasks, collaboration for the development and evaluation of multiple perspectives, and abundance of tools to enhance communication and access to real-world examples and problems, reflective thinking, modeling of problem solving by experts in the content domain, and apprenticeship mentoring relationships to guide learning (p. 132).

As noted above, my own vital concern for the *integration* of cognitive and affective dimensions of learning has led me to write in terms of "impassioned scholarly apprenticeship," contrasted with a mere "cognitive apprenticeship" that could be interpreted as being detached from the emotions or "objective" in its methods and conclusions. In an update of my 1976 dissertation (Hackbarth 1996a), I concluded that:

Special steps must be taken if students are successfully to investigate the world as embodied in the curriculum in the same spirit as they spontaneously expand the horizons of their daily lives. Engagement of students in the reflective investigation of particular phenomena by means of discipline-based methods might serve to foster this spirit of adventure. Teachers wishing to participate with their students in such inquiry . . . could:

- Meditate upon the nature of knowledge, how it evolves, and of what value it is to learn.

- Study the methods actually used to gain new knowledge and the criteria by which evidence and claims to truth are assessed in each subject area.

- Design, implement, assess, and revise inquiry activities that their students are capable of engaging in fruitfully.

- Encourage students' creative expression in the pursuit of personally significant knowledge that enhances efficacy within their daily lives.

- Model the quest for knowledge in the service of humanity (pp. 38-39).

Active engagement by teachers of their students in scholarly apprenticeships that draw upon human, print, Web, and other resources may serve well to impart valuable insights into the nature of knowing per se, and thus may serve as good preparation for those who ultimately contribute to the advance of knowledge.

M. D. Roblyer, Oare Dozier-Henry, and Ada Burnette (1996) acknowledged that computer-mediated communications could help students become familiar with the diverse cultures across the globe. However, they suggested that:

> [The goals of] accepting, learning from, and appreciating people with different value systems, beliefs, and behaviors . . . require deeper study and interpersonal experiences with members of the groups being studied. We must build upon the relatively superficial activities of "telepals" and of learning about various foods and holidays in other cultures. In this deeper and more meaningful study, technology [in the product sense] may have a greatly attenuated role (p. 11).

My own observations while serving as a student teacher confirmed this need for greater depth. After engaging upper elementary students in a cross-town pen-pal exchange, my supervising teacher arranged a visit. The gaps in facilities and race were readily apparent. Though the enterprising teachers did much to encourage friendly interaction between the mixed-race, mixed-gender couples, when the artificial ties were removed, the students quickly regrouped, all with members of their own class. An unintended no-show for the scheduled second meeting a month later did little to enhance the bonds of friendship. If such a promising project can sour over such a short distance, what are the prospects for keypal meetings? And if distant keypals are never to meet, where and how are students going to learn to love?

Two decades ago, in an assessment of the scope and promise of the then highly touted programmed instruction, my UCLA mentor, George Kneller and I (1977) observed that:

> If the material base of our civilization is to be maintained and improved, a good deal of . . . knowledge must be transferred from generation to generation. Much may be transmitted by technological means. . . . But the moral and intellectual heritage of our civilization consists in large part of inexact knowledge, values, and works of art and thought. Such content is learned better through the active inquiry of the student, guided and encouraged by his [or her] teacher. . . , [because] education [in its richest sense is] a meeting of persons, in which the teacher personalizes knowledge, bringing it to life in his [or her] own way, and the student appropriates knowledge [from many sources], using it so that it both reflects and contributes to the growth of his [or her] own personality [as well as intellect and character] (p. 186).

Surely, WBL activities can be crafted in such ways as to be integrated effectively into more human-relation-centered, inquiry-based, and open-ended curriculums that are responsive to these challenges.

CONCLUDING REMARKS

Today's students and teachers have access to vast resources. Classrooms are filled with books, audiotapes, and videos. Nearby libraries and computer labs offer more opportunities for learning. The virtues of Web-based learning activities need to be assessed in relation to what they offer more effectively and efficiently than more traditional sources. Educators need to reflect on the merits and costs of E-mail versus snail mail and telephone, online browsing versus opening a book or viewing a video, singing and dancing versus sitting, hands-on experiences versus simulated ones. Much random exploration of online services can be justified in terms of students gaining familiarity with an exciting and empowering medium. However, *time spent online needs to be made at least as productive in achieving aims of education as activities it displaces.* And this pertains to financing and extracurricular efforts as well. Thus, I agreed wholeheartedly when Judy Salpeter (1996), editor-in-chief of *Technology & Learning*, tempered her enthusiasm for NetDay 96, California's " 'high-tech barnraising' designed to wire at least one-fifth of the state's 13,000 schools for Internet access" with:

> Nationally, I'd love to see millions of volunteers heading for schools every weekend with the sense of purpose that motivated NetDay organizers. This week we might rebuild unsafe playgrounds. Next week, the focus might be on filling school shelves with books and mobilizing volunteer adults to listen to kids read. The week after, we'd bring in painters, musicians, and poets, and find ways for every school to have an "artists in residence" program (p. 5).

Getting the most out of WBL activities requires much offline effort (McKenzie 1995; Rowland and Kinnaman 1995; Dyrli and Kinnaman 1996b). First, we have to become familiar with the hardware, features, and navigation tools. Then we have to engage our students in planning. Problems need to be found and defined and hypotheses proposed before decisions about the best sources can be made. Inquiries ultimately need to be discipline-based, not random or merely whimsical. Interdisciplinary study at its best evolves out of knowledge of how historians, economists, mathematicians, artists, and scientists conduct their distinctive enterprises. This holds as well, I believe, when one is in pursuit of "expert knowledge" in accord with "cognitive flexibility theory" (as described by Spiro, Feltovich, and Coulson at: gwis2.circ.gwu.edu/~kearsley/spiro.html; and in Spiro, Feltovich, Jacobson, and Coulson 1992).

Except during "chat" and informal keypal E-mail exchanges, and for "print phobic" and motor-impaired students, the quality of written communications is enhanced by first being drafted by hand. Recall the classic admonition: "If it is worth doing, it is worth doing well." The process-writing activities of brainstorming, prioritizing, outlining, elaborating, editing, sharing, and revising are no less important in online communications than in producing term papers and newsletters.

In their use of Internet resources, teachers need to exercise caution. Though commercial online services permit restricting access to the "pink" bulletin boards with their racy content, the Internet abounds with pornographic, sexist, and racist material. The commercial bulletin boards are monitored, but students could read from Internet "usenet newsgroups" of every conceivable persuasion. Worst, unless they are warned, students can be enticed to meet adult strangers posing as peers. As a safeguard, schools are well-advised to prepare and discuss with students an "acceptable use policy" that must be signed by students and parents as a condition of well-monitored, electronically limited Internet access.

As a computer specialist teacher (but a "multimedia learning generalist" at heart) in Manhattan, it has been my job to integrate computer technology into elementary school classrooms. Students generally react to computer time with glee. Teachers' attitudes span the range, and their practices often are at odds with constructive use of computer technology. I can understand why.

Judy Salpeter (1995), with all her access to the finest in computers and technical support, still laments the shortcomings. Empathizing with teachers who face ever increasing challenges, she asked "Who's to blame?" for the lagging effective use of computers in schools. Rightly, she noted that:

> How many lawyers or business executives do you know who not only use computers but also are expected to set up and repair their own machines, and install and customize their own software? Far too often, teachers are left on their own to do just that (p. 6).

Larry Cuban (1995), in his analysis of why many teachers reject computers, as they did television before, rightly identified perceived *efficiency* as a core criterion. He rightly gave teachers credit for setting justified priorities and for devising effective means of achieving both the mundane and highest aims of education. The truths of Salpeter's and Cuban's observations have been revealed to me over the past few years in my daily encounters with bright, dedicated, and knowledgeable teachers.

In teacher education programs across the world, candidates are admonished to validate their students' feelings and ideas and to focus on their strengths. But in discussions about "educational technology" (too often in that limited sense of hardware and software), teachers are commonly portrayed as resistant and ignorant, and are pushed to "get wired." Thus, all the wondrous things they do from day to day are invalidated, and *training* in computer skills is advocated to remediate their deficiencies. How ironic!

My approach has been to ground the *process* of educational technology, and its superb products, in what successful teachers already do well: needs analyses in relation to ambitious objectives and student characteristics, conscientious instructional planning and implementation, multidimensional evaluation of learning processes and products, and careful revision in light of results. And I am ever-present to assist with installing new software and in handling oft-needed repairs. Only within this context can computer technology generally, and WBL in particular, be integrated effectively and selectively into world-class curriculums.

WEB K-12 RESOURCES

The following annotated list of recommended Web sites of interest primarily to K-12 educators was compiled by Laurie A. Quinlan, Communications Instructor, Lakeville High School, Lakeville, MN. She graciously agreed to let me publish it here (with nonexclusive rights) and invited readers to contact her for updates (laurieq@vax1.mankato.msus.edu) and to read her K-12 teacher-oriented column in *TechTrends*, an informative periodical included with our membership in the Association for Educational Communications and Technology (aect@aect.org).

AskERIC Home Page: http://ericir.syr.edu
> The Educational Resources Information Center (ERIC) provides a variety of services and products for educators at all levels.

B.E.S.T.: http://eyecatchers.com/eyecat/BEST
> Archive of the best educational sites on the WWW.

Busy Teacher Web Site: http://www.ceismc.gatech.edu/BusyT
> Reviews of educational materials on the Web, lesson plans, and classroom projects.

Classroom Connect: http://www.classroom.net
> Provides information on Internet searching, educational conferences, school Web sites, and Web resources.

Educational Site of the Week: http://www.cyberstation.net/~may/surprise.htm
> Every Wednesday, a new educational site is chosen; also has archives of past sites.

EdWeb: http://K12.cnidr.org:90
> Online educational resources and information about trends in education.

GNA Teacher's Guide: http://uu-gna.mit.edu:8001/HyperNews/get/text/guide/index.html
> Resources for online educators including databases, directories, hotlists, and periodicals.

Hotlist of K-12 Internet Sites: http://www.sendit.nodak.edu/k12
> Index of elementary and secondary schools with Web sites.

InSITE: http://curry.edschool.Virginia.EDU/insite
> Provides educational resources and discusses teacher education issues.

Instructional Technology Connections: http://www.cudenver.edu/~mryder/itcon.html
> Excellent collection of listservs, E-journals, and K-12 links for teachers.

Kathy Schrock's Guide for Educators: http://www.capecod.net/Wixon/wixon.htm
A thorough list of resources arranged by discipline.

Teacher Tool Box: http://www.trc.org
Impressive list of resources for the K-12 curriculum.

Teacher's Edition Online: http://www.teachnet.com
Information on lesson plans, bulletin board ideas, and classroom themes and projects.

Web66: A K12 WWW Project: http://web66.coled.umn.edu
Information on setting up a server and finding K-12 resources.

World Lecture Hall Home Page: http://www.utexas.edu/world/lecture
Syllabi, assignments, lecture notes, exams, and calendars from many online courses. (See also /world/instruction/index.html.)

To these I would add:

American Federation of Teachers: http://www.aft.org
Explores issues of professional concern that extend well beyond the classroom walls.

ArtsEdNet: http://www.artsednet.getty.edu
Information about "discipline-based arts education."

Assessing WWW Sites for Education: http://www. capecod.net/wixon/wixon.htm
Kathy Schrock's Web site evaluation tool for students.

Berit's Best Sites for Children: http://www.cochran.com/theosite/ksites.html
Another regularly updated source.

CCCnet: http://www.cccnet.com
An interactive online K-12 curriculum, and a showcase for student projects.

CyberKids (and Cyberteens): http://www.woodwind.com:80/cyberkids
An online magazine with stories and articles by children.

Delivering Instruction on the World Wide Web: http://www.edb.utexas.edu/coe/depts/ci/it/projects/wbi/wbi.html
Includes hardware and software requirements, HTML tutorials, discussion of design models, and links to other resources.

The Discovery Channel: http://www.discovery.com
Billed as a "gateway to exploration and adventure."

Electronic Learning: http://scholastic.com/EL
Describes top sites for educators.

Global SchoolNet Foundation: http://www.gsn.org
A Microsoft-sponsored provider of information about educational uses of the Internet, and a host for school home pages.

Heritage Online: http://www.hol.edu
Antioch University credit courses to help educators use the Internet.

Hot Sheet: http://www.tstimpreso.com/hotsheet
Lists and provides links to popular sites by category—search engines, news, government, education, etc.

Impact II—The Teachers Network (TeachNet): http://www.teachnet.org
A searchable database of award-winning classroom projects, funding opportunities, and bulletin boards, and an introduction to the Web course.

Internet High School: http://www.caso.com
Describes providers of online high school and equivalency courses, and The Internet University area lists college-level courses.

Kidscom: http://www.kidscom.com
Describes Internet projects for children in English, French, German, and Spanish.

KidsConnect: AskKC@iconnect.syr.edu
A Microsoft-funded service for students wishing to pose questions. (Now that should give parents and teachers a break!)

KIDLINK: http://www.kidlink.org
Helps link up keypals across the world.

KidsWeb: http://www.npac.syr.edu/textbook/kidsweb
Has links to Web sites of interest to children, identified by category (arts, sciences, social studies, reference, etc.).

Ligature Gateway Academy: http://academy3.ligature.com
Provider of Internet-based core curriculum for middle schools.

The Magellan Internet Guide: http://www.mckinley.com
Permits limiting search to those Web sites that have been "rated and reviewed."

Media Literacy Project: http://interact.uoregon.edu/MediaLit/HomePage
Describes resources that help develop critical thinking about media.

NASA's K-12 Internet Initiative: http://quest.arc.nasa.gov
Provides guidance in educational uses of Internet.

National Education Association: http://www.nea.org
Has links to K-12 newsgroups and listservs.

The Open University: http://www.open.ac.uk
Describes course offerings at this leading distance education institution.

Optical Data Corporation: http://www.infomall.org/Showcase/opticaldata
Much about the company's products, but also has suggestions for educational uses of the Internet.

Scholastic Network: http://scholastic.com/network
Has curriculum guides, projects, and libraries.

SubmitAll: http://www.hometeam.com
Provides site for free home page and links your URL to search sites and directory services.

TeachNet: http://www.teachnet.org
A searchable database of award-winning classroom projects, funding opportunities, bulletin boards, and an introduction to the Web course.

Top Ed Sites: http://www.pointcom.com
Provides reviews of education-related Web sites.

Uncle Bob's Kids' Page: http://gagme.wwa.com/~boba/kids.html
Best of the Web for children.

WebCATS: Library Catalogues on the World Wide Web: http://library.USask.ca/hywebcat
Has links to "all" libraries with Web-based online public-access catalogs.

WebEd K12 Curriculum Links: http://badger.state.wi.us/agencies/dpi/www/WebEd.html
Provides links to exemplary school Web sites.

World Wide Web Courseware Developers Listserv Home Page: http://www.unb.ca/web/wwwdev
A source for developers of WBL activities; also lists Web-based "continuing education" courses in a wide variety of fields.

WWLib: http://www.scit.wlv.ac.uk/wwlib
An indexed catalog of Web sites in the United Kingdom.

Yahoo Maps: http://maps.yahoo.com/yahoo
Provides maps as per input of U.S. cities, streets, zip codes.

Yahooligans: http://www.yahooligans.com
"Yet another hierarchically organized oracle" for locating hot sites, but for 8-14 year olds.

Yahoo People Search: http://www.yahoo.com/search/people
Provides telephone numbers and street addresses.

KEEPING UP TO DATE

Regularly updated, annotated lists of books about the Internet and its World Wide Web are available from:

listserv@ubvm.cc.buffalo.edu
> message: Get newusers FAQ nettrain F=mail
> or for reviews, message: Get nettrain revs_1nettrain F=mail
> Substitute 2, 3, 4, and 5 for the number one to obtain all five parts of the list.

Another great source is The Unofficial Internet Book List: http://www.northcoast.com/savetz/booklist

Edupage is a summary of news items on information technology, provided online three times a week as a service of Educom, a consortium of colleges "seeking to transform education through the use of information technology." Written by John Gehl and Suzanne Douglas, it is available in English as well as several other languages. For translations and archives see:
> http://www.educom.edu
> or E-mail: translations@educom.unc.edu.

InfoList for Teachers is another great source of Internet sites. It is a listserv-delivered, regularly updated publication by Rick Lakin, Yvonne Andres, Al Rogers, and Erica Rogers, and hosted by the Global Schoolnet Foundation.
> http://www.electriciti.com/~rlakin

The Scout Report is a weekly online publication that describes Internet resources of interest to researchers and educators. It is prepared by Net Scout Services in the Computer Science Department, University of Wisconsin, and is sponsored by InterNIC, the National Science Foundation, AT&T, and Network Solutions, Inc.
> http://rs.internic.net/scout_report-index.html
> or E-mail: admin@ds.internic.net.

Edupage, InfoList for Teachers, and *The Scout Report* may conveniently be received, along with other items of interest, by subscribing to the Minnesota Educational Media Organization's listserv, MEMO-net (administrator Don Descy). Simply E-mail:
> listserv@vax1.mankato.msus.edu,
> Leave the subject line blank, and type the message: subscribe memo-net Your Name

Videos about Web-Based Learning may be obtained from:
> AECT: 1-202-347-7834; aect@aect.org
> ASCD: 1-800-933-ASCD; 1-703-549-9110; member@ascd.org
> Chip Taylor Communications: 1-800-876-CHIP; 1-603-434-9262; chiptaylor@chiptaylor.com
> Educational Activities: 1-800-645-3739; 1-516-223-4666; edact@panix.com
> ISTE: 1-800-336-5191; 1-503-346-4414; iste@oregon.uoregon.edu
> PC-TV: 1-603-863-9322; 1-415-574-6233; 74774.13@compuserve.com
> RMI Media Productions: 1-800-745-5480; rmimedia@aol.com
> University of Delaware: 1-302-831-8162; podium@udel.edu
> The Video Journal of Education: 1-800-572-1153; 1-801-566-6500; http://www.videojournal.com
> Wentworth Worldwide Media: 1-800-638-1639; 1-717-393-1000; connect@wentworth.com
> Winnebago: 1-800-533-5430; 1-507-724-5411; sales@winnebago.com

REFERENCES AND RELATED READINGS

Armstrong, S. (1995). *Telecommunications in the classroom*, 2d ed. Eugene, OR: International Society for Technology in Education.

Aronson, L. (1995). *HTML3 manual of style*. New York: Macmillan Computer Publishing.

Berge, Z. L., and Collins, M. P., eds. (1995). *Computer-mediated communication and the online classroom*. Cresskill, NJ: Hampton Press.

Berge, Z. L., and Collins, M. P., eds. (1996). *The online classroom K-12*. Cresskill, NJ: Hampton Press.

Boe, T., Graubart, C., and Cappo, M. (1995). *World desk: A student handbook to Gopher and the World Wide Web*. Santa Cruz, CA: Learning in Motion.

Braden, R. (1996). The case for linear instructional design and development: A commentary on models, challenges, and myths. *Educational Technology 36*(2), 5-23.

Burbules, N. C., and Callister, T. A., Jr. (1996). Knowledge at the crossroads: Some alternative futures of hypertext learning environments. *Educational Theory 46*(1), 23-50.

Campbell, D., and Campbell, M. (1995). *The student's guide to doing research on the Internet.* Reading, MA: Addison-Wesley.

Cennamo, K. S., Abell, S. K., and Chung, M. (1996). A "layers of negotiation" model for designing constructivist learning materials. *Educational Technology 36*(4), 39-54.

Clark, D. (1995). *The student's guide to the Internet.* Indianapolis, IN: Alpha Books.

Cornish, M., and Monahan, B. (1996). A network primer for educators. *Educational Technology 36*(2), 55-57.

Cotton, E. G. (1996). The online classroom: Teaching with the Internet. Syracuse, NY: ERIC/EdInfo Press.

Crawford, L. (1995). Kids in cyberspace: A smart, safe guide to online services. *The Computing Teacher 22*(6), 12-14.

Cuban, L. (1995). Déjà vu all over again? *Electronic Learning 15*(2), 34-37, 61.

Cummins, J., and Sayers, D. (1995). *Brave new schools: Challenging cultural literacy through global learning networks.* New York: St. Martin's Press.

Davidson, H. (1996). Casting the Web. *Technology & Learning 16*(6), 22.

Descy, D. E. (1995). Making a World-Wide Web page. *TechTrends 40*(5), 9-11.

Descy, D. E. (1996). *NCSA Mosaic, Netscape,* and *Java/HotJava!! TechTrends 41*(1), 6-8.

Descy, D. E. (in press). The Internet and education: Privacy and pitfalls. *Educational Technology.*

Dick, W., and Carey, L. M. (1996). *The Systematic Design of Instruction,* 4th ed. New York: HarperCollins.

Duffy, T. M., and Bednar, A. K. (1992). Attempting to come to grips with alternative perspectives. In *Constructivism and the technology of instruction: A conversation,* ed. T. M. Duffy and D. H. Jonassen. Hillsdale, NJ: Lawrence Erlbaum.

Dyrli, O. E. (1995). Personalizing politics. *Technology & Learning 16*(3), 10.

Dyrli, O. E., and Kinnaman, D. E. (1995). Connecting classrooms: School is more than a place. *Technology & Learning 15*(8), 82-88.

Dyrli, O. E., and Kinnaman, D. E. (1996a). Part 2: Energizing the classroom curriculum through telecommunications. *Technology & Learning 16*(4), 65-70.

Dyrli, O. E., and Kinnaman, D. E. (1996b). Part 3: Teaching effectively with telecommunications. *Technology & Learning 16*(5), 57-62.

Dyrli, O. E., and Kinnaman, D. E. (1996c). Part 4: Connecting with the world through successful telecommunications projects. *Technology & Learning 16*(6), 57-62.

Dyrli, O. E., and Kinnaman, D. E. (1996d). Part 5: The changing face of telecommunications: What's next for schools? *Technology & Learning 16*(7), 56-61.

Eckols, S. L., and Rossett, A. (1989). *HyperCard* for the design, development, and delivery of instruction. *Performance Improvement Quarterly 2*(4), 2-20.

Elliot, G. J., Jones, E., Cooke, A., and Baker, P. (1995). Making sense: A review of hypermedia in higher education. In *Educational Multimedia and Hypermedia, 1995: Proceedings of ED-MEDIA 95,* H. Maurer, ed. Charlottesville, VA: Association for the Advancement of Computing in Education.

Ellsworth, J. H. (1994). *Education on the Internet: A hands-on book of ideas, resources, projects, and advice.* Indianapolis, IN: Sams Publishing.

Fetterman, D. M. (1996). Videoconferencing on-line: Enhancing communication over the Internet. *Educational Researcher 25*(4), 23-27.

Frazier, D., with Kurshan, B., and Armstrong, S. (1995). *Internet for kids.* Alameda, CA: SYBEX.

Frazier, G., and Frazier, D. (1995). *Telecommunications and education: Surfing and the art of change.* Alexandria, VA: National School Boards Association.

Gardner, D. C., Beatty, G. J., and Sauer, D. (1995). *Internet for Windows: America Online Edition.* Rocklin, CA: Prima Publishing.

Giagnocavo, G., McLain, T., and DiStefano, V. (1995). *Educator's Internet companion—Classroom Connect's complete guide to educational resources on the Internet.* Lancaster, PA: Wentworth Worldwide Media.

Hackbarth, S. (1986). Instructional systems design: An appropriate technology for developing nations. *Programmed Learning and Educational Technology 22,* 35-38.

Hackbarth, S. (1996a). Confluent education: An analysis from the perspective of Merleau-Ponty's philosophy. In *Confluence in education: Integrating consciousness for human change,* ed. J. H. Brown. Greenwich, CT: JAI Press. 17-42.

Hackbarth, S. (1996b). *The educational technology handbook: A comprehensive guide: Process and products for learning.* Englewood Cliffs, NJ: Educational Technology Publications.

Hackbarth, S. (1996c). Exploiting educational features of commercial online services. In *Wired together: The online classroom K-12,* ed. Z. L. Berge and M. P. Collins. Cresskill, NJ: Hampton Press.

Halliday, C. M. (1995). *The trail guide to Prodigy: A rapid-reading reference to using and cruising the Prodigy online service.* Reading, MA: Addison-Wesley.

Harmon, C. (1996). *Using the Internet, online services, & CD-ROMs for writing research and term papers.* New York: Neal-Schuman.

Harris, J. (1995a). Educational telecomputing activities: Problem-solving projects. *Learning and Leading with Technology 22*(8), 59-63.

Harris, J. (1995b). *Way of the ferret: Finding and using educational resources on the Internet,* 2d ed. Eugene, OR: International Society for Technology in Education.

Harris, J. (1995-1996). Telehunting, telegathering, teleharvesting. *Learning and Leading with Technology 23*(4), 36-39.

Heide, A., and Stilborne, L. (1996). *The teacher's complete and easy guide to the Internet.* Buffalo, NY: Trifolium Books.

Hill, J., and Buerger, B. (1996). Hypermedia as a bridge between education and profession. *Educational Technology Review, Winter*(5), 21-25.

Johnson, N. B. (1995). *Navigating the Internet with Prodigy.* Indianapolis, IN: Sams.net Publishing.

Jonassen, D. H. (1996). *Computers in the classroom: Mindtools for critical thinking.* Englewood Cliffs, NJ: Prentice-Hall.

Joseph, L. (1995). *World Link.* Columbus, OH: Greyden Press.

Junion-Metz, G. (1996). *K-12 resources on the Internet: An instructional guide.* Berkeley, CA: Library Solutions Press.

Kaufeld, J. (1995). *America Online for dummies.* Indianapolis, IN: IDG Books.

Kearsley, G. (1996). The World Wide Web: Global access to education. *Educational Technology Review, Winter*(5), 26-30.

Kemp, J. E., Morrison, G. R., and Ross, S. M. (1994). *Designing effective instruction.* New York: Merrill.

Kimeldorf, M. (1995). Teaching online—techniques and methods. *Learning and Leading with Technology 23*(1), 26-31.

Kneller, G. F., and Hackbarth, S. L. (1977). An analysis of programmed instruction. *The Educational Forum 41*(2), 181-87.

Krol, E., and Klopfenstein, B. (1996). *The whole Internet,* academic ed. Sebastopol, CA: O'Reilly.

Kurshan, B. (1996). Virtual communities: The Web of life and learning. *MultiMedia Schools 3*(3), 24-26.

Lamb, A. C. (1996). *Spin your own Web site using HTML.* Evansville, IN: Vision To Action.

Lamb, A. C., and Johnson, L. (1995). *Cruisin' the information highway: Internet and the K-12 classroom.* Evansville, IN: Vision To Action.

Landeck, T. (1995). Curriculum and technology: Levels of integration. *Windows K-12 Classroom Resource 1*(1), 14-15.

Laughon, S., and Hanson, W. R. (1996). Potholes on the Infobahn. *MultiMedia Schools 3*(3): 14-23.

Leshin, C. B. (1995a). *Internet adventures: Visiting virtual communities: A step-by-step guide for educators.* Phoenix, AZ: XPLORA Publishing.

Leshin, C. B. (1995b). *Netscape adventures: Step-by-step guide to Netscape Navigator and the World Wide Web.* Phoenix, AZ: XPLORA Publishing.

Leshin, C. B. (1996). *Internet adventures: Step-by-step guide for finding and using educational resources.* Boston: Allyn & Bacon.

Linn, M. C., and Muilenburg, L. (1996). Creating lifelong science learners: What models form a firm foundation? *Educational Researcher 25*(5), 18-24.

Margolis, P. E. (1996). *Random House personal computer dictionary*, 2d ed. New York: Random House.

McClain, T. (1995). *Educator's Internet companion.* Lancaster, PA: Wentworth Worldwide Media.

McClain, T., and DiStefano, V. (1995). *Educator's World Wide Web tour guide.* Lancaster, PA: Wentworth Worldwide Media.

McClain, T., and DiStefano, V. (1996). *Educator's essential Internet training system.* Lancaster, PA: Wentworth Worldwide Media.

McKenzie, J. (1995). Beforenet and afternet. *MultiMedia Schools 2*(3), 6-8.

McManus, T. F. (1996). Delivering instruction on the World Wide Web [online]. Available at: http://www.edb.utexas.edu/coe/depts/ci/it/projects/wbi/wbi.html.

Merrill, M. D. (1996). What new paradigms of ISD? *Educational Technology 36*(4), 57-58.

Meyers, E., and McIsaac, P. (1996). *Teacher's guide to cyberspace.* New York: Impact II—The Teachers Network.

Miller, E. B. (1996). *The Internet resource directory for K-12 teachers and librarians, 95/96 edition.* Englewood, CO: Libraries Unlimited.

Milone Jr., M. N., and Salpeter, J. (1996). Technology and equity issues. *Technology & Learning 16*(4), 38-47.

Moody, G. (1995). *The Internet with Windows.* Newton, MA: Butterworth-Heinemann.

O'Loughlin, L. (1995a). *Free stuff from America Online: Your guide to getting hundreds of valuable goodies.* Scottsdale, AZ: Coriolis Group Books.

O'Loughlin, L. (1995b). *Free stuff from CompuServe: Your guide to getting hundreds of valuable goodies.* Scottsdale, AZ: Coriolis Group Books.

Peters, M., and Lankshear, C. (1996). Critical literacy and digital texts. *Educational Theory 46*(1), 51-70.

Pfaffenberger, B. (1993). *Que's computer user's dictionary*, 4th ed. Indianapolis, IN: Que.

Pfaffenberger, B. (1995). *Que's computer and Internet dictionary*, 6th ed. Indianapolis, IN: Que.

Pfaffenberger, B. (1996). *Publish it on the Web! Macintosh version.* Boston: AP Professional.

Pivovarnick, J. (1995). *The complete idiot's guide to America Online.* Indianapolis, IN: Alpha Books.

Place, R., Dimmler, K., and Powell, T. (1996). *Educator's Internet yellow pages.* Englewood Cliffs, NJ: PTR Prentice Hall.

Pogrow, S. (1996). Reforming the wannabe reformers: Why education reforms almost always end up making things worse. *Phi Delta Kappan 77*, 656-63.

Polly, J. A. (1996). *The Internet kids yellow pages special edition.* Berkeley: Osborne McGraw-Hill.

Postman, N. (1995). *The end of education: Redefining the value of school.* New York: Alfred A. Knopf.

Powell, N. (1996). Ready to be a cybernaut? In *Teachers guide to cyberspace*, ed. E. Meyers and P. McIsaac. New York: Impact II—The Teachers Network.

Price, J. (1995). *The trail guide to America Online: A rapid-reading reference to using and cruising the America Online service.* Reading, MA: Addison-Wesley.

Quinlan, L. (1996). Customizing Web documents for the classroom: An example from Lakeville High School's advanced composition class. *TechTrends 41*(2), 27-30.

Quinlan, L. (in press). Creating a classroom kaleidoscope. *Educational Technology.*

Reigeluth, C. M. (1996). Of paradigms lost and gained. *Educational Technology 36*(4), 58-61.

Reiser, R. A., and Dick, W. (1996). *Instructional planning: A guide for teachers.* Boston: Allyn & Bacon.

Roblyer, M. D., Dozier-Henry, O., and Burnette, A. P. (1996). Technology and multicultural education: The "uneasy alliance." *Educational Technology, 36*(3), 5-12.

Rowland R., and Kinnaman, D. (1995). *Researching on the Internet: The complete guide to finding, evaluating, and organizing information effectively.* Rocklin, CA: Prima.

Salpeter, J. (1995). Quit blaming teachers. *Technology & Learning 16*(3), 6.

Salpeter, J. (1996). Why NetDay? *Technology & Learning 16*(7), 5.

Sanchez, B., and Harris, J. (1996). Online mentoring: A success story. *Learning and Leading with Technology 23*(8), 57-60.

Schofield, J. W. (1995). *Computers and classroom culture.* New York: Cambridge University Press.

Shafran, A. (1995). *The complete idiot's guide to CompuServe.* Indianapolis, IN: Que.

Shanker, A. (1995). A reflection on 12 studies of education reform. *Phi Delta Kappan 77*, 81-83.

Shotsberger, P. G. (1996). Instructional uses of the World Wide Web: Exemplars and precautions. *Educational Technology 36*(2), 47-50.

Simpson, C. M. (1995). *Internet for library media specialists.* Worthington, OH: Linworth Publishing.

Spiro, R. J., Feltovich, P. J., Jacobson, M. J., and Coulson, R. L. (1992). Cognitive flexibility, constructivism, and hypertext: Random access instruction for advanced knowledge acquisition in ill-structured domains. In *Constructivism and the technology of instruction: A conversation*, ed. T. M. Duffy and D. H. Jonassen. Hillsdale, NJ: Lawrence Erlbaum, 57-75.

Starr, R. M. (in press). Delivering instruction on the World Wide Web: Overview and basic design principles. *Educational Technology.*

Steen, D. R., Roddy, M. R., Sheffield, D., and Stout, M. B. (1995). *Teaching with the Internet: Putting teachers before technology.* Bellevue, WA: Resolution Business Press.

Steinberg, G. (1995). *Special edition using America Online.* Indianapolis, IN: Que.

Tsikalas, K. (1995). Internet-based learning? *Electronic Learning 14*(7), 14-15.

Tyre, T. (1995). Commercial online services: Benefits for educators. *T.H.E. Journal 23*(1), 44-45.

Valauskas, E. J., and Ertel, M. (1996). *The Internet for teachers and school library media specialists: Today's applications, tomorrow's prospects.* New York: Neal-Schuman.

Wagner, R. (1995). *Inside CompuServe,* 3d ed. Indianapolis, IN: New Riders Publishing.

Warschauer, M. (1995). *E-mail for English teaching: Bringing the Internet and computer learning networks into the language classroom.* Alexandria, VA: TESOL.

Wentworth Worldwide Media (1995). *Educator's Internet companion: Classroom Connect's complete guide to educational resources on the Internet.* Lancaster, PA: Author.

Wentworth Worldwide Media. (1996). *Educator's World Wide Web tourguide,* rev. ed. Lancaster, PA: Author.

Wiggins, R. R., and Tittle, E. (1995). *The trail guide to CompuServe: A rapid-reading reference to using and cruising the CompuServe online service.* Reading, MA: Addison-Wesley.

Williams, B. (1995). *The Internet for teachers.* Indianapolis, IN: IDG Books.

Willis, J. (1995). A recursive, reflective, instructional design model based on constructivist-interpretivist theory. *Educational Technology 35*(6), 5-23.

ACKNOWLEDGMENTS

Thanks to Laurie Quinlan and Lori McConkey for their careful reading of this chapter and for providing many constructive suggestions.

Educational Technologists, Chameleons, and Systemic Thinking

Charles M. Reigeluth
Dale Avers
Indiana University

Reiser and Salisbury (1991) report several studies that reveal educational technology having relatively little effect on public education in the United States. Similarly, a report by the Alberta Department of Education (1987) noted that:

> Historically, the role of technology in education has been incremental and peripheral, with new technologies being added to the traditional teacher-centered model of instruction. This process has resulted in large expenditures and increases in teacher workload with no significant improvement to the performance of the education system (p. 26).

Meanwhile, we educational technologists are being confronted with an accelerating rate and magnitude of change. This change has two driving forces. One is the change in needs that educators and trainers must serve. As we evolve from the industrial age into the information age, the educational needs of society are dramatically changing (as are the training needs of corporations), requiring educational technology to dramatically change to meet those new needs.

The other driving force is changes in technology. As educational technologists, we now have tools at our disposal that are far more powerful, numerous, and complicated than just a decade ago. Like the chameleon, as this "environment" in which we work changes, we must adapt to those changes if we are to succeed. If we don't change, we will likely find ourselves, in an age of CDs, either still using Victrolas or committing ourselves to 8-track audiotapes.

Under these circumstances, how can we make good decisions about changes for our schools or training departments?

Systemic thinking is a powerful tool that can help us to understand why educational technology has had relatively little effect on education and training, and to understand the changes that are swirling around us, so that we can respond to those changes in ways that will enhance our success. This article will explore what systemic thinking is and how it can help educational technologists in these turbulent times.

WHAT IS SYSTEMIC THINKING?

Hall and Fagen (1968 in Weinberg 1975) define a system as "a set of objects together with relationships between objectives and between their attributes" (p. 63) whose function as a whole is to achieve a common purpose (Betts 1992). Ackoff (1981) describes a system as having a set of two or more elements that satisfy the following three conditions:

1. The behavior of each element has an effect on the behavior of the whole;

2. The behavior of the elements and their effects on the whole are interdependent (no element has an independent effect on the whole); and

3. However subgroups of the elements are formed, each has an effect on the behavior of the whole, and none has an independent effect on it.

Therefore, when a system is taken apart, it loses its essential properties. Because of this, analysis and reductionism do not work in understanding systems.

Systems thinking is a process through which all aspects of a situation or problem are considered, including the objectives, functions, personnel, and available resources (Tiffin 1978) with the primary purpose of understanding the *whole* (Weinberg 1975). It is a holistic approach to problem-solving (Bawden 1991) further described by Ackoff (1981) as synthesis, the act of putting things together, the opposite of reductionism. The reductionist view was the prevailing mechanism for understanding problems in the industrial age. It reduces problems to their smallest elements in an attempt to analyze and understand each piece. Complex and dynamic questions go unanswered and problems unresolved when reductionism and analysis are employed, because these methods inhibit understanding the whole (Ackoff 1981).

Systems thinking combines the complementary processes of analysis and synthesis in a new way. Ackoff (1981) describes three steps that reverse the analytical (reductionistic) thinking of the machine age:

1. Identify a containing whole of which the thing to be explained is a part;

2. Explain the behavior or properties of the containing whole; and

3. Explain the behavior or properties of the thing to be explained in terms of its role or function within its containing whole.

In this sequence, synthesis precedes analysis. Analysis focuses on structure, while synthesis focuses on function, for it reveals why things operate as they do. Synthesis yields understanding and enables us to explain. The purpose of systems thinking is, then, to understand the *function* of the system within the context of its environment. An application of systems thinking would be to understand the function and roles of educational technology within the context of the larger educational system, not in isolation.

HOW SYSTEMIC THINKING CAN HELP
EDUCATIONAL TECHNOLOGISTS

The "containing whole" (or supersystem) for an educational system is the society (or community) it serves. Similarly, for a training system, it is the company (or organization) it serves. When the suprasystem changes in significant ways, the educational (or training) system must change in equally significant ways. For example, as has been described in more detail by Reigeluth (1994), in the Agrarian Age, the horse was the predominant and most appropriate mode of transportation. But as we began to evolve into the Industrial Age, the transportation needs of society changed dramatically. It became necessary to ship large quantities of raw materials and finished goods to and from factories. The transportation system responded with a systemic change, or paradigm shift, in which the railroad became the predominant mode of transportation, and it afforded a quantum improvement in the ability to meet the new transportation needs. Now, as we are evolving into the information age, we find our transportation needs have again dramatically changed, and a new, more complex, and diverse paradigm has emerged: a combination of the automobile and airplane, which has similarly afforded a quantum improvement in meeting our new needs.

Educational systems are like transportation systems in some important ways. The one-room schoolhouse was much like the horse in that it was personalized and flexible. And our current educational system is much like the railroad in that everyone must leave from the same place at the same time and travel at the same speed to the same destination, or be dropped off along the way (Reigeluth 1994).

We have seen similar paradigm shifts in other major systems in our society, as table 1, page 134, illustrates. This helps us, as educational technologists, to understand that our educational and training systems are at a point where a true paradigm shift is necessary, and we have a particularly important role to play in shaping the systemic changes that will inevitably occur within our organizations.

Table 1

Major Paradigm Shifts in Society

Society:	Agrarian	Industrial	Information
Transportation:	Horse	Train	Plane & car
Family:	Extended family	Nuclear family	Single-parent family
Business:	Family	Bureaucracy	Team
Education:	One-room schoolhouse	Current system	?

Source: From Reigeluth 1994.

To help prepare for our role in the systemic change process, we educational technologists must understand the ways that education is likely to change, which of course depends on the ways in which the educational needs of our supersystems are changing, as well as the advances in tools that are available to help meet those new needs. Reigeluth (1994) describes in some detail the ways that society and its various systems are changing (see table 2) and explores the educational implications of those changes.

Table 2

Major Differences Between the Industrial Age
and the Information Age That Affect Education

Industrial Age	Information Age
Mass production, etc.	Customized production, etc.
Adversarial relationships	Cooperative relationships
Bureaucratic organization	Team organization
Autocratic leadership	Shared leadership
Centralized control	Autonomy with accountability
Uniformity	Diversity
Autocracy	Democracy
Compliance	Initiative
One-way communications	Networking
Compartmentalization (Division of Labor)	Holism (Integration of tasks)

Perhaps of most significance to educational technologists is the move from mass to customized: mass production to customized production, mass transportation to customized, mass communication to customized, and so forth. In education, we certainly use a mass approach, as reflected by the railroad analogy. We teach a large group of learners a fixed amount of content in a fixed amount of time. But if there is one thing educators can agree on, it's that people learn at different rates and have different learning needs. So, if we hold time constant, we force achievement to vary. If we truly want all learners to succeed, we need to allow time to vary.

Having an attainment-based system rather than a time-based system has tremendous implications for our whole educational system, in that it truly represents a paradigm shift. It means having personal learning plans, rather than group-based progress, which means doing away with classes and grade levels as we know them. Because the teacher cannot be teaching different things to each learner all at the same time, it also means a different role for the teacher—more of a guide on the side than a sage on the stage. Teachers are freed from their role as sole disseminators of content and allowed to develop a more personal relationship with the learner, leading to the development of a personalized learning plan for each, and more time spent guiding and motivating learners (Frick 1991). It also requires more reliance on team-based learning, as well as a more central—rather than peripheral—role for technological tools, which interestingly are becoming far more powerful than ever. The very information technologies that are making a paradigm shift in education necessary are also providing the tools to make it possible, just like the industrial technologies that made the railroad necessary also provided the tools to make it possible.

Reigeluth (1994) and Reigeluth and Garfinkle (1994) provide considerable discussion of the kinds of changes that seem likely as we evolve to Information Age systems of education and training. Some of those are summarized in table 3.

Table 3

Emerging Picture of Features for an Information-Age
Educational System Based on Changes in the Work Place

Industrial Age	Information Age
Grade levels	Continuous progress
Covering the content	Outcomes-based learning
Norm-referenced testing	Individualized testing
Non-authentic assessment	Performance-based assessment
Group-based content delivery	Personal learning plans
Adversarial learning	Cooperative learning
Classrooms	Learning centers
Teacher as dispenser of knowledge	Teacher as coach or facilitator of learning
Memorization of meaningless facts	Thinking, problem-solving skills and meaning making
Isolated reading, writing skills	Communication skills
Books as tools	Advanced technologies as tools

Source: From Reigeluth 1994.

But here we would like to focus on how the use of media and technology is likely to change as the educational paradigm shifts. We envision the changes shown in table 4, page 136.

Table 4

Changing Use of Media and Technology

Industrial Age	Information Age
Primarily used by teachers	Primarily used by students
Adjunct to the teacher	Stand-alone
Used individually by students	Used collaboratively by students
Instructs all learners in the same way	Customized for learner's needs, style

These changes in the use of media and technology will have a significant impact on the educational technologist's methods, role, and expertise. Our success in these turbulent times will depend to a large extent on whether we anticipate and prepare for these kinds of changes.

Furthermore, given the more central role of educational technologies in our future instructional systems, it is imperative that we educational technologists become actively involved in the change processes that our organizations undertake. As with the change from the record player to the CD player, systemic changes are driven not only by changing educational needs but also by advances in technological tools available for meeting those needs. As those tools become more and more powerful, they make new ways of teaching possible. Our input is essential to successful change efforts in our organizations. In fact, we should be playing leadership roles in those change efforts.

This raises the issue of how to help your organization engage in a systemic change process. Educational technologists can play a significant role in a systemic change effort through an awareness of the systemic effect of any changes being considered. You can communicate this awareness to other educational professionals, creating a grassroots activity that can lead, facilitate, and support a systemic change effort. The most important activity in any systemic change effort is fostering an evolution in mindsets. We educational technologists, typically on the cutting edge of change, are in optimal positions to facilitate this process. For more information about how to enhance the success of a systemic change effort, see Jenlink, Reigeluth, Carr, and Nelson (1996); Fullan (1991); and Banathy (1991, 1994).

CONCLUSION

Systemic thinking is a powerful tool that can help us to understand why educational technology has had relatively little effect on education and training. And it can help us to understand the forces for educational change around us that are driven by the changing educational needs of society and the changing technological tools at our disposal, both of which become more pronounced as we evolve deeper into the Information Age. We have looked at what systemic thinking is and how it can be helpful to educational technologists, so we may adapt, like the chameleon, to changes in our environment (supersystem). Systems thinking can be used to synthesize and analyze current instructional problems and to design solutions. If it is used appropriately, we can end up with CDs, which became the predominant paradigm of music medium, rather than ending up with 8-track audiotapes, which obviously didn't. It seems likely that time-based, teacher-centered instruction will give way to customized, learner-focused instruction in which educational technology assumes a more central role. But for this to happen, we educational technologists must learn more about systemic thinking and the systemic change process so that we can provide the kind of leadership and vision so sorely needed in education and training today.

REFERENCES

Ackoff, R. L. (1981). *Creating the corporate future.* New York: John Wiley.

Alberta Department of Education. (1987). *Visions 2000: A vision of educational technology in Alberta by the year 2000.* Edmonton, Alberta, Canada: Technology and Education Committee. (ED 291 364)

Banathy, B. (1991). *Systems design of education.* Englewood Cliffs, NJ: Educational Technology Publications.

Banathy, B. (1994). Designing educational systems: Creating our future in a changing world. In *Systemic change in education,* ed. C. M. Reigeluth and R. J. Garfinkle. (Englewood Cliffs, NJ: Educational Technology Publications), 27-34.

Bawden, R. (1991). Towards action research systems. In *Action research for change and development,* ed. O. Zuber-Skerritt (New York: HarperCollins).

Betts, F. (1992, November). How systems thinking applies to education. *Educational Leadership 50*(3), 38-41.

Frick, T. W. (1991). *Restructuring education through technology.* Bloomington, IN: Phi Delta Kappa Educational Foundation.

Fullan, M. G. (1991). *The new meaning of educational change.* New York: Teachers College Press.

Jenlink, P. M., Reigeluth, C. M., Carr, A. A., and Nelson, L. M. (1996, January-February). An expedition for change: Facilitating the systemic change process in school districts. *TechTrends 41*(1), 21-30.

Reigeluth, C. M. (1994). The imperative for systemic change. In *Systemic change in education,* ed. C. M. Reigeluth and R. J. Garfinkle (Englewood Cliffs, NJ: Educational Technology Publications).

Reigeluth, C. M., and Garfinkle, R. J. (1994). Envisioning a new system of education. In *Systemic change in education,* ed. C. M. Reigeluth and R. J. Garfinkle (Englewood Cliffs, NJ: Educational Technology Publications).

Reiser, R. A., and Salisbury, D. F. (1991). Instructional technology and public education in the United States. In *Instructional technology. Past, present and future,* ed. G. J. Anglin (Englewood, CO: Libraries Unlimited).

Tiffin, J. (1978). Problems in instructional television in Latin America. *Revista de Tecnologia Educativa 4*(2), 163-235.

Weinberg, G. M. (1975). *An introduction to general systems thinking.* New York: John Wiley.

Revisiting Cable TV in the Classroom*

Glen A. Holmes
John Wenrich
Virginia Polytechnic Institute and State University

INTRODUCTION

People of all ages learn from cable TV—in the classroom, at work, and in the home. Together with schools, universities, and other public service agencies, public TV stations currently offer programming that gives learners of all ages equality of educational opportunity. Cable TV, in its ongoing commitment to lifelong learning, is helping achieve our nation's educational goals and has made a significant impact toward reaching them by bringing together teachers, subject matter experts, and students who can't all be in the same place at the same time. The opportunity to combine the skills of content specialists, educators, and television professionals allows people to learn in a variety of settings and different modes (e.g., individual, small or large groups, live vs. delayed programming).

The use of cable TV is widespread among all academic levels. Cable TV stations reach nearly two-thirds of the nation's elementary and secondary schools, constituting an average broadcast time of 5.5 hours per day. Colleges and universities also incorporate cable TV into their instruction by targeting adult populations and delivering telecourses, live interactive video conferences, and other resource programming in order to provide numerous learning opportunities at a distance. Finally, learners benefit in the home in both formal and informal settings as they watch and glean from a variety of daytime and prime-time evening programs that have significant educational value (Office of Instructional Technology 1995).

CHARACTERISTICS OF CABLE TV IN THE CLASSROOM

Cable TV use in the classroom is a form of distance learning. One classic definition of distance learning is "any formal approach to learning in which the majority of the instruction occurs while the educator and learner are at a distance from each other" (Grimes 1993). Cable TV satisfies these criteria by providing educational programming that originates at one or several sites and is then delivered over the air by satellite or via cable to elementary and secondary schools, colleges, universities, businesses, homes, and other locations throughout the land.

The Office of Instructional Technology (1995) denotes several factors that should be taken into account when considering issues related to any distance learning environment—not to mention the particular uses of cable TV for educational purposes. These factors include:

- The nature of the learning environment;
- The design, preparation, and delivery of the instructional material;
- The nature of teacher-learner interactions;

*Special thanks are extended to the following students who contributed to the development of this manuscript: Bader Ali, Ali Alkandari, Juone Brown, Mohammad Qadiri, Ahmad Shaari, and Carmel Vaccare, all of whom are enrolled in the Instructional Technology doctoral program at Virginia Tech.

- The infrastructures necessary to deliver instruction and their physical specifications; and

- The associated cost.

This document will explore several of these issues within the context of educational television.

The Learning Environment

Any distance learning environment should, at a minimum, satisfy several general criteria. These criteria include:

- Separation of the teacher and learner during at least a majority of the instructional process;

- The influence of an educational organization;

- Means for student evaluation;

- The use of educational media to bring teachers and learners closer together in either real or virtual proximity; and

- A mechanism for one-way or two-way communication between teacher, tutor, or educational agency and learner (Keegan 1986).

Participants in cable TV-based learning environments (e.g., teachers, students, school systems) receive numerous instructional as well as other practical benefits, including:

- Sharing of resources that enable those at one site to be used at another;

- Improved access to instructors—that is, as more instructors become available to deliver courses, students compete less for instructor time;

- Greater student access to information—that is, one student per multiple resource locations;

- Enhanced curricula to broaden and enrich the learning experience; and

- Reduced cost of delivery and, possibly, an enlarged revenue base for delivery of a course (Grimes 1993).

Teaching and learning typically involves either a one-way or two-way exchange of information among participants. The traditional classroom offers a variety of stimuli that can be used to attract the attention of learners or provide feedback to the instructor. Communication is multidimensional and can occur directly among teacher and students or in combination with various other visual, auditory, or computer-controlled media.

In the case of cable TV, this information must be exchanged over a distance—a phenomenon made possible through the use of transmitters, satellites, and other forms of sophisticated technology. However, in most situations, teachers and students at different locations cannot see and hear each other directly. The media used in these situations (e.g., video and audio channels) are quite adept at facilitating the communication, yet they lack the ability to deliver information at degrees of fidelity comparable to those typical of a conventional classroom. Perhaps this will soon no longer be a major issue, as improvements in technology (increased bandwidth, throughput, and the like) continue to emerge, and as costs to deliver instruction continue to decline.

Design, Preparation, and Delivery of Instruction

Teaching via cable demands that special attention be given to the possibilities and limitations of the technologies involved, from both a design and a delivery perspective. Issues such as preparation, presentation style, classroom layout, student-teacher interaction, and assignments, which are often taken for granted in traditional classroom settings, must be carefully planned and adapted for cable TV.

Spontaneity is essentially absent from a distance learning environment, in spite of the rate of transmission available to us today. Veteran teachers often make decisions to alter instruction based upon immediate feedback obtained from students during class—an option essentially unavailable to users of this medium. Consequently, instructors must discover ways to allow for changes in pace and sequence without the benefit of immediate student feedback.

By comparison to the conventional classroom, the space allocated for delivery of instruction to educational TV audiences is limited to a single (or, perhaps, multiple) two-dimensional screen(s). Teachers are required to prepare clearly written and exhaustive notes in advance of live or prerecorded instruction. There are few or no opportunities to pass out materials during class unless, of course, materials are sent in advance to remote sites and distributed by local facilitators.

Instructors are often placed at a disadvantage in that the cumulative size of classes at remote sites tends to be significantly larger than it might be otherwise. This becomes problematic, particularly in those situations where courses may not have been taught before— allowing little or no opportunity to work out most of the bugs at a more comfortable pace.

The traditional classroom culture that most learners have grown accustomed to over the years is radically changed in a cable TV-based learning environment. No longer can the behavior of participants be predicted with accuracy based on previous norms. The teacher is deprived of the typical movement zone. Students are no longer obligated to remain silent and attentive until the teacher calls upon them. Nor is the interaction between and among students controlled or monitored by the instructor. Regularity and frequency of class meetings are altered as students gain much more flexibility as to when and how long they participate in a learning session or activity.

Questions regarding time, place, and mode of instructional delivery are constantly important. The ability (or lack thereof) to hear and see students becomes pivotal in determining how instruction will be provided. How much the limited mobility of the teacher impacts the quality of the learning experience is also a factor. Should students enjoy the freedom to come and go as they please? What is the nature of the relationship between students and teachers? Or is there any relationship at all?

In a cable TV-based learning environment, audio and visual presentation techniques heavily affect the overall learning experience. Teachers are required to work with smaller areas for projection and only to the extent that such an area or workspace can be seen by a camera. Taking the entire class in at a glance is nearly impossible, and if attempted at all, lacks sufficient detail to gather salient information that might positively alter the learning experience. In other words, peripheral vision does not exist in a cable TV-based learning environment. Students as well as teachers must discover some other way to get the attention of one another.

Teacher-Learner Interactions

The complexity of cable TV communications systems depends on a number of factors, including the kind of interaction that is needed or desired among teachers and students, and whether or not the interaction takes place in real time. Optimal use of cable TV for instructional purposes can be described as collaboratory, because many systems support two-way, multiple site transmission. That is, the medium is broadcast simultaneously from every site to every other site. In this type of interaction, the teacher and students can exchange information while using full-motion video and audio in a multisite (three or more site) mode. In more elaborate systems, the interaction is often real-time, rather than delayed. In addition, multiple sites can employ more than one teacher at any given time. Instructors reserve the option to alternate between lessons, presentation styles, modes of interaction, and the like.

It is also important to consider how "in-class" and "out-of-class" interaction styles are changed when delivering instruction via cable TV. Whereas interaction styles within a conventional classroom remain fluid and are subject to change dynamically as well as frequently, such is not the case when using cable TV. Traditionally student-centered interaction styles tend to suffer when teachers are forced to use the more faculty-centered approach characteristic of cable TV-based learning environments.

EXAMPLES OF CABLE TV USE
IN THE CLASSROOM

Cable in the Classroom is one of the largest initiatives ever launched among cable companies, national cable networks, and teachers and parents to provide commercial-free educational programming to schools across the country at no cost. Cable in the Classroom is a consortium of more than 7,200 cable companies and 32 national cable programming networks (e.g., CNN, BET, Nickelodeon, A&E, Discovery); it provides free cable connections to all schools and delivers more than 525 hours per month of educational, commercial-free programming into classrooms. Programming covers all subjects and disciplines and a variety of other educational issues. Teachers are at liberty to use the educational programming in any way they choose as there are no viewing requirements. Three examples of programs are shown in table 1.

Program Development

Most instructional cable TV is designed specifically for use in the classroom environment. Program development teams are generally composed of instructional designers, curriculum advisors, and other professionals who have expertise in specific areas commensurate with the audiences that will ultimately receive instruction (e.g., K-12, college and university, math, science). Content is generally presented as a supplement, rather than a substitute, to traditional classroom instruction, as it is designed to be integrated with existing educational plans to enhance effective teaching and learning.

Table 1

Some Examples of Cable TV Use in the Classroom

Program	Audience	Content
The Business Channel (TBC)	Adults	Emphasis on business education, training, and skills development that promote "quality work and encourage productivity."
Electronic Field Trips	K-12	"Transports" or "translates" students to exciting locations via broadcast, satellite, cable, and other computer technologies.
The Ready to Learn Service	Ages 2-12	Designed to help children build skills necessary to become independent learners (for example, negotiation, experimentation, and task completion).

Instructor Assistance

Teachers who use cable TV in the classroom can receive assistance through use of the curriculum or study guides that accompany each program prepared for broadcast. Some organizations such as Cable in the Classroom publish a complimentary monthly program guide for teachers. The magazine helps teachers select programs suitable for activities conducted in their own classrooms, offers suggestions for follow-up activities, and includes discussion questions for learning enrichment.

In addition, some local public TV stations provide professional development for teachers, community resources, and much more. For example, the Public Broadcasting Service's (PBS) Mathline's Middle School Math Project (MSMP) focuses on professional development for math teachers—specifically, teachers in grades 5-8. MSMP participants have access to video modules of other teachers delivering instruction based on national and regional mathematics standards. Participants also hold membership—and regularly interact with their peers—in an online learning community devoted to improving math education nationwide (Public Broadcasting Service 1995b).

EQUIPMENT INFRASTRUCTURE

Nowadays, cable TV systems rarely employ a single type of equipment to provide programming to customers. Such systems are often complex and may consist of many unique pieces of telecommunications equipment, including satellites, antennas, coaxial or fiber cable, and the like. However, a typical broadband cable distance learning environment will use two-way, multiple-site video and audio communicated via a common broadband coaxial cable to/from each site. In this arrangement, each site has its own one-to-many TV channel (video and audio) that every other site in the network can access. Because every site must have as many monitors as there are sites in the mix, three to four active sites represent a practical limit.

The more commonly used approach in K-12 classrooms is not as flexible. Here the transmission is one-way. The medium is communicated in only one direction and is broadcast simultaneously to any number of other sites capable of receiving the transmission. Learners at all remote sites can observe (see and hear) the instructor; however, the instructor cannot see or interact with any students at the various sites.

Cameras may also be used at remote sites to capture visual information. This information (e.g., a student's reactions to the presentation) can be returned to the teacher and used as feedback to adjust subsequent delivery of instruction. Microphones may be used to gather any verbal information expressed at either site. Audio channels could then be used to transmit information to the students at remote sites.

Quantity of Sites

Cable TV in the classroom can be described as an instructional medium/method used to simultaneously link teachers and learners in more than one geographic location or site. Effective use of cable TV for this purpose involves a minimum of two sites. The instructor or facilitator is located at one of the sites. Learners are at the other sites and may or may not be at the instructor site. Depending on interactivity requirements (which tend to stay low in most public school settings), the maximum number of sites can be unlimited. A good example is *Sesame Street,* one of several educational programs broadcast on a daily basis to thousands of elementary classrooms across the country. The programs originate in Chicago, typically employ one or several characters (instructors/facilitators) at a time, and are transmitted via satellite to hundreds of thousands of children simultaneously.

The distance learning model often employed when using cable TV for instruction in elementary and secondary schools uses one instructor site and multiple learner sites. That is, an instructor at one location lectures to a large number of classes, with each class situated in a different location. In this approach, visual contact need not be established between the instructor and learner other than that required for learners to see the instructor and any other media the instructor wishes to use. Student questions are presented to the local teacher/facilitator, one at a time, and are often queued until all have been addressed or until time runs out. There is no limit on the number of sites; however, an optimum number of students per site is approximately 20.

Costs

The current infrastructure necessary to deliver instruction to K-12 classrooms via cable represents an investment upwards of nearly $320 million. The costs associated with using cable TV to deliver instruction as well as any other form of distance learning facility depends on factors such as the type of the interaction (e.g., one-way vs. two-way audio or video transmission); the quantity and geographic location of the classroom sites; the frequency and duration of each class transmission; the fidelity of the media; and the telecommunications facilities, services, and internal networks required to interconnect the sites (Office of Instructional Technology 1995). Because of this, costs can range anywhere from a few hundred dollars per class-hour to more than a thousand dollars per class-hour.

There are essentially two kinds of cable TV networks: private systems and public systems. In private systems, a limited number of sites can appear on the network at any given time. Also, a private and dedicated hardware network is used to link the sites. Such systems are typically found in small geographic areas including school campuses, school districts, or one or more smaller counties. In addition, some larger corporations may have their own private national or international system.

The number of sites that can be accommodated in a public system is much larger. Furthermore, public telecommunications services (e.g., cable TV providers, telephone companies) are used to link sites together. Sophisticated equipment must be installed at each site, yet it is much more plentiful in public systems than in the private sector. Consequently, a much wider variety of cable TV learning opportunities are possible when using a public system. In general, public systems can and do extend beyond local geographic boundaries and, in some cases, reach into multiple countries simultaneously.

Current Trends and Legislation

At the time of this writing, one might argue that the public broadcasting industry is in a unique position to help direct its own future away from federal appropriations and towards self-sufficiency. However, the extent to which such a move might affect educational uses of the medium is not clear. Although currently proposed legislation calls for a minimum of three hours per week of educational programming to be provided by commercial broadcast interests, it is apparent that commercial broadcasters oppose the FCC rule-making on children's television and openly reject assuming such a responsibility.

Instructional television (cable TV) needs resources to deliver quality programming to its audiences. In the absence of federal dollars to support such initiatives, no guarantees can be given that "quality," or any other form of educational programming, would be available to users. Whereas an ultimate decentralization of public television's infrastructure may foster creativity, freedom of expression, and competitiveness, current efforts to become self-sufficient fall short in guaranteeing long-term viability for public broadcasting as a whole, and educational programming in particular.

CONCLUSIONS

Educators continue to espouse the use of cable television in the classroom. The impetus is characterized by a steadily increasing number of U.S. schools that are either ready or becoming equipped to deliver and receive instruction via TV. The number of capable schools rose from 45,000 to 71,000 (or 69 percent of all K-12 schools in the United States) between 1991 and 1995—an increase of 58 percent in just four years (Cable in the Classroom 1995). Furthermore, of the nation's total student population in K-12 (48,000,000), an estimated 38,000,000 (80 percent) are reached by cable TV on an annual basis. These remarkable statistics demand that professionals (e.g., teachers, administrators, programmers, researchers) as well as consumers (students and parents) associated with the cable TV industry launch and maintain ongoing investigations of issues, policies, and practices governing the use of cable TV for instructional purposes.

The potential for instruction provided by cable in the classroom is eclipsed, however, by the number of educational practitioners who remain uninformed about the concept or who lack proficiency in the use of the medium to deliver instruction. All educators can benefit by maximizing their knowledge and use of the medium.

REFERENCES

America's Public Television, Inc. (1995). *Harnessing the power of television for education.* An unpublished Internet manuscript.

Cable in the Classroom. (1995). *Cable in the Classroom: Partners in learning.* Circular prepared by CCI/Crosby Publishing, Cambridge, MA.

Cable in the Classroom Fact Sheet. (1996). *Cable in the Classroom.* Alexandria, VA: Author.

Grimes, G. (1993). Going the distance with technology . . . Happy 100th anniversary to distance education. *'etin,* May, 6-8.

Holmes, G. A., and Branch, R. C. (1994). *Cable television in the classroom.* Syracuse, NY: ERIC Clearinghouse on Information & Technology. (ERIC Digest, EDO-IR-94-5; ED 371-727).

Keegan, D. (1986). *The foundations of distance education.* London: Croom Helm.

Office of Instructional Technology. (1995). *Factors that characterize a distance learning application.* Unpublished manuscript. Regents of the University of Michigan.

Public Broadcasting Service. (1995a). *Learning services: Instructional television.* Washington, DC: Author.

Public Broadcasting Service. (1995b). *Learning services: Middle school math project (MSMP).* Washington, DC: Author.

Public Broadcasting Service. (1995c). *Learning services: Overview of services.* Washington, DC: Author.

K-12 Technology Planning at State, District, and Local Levels*

Larry S. Anderson
Founder/Director, National Center for Technology Planning
Mississippi State University

INTRODUCTION

In the early 1990s, the Council of Chief State School Officers (CCSSO), a professional organization of state superintendents of education, released a position paper (Improving . . . 1991) advocating that all states develop and maintain written plans for integrating technology in the education curriculum. In the ensuing years, with the added incentive provided by Goals 2000 legislation (Congress . . . 1993), many states have completed, or are currently working on, technology plans.

KEY PRINCIPLES OF TECHNOLOGY PLANNING

- *Include people in the community.* Planners need to involve all school and community "stakeholders" in the planning process. This is probably the most important advice one can receive related to technology planning.

- *Establish timelines and monitor them often.* Planning will be far more successful if key participants work from a mutually understood timeline. It is a good idea to print the timeline and display it prominently. The timeline should be addressed and monitored often. This will help keep planners on task and ensure that goals are reached in a timely fashion.

- *Delegate responsibilities for planning.* The chairperson of the planning committee should make use of the particular expertise and talents of each committee member when assigning responsibilities. It is important to compliment committee members when they perform admirably.

- *Evaluate.* Technology planning experts often say that there are three things to remember when building and implementing a technology plan: "evaluate, evaluate, evaluate." Planners will need to monitor all planning activities and include an evaluation program that will help them track the success of their activities.

LOCAL PLANNING

A local or building-level technology plan is more specific than a district or state plan. A local plan focuses on the learner and the associated activities, principles, and materials required to ensure that the desired instructional activities occur. Teachers and administrators who develop local plans will need to pay strict attention to the curriculum issues in the school.

*This ERIC Digest was prepared by Dr. Larry S. Anderson, Founder/Director National Center for Technology Planning, P.O. Box 5425, Mississippi State, MS 39762, (601) 325-2281; FAX (601) 325-7599; E-mail LSA1@Ra.MsState.Edu

ERIC Digests are in the public domain and may be freely reproduced and disseminated.

This publication was prepared with funding from the Office of Educational Research and Improvement, U.S. Department of Education, contract no. RR93002009. The opinions expressed in this report do not necessarily reflect the positions or policies of OERI or the Department of Education.

Technologies will support curriculum delivery and learning activities. A local technology plan will need a vision statement, a mission statement, and goals for how technology will be used in teaching and learning.

DISTRICT PLANNING

School district technology plans provide strategies for incorporating technological solutions in all local schools. A district plan provides an overview of what local schools wish to accomplish. District planners should remember to involve a cross-section of leaders from various schools in the district in the planning process. The committee needs to hold periodic "town meetings" to explain the plan, report progress, and explain related activities. The district planning committee should seek and acquire "buy-in" throughout the process from all members of the community.

The scope of planning is much broader at the district level than at the local level. Curriculum concerns, for example, will span a greater breadth of subject matter. Districts need to plan for great diversity as they consider the ages of students, teaching delivery methods, and assessment techniques. Because there may be local variance in some of the key elements that go into a district plan, it is important that planners incorporate input from local schools in their technology plans.

A district plan will include, and address in detail, elements that may not appear in a local plan at all. For example, a district plan might include district funding strategies, public relations tactics, and strategies for using technology in administration, transportation, food service, guidance, and student services. Most importantly, the district needs to outline how it will provide leadership and guidance for those who will implement and benefit from the plan.

STATE PLANNING

Just as a district technology plan is more general and less specific than a local plan, so a state plan is more general and less specific than a district plan. While some parts of a state plan will have elements that are specific, their specificity will deal with principles that are general in nature. A state-level plan addresses many issues mentioned in school district plans, and may provide a compilation of concerns and desires illuminated by the district plans. A state may want to describe how its financial support for districts will enable schools to integrate technologies into instruction and administration. A state may also want to describe the process by which districts will be accountable to the state for the funds given them.

DOVETAILED ELEMENTS

While local, district, and state plans are significantly different in certain areas, several similarities exist. Planners use the term "dovetail" to describe the manner in which these plans fit with each other.

State-level planners need to decide whether they will adopt a top-down or bottom-up scheme. If a top-down approach is taken, the state will fashion a plan, then ask districts to follow the state's guidelines. In some cases, where the state uses a top-down technique, the district may employ a bottom-up method. For example, the district might craft its vision statement only after it has compiled vision statements from all schools within the district.

A state plan will, most likely, define a framework into which district plans should fit. Often, statewide technology coordinators will develop a handbook that district planners will use as a guide for building the district plan. In this way, the district plan will "fit," or dovetail into the state plan. The district, then, will use input from local plans to dovetail into the district plan.

REALITIES OF PLANNING

- *Financial.* A technology plan needs to address the amount of money that will be required to implement and maintain whatever the plan proposes; how matching money, if necessary, will be sought; how leveraged money might be needed in the future; how finances will be managed; what the contingency plans might be if additional funding is secured or if a shortfall occurs; and how funds will be allocated to pay for planned obsolescence. Planners need to remember that public funds are employed in the infusion of technologies into instruction; therefore, strong accountability to the community is necessary.

- *Technical.* As state, district, and local groups consider and include the technical components of their plans, they need to recognize the impact of rapid technological change and growth. Plans need not focus on, but should certainly include, hardware and software. Inclusion of a detailed technical plan that addresses technological obsolescence will help to plan for future equipment upgrades.

- *Human capital.* A technology plan needs to outline the ways in which human talent will be incorporated. Many models show effective employment of human capital, and planners need to examine existing technology plans that demonstrate how this is done.

- *Architectural.* When planners specify the design of structures or areas where technology will be used, careful attention needs to be devoted to eliminating any obstacles that will obstruct or hinder teaching and learning. Consulting with an experienced architect is well worth the time and money.

- *Legal.* At all levels of planning, legal concerns are important. Not only do planners need to consider protection for the "system," but strategies need to be outlined for the protection of students and other learners. Consult with community resources for legal advice.

SUMMARY

Although technology planning occurs at multiple levels, many principles are identical. Planners need to engage the services, creativity, and assistance of all stakeholders. Efforts of all participants in the planning process need to be marshaled to meet established timelines, to accept delegated responsibilities, and to evaluate progress along the way. Planners at the local, district, and state levels are encouraged to share the work they create. Through open, willing sharing, all learners will benefit.

FURTHER READING

Anderson, L. S. (1995, November-December). Making dreams come true! How to write a technology plan. *Multimedia Schools* 2(5), 14-19. (EJ 513 826)

Anderson, L. S. (1996, February). *The role of the school business manager in technology planning.* Internet WWW page at URL: http://www2.msstate.edu/~lsa1/nctp/Sch.Bus.Mgr.html (version current as of February 1996).

Anderson, L. S., and Perry, J. F., Jr. (1996, February 24). *Technology planning: Recipe for success.* Internet WWW page at URL: http://www2.msstate.edu/~lsa1/nctp/tp.recipe.html (version current as of February 24, 1996).

Building a system to invest in people: States on the cutting edge. (1995). Rochester, NY: National Center on Education and the Economy. (ED 384 971)

Challenges, opportunities, successes: 1995-1997 biennial report. (1995). North Carolina Department of Public Instruction, State Board of Education. (ED 384 119)

Congress of the United States. (1993). *Goals 2000: Educate America Act.* Report from the Committee on Education and Labor, Together with Dissenting and Supplemental Dissenting Views [to Accompany H.R. 1804]. House of Representatives, 103d Congress, 1st Session. (ED 361 834)

Hunter, B. M. (1995). *From here to technology. How to fund hardware, software, and more.* Arlington, VA: American Association of School Administrators. (ED 385 000)

Improving student performance through learning technologies: 1991 policy statement of the Council of Chief State School Officers. (1994). In *Educational Media and Technology Yearbook, Vol. 20,* ed. Donald P. Ely and Barbara B. Minor. Englewood, CO: Libraries Unlimited.

Johnson, D. (1995). The new and improved school library: How one district planned for the future. *School Library Journal 41*(6), 36-39. (EJ 505 448)

National Center for Technology Planning. (1996, April). Internet WWW page at URL: http://www2.msstate.edu/~lsa1/nctp/index.html (version current as of April 1996).

Orwig, A. H. (1996, April). *Strategic planning for technology: Is your school really ready?* Internet WWW page at URL: http://gnn.com/gnn/meta/edu/features/archive/atechpla.html (version current as of April 1996).

Rural and urban school finance: Districts and experts speak out. Policy briefs. Report 1. (1995). Oak Brook, IL: North Central Regional Educational Laboratory. (ED 384 121)

See, J. *Developing effective technology plans.* (1996, February 19). Internet WWW page at URL: http://www2.msstate.edu/~lsa1/nctp/john.see.html (version current as of February 19, 1996).

Solomon, G. (1992, September). *Teacher training—Reaching out.* Internet WWW page at URL: http://www2.msstate.edu/~lsa1/nctp/tea.tng.gwen.html (version current as of April 1996). Adapted from *Scholastic's Electronic Learning,* September 1992.

Wilson, B. G., Teslow, J. L., Cyr, T. A., and Hamilton, R. H. (1994). *Technology making a difference: The Peakview Elementary School study.* Syracuse, NY: ERIC Clearinghouse on Information & Technology. (ED 381 149)

Local Area Networks
for K-12 Schools*

Timoth C. Lederman
Department of Computer Science
Siena College

WHAT IS A LAN?

A Local Area Network (LAN) allows computing equipment to share information from any device on a network with other devices on the same network, and includes cabling, network transmission devices, network interfaces, and computing devices. Some examples of computing devices on a LAN include:

- **File Servers**—Computers that serve as central storage facilities for data and program files.

- **Print Servers**—Computers with one or more printers attached that provide printing services to other computers on the LAN. Some printers have special interfaces that allow the printer itself to act as a print server on a network.

- **Modem/Fax/Communications Servers**—Devices that allow computers on the LAN to communicate outside the network through a standard local telephone system. It is also possible, with appropriate communications servers and software, to allow external computers to dial in to a LAN and communicate (data or faxes) with devices on the LAN.

Computer Communications

Different kinds of computers use different methods, or protocols, to communicate with each other. Macintosh computers use the AppleTalk protocol. Macintosh as well as PCs can use TCP/IP to share information on the Internet. Some PCs require a Network Operating System (NOS) to communicate. For example, Novell Netware is a popular NOS with PC users.

Servers and Clients

A server computer provides a special service (examples described above), while a client computer requests and receives a service from a server. The same computer could be a client or a server, depending upon the type of data communications taking place. For example, a computer could serve one of its files to another computer, but it could also receive a file from that computer.

---

*Timoth Lederman is a Professor of Computer Science, Siena College, Loudonville, New York. lederman@siens.edu

ERIC Digests are in the public domain and may be freely reproduced and disseminated.

This publication was prepared with funding from the Office of Educational Research and Improvement, U.S. Department of Education, under contract no. RR93002009. The opinions expressed in this report do not necessarily reflect the positions of OERI or ED.

Uses for LANs in a School Building

- sharing printers
- sharing programs
- centralized file sharing
- access to the library card catalog
- cost-effective connection to external networks
- school information system for administrators, teachers, students, parents and the community

- electronic mail
- school bulletin boards
- access to library databases
- sending and receiving faxes

Uses for LANs District Wide

District uses for LANs include all of the above, but in particular:

- file sharing (student information)
- transmission of records (attendance, grades, discipline)
- electronic mail
- shared use of one district connection to the Internet

Note: The interconnection of multiple building LANs is often accomplished by Wide Area Networking (WAN) through radio transmission or through leased data lines from a telephone company.

Types of LANs

Common types of LAN hardware are Ethernet and Token Ring. Ethernet predominates because it is easily designed and is composed of data transfer devices that are less expensive than similar Token Ring devices. The performance of Ethernet and Token Ring are roughly the same in most situations. While it is possible to interconnect Ethernet and Token Ring networks in the same location, such an interconnection adds to cost and complexity. It is best to keep the configuration of a school's data communication infrastructure as simple as possible.

Another standard for data communication is ATM (Asynchronous Transfer Mode). It is more expensive than Ethernet or Token Ring but allows higher speeds and will eventually allow better integration of computer-data, digitized voice (telephone), and video. Some suggestions for choosing a LAN include:

- If a school does not have an existing high speed data network, choose Ethernet.
- If a school has an extensive Ethernet or Token Ring LAN, continue with that standard.
- If a school has a small Token Ring LAN and a significant extension of the LAN is being proposed, two cost projections should be made. One estimate should include costs for extending the existing Token Ring LAN, and the other should consider the price of replacing the entire LAN with Ethernet.
- If a school or district receives maintenance assistance from an organization that only supports Token Ring, it is sometimes appropriate, if not necessary, to choose Token Ring.

Design Considerations

Cabling medium. The most cost-effective cabling is Category 5 twisted-pair cable. This cable works with standard Ethernet (10 Million bits per second, 10 Mbps) and "fast" Ethernet (100 Mbps), and is capable of speeds up to 150 Mbps with existing technology. This has become the cable of choice in most LAN designs. Fiber-optic cable transmits more data, but materials and installation are much more expensive. Proper installation of fiber-optic cable is difficult in an old building because the cable should not be bent during installation or when finally terminated (an 8″ minimum bending radius is allowed).

Wiring plan. The location of wiring cabinets/closets is dependent on suitable locations in the building and distances between computers. The maximum distance between a computer and a network wiring cabinet/closet is 10 meters. A refrigerator-sized cabinet where cables come together and network transmission equipment (and sometimes servers) are stored can be enclosed with doors and stand in a large room, or it can be placed as an open rack in a small room or closet. Wiring cabinets/closets can be interconnected with twisted-pair cable, but fiber-optic cable is a better choice for a variety of reasons, especially higher speed.

Number of network connections (plug-in points) per room. Every computer needs a network connection and each connection is comprised of (1) a plug-in point in the wall of the room and (2) wiring from this point to the wiring cabinet/closet. Short- and long-term technology goals need to be considered when planning the number of network connections per room.

Regular classrooms. Provide from one to six network connections per regular classroom.

Special classrooms. A minimum of one network connection should be provided in home economics, physical education, music, and art rooms. Some schools equip these rooms, and special education and reading rooms, just like regular classrooms and provide up to six network connections.

Technology classrooms. This room could be equipped like a regular classroom, but some districts place emphasis on computer and communication technology in their technology curricula, especially at the middle school level, and may often provide a network connection ratio of one connection per two students (15 connections in a room that holds up to 30 students).

Computing classrooms. It is advantageous to maintain at least one classroom per school that provides one computer per student (30 network connections for classes of up to 30 students).

Library. The library can become an even more versatile center for access to information, research, and creative endeavors if it is wired with network connections. Networked computers can be used to access an online card catalog within the school, or online catalogs from other schools in the district. If the school has a connection to external networks, a LAN allows every computer in the library (and in the school) to access online catalogs and databases from a variety of locations. A connection to the Internet, for example, provides access to college, university, and government libraries throughout the world. Networked multimedia workstations in libraries allow students to access multimedia databases, encyclopedias, and other graphic/visual-oriented resources.

Many school libraries locate network connections in as many places as possible in the library. Librarians recognize that computers will become increasingly prevalent in libraries as cost-effective replacements for expensive and space-consuming resources like serials, periodicals, newspapers, and reference books.

Administrative offices. At least one network connection per person should be provided for administrative purposes. Two connections per person will allow for the connection of printers and other network devices.

Other offices. The offices of school nurses, psychologists, career/guidance counselors, home/school counselors, and other academic support personnel should have at least one network connection per person.

**Additional Things to Remember When
Designing a School's LAN**

Network outlets. Locate near the area where the computers are or will be located.

Electrical outlets. Locate near the network outlets. If electrical outlets are installed for future use, be sure the building's power supply and power distribution infrastructure are adequate to handle the added computers. Because the cost of providing electrical service can be substantial (as much as half of the cost of a LAN itself), it is prudent to consider this cost at the same time as estimating the cost of the LAN.

Furniture and fixtures location. When developing a wiring plan, consider the placement of furniture and stationary fixtures.

Wiring. When wiring for a LAN, run additional cabling for other purposes at the same time because the cost benefits are often substantial. The installation of cabling for the following purposes should be considered when installing LAN cabling:

cable TV	telephone and intercom
alarms/security	environmental sensors

Potential use of space. Include every room in the LAN design that might ever house a class, group, or office. It is much less expensive to design and install a network for an entire building than it is to "modularize" into smaller LAN projects (classrooms in one project and offices in another project). Room use may change over the years (e.g., large closets may become offices or small classrooms).

SUMMARY

There are many aspects of LAN design to consider when developing a technology plan for a school building or school district. This digest has indicated several key design issues; however, one should contact an experienced consultant or network designer before finalizing a LAN design.

FURTHER READING

Brennan, M. A. (1991, November). *Trends and issues in library and information science 1990.* ERIC Digest. Syracuse, NY: ERIC Clearinghouse on Information Resources. (ED 340 389)

Charp, S., ed. (1994). Networking and telecommunications. *T.H.E. Journal 21*(10). (EJ 483 802-807)

Charp, S., ed. (1995). Networking and telecommunications. *T.H.E. Journal 22*(9). (EJ 501 732-735)

Communications, computers, and networks. (1991). *Scientific American 265*(3). [Special issue].

Ellis, T. I. (1984). *Microcomputers in the school office.* ERIC Digest. Eugene, OR: ERIC Clearinghouse on Education Management. (ED 259 451)

Klausmeier, J. (1984). *Networking and microcomputers.* ERIC Digest. Syracuse, NY: ERIC Clearinghouse on Information Resources. (ED 253 256)

Neubarth, M., ed. (1995, October). The Internet in education. *Internet World 6*(10). [Special issue]. (EJ 510 430-437)

Rienhold, F. (1989). *Use of local area networks in schools.* ERIC Digest. Syracuse, NY: ERIC Clearinghouse on Information Resources. (ED 316 249)

Tennant, R. (1992). *Internet basics.* ERIC Digest. Syracuse, NY: ERIC Clearinghouse on Information Resources. (ED 348 054)

Computer Skills for Information Problem-Solving
Learning and Teaching Technology in Context*

Michael B. Eisenberg
Syracuse University

Doug Johnson
Mankato Public Schools

There seems to be clear and widespread agreement among the public and educators that students need to be proficient computer users—students need to be "computer literate." However, while districts are spending a great deal of money on technology, there seems to be only a vague notion of what computer literacy really means.

- Can the student who operates a computer well enough to play Doom be considered computer literate?

- Will a student who has used computers in school only for running tutorials or an integrated learning system have the skills necessary to survive in our society?

- Will the ability to do basic word processing be sufficient for students entering the workplace or postsecondary education?

Clearly not. In too many schools, most teachers and students still use computers only as the equivalent of expensive flash cards or electronic worksheets. The productivity side of computer use in the general content area curriculum is neglected or grossly underdeveloped (Moursund 1995).

There are, however, some encouraging signs concerning computers and technology in education. For example, it is becoming increasingly popular for educational technologists to advocate integrating computers into the content areas. Teachers and administrators are recognizing that computer skills should not be taught in isolation, and that separate "computer classes" do not really help students learn to apply computer skills in meaningful ways. This is an important shift in approach and emphasis. And it's a shift with which library media specialists have a great deal of familiarity.

Library media specialists know that moving from isolated skills instruction to an integrated approach is an important step that takes a great deal of planning and effort. Over the past 20 years, library media professionals have worked hard to move from teaching isolated "library skills" to teaching integrated information skills. Effective integration of information skills has two requirements:

1. The skills must directly relate to the content area curriculum and to classroom assignments, and

---

*Michael B. Eisenberg is the Director of the ERIC Clearinghouse on Information and Technology and Professor of Information Studies, Syracuse University, Syracuse, New York. Doug Johnson is the District Media Supervisor for Mankato Public Schools, Mankato, Minnesota. Robert E. Berkowitz is Library Media Specialist at Wayne Central High School and an Adjunct Professor in the School of Information Studies, Syracuse University.

ERIC Digests are in the public domain and may be freely reproduced and disseminated.

This publication was prepared with funding from the Office of Educational Research and Improvement, U.S. Department of Education, under contract no. RR93002009. The opinions expressed in this report do not necessarily reflect the positions of OERI or ED.

2. The skills themselves need to be tied together in a logical and systematic information process model.

Schools seeking to move from isolated computer skills instruction will also need to focus on both of these requirements. Successful integrated information skills programs are designed around collaborative projects jointly planned and taught by teachers and library media professionals. Computer skills instruction can follow the same approach. Library media specialists, computer teachers, and classroom teachers need to work together to develop units and lessons that will include both computer skills, general information skills, and content-area curriculum outcomes.

A meaningful, unified computer literacy curriculum must be more than "laundry lists" of isolated skills, such as:

- knowing the parts of the computer
- writing drafts and final products with a word processor
- searching for information using a CD-ROM database

While these specific skills are certainly important for students to learn, the "laundry list" approach does not provide an adequate model for students to transfer and apply skills from situation to situation. These curricula address the *how* of computer use, but rarely the *when* or *why*. Students may learn isolated skills and tools, but they will still lack an understanding of how those various skills fit together to solve problems and complete tasks.

Students need to be able to use computers flexibly, creatively, and purposefully. All learners should be able to recognize what they need to accomplish, determine whether a computer will help them to do so, and then be able to use the computer as part of the process of accomplishing their task. Individual computer skills take on new meanings when they are integrated within this type of information problem-solving process, and students develop true computer literacy because they have genuinely applied various computer skills as part of the learning process.

The appended curriculum, "Computer Skills for Information Problem-Solving," demonstrates how computer literacy skills can fit within an information literacy skills context (American Association of School Librarians 1995). The baseline information literacy context is the Big Six Skills process (see sidebar and Eisenberg and Berkowitz citations). The various computer skills are adapted from curricula developed by the state of Minnesota (Minnesota Department of Education 1989) and the Mankato Area Public Schools (Mankato Schools Information Literacy Curriculum Guideline). These basic computer skills are those that all students might reasonably be expected to authentically demonstrate before graduation. Because Internet-related skills are increasingly important for information problem-solving, they are included in this curriculum, and are noted by double asterisks (**).

Some computer literacy "skills" competencies that do not seem to fit into this information processing model, and that may or may not be important to have stated, include:

- Knowing the basic operation, terminology, and maintenance of equipment
- Knowing how to use computer-assisted instructional programs
- Having knowledge of the impact of technology on careers, society, and culture
- Computer programming
- Specialized computer applications like music composition software, computer assisted drawing and drafting programs, and mathematics modeling software.

Listing computer skills is only a first step in assuring that all our children become proficient information and technology users. A teacher-supported scope and sequence of skills, well-designed projects, and effective assessments are also critical. Many library media specialists will need to hone their own technology skills in order to remain effective information skills teachers. But such a curriculum holds tremendous opportunities for library media specialists to become vital, indispensable staff members, and for all children to master the skills they will need to thrive in an information-rich future.

REFERENCES AND SUGGESTED READING

American Association of School Librarians. (1995, November). Information literacy: A position paper on information problem solving. *Emergency Librarian* 23(2), 20-23. (EJ 514998). Also available from the American Association of School Librarians.

California Media and Library Educators Association Staff. (1993). *From library skills to information literacy: A handbook for the 21st century.* Englewood, CO: Libraries Unlimited.

Coulehan, J. L. (1995). Using electronic mail for a small-group curriculum in ethical and social issues. *Academic Medicine 70*(2), 158-63. (EJ 499 651)

Doyle, C. S. (1994). *Information literacy in an information society: A concept for the information age.* Syracuse, NY: ERIC Clearinghouse on Information and Technology. (ED 372 763)

Eisenberg, M., and Berkowitz, B. (1988). *Curriculum initiative: An agenda and strategy for library media programs.* Norwood, NJ: Ablex.

Eisenberg, M. B., and Berkowitz, R. E. (1992). Information problem-solving: The big six skills approach. *School Library Media Activities Monthly 8*(5), 27-29, 37, 42. (EJ 438 023)

Eisenberg, M. B., and Ely, D. P. (1993). Plugging into the "Net." *Emergency Librarian 21*(2), 8-16. (EJ 471 260)

Eisenberg, M. B., and Small, R. V. (1993). Information-based education: An investigation of the nature and role of information attributes in education. *Information Processing and Management 29*(2), 263-75. (EJ 462 841)

Eisenberg, M. B., and Spitzer, K. L. (1991). Information technology and services in schools. In *Annual Review of Information Science and Technology: Vol. 26,* ed. M. E. Williams. Medford, NJ: Learned Information. (EJ 441 688)

Garland, K. (1995). The information search process: A study of elements associated with meaningful research tasks. *School Libraries Worldwide 1*(1), 41-53. (EJ 503 407)

Johnson, D. (1995). Captured by the web: K-12 schools and the World Wide Web. *MultiMedia Schools 2*(2), 24-30. (EJ 499 841)

Johnson, D. (1995). The new and improved school library: How one district planned for the future. *School Library Journal 41*(6), 36-39. (EJ 505 448)

THE BIG SIX SKILLS APPROACH TO INFORMATION PROBLEM-SOLVING

Copyright ©
Eisenberg and Berkowitz, 1988.

The Big Six is an information literacy curriculum, an information problem-solving process, and a set of skills that provide a strategy for effectively and efficiently meeting information needs. The Big Six Skills approach can be used whenever students are in a situation, academic or personal, that requires information to solve a problem, make a decision, or complete a task. This model is transferable to school, personal, and work applications, as well as all content-areas, and the full range of grade levels. When taught collaboratively with content area teachers in concert with content-area objectives, it serves to ensure that students are information literate.

The Big Six:

1. Task Definition
   1.1 Define the task (the information problem)
   1.2 Identify information needed in order to complete the task (to solve the information problem)

2. Information-Seeking Strategies
   2.1 Brainstorm all possible sources
   2.2 Select the best sources

3. Location and Access
   3.1 Locate source
   3.2 Find information within the source

4. Use of Information
   4.1 Engage in the source (read, hear, view, touch)
   4.2 Extract relevant information

5. Synthesis
   5.1 Organize information from multiple sources
   5.2 Present the information

6. Evaluation
   6.1 Judge the process (efficiency)
   6.2 Judge the product (effectiveness)

Johnson, D. (1995). Student access to the Internet: Librarians and teachers working together to teach higher level survival skills. *Emergency Librarian 22*(3), 8-12. (EJ 497 895)

Kuhlthau, C. C. (1993). Implementing a process approach to information skills: A study identifying indicators of success in library media programs. *School Library Media Quarterly 22*(1), 11-18. (EJ 473 063)

Kuhlthau, C. C. (1995). The process of learning from information. *School Libraries Worldwide 1*(1), 1-12. (EJ 503 404)

Mankato Schools Information Literacy Curriculum Guideline. Internet WWW page at URL: http://www.isd77.k12.mn.us/resources/infolit.html (version current as of March 11, 1996).

McNally, M. J., and Kuhlthau, C. C. (1994). Information search process in science education. *Reference Librarian 44*, 53-60. (EJ 488 273)

Minnesota Department of Education. (1989). *Model learner outcomes for educational media and technology.* St. Paul, MN: Author. (ED 336 070)

Moursund, D. (1995, December). Effective practices (part 2): Productivity tools. *Learning and Leading with Technology 23*(4), 5-6.

Pappas, M. L. (1993, September). A vision of school library media centers in an electronic information age. *School Library Media Activities Monthly 10*(1), 32-34, 38. (EJ 469 122)

Pappas, M. L. (1995). Information skills for electronic resources. *School Library Media Activities Monthly 11*(8), 39-40. (EJ 499 875)

Todd, R. J. (1995). Information literacy: Philosophy, principles, and practice. *School Libraries Worldwide 1*(1), 54-68. (EJ 503 408)

Todd, R. J. (1995). Integrated information skills instruction: Does it make a difference? *School Library Media Quarterly 23*(2), 133-138. (EJ 497 921)

Wisconsin Educational Media Association. (1993). *Information literacy: A position paper on information problem-solving.* Madison, WI: WEMA Publications. (ED 376 817). (Portions adapted from Michigan State Board of Education's *Position Paper on Information Processing Skills,* 1992).

APPENDIX A
Computer Skills for Information Problem-Solving:
A Curriculum Based on the Big Six Skills Approach

Copyright © Michael B. Eisenberg, Doug Johnson, and Robert E. Berkowitz

1. **Task Definition:**
   The first step in the information problem-solving process is to recognize that an information need exists, to define the problem, and to identify the types and amount of information needed. In terms of technology, students will be able to:

   A. Use e-mail and online discussion groups (e.g., listservs, newsgroups) on the Internet to communicate with teachers regarding assignments, tasks, and information-problems.**

   B. Use e-mail and online discussion groups (e.g., listservs, newsgroups) on the Internet to generate topics and problems and to facilitate cooperative activities among groups of students locally and globally.**

   C. Use desktop conferencing, e-mail, and groupware software on local area networks to communicate with teachers regarding assignments, tasks, and information problems.

   D. Use desktop conferencing, e-mail, and groupware software on local area networks to generate topics and problems and to facilitate cooperative activities among groups of students locally.

** Items are specific to Internet use.

E. Use computer brainstorming or idea generating software to define or refine the information problem. This includes developing a research question or perspective on a topic.

2. **Information Seeking Strategies:**
    Once the information problem has been formulated, the student must consider all possible information sources and develop a plan for searching. Students will be able to:

    A. Assess the value of various types of electronic resources for data gathering, including databases, CD-ROM resources, commercial and Internet online resources, electronic reference works, community and government information electronic resources.**

    B. Identify and apply specific criteria for evaluating computerized electronic resources.

    C. Assess the value of e-mail, and online discussion groups (e.g., listservs, newsgroups) on the Internet as part of a search of the current literature or in relation to the information task.

    D. Use a computer to generate modifiable flow charts, Gantt charts, time lines, organizational charts, project plans and calendars that will help the student plan and organize complex or group information problem-solving tasks.

3. **Location and Access:**
    After students determine their priorities for information seeking, they must locate information from a variety of resources and access specific information found within individual resources. Students will be able to:

    A. Locate and use appropriate computer resources and technologies available within the school library media center, including those on the library media center's local area network (e.g., online catalogs, periodical indexes, full-text sources, multimedia computer stations, CD-ROM stations, online terminals, scanners, digital cameras).

    B. Locate and use appropriate computer resources and technologies available throughout the school including those available through local area networks (e.g., full-text resources, CD-ROMs, productivity software, scanners, digital cameras).

    C. Locate and use appropriate computer resources and technologies available beyond the school through the Internet (e.g., newsgroups, listservs, WWW sites via Netscape, Lynx or another browser, gopher, ftp sites, online public access library catalogs, commercial databases and online services, other community, academic, and government resources).**

    D. Know the roles and computer expertise of the people working in the school library media center and elsewhere who might provide information or assistance.

    E. Use electronic reference materials (e.g., electronic encyclopedias, dictionaries, biographical reference sources, atlases, geographic databanks, thesauri, almanacs, fact books) available through local area networks, stand-alone workstations, commercial online vendors, or the Internet.

    F. Use the Internet or commercial computer networks to contact experts and help and referral services.**

    G. Conduct self-initiated electronic surveys through e-mail, listservs, or newsgroups.**

H. Use organizational systems and tools specific to electronic information sources that assist in finding specific and general information (e.g., indexes, tables of contents, user's instructions and manuals, legends, boldface and italics, graphic clues and icons, cross-references, Boolean logic strategies, time lines, hypertext links, knowledge trees, URLs, etc.) including the use of:

   1. Search tools and commands for stand-alone, CD-ROM, and online databases and services (e.g., DIALOG commands, America Online, UMI, Mead);

   2. Search tools and commands for searching the Internet (e.g., Yahoo, Lycos, WebCrawler, Veronica, Archie).**

4. Use of Information:

After finding potentially useful resources, students must engage (read, view, listen) the information to determine its relevance and then extract the relevant information. Students will be able to:

A. Connect and operate the computer technology needed to access information, and read the guides and manuals associated with such tasks.

B. View, download, decompress, and open documents and programs from Internet sites and archives.**

C. Cut and paste information from an electronic source into a personal document complete with proper citation.

D. Take notes and outline with a word processor or similar productivity program.

E. Record electronic sources of information and locations of those sources to properly cite and credit in footnotes, endnotes, and bibliographies.

F. Use electronic spreadsheets, databases, and statistical software to process and analyze statistical data.

G. Analyze and filter electronic information in relation to the task, rejecting non-relevant information.

5. Synthesis:

Students must organize and communicate the results of the information problem-solving effort. Students will be able to:

A. Classify and group information using a word processor, database, or spreadsheet.

B. Use word processing and desktop publishing software to create printed documents, applying keyboard skills equivalent to at least twice the rate of handwriting speed.

C. Create and use computer-generated graphics and art in various print and electronic presentations.

D. Use electronic spreadsheet software to create original spreadsheets.

E. Generate charts, tables, and graphs using electronic spreadsheets and other graphing programs.

F. Use database/file management software to create original databases.

G. Use presentation software (e.g., PowerPoint, HyperStudio, Aldus Persuasion) to create electronic slide shows and to generate overheads and slides.

    H. Create hypermedia and multimedia productions with digital video and audio.

    I. Create World Wide Web pages and sites using hypertext markup language (HTML).**

    J. Use e-mail, ftp, and other telecommunications capabilities to share information, products, and files.**

    K. Use specialized computer applications as appropriate for specific tasks, e.g., music composition software, computer-assisted drawing and drafting programs, mathematics modeling software.

    L. Properly cite and credit electronic sources of information in footnotes, endnotes, and bibliographies.

6. **Evaluation:**
Evaluation focuses on how well the final product meets the original task (effectiveness) and the process of how well students carried out the information problem-solving process (efficiency). Students may evaluate their own work and process or be evaluated by others (i.e., classmates, teachers, library media staff, parents). Students will be able to:

    A. Evaluate electronic presentations in terms of both the content and format.

    B. Use spell and grammar checking capabilities of word processing and other software to edit and revise their work.

    C. Apply legal principles and ethical conduct related to information technology regarding copyright and plagiarism.

    D. Understand and abide by telecomputing etiquette when using e-mail, newsgroups, listservs and other Internet functions.**

    E. Understand and abide by acceptable use policies in relation to use of the Internet and other electronic technologies.

    F. Use e-mail and online discussion groups (e.g., listservs, newsgroups) on local area networks and the Internet to communicate with teachers and others regarding their performance on assignments, tasks, and information-problems.**

    G. Use desktop conferencing, e-mail, and groupware software on local area networks to communicate with teachers and others regarding student performance on assignments, tasks, and information problems.

    H. Thoughtfully reflect on the use of electronic resources and tools throughout the process.

Addendum:
Included here are skills and knowledge related to technology that are not part of the computer and information technology curriculum. These items should be learned in context, i.e., as students are working through various assignments and information problems using technology. Students will be able to:

    A. Know and use basic computer terminology.

    B. Operate various pieces of hardware and software—particularly operating systems— and be able to handle basic maintenance.

    C. Understand the basics of computer programming. Specific courses in computer programming should be part of the school's curricular offerings.

D. Understand and articulate the relationship and impact of information technology on careers, society, culture, and their own lives.

This curriculum guide is an excerpt from *Computer Skills for Information Problem-Solving: Learning and Teaching Technology in Context,* ERIC Digest (1996, March), prepared by Michael B. Eisenberg and Doug Johnson for the ERIC Clearinghouse on Information and Technology, Syracuse, New York. (ED 392 463)

Electronic Portfolios
A New Idea in Assessment*

Anna Maria D. Lankes
OCM BOCES
Syracuse, New York

INTRODUCTION

Teachers and administrators are showing increased interest in becoming part of a new wave of assessment in the classroom—assessment that includes authentic and performance-based measures. These methods of assessment allow students to demonstrate desired performance through real-life situations (Meyer 1992). Such methods of assessment are not limited to multiple-choice and standardized tests, but include projects that require students to demonstrate their problem-solving skills as well as their skills in analyzing and synthesizing information. Several school districts across the United States have reported improved student performance associated with new assessment programs (Herman 1992). Many schools are developing new methods for measuring students' progress in both the elementary and secondary classroom. One of these new assessment measures, the portfolio, has become increasingly popular, and technology is helping with its creation and management.

WHAT IS A PORTFOLIO?

A portfolio at the K-12 education level is essentially a collection of a student's work that can be used to demonstrate skills and accomplishments. An educational portfolio is more than just a group of projects and papers stored in a file folder. It includes other features such as teachers' evaluations and student self-reflections. According to the Northwest Evaluation Association, a portfolio is "a purposeful collection of student work that exhibits the student's efforts, progress, and achievements. The collection must include student participation in selecting contents, the criteria for selection, the criteria for judging merit, and evidence of student self-reflection" (Paulson, Paulson, and Meyer 1991). A portfolio may be used to demonstrate a student's achievements in specific subject areas such as mathematics and science, or it may be used across the curriculum to assess abilities in all subject areas.

WHY USE A PORTFOLIO?

Developmental portfolios. A teacher who is interested in documenting a student's improvements in writing or mathematics throughout a school year can have the student keep a developmental portfolio containing samples of the student's work along with self-evaluations of specific assignments. Such a portfolio provides specific documentation that can be used for student evaluations and parent conferences.

Teacher planning. Teachers may use an existing portfolio system in order to receive information about an incoming class of students. The teacher may gain a better understanding of the ability levels of the students prior to the start of the school year and plan accordingly.

*Anna Maria D. Lankes is Systems Consultant—Computer Assisted Instruction, OCM BOCES (Onondaga-Cortland-Madison Board of Cooperative Educational Services), P.O. Box 4754, Syracuse, NY 13221. amlankes@ericir.syr.edu

ERIC Digests are in the public domain and may be freely reproduced and disseminated.

This publication was prepared with funding from the Office of Educational Research and Improvement, U.S. Department of Education, under contract no. RR93002009. The opinions expressed in this report do not necessarily reflect the positions of OERI or ED.

Proficiency portfolios. Central Park East Secondary School in New York City uses portfolios as a means for determining graduation eligibility. Students at this school are required to complete 14 portfolios that demonstrate their competence and performance in areas such as science and technology, ethics and social issues, community service, and history (Gold and Lanzoni 1993).

Showcase portfolios. A showcase portfolio can document a student's best work accomplished during an entire educational career. It can include the research papers, artwork, and science experiments that best represent the student's skills and abilities.

Employment skills portfolios. Businesses across the country are increasingly interested in viewing student portfolios in order to evaluate a prospective employee's work readiness skills. Students in the Michigan public schools, for example, are creating employability skills portfolios to demonstrate their skills to prospective employers (Stemmer, Brown, and Smith 1992).

College admission portfolios. Colleges and universities are using showcase portfolios to determine eligibility for admission. By requiring portfolios from prospective students, college and university admissions officers are better able to assess applicants' potential for success at their institutions.

TECHNOLOGY AND THE CREATION OF COMPUTER-BASED PORTFOLIOS

How to store and manage portfolio materials is a concern shared by many educators interested in implementing portfolio programs. In order to keep portfolios that would include papers, projects, and video and audiotapes for a class of students for 13 years (K-12), a school would need several additional classrooms to store this wealth of information. Many educators have been reluctant to implement portfolio assessment programs in their schools because of such storage concerns. A likely solution to this problem is the creation and storage of portfolios using computer technology.

The terms *computer-based portfolio* and *electronic portfolio* are used to describe portfolios saved in electronic format. Electronic portfolios contain the same types of information as the portfolios discussed earlier, but the information is collected, stored, and managed electronically. Because current technology allows for the capture and storage of information in the form of text, graphics, sound, and video, students can save writing samples, solutions to mathematics problems, samples of art work, science projects, and multimedia presentations in one coherent document. A single computer with a large storage capacity can store portfolios for all of the students in a class. With more students creating multimedia projects, however, a floppy or even a hard disk might not suffice for storage. An alternative is to store student portfolios on a CD-ROM. A CD-ROM can store approximately 650 MB of information or 300,000 sheets of typed text. This might include all of the portfolios for an entire grade level of students. A computer-based portfolio program also allows for easy transfer of information. An individual computer disk or CD-ROM could be created to transport a student's documents from teacher to teacher or school to school.

SOLUTIONS AND EXAMPLES

Several commercially available portfolio programs offer teachers the ability to track student achievement. Aurbach's Grady Profile is one program that provides a template for teachers and students to enter work samples. Programs may include writing samples, standardized test scores, oral communication skills, and mathematics assessments. Other software programs, such as Roger Wagner Publishing's HyperStudio and Claris's FileMaker Pro, allow teachers to create their own templates for portfolio assessment. Educators can use these programs to customize portfolios to suit the needs of their classes. For example, one high school

English portfolio might include outlines and drafts for each writing assignment, while another might include only the finished product along with self-reflections by the student.

One school involved in creating electronic portfolios for all its students is East Syracuse-Minoa High School in East Syracuse, New York. Students at this high school are creating electronic portfolios that can be sent to colleges as part of the admissions process, and to potential employers to determine workplace readiness. This electronic portfolio, called "The Portfolio Manager," was created in HyperStudio and contains traditional information about students (transcripts, letters of recommendation, and work history) as well as student-selected work samples (writing samples, multimedia research papers, artwork, and video clips from a performance in the school play). The students are responsible for updating and selecting the work samples they include in the portfolio and can select virtually any piece of work that they believe best represents their skills and abilities. Currently, students begin creating portfolios during their sophomore year and continue updating and revising the work samples throughout their high school careers. Upon completion, the portfolio can be distributed in floppy disk, CD-ROM, videotape, or print versions.

SUMMARY

The implementation of computer-based portfolios for student assessment is an exciting educational innovation. This method of assessment not only offers an authentic demonstration of accomplishments but also allows students to take responsibility for the work they have done. In turn, this motivates them to accomplish more in the future. A computer-based portfolio system offers many advantages for both the education and the business communities and should continue to be a popular assessment tool in the Information Age.

REFERENCES

Alternative assessment and technology. (1993). ERIC Digest. Syracuse, NY: ERIC Clearinghouse on Information and Technology. (ED 365 312)

Barrett, H. C. (1994). Technology-supported assessment portfolios. *Computing Teacher 21*(6), 9-12. (EJ 479 843)

Brewer, G. (1994). *FileMaker Pro* [Computer program]. Santa Clara, CA: Claris.

Gold, J. (Producer and Director), and Lanzoni, M., ed. (1993). *Graduation by portfolio—Central Park East Secondary School* [Videotape]. New York: Post Production, 29th Street Video.

Grady, M. P. (1991). *Grady Profile* [Computer program]. St. Louis, MO: Aurbach.

Herman, J. L. (1992). What research tells us about good assessment. *Educational Leadership 49*(8), 74-78. (EJ 444 324)

Hunter, B., et al. (1993). Technology in the classroom: Preparing students for the information age. *Schools in the Middle 2*(4), 3-6. (EJ 465 259)

McLellan, H. (1993). Evaluation in a situated learning environment. *Educational Technology 33*(3), 39-45. (EJ 461 596)

Meyer, C. A. (1992). What's the difference between "authentic" and "performance" assessment? *Educational Leadership 49*(8), 39-40. (EJ 444 312)

Paulson, L. F., Paulson, P. R., and Meyer, C. (1991). What makes a portfolio a portfolio? *Educational Leadership 48*(5), 60-63. (EJ 421 352)

Saylor, K., and Overton, J. (1993). *Kentucky writing and math portfolios.* Middlesboro, KY: Middlesboro Intermediate School. (ED 361 382)

Stemmer, P., Brown, B., and Smith, C. (1992). The employability skills portfolio. *Educational Leadership 49*(6), 32-35. (EJ 441 170)

Wagner, R. (1993). *HyperStudio* [Computer program]. El Cajon, CA: Roger Wagner Publishing.

Part Four
Leadership Profiles

Introduction

The purpose of this section is to profile individuals who have made significant contributions to the field of educational media and technology. There is no formal survey or popularity contest to determine the persons for whom the profiles are written, but those selected are usually still active in the field. Please direct any comments, questions, and suggestions about the selection process to the Senior Editor.

Leaders profiled in the *Yearbook* have either held prominent offices, written important works, or made significant contributions that have in some way influenced the contemporary vision of the field. They have often been directly responsible for mentoring individuals who have themselves become recognized for their contributions. There are special reasons to feature people of national and international renown, and the editors of this volume of the *Educational Media and Technology Yearbook* believe Donald P. Ely, James Okey, and Constance Dorothea Weinman are worthy of such distinction.

Donald P. Ely
The Consummate Professor

Norman C. Higgins
Professor of Education, Dowling College

Rightly or wrongly, we judge people by the impression they make on their initial encounters with us. My first experience with Dr. Ely came during a graduate student orientation in the Newhouse Communications Center at Syracuse University. Dr. Ely's portrait was projected onto a six-foot screen, and he addressed the 1965 cohort of graduate students from an audiotape. After introducing himself and explaining where he was and why he was unable to welcome us in person, he gave his assessment of the state of the field, which began with the phrase, "These are the best of times and the worst of times in Educational Communications." I was impressed. Here was a man at the height of his professional career as President of the Department of Audio-Visual Instruction (DAVI), who had taken the time to prepare and record a welcoming address for those of us who were just entering the field. He borrowed a literary phrase that captured the essence of a field that is always in the act of becoming, and he removed the barriers of time and place by using technology to inform and inspire his students. Some 30 years later he is as active as ever: analyzing trends in the field, using technology to transcend time and place, and informing and inspiring yet another generation of graduate students entering what is currently known as the field of Educational Technology.

Don Ely joined the faculty of Syracuse University as an instructor in 1956. He moved upward through the academic and administrative ranks at Syracuse to become a Professor of Education, a department chair, a division director, and Director of the ERIC Clearinghouse on Information and Technology. He also traveled from Syracuse as a Fulbright scholar, a visiting professor on five continents, an officer in the Association for Educational Communications and Technology (AECT), and an educational consultant to foreign governments. Throughout his professional career he has been at the forefront of a dynamic field, working hard to maintain a sense of balance among the activities by which university professors are evaluated: teaching, research, and service.

Don Ely's service to the profession is well known both in the United States and abroad. His concerns for the uses of technology to create and disseminate information have transcended the boundaries that separate the library information and media technology professions in the United States. He moves among the leaders of AECT as comfortably as he moves among the leaders of the American Association of School Librarians, the American Library Association, and the American Society for Information Science. He has been called upon by political leaders to testify before committees of the U.S. Congress about educational legislation and to serve on the New York governor's and the White House conferences on library and information services.

Abroad, Don is the profession's Ambassador-at-Large, serving, at last count, on four continents. He has held three Fulbright Fellowships in South America (Chile, Peru, and one for research in the American Republics). In southeast Asia he participated in the planning of the Indonesian Open University. He also assisted in establishing the Center for Communications Technology in the Indonesia Ministry of Education and Culture. Prior to the revolution in Iran he helped with planning and training the staff for Educational Radio and Television of Iran. In Europe he has been actively involved in developing the educational technology curriculum at the University of Twente in the Netherlands. In Africa he served as a visiting professor in the Soweto College of Education. (As might be expected, Don can order dinner in Spanish, Dutch, and more than one Indonesian language.)

In the publish-or-perish world of a university professor, Don has not just survived; he has thrived. He is the coauthor of two leading education textbooks that span media technology and library science: *Teaching and Media: A Systematic Approach* and *Media Personnel in Education: A Competency Approach.* He served as editor of *Educational Media and Technology Yearbook* in 1988 and from 1992 to 1996. He coedited the educational technology entries in the 2d edition of the *International Encyclopedia of Education.* But he is not one to rest on his laurels; his *Classic Readings in Instructional Technology* has recently been published, and the 2d edition of the *International Encyclopedia of Educational Technology* is in press. Don also serves on the editorial boards of leading educational technology journals in the United States and abroad: *Educational Technology Research and Development* (U.S.), *British Journal of Educational Technology* (U.K.), *Educational and Training Technology International* (U.K.), and *Tecnologia Educativa* (Chile).

Don's reputation of service and publications is well founded, but it is as a teacher that he truly excels. Some professors expect their students to do as they say. Some expect their students to do as they do. But for a few professors, like Don Ely, there is little difference between what they say and what they do. These are the professors who practice what they teach. Don has the ability to look at complex situations, analyze strengths and weaknesses, cut to the heart of issues, and craft memorable phrases that summarize his assessments of situations. Whether he is teaching principles of educational media administration or concepts concerning the uses of distance learning, you always know he is speaking as one who has been there and has used the concepts and principles of which he speaks. His teaching is grounded in his own real-world experiences.

Those whom Don has taught are doubly blessed. They have increased their knowledge of a subject, and they have also gained by knowing a kind, caring, and considerate man with high expectations for himself and his students.

One of Don's unheralded accomplishments as teacher and administrator has been his ability to arrange financial support for graduate students at Syracuse University. Over the years he has secured more than a million dollars to support graduate students through government-funded fellowships, institutes, and scholarships. He has created partnerships with other divisions within the university to provide assistantships and tuition waivers for graduate students to attend Syracuse. He has forged ties between Syracuse and foreign universities and governments that have provided opportunities for students from other countries to study educational technology with leaders in the field. Through Don's efforts, many students who would have been unable to obtain a graduate education have been given that opportunity. As a tribute to his teaching, Don's students can be found in instructional positions at major universities throughout the country, in administrative positions in educational agencies around the world, and in leadership positions in international professional organizations.

Such a full and distinguished professional career has consumed many an ordinary man, but Don Ely is no ordinary man. He has always found time to meet his responsibilities and commitments to his community and his family. He serves as a Trustee of the Onondaga County (New York) Public Library and as an Elder in the Pebble Hill Presbyterian Church. Whether at home in Dewitt, New York, or on assignment elsewhere, Don, his wife Martha, and his sons have trekked together, taking advantage of every opportunity to meet people, experience different communities, and strengthen the ties that bind them as a family. Since disengaging from full-time teaching at Syracuse (*retirement* is not in his vocabulary), Don has more time to enjoy traveling and hiking in the Adirondack Mountains with Martha.

James Okey

Kent L. Gustafson
*Department of Instructional Technology
University of Georgia*

Dr. James Okey is one of the most fascinating individuals with whom one could ever have the privilege to work. To say he is inquisitive and multifaceted is an understatement. After all, how many people do you know who have personally constructed a beautiful log home (including all the cabinetry), taught themselves complex computer languages, led many successful instructional development teams, administered an academic department, and won a major teaching award? Jim Okey has done all of these things and more, including his most recent adventure: study in a culinary school in New York City. This newest chapter in his life follows his retirement from the University of Georgia, where he spent 20 years on the faculty and influenced many students, colleagues, and administrators.

Jim began life on a small farm in Wisconsin and, as a result, has always appreciated both the value of work and the importance and beauty of nature. His philosophy and work ethic dictate that every day should include productive activities and, especially, some new learning. For example, I remember his taking classes in Italian a couple of years before he retired. When I asked him why Italian, his reply was, in essence, "Well, I don't know much about it and decided to find out." This insatiable curiosity led him to study everything from beekeeping to Pascal to instructional design research.

After graduating from the University of Wisconsin in 1961 with a B.S. degree, Jim took his first teaching position as a science teacher in Wisconsin. But even before that he was already paying close attention to his students, a trait he would carry with him through his academic career. I still vividly recall the day a couple of years ago when we were in a meeting with a group of research meteorologists and, at the first break, he said to one of them, "I know you from some place." The researcher said he had no such recollection. However, after a little "Did you ever . . ." and "Do you know so-and-so," Jim said, "I had you as a student!" And, as it turned out, the researcher had been a high school student in the school where Jim had done his student teaching. On the basis of that limited contact, Jim still remembered him after more than 30 years. Needless to say, I was amazed (and somewhat chagrined), especially as I can't always remember students from a previous quarter.

Jim returned to school and obtained an M.Ed. from Texas A&M in 1965 and a Ph.D. from Florida State University in 1968. Although his major at Florida State was in science education, Jim's insatiable curiosity and interest in instructional technology resulted in his taking all the major courses in instructional systems design as well. Following graduation, Jim went to Berkeley to do postdoctoral study with Robert Gagné because of his keen interest in hierarchical knowledge structures and how they might relate to Gagné's hierarchies of learning. Jim's higher education positions included a one-year stay at the University of California, Santa Barbara, and five years at Indiana University, where he achieved the rank of associate professor. Coming to the University of Georgia in 1975, Jim spent 11 years in science education, and in 1986 joined the then recently created Department of Instructional Technology, where he worked until his retirement in 1995.

Perhaps Jim's most defining professional characteristic is his extraordinary foresight. He has an almost uncanny ability to see new directions and trends before anyone around him. As a science educator, he was exploring topics like mastery learning long before they became popular subjects for research and experimentation. He was also the first faculty member in the College of Education to obtain microcomputers so as to explore their application to instruction. The Commodore Pets he acquired were little more than objects of curiosity to his colleagues, but to him (and later to others) they represented the wave of the future. In recent years he recognized that distance education would become of much greater prominence and began to develop his knowledge and skill in this area—again, long before most of his colleagues.

Another of Jim's notable academic strengths is combining rigorous analysis with action and evaluation. His belief that the only good analysis was one that was followed by action led him to experiment with various forms of emerging technology throughout his career. Although a superb scholar with many publications and presentations to his credit, Jim has always been interested in exploring the practical benefits of technology in the classroom. Translating research results into real instruction focused on real learners, and carefully evaluating the consequences, is one of his major passions. No theoretical ideologue, Jim nonetheless clearly belongs to the instructivist tradition that says objectives can be specified, and the teacher's task is to create a rich array of learning environments that assure that students achieve those objectives. As a strong proponent of the systematic design process, he applied it every day to his teaching, not by lecturing but by searching for and trying a variety of teaching and learning strategies and adapting them to his classroom and laboratory courses.

In recognition of his teaching excellence, Jim received the Superior Teaching Award from the University of Georgia in 1989. This is one of the university's most prestigious awards and is given to only four or five faculty each year. Subsequently he was asked to serve as a Senior Fellow for one year in the Office of Instructional Development at the university. In this role he served as a resource and teaching mentor to selected young faculty who showed particular promise in the classroom. Although not given to pride, Jim felt greatly honored for having been selected for the teaching award, and—perhaps even more importantly—for being selected to work with these outstanding young faculty from across the university.

Jim was also an exceptional mentor and advisor to graduate students. He was eagerly sought as an advisor by both master's and doctoral students, not because he was "easy" but because of his concern that they get the best possible educational experience. A review of his extensive publications and presentations reveals that he made a practice of including students in his work and sharing the experience of writing and presenting with them. This caring and involving attitude is now being continued by his many advisees, who themselves are college faculty around the country and, indeed, around the world.

I have had several opportunities to observe Jim in the classroom, including once recently for an entire quarter. This opportunity arose because the university had made a significant investment in two-way audio/video interactive technology that opens new opportunities for distance education courses across the state of Georgia. Jim immediately volunteered to teach a course using this system even though he had no previous experience with such technology. Because I too planned to use the system in a subsequent quarter, Jim invited me to sit in on his course, an invitation I quickly accepted. Despite his lack of familiarity with this complex technology, Jim informed the class he would be experimenting with a variety of instructional strategies and encouraged their feedback. His rapport with the students at each site was wonderful, and both he and I learned a great deal about the promises and pitfalls of this delivery system.

Another example of his teaching excellence was revealed a number of years ago when, at the end of a master's oral exam, a student was asked what was the best course in her program. The student, who had majored in the school library media program, chose her required research course with Dr. Okey. She indicated that he had made the course extremely interesting and relevant and that she was excited about doing more research after graduation. Having taught this course myself, this came as somewhat of a surprise, as it seemed unlikely that one of my students would have made such a comment. I reported her comments to Dr. Okey (he was not present at the oral) and inquired as to what he was doing to create such positive attitudes along with the skills needed to do research. He then described a variety of strategies that I have since incorporated into the course with similar (but, alas, not as great) results. It is interesting to note that this student's comments were not a one-time phenomenon; similar comments were heard from other students in subsequent quarters.

Although always curious about the potential of new technological devices, Jim is no techno-junkie interested in the technology purely for its own sake. His abiding interest has always been in identifying its useful applications. For example, Jim was an active promoter of the idea of acquiring microcomputers back when they first made their appearance in education. The University of Georgia purchased a special model of the Apple II (often referred to as the "Black Apple" due to the color of the case) to equip a laboratory partially at the behest of Dr. Okey. While others immediately began to teach BASIC, which was all the rage at the time, Jim was far more interested in instructional software and its classroom use. Idolizing the computer was another fad he avoided.

Another notable contribution of Jim Okey to the university was his ready willingness to assist others in a variety of ways. Whether it was serving on a committee, offering a faculty development seminar at the campus-wide series, or working with administrators in solving some knotty problem, Jim could always be counted on as a thoughtful and insightful partici- pant. No shrinking violet, he would offer his analysis of the situation and suggest ideas for a course of action. However, he had no need to dominate the discourse or have his suggestions acted upon. In the spirit of collaborative analysis and decision-making, he freely entered into the discussion and would support the results. He also had the ability to see the big picture on an issue and not get sidetracked by personal or departmental interests. It was these attributes that resulted in his being selected by the president of the University of Georgia to serve for several years on a small advisory committee that met regularly with him. Jim always repre- sented the needs of students first, faculty second, and the bureaucracy third (or last if there were other affected constituencies besides students and faculty).

Dr. Okey served as Chair of the Department of Instructional Technology at Georgia for two years, but—typical of his intense interest in teaching and inquiry—he stepped down the year before his retirement because "I don't want to spend my last year that way." Not that he disparaged administration. In fact, he admired those who could manage well. It was just that he had his own sense of what he wanted to be as a professor, and being "in charge" was not one of them. His leadership in the profession has always been derived much more from his intellect, energy, and enthusiasm than from status or formal power.

Jim has been active in service to, and made presentations at, the conferences of several professional organizations, including the Association for Educational Communications and Technology, the National Association of Science Teachers, the American Educational Re- search Association, and the National Association for Research in Science Teaching. He was elected president of this last group early in his career but much preferred to deal with the substance and contents of the various professional groups rather than with their political sides.

As of this writing (spring of 1996), Jim is enrolled full-time in a culinary school in New York City. Typical of his boundless energy and enthusiasm, his year-long program includes working in restaurants in the city and a possible internship in a four-star restaurant in Paris. Where he is likely to go from there is anybody's guess, but one can be sure it will not be into sedentary retirement. Perhaps he will combine his teaching skills, his longtime interest in instructional design and technology, and his new culinary skills to create some form of cooking education activity. Whether he will become the next Julia Child, develop a distance education cooking school, or put out a cooking CD-ROM, I am not sure. But I am quite certain we have not seen the last of him in the instructional technology profession.

Constance Dorothea Weinman (1907-1985)
Pioneer - Educator - Philanthropist

Deborah Tyksinski*
SUNY Institute of Technology

We picture American pioneers as flamboyant characters, rugged and larger than life. In truth, most are ordinary citizens distinguished by clear personal vision and unwavering determination. Constance Weinman was such a person. She believed that the key to improved learning was through the informed use of media. She shaped the world we live in through her innovative thoughts and actions, day by day, lesson by lesson. This is the story of a quiet pioneer.

Constance Dorothea Weinman was born on July 27, 1907, in Portland, Oregon, where she lived until moving with her parents to the family homestead in Lake Labish, a rural area outside Salem, Oregon. Though she later moved away to attend high school and college, her early career found her back in Salem. She lived there in her family home and cared for her disabled mother for many years while devoting herself to the study and development of instructional technology. Dr. Weinman passed away in Salem on March 12, 1985, at the age of 77.

A lifelong scholar, Weinman completed her B.A. in mathematics in 1929 and M.A. in education in 1932, both from the University of Oregon. Later, while employed by the Salem Public School System, she pursued advanced graduate studies during the summers. In 1963, she enrolled in the doctoral program at New York University, where she continued to study part-time for 10 years before completing her Ed.D. in 1973 at the age of 65.

Constance Weinman endeavored to improve instruction through the informed use of media. She began her career as a mathematics and science teacher. In 1935, while employed at Parrish Junior High School in Salem, she also served as the Audio/Visual Coordinator in charge of the distribution of AV resources and "running the noon movies." At that time, the audiovisual collection consisted of several film and slide projectors located in a cupboard in her classroom. During the next several years her attention shifted from the content to the methods of instruction. In 1947, through the University of Oregon, she became certified as a specialist in audiovisual instruction. Five years later she became the first full-time audiovisual aids consultant for the Salem School System, and held that position for more than 20 years.

During the 1950s and 1960s, Weinman became an innovator in the fledgling field of instructional technology. She believed that visual learning was central to proper education and developed a system to produce visually based instructional materials when commercial products were not yet commonly available. She recognized that children needed more than

*The author gratefully acknowledges the contributions of the Marion County Historical Society; the University of Oregon; New York University; Bruce Williams; James Perry; and Dr. Weinman's family, friends, and coworkers who shared memories of their experiences.

books and lectures to learn about the world—that learning was enhanced through the use of visuals to support lessons. What began with a few slide projectors in a closet in her classroom eventually grew into a sophisticated media system around which, in 1974, an experimental school was designed.

Constance Weinman was an accomplished agent of change, carefully clearing the way for early institutional adoption of emerging instructional media. The Salem Public School System routinely used overhead projectors for classroom instruction in 1961 when, according to a survey commissioned by the U.S. Department of Education, school systems using overhead projectors at that time were considered early adopters (BSSR 1965). When commercially available overhead transparencies were scarce, the Salem media department filled the void by researching topics and creating attractive materials custom-designed for the teacher.

In 1964, Weinman's media department featured an impressive 15 employees, a state-of-the-art cataloging system, and a complete darkroom. Graphic artists designed visuals and produced instructional materials using a large type machine and hand lettering. Color transparencies were produced by applying individual colors one at a time. Weinman personally researched and selected the equipment and instructional materials used by the Salem School System.

In 1974 Salem opened an experimental elementary school designed to integrate instructional media into the classroom. The school system design, strongly influenced by Weinman, was literally built around the media department, with open classrooms located within easy access of the instructional media center. Each classroom was equipped with an overhead projector and other media as requested by the teacher. Media staff were located in the elementary school rather than in their customary quarters in the district administration building. The proximity was designed to encourage teachers to collaborate with the media staff to develop materials for use in their lessons. Though the alternative school experienced a number of organizational difficulties, the convenient access to media was considered a success.

Throughout her career, Constance Weinman was active in the development of a new profession dedicated to the study and uses of instructional media. She worked with the National Education Association (NEA) to help foster the creation of the Department of Audio-Visual Instruction (DAVI), the ancestor of the Association for Educational Communications and Technology (AECT). She twice served as the president of the Oregon Audio-Visual Association. She was a chair of the Salem Programs for the Department of Audio-Visual Instruction and a life member of the NEA. Weinman was also involved with national and international organizations: Pi Lambda Theta, Pi Mu Epsilon, Kappa Delta Pi, Delta Kappa Gamma, International Toastmistress Clubs (president and council chairperson), Business and Professional Woman's Club (vice president) and the American Association of University Women.

Family and coworkers remember Connie as a serious, often intense woman. She was as devoted to learning as she was to helping others to learn. She believed the best way to improve one's position in life was through higher education, "the higher, the better." She stated that learning should be a continuous process, with formal degrees representing important plateaus but not the ultimate experience. Though her former employees remember her as a tough taskmistress, they also recall her philosophy that parents' first priority was to care for their children. They appreciated her allowing them to leave work to attend a school play or to meet with a teacher. She also was generous, lending financial or personal assistance to struggling adults trying to balance work, school, and family demands.

Constance Weinman was considered a woman ahead of her time. She was an independent thinker: innovative and fiercely committed to her ideas. Some colleagues, particularly male administrators in the Salem School System, found her freethinking approach to life unbecoming of a woman and perhaps threatening. Others found her difficult to negotiate with once she made up her mind. But many appreciated her innovative ideas and determined spirit. She was considered a deep thinker and activist for continuous improvement, particularly regarding the field of education.

Dr. Weinman loved local and family history. Her family, the Leedy clan, is said to have established their onion farm in Lake Labish during the homestead period in the Pacific Northwest. Colleagues recall her passion for uncovering new bits of information about her family's settlement. Her master's thesis was based on a history of the Salem Public School System from 1893 to 1916. She believed that documenting the past would enable future generations to learn from their predecessors. Her doctoral dissertation, *A Unit of Correlated Audio/Visual Instructional Materials for Use in Teaching Local History in Grades 4 & 8 in Salem Oregon Public Schools,* reflected her passion for both history and instructional technology.

Constance Weinman established a scholarship for graduate students in the field of instructional media to support the continuation of her vision for improved classroom instruction and to aid struggling graduate students by easing their financial burden. The Constance Dorothea Weinman Scholarship was established in 1986 and continued until 1994, when her estate was distributed to the Marion County Historical Society and the University of Oregon. Her generous legacy assisted over 250 award recipients during the life of the scholarship.

The annual scholarship competition was administered cooperatively by the U.S. National Bank of Oregon and the School of Education at the University of Oregon. Seventy-five percent of recipients were doctoral students, and 25 percent master's students. Annual awards were offered for up to $5,000 to individuals "who demonstrated genuine interest, aptitude, excellence in scholarship and the potential for leadership in research, teaching and practice within the professional field of instructional systems technology." Though the competition favored students from Oregon, awards were made to students attending institutions throughout the United States.

Former awardees report that the scholarship offered critical assistance when it was most desperately needed. Awards funded "a first good computer," travel for an extensive literature search, development of instructional materials, and attendance at national conferences. Several recipients reported that the financial assistance helped foster their first big break into their chosen profession. In other cases, the support helped balance the financial demands of higher education with those of the family.

The impact of Dr. Weinman's scholarship lives on though the scholarship program has ended. Recipients engage in activities where they, too, may effect change in the field of education. Awardees are found directing a learning center for a college, fostering community involvement in school reform, designing museum exhibits, training educators in the use of instructional technology, and developing systems for collaboration through computer-assisted visualization. Several recipients are conducting research, developing technology, or evaluating the effects of various technologies on learning. Through the recipients of her scholarship, Dr. Weinman continues to support innovation in the field of education.

Was Constance Weinman a woman ahead of her time? Perhaps. She clearly recognized the impact of visual communication on learning. Her creative instructional materials of the 1960s bring to mind contemporary innovations using personal computers, multimedia, and the World Wide Web. Her early use of instructional media, her advocacy for the national development of instructional technology, and the creation of her scholarship fund certainly advanced the state of the profession. Guided by her vision for improved instructional methods, Dr. Weinman devoted herself day by day, lesson by lesson, to the improvement of education in the classroom. She was a modest, hardworking woman, seldom drawing attention to herself. She was a quiet pioneer.

REFERENCE

Bureau of Social Service Research. (1995). *Audiovisual media in the public school, 1961-1964: A profile of change.* Washington, DC: Author.

Part Five
The Year in Review

Introduction

There are many professional associations in the field of educational media and technology. We have furnished reports on the current status of seven associations in each edition for several years, and regretfully announced the demise of one of them in the 1995-1996 edition—the Association for the Development of Computer-based Instructional Systems (ADCIS) together with its major journal, *The Journal of Computer-Based Instruction (JCBI).* In this edition we note that one of the six remaining associations has changed its name from National Society for Performance and Instruction (NSPI) to International Society for Performance Improvement (ISPI).

These six associations are still considered to be the major organizations in this field in North America. Their inclusion is based on longevity, number of members, professional journals published, and visibility. A number of additional professional associations are listed in Part 6, Organizations and Associations in North America.

The current status of the six featured groups is reported here with the most recent conference dates available at the time of publication, their new publications, and, in most cases, current officers. All of these associations have received recognition for their contributions to the advancement of educational media and technology.

AECT
Association for Educational Communications and Technology

Established in 1923, the Association for Educational Communications and Technology is an international professional association dedicated to the improvement of instruction through the utilization of media and technology. The mission of the association is to provide leadership in educational communications and technology by linking professionals holding a common interest in the use of education technology and its application to the learning process. In the past few years, convention topics have focused on hypermedia, teleconferencing, and converging technologies, and AECT cosponsored the teleconference, "Teaching and Technology: A Critical Link," which addressed issues on the restructuring of public schools and the role of technology. AECT also honors outstanding individuals or groups making significant contributions to the field of educational communications and technology or to the association. (See the separate listing for full information on these awards.)

MEMBERSHIP

AECT members include instructional technologists; media or library specialists; university professors and researchers; industrial/business training specialists; religious educators; government media personnel; school, school district, and state department of education media program administrators and specialists; educational/training media producers; and numerous others whose professional work requires improvement of media and technology in education and training. AECT members also work in the armed forces, in public libraries, in museums, and in other information agencies of many different kinds, including those related to the emerging fields of computer technology.

MEMBERSHIP SERVICES

AECT serves as a central clearinghouse and communications center for its members. The association maintains TechCentral, a national electronic mail network and bulletin board service. Through its various committees and task forces, it compiles data and prepares recommendations to form the basis of guidelines, standards, research, and information summaries on numerous topics and problems of interest to the membership. AECT professional staff members report on government activities of concern to the membership and provide current data on laws and pending legislation relating to the educational media/technology field. AECT also maintains the ECT Foundation, through which it offers a limited number of financial grants to further the association's work. Archives are maintained at the University of Maryland.

CONFERENCES

The 1996 Annual Convention and International Computing and Instructional Technology Exposition (InCITE) was held February 14-18 in Indianapolis, IN. The theme was "Exploring the Information Kaleidoscope." The 1997 Convention and InCITE will be held February 13-15 in Albuquerque, NM.

PUBLICATIONS

AECT maintains an active publication program which includes *TechTrends for Leaders in Education and Training* (6/yr., free with membership); *Educational Technology Research & Development* (4/yr.); various division publications; and a number of books and videotapes, including the following recent titles: *School Change: Students Make It Happen* (1996); *A School Changes* (1995); *Educational Technology: A Review of the Research, 2d ed.* (1996); *Degree Curricula in Educational Communications and Technology, 5th ed.* (1995); *Instructional Technology: The Definition and Domains of the Field* (1994).

AFFILIATED ORGANIZATIONS

Because of similarity of interests, a number of organizations have chosen to affiliate with AECT. These include the Association for Media and Technology in Education in Canada (AMTEC); Community College Association for Instruction and Technology (CCAIT); Consortium of University Film Centers (CUFC); Federal Educational Technology Association (FETA); Health Science Communications Association (HeSCA); International Association for Learning Laboratories (IALL); International Visual Literacy Association (IVLA); Minorities in Media (MIMS); National Association of Regional Media Centers (NARMC); National Instructional Television Fixed Services (NITFS); New England Educational Media Association (NEEMA); and Southern Regional Media Leadership Council (SRMLC).

Two additional organizations are also related to the Association for Educational Communications and Technology: the AECT Archives and the AECT ECT Foundation.

AECT DIVISIONS

AECT has 11 divisions: Division for Systemic Change in Education (CHANGE); Division of Educational Media Management (DEMM); Division of Instructional Development (DID); Division of Interactive Systems and Computers (DISC); Division of Learning and Performance Environments (DLPE); Division of School Media Specialists (DSMS); Division of Telecommunications (DOT); Industrial Training and Education Division (ITED); International Division (INTL); Media Design and Production Division (MDPD); and Research and Theory Division (RTD).

CURRENT OFFICERS/MEMBERS OF THE AECT BOARD OF DIRECTORS

Stanley D. Zenor, Executive Director; Lynn Milet, Past President; William J. Burns, President; Franz J. Frederick, President-Elect; Connie Bakker, Secretary-Treasurer; and Ed Caffarella, Victoria DeFields, Marcy P. Driscoll, Mary James, Robin Taylor-Roth, David Tiedemann, Joan Wallin, and Charles R. White, Board Members.

Further information is available from AECT, 1025 Vermont Avenue NW, Suite 820, Washington, DC 20005. (202) 347-7834. Fax (202) 347-7839.

AMTEC
Association for Media and Technology in Education in Canada
L'Association des Media et de la Technologie en Education au Canada

PURPOSE

Canada's national association for educational media and technology professionals, AMTEC is a forum concerned with the impact of media and technology on teaching, learning, and society. As an organization, AMTEC provides national leadership through annual conferences, publications, workshops, media festival awards, ongoing reaction to media and technology issues at the international, national, provincial, and local levels, and linkages with other organizations with similar interests.

MEMBERSHIP

AMTEC's membership is geographically dispersed and professionally diversified. Membership stretches from St. John's, Newfoundland, to Victoria, British Columbia, and from Inuvik, Northwest Territories, to Niagara Falls, Ontario. Members include teachers, consultants, broadcasters, media managers, photographers, librarians/information specialists, educational technology specialists, instructional designers/trainers, technology specialists, artists, and producers/distributors. They represent all sectors of the educational media and technology fields: elementary and secondary schools, colleges, institutes of technology, universities, provincial governments, school boards, military services, health services libraries, and private corporations.

ACTIVITIES

Workshops. AMTEC offers workshops in cooperation with other agencies and associations based on AMTEC members' needs, in addition to the in-depth workshops at the AMTEC annual conference.

Annual Conference. The AMTEC annual conference provides opportunities to meet delegates from across the nation and to attend sessions on the latest issues and developments in such areas as copyright law, instructional design, distance education, library standards, media production, broadcasting and educational technology, media utilization, and visual literacy. The 1996 annual conference was held in Vancouver, BC, in June; and AMTEC 97 will be held in Saskatoon, SK.

Awards. AMTEC annually recognizes outstanding individual achievement and leadership in the field through the EMPDAC (Educational Media Producers and Distributors Association of Canada) Achievement Award, the AMTEC Leadership Award, and the Telesat Educational Telecommunications Award.

Annual Media Festival. AMTEC conducts a national showcase for educational media and technology productions. Awards are presented annually at the AMTEC conference in recognition of outstanding achievement in areas such as television, radio, film, slide, and computer software.

Reaction to Issues. AMTEC provides opportunities for members to contribute to educational media and technology issues and their solutions. The association frequently communicates with other associations and levels of government to resolve issues of concern to the membership.

PUBLICATIONS

- *The Canadian Journal of Educational Communication (CJEC)*, a quarterly covering the latest in research, application, and periodical literature. It also publishes reviews on significant books and films and critiques on computer programs.

- *Media News*, a quarterly newsletter that covers the news in the field, including helpful tips, future conferences, comments on current projects, and information about AMTEC members and the AMTEC Board.

- *Membership Directory*, which expands the professional network of members.

In addition, occasional publications are produced to assist members in keeping abreast in the field. These include directories, guidelines, and monographs. AMTEC also operates a mailserv on the Internet.

CURRENT OFFICERS

The AMTEC Board of Directors includes the association's President, Gary Karlsen; Past President, Allen LeBlanc; President-Elect, Rick Schwier; Secretary/Treasurer, Mary Anne Epp; and Director, Danielle Fortosky. Additional information may be obtained from AMTEC, 3-1750 The Queensway, Suite 1318, Etobicoke, ON, Canada M9C 5H5; Attn. Ms. Mary Anne Epp, Secretary/Treasurer.

ISPI

International Society for Performance Improvement
(formerly the National Society for Performance and Instruction-NSPI)

ISPI is an international association dedicated to increasing productivity in the workplace through the application of performance and instructional technologies. Founded in 1962, the society promotes the improvement of human performance among governmental, legislative, business, corporate, and educational leaders, and through the national media.

MEMBERSHIP

The 5,500 members of ISPI are located throughout the United States, Canada, and 33 other countries. Members include performance technologists, training directors, human resource managers, instructional technologists, change agents, human factors practitioners, and organizational development consultants. They work in a variety of settings, including business, industry, universities, governmental agencies, health services, banks, and the armed forces.

SERVICES TO ISPI MEMBERS

ISPI offers its members opportunities to grow professionally and personally, to meet and know leaders in the field and learn about new things before they are published for the world at large, to make themselves known in the field, and to pick up new ideas on how to deal with their own political and technical challenges on the job. Membership benefits include subscriptions to *Performance & Instruction* and *News & Notes*; the *Annual Membership Directory*; participation in the annual conference and exposition; access to a variety of resources and individuals to help improve professional skills and marketability; a variety of insurance programs at group rates; leadership opportunities through participation in special projects, 12 major committees, and task forces, or serving as national or chapter officers; an executive referral service; and discounts on publications, advertising, conference registration and recordings, and other society services.

CONFERENCES

Annual Conference and Expo: 1997, April 14-18, Anaheim, CA; 1998, March 23-28, Chicago, IL.

PUBLICATIONS

ISPI publications include *Performance & Instruction Journal* (10/yr.); *Performance Improvement Quarterly*; *News & Notes* (10/yr.); and the *Annual Membership Directory*.

CURRENT OFFICERS

Carol Valen, President; Ruth Colvin Clark, President-Elect; Lori Gillespie, Treasurer; Rob Foshay, Ed Blankenhagen, and Mark M. Greene, Directors; and Richard D. Battaglia, Executive Director.

Annual dues: active member, $125; student, $40. Further information is available from ISPI, 1300 L Street NW, Suite 1250, Washington, DC 20005. (202) 408-7969. Fax (202) 408-7972.

ISTE
International Society for Technology in Education

PURPOSE

The International Society for Technology in Education is a nonprofit professional society of educators. Its goals include the improvement of education through the appropriate use of computer-related technology and the fostering of active partnerships between businesses and educators involved in this field. The majority of ISTE's efforts are aimed at precollege education and teacher preparation.

MEMBERSHIP

ISTE members are teachers, administrators, computer coordinators, curriculum coordinators, teacher educators, information resource managers, and educational technological specialists. Approximately 85 percent of the 10,000-person membership is in the United States, 10 percent is in Canada, and the remainder is scattered throughout nearly 100 other countries.

ACTIVITIES

ISTE works to achieve its mission through its publication program, which includes 12 periodicals as well as a wide range of books and courseware, cosponsorship or sponsorship of a variety of conferences and workshops, and its extensive network of regional affiliates, a Private Sector Council, a distance education program, and membership in NCATE (National Council for the Accreditation of Teacher Education).

PUBLICATIONS

Periodical publications include membership periodicals: *Learning and Leading with Technology: The ISTE Journal of Educational Technology Practice and Policy* (formerly *The Computing Teacher* (8/yr.); the *Journal of Research on Computing in Education* (quarterly); and *ISTE Update: People, Events, and News in Education Technology* (newsletter, 8/yr.). Quarterly periodicals for special-interest groups include: *Logo Exchange*, for the SIG Logo; the *Journal of Computing in Teacher Education*, for the Teacher Educators SIG; *HyperNEXUS*, for the Hyper/Multi-Media SIG; the *Journal of Computer Science Education*, for the Computer Science SIG; *T.I.E. News*, for the Telecommunications SIG; and *SIGTC Connections*, for the Technology Coordinator SIG. Other periodicals include *Microsoft Works in Education*, a quarterly for users of Microsoft Works; and *CAELL Journal* (Computer Assisted English Language Learning Journal), quarterly for teachers of English, foreign languages, and adult literacy.

ISTE also publishes a variety of books and courseware.

CONFERENCES

ISTE is the administrative house for the National Educational Computing Conference (NECC). NECC '96 was held in Minneapolis, MN, June 9-13; NECC '97 will be held in Seattle, WA, June 30-July 2.

CURRENT OFFICERS

The current ISTE Board includes David Brittain, President; Lynne Schrum, President-Elect; Terrie Gray, Secretary; Terry Killion, Treasurer; Dennis Bybee, Associate Executive Officer; David Moursund, Executive Officer; Kathy Edwards; Cheryl Lemke; Chip Kimball; Paul O'Driscoll; Carla Schutte; Gwen Solomon; Neal Strudler; Harriet Taylor; Michael Turzanski; and Peter Wholihan.

For further information, contact Maia Howes, ISTE Executive Secretary, at 1787 Agate Street, Eugene, OR 97403-1923. (503) 346-2414. Fax (503) 346-5890. Internet iste@oregon.

IVLA
International Visual Literacy Association

PURPOSE

IVLA, Inc., a nonprofit international association, was established in 1968 to provide a multidisciplinary forum for the exploration, presentation, and discussion of all aspects of visual communication and their applications through visual images, visual literacy, and literacies in general. The association serves as the organizational bond for professionals from many diverse disciplines who are creating and sustaining the study of the nature of visual experiences and literacies and their cognitive and affective bases, and who are developing new means for the evaluation of learning through visual methods.

MEMBERSHIP

IVLA members represent a diverse group of disciplines, including fine and graphic artists, photographers, researchers, scientists, filmmakers, television producers, graphic and computer-graphic designers, phototherapists, business communication professionals, school administrators, classroom teachers, visual studies theorists and practitioners, educational technologists, photojournalists, print and electronic journalists, and visual anthropologists.

MEMBER SERVICES

Members of IVLA benefit from opportunities to interact with other professionals whose ideas may be challenging or reinforcing. Such opportunities are provided by the annual conference, information exchanges, research programs, workshops, seminars, presentation opportunities as an affiliate of the Association for Educational Communications and Technology (AECT), and access to the Visual Literacy Collection located at Arizona State University.

PUBLICATIONS

IVLA publishes two periodicals: the *Journal of Visual Literacy* (2/yr.) and the *Review*, a visual literacy newsletter. It also publishes an annual book of selected conference readings.

CONFERENCES

The 1996 conference was held in Cheyenne, WY, October 2-6, with the theme, "Vision Quest: Journey Toward Visual Literacy."

CURRENT OFFICERS

Nancy Knupfer, President; Richard Couch, President-Elect; Landra Rezabek, Immediate Past President; Barbara I. Clark, Executive Treasurer; and Beth Wiegmann, Recording Secretary.

Further information may be obtained from Barbara I. Clark, Treasurer, Gonzaga University, E 502 Boone, AD25, Spokane, WA 99258-0001. (509) 328-4220 X3478; e-mail bclark@soe.gonzaga.edu.

SALT
Society for Applied Learning Technology

PURPOSE

The Society for Applied Learning Technology (SALT) is a nonprofit professional membership organization that was founded in 1972. Membership in the society is oriented to professionals whose work requires knowledge and communication in the field of instructional technology. The society provides members a means to enhance their knowledge and job performance by participation in society-sponsored meetings, through subscriptions to society-sponsored publications, by association with other professionals at conferences sponsored by the society, and through membership in special-interest groups and special society-sponsored initiatives and projects.

The society sponsors conferences that are educational in nature and cover a wide range of application areas, such as interactive videodisc in education and training, development of interactive instructional materials, CD-ROM applications in education and training, interactive instruction delivery, and learning technology in the health care sciences. These conferences provide attendees with an opportunity to become familiar with the latest technical information on application possibilities, on technologies, and on methodologies for implementation. In addition, they provide an opportunity for interaction with other professional and managerial individuals in the field.

The society also offers members discounts on society-sponsored journals, conference registration fees, and publications.

PUBLICATIONS

- *Journal of Interactive Instruction Development*. This established quarterly journal meets the needs of instructional systems developers and designers by providing important perspectives on emerging technologies and design technologies.

- *Journal of Medical Education Technologies*. This exciting quarterly journal helps keep readers abreast of developments utilizing technology-based learning systems to train health care professionals and educate students involved in the various health care disciplines.

- *Journal of Educational Technology Systems*. This quarterly publication deals with systems in which technology and education interface, and is designed to inform educators who are interested in making optimum use of technology.

- *Journal of Instruction Delivery Systems.* Published quarterly, this journal covers interactive multimedia applications. It is devoted to enhancing productivity through appropriate applications of technology in education, training, and job performance.

CONFERENCES

Conferences in 1996 were held in Kissimmee, FL, February 21-23, "Orlando Multimedia '96," and Arlington, VA, August 21-23, "Interactive Multimedia '96." Conferences in 1997 will be held in Kissimmee, FL, February 19-21, "Orlando Multimedia '97," and Arlington, VA, August 20-22, "Interactive Multimedia '97."

CURRENT OFFICERS

Dr. Nathaniel Macon, Chairman; Raymond G. Fox, President; Dr. Stanley Winkler, Vice President; and Dr. Carl R. Vest, Secretary/Treasurer.

Further information is available from the Society for Applied Learning Technology, 50 Culpeper Street, Warrenton, VA 22186. (540) 347-0055. Fax (540) 349-3169. E-mail info@salt.org.

Part Six
Organizations and Associations in North America

Introduction

This part of *EMTY* includes annotated entries for several hundred associations and organizations headquartered in North America whose interests are in some manner significant to the fields of instructional technology/educational media, library and information science, communication, computer technology, training/management in business/industry, publishing, and others. They are organized into two general geographic areas: the United States and Canada. The section on the United States includes a classified list with headings designed to be useful in finding subject leads to the alphabetical list. Readers who know only the acronym for an association or organization of interest may refer to the index to obtain its full name.

It was not deemed necessary to include a classified list for Canada because the overall number of organizations listed is considerably smaller than for the United States.

All organizations listed in part 6 were sent a copy of the entry describing the organization that appeared in *EMTY 1995-1996*. Respondents were invited to update and edit these entries, with the proviso that, if no response was received, the entry would be omitted from *EMTY 1997*. However, information on organizations from which a response was received for the 1995-1996 edition are included in this list with an asterisk (*) to indicate that the information is a year old. Organizations for which no response has been received since before 1995 have been omitted. Any organization that has had a name change since the 1995-1996 edition is listed under the new name; a note referring the user to the new name appears under the former name. If information was received that an organization had ceased operations, a note to this effect appears under the organization name in the alphabetical listing.

The reader is reminded that changes in communications and media are frequent and extensive and that the information in this directory is as accurate as possible at the time of publication.

United States

CLASSIFIED LIST

Adult, Continuing, Distance Education
(ALA) Reference and Adult Services Division (RASD)
(ALA Round Table) Continuing Library Education Network and Exchange (CLENE)
Association for Continuing Higher Education (ACHE)
Association for Educational Communications and Technology (AECT)
ERIC Clearinghouse on Adult, Career, and Vocational Education (CE)
National Education Telecommunications Organization & Education Satellite Company (NETO/EDSAT)
National University Continuing Education Association (NUCEA)
Network for Continuing Medical Education (NCME)
Superintendent of Documents

Audio (Records, Audiocassettes and Tapes, Telephone, Radio); Listening
Clearinghouse on Development Communication
Federal Communications Commission (FCC)

Audiovisual (General)
Association for Educational Communications and Technology (AECT)
(AECT) Division of Educational Media Management (DEMM)
(AECT) Division of School Media Specialists (DSMS)
Association of AudioVisual Technicians (AAVT)
HOPE Reports
National Audiovisual Center

Children-, Youth-Related Organizations
(ALA) Association for Library Service to Children (ALSC)
(ALA) Young Adult Library Services Association (YALSA)
Association for Childhood Education International (ACEI)
Children's Television International, Inc.
Close Up Foundation
Council for Exceptional Children (CEC)
(CEC) Technology and Media Division (TAM)
ERIC Clearinghouse on Elementary and Early Childhood Education (PS)
ERIC Clearinghouse on Disabilities and Gifted Education (EC)
National Association for the Education of Young Children (NAEYC)
National PTA

Communication
Clearinghouse on Development Communication
ERIC Clearinghouse on Information & Technology (IR)
ERIC Clearinghouse on Languages and Linguistics (FL)
ERIC Clearinghouse on Reading, English, and Communication (CS)
International Association of Business Communicators (IABC)
National Council of the Churches of Christ Communication Unit
Speech Communication Association (SCA)

Computers, Computer Software, Computer Hardware
(AECT) Division of Interactive Systems and Computers (DISC)
Association for the Advancement of Computing in Education (AACE)
International Society for Technology in Education (ISTE) (formerly International Council for Computers in Education)
OCLC (Online Computer Library Center)
Society for Computer Simulation (SCS)
SpecialNet

Copyright
International Copyright Information Center (INCINC)

Databases; Networks
ERIC (Educational Resources Information Center) (See separate entries for the various clearinghouses.)
ERIC Document Reproduction Service (EDRS)
ERIC Processing and Reference Facility
SpecialNet

Education (General)
American Association of School Administrators (AASA)
American Society of Educators (ASE)
Association for Childhood Education International (ACEI)
(AECT) Minorities in Media (MIM)
Association for Experiential Education (AEE)
Center for Instructional Research and Curriculum Evaluation
Council for Basic Education
Education Development Center, Inc.
ERIC Clearinghouse on Counseling and Student Services (CG)

ERIC Clearinghouse on Educational
Management (EA)
ERIC Clearinghouse on Elementary and Early
Childhood Education (PS)
ERIC Clearinghouse on Disabilities and Gifted
Education (EC)
ERIC Clearinghouse on Rural Education and
Small Schools (RC)
ERIC Clearinghouse for Science, Mathematics,
and Environmental Education (SE)
ERIC Clearinghouse for Social Studies/Social
Science Education (ERIC/ChESS)
ERIC Clearinghouse on Teaching and Teacher
Education (SP)
ERIC Clearinghouse on Urban Education (UD)
National Association of State Educational Media
Professionals (NASTEMP)
National Association of State Textbook Adminis-
trators (NASTA)
National Center for Appropriate Technology
(NCAT)
National Clearinghouse for Bilingual Education
National Council for Accreditation of Teacher
Education (NCATE)
National Science Teachers Association (NSTA)

Education (Higher)
American Association of Community Colleges
(AACC)
American Association of State Colleges and
Universities
Association for Continuing Higher Education
(ACHE)
Association of Teacher Educators (ATE)
(AECT) Community College Association for
Instruction and Technology (CCAIT)
(AECT) Northwest College and University
Council for the Management of Educa-
tional Technology
Association for Library and Information Science
Education (ALISE)
Consortium of College and University Media
Centers
ERIC Clearinghouse for Community Colleges
(JC)
ERIC Clearinghouse on Higher Education (HE)

**Equipment (Manufacturing, Maintenance,
Testing, Operating)**
(ALA) Library and Information Technology
Association (LITA)
Association of AudioVisual Technicians
(AAVT)
EPIE Institute
ERIC Clearinghouse on Assessment and
Evaluation (TM)
ITA (formerly International Tape/Disc
Association [ITA])
National School Supply and Equipment
Association (NSSEA)
Society of Cable Television Engineers
(SCTE)

ERIC-Related
ACCESS ERIC
Adjunct ERIC Clearinghouse for Art Education
(ADJ/AR)
Adjunct ERIC Clearinghouse for ESL Literacy
Education (ADJ/LE)
Adjunct ERIC Clearinghouse for Law Related
Education (ADJ/LR)
Adjunct ERIC Clearinghouse for the Test
Collection (ADJ/TC)
Adjunct ERIC Clearinghouse for United States-
Japan Studies (ADJ/JS)
Adjunct ERIC Clearinghouse on Chapter 1 (Com-
pensatory Education) (ADJ/Chapter 1)
Adjunct ERIC Clearinghouse on Clinical Schools
(ADJ/CL)
Adjunct ERIC Clearinghouse on Consumer
Education (ADJ/CN)
ERIC (Educational Resources Information
Center)
ERIC Clearinghouse on Adult, Career, and
Vocational Education (CE)
ERIC Clearinghouse on Assessment and
Evaluation (TM)
ERIC Clearinghouse for Community Colleges
(JC)
ERIC Clearinghouse on Counseling and Student
Services (CG)
ERIC Clearinghouse on Educational Manage-
ment (EA)
ERIC Clearinghouse on Elementary and Early
Childhood Education (PS)
ERIC Clearinghouse on Disabilities and Gifted
Education (EC)
ERIC Clearinghouse on Higher Education (HE)
ERIC Clearinghouse on Information &
Technology (IR)
ERIC Clearinghouse on Languages and
Linguistics (FL)
ERIC Clearinghouse on Reading, English, and
Communication Skills (CS)
ERIC Clearinghouse on Rural Education and
Small Schools (RC)
ERIC Clearinghouse for Science, Mathematics,
and Environmental Education (SE)
ERIC Clearinghouse for Social Studies/Social
Science Education (SO)
ERIC Clearinghouse on Teaching and Teacher
Education (SP)
ERIC Clearinghouse on Urban Education (UD)
ERIC Document Reproduction Service (EDRS)
ERIC Processing and Reference Facility

**Films—Educational/Instructional/
Documentary**
Anthropology Film Center (AFC)
Association of Independent Video and
Filmmakers/Foundation for Independent
Video and Film (AIVF/FIVF)
Children's Television International, Inc.
CINE
CINE Information

Council on International Non-theatrical Events
(see CINE)
Film Arts Foundation (FAF)
National Aeronautics and Space Administration
(NASA)
National Alliance for Media Arts and Culture
(NAMAC)
National Audiovisual Center (NAC)
National Film Board of Canada (NFBC)
National Information Center for Educational
Media (NICEM)
Pacific Film Archive (PFA)
PCR: Films and Video in the Behavioral Sciences
University Film and Video Association

**Films—Theatrical (Film Study, Criticism,
Production)**
Academy of Motion Picture Arts and Sciences
(AMPAS)
American Society of Cinematographers
Film Arts Foundation (FAF)
Hollywood Film Archive
National Film Information Service (offered by
AMPAS)
The New York Festivals (formerly International
Film and TV Festival of New York)

Films—Training
(AECT) Industrial Training and Education
Division (ITED)
Association of Independent Video and
Filmmakers/Foundation for Independent
Video and Film (AIVF/FIVF)
Council on International Non-theatrical Events
Great Plains National ITV Library (GPN)
National Audiovisual Center (NAC)
National Film Board of Canada (NFBC)
Training Media Association

Futures
Office of Technology Assessment (OTA)
World Future Society (WFS)

**Games, Toys, Drama, Play, Simulation,
Puppetry**
Society for Computer Simulation (SCS)
USA-Toy Library Association (USA-TLA)

Health-Related Organizations
Health Science Communications Association
(HeSCA)
Lister Hill National Center for Biomedical
Communications of the National Library
of Medicine
Medical Library Association (MLA)
National Association for Visually Handicapped
(NAVH)
Network for Continuing Medical Education
(NCME)

Information Science
International Information Management Congress
(IMC)

**Instructional Technology/Design/
Development**
Agency for Instructional Technology (AIT)
Association for Educational Communications and
Technology (AECT)
(AECT) Community College Association for
Instruction and Technology (CCAIT)
(AECT) Division of Educational Media Manage-
ment (DEMM)
(AECT) Division of Instructional Development
(DID)
National Society for Performance and Instruction
(NSPI)
Office of Technology Assessment (OTA)
Professors of Instructional Design and Technol-
ogy (PIDT)
Society for Applied Learning Technology (SALT)

International Education
(AECT) International Division (INTL)
(AECT) International Visual Literacy Associa-
tion, Inc. (IVLA)
East-West Center

Libraries—Academic, Research
American Library Association (ALA)
(ALA) Association of College and Research
Libraries (ACRL)
ERIC Clearinghouse on Information &
Technology (IR)

Libraries—Public
American Library Association (ALA)
(ALA) Association for Library Service to
Children (ALSC)
(ALA) Library Administration and Management
Association (LAMA)
(ALA) Library and Information Technology
Association (LITA)
(ALA) Public Library Association (PLA)
(ALA) Reference and Adult Services Division
(RASD)
(ALA) Young Adult Library Services Associa-
tion (YALSA)
ERIC Clearinghouse on Information &
Technology (IR)

Libraries—Special
American Library Association (ALA)
(ALA) Association for Library Service to
Children (ALSC)
(ALA) Association of Specialized and
Cooperative Library Agencies (ASCLA)
ERIC Clearinghouse on Information &
Technology (IR)

Medical Library Association (MLA)
Theater Library Association
USA Toy Library Association (USA-TLA)

Libraries and Media Centers—General, School

American Library Association (ALA)
(ALA) American Association of School
Librarians (AASL)
(ALA) American Library Trustee Association
(ALTA)
(ALA) Association for Library Collections and
Technical Services (ALCTS)
(ALA) Association for Library Service to
Children (ALSC)
(ALA Round Table) Continuing Library Educa-
tion Network and Exchange (CLENE)
Association for Educational Communications
and Technology (AECT)
(AECT) Division of School Media Specialists
(DSMS)
(AECT) National Association of Regional Media
Centers (NARMC)
Catholic Library Association (CLA)
Consortium of College and University Media
Centers
ERIC Clearinghouse on Information &
Technology (IR)
International Association of School Librarianship
(IASL)
Library of Congress
National Alliance for Media Arts and Culture
(NAMAC)
National Commission on Libraries and Informa-
tion Science (NCLIS)
National Council of Teachers of English
(NCTE), Commission on Media
On-Line Audiovisual Catalogers (OLAC)
Southeastern Regional Media Leadership Council
(SRMLC)

Microforms; Micrographics

See ERIC-related entries.

Museums; Archives

(AECT) Archives
Association of Systematics Collections
George Eastman House (formerly International
Museum of Photography at George
Eastman House)
Hollywood Film Archive
Museum of Modern Art
National Gallery of Art (NGA)
National Public Broadcasting Archives (NPBA)
Pacific Film Archive (PFA)
Smithsonian Institution

Photography

George Eastman House (formerly International
Museum of Photography at George
Eastman House)
International Center of Photography (ICP)

National Press Photographers Association, Inc.
(NPPA)
Photographic Society of America (PSA)
Society for Imaging Science and Technology
(IS&T)
Society for Photographic Education (SPE)
Society of Photo Technologists (SPT)

Print—Books

American Library Association (ALA)
Association for Educational Communications
and Technology (AECT)
Smithsonian Institution

Production (Media)

American Society of Cinematographers (ASC)
Association for Educational Communications
and Technology (AECT)
(AECT) Media Design and Production Division
(MDPD)
Association of Independent Video and
Filmmakers/Foundation for Independent
Video and Film (AIVF/FIVF)
Film Arts Foundation (FAF)

Publishing

Magazine Publishers of America (MPA)
National Association of State Textbook
Administrators (NASTA)

Religious Education

Catholic Library Association (CLA)
National Religious Broadcasters (NRB)

Research

American Educational Research Association
(AERA)
Appalachia Educational Laboratory, Inc. (AEL)
(AECT) ECT Foundation
(AECT) Research and Theory Division (RTD)
Center for Advanced Visual Studies (CAVS)
Center for Technology in Education (CTE)
Center for Instructional Research and Curriculum
Evaluation
Clearinghouse on Development Communication
Council for Educational Development and
Research (CEDaR)
Education Development Center, Inc.
ERIC Clearinghouses. See ERIC-related entries.
Far West Laboratory for Educational Research
and Development (FWL) (see WestEd)
HOPE Reports
Mid-continent Regional Educational Laboratory
(McREL)
National Center for Improving Science Education
National Center for Research in Mathematical
Sciences Education
National Center for Science Teaching and
Learning
The NETWORK
North Central Regional Educational Laboratory
(NCREL)

Northwest Regional Educational Laboratory
(NWREL)
Office of Technology Assessment (OTA)
Pacific Regional Educational Laboratory (PREL)
Regional Laboratory for Educational Improve-
ment of the Northeast and Islands
Research for Better Schools, Inc.
SouthEastern Regional Vision for Education
(SERVE)
Southwest Educational Development Laboratory
(SEDL)
WestEd

Selection, Collections, Processing (Materials)
National Information Center for Educational
Media (NICEM)

Special Education
(CEC) Council for Exceptional Children, Tech-
nology and Media Division (TAM)
Council for Exceptional Children (CEC)
ERIC Clearinghouse on Disabilities and Gifted
Education (EC)
National Association for Visually Handicapped
(NAVH)
National Center to Improve Practice (NCIP)
.National Technology Center (NTC)

Training
American Management Association (AMA)
American Society for Training and Development
(ASTD)
Association for Educational Communications and
Technology (AECT)
(AECT) Federal Educational Technology
Association (FETA)
(AECT) Industrial Training and Education
Division (ITED)
ERIC Clearinghouse on Adult, Career, and
Vocational Education (CE)

International Society for Performance Improvement (ISPI)
Training Media Association

**Video (Cassette, Broadcast, Cable, Satellite,
Videodisc, Videotex)**
Agency for Instructional Technology (AIT)
Association for Educational Communications and
Technology (AECT)
(AECT) Division of Telecommunications (DOT)
(AECT) National ITFS Association (NIA/ITFS)
Association of Independent Video and
Filmmakers/Foundation for Independent
Video and Film (AIVF/FIVF)
Cable in the Classroom
Central Educational Network (CEN)
Children's Television International, Inc.
Close Up Foundation
Community College Satellite Network
Federal Communications Commission (FCC)
Great Plains National ITV Library (GPN)
International Teleconferencing Association
(ITCA)
International Television Association (ITVA)
ITA (formerly International Tape/Disc
Association [ITA])
National Aeronautics and Space Administration
(NASA)
National Association of Broadcasters (NAB)
National Education Telecommunications Organi-
zation & Education Satellite Company
(NETO/EDSAT)
National Telemedia Council, Inc. (NTC)
PBS Adult Learning Service (ALS)
PBS ENCORE
PBS VIDEO
Public Broadcasting Service (PBS)
Society of Cable Television Engineers (SCTE)
Society of Motion Picture and Television Engi-
neers (SMPTE)
University Film and Video Association (UFVA)

ALPHABETICAL LIST

*Academy of Motion Picture Arts and Sciences (AMPAS). 8949 Wilshire Blvd., Beverly Hills, CA 90211. (310) 247-3000. Fax (310) 859-9351. Bruce Davis, Exec. Dir. An honorary organization composed of outstanding individuals in all phases of motion pictures. Seeks to advance the arts and sciences of motion picture technology and artistry. Presents annual film awards; offers artist-in-residence programs; operates reference library and National Film Information Service. *Membership:* 5,300. *Publications: Annual Index to Motion Picture Credits; Academy Players Directory.*

*Agency for Instructional Technology (AIT). Box A, Bloomington, IN 47402-0120. (812) 339-2203. Fax (812) 333-4218. Michael F. Sullivan, Exec. Dir., Mardell Raney, Editor-in-Chief. AIT is a nonprofit U.S.-Canadian organization established in 1962 to strengthen education through technology. The Agency provides leadership and service through the development, acquisition, and distribution of technology-based instructional materials. AIT pioneered the consortium process to develop instructional series that meet learners' needs. It has cooperatively produced more than 32 series since 1970. Today, major funding comes from state and provincial departments of education, federal and private institutions, corporate sponsors, and other partners. *Publications: TECHNOS: Quarterly for Education and Technology* is the journal of the Agency for Instructional Technology. It is a forum for the discussion of ideas about the use of technology in education, with a focus on reform. A think piece for decision makers, *TECHNOS Quarterly* focuses on the policy and pedagogical implications of the electronic revolution. ISSN 1060-5649. $20/yr. (four issues). AIT also publishes two product catalogs, one for audiovisual and one for broadcast customers. Materials include video programming, interactive videodiscs, computer software, and supporting print. Its series are broadcast on six continents, reaching nearly 34 million students in North American classrooms each year. Catalogs are available free on request.

*American Association of Community Colleges (AACC). One Dupont Cir. NW, Suite 410, Washington, DC 20036. (202) 728-0200. Fax (202) 833-2467. David Pierce, Pres. AACC serves the nation's 1,211 community, technical, and junior colleges through advocacy, professional development, publications, and national networking. The annual convention draws more than 4,000 mid- and top-level administrators of two-year colleges. Staff and presidents offer expertise in all areas of education. Sixteen councils and six commissions address all areas of education. AACC also operates the Community College Satellite Network, providing programming and assistance to colleges. *Membership:* 1,110 institutional, 16 international, 3 foundation, 65 corporate, 75 individual, and 80 educational associate members. *Dues:* Vary for each category. *Meetings:* Annual Convention, April 22-25, 1995, Minneapolis, MN, "New Thinking for a New Century." *Publications: Community College Journal* (bi-mo.); *Community College Times* (bi-weekly newspaper); *College Times*; Community College Press (books and monographs).

*(AACC) Community College Satellite Network (CCSN). One Dupont Cir. NW, Suite 410, Washington, DC 20036. (202) 728-0200. Fax (202) 833-2467. Monica W. Pilkey, Dir. An affiliate of AACC, CCSN provides leadership and facilitates distance education, teleconferencing, and satellite training to the nation's community colleges. CCSN offers discounted teleconferences, free program resources, and general informational assistance in telecommunications. It also coordinates community college satellite downlinks nationally for teleconference users and producers. CCSN meets with its members at various industry trade shows and is very active in the AACC annual convention held each spring. *Membership:* 170 educational institutions. *Dues:* Vary by enrollment numbers. *Publications: Schedule of Programming*, 2/yr., contains listings of live and taped teleconferences for training and staff development; several other publications (free catalog available).

American Association of State Colleges and Universities (AASCU). One Dupont Cir. NW, Suite 700, Washington, DC 20036-1192. (202) 293-7070. Fax (202) 296-5819. James B. Appleberry, Pres. Membership is open to regionally accredited institutions of higher education, and those in the process of securing accreditation, that offer programs leading to the degree of bachelor, master, or doctor, and that are wholly or partially state-supported and state-controlled. Organized and operated exclusively for educational, scientific, and literary purposes, its particular purposes are to improve higher education within its member institutions through cooperative planning, studies, and research on common educational problems and the development of a more unified program of action among its members; and to provide other needed and worthwhile educational services to the colleges and universities it may represent. *Membership:* 375 institutions (university), 28 system, and 7 associate members. *Dues:* Based on current student enrollment at institution. *Publications: MEMO: To the President*; *The Center Associate*; *Office of Federal Program Reports*; *Office of Federal Program Deadlines.* (Catalogs of books and other publications available upon request.)

*American Educational Research Association (AERA). 1230 17th St. NW, Washington, DC 20036. (202) 223-9485. Fax (202) 775-1824. William J. Russell, Exec. Dir. AERA is an international professional organization with the primary goal of advancing educational research and its practical application. Its members include educators; administrators; directors of research, testing, or evaluation in federal, state, and local agencies; counselors; evaluators; graduate students; and behavioral scientists. The broad range of disciplines represented includes education, psychology. statistics, sociology, history, economics, philosophy, anthropology, and political science. *Membership:* 20,000. *Dues:* Vary by category—voting, active, student, and international affiliate. *Meetings:* 1994 Annual Convention, April 4-8, New Orleans, LA; 1995 Convention, April 17-21, San Francisco, CA. *Publications: Educational Researcher*; *American Educational Research Journal*; *Journal of Educational Statistics*; *Educational Evaluation and Policy Analysis*; *Review of Research in Education*; *Review of Educational Research.*

*American Library Association (ALA). 50 E. Huron St., Chicago, IL 60611. (312) 944-6780. Fax (312) 440-9374. Carol Henderson, Exec. Dir. The ALA is the oldest and largest national library association. Its 55,000 members represent all types of libraries—state, public, school, and academic—as well as special libraries serving persons in government, commerce, the armed services, hospitals, prisons, and other institutions. Chief advocate of achievement and maintenance of high-quality library information services through protection of the right to read, educating librarians, improving services, and making information widely accessible. *Membership:* 55,000. *Dues:* Basic dues $38 first year, $75 renewing members. *Meetings*: 1997: Midwinter Meeting, February 14-20, Washington, DC; Annual Conference, June 26-July 3, San Francisco, CA; 1998: Midwinter Meeting, January 9-15, New Orleans, LA; Annual Conference, June 25-July 2, Washington, DC. *Publications: American Libraries*; *Booklist*; *Choice*; *Book Links.*

    (ALA) American Association of School Librarians (AASL). 50 E. Huron St., Chicago, IL 60611. (312) 280-4386. Fax (312) 664-7459. Ann Carlson Weeks, Exec. Dir. Interested in the general improvement and extension of school library media services for children and youth. Activities and projects of the association are divided among 55 committees and 3 sections. *Membership*: 7,690. *Dues:* Membership in ALA plus $40; retired memberships and student membership rates available. *Meetings*: National Conference, April 2-6, 1997, Portland, OR. *Publications: School Library Media Quarterly* (journal, q.); *Hotline Connections* (newsletter, 4/yr.).

    *(ALA) American Library Trustee Association (ALTA). 50 E. Huron St., Chicago, IL 60611. (312) 280-2160. Fax (312) 280-3257. Susan Roman, Exec. Dir. Interested in the development of effective library service for people in all types of communities and libraries. Members, as policymakers, are concerned with organizational patterns of service, the development of competent personnel, the provision of adequate financing, the passage of suitable legislation and the encouragement of citizen support for libraries. *Membership:* 1,710. *Dues:* $40 plus membership in ALA. *Publications: ALTA Newsletter*; professional monographs and pamphlets.

(ALA) Association for Library Collections and Technical Services (ALCTS). 50 E. Huron St., Chicago, IL 60611. (312) 944-6780. Karen Muller, Exec. Dir; David Farrell, Pres., June 1996-July 1997. Dedicated to acquisition, identification, cataloging, classification, and preservation of library materials, the development and coordination of the country's library resources, and aspects of selection and evaluation involved in acquiring and developing library materials and resources. Sections include Acquisitions, Cataloging and Classification, Collection Management and Development, Preservation and Reformatting, and Serials. *Membership:* 5,445. *Dues:* $45 plus membership in ALA. *Meetings:* Annual conference and midwinter meeting with ALA. *Publications: Library Resources & Technical Services* (q.); *ALCTS Newsletter* (6/yr.); *ALCTS Network News (AV 2)*, electronic newsletter issued irregularly.

*****(ALA) Association for Library Service to Children (ALSC)**. 50 E. Huron St., Chicago, IL 60611. (312) 280-2163. (800) 545-2433. Fax (312) 280-3257. Susan Roman, Exec. Dir. Interested in the improvement and extension of library services for children in all types of libraries, evaluation and selection of book and nonbook library materials, and improvement of techniques of library services for children from preschool through the eighth grade or junior high school age. Annual conference and midwinter meeting with the ALA. Committee membership open to ALSC members. *Membership:* 3,600. *Dues:* $35 plus membership in ALA. *Meetings:* ALA Midwinter Meeting, February 3-9, 1995, Philadelphia, PA; ALA Annual Conference June 22-29, 1995, Chicago, IL. *Publications: Journal of Youth Services in Libraries* (q.); *ALSC Newsletter* (q.).

(ALA) Association of College and Research Libraries (ACRL). 50 E. Huron St., Chicago, IL 60611-2795. (312) 280-3248. Fax (312) 280-2520. E-mail Althea. Jenkins@ala.org. Althea H. Jenkins, Exec. Dir. ACRL provides leadership for development, promotion, and improvement of academic and research library resources and services to facilitate learning, research, and the scholarly communications process. It has available library standards for colleges, universities, and two-year institutions, and publishes statistics on academic libraries. Committees include Academic Status, Colleagues Committee, Copyright, Council of Liaisons, Government Relations, Image Enhancement, Intellectual Freedom, International Relations, Media Resources, Professional Education, Publications, Racial and Ethnic Diversity, Research, Standards and Accreditation, and Statistics. A free list of materials is available. The association administers 13 different awards, most of which are given annually. *Membership:* over 10,000. *Dues:* $35 (in addition to ALA membership). *Meetings:* 1997 National Conference, April 11-14, Nashville, TN, "Choosing Our Futures." *Publications: College & Research Libraries* (6/yr.); *College & Research Libraries News* (11/yr.); *CLIP Notes* (current issues are #20-22). Recent titles include: *Teaching Information Retrieval and Evaluation Skills to Education Students and Practitioners: A Casebook of Applications; Internet Resources: A Subject Guide, Science and Engineering Conference Proceedings; A Guide to Sources for Identification and Verification; Vocational and Technical Resources for Community College Libraries;* and *Continuity and Transformation: The Promise of Confluence,* proceedings of the 7th ACRL National Conference.

*****(ALA) Association of Specialized and Cooperative Library Agencies (ASCLA)**. 50 E. Huron St., Chicago, IL 60611. (800) 545-2433, ext. 4399. Fax (312) 944-8085. Cathleen Bourdon, Exec. Dir. Represents state library agencies, multitype library cooperatives, and libraries serving special clienteles to promote the development of coordinated library services with equal access to information and material for all persons. The activities and programs of the association are carried out by 21 committees, 3 sections, and various discussion groups. Write for free checklist of materials. *Membership:* 1,300. *Dues:* (in addition to ALA membership) $30 for personal members, $50 for organizations, $500 for state library agencies. *Meetings:* Midwinter: 1997, Washington, DC, February 14-20. Annual Conferences: 1997, San Francisco, CA, June 26-July 3; 1998, Washington, DC, June 25-July 2. *Publications: Interface* (q.). Recent titles include: *The Americans with Disabilities Act: Its Impact on Libraries*; *Deafness: An Annotated Bibliography and Guide to Basic Materials*; *Library Standards for Adult Correctional Institutions 1992.*

(ALA) Library Administration and Management Association (LAMA). 50 E. Huron St., Chicago, IL 60611. (312) 280-5038. Karen Muller, Exec. Dir.; John J. Vasi, Pres., June 1995-July 1996. Provides an organizational framework for encouraging the study of administrative theory, for improving the practice of administration in libraries, and for identifying and fostering administrative skills. Toward these ends, the association is responsible for all elements of general administration that are common to more than one type of library. These may include: Buildings and Equipment Section (BES); Fundraising & Financial Development Section (FRFDS); Library Organization & Management Section (LOMS); Personnel Administration Section (PAS); Public Relation Section (PRS); Systems & Services Section (SASS); Statistic Section (SS). *Membership:* 5,138. *Dues:* $35 (in addition to ALA membership); $15 library school students. *Meetings:* ALA Annual Conference: 1997, San Francisco, CA, June 26-July 3; 1998, Washington, DC, June 25-July 2. LITA/LAMA National Conference: 1996, Pittsburgh, PA, October 13-16. *Publication: Library Administration & Management* (q.).

*(ALA) Library and Information Technology Association (LITA). 50 E. Huron St., Chicago, IL 60611. (312) 280-4270; (voice) (800) 545-2433, ext. 4270. Fax (312) 280-3257. Linda J. Knutson, Exec. Dir. Concerned with library automation, the information sciences, and the design, development, and implementation of automated systems in those fields, including systems development, electronic data processing, mechanized information retrieval, operations research, standards development, telecommunications, video communications, networks and collaborative efforts, management techniques, information technology, optical technology, artificial intelligence and expert systems, and other related aspects of audiovisual activities and hardware applications. *Membership:* 5,800. *Dues:* $35 plus membership in ALA, $15 for library school students, $25 first year, new members. *Meetings:* 1996, LITA/LAMA National Conference, Pittsburgh, PA, October 13-16. *Publications: Information Technology and Libraries*; *LITA Newsletter.*

(ALA) Public Library Association (PLA). 50 E. Huron St., Chicago, IL 60611. (312) 280-5PLA. Fax (312) 280-5029. E-mail George.Needham@ala.org. George M. Needham, Exec. Dir.; Judith Drescher, Pres., 1994-95; LaDonna Kienitz, Pres., 1995-96. Concerned with the development, effectiveness, and financial support of public libraries. Speaks for the profession and seeks to enrich the professional competence and opportunities of public libraries. Sections include Adult Lifelong Learning; Community Information; Metropolitan Libraries; Public Library Systems; Small and Medium-sized Libraries; Public Policy for Public Libraries; Planning, Measurement and Evaluation; and Marketing of Public Library Services. *Membership:* 7,800. *Dues:* $50, open to all ALA members. *Meetings:* National Conference, PLA National Conference, March 26-30, 1996, Portland, OR. "Access for All: The Public Library Promise." *Publication: Public Libraries* (bi-mo.).

(ALA) Reference and Adult Services Division (RASD). 50 E. Huron St., Chicago, IL 60611. (800) 545-2433, ext. 4395. Fax (312) 944-8085. Cathleen Bourdon, Exec. Dir. Responsible for stimulating and supporting in every type of library the delivery of reference information services to all groups and of general library services and materials to adults. *Membership:* 5,500. *Dues:* $35 plus membership in ALA. *Publications: RQ* (q.); *RASD Update*; others.

*(ALA) Young Adult Library Services Association (YALSA) (formerly Young Adult Services Division). 50 E. Huron St., Chicago, IL 60611. (312) 280-4390. Fax (312) 664-7459. Linda Waddle, Deputy Exec. Dir.; Jennifer Jung Gallant, Pres. Seeks to advocate, promote, strengthen service to young adults as part of the continuum of total library services, and assumes responsibility within the ALA to evaluate and select books and nonbook media, and to interpret and make recommendations regarding their use with young adults. Committees include Best Books for Young Adults, Recommended Books for the Reluctant Young Adult Reader, Media Selection and Usage, Publishers' Liaison, and Selected Films for Young Adults. *Membership:* 2,223. *Dues:* $40 (in addition to ALA membership), $15 for students. *Publication: Journal of Youth Services in Libraries* (q.).

*(ALA) Continuing Library Education Network and Exchange Round Table (CLENERT). 50 E. Huron St., Chicago, IL 60611. (312) 280-4278. Kenna J. Forsythe, Pres.; Duncan F. Smith, Pres.-Elect. Seeks to provide access to quality continuing education opportunities for librarians and information scientists and to create an awareness of the need for such education in helping individuals in the field to respond to societal and technological changes. *Membership:* 350. *Dues:* Open to all ALA members; individual members $15, $50 for organizations. *Publication: CLENExchange* (q.), available to nonmembers by subscription at $20/yr. U.S. zip, $25 non-U.S. zip.

American Management Association (AMA). 135 W. 50th St., New York, NY 10020-1201. (212) 586-8100. Fax (212) 903-8168. David Fagiano, Pres. and CEO. Founded in 1923, the AMA provides educational forums worldwide where members and their colleagues learn superior, practical business skills and explore best practices of world-class organizations through interaction with each other and expert faculty practitioners. Its publishing program provides tools individuals use to extend learning beyond the classroom in a process of life-long professional growth and development through education. The AMA operates eight management centers and offices in the United States and, through AMA/International, in Brussels, Belgium, and Tokyo, Japan; it also has affiliated centers in Toronto, Canada, and Mexico City, Mexico. AMA offers conferences, seminars, and membership briefings where there is an interchange of information, ideas, and experiences in a wide variety of management topics. AMA publishes approximately 60 books per year, as well as numerous surveys and management briefings. *Membership:* approx. 70,000. *Dues:* corporate, $550-1,495; growing company, $475-1,675; individual, $160 plus $40 per division. *Publications* (periodicals): *Management Review* (membership); *Compensation and Benefits Review*; *CompFlash®*; *Organizational Dynamics*; *HR Focus*; *The President*; *Small Business Reports*; *Supervisory Management*; *The Take Charge Assistant*; and *Trainer's Workshop*. Catalogs of self-study products, training resources, and business books are available. Other services offered by AMA include AMA Video; Extension Institute (self-study programs in both print and audio formats); Operation Enterprise (young adult program); AMA On-Site (seminars delivered at site of the company's choice); AMA by Satellite (videoconferences); the Information Resources Center (for AMA members only); a management information and library service; and five AMA bookstores. It also cooperates with management associations around the world through correspondent association agreements.

American Society for Training and Development (ASTD). 1640 King St., Box 1443, Alexandria, VA 22313. (703) 683-8100. Fax (703) 683-8103. Curtis E. Plott, Pres. and CEO. Founded in 1944, ASTD is the world's premiere professional association in the field of workplace learning and performance. ASTD's membership includes more than 58,000 people in organizations from every level of the field of workplace performance in more than 100 countries. Its leadership and members work in more than 15,000 multinational corporations, small- and medium-sized businesses, government agencies, colleges, and universities. ASTD is the leading resource on workplace learning and performance issues, providing information, research, analysis, and practical information derived from its own research, the knowledge and experience of its members, its conferences and publications, and the coalitions and partnerships it has built through research and policy work. *Membership:* 58,000 National and Chapter members. *Dues:* $150/yr., National. *Meetings:* 1996, International Conference, Orlando, FL, June 2-6; Technical and Skills Training Conference, Cincinnati, OH, October 18-20. *Publications: Training & Development Magazine; Technical & Skills Training Magazine; Info-Line; The American Mosaic: An In-Depth Report of Diversity on the Future of Diversity at Work; ASTD Video Directories; ASTD Directory of Academic Programs in T&D/HRD; Training and Development Handbook; Technical & Skills Training Handbook.* Quarterly publications: *National Report on Human Resources; Washington Policy Report.* ASTD also has recognized professional forums, most of which produce newsletters.

American Society of Educators (ASE). 1429 Walnut St., 10th Fl., Philadelphia, PA 19102. (215) 563-6005. Fax (215) 587-4706. E-mail Micheles@media-methods.com. Michele Sokolof, Editorial Dir. ASE services the information needs of K-12 teachers, librarians, media specialists, curriculum directors, and administrators in evaluating the practical applications of today's multimedia/technology resources for teaching and learning purposes. *Membership:* 42,000. *Dues:* $29/yr., $48/yr. foreign. *Publication: Media and Methods,* bi-mo. magazine.

Anthropology Film Center (AFC). 1626 Canyon Rd., Santa Fe, NM 87501. (505) 983-4127. Carroll Williams, Dir. Offers the Documentary Film Program, a 30-week full-time course in 16mm film in documentary and ethnographic film production, CD-I and theory, and summer workshops. Also provides consultation, research, 16mm film equipment sales and rental, facilities rental, occasional seminars and workshops, and a specialized library.

*Appalachia Educational Laboratory, Inc. (AEL). 1031 Quarrier St., P.O. Box 1348, Charleston, WV 25325. (304) 347-0400; (800) 624-9120 (outside WV), (800) 344-6646 (in WV). Fax (304) 347-0487. E-mail eidellt@ael.org. Terry L. Eidell, Exec. Dir. One of 10 Office of Educational Research and Improvement (OERI) regional educational laboratories designed to help educators and policymakers solve educational problems in their schools. Using the best available information and the experience and expertise of professionals, AEL seeks to identify solutions to education problems, tries new approaches, furnishes research results, and provides training to teachers and administrators. AEL serves Kentucky, Tennessee, Virginia, and West Virginia.

Association for Childhood Education International (ACEI). 11501 Georgia Ave., Suite 315, Wheaton, MD 20902. (301) 942-2443. Fax (301) 942-3012. E-mail ACEIHQ@aol.com. Anne W. Bauer, Ed. and Dir. of Publications. Concerned with children from infancy through early adolescence. ACEI publications reflect careful research, broad-based views, and consideration of a wide range of issues affecting children. Many are media-related in nature. The journal (*Childhood Education*) is essential for teachers, teachers-in-training, teacher educators, day care workers, administrators, and parents. Articles focus on child development and emphasize practical application. Regular departments include book reviews (child and adult); reviews of films, pamphlets, and software; research; and classroom idea-sparkers. Articles address timely concerns. Five issues are published yearly, including a theme issue devoted to critical concerns. *Membership:* 12,000. *Dues:* $45/yr., prof.; $26/yr., student; $23/yr., retired; $78/yr., institutional. *Meeting:* 1996, Annual International Study Conference, Minneapolis, MN, April 10-13, "The Spirit of '96: To Dream, To Dare, To Do." *Publications: Childhood Education* (official journal) with *ACEI Exchange* (insert newsletter); *Journal of Research in Childhood Education;* professional division newsletters (*Focus on Infancy, Focus on Early Childhood,* and *Focus on Later Childhood/Early Adolescence*); *Celebrating Family Literacy Through Intergenerational Programming; Selecting Educational Equipment for School and Home; Developmental Continuity Across Preschool and Primary Grades; Implications for Teachers; Developmentally Appropriate Middle Level Schools; Common Bonds: Antibias Teaching in a Diverse Society; Childhood 1892-1992; Infants and Toddlers with Special Needs and Their Families* (position paper); and pamphlets.

Association for Continuing Higher Education (ACHE). Continuing Education, Trident Technical College, P.O. Box 118067, CE-P, Charleston, SC 29423-8067. (803) 722-5546. Fax (803) 722-5520. Wayne Whelan, Exec. Vice Pres. The association is an institution-based organization of colleges, universities, and individuals dedicated to the promotion of lifelong learning and excellence in continuing higher education. ACHE encourages professional networks, research, and exchange of information for its members and advocates continuing higher education as a means of enhancing and improving society. *Membership:* 1,622 individuals in 674 institutions. *Dues:* $60/yr. professionals, $240/yr. institutional. *Meetings:* 1996 Annual Meeting, Palm Desert, CA, October 26-29, "Repositioning the Continuing Higher Education Agenda." 1997 Annual Meeting, Pennsylvania State University, October 25-28; 1998 Annual Meeting, Fort Worth, TX, October 30-November 3. *Publications: Journal of Continuing Higher Education* (3/yr.); *Five Minutes with ACHE* (newsletter, 10/yr.); *Proceedings* (annual).

Association for Educational Communications and Technology (AECT). 1025 Vermont Ave. NW, Suite 820, Washington, DC 20005. (202) 347-7834. Fax (202) 347-7839. Stanley Zenor, Exec. Dir; William Burns, Pres. AECT is an international professional association concerned with the improvement of learning and instruction through media and technology. It serves as a central clearinghouse and communications center for its members, who include instructional technologists; media or library specialists; religious educators; government media personnel; school, school district, and state department of education media program administrators and specialists; and educational/training media producers. AECT members also work in the armed forces, in public libraries, in museums, and in other information agencies of many different kinds, including those related to the emerging fields of computer technology. *Membership:* 4,500, plus 9,000 additional subscribers, 11 divisions, 15 national affiliates, 46 state and territorial affiliates, and more than 30 national committees and task forces. *Dues:* $75/yr. regular, $35/yr. student and retired. *Meetings:* 1995 Annual Convention and InCITE Exposition, February 8-12, Anaheim, CA; 1996 Annual Convention and InCITE Exposition, February 14-18 in Indianapolis, IN. *Publications: TechTrends* (6/yr., free with membership; $36/yr. nonmembers); *Report to Members* (6/yr., newsletter); *Educational Technology Research and Development* (q., $40/yr. members; $55/yr. nonmembers); various division publications; several books; videotapes.

Because of similarity of interests, the following organizations have chosen to affiliate with the Association for Educational Communications and Technology. (As many as possible have been polled for inclusion in *EMTY*.)

- Community College Association for Instruction and Technology (CCAIT)
- Consortium of College and University Media Centers (CCUMC)
- Federal Educational Technology Association (FETA)
- Health Sciences Communications Association (HeSCA)
- International Association for Learning Laboratories (IALL)
- International Council for Educational Media (ICEM)
- International Visual Literacy Association, Inc. (IVLA)
- Minorities in Media (MIM)
- National Association of Regional Media Centers (NARMC)
- National Instructional Television Fixed Service Association (NIA/ITFS)
- New England Educational Media Association (NEEMA)
- Northwest College and University Council for the Management of Educational Technology (NW/MET)
- Southeastern Regional Media Leadership Council (SRMLC)

Two additional organizations are also related to the Association for Educational Communications and Technology:

- AECT Archives
- AECT ECT Foundation

Association for Educational Communications and Technology (AECT) Divisions:

(AECT) Division of Educational Media Management (DEMM). 1025 Vermont Ave. NW, Suite 820, Washington, DC 20005. (202) 347-7834. Robert A. Harrell, Pres. Seeks to develop an information exchange network and to share information about common problems, solutions, and program descriptions of educational media management. Develops programs that increase the effectiveness of media managers; initiates and implements a public relations program to educate the public and administrative bodies as to the use, value, and need for educational media management; and fosters programs that will help carry out media management responsibilities effectively. *Membership:* 780. *Dues:* One division membership included in the basic AECT membership; additional division memberships $10/yr. *Publication: Media Management Journal.*

(AECT) Division of Instructional Development (DID). 1025 Vermont Ave. NW, Suite 820, Washington, DC 20005. (202) 347-7834. Thomas M. Duffy, Pres. DID is composed of individuals from business, government, and academic settings concerned with the systematic design of instruction and the development of solutions to performance problems. Members' interests include the study, evaluation, and refinement of design processes; the creation of new models of instructional development; the invention and improvement of techniques for managing the development of instruction; the development and application of professional ID competencies; the promotion of academic programs for preparation of ID professionals; and the dissemination of research and development work in ID. *Membership:* 726. *Dues:* One division membership included in the basic AECT membership; additional division memberships $10/yr. *Publications: DID Newsletter*; occasional papers.

(AECT) Division of Interactive Systems and Computers (DISC). 1025 Vermont Ave. NW, Suite 820, Washington, DC 20005. (202) 347-7834. Jim Stonge, Pres. Concerned with the generation, access, organization, storage, and delivery of all forms of information used in the processes of education and training. DISC promotes the networking of its members to facilitate sharing of expertise and interests. *Membership:* 883. *Dues:* One division membership included in the basic AECT membership; additional division memberships $10/yr. *Publication:* Newsletter.

*****(AECT) Division of Learning and Performance Environments (DLPE).** 1025 Vermont Ave. NW, Suite 820, Washington, DC 20005. (202) 347-7834. Rod Sims, Pres. Seeks to provide continuing education and leadership in the field of learning and human performance using computer-based technologies. The Division is composed of individuals from business, academic settings, and government who are looking for a forum for sophisticated discussions of the issues they face. Member interests include scholarly research, the application of theory to practice, design, development, evaluation, assessment, and implementation of learning and performance support systems for adults. *Membership:* New division; data not provided. *Dues:* One division membership included in the basic AECT membership; additional division memberships $10/yr.

(AECT) Division of School Media Specialists (DSMS). 1025 Vermont Ave. NW, Suite 820, Washington, DC 20005. (202) 347-7834. Paula Galland, Pres. DSMS promotes communication among school media personnel who share a common concern in the development, implementation, and evaluation of school media programs; and strives to increase learning and improve instruction in the school setting through the utilization of educational media and technology. *Membership:* 902. *Dues:* One division membership included in the basic AECT membership; additional division memberships $10/yr. *Publication:* Newsletter.

(AECT) Division of Telecommunications (DOT). 1025 Vermont Ave. NW, Suite 820, Washington, DC 20005. (202) 347-7834. Cynthia Elliott, Pres. Seeks to improve education through use of television and radio, video and audio recordings, and autotutorial devices and media. Aims to improve the design, production, evaluation, and use of telecommunications materials and equipment; to upgrade competencies of personnel engaged in the field; to investigate and report promising innovative practices and technological developments; to promote studies, experiments, and demonstrations; and to support research in telecommunications. Future plans call for working to establish a national entity representing instructional television. *Membership:* 607. *Dues:* One division membership included in the basic AECT membership; additional division memberships $10/yr. *Publication:* Newsletter.

(AECT) Industrial Training and Education Division (ITED). 1025 Vermont Ave. NW, Suite 820, Washington, DC 20005. (202) 347-7834. Andrew R. J. Yeaman, Pres. Seeks to promote the sensitive and sensible use of media and techniques to improve the quality of education and training; to provide a professional program that demonstrates the state of the art of educational technology as a part of the AECT convention; to improve communications to ensure the maximum use of educational techniques and media that can give demonstrable, objective evidence of effectiveness. *Membership:* 273. *Dues:* One division membership included in the basic AECT membership; additional division memberships $10/yr. *Publication:* Newsletter.

(AECT) International Division (INTL). 1025 Vermont Ave. NW, Suite 820, Washington, DC 20005. (202) 347-7834. Marina Stock McIsaac, Pres. Seeks to improve international communications concerning existing methods of design; to pretest, use, produce, evaluate, and establish an approach through which these methods may be improved and adapted for maximum use and effectiveness; to develop a roster of qualified international leaders with experience and competence in the varied geographic and technical areas; and to encourage research in the application of communication processes to support present and future international social and economic development. *Membership:* 295. *Dues:* One division membership included in the basic AECT membership; additional division memberships $10/yr. *Publication:* Newsletter.

(AECT) Media Design and Production Division (MDPD). 1025 Vermont Ave. NW, Suite 820, Washington, DC 20005. (202) 347-7834. Keith A. Danielson, Pres. Seeks to provide formal, organized procedures for promoting and facilitating interaction between commercial and noncommercial, nontheatrical filmmakers, and to provide a communications link for filmmakers with persons of similar interests. Also seeks to provide a connecting link between creative and technical professionals of the audiovisual industry. Advances the informational film producer's profession by providing scholarships and apprenticeships to experimenters and students and by providing a forum for discussion of local, national, and universal issues. Recognizes and presents awards for outstanding films produced and for contributions to the state of the art. *Membership:* 318. *Dues:* One division membership included in the basic AECT membership; additional division memberships $10/yr. *Publication:* Newsletter.

(AECT) Research and Theory Division (RTD). 1025 Vermont Ave. NW, Suite 820, Washington, DC 20005. (202) 347-7834. Patricia L. Smith, Pres. Seeks to improve the design, execution, utilization, and evaluation of educational technology research; to improve the qualifications and effectiveness of personnel engaged in educational technology research; to advise the educational practitioner as to use of the research results; to improve research design, techniques, evaluation, and dissemination; to promote both applied and theoretical research on the systematic use of educational technology in the improvement of instruction; and to encourage the use of multiple research paradigms in examining issues related to technology in education. *Membership:* 452. *Dues:* One division membership included in the basic AECT membership; additional division memberships $10/yr. *Publication:* Newsletter.

(AECT) Systemic Change in Education Division (CHANGE). 1025 Vermont Ave. NW, Suite 820, Washington, DC 20005. (202) 347-7834. Alison A. Carr, Pres. Serves those who are interested in systemic change in a wide variety of settings, including public and private schools. Fosters the belief that systemic change is necessary in educational settings for meeting learners' needs and for dramatically improving the quality of education. *Membership:* New division; data not provided. *Dues:* One division membership included in the basic AECT membership; additional division memberships $10/yr. *Publication:* Newsletter.

Association for Educational Communications and Technology (AECT)

Affiliate Organizations:

(AECT) Community College Association for Instruction and Technology (CCAIT). Truckee Meadows Community College, 4001 S. Virginia St., Reno, NV 89502. (702) 674-7534. Fax (702) 673-7108. E-mail pmills@scs.unrdu. Peggy Mills, Pres. A national association of community and junior college educators interested in the discovery and dissemination of information about problems and processes of teaching, media, and technology in community and junior colleges. Facilitates member exchange of data, reports, proceedings, personnel, and other resources; sponsors AECT convention sessions and social activities. *Membership:* 250. *Dues:* $15. *Meeting:* February 1996, Albuquerque, NM. *Publications:* Regular newsletter; irregular topical papers.

(AECT) Consortium of College and University Media Centers (CCUMC). See separate listing.

(AECT) Federal Educational Technology Association (FETA). FETA Membership, Sara Shick, FETA, P.O. Box 3412, McLean, VA 22103-3412. (703) 406-3040 (Clear Spring, Inc.). Minx Olsen, Pres. FETA is dedicated to the improvement of education and training through research, communication, and practice. It encourages and welcomes members from all government agencies, federal, state, and local; from business and industry; and from all educational institutions and organizations. FETA encourages interaction among members to improve the quality of education and training in any arena, but with specific emphasis on government-related applications. *Membership:* 150. *Dues:* $20/yr. *Meetings:* Meets in conjunction with AECT InCITE, concurrently with SALT's Washington meeting in August, and periodically throughout the year in Washington, DC. *Publication:* Newsletter (occasional).

(AECT) Health Sciences Communications Association (HeSCA). See separate listing.

International Association for Learning Laboratories (IALL). IALL c/o IALL Business Manager, Malacester College, 1600 Grand Ave., St. Paul, MN 55105. (612) 696-6336. E-mail browne@macalstr.edu. Robert Henderson, Pres. Thomas Browne, Bus. Mgr. IALL is a professional organization working for the improvement of second language learning through technology in learning centers and classrooms. *Meetings:* 1977, Victoria, BC, Canada, August.

International Council for Educational Media (ICEM). ICEM, c/o Robert LeFranc, ICEM Secretariat, 29 rue d'Ulm, 25230 Paris, Cedex 05, France. 33-1-46. Fax 33-1-46-35-78-89. Asgeir Godmundsmon, Pres. Richard Cornell, U.S. member, University of Central Florida, Education Room 310, Orlando, FL 32816-0992. (407) 823-2053. Fax (407) 823-5135. E-mail cornell@pogasus.cc.ucf.edu. The objective of ICEM is to provide a channel for the international exchange of information and experience in the field of educational technology, with particular reference to preschool, primary, and secondary education, technical and vocational training, and teacher and continuing education; to encourage organizations with a professional responsibility for the design, production, promotion, distribution, and use of educational media in member countries; to promote an understanding of the concept of educational technology on the part of both educators and those involved in their training; to contribute to the pool of countries by the sponsorship of practical projects involving international cooperation and co-production; to advise manufacturers of hardware and software on the needs of an information service on developments in educational technology; to provide consultancy for the benefit of member countries; and to cooperate with other international organizations in promoting the concept of educational technology. ICEM is a Class B Affiliate of UNESCO.

(AECT) International Visual Literacy Association, Inc. (IVLA). Gonzaga University, E. 502 Boone AD25, Spokane, WA 99258-0001. (509) 328-4220 ext. 3478. Fax (509) 324-5812. E-mail bclark@soe.gonzaga.edu. Dr. Barbara I. Clark, Exec. Treas. Provides a multidisciplinary forum for the exploration of modes of visual communication and their application through the concept of visual literacy; promotes development of visual literacy, and serves as a bond between the diverse organizations and groups working in that field. *Dues:* $40 regular; $20 student, retired; $45 outside U.S. *Meeting:* Annual Meeting 1996, Cheyenne, WY, October 2-6, "VisionQuest: Journeys Toward Visual Literacy." *Publications: Journal of Visual Literacy; Readings from Annual Conferences.*

(AECT) Minorities in Media (MIM). Arizona State University, P.O. Box 970111, Tempe, AZ 85287-0111. (602) 965-1832. Dr. Benjamin Kinard, Pres. Seeks to encourage the effective use of educational media in the teaching/learning process; provide leadership opportunities in advancing the use of technology as an integral part of the learning process; provide a vehicle through which minorities might influence the use of media in institutions; develop an information exchange network to share information common to minorities in media; study, evaluate, and refine the educational technology process as it relates to the education of minorities; and encourage and improve the production of materials for the education of minorities. *Membership:* 100. *Dues:* $10. *Publication:* Annual newsletter.

(AECT) National Association of Regional Media Centers (NARMC). NARMC, Education Service Center, Region 20, 1314 Hines Ave., San Antonio, TX 78206-1816. E-mail jtaylor@tenet.edu. Lynn Bennett, Pres; James H. Taylor, Treasurer. Seeks to foster the exchange of ideas and information among educational communications specialists responsible for the administration of regional media centers, through workshops, seminars, and national meetings. Studies the feasibility of developing joint programs that could increase the effectiveness and efficiency of regional media services. Disseminates information on successful practices and research studies conducted by regional media centers. Member institutions serve more than 20 million students. *Membership:* 285 regional centers (institutions), 70 corporations. *Dues:* $55 institutions, $250 corporations. *Meetings:* National Conference, affiliated with AECT National Conference, Anaheim, CA, February 8-12, 1995. Theme: "Information Technology— Expanding Frontiers." *Publications: N.A.R.M.C.—Highlights; N.A.R.M.C.— 'etin; Annual Membership Report; Biannual Survey Report of Regional Media Centers.*

(AECT) National ITFS Association (NIA). National ITFS Association, Box #1130, 3421 M Street, NW, Washington, DC 20007. Theodore Steinke, Chair, Bd. of Dirs.; Frederick M. Hurst, Pres. Established in 1978, NIA/ITFS is a nonprofit, professional organization of Instructional Television Fixed Service (ITFS) licensees, applicants, and others interested in ITFS broadcasting. The goals of the association are to gather and exchange information about ITFS, to gather data on utilization of ITFS, and to act as a conduit for those seeking ITFS information or assistance. The NIA represents ITFS interests to the FCC, technical consultants, and equipment manufacturers. The association provides its members with a quarterly newsletter and an FCC regulation update as well as information on excess capacity leasing and license and application data. *Meeting:* Meets with AECT and InCITE. *Publications: National ITFS Association Newsletter* (q.); FCC regulation update.

New England Educational Media Association (NEEMA). NEEMA, c/o Jean Keilly, 58 South Mammoth Road, Manchester, NH 03109. (603) 622-9626. Fax (603) 424-6229. Dorothy Crazler, Pres. NEEMA is a regional professional association dedicated to the improvement of instruction through the effective utilization of school library media services, media, and technology applications. For over 75 years, it has represented school library media professionals through activities and networking efforts to develop and polish the leadership skills, professional representation, and informational awareness of the membership. The Board of Directors consists of Departments of Education as well as professional leaders of the region. An annual conference program and Leadership Program are offered in conjunction with the various regional state association conferences.

(AECT) Northwest College and University Council for the Management of Educational Technology (NW/MET). Learning Resources Center, Willamette University, 900 State St., Salem, OR 97301. (503) 370-6054. Fax (503) 370-6148. E-mail mmorandi@willamette.edu. Listserv NW-MET@willamette.edu. Kees Hof, Pres. Marti Morandi, Membership Chair. The first regional group representing institutions of higher education in Alberta, Alaska, British Columbia, Idaho, Montana, Oregon, Saskatchewan, and Washington to receive affiliate status in AECT. Membership is restricted to media managers with campus-wide responsibilities for educational technical services in the membership region. Corresponding membership is available to those who work outside the membership region. An annual conference and business meeting are held the last weekend of October each year, rotating throughout the region. Current issues under consideration include managing emerging telecommunication technologies, copyright, accreditation, and certification. Organizational goals include identifying the unique status problems of media managers in higher education and improving the quality of the major publication. *Membership:* approx. 85. *Dues:* $35. *Publications:* Two annual newsletters and a single *NW/MET Journal.*

Southeastern Regional Media Leadership Council (SRMLC). Auburn University, 3402 Haley Center, Auburn, AL 36849-5216. (334) 844-4291. Fax (334) 844-5785. E-mail bannosh@mail.auburn.edu. Susan Bannon, Dir. The purpose of the SRMLC is to strengthen the role of the individual state AECT affiliates with the Southeastern region; to seek positive change in the nature and status of instructional technology as it exists within the Southeast; to provide opportunities for the training and development of leadership for both the region and the individual affiliates; and to provide opportunities for the exchange of information and experience among those who attend the conference.

Other AECT-Related Organizations:

(AECT) Archives. University of Maryland at College Park, Hornbake Library, College Park, MD 20742. Thomas Connors, Archivist, National Public Broadcasting Archives. (301) 405-9988. Fax (301) 314-9419. A collection of media, manuscripts, and related materials representing important developments in visual and audiovisual education and in instructional/educational technology. The collection is housed as part of the National Public Broadcasting Archives. Maintained by the University of Maryland at College Park in cooperation with AECT. Open to researchers and scholars.

*(AECT) ECT Foundation. c/o AECT, 1025 Vermont Ave. NW, Suite 820, Washington, DC 20005. Hans-Erik Wennberg, Pres. The ECT Foundation is a nonprofit organization whose purposes are charitable and educational in nature. Its operation is based on the conviction that improvement of instruction can be accomplished, in part, by the continued investigation and application of new systems for learning and by periodic assessment of current techniques for the communication of information. In addition to awarding scholarships, internships, and fellowships, the foundation develops and conducts leadership training programs for emerging professional leaders.

Association for Experiential Education (AEE). 2885 Aurora Ave., Suite 28, Boulder, CO 80303-2252. (303) 440-8844 ext. 3. Fax (303) 440-9581. E-mail AEEMikal@Nile.com. Mikal Evan Belicove, Mgr. Membership Services. AEE is a not-for-profit, international, professional organization with roots in adventure education, committed to the development, practice, and evaluation of experiential learning in all settings. Our vision is to be a leading international organization for the development and application of experiential education principles and methodologies. Our intent is to create a just and compassionate world by transforming education and promoting positive social change. *Membership:* More than 2,000 members in over 25 countries. Membership consists of individuals and organizations with affiliations in education, recreation, outdoor adventure programming, mental health, youth service, physical education, management development training, corrections, programming for people with disabilities, and environmental education. *Dues:* $50-$250/yr. Types of membership are individual, family, corporate/organizational. *Meetings:* 1996, Annual AEE International Conference, Spokane, WA, September 26-29. Regional Conferences: Northwest, Willsonville, OR, February 29-March 3; Heartland, Marquette, MI, March 15-17; Southeast, Seabrook Isle, SC, March 29-31; Mid-South, Robbers Cave State Park, OK, April 11-14; Mid-Atlantic, Palmyra, VA, April 11-14; Northeast, Durham, NH, April 12-14; West and Rocky Mountain Regional Conferences, TBA. *Publications: Jobs Clearinghouse* (mo.); *The Journal of Experiential Education* (3/yr.); *Experience and the Curriculum; Adventure Therapy; Therapeutic Applications of Adventure Programming; Manual of Accreditation Standards for Adventure Programs; The Theory of Experiential Education, Third Edition; Experiential Learning in Schools and Higher Education; Ethical Issues in Experiential Education, Second Edition; Book of Metaphors, Volume II*; bibliographies, directories of programs and membership directory.

Association for Library and Information Science Education (ALISE). 4101 Lake Boone Tr., Suite 201, Raleigh, NC 27607. Penney DePas, CAE, Exec. Dir.   Seeks to advance education for library and information science and produces annual *Library and Information Science Education Statistical Report.* Open to professional schools offering graduate programs in library and information science; personal memberships open to educators employed in such institutions; other memberships available to interested individuals. *Membership:* 650 individuals, 85 institutions. *Dues:* institutional, $250 full; $150 associate; $75 international; personal, $60 full-time; $25 part-time, student, retired. *Publications: Journal of Education for Library and Information Science*; directory; *Library and Information Science Education Statistical Report; ALISE Alert* (newsletter).

Association for the Advancement of Computing in Education (AACE). P.O. Box 2966, Charlottesville, VA 22902. (804) 973-3987. Fax (804) 978-7449. E-mail aace@virginia.edu; http://aace@virginia.edu/aace. Gary H. Marks, Exec. Dir.; April Ballard, contact person. AACE is an international educational professional organization whose purpose is to bring professionals from around the world to share knowledge and ideas on research, development, and application in information technology and education. It publishes major journals, books, and CD-ROMs on the subject, and organizes major conferences. Members include educators at all levels, technology center coordinators, and administrators in business and industry. *Membership:* 5,000. *Dues:* Basic membership $65 includes one journal. *Meetings:* 1997: Society for Information Technology and Teacher Education International Conference, March 31-April 6, Orlando, FL; ED-MEDIA/ED-TELECOM 97, World Conferences on Educational Multimedia and Hypermedia and Educational Telecommunications, June 14-19, Calgary, AB, Canada; AI-ED 97, World Conference on Artificial Intelligence in Education, August 19-22, Kobe, Japan; WEBNET 97, World Conference of the Web Society, dates in October TBA, Toronto, ON, Canada; ICCE 97, International Conference on Computers in

Education (Asia-Pacific Chapter), dates in December TBA, Kuching, Malaysia. *Publications: Educational Technology Review* (3/yr.); *Journal of Educational Multimedia and Hypermedia* (q.); *International Journal of Educational Telecommunications* (q.); *Journal of Computers in Mathematics and Science Teaching* (q.); *Journal of Technology and Teacher Education* (q.); *Journal of Artificial Intelligence in Education* (q.); *Journal of Computing in Childhood Education* (q.). A catalog of books and CD-ROMs is available on request.

Association of American Publishers (AAP). 1718 Connecticut Ave. NW, Washington, DC 20009. (202) 232-3335. Fax (202) 745-0694. E-mail 250-5318@mcimail.com; 71 Fifth Ave., New York, NY 10003. (212) 255-0200. Fax (202) 255-7007. Nicholas A. Veliotes, Pres. (DC); Judith Platt, Dir., Communications and PA (DC). AAP is the principal trade association of the book publishing industry. Association members publish hardcover and paperback books in every field, including general fiction and nonfiction; poetry; children's books; textbooks; Bibles and other religious books; reference works; scientific, medical, technical, professional and scholarly books and journals; and classroom instructional and testing materials. They also produce computer software and electronic products and services, such as online databases, CD-ROM, and CD-I. AAP has five divisions: Trade Division, School Division (K-12), Higher Education Division, Professional and Scholarly Publishing Division, and International Division. The Association's highest priorities are expending domestic and foreign markets for American books, journals, and electronic publishing products; promoting the status of publishing in the United States and abroad; defending intellectual freedom at home and the freedom of written expression worldwide; keeping AAP members informed on legislative, regulatory, and policy issues* that affect our industry and serving as the industry's voice on these issues; and protecting the rights of creators through ongoing efforts in defense of copyright. [*Key issues include copyright, postal rates and regulations, First Amendment concerns, international freedom to publish, tax and trade policy, education and library funding, literacy, and new technology.] *Membership:* 200 corporate members—regular membership; university press associate; not-for-profit associate; affiliate membership. *Meetings:* 1996, Annual Meeting, Palm Beach, FL, March; for divisional annual meetings, contact Communications and Public Affairs Dept., (202) 232-3335, ext. 236. *Publications: Book Publishing and the First Amendment* (AAP DC); *Annual Industry Statistics* (NY office); *New Media Market Trends Survey* (AAP DC); *Copyright Management and the NII* (AAP DC). Contact Communications and Public Affairs for a current list of publications.

Association of Independent Video and Filmmakers/Foundation for Independent Video and Film (AIVF/FIVF). 304 Hudson St., 6th Floor, New York, NY 10013. (212) 807-1400. Fax (212) 463-8519. Ruby Lerner, Exec. Dir. The national trade association for independent video and filmmakers, representing their needs and goals to industry, government, and the public. Programs include screenings and seminars, insurance for members and groups, and information and referral services. Recent activities include advocacy for public funding of the arts, public access to new telecommunications systems, and monitoring censorship issues. *Dues:* $45 individuals, $75 libraries, $100 nonprofit organizations, $150 business/industry, $25 students. *Publications: The Independent Film and Video Monthly; The AIVF Guide to International Film and Video Festivals; The AIVF Guide to Film and Video Distributors; The Next Step: Distributing Independent Films and Videos; Alternative Visions: Distributing Independent Media in a Home Video World; Directory of Film and Video Production Resources in Latin America and the Caribbean.*

*Association of Systematics Collections (ASC). 730 11th St. NW, 2d Floor, Washington, DC 20001. (202) 347-2850. Fax (202) 347-0072. K. Elaine Hoagland, Exec. Dir. Fosters the care, management, and improvement of biological collections and promotes their utilization. Institutional members include private, free-standing museums, botanical gardens, zoos, college and university museums, and public institutions, including state biological surveys, agricultural research centers, the Smithsonian Institution, and the U.S. National Biological Survey. The ASC also represents affiliate societies, keeps members informed about funding and legislative issues, and provides technical consulting for such subjects as collection permits, care of collections, and taxonomic expertise. *Membership:* 82 institutions, 22 societies, 1,200 newsletter subscribers. *Dues:* Depend on the size of collections. *Publications: ASC Newsletter* (for members and nonmember subscribers, bi-mo.); *Guidelines for Institutional Policies and Planning in Natural History Collections; Biogeography of the Tropical Pacific; Collections of Frozen Tissues; Guidelines for Institutional Database Policies.*

Cable in the Classroom. 1900 N. Beauregard St., Suite 108, Alexandria, VA 22311. (703) 845-1400. Fax (703) 845-1409. E-mail cicbobbi@aol.com. Dr. Bobbi L. Kamil, Exec. Dir. Cable in the Classroom is the cable industry's $400 million public service initiative to enrich education. It provides free cable connections to more than 70,000 schools (approximately 70% of all public and private schools K-12), reaching more than 85% of all U.S. students with commercial-free, quality educational programming. It also provides curriculum-related support materials for its programming and conducts Teacher Training and Media Literacy workshops throughout the country. *Membership:* Cable in the Classroom is a consortium of more than 75 multiple system operators, more than 8,400 local cable companies, and 32 national cable programming networks. *Meetings:* Cable in the Classroom exhibited at 12 major education conferences in 1996. *Publications: "Delivering the Future": Cable and Education Partnerships for the Information Age* (Dr. Bobbi Kamil); *Cable in the Classroom Magazine* (mo.); *"Taking Charge of Your TV": A Guide to Critical Viewing for Parents and Children* (booklet, available on request).

Catholic Library Association (CLA). St. Joseph's Central High School, 22 Maplewood Ave., Pittsfield, MA 01201-4780. (413) 443-2CLA. Fax (413) 442-7020. E-mail jbostley@k12.oit. wmass.edu. Sr. Jean R. Bostley, SSJ, Pres. and Exec. Dir. Provides educational programs, services, and publications for Catholic libraries and librarians. *Membership:* approx. 1,000. *Dues:* $45 individuals; special rates for students and retirees. *Meetings:* Meetings are held in conjunction with the National Catholic Educational Association: 1996, April 9-12, Philadelphia, PA; 1997, April 1-4, Minneapolis, MN; 1998, April 14-17, Los Angeles, CA; 1999, April 6-9, New Orleans, LA. *Publications: Catholic Library World* (q.); *Catholic Periodical and Literature Index* (q. with annual cumulations).

*Center for Children and Technology. Education Development Center, Inc., 96 Morton St., New York, NY 10014. (212) 222-6700. Dr. Jan Hawkins, Dir. One of 25 university-based national education and development centers supported by the Office of Educational Research and Improvement (OERI) in the U.S. Office of Education to help strengthen student learning in the United States. These centers conduct research on topics that will help policy makers, practitioners, and parents meet the national education goals by the year 2000. In addition to addressing specific topics, most of these centers focus on children at risk. Many are also cooperating with other universities, and many work with elementary and secondary schools. All have been directed by OERI to make sure the information they produce reaches parents, teachers, and others who can use it to make meaningful changes in America's schools.

Children's Television International (CTI)/GLAD Productions, Inc. 14512 Lee Road, Chantilly, VA 22021. (703) 502-3006; (800) CTI-GLAD (284-4523). Fax (703) 502-3009. Ray Gladfelter, Pres. and Dir. of Customer Services. An educational organization that develops, produces, and distributes a wide variety of color television and video programming and related publications as a resource to aid the social, cultural, and intellectual development of children and young adults. Program areas cover language arts, science, social studies, history, and art for home, school, and college viewing. *Publications: The History Game: A Teacher's Guide;* other teacher guides for instructional series; and a complimentary catalog for educational videos.

CINE. 1001 Connecticut Ave. NW, Suite 638, Washington, DC 20036. (202) 785-1136. Fax (202) 785-4114. Christine Reilly, Exec. Dir. CINE coordinates the selection and placement of documentary, instructional, informational, and interactive films and videos in 100 international competitions and festivals annually. Approximately 1,200 entries are received each year; of these, about 25% are selected for awards. Professional productions receive the Golden Eagle and productions by pre-professionals and amateurs receive the Eagle. *Meeting:* 1996, CINE Showcase and Awards, February 29-March 1, Washington, DC. *Publications: 1995-96 Worldwide Directory of Film and Video Festivals and Events*; *CINE Annual Yearbook of Film and Video Awards*.

*Clearinghouse on Development Communication. 1815 N. Fort Myer Dr., 6th Floor, Arlington, VA 22209. (703) 527-5546. Fax (703) 527-4661. Valerie Lamont, Acting Dir. A center for materials and information on applications of communication technology to development problems. Operated by the Institute for International Research and funded by the Bureau for Research and Development of the U.S. Agency for International Development. Visitors and written requests for information are welcome, and an electronic bulletin board, CDCNET, is available to individuals with computer communications software and modems. *Dues:* Subscription, $10. *Publications: Development Communication Report* (q.); other special reports, information packages, project profiles, books, bulletins, and videotapes.

*Close Up Foundation. 44 Canal Center Plaza, Alexandria, VA 22314. (703) 706-3300; (800) 765-3131. Fax (703) 706-0002. Stephen A. Janger, Pres. A nonprofit, nonpartisan civic education organization promoting informed citizen participation in public policy and community service. Programs reach more than a million participants a year. *Publications: Current Issues*; *The Bill of Rights: A User's Guide*; *Perspectives*; *International Relations*; *The American Economy*; documentary videotapes on domestic and foreign policy issues. Close Up brings 24,000 secondary and middle school students and teachers and older Americans each year to Washington for week-long government studies programs, and produces television programs on the C-SPAN cable network for secondary school and home audiences.

Computer Using Educators, Inc. (CUE). 1210 Marina Village Parkway, Suite 100, Alameda, CA 94501. (510) 814-6630. Fax (520) 814-0195. E-mail cueinc@aol.com. Gloria Gibson, Dir. of Program Development. CUE, a California non-profit corporation, was founded in 1976 by a group of teachers interested in exploring the use of technology to improve learning in their classrooms. The organization has never lost sight of this mission. Today it has an active membership of 10,000 professionals world-wide in school, community colleges, colleges, and universities. CUE's 23 affilitates in California provide members with local year-round support through meetings, grants, events, and mini-conferences. SIGs support members interested in a variety of special topics. CUE's annual conference, newsletter, advocacy, web page, and other programs help the technology-using educator connect with other professionals. *Membership:* 10,000 including individual, corporate, and institutional members. *Dues:* $30/yr. *Meetings:* 1996, Spring Conference, May 9-11, Palm Springs, CA, "Building Blocks for the Future"; Fall Conference, October 24-26, Santa Clara, CA, "Elect Technology: Platform for the Future." *Publication: CUE Newsletter*.

Consortium of College and University Media Centers. 121 Pearson Hall-MRC, Iowa State University, Ames, IA 50011-2203. (515) 294-1811. Fax (515) 294-8089. E-mail donrieck@iastate. edu; ccumc@ccumc.org. Don Rieck, Exec. Dir. A professional group of higher education media personnel whose purpose is to improve education and training through the effective use of educational media. Assists educational and training users in making films, video, and educational media more accessible. Fosters cooperative planning among university media centers. Gathers and disseminates information on improved procedures and new developments in instructional technology and media center management. *Membership:* 400. *Dues:* $160/yr. constituents; $60 active; $160 sustaining (commercial); $25 students; $100 associates. *Meetings:* 1996, Spring Conference, April 12-14, San Diego, CA; Fall Conference, October 18-22, Kansas City, MO. 1997, Spring Conference, April 18-20, Dallas, TX. *Publications: Leader* (newsletter to members); *University and College Media Review* (journal).

*Council for Basic Education. 1319 F St. NW, Suite 900, Washington, DC 20004-1152. (202) 347-4171. Fax (202) 347-5047. Christopher T. Cross, Pres. CBE's mission is to strengthen teaching and learning of the basic subjects—English, history, government, geography, mathematics, the sciences, foreign languages, and the arts—in order to develop the capacity for lifelong learning and foster responsible citizenship. CBE advocates this goal by publishing analytical periodicals and administering practical operational programs as examples to strengthen content in curriculum and teaching at the pre-college level. The Council also sponsors independent summer study fellowship programs for teachers in the humanities, arts, and sciences, and is currently involved in offering program assistance to school districts who are setting curriculum standards in academic subjects consonant with Goals 2000. *Membership:* 4,000. *Dues:* $100 Friends; $40 members; $25/yr. subscribers. *Publications: Basic Education* (monthly periodical on educational issues); *Perspective* (quarterly that treats current educational issues in depth).

*Council for Educational Development and Research (CEDaR). 2000 L St. NW, Suite 601, Washington, DC 20036. (202) 223-1593. Dena G. Stoner, Exec. Dir. Members are educational research and development institutions. Aims to advance the level of programmatic, institutionally based educational research and development and to demonstrate the importance of research and development in improving education. Provides a forum for professional personnel in member institutions. Coordinates national dissemination program. Other activities include research, development, evaluation, dissemination, and technical assistance on educational issues. *Membership:* 15. *Publication: R&D Preview.*

Council for Exceptional Children (CEC). 1920 Association Dr., Reston, VA 22091. (703) 620-3660. Fax (703) 264-9494. Nancy Safer, Interim Exec. Dir. An international professional membership organization dedicated to improving educational outcomes for individuals with exceptionalities—those with disabilities and/or those who are gifted. Maintains a library and database on literature on special education; prepares books, monographs, digests, films, cassettes, and journals; sponsors annual conventions and conferences on special education; provides on-site and regional training on various topics and at varying levels; provides information and assistance to lawmakers on the education of individuals with disabilities and those who are gifted; coordinates a political action network on the rights of exceptional persons. *Membership:* 55,000. *Dues:* Professionals, $69-77, depending on state of residence; students, $30-30.50, depending on state of residence. *Publications: Exceptional Children; Teaching Exceptional Children; Exceptional Child Educational Resources;* numerous other professional publications dealing with the education of exceptional individuals. (*See also* the ERIC Clearinghouse on Disabilities and Gifted Education.)

> **(CEC) Technology and Media Division (TAM)**. Council for Exceptional Children. The Technology and Media Division (TAM) of The Council for Exceptional Children (CEC) encourages the development of new applications, technologies, and media for use as daily living tools by special populations. This information is disseminated through professional meetings, training programs, and publications. TAM members receive four issues annually of the *Journal of Special Education Technology* containing articles on specific technology programs and applications, and five issues of the TAM newsletter, providing news of current research, developments, products, conferences, and special programs information. *Membership:* 1,700. *Dues:* $10 in addition to CEC membership.

Council on International Non-theatrical Events (CINE). See listing for CINE.

East-West Center. 1777 East-West Rd., Honolulu, HI 96848. (808) 944-7666. Fax (808) 944-7333. E-mail culture@ewc. Kenji Sumida, Pres.; Grant Otoshi, Adminis. Officer. The U.S. Congress established the East-West Center in 1960 with a mandate to foster mutual understanding and cooperation among the governments and peoples of Asia, the Pacific, and the United States. Officially known as the Center for Cultural and Technical Interchange Between East and West, it is a public, non-profit institution with an international board of governors. Principal funding for the center comes from the U.S. government, with additional support provided by private agencies, individuals, and corporations, and more than 20 Asian and Pacific governments, private agencies, individuals, and corporations. The center, through research, education, dialog, and outreach, provides a neutral meeting ground where people with a wide range of perspectives exchange views on topics of regional concern. Some 2,000 scholars, government and business leaders, educators, journalists, and other professionals from throughout the region annually work with Center staff to address issues of contemporary significance in such areas as international economics and politics, the environment, population, energy and mineral resources, cultural studies, communications, the media, and Pacific islands development.

Education Development Center, Inc. 55 Chapel St., Newton, MA 02160. (617) 969-7100. Fax (617) 244-3436. Janet Whitla, Pres. Seeks to improve education at all levels, in the United States and abroad, through curriculum development, institutional development, and services to the school and the community. Produces filmstrips and videocassettes, primarily in connection with curriculum development and teacher training. *Publications: Annual Report*; *EDC News* (newsletter, 2/yr.).

Educational Film Library Association. See listing for American Film and Video Association (AFVA).

Eisenhower National Clearinghouse for Mathematics and Science Education. 1929 Kenny Road, Columbus, OH 43210-1079. (800) 621-5785; (614) 292-7784. Fax (614) 292-2066. E-mail info@enc.org. Dr. Len Simutis, Dir. The Eisenhower National Clearinghouse for Mathematics and Science Education (ENC) is located at The Ohio State University and funded by the U.S. Department of Education's Office of Educational Research and Improvement (OERI). ENC provides K-12 teachers and other educators a central source of information on mathematics and science curriculum materials, particularly those which support education reform. Among ENC's products and services are ENC Online, which is available through a toll-free number and via Internet; 12 demonstration sites located throughout the nation; and a variety of publications, including the *Guidebook to Excellence*, which lists federal resources in mathematics and science education. In 1996, ENC will produce CD-ROMs that include curriculum resources and the ENC Resource Finder, which is the same searchable catalog of curriculum resources that is found through ENC Online. *Membership:* Users include K-12 teachers, other educators, policy makers, and parents. *Publications: ENC Update* (newsletter); *ENC Focus* (print catalog on selected topics); *ENC Online Brochure*; *Guidebook to Excellence* (federal programs in mathematics and science education). ENC Online is available online via a toll-free number (1-800-362-4448) or via Internet at enc.org.

*EPIE Institute (Educational Products Information Exchange). 103 W. Montauk Highway, Hampton Bays, NY 11946. (516) 728-9100. Fax (516) 728-9228. E-mail komoski@ bnlcl6.bnl.gov. P. Kenneth Komoski, Exec. Dir. Involved primarily in assessing educational materials and providing product descriptions/citations of virtually all educational software. All of EPIE's services, including its Curriculum Alignment Services for Educators, are available to schools and state agencies as well as individuals. *Publications: The Educational Software Selector (T.E.S.S.)* (annual); *The Educational Software Selector Database: TESS*, available to members of the States Consortium for Improving Software Selection.

ERIC (Educational Resources Information Center). National Library of Education (NLE), Office of Educational Research and Improvement (OERI), 555 New Jersey Ave. NW, Washington, DC 20208-5720. (202) 219-2289. Fax (202) 219-1817. Internet eric@inet.ed.gov. Keith Stubbs, Dir. ERIC is a federally-funded nationwide information network that provides access to the English-language education literature. The ERIC system consists of 16 Clearinghouses, 9 Adjunct Clearinghouses, and system support components that include ACCESS ERIC, the ERIC Document Reproduction Service (EDRS), and the ERIC Processing and Reference Facility. ERIC actively solicits papers, conference proceedings, literature reviews, and curriculum materials from researchers, practitioners, educational associations and institutions, and federal, state, and local agencies. These materials, along with articles from nearly 800 different journals, are indexed and abstracted for entry into the ERIC database. The ERIC database—the largest education database in the world—now contains more than 850,000 records of documents and journal articles. Users can access the ERIC database online, on CD-ROM, or through print and microfiche indexes. ERIC microfiche collections, which contain the full text of most ERIC documents, are available for public use at more than 1,000 locations worldwide. Reprints of ERIC documents, on microfiche or in paper copy, can also be ordered from EDRS. Copies of journal articles can be found in library periodical collections, through interlibrary loan, or from article reprint services. A list of the ERIC Clearinghouses, together with full addresses, telephone numbers, and brief scope notes describing the areas they cover, follows here. *Dues:* None. *Publications: Resources in Education* (U.S. Government Printing Office); *Current Index to Journals in Education* (Oryx Press).

ERIC Clearinghouse for Community Colleges (JC) (formerly Junior Colleges). University of California at Los Angeles (UCLA), 3051 Moore Hall, P.O. Box 95121, Los Angeles, CA 90024-1521. (310) 825-3931; (800) 832-8256. Fax (310) 206-8095. E-mail ericcc@ucla.edu. Arthur M. Cohen, Dir. Development, administration, and evaluation of two-year public and private community and junior colleges, technical institutes, and two-year branch university campuses. Two-year college students, faculty, staff, curricula, programs, support services, libraries, and community services. Linkages between two-year colleges and business/industrial/community organizations. Articulation of two-year colleges with secondary and four-year postsecondary institutions.

ERIC Clearinghouse for Social Studies/Social Science Education (SO). Indiana University, Social Studies Development Center, 2805 E. Tenth St., Suite 120, Bloomington, IN 47408-2698. (812) 855-3838; (800) 266-3815. Fax (812) 855-0455. E-mail ericso@indiana.edu. John Patrick, Dir. All levels of social studies and social science education; the contributions of history, geography, and other social science disciplines; applications of theory and research to social science education; education as a social science; comparative education (K-12); content and curriculum materials on social topics such as law-related education, ethnic studies, bias and discrimination, aging, and women's equity. Music and art education are also covered. Includes input from the Adjunct ERIC Clearinghouses for Law-Related Education, for U.S.-Japan Studies, and on Art Education.

ERIC Clearinghouse on Adult, Career, and Vocational Education (CE). The Ohio State University, Center on Education and Training for Employment, 1900 Kenny Rd., Columbus, OH 43210-1090. (614) 292-4353; (800) 848-4815. Fax (614) 292-1260. E-mail ericacve@magnus.acs.ohio-state.edu. Susan Imel, Dir. All levels and settings of adult and continuing, career, and vocational/technical education. Adult education, from basic literacy training through professional skill upgrading. Career awareness, career decision making, career development, career change, and experience-based education. Vocational and technical education, including new subprofessional fields, industrial arts, corrections education, employment and training programs, youth employment, work experience programs, education/business partnerships, entrepreneurship, adult retraining, and vocational rehabilitation for individuals with disabilities. Includes input from the Adjunct ERIC Clearinghouse on Consumer Education.

ERIC Clearinghouse on Assessment and Evaluation (TM) (formerly Tests, Measurement and Evaluation). The Catholic University of America, 210 O'Boyle Hall, Washington, DC 20064-4035. (202) 319-5120; (800) 464-3742. Fax (202) 319-6692. E-mail eric_ae@cua.edu. Lawrence M. Rudner, Dir. Tests and other measurement devices; methodology of measurement and evaluation; application of tests, measurement, or evaluation in educational projects and programs; research design and methodology in the area of assessment and evaluation; and learning theory. Includes input from the Adjunct Test Collection Clearinghouse.

ERIC Clearinghouse on Counseling and Student Services (CG) (formerly Counseling and Personnel Services). University of North Carolina at Greensboro, School of Education, 101 Park Building, Greensboro, NC 27412-5001. (919) 334-4114; (800) 414-9769. Fax (919) 334-4116. E-mail ericcass@iris.uncg.edu. Garry R. Walz, Dir. Preparation, practice, and supervision of counselors at all educational levels and in all

settings; theoretical development of counseling and student services; personnel procedures such as testing and interviewing and the analysis and dissemination of the resultant
information; group and case work; nature of pupil, student, and adult characteristics;
and personnel workers and their relation to career planning, family consultations, and
student orientation activities.

ERIC Clearinghouse on Disabilities and Gifted Education (EC) (formerly Handicapped and Gifted Children). Council for Exceptional Children (CEC), 1920 Association Dr., Reston, VA 22091-1589. (703) 264-9474; (800) 328-0272. Fax (703)
264-9494. E-mail ericec@inet.ed.gov. Sheila Mingo, Dir. All aspects of the education
and development of the disabled and gifted, including identification, assessment, intervention, and enrichment, both in special settings and within the mainstream.

ERIC Clearinghouse on Educational Management (EA). University of Oregon
(Dept. 5207), 1787 Agate St., Eugene, OR 97403-5207. (503) 346-5043; (800) 438-
8841. Fax (503) 346-2334. E-mail ppiele@oregon.uoregon.edu. Philip K. Piele, Dir.
The leadership, management, and structure of public and private education organizations;
practice and theory of administration; preservice and inservice preparation of administrators; tasks and processes of administration; methods and varieties of organization and organizational change; and the social context of education organizations.
Sites, buildings, equipment for education; planning, financing, constructing, renovating,
equipping, maintaining, operating, insuring, utilizing, and evaluating educational
facilities.

ERIC Clearinghouse on Elementary and Early Childhood Education (PS). University of Illinois, 805 W. Pennsylvania Ave., Urbana, IL 61801-4897. (217) 333-1386;
(800) 583-4135. Fax (217) 333-3767. E-mail ericeece@uiuc.edu. Lilian G. Katz, Dir.
The physical, cognitive, social, educational, and cultural development of children from
birth through early adolescence; prenatal factors; parents, parenting, and family relationships that impinge on education; learning theory research and practice related to the
development of young children, including the preparation of teachers for this educational level; interdisciplinary curriculum and mixed-age teaching and learning; educational, social, and cultural programs and services for children; the child in the context
of the family and the family in the context of society; theoretical and philosophical issues
pertaining to children's development and education. Includes input from the Adjunct
ERIC Clearinghouse for Child Care.

ERIC Clearinghouse on Higher Education (HE). George Washington University, One
Dupont Cir. NW, Suite 630, Washington, DC 20036-1183. (202) 296-2597; (800)
773-3742. Fax (202) 296-8379. E-mail eriche@inet.ed.gov. Jonathan D. Fife, Dir.
Topics relating to college and university conditions, problems, programs, and students.
Curricular and instructional programs, and institutional research at the college or
university level. Federal programs, professional education (medicine, law, etc.), professional continuing education, collegiate computer-assisted learning and management,
graduate education, university extension programs, teaching and learning, legal issues
and legislation, planning, governance, finance, evaluation, interinstitutional arrangements, management of institutions of higher education, and business or industry educational programs leading to a degree.

ERIC Clearinghouse on Information & Technology (IR) (formerly Information
Resources). Syracuse University, 4-194 Center for Science and Technology, Syracuse,
NY 13244-4100. (315) 443-3640; (800) 464-9107. Fax (315) 443-5448. E-mail
eric@ericir.syr.edu. AskERIC (question-answering service via Internet) askeric@ericir.
syr.edu. Michael B. Eisenberg, Dir. Educational technology and library and information
science at all levels. Instructional design, development, and evaluation within educational technology, along with the media of educational communication: computers and
microcomputers, telecommunications, audio and video recordings, film and other

audiovisual materials as they pertain to teaching and learning. The focus is on the operation and management of information services for education-related organizations. Includes all aspects of information technology related to education.

ERIC Clearinghouse on Languages and Linguistics (FL). Center for Applied Linguistics, 1118 22d St. NW, Washington, DC 20037-0037. (202) 429-9292; (800) 276-9834. Fax (202) 659-5641. E-mail eric@cal.org. Joy Peyton, Dir. Languages and language sciences. All aspects of second language instruction and learning in all commonly and uncommonly taught languages, including English as a second language. Bilingualism and bilingual education. Cultural education in the context of second language learning, including intercultural communication, study abroad, and international education exchange. All areas of linguistics, including theoretical and applied linguistics, sociolinguistics, and psycholinguistics. Includes input from the Adjunct ERIC Clearinghouse on Literacy Education.

ERIC Clearinghouse on Reading, English, and Communication (CS) (formerly Reading and Communication Skills). Indiana University, Smith Research Center, Suite 150, 2805 E. 10th St., Bloomington, IN 47408-2698. (812) 855-5847; (800) 759-4723. Fax (812) 855-4220. E-mail ericcs@ucs.indiana.edu. Carl B. Smith, Dir. Reading, English, and communication (verbal and nonverbal), preschool through college; research and instructional development in reading, writing, speaking, and listening; identification, diagnosis, and remediation of reading problems; speech communication (including forensics), mass communication, interpersonal and small group interaction, interpretation, rhetorical and communication theory, speech sciences, and theater. Preparation of instructional staff and related personnel. All aspects of reading behavior with emphasis on physiology, psychology, sociology, and teaching; instructional materials, curricula, tests/measurement, and methodology at all levels of reading; the role of libraries and other agencies in fostering and guiding reading; diagnostics and remedial reading services in schools and clinical settings. Preparation of reading teachers and specialists.

ERIC Clearinghouse on Rural Education and Small Schools (RC). Appalachia Educational Laboratory (AEL), 1031 Quarrier St., P.O. Box 1348, Charleston, WV 25325-1348. (304) 347-0465; (800) 624-9120. Fax (304) 347-0487. E-mail lanhamb@ael.org. Craig Howley, Dir. Economic, cultural, social, or other factors related to educational programs and practices for rural residents; American Indians/Alaska Natives, Mexican Americans, and migrants; educational practices and programs in all small schools; and outdoor education.

ERIC Clearinghouse on Science, Mathematics, and Environmental Education (SE). Ohio State University, 1929 Kenny Road, Columbus, OH 43210-1080. (614) 292-6717; (800) 276-0462. Fax (614) 292-0263. E-mail ericse@osu.edu. David L. Haury, Dir. Science, mathematics, and environmental education at all levels, and within these three broad subject areas, the following topics: development of curriculum and instruction materials; teachers and teacher education; learning theory/outcomes (including the impact of parameters such as interest level, intelligence, values, and concept development upon learning in these fields); educational programs; research and evaluative studies; media applications; computer applications.

ERIC Clearinghouse on Teaching and Teacher Education (SP) (formerly Teacher Education). American Association of Colleges for Teacher Education (AACTE), One Dupont Cir. NW, Suite 610, Washington, DC 20036-1186. (202) 293-2450; (800) 822-9229. Fax (202) 457-8095. E-mail ericsp@inet.ed.gov. Mary E. Dilworth, Dir. School personnel at all levels. Teacher recruitment, selection, licensing, certification, training, preservice and inservice preparation, evaluation, retention, and retirement. The theory, philosophy, and practice of teaching. Curricula and general education not specifically covered by other clearinghouses. Organization, administration, finance, and legal issues relating to teacher education programs and institutions. All aspects of health, physical, recreation, and dance education. Includes input from the Adjunct ERIC Clearinghouse on Clinical Schools.

ERIC Clearinghouse on Urban Education (UD). Teachers College, Columbia University, Institute for Urban and Minority Education, Main Hall, Rm. 303, Box 40, 525 W. 120th St., New York, NY 10027-9998. (212) 678-3433; (800) 601-4868. Fax (212) 678-4012. E-mail eric-cue@columbia.edu. Erwin Flaxman, Dir. Programs and practices in public, parochial, and private schools in urban areas and the education of particular racial/ethnic minority children and youth in various settings—local, national, and international; the theory and practice of educational equity; urban and minority experiences; and urban and minority social institutions and services.

ACCESS ERIC. Aspen Systems Corp., 1600 Research Blvd., Rockville, MD 20850-3172; 1-800-LET-ERIC [538-3742]. Fax (301) 309-2084. E-mail acceric@inet.ed.gov. Beverly Swanson, ERIC Project Exec. ACCESS ERIC coordinates ERIC's outreach and systemwide dissemination activities; develops new ERIC publications; and provides general reference and referral services. Its publications include several reference directories designed to help the public understand and use ERIC as well as provide information about current education-related issues, research, and practice. *Publications: A Pocket Guide to ERIC*; *All About ERIC*; *The ERIC Review*; the Conclusion Brochure series; *Catalog of ERIC Clearinghouse Publications*; *ERIC Calendar of Education-Related Conferences*; *ERIC User's Interchange*; *Directory of ERIC Information Service Centers*. *Databases*: ERIC Digests Online (EDO); Education-Related Information Centers; ERIC Information Service Providers; ERIC Calendar of Education-Related Conferences. (The databases are available through GTE Education Services on a subscription basis.)

> **Adjunct ERIC Clearinghouse for Art Education**. Indiana University, Social Studies Development Center, 2805 East 10th St., Suite 120, Bloomington, IN 47408-2698. (812) 855-3838; (800) 266-3815. Fax (812) 855-0455. E-mail clarkgil@indiana.edu; zimmerm@ucs.indiana.edu. Gilbert Clark and Enid Zimmerman, Co-Directors. Adjunct to the ERIC Clearinghouse on Social Studies/Social Science Education.

> **Adjunct ERIC Clearinghouse for Consumer Education (ADJ/CN)**. National Institute for Consumer Education, 207 Rackham Bldg., West Cir. Dr., Eastern Michigan University, Ypsilanti, MI 48197-2237. (313) 487-2292; (800) 336-6423. Fax (313) 487-7153. E-mail nice@emuvax.emich.edu. Rosella Bannister, Dir. Adjunct to the ERIC Clearinghouse on Adult, Career, and Vocational Education.

> **Adjunct ERIC Clearinghouse for Child Care (ADJ/CC)**. Adjunct ERIC Clearinghouse for Child Care (ADJ/CC). National Child Care Information Center, 301 Maple Ave., Suite 602, Vienna, VA 22180. (703) 938-6555; (800) 616-2242. Fax (800) 716-2242. E-mail agoldstein@acf.dhhs.gov. Anne Goldstein, Proj. Dir. Adjunct to the ERIC Clearinghouse on Elementary and Early Childhood Education.

> **Adjunct ERIC Clearinghouse for ESL Literacy Education (ADJ/LE)**. National Clearinghouse for Literacy Education, Center for Applied Linguistics (CAL), 1118 22d St. NW, Washington, DC 20037-0037. (202) 429-9292, Ext. 200. Fax (202) 659-5641. E-mail ncle@cal.org. Joy Peyton, Dir. Adjunct to the ERIC Clearinghouse on Languages and Linguistics.

Adjunct ERIC Clearinghouse for Law-Related Education (ADJ/LR). Indiana University, Social Studies Development Center, 2805 East 10th St., Suite 120, Bloomington, IN 47408-2698. (812) 855-3838; (800) 266-3815. Fax (812) 855-0455. E-mail patrick@indiana.du; rleming@ucs.indiana.edu; temchkame@indiana.edu. John Patrick and Robert Leming, Co-Directors. Adjunct to the ERIC Clearinghouse on Social Studies/Social Sciences Education.

Adjunct ERIC Clearinghouse for the Test Collection (ADJ/TC). Educational Testing Service (ETS), ETS Test Collection, Rosedale and Carter Roads, Princeton, NJ 08541. (609) 734-5737. Fax (609) 683-7186. E-mail mhalpern@ets.org. Marilyn Halpern, Mgr., Library, Text Collection. Adjunct to the ERIC Clearinghouse on Assessment and Evaluation.

Adjunct ERIC Clearinghouse for United States-Japan Studies (ADJ/JS). Indiana University, Social Studies Development Center, 2805 E. 10th St., Suite 120, Bloomington, IN 47408-2698. (812) 855-3838; (800) 266-3815. Fax (812) 855-0455. E-mail eabrooks@indiana.edu. C. Frederick Risinger, Dir. Adjunct to the ERIC Clearinghouse on Social Studies/Social Science Education.

Adjunct ERIC Clearinghouse on Chapter 1 (Compensatory Education) (ADJ/CHP1). Chapter 1 Technical Assistance Center, PRC Inc., 2601 Fortune Cir. E., One Park Fletcher Bldg., Suite 300-A, Indianapolis, IN 46241-2237. (317) 244-8160; (800) 456-2380. Fax (317) 244-7386. E-mail prcinc@delphi.com. Jean M. Williams, Coord. Adjunct to the ERIC Clearinghouse on Urban Education.

Adjunct ERIC Clearinghouse on Clinical Schools (ADJ/CL). American Association of Colleges for Teacher Education, One Dupont Cir. NW, Suite 610, Washington, DC 20036-1186. (202) 293-2450; (800) 822-9229. Fax (202) 457-8095. E-mail iabdalha@inet.ed.gov. Ismat Abdal-Haqq, Coord. Adjunct to the ERIC Clearinghouse on Teaching and Teacher Education.

ERIC Document Reproduction Service (EDRS). 7420 Fullerton Rd., Suite 110, Springfield, VA 22153-2852. (703) 440-1400; (800) 443-ERIC (3742). Fax (703) 440-1408. E-mail edrs@inet.ed.gov. Peter M. Dagutis, Dir. Produces and sells microfiche and paper copies of documents abstracted in ERIC. Back collections of ERIC documents, annual subscriptions, cumulative indexes, and other ERIC-related materials are also available. ERIC documents can be ordered by toll-free phone call, fax, mail, or online (DIALOG, BRS, and OCLC).

ERIC Processing and Reference Facility. 1100 West Street, 2nd Floor, Laurel, MD 20707-3598. (301) 497-4080; (800) 799-ERIC (3742). Fax (301) 953-0263. E-mail ericfac@inet.ed.gov. Ted Brandhorst, Dir. A central editorial and computer processing agency that coordinates document processing and database building activities for ERIC; performs acquisition, lexicographic, and reference functions; and maintains systemwide quality control standards. The ERIC Facility also prepares *Resources in Education (RIE)*, ERIC Ready References, and other products.

Far West Laboratory for Educational Research and Development (FWL). See listing for WestEd.

*Federal Communications Commission (FCC). 1919 M St. NW, Washington, DC 20554. Patti Grace Smith, Deputy Dir. of Policy/Public Information and Reference Services. The FCC is a federal government agency regulating interstate and international communications by radio, television, wire, satellite, and cable in the United States and its territories and possessions. It allocates frequencies and channels for different types of communication activities, issues amateur and commercial radio operators' licenses, and regulates rates of many types of interstate communication services. Public Service Division: Consumer Assistance Branch

(202) 632-7000. Fax (202) 632-0274. TT (202) 632-6999. Public Policy Planning Branch (202) 632-0244. Martha Contee, Chief, Public Service Div. (PSD). *Publications:* Fact Sheets, Information Bulletins, and Public Notices pertaining to FCC-regulated services.

Film Arts Foundation (FAF). 346 9th St., 2d Floor, San Francisco, CA 94103. (415) 552-8760. Fax (415) 552-0882. Gail Silva, Dir. Service organization designed to support and promote independent film and video production. Services include low-cost 16mm and Super-8 editing facility, festivals file, resource library, group legal plan, association health options, seminars, workshops, annual film and video festival, grants program, monthly publication, work-in-progress screenings, proposal and distribution consultation, nonprofit sponsorship of selected film and video projects, and advocacy for independent film and video. *Membership:* 3,200 plus. *Dues:* $35. *Publications: Release Print*; *AEIOU (Alternative Exhibition Information of the Universe)*; *Media Catalog* (over 200 titles of independent media projects completed with FAF's nonprofit fiscal sponsorship).

George Eastman House (formerly International Museum of Photography at George Eastman House). 900 East Ave., Rochester, NY 14607. (716) 271-3361. Fax (716) 271-3970. Marianne Fullon, Acting Dir. World-renowned museum of photography and cinematography established to preserve, collect, and exhibit photographic art and technology, film materials, and related literature. Services include archives, traveling exhibitions, research library, center for the conservation of photographic materials, and photographic print service. Educational programs, films, symposia, and internship stipends offered. *Dues:* $40 libraries; $50 families; $40 individuals; $36 students; $30 senior citizens; $75 Contributors; $125 Sustainers; $250 Patrons; $500 Benefactors; $1,000 George Eastman Society. *Publications: IMAGE*; *Microfiche Index to Collections*; *Newsletter*; *Annual Report: The George Eastman House and Gardens*; *Masterpieces of Photography from the George Eastman House Collections*; and exhibition catalogues.

The George Lucas Educational Foundation. P.O. Box 3494, San Rafael, CA 94912. (415) 662-1600. Fax (415) 662-1605. E-mail edutopia@glef.org; America Online edutopia; gopher glef.org; URL http://glef.org. The Foundation was formed to create a vision of a technology-rich effective educational system. More than four years after its creation, the Foundation's current activities focus on spreading the word about the work that others are doing to improve teaching and learning. The focus is still on how the power of technology can best be harnessed in education, but the Foundation also champions other education reforms that many believe are critical. A documentary and a resource book are being developed to show what effective education looks like today around the country. The target audience is elected officials, corporate executives, community and opinion leaders, media, and parents. We hope to give educators useful tools as they work to change teaching and learning. Subscribers to the newsletter, *EDUTOPIA*, include educators, parents, the media, elected officials, corporate executives, community and opinion leaders. The work in which we are involved is targeted at the same diverse audience. The George Lucas Educational Foundation is a private operating foundation; it is not a grant-making organization. *Publication: EDUTOPIA* (bi-annual newsletter).

Great Plains National ITV Library (GPN). PO Box 80669, Lincoln, NE 68501-0669. (402) 472-2007; (800) 228-4630. Fax (402) 472-4076. E-mail gpn@unl.edu. Lee Rockwell, Dir. Acquires, produces, promotes, and distributes educational video series and singles. Offers more than 200 videotape (videocassette) courses and related teacher utilization materials. Available for purchase or, in some instances, lease. Also distributes instructional videodiscs and CD-ROMs. *Publications: GPN Educational Video Catalogs* by curriculum areas; periodic brochures.

Health Sciences Communications Association (HeSCA). One Wedgewood Dr., Suite 28, Jewett City, CT 06351-2428. (860) 376-5915. Fax (860) 376-6621. E-mail 75323.3163@compuserve.com. Ronald Sokolowski, EA. HeSCA is an international nonprofit organization dedicated to the promotion and sharing of ideas, skills, resources, and techniques to enhance communication and education in the health sciences. HeSCA is actively supported by leading medical and veterinary schools, hospitals, medical associations, and businesses. *Membership:* 150. *Dues:* $150 individual; $195 institutional ($150 additional institutional dues); $60 retirees; $75 students; $1,000 sustaining; (all include subscriptions to the journal and newsletter). *Meeting:* Health Sciences Communication Association, July 31-August 4, 1996, Milwaukee, WI. *Publications: Journal of Biocommunications; Feedback* (newsletter); *Patient Education Sourcebook Vol. II; 1995 Media Festivals and LRC Catalogue.*

Hollywood Film Archive. 8391 Beverly Blvd., #321, Hollywood, CA 90048. (213) 933-3345. D. D. Richard Baer, Dir. Archival organization for information about feature films produced worldwide, from the early silents to the present. Offers comprehensive movie reference works for sale, including *Variety Film Reviews* (1907-1994) and the *American Film Institute Catalogs* (1911-20, 1921-30, 1931-40, 1961-70), as well as the *Film Superlist* (1894-1939, 1940-1949, 1950-1959) volumes, which provide information both on copyrights and on motion pictures in the public domain, and *Harrison's Reports and Film Reviews* (1919-1962). *Publications:* Reference books.

HOPE Reports, Inc. 58 Carverdale Dr., Rochester, NY 14618-4004. (716) 442-1310. Fax (716) 442-1725. Thomas W. Hope, Pres., Chair, and CEO; Mabeth S. Hope, Vice Pres. Supplies statistics, marketing information, trends, forecasts, and salary and media studies to the visual communications industries in printed reports, in custom studies, or by consulting, or by telephone. Clients/users in the United States and abroad include manufacturers, dealers, producers, and media users in business, government, health sciences, education, and community agencies. *Publications: Hope Reports AV Events Calendar* (annual); *Hope Reports Industry Quarterly; Contract Production for the '90s; Video Post-Production; Media Market Trends; Educational Media Trends through the 1990's; LCD Panels and Projectors; Overhead Projection System; Presentation Slides; Producer & Video Post Wages & Salaries; Noncommercial AV Wages & Salaries; Corporate Media Salaries; Digital Photography: Pictures of Tomorrow; Hope Reports Top 100 Contract Producers.*

*International Association of Business Communicators (IABC). One Hallidie Plaza, Suite 600, San Francisco, CA 94102. (415) 433-3400. Fax (415) 362-8762. David Paulus, Pres. and CEO. IABC is the worldwide association for the communication and public relations profession. It is founded on the principle that the better an organization communicates with all its audiences, the more successful and effective it will be in meeting its objectives. IABC is dedicated to fostering communication excellence, contributing more effectively to organizations' goals worldwide, and being a model of communication effectiveness. *Membership:* 11,000 plus. *Dues:* $180 in addition to local and regional dues. *Meetings:* 1995, June 11-14, Toronto, ON; 1996, June 16-19, Dallas, TX. *Publication: Communication World.*

*International Association of School Librarianship (IASL). Box 19586, Kalamazoo, MI 49019. (616) 343-5728. Dr. Jean E. Lowrie, Exec. Sec. Seeks to encourage development of school libraries and library programs throughout the world, to promote professional preparation of school librarians and continuing education programs, to achieve collaboration among school libraries of the world, and to facilitate loans and exchanges in the field. *Membership:* 900 plus. *Dues:* $25/yr. personal and institution for North America, Western Europe, Japan, and Australia; $15/yr. for all other countries; $30-$100/yr. associations (based on membership). *Meetings:* July 17-22, 1995, Worcester, UK. *Publications: IASL Newsletter* (q.); *Annual Proceedings; Connections: School Library Associations and Contact People Worldwide; Indicators of Quality for School Library Media Programs; Books and Borrowers; School Libraries Worldwide; Conference Proceedings Index 1972-1984.*

International Center of Photography (ICP). 1130 Fifth Ave., New York, NY 10128. (212) 860-1777. Fax (212) 360-6490. ICP Midtown, 1133 Avenue of the Americas, New York, NY 10036. (212) 768-4680. Fax (212) 768-4688. Willis Hartshorn, Dir.; Phyllis Levine, Dir. of Public Information. A comprehensive photographic institution whose exhibitions, publications, collections, and educational programs embrace all aspects of photography from aesthetics to technique; from the 18th century to the present; from master photographers to newly emerging talents; from photojournalism to the avant garde. Changing exhibitions, lectures, seminars, workshops, museum shops, and screening rooms make ICP a complete photographic resource. ICP offers a two-year NYU-ICP Master of Arts Degree in Studio Art with Studies in Photography and one-year certificate programs in Documentary Photography and Photojournalism and General Studies in Photography. *Membership:* 5,800. *Dues:* $50 individual membership, $60 double membership, $125 Supporting Patron, $250 Photography Circle, $500 Silver Card Patron, $1,000 Gold Card Patron; corporate memberships available. *Meetings:* ICP Infinity Awards, April 1996. *Publications: A Singular Elegance: The Photographs of Baron Adolph de Meyer; Talking Pictures: People Speak about the Photographs That Speak to Them; Library of Photography; Encyclopedia of Photography Master Photographs from PFA Collection; Man Ray in Fashion; Quarterly Program Guide; Quarterly Exhibition Schedule.*

International Copyright Information Center (INCINC). c/o Association of American Publishers, 1718 Connecticut Ave. NW, 7th Floor, Washington, DC 20009-1148. (202) 232-3335. Fax (202) 745-0694. E-mail 250-5318@mcimail.com. Carol A. Risher, Dir. Assists developing nations in their efforts to secure permission to translate and/or reprint copyrighted works published in the United States.

International Council for Computers in Education (ICCE). See listing for International Society for Technology in Education (ISTE).

International Film and TV Festival of New York. See listing for The New York Festivals.

*International Information Management Congress (IMC). 1650 38th St., 205W, Boulder, CO 80301. (303) 440-7085. Fax (303) 440-7234. John A. Lacy, Pres. and CEO. Promote understanding and cooperation among organizations of the world engaged in furthering the progress and application of document-based information systems. Provide an international clearinghouse for information and advancement in systems and technology. Conduct conferences and exhibitions for the exchange of information. Provide document-based information through the publication of the *IMC Journal.* Encourage and assist in the establishment and use of document-based standards. *Membership:* 30 associations, 70 sustaining company members. *Dues:* $85/yr. affiliates (any individual with an interest in the document-based information systems field); $200 associate (any association or society with common goals within the industry); $350-$5,100/yr. sustaining (any corporate organization with a common interest in the industry; includes major computer companies, major photographic companies, and numerous smaller specialized companies). *Meeting:* 1996, "MC Document Imaging '96," June 3-6, Paris, France. *Publication: IMC Journal* (bi-mo.).

International Museum of Photography at George Eastman House. See listing for George Eastman House.

International Society for Performance Improvement (ISPI). 1300 L St. NW, Suite 1250, Washington, DC 20005. (202) 408-7969. Fax (202) 408-7972. Richard D. Battaglia, Exec. Dir. ISPI is an international association dedicated to increasing productivity in the workplace through the application of performance and instructional technologies. Founded in 1962, its members are located throughout the United States, Canada, and 30 other countries. The society offers an awards program recognizing excellence in the field. *Meetings:* The Annual Conference and Expo are held in the spring. *Membership:* 10,000. *Dues:* $125, active members; $40, students and retirees. *Meetings:* 1996, April 15-19, Dallas, TX; 1997, April 14-18, Anaheim, CA; 1998, March 23-28, Chicago, IL. *Publications: Performance & Instruction Journal* (10/yr.); *Performance Improvement Quarterly; News & Notes* (newsletter, 10/yr.); *Annual Membership Directory.*

*International Society for Technology in Education (ISTE) (formerly International Council for Computers in Education [ICCE]). 1787 Agate St., Eugene, OR 97403-1923. (503) 346-4414. Fax (503) 346-5890. Internet iste@oregon.uoregon.edu. David Moursund, CEO; Maia S.

Howes, Exec. Secy. The largest nonprofit professional organization dedicated to the improvement of all levels of education through the use of computer-based technology. Technology-using educators from all over the world rely on ISTE for information, inspiration, ideas, and updates on the latest electronic information systems available to the educational community. ISTE is a prominent information center and source of leadership to communicate and collaborate with educational professionals, policy makers, and other organizations worldwide. *Membership:* 12,000 individual members, 75 organizational affiliates, 25 Private Sector Council members. *Dues:* $55 individuals, $215 all-inclusive memberships (U.S.); $420 institutions; $1,500 to $5,000, Private Sector Council members. *Meeting:* 1995 National Educational Computing Conference (NECC '95), June 17-19, Baltimore, MD, "Emerging Technologies—Lifelong Learning." *Publications: Learning and Leading with Technology: The ISTE Journal of Educational Technology Practice and Policy* (formerly *The Computing Teacher*) (8/yr.); *The Update Newsletter* (7/yr.); *The Journal of Research on Computing in Education* (q.); guides to instructional uses of computers at the precollege level and in teacher training, about 80 books, and a range of distance education courses that carry graduate-level credit.

International Tape/Disc Association. See listing for ITA.

International Teleconferencing Association (ITCA). 1650 Tysons Blvd., Suite 200, McLean, VA 22102. (703) 506-3280. Fax (703) 506-3266. Fax on demand (800) 891-8633. E-mail dasitca@aol.com. Tom Gibson, Exec. Dir.; Christie Scott, Mgr., Publications and Programming. ITCA, an international nonprofit association, is dedicated to the growth and development of teleconferencing as a profession and an industry. ITCA provides programs and services which foster the professional development of its members; champions teleconferencing and related technologies as primary communications tools; recognizes and promotes broader applications and the development of teleconferencing and related technologies; and serves as the authoritative resource for information and research on teleconferencing and related technologies. *Membership:* ITCA represents over 1,900 teleconferencing professionals throughout the world. ITCA members use teleconferencing, manage business television and teleconferencing networks, design the technology, sell products and services, advise customers and vendors, conduct research, teach courses via teleconference, and teach about teleconferencing. They represent such diverse industry segments as health care, aerospace, government, pharmaceutical, education, insurance, finance and banking, telecommunications, and manufacturing. *Dues:* $2,000 gold sustaining; $1,000 sustaining; $500 organizational; $250 small business; $100 individual; and $30 student. *Meetings:* Annual trade show and convention: ITCA '96, May 21-24, Washington, DC (for more information, call (703) 506-3283). *Publications: ITCA Connections Newsletter* (mo.); *Videoconferencing Room Directory*; *Member Directory; Yearbook*; *Classroom of the Future*; *Teleconferencing in State Government Guide*; *Teleconferencing Success Stories*.

*****ITA** (formerly International Tape/Disc Association [ITA]). 505 Eighth Ave., New York, NY 10018. (212) 643-0620. Fax (212) 643-0624. Charles Van Horn, Exec. V.P.; Charles Riotto, Exec. Dir. of Operations. An international association providing a forum for the exchange of management information on global trends and innovations which drive the magnetic/optical recording media and associated industries. Members include magnetic and optical recording media manufacturers, rights holders to video programs, recording and playback equipment manufacturers, and audio and video duplicators/replicators. For more than 24 years, ITA has provided vital information and educational services throughout the magnetic and optical recording media industries. By promoting a greater awareness of marketing, merchandising, and technical developments, the association serves all areas of the entertainment, information, and delivery systems industries. *Membership:* 450 corporations. *Dues:* Corporate membership dues based on sales volume. *Meetings:* 25th Annual Seminar, March 8-12, 1995, Rancho Mirage, CA; REPLItech Europe, April 4-6, 1995, Vienna, Austria; REPLItech International, June 13-15, 1995, Santa Clara, CA; REPLItech Asia, October 24-26, 1995, Singapore. (REPLItech is a seminar and trade show aimed at duplicators and replicators of magnetic and optical media.) *Publications: ITA Membership Newsletter; Seminar Proceedings; 1995 International Source Directory.*

ITVA (International Television Association). 6311 N. O'Connor Rd., Suite 230, Irving, TX 75039. (214) 869-1112. Fax (214) 869-2980. Fred M. Wehrli, Exec. Dir. Founded in 1968, ITVA's mission is to advance the video profession, to serve the needs and interests of its members, and to promote the growth and quality of video and related media. Association members are video professionals working in or serving the corporate, governmental, institutional, or educational markets. ITVA provides professional development opportunities through local, regional, and national workshops, video festivals, and publications. The networking opportunities available to members are another principal benefit. ITVA welcomes anyone who is interested in professional video and is seeking to widen his/her horizons either through career development or networking. ITVA offers its members discounts on major medical insurance, production/liability insurance; hotel, car rental, and long distance telephone discounts; and a MasterCard program. The association is also a member of the Small Business Legislative Council. *Membership:* 9,000, 77 commercial member companies. *Dues:* $150 individuals; $425 organizational (includes 3 individuals); $1,750 commercial silver; $750 commercial bronze. *Meetings:* 1996, Annual International Conference, June 11-15, Philadelphia, PA (meetings are in conjunction with INFOCOMM International). *Publications: ITVA News* (6/yr.); *Membership Directory* (annual); *Handbook of Treatments; It's a Business First . . . and a Creative Outlet Second; Handbook of Forms; How To Survive Being Laid Off; Employment Tax Procedures: Classification of Workers Within the Television Commercial Production and Professional Video Communication Industries; A Report on the IRS Guidelines Classifying Workers in the Video Industry.*

*Library of Congress. James Madison Bldg., 101 Independence Ave. SE, Washington, DC 20540. (202) 707-5000. Fax (202) 707-1389. Contact the National Reference Service, (202) 707-5522. The Library of Congress is the major source of research and information for the Congress. In its role as the national library, it catalogs and classifies library materials in some 470 languages, distributes the data in both printed and electronic form, and makes its vast collections available through interlibrary loan and on-site to anyone over high school age. It contains the world's largest television and film archive, acquiring materials through gift, purchase, and copyright deposit. The collections of the Motion Picture, Broadcasting, and Recorded Sound Division include 994,188 moving images and 2,118,881 recordings. Bibliographic data in the computerized Library of Congress Information System is now available for online searching over the Internet. The Internet address for telnet (connecting) to LOCIS is locis.loc.gov. The numeric address is 140.147.254.3. In 1993, the library had 900,000 readers and visitors and performed 1,400,000 direct reference services. *Publications:* Listed in *Library of Congress Publications in Print* (free from Office Systems Services).

*Lister Hill National Center for Biomedical Communications. National Library of Medicine, 8600 Rockville Pike, Bethesda, MD 20894. (301) 496-4441. Fax (301) 402-0118. Harold M. Schoolman, M.D., Acting Dir. The center conducts research and development programs in three major categories: Computer and Information Science; Biomedical Image and Communications Engineering; and Educational Technology Development. Major efforts of the center include its involvement with the Unified Medical Language System (UMLS) project; research and development in the use of expert systems to embody the factual and procedural knowledge of human experts; research in the use of electronic technologies to distribute biomedical information not represented in text and in the storage and transmission of x-ray images over the Internet; and the development and demonstration of new educational technologies, including the use of microcomputer technology with videodisc-based images, for training health care professionals. A Learning Center for Interactive Technology serves as a focus for displaying new and effective applications of educational technologies to faculties and staff of health sciences educational institutions and other visitors, and health professions educators are assisted in the use of such technologies through training, demonstrations, and consultations.

Magazine Publishers of America (MPA). 919 Third Ave., 22nd Floor, New York, NY 10022. (212) 872-3700. Fax (212) 888-4217. Donald D. Kummerfeld, Pres. MPA is the trade association of the consumer magazine industry. MPA promotes the greater and more effective use of magazine advertising, with ad campaigns in the trade press and in MPA member magazines, presentations to advertisers and their ad agencies, and magazine days in cities around the United States. MPA runs educational seminars, conducts surveys of its members on a variety of topics, represents the magazine industry in Washington, D.C., maintains an extensive library on magazine publishing, and carries on other activities. *Membership:* 230 publishers representing more than 1,200 magazines. *Meetings:* American Magazine Conferences: 1996, October 13-16, Southampton Princess, Bermuda; 1997, October 23-26, Scottsdale Princess, AZ. *Publications: Newsletter of Consumer Marketing*; *Newsletter of Research*; *Newsletter of International Publishing*; *Magazine*; *Washington Newsletter*.

Medical Library Association (MLA). 6 N. Michigan Ave., Suite 300, Chicago, IL 60602. (312) 419-9094. Fax (312) 419-8950. E-mail info@mlahg.org; web site http://www.kumc. edu/mla/. Dr. Nana Bradley, Pres.; Carla J. Funk, Exec. Dir. MLA is a professional organization of 5,000 individuals and institutions in the health sciences information field, dedicated to fostering medical and allied scientific libraries, promoting professional excellence and leadership of its members, and exchanging medical literature among its members. *Membership:* 3,743 individuals, 1,281 institutions. *Dues:* $65-$110 individuals, $25 students; $175-$410 institutional dues depend on number of periodical subscriptions. *Meeting:* 1996, May 31-June 5, Kansas City, MO, "The Information Frontier." *Publications: MLA News* (newsletter, 10/yr.); *Bulletin of the Medical Library Association* (q.); monographs.

*Mid-continent Regional Educational Laboratory (McREL). 2550 S. Parker Rd., Suite 500, Aurora, CO 80014. (303) 337-0990. Fax (303) 337-3005. E-mail twaters@mcrel.org. J. Timothy Waters, Exec. Dir. One of 10 Office of Educational Research and Improvement (OERI) regional educational laboratories designed to help educators and policymakers solve educational problems in their schools. Using the best available information and the experience and expertise of professionals, McREL seeks to identify solutions to education problems, tries new approaches, furnishes research results, and provides training to teachers and administrators. McREL serves Colorado, Kansas, Missouri, Nebraska, North Dakota, South Dakota and Wyoming. Its specialty areas are curriculum, learning, and instruction. An affiliate organization, McREL Institute, works nationwide and markets curriculum products and training.

Museum of Modern Art, Circulating Film and Video Library. 11 W. 53d St., New York, NY 10019. (212) 708-9530. Fax (212) 708-9531. William Sloan, Libr. Sponsors film study programs and provides film and video rentals and sales. *Publications: Circulating Film and Video Catalog Vols. 1 and 2.*

National Aeronautics and Space Administration (NASA). NASA Headquarters, Code FE, Washington, DC 20546. (202) 358-1110. Fax (202) 358-3048. E-mail mphelps@hr.hq. nasa.gov. Dr. Malcom V. Phelps, Asst. Dir.; Frank C. Owens, Dir., Education Division. From elementary through postgraduate school, NASA's educational programs are designed to capture students' interests in science, mathematics, and technology at an early age; to channel more students into science, engineering, and technology career paths; and to enhance the knowledge, skills, and experiences of teachers and university faculty. NASA's educational programs include NASA Spacelink (an electronic information system); videoconferences (60-minute interactive staff development videoconferences to be delivered to schools via satellite); and NASA Television (informational and educational television programming). Additional information is available from the Education Division at NASA Headquarters and counterpart offices at the nine NASA field centers. Over 200,000 educators make copies of Teacher Resource Center Network materials each year, and thousands of teachers participate in interactive video teleconferencing, use Spacelink, and watch NASA Television. Additional information may be obtained from Spacelink (spacelink.msfc.nasa.gov or http://spacelink.msfc.nasa.gov).

National Alliance for Media Arts and Culture (NAMAC). 655 13th St., Suite 201, Oakland, CA 94612. (510) 451-2717. Fax (510) 451-2715. E-mail namac@aol.com. Julian Low, Dir. A nonprofit organization dedicated to increasing public understanding of and support for the field of media arts in the United States. Members include media centers, cable access centers, universities, and media artists, as well as other individuals and organizations providing services for production, education, exhibition, distribution, and preservation of video, film, audio, and intermedia. NAMAC's information services are available to the general public, arts and nonarts organizations, businesses, corporations, foundations, government agencies, schools, and universities. *Membership:* 200 organizations, 150 individuals. *Dues:* Institutional ranges from $50 to $250/yr. depending on annual budget; $30/yr. individual. *Publications: Media Arts Information Network; NAMAC Directory* (published biennially, available for $25 to nonmembers).

National Association for the Education of Young Children (NAEYC). 1509 16th St. NW, Washington, DC 20036-1426. (202) 232-8777; (800) 424-2460. Fax (202) 328-1846. Marilyn M. Smith, Exec. Dir.; Pat Spahr, contact person. Dedicated to improving the quality of care and education provided to young children (birth-8 years). *Membership:* Nearly 95,000. *Dues:* $25. *Meeting:* 1996 Annual Conference, November 20-23, Dallas, TX. *Publications: Young Children* (journal); more than 60 books, posters, videos, and brochures.

National Association for Visually Handicapped (NAVH). 22 W. 21st St., 6th Floor, New York, NY 10010. (212) 889-3141. Fax (212) 727-2931. Lorraine H. Marchi, Founder/Exec. Dir.; Eva Cohen, Asst. to Exec. Dir. (or) 3201 Balboa St., San Francisco, CA 94121. (415) 221-3201. Serves the partially sighted (not totally blind). Offers informational literature for the layperson and the professional, most in large print. Newsletters for adults *Seeing Clearly* and for children *In Focus* are published at irregular intervals and distributed free throughout the English-speaking world. Maintains a loan library of large-print books. Provides counseling and guidance for the visually impaired and their families and the professionals and paraprofessionals who work with them. *Membership:* 12,000. *Dues:* Full membership $40/yr. for individuals. *Publications: Visual Aids and Informational Material Catalog; Large Print Loan Library;* two newsletters; informational pamphlets on topics ranging from *Diseases of the Macula* to knitting and crochet instructions.

National Association of State Textbook Administrators (NASTA). Textbook Adoption Services, North Carolina Department of Public Instruction, 301 North Wilmington St., Raleigh, NC 27601-2825. (919) 715-1893. Fax (919) 715-2299. Ann Fowler, Pres. NASTA's purposes are (1) to foster a spirit of mutual helpfulness in adoption, purchase, and distribution of instructional materials; (2) to arrange for study and review of textbook specifications; (3) to authorize special surveys, tests, and studies; and (4) to initiate action leading to better quality instructional materials. Services provided include a working knowledge of text construction, monitoring lowest prices, sharing adoption information, identifying trouble spots, and discussions in the industry. The members of NASTA meet to discuss the textbook adoption process and to improve the quality of the instructional materials used in the elementary, middle, and high schools. NASTA is not affiliated with any parent organization and has no permanent address. Meetings are conducted with the American Association of Publishers and the Book Manufacturers' Institute. *Membership:* The textbook administrator from each of the 23 states that adopts textbooks at the state level. *Dues:* $25/yr. individual. *Publications:* none.

National Audiovisual Center (NAC). National Archives and Records Administration, 8700 Edgeworth Dr., Capitol Heights, MD 20743. (301) 763-1896; (800) 788-6282. Fax (301) 763-6025. George Ziener, Dir. Central information and distribution source for more than 8,000 audiovisual programs produced by or for the U.S. government. Materials are made available for sale or rent on a self-sustaining basis, at the lowest price possible. *Publications: Media Resource Catalog* (1991), listing 600 of the latest and most popular programs, is available free. Also available free are specific subject listings such as science, history, medicine, and safety and health. There is a free quarterly update that lists significant additions to the collection. A computer bulletin board has been available for information searches and production orders since late 1993.

The National Center for Improving Science Education. 2000 L St. NW, Suite 603, Washington, DC 20036. (202) 467-0652. Fax (202) 467-0659. BITNET info@ncise.org. Senta A. Raizen, Dir., 300 Brickstone Square, Suite 900, Andover, MA 01810. (508) 470-1080. (508) 475-9220. A division of The NETWORK, Inc. (a nonprofit organization dedicated to educational reform) that works to promote changes in state and local policies and practices in science curriculum, teaching, and assessment through research and development, evaluation, technical assistance, and dissemination. *Publications: Science and Technology Education for the Elementary Years: Frameworks for Curriculum and Instruction; Developing and Supporting Teachers for Elementary School Science Education; Assessment in Elementary School Science Education; Getting Started in Science: A Blueprint Elementary School Science Education; Elementary School Science for the 90s; Building Scientific Literacy: Blueprint for the Middle Years; Science and Technology Education for the Middle Years: Frameworks for Curriculum and Instruction; Assessment in Science Education: The Middle Years; Developing and Supporting Teachers for Science Education in the Middle Years; The High Stakes of High School Science; Future of Science in Elementary Schools: Educating Prospective Teachers; Technology Education in the Classroom: Understanding the Designed World; What College-Bound Students Abroad Are Expected to Know About Biology* (with AFT); *Examining the Examinations: A Comparison of Science and Mathematics Examinations for College-Bound Students in Seven Countries.* A publications catalog and project summaries are available on request.

*National Center for Research in Mathematical Sciences Education (NCRMSE). Wisconsin Center for Education Research, School of Education, University of Wisconsin-Madison, 1025 West Johnson St., Madison, WI 53706. (608) 263-4285. Fax (608) 263-3406. E-mail romberg@ums.macc.wisc.edu. Dr. Thomas A. Romberg, Dir. One of 25 university-based national education and development centers supported by the Office of Educational Research and Improvement (OERI) in the U.S. Department of Education to help strengthen student learning in the United States. The mission of this Center is to provide a research base for the reform of school mathematics. The changes needed in the teaching and learning of mathematics in the United States are a consequence of several factors: development of new technologies; changes in mathematics itself; new knowledge about teachers, learning, teaching, and schools as institutions; and renewed calls for equity in learning mathematics regardless of race, class, gender, or ethnicity. To accomplish its mission, the 5-year-old Center has created national networks of scholars who will collaborate on the identification of reform goals as they develop a long-range research plan designed to improve mathematics in U.S. schools. *The Curriculum and Evaluation Standards for School Mathematics* (1989) and the *Professional Standards for Teaching Mathematics* (1992), published by the National Council of Teachers of Mathematics, provide a foundation for Center research. The Center is organized around seven working groups. The working groups involve more than 300 scholars, classroom teachers, and Ph.D. students in research on teaching and learning in K-12 mathematics. *Meetings:* Numerous meetings are scheduled at AERA and NCTM conferences to present research findings. Members of working groups meet one or two times annually to review and critique their research. *Publications: NCRMSE Research Review: The Teaching and Learning of Mathematics* (quarterly newsletter), and numerous books, chapters, articles, and working papers. A 43-page bibliography of publications is available.

National Center for Science Teaching and Learning (NCSTL). The Ohio State University, 1929 Kenny Road, Columbus, OH 43210. (614) 292-3339. Fax (614) 292-1595. E-mail awhite@magnus.acs.ohio-state.edu. Dr. Arthur L. White, Dir.; Michael Aiello, Prog. Dir., contact person. Since 1990, as part of a national effort to reform our country's science education system, with the goal of making science, mathematics, and technology education one of America's highest priorities, Ohio State has housed the NCSTL. Funded by the Office of Educational Research and Improvement of the U.S. Department of Education, the Center supports improvements in science teaching and learning by initiating, promoting, and facilitating research and disseminating the research findings to all those with an interest in science education. The NCSTL studies the impact of non-curricular factors in science teaching and learning in America's schools by collaborating with teachers in the classroom to enhance the science learning experience. These factors include social and cultural influences on science teaching and learning such as language; public expectations and societal incentives including the role of partnerships for fostering science teaching and learning; economic, political, and administrative forces at play in the science teaching and learning endeavor including reform processes; the influences of educational technology on the teaching and learning of science with emphases on instruction and assessment environments; examination of the relationship of science learning to other content areas with particular focus on mathematics; and models for evaluation and assessment. The Center also has a sizable evaluation component which looks at the overall operation of the NCSTL and also participates in projects related to authentic and alternate assessment. The underlying philosophy of the Center is that science educators alone should not, and indeed cannot, define science education. Science teaching and learning research must be a product of a diverse group of individuals including educators, scientists, researchers, policy makers, business and community leaders, parents, and students. In accordance with this philosophy, the Center encourages the participation of and promotes discourse among individuals from these groups. The NCSTL networks that have already been established include faculty, administration, business, and governmental persons within the University, across the state of Ohio, nationally, and internationally. More than 50 individuals in five Colleges at The Ohio State University (Agriculture, Education, Engineering, Mathematical and Physical Sciences, and Medicine) participate in Center projects. The Center has also established on-going collaborative relationships with Clark-Atlanta University (GA), the University of California at Santa Cruz, East Carolina University (NC), the Southeastern Regional Vision for Education (NC), the University of Michigan, the Far West Laboratory for Educational Research and Development (CA), the University of California at Riverside, the Coalition of Essential Schools at Brown University (RI), the AIMS Education Foundation (CA), and Florida Atlantic University. Users include educators, parents, researchers, education agencies, students, policy makers, and the general public. *Publications: COGNOSOS* (q.); *NSF/SSMA Wingspread Conference: A Network for Integrated Science and Mathematics Teaching and Learning. Conference Plenary Papers*; *Advanced Technologies as Educational Tools in Science*; *Integration of Science and Mathematics: What Parents Can Do*; *A Review of Educational Technology in Science Assessment*; *Assessment of Science Teaching and Learning Outcomes*; *Hypermedia: A Conceptual Framework for Science Education and Review of Recent Findings*; *Authentic Assessment Strategies for Elementary Science & Mathematics: A Beginning.*

National Center to Improve Practice (NCIP). Education Development Center, 55 Chapel St., Newton, MA 02158-1060. (617) 969-7100 ext. 2387. TTY (617) 969-4529. Fax (617) 969-3440. E-mail ncip@edc.org; WWW: http://www.edc.org/FSC/NCIP. NCIP, a five-year project funded by the U.S. Department of Education's Office for Special Education Programs (OSEP), is located at Education Development Center, Inc. (EDC) in Newton, MA. The mission of NCIP is to promote the effective use of technology to enhance educational outcomes for students with sensory, cognitive, physical, and social emotional disabilities. Through its telecommunications network, NCIPnet, NCIP links a national community of educators—staff developers, technology coordinators, teachers, specialists, administrators, clinicians, advocates, and consumers—who share their knowledge, experience, and questions about assistive and instructional technologies through online discussions. NCIPnet participants have access to a range of topical discussion folders facilitated by experts in the field. An extensive set of resources related to technology and special education is also available on NCIPnet. NCIP supports this knowledge building process with additional resources and materials in print and video formats. It has developed and disseminates a series of Video Profiles, which vividly illustrate how students with differing disabilities use a range of assistive and instructional technologies to improve their learning. Each video is accompanied by supporting print materials which explore topics more broadly and provide an excellent context for video viewing. *Publications:* Video Profile Series: *Multimedia and More: Help for Students with Learning Disabilities*; *Jeff with Expression: Writing in the Word Prediction Software*; *"Write"*

Tools for Angie: Technology for Students Who Are Visually Impaired; *Telling Tales in ASC and English: Reading, Writing and Videotapes.*

*National Clearinghouse for Bilingual Education (NCBE). The George Washington University, 1118 22d St. NW, Washington, DC 20037. (202) 467-0867; (800) 321-NCBE. Fax (800) 531-9347; (202) 467-4830. E-mail askncbe@ncbe.gwu.edu; gopher gopher.ncbe.gwu.edu; http://www.ncbe.gwu.edu. Joel Gomez, Dir. NCBE is funded by the U.S. Department of Education's Office of Bilingual Education and Minority Languages Affairs (OBEMLA) to collect, analyze, synthesize, and disseminate information relating to the effective education of linguistically and culturally diverse students in the United States. Operated by The George Washington University in Washington, DC, NCBE provides information services through its online services, which include a World Wide Web server, the NCBE Gopher, and a Majordomo list server; through a toll-free fax service; and a telephone reference and referral service.

*National Commission on Libraries and Information Science (NCLIS). 1110 Vermont Ave. NW, Suite 820, Washington, DC 20005-3522. (202) 606-9200. Fax (202) 606-9203. E-mail py_nclis@inet.ed.gov. Peter R. Young, Exec. Dir. A permanent independent agency of the U.S. government charged with advising the executive and legislative branches on national library and information policies and plans. The commission reports directly to the White House and the Congress on the implementation of national policy; conducts studies, surveys, and analyses of the nation's library and information needs; appraises the inadequacies and deficiencies of current resources and services; promotes research and development activities; conducts hearings and issues publications as appropriate; and develops overall plans for meeting national library and information needs and for the coordination of activities at the federal, state, and local levels. *Membership:* 15 commissioners, 14 appointed by the president and confirmed by the Senate; ex-officio, the Librarian of Congress. *Publication: Annual Report.*

National Council for Accreditation of Teacher Education (NCATE). 2010 Massachusetts Ave. NW, Suite 500, Washington, DC 20036. (202) 466-7496. Fax (202) 296-6620. Arthur E. Wise, Pres. A consortium of professional organizations that establishes standards of quality and accredits professional education units in schools, colleges, and departments of education. Interested in the self-regulation and improvement of standards in the field of teacher education. *Membership:* 500 colleges and universities, 29 educational organizations. *Publications: Standards, Procedures and Policies for the Accreditation of Professional Education Units*; *Teacher Education: A Guide to NCATE-Accredited Colleges and Universities*; *Quality Teaching* (newsletter, 3/yr.).

National Council of Teachers of English (NCTE), Commission on Media. 1111 W. Kenyon Rd., Urbana, IL 61801-1096. (217) 328-3870. Fax (217) 328-9645. Miles Myers, Exec. Dir.; Lawrence B. Fuller, Commission Dir. The functions of NCTE are to study emerging technologies and their integration into English and language arts curricula and teacher education programs; to identify the effects of such technologies on teachers, students, and educational settings, with attention to people of color, handicapped, and other students who are not well-served in current programs; to explore means of disseminating information about such technologies to the NCTE membership; to serve as liaison between NCTE and other groups interested in computer-based education in English and language arts; and to maintain liaison with the NCTE Commission on Media and other Council groups concerned with instructional technology. *Membership:* 68,000 individual, 110,000 subscribers. *Dues:* $40 individual. *Meeting:* 1996, NCTE Annual Convention, November 21-26, Chicago, IL; "Honoring All Our Stories." *Publications: English Journal* (8/yr.); *College English* (8/yr.); *Language Arts* (8/yr.); *English Education* (q.); *Research in the Teaching of English* (q.); *Teaching English in the Two-Year College* (q.); *College Composition and Communication* (q.); *English Leadership Quarterly* (q.); *Quarterly Review of Doublespeak* (q); *Primary Voices* (q.); *Voices from the Middle* (q.).

National Council of the Churches of Christ in the U.S.A. Communication Commission, 475 Riverside Dr., New York, NY 10115. (212) 870-2574. Fax (212) 870-2030. Mike Maus, Dir. Ecumenical arena for cooperative work of Protestant and Orthodox denominations and agencies in broadcasting, film, cable, and print media. Offers advocacy to government and industry structures on media services. Services provided include liaison to network television and radio programming; film sales and rentals; distribution of information about syndicated religious programming; syndication of some programming; cable television and emerging technologies information services; news and information regarding work of the National Council of Churches, related denominations, and agencies. Works closely with other faith groups in Interfaith Broadcasting Commission. Online communication via Ecunet/NCCLink. *Membership:* 32 denominations. *Publication: EcuLink.*

*National Education Telecommunications Organization & Education Satellite Company (NETO/EDSAT). 1735 I Street NW, Suite 601, Washington, DC 20006. (202) 293-4211; (800) 220-1235. Fax (202) 293-4210. Shelly Weinstein, Pres. and CEO. NETO/EDSAT is a not-for-profit organization bringing together the users and providers of telecommunications to deliver education, instruction, and training in America's classrooms, colleges, workplaces, and other distance education centers. NETO/EDSAT facilitates and collaborates with key stakeholders in the education and telecommunications fields. Programs and services include research and education, outreach, seminars and conferences, and satellite services and scheduling. The NETO/EDSAT mission is to help create an integrated nationwide multitechnology infrastructure, a dedicated satellite that links space and existing secondary access roads—i.e., telephone and cable—over which teaching and education resources are delivered and shared in a user friendly format with students, teachers, workers, and individuals. "A transparent I-95." A modern-day "learning place" for the rural, urban, migrant, suburban, disadvantaged, and youths-at-risk which provides equal and affordable access to and utilization of educational resources, and teaching and learning tools. A U.S. technologically integrated telecommunications system which transports educational resources to all children and adults regardless of the wealth and geography of their community. *Membership:* Members include school districts, colleges, universities, state agencies, public/private educational consortia, libraries, and other distance education providers. *Publications: NETO/EDSAT "UPDATE"* (newsletter, q.); *Analysis of a Proposal for an Education Satellite, EDSAT Institute.*

National Film Board of Canada (NFBC). 1251 Avenue of the Americas, 6th Floor, New York, NY 10020. (212) 596-1770. Fax (212) 595-1779. E-mail gsem78a@prodigy.com. John Sirabella, U.S. Marketing Mgr./Nontheatrical Rep. Established in 1939, the NFBC's main objective is to produce and distribute high-quality audiovisual materials for educational, cultural, and social purposes.

*National Film Information Service (offered by the Academy of Motion Picture Arts and Sciences). 8949 Wilshire Blvd., Beverly Hills, CA 90211-1972. (310) 247-3000. The purpose of this organization is to provide an information service on film. The service is fee-based and all inquiries must be accompanied by a self-addressed stamped envelope.

National Gallery of Art (NGA). Department of Education Resources: Art Information and Extension Programs, Washington, DC 20565. (202) 842-6273. Ruth R. Perlin, Head. This department of NGA is responsible for the production and distribution of educational audiovisual programs, including interactive technologies. Materials available (all loaned free to schools, community organizations, and individuals) range from films, videocassettes, and color slide programs to videodiscs. A free catalog of programs is available upon request. Two videodiscs on the gallery's collection are available for long-term loan. *Publication: Extension Programs Catalogue.*

*National Information Center for Educational Media (NICEM). P.O. Box 40130, Albuquerque, NM 87196. (505) 265-3591; (800) 926-8328. E-mail tnaccessi@technet.nm.org. Marjorie M. K. Hlava, Pres., Access Innovations, Inc.; Patrick Sauer, Mng. Dir., NICEM; C. J. Donnelly, Marketing. In conjunction with the Library of Congress, NICEM is a centralized facility that collects, catalogs, and disseminates information about nonbook materials of many different kinds. Its mission is to build and expand the database to provide current and archival information about nonbook educational materials; to apply modern techniques of information dissemination that meet user needs; and to provide a comprehensive, centralized nonbook database used for catalogs, indexes, multimedia publications, special search services, machine-readable tapes, and online access. NICEM services include NICEM EZ (user-defined searches of the database, fee set at editorial time rate, one-day turnaround) and AVxpress ("Document" delivery of any media title [in print] found in NICEM or in any other listing of media material, in cooperation with Dynamic Information in Burlingame, CA). The NICEM masterfile is also available on DIALOG File 46, via CompuServe as the Knowledge Index, and on CD-ROM (AVOnline via SilverPlatter); (NICEM AVmarc via BiblioFile). A 45,000 unit subset of NICEM titles is carried on the Human Resource Information Network, via National Standards Association. *Clients, Users:* College and university media centers, school districts, BOCES, libraries, corporate researchers, students, and filmmakers. Nonmembership organization—no change to catalog. *Publications: Film & Video Finder, 4th ed., 1994-95; Index to AV Producers & Distributors, 9th ed., 1994-95; Audiocassette & CD Finder, 1995.*

National PTA. 330 N. Wabash, Suite 2100, Chicago, IL 60611. (312) 670-6782. Fax (312) 670-6783. Joan Dykstra, Pres.; Patty Yoxall, Public Relations Mgr. Advocates for the education, health, safety, and well-being of children and teens. Provides parenting education and leadership training to PTA volunteers. *Membership:* 6.8 million. *Dues:* Varies by local unit. *Sample Publications: Our Children* (magazine); *PTA Today* (magazine); *What's Happening in Washington* (legislative newsletters); numerous brochures for parents in English and Spanish. Catalog available.

National Press Photographers Association, Inc. (NPPA). 3200 Croasdaile Dr., Suite 306, Durham, NC 27705. (919) 383-7246. Fax (919) 383-7261. E-mail 72640.21@compuserve.com. Charles H. Cooper, Exec. Dir. An organization of professional news photographers who participate in and promote photojournalism in publications and through television and film. Sponsors workshops, seminars, and contests; maintains an audiovisual library of subjects of media interest. *Membership:* 11,000. *Dues:* $75/yr. (domestic); $105 (international); $40 student. *Meetings:* 1996, Annual Convention and Education Days, June 26-29, Indianapolis, IN (NPPA's 51st Annual Convention). An extensive array of other conferences, seminars, and workshops are held throughout the year. *Publications: News Photographer* magazine (m.); *The Best of Photojournalism PJ021* (annual book).

*National Public Broadcasting Archives (NPBA). Hornbake Library, University of Maryland at College Park, College Park, MD 20742. (301) 405-9255. Thomas Connors, Archivist. NPBA brings together the archival record of the major entities of noncommercial broadcasting in the United States. NPBA's collections include the archives of the Corporation for Public Broadcasting (CPB), the Public Broadcasting Service (PBS), and National Public Radio (NPR). Other organizations represented include the Midwest Program for Airborne Television Instruction (MPATI), the Public Service Satellite Consortium (PSSC), America's Public Television Stations (APTS), and the Joint Council for Educational Telecommunications (JCET). NPBA also makes available the personal papers of many individuals who have made significant contributions to public broadcasting, and its reference library contains basic studies of the broadcasting industry, rare pamphlets, and journals on relevant topics, plus up-to-date clippings from the PBS press clipping service. NPBA also collects and maintains a selected audio and video program record of public broadcasting's national production and support centers and of local stations. Oral history tapes and transcripts from the NPR Oral History Project are also available at the archives. The archives are open to the public from 9 am to 5 pm, Monday through Friday. Research in NPBA collections should be arranged by prior appointment. For further information, call (301) 405-9988.

National Religious Broadcasters (NRB). 7839 Ashton Ave., Manassas, VA 22110. (703) 330-7000. Fax (703) 330-7100. E. Brandt Gustavson, Pres. NRB essentially has two goals: (1) to ensure that religious broadcasters have access to the radio and television airwaves, and

(2) to encourage broadcasters to observe a high standard of excellence in their programming and station management for the clear presentation of the gospel. Holds national and regional conventions. *Membership:* 800 organizational stations, program producers, agencies, and individuals. *Dues:* Based on income. *Meetings:* 1996, 53rd Annual Convention, February 3-6, Indianapolis, IN. *Publications: Religious Broadcasting Magazine* (mo.); *Annual Directory of Religious Media; Religious Broadcasting Resources Library Brochure; Religious Broadcasting Cassette Catalog.*

National School Supply and Equipment Association (NSSEA). 8300 Colesville Rd., Suite 250, Silver Spring, MD 20910. (301) 495-0240. Fax (301) 495-3330. E-mail nssea@aol.com. Tim Holt, Exec. V.P. A service organization of more than 1,600 manufacturers, distributors, retailers, and independent manufacturers' representatives of school supplies, equipment, and instructional materials. Seeks to maintain open communications between manufacturers and dealers in the school market, to find solutions to problems affecting schools, and to encourage the development of new ideas and products for educational progress. *Meetings:* 1996, The School Equipment Show, February 22-24, Tampa, FL; Ed Expo '96, March 28-31, Tampa, FL; 80th Annual NSSEA Fall Show, November 14-17, Dallas, TX. *Publications: Tidings; Annual Membership Directory.*

*National Science Teachers Association (NSTA). 1840 Wilson Blvd., Arlington, VA 22201. (703) 243-7100. Fax (703) 243-7177. E-mail alex.mondale@nsta.org. Bill Aldridge, Exec. Dir. A national nonprofit association of science teachers ranging from kindergarten through university level. NSTA conducts one national and three regional conventions and provides numerous programs and services, including awards and scholarships, inservice teacher workshops, professional certification, a major curriculum reform effort, and more. It has position statements on many issues, such as teacher preparation, laboratory science, and the use of animals in the classroom. It is involved in cooperative working relationships in a variety of projects with educational organizations, government agencies, and private industries. *Membership:* 50,000. *Dues:* $52/yr. individual or institutional (includes one journal and other benefits). *Meetings:* 1996, National, March 28-31, St. Louis, MO. *Publications: Science and Children* (8/yr., journal for elementary teachers); *Science Scope* (8/yr., journal for middle-level teachers); *The Science Teacher* (9/yr., for high school teachers); *Journal of College Science Teaching* (6/yr., journal for college teachers); *NSTA Reports!* (6/yr., newspaper for K-college teachers, free to all NSTA members); *Quantum* (magazine for physics and math high school students); books (free catalog available).

National Society for Performance and Improvement (NSPI). See listing for International Society for Performance Improvement (ISPI).

National Telemedia Council Inc. (NTC). 120 E. Wilson St., Madison, WI 53703. (608) 257-7712. Fax (608) 257-7714. E-mail NTelemedia@aol.com. Dr. Martin Rayala, Pres.; Marieli Rowe, Exec. Dir. The NTC is a national not-for-profit professional organization dedicated to promoting media literacy, or critical television viewing skills. This is done primarily through work with teachers, parents, and caregivers. NTC activities include the development of the Media Literacy Clearinghouse and Center; the Teacher Idea Exchange (T.I.E.); national conferences and regional and local workshops; the Jessie McCanse Award for individual contribution to media literacy. *Dues:* $30 basic membership; $50 contributing; $100 patron. *Publications: Telemedium; The Journal of Media Literacy* (newsletter, q.).

*National University Continuing Education Association (NUCEA). One Dupont Cir. NW, Suite 615, Washington, DC 20036. (202) 659-3130. Fax (202) 785-0374. Edward Simpson, Pres. 1995-96; Kay J. Kohl, Exec. Dir.; Susan Goewey, Dir. of Pubs.; J. Noah Brown, Dir. of Govt. Relations & Public Affairs. An association of public and private institutions concerned with making continuing education available to all population segments and to promoting excellence in the continuing higher education community. NUCEA has an annual national conference and several professional development seminars throughout the year, and many institutional members offer university and college film rental library services. *Membership:*

425 institutions; 2,000 professionals. *Dues:* Vary according to membership category. *Publications:* Monthly newsletter; quarterly occasional papers; scholarly journal; *Independent Study Catalog*; *The Electronic University. A Guide to Distance Learning Programs*; *Guide to Certificate Programs at American Colleges and Universities*; NUCEA-ACE/Oryx Continuing Higher Education book series; *Lifelong Learning Trends* (a statistical factbook on continuing higher education); organizational issues series; membership directory; other publications relevant to the field.

*The NETWORK, Inc. 300 Brickstone Square, Suite 900, Andover, MA 01810. (508) 470-1080. Fax (508) 475-9220. Internet suem@neirl.org. Sue Martin, Pub. Mgr. A research and service organization providing training, research and evaluation, technical assistance, and materials to schools, educational organizations, and private sector firms with educational interests. *Publications: Portrait of Our Mothers: Using Oral History in the Classroom*; *Juggling Lessons: A Curriculum for Women Who Go to School, Work, and Care for Their Families*; *An Action Guide for School Improvement*; *Making Change for School Improvement: A Simulation Game*; *Report on National Dissemination Efforts: Volumes I-X*; *The Effective Writing Teacher*; *Cumulative Writing Folder*; *Developing Writing and Thinking Skills Across the Curriculum: A Practical Program for Schools*; *Five Types of Writing Assignments*. Publications catalog is available upon request.

*Network for Continuing Medical Education (NCME). One Harmon Plaza, 7th Floor, Secaucus, NJ 07094. (201) 867-3550. Fax (201) 867-2491. Produces and distributes videocassettes to hospitals for physicians' continuing education. Programs are developed for physicians in the practice of General Medicine, Anesthesiology, Emergency Medicine, Gastroenterology, and Surgery. Physicians who view all the programs can earn up to 25 hours of Category 1 (AMA) credit and up to 20 hours of Prescribed (AAFP) credit each year. *Membership:* More than 1,100 hospitals provide NCME programs to their physicians. *Dues:* Subscription fees: VHS-$l,920/yr. Sixty-minute videocassettes are distributed to hospital subscribers every three weeks.

North Central Regional Educational Laboratory (NCREL). 1900 Spring Rd., Suite 300, Oak Brook, IL 60521-1480. (708) 571-4700; (800) 356-2735. Fax (708) 571-4716. E-mail info@ncrel.org. Jan Bakker, Resource Center Dir. NCREL's work is guided by a focus on comprehensive and systemic school restructuring that is research-based and learner-centered. One of 10 Office of Educational Research and Improvement (OERI) regional educational laboratories, NCREL disseminates information about effective programs, develops educational products, holds conferences, provides technical assistance, and conducts research and evaluation. In addition to conventional print publications, NCREL uses computer networks, videoconferencing via satellite, and video and audio formats to reach its diverse audiences. NCREL operates the Midwest Consortium for Mathematics and Science Education which works to advance systemic change in mathematics and science education. Persons living in Illinois, Indiana, Iowa, Michigan, Minnesota, Ohio, and Wisconsin are encouraged to call NCREL Resource Center with any education-related questions. *Publications: Clipboard* (q.); a catalog of print, video, and other media products is available by calling the main number.

Northwest Regional Educational Laboratory (NWREL). 101 SW Main St., Suite 500, Portland, OR 97204. (503) 275-9500. Fax (503) 275-9489. Dr. Ethel Simon-McWilliams, Exec. Dir. One of 10 Office of Educational Research and Improvement (OERI) regional educational laboratories, NWREL works with schools and communities to improve educational outcomes for children, youth, and adults. NWREL provides leadership, expertise, and services based on the results of research and development. The specialty area of NWREL is school change processes. It serves Alaska, Idaho, Oregon, Montana, and Washington. *Membership:* 817. *Dues:* None. *Publication: Northwest Report* (newsletter).

OCLC Online Computer Library Center, Inc. 6565 Frantz Rd., Dublin, OH 43017-3395. (614) 764-6000. Fax (614) 764-6096. Internet nita_dean@oclc.org. K. Wayne Smith, Pres. and CEO. Nita Dean, Mgr., Public Relations. A nonprofit membership organization that engages in computer library service and research and makes available computer-based processes, products, and services for libraries, other educational organizations, and library users. From its facility in Dublin, Ohio, OCLC operates an international computer network that libraries use to catalog books, order custom-printed catalog cards and machine-readable records for local catalogs, arrange interlibrary loans, and maintain location information on library materials. OCLC also provides online and offline reference products and services for the electronic delivery of information. More than 22,000 libraries contribute to and/or use information in the OCLC Online Union Catalog. *Publications: OCLC Newsletter* (6/yr.); *OCLC Reference News* (4/yr.); *Annual Report; Annual Review of Research.*

*Office of Technology Assessment (OTA). U.S. Congress, Washington, DC 20510-8025. (202) 228-6938. Fax (202) 228-6293. E-mail kfulton@ota.gov. Kathleen Fulton, Proj. Dir. (contact for education). (Education in now part of the Education and Human Resources Program, Denise Dougherty, Dir.) Established by Congress to study, report on, and assess the significance and probable impact of new technological developments on U.S. society and to advise Congress on public policy implications and options. Recent assessments focusing on technology and education issues include *Elementary and Secondary Education for Science and Engineering, A Technical Memorandum* (1989); *Higher Education for Science and Engineering, A Background Paper* (1989); *Linking for Learning: A New Course for Education* (1989); *Critical Connections: Communication for the Future* (1990); *Computer Software and Intellectual Property, A Background Paper* (1990); the assessment, *Power On! New Tools for Teaching & Learning* (1988), includes an interim staff paper on "Trends and Status of Computers in Schools: Use in Chapter 1 Programs and Use with Limited English Proficient Students" (March 1987); *Testing and Assessment in Vocational Education; Risks to Students in School* (January 1995); *Teachers and Technology* (February 1995); *Technology and Work-Based Learning* (Spring 1996). *Publications:* For a list, contact the publishing office at (202) 224-8996.

On-line Audiovisual Catalogers (OLAC). c/o Columbia University Health Sciences Library, 701 West 168th St., New York, NY 10032. (212) 305-1406. Fax (212) 234-0595. Johanne LaGrange, Treas. Formed as an outgrowth of the ALA conference, OLAC seeks to permit members to exchange ideas and information, and to interact with other agencies that influence audiovisual cataloging practices. *Membership:* 725. *Dues:* Available for single or multiple years, ranges from \$10 to \$27 individual, \$16 to \$45 institutional. *Publication: OLAC Newsletter.*

Pacific Film Archive (PFA). University Art Museum, 2625 Durant Ave., Berkeley, CA 94720-2250. (510) 642-1437 (library); (510) 642-1412 (general). Fax (510) 642-4889. Edith Kramer, Dir. and Curator of Film; Nancy Goldman, Head, PFA Library and Film Study Center. Sponsors the exhibition, study, and preservation of classic, international, documentary, animated, and avant-garde films. Provides on-site research screenings of films in its collection of over 6,000 titles. Provides access to its collections of books, periodicals, stills, and posters (all materials are noncirculating). Offers UAM members and University of California, Berkeley, affiliates reference and research services to locate film and video distributors, credits, stock footage, etc. Library hours are 1 p.m.-5 p.m. weekdays. *Membership:* Through parent organization, the University Art Museum. *Dues:* \$40 individual and nonprofit departments of institutions. *Publication: UAM/PFA Calendar* (6/yr.).

Pacific Region Educational Laboratory (PREL). 828 Fort Street Mall, Suite 500, Honolulu, HI 96813-4321. (808) 533-6000. Fax (808) 533-7599. John W. Kofel, Exec. Dir. One of 10 Office of Educational Research and Improvement (OERI) regional educational laboratories designed to help educators and policymakers solve educational problems in their schools. Using the best available information and the experience and expertise of professionals, PREL seeks to identify solutions to education problems, tries new approaches, furnishes research results, and provides training to teachers and administrators. The specialty area of PREL is language and cultural diversity. It serves American Samoa, Commonwealth of the Northern Mariana Islands, Federated States of Micronesia, Guam, Hawaii, Republic of the Marshall Islands, and Republic of Palau.

*PCR: Films and Video in the Behavioral Sciences. Special Services Bldg., Pennsylvania State University, University Park, PA 16802. (814) 863-3102; purchasing info, (800) 826-0132. Fax (814) 863-2574. E-mail tjm@psulias.psu.edu. Thomas McKenna, Mng. Ed. Collects and makes available to professionals 16mm films and video in the behavioral sciences judged to be useful for university teaching and research. A free catalog of the films in PCR is available. The PCR catalog now contains some 1,400 films in the behavioral sciences (psychology, psychiatry, anthropology, animal behavior, sociology, teaching and learning, and folklife). Some 7,000 professionals now use PCR services. Films and tapes are available on loan for a rental charge. Many films may also be purchased. Films may be submitted for international distribution. Contact the managing editor through PCR.

Photographic Society of America (PSA). 3000 United Founders Blvd., Suite 103, Oklahoma City, OK 73112. (405) 843-1437. Jacque Noel, Operations Mgr. A nonprofit organization for the development of the arts and sciences of photography and for the furtherance of public appreciation of photographic skills. Its members, largely amateurs, consist of individuals, camera clubs, and other photographic organizations. Divisions include color slide, motion picture, nature, photojournalism, travel, pictorial print, stereo, and techniques. Sponsors national, regional, and local meetings, clinics, and contests. Request dues information from preceding address. *Meetings:* 1996, International Conference, September 2-7, Tucson, AZ; Regional Convention, April 25-27, Palm Beach Gardens, FL. 1997, International Conference, September 1-6, St. Charles, IL. *Publication: PSA Journal.*

Public Broadcasting Service (PBS). 1320 Braddock Pl., Alexandria, VA 22314-1698. (703) 739-5000. Ervin S. Duggan, CEO and Pres. National distributor of public television programming, obtaining all programs from member stations, American independent producers, or foreign sources. PBS also offers educational services for teachers, students, and parents including: PTV, The Ready to Learn Service on PBS; Going the Distance; PBS MATHLINE; and PBS ONLINE. Owned and operated by local public television organizations through annual membership fees. PBS services include program acquisition, distribution, and scheduling; development and fundraising support; and engineering and technical development. Of special interest are: the PBS Adult Learning Service, which offers telecourses through college/public television station partnerships; PBS K-12 Learning Services, providing learning resources for elementary and secondary school teachers and students; and PBS VIDEO, which offers videotapes of PBS programs for rent or sale to educational institutions. PBS is governed by a board of directors elected by PBS members for three-year terms. *Membership:* 198 organizations operating 346 stations.

*PBS Adult Learning Service (ALS). 1320 Braddock Pl., Alexandria, VA 22314-1698. (800) 257-2578. Fax (703) 739-8495. Will Philipp, Dir. Contact ALS Customer Service. The mission of ALS is to help colleges, universities, and public television stations increase learning opportunities for distance learners; enrich classroom instruction; update faculty; train administrators, management, and staff; and provide other educational services for local communities. A pioneer in the widespread use of video and print packages incorporated into curricula and offered for credit by local colleges, ALS began broadcasting telecourses in 1981. Since that time, over 2 million students have earned college credit through telecourses offered in partnership with more than two-thirds of the nation's colleges and universities. In 1988, ALS established the Adult Learning Satellite Service (ALSS) to provide colleges, universities, businesses, hospitals, and other organizations with a broad range of educational programming via direct satellite. *Membership:* 500-plus colleges, universities, hospitals, government agencies, and Fortune 500 businesses are now ALSS Associates. Organizations that are not Associates can still acquire ALS programming, but at higher fees. *Dues:* $1,500/yr.; multisite and consortia rates are available. *Publications: ALSS Programming Line-Up* (catalog of available programming, 3/yr.); *The Agenda* (news magazine about issues of interest to distance learning and adult learning administrators); and *Changing the Face of Higher Education* (an overview of ALS services).

*PBS ENCORE. 1320 Braddock Pl., Alexandria, VA 22314. (703) 739-5225. Bonnie Green, Prog. Assoc. Distributes PBS programs with extant broadcast rights to public television stations. *Publication: PBS Encore A to Z Listing.*

PBS VIDEO. 1320 Braddock Pl., Alexandria, VA 22314. (703) 739-5380; (800) 344-3337. Fax (703) 739-5269. Jon Cecil, Dir., PBS VIDEO Marketing. Markets and distributes PBS television programs for sale on videocassette or videodisc to colleges, public libraries, schools, governments, and other organizations and institutions. *Publications: PBS VIDEO Resource Catalog*; *PBS VIDEO Catalogs of New and Popular Videos* (6/yr.); and the *PBS VIDEO Elementary Catalog.*

The Regional Laboratory for Educational Improvement of the Northeast and Islands. 300 Brickstone Square, Suite 950, Andover, MA 01810. (508) 470-0098. Fax (508) 475-9220. E-mail info@neirl.org. Glen Harvey, Exec. Dir. NEIRL—one of 10 regional laboratories sponsored in part by the U.S. Department of Education—works to ensure that all students succeed in school through applied research and development, training and technical assistance, dissemination of proven practices, evaluation assistance, and overall guidance to and collaboration with schools, districts, and states throughout New England, New York, Puerto Rico, and the Virgin Islands. *Membership:* Open to individuals, schools, or other organizations committed to improving education. *Meetings:* Upcoming events are announced on NEIRL's World Wide Web and/or Gopher servers: http://www.neirl.org and gopher.neirl.org. *Publications: Hand in Hand: How Nine Urban Schools Work with Families and Community Services*; *Being Prepared: The School Emergency Response Plan Handbook*; *Mentoring: A Resource and Training Guide for Educators*; *Genuine Reward: Community Inquiry into Connecting Learning, Teaching, and Assessing*; *Building Systems for Professional Growth: An Action Guide*; *Continuing to Learn: A Guidebook for Teacher Development*; *Kindle the SPARK: An Action Guide Committed to the Success of Every Child*; *Education by Charter: Restructuring School Districts*; *CaMaPe: An Organizational and Educational Systems Approach to Secondary School Development.* A publications catalog is available upon request.

Research for Better Schools, Inc. (RBS). 444 North Third St., Philadelphia, PA 19123-4107. (215) 574-9300. Fax (215) 574-0133. John E. Hopkins, Exec. Dir. One of 10 Office of Educational Research and Improvement (OERI) regional educational laboratories designed to help educators and policymakers solve educational problems in their schools. Using the best available information and the experience and expertise of professionals, RBS seeks to identify solutions to education problems, tries new approaches, furnishes research results, and provides training to teachers and administrators. RBS serves Delaware, Maryland, New Jersey, Pennsylvania, and the District of Columbia.

*Smithsonian Institution. 1000 Jefferson Drive SW, Washington, DC 20560. (202) 357-2700. Fax (202) 786-2515. Robert McCormick Adams, Secy. An independent trust instrumentality of the United States that conducts scientific, cultural, and scholarly research; administers the national collections; and performs other educational public service functions, all supported by Congress, trusts, gifts, and grants. Includes 16 museums, including the National Museum of Natural History, the National Museum of American History, the National Air and Space Museum, and the National Zoological Park. Museums are free and open daily except December 25. The Smithsonian Institution Traveling Exhibition Service (SITES) organizes exhibitions on art, history, and science and circulates them across the country and abroad. *Membership:* Smithsonian Associates (Resident and National Air and Space). *Dues:* Vary. *Publications: Smithsonian*; *Air & Space/Smithsonian*; *The Torch* (staff newsletter, mo.); *Research Reports* (semitechnical, q.); *Smithsonian Runner* (for and about American Indians and Smithsonian-related activities, 6/yr.); Smithsonian Institution Press Publications, 470 L'Enfant Plaza, Suite 7100, Washington, DC 20560.

Society for Applied Learning Technology (SALT). 50 Culpeper St., Warrenton, VA 22186. (540) 347-0055. Fax (540) 349-3169. E-mail info@salt.org. Raymond G. Fox, Pres. The society is a nonprofit, professional membership organization that was founded in 1972. Membership in the society is oriented to professionals whose work requires knowledge and communication in the field of instructional technology. The society provides members a means to enhance their knowledge and job performance by participation in society-sponsored meetings, through subscription to society-sponsored publications, by association with other professionals at conferences sponsored by the society, and through membership in special interest groups and special society-sponsored initiatives/projects. In addition, the society offers members discounts on society-sponsored journals, conferences, and publications. *Membership:* 1,000. *Dues:* $45. *Meetings:* 1996: "Orlando Multimedia '96," February 21-23, Kissimmee, FL; "Interactive Multimedia '96," August 21-23, Arlington, VA. *Publications: Journal of Educational Technology Systems*; *Journal of Instruction Delivery Systems*; *Journal of Interactive Instructional Development*; *Journal of Medical Education Technologies*. Send for list of books.

Society for Computer Simulation (SCS). P.O. Box 17900, San Diego, CA 92177-7900. (619) 277-3888. Fax (619) 277-3930. Bill Gallagher, Exec. Dir. Founded in 1952, SCS is a professional-level technical society devoted to the art and science of modeling and simulation. Its purpose is to advance the understanding, appreciation, and use of all types of computer models for studying the behavior of actual or hypothesized systems of all kinds. Sponsors standards and local, regional, and national technical meetings and conferences, such as the Western Simulation Multi-conference, Summer Computer Simulation Conference, Winter Simulation Conference, International Simulation Technology Conference (SIMTEC), National Educational Computing Conference (NECC), and others. *Membership:* 1,900. *Dues:* $60. *Publications: Simulation* (mo.); Simulation series (q.); *Transactions of SCS* (q.). Additional office in Ghent, Belgium.

*Society for Photographic Education (SPE). P.O. Box 222116, Dallas, TX 75222-2116. (817) 273-2845. Fax (817) 273-2846. M. L. Hutchins, Exec. Dir. An association of college and university teachers of photography, museum photographic curators, writers, and publishers. Promotes higher standards of photographic education. *Membership:* 1,700. *Dues:* $55. *Meetings:* March 1995, Atlanta; March 21-24, 1996, Los Angeles, CA. *Publications: Exposure*; newsletter.

Society of Cable Television Engineers (SCTE). 140 Philips Rd., Exton, PA 19341-1318. (610) 363-6888. Fax (363) 363-5898. William W. Riker, Pres. SCTE is dedicated to the technical training and further education of members. A nonprofit membership organization for persons engaged in engineering, construction, installation, technical direction, management, or administration of cable television and broadband communication technologies. Also eligible for membership are students in communications, educators, government and regulatory agency employees, and affiliated trade associations. SCTE provides technical training and certification, and is an American National Standards Institute (ANSI)-approved standards developer for the cable television industry. *Membership:* 14,500. *Dues:* $40/yr. *Meetings:* 1996, Conference on Emerging Technologies, January 8-10, San Francisco, CA; Cable-Tec Expo, June 10-13, Nashville, TN (hardware exhibits and engineering conference). *Publication: The Interval.*

Society of Photographic Engineering. See listing for Society for Imaging Science and Technology (IS&T).

*SouthEastern Regional Vision for Education (SERVE). P.O. Box 5367, Greensboro, NC 27435-3277. (910) 334-3211; (800) 755-3277. Fax (910) 334-3268. E-mail rforbes@serve.org. Dr. Roy H. Forbes, Exec. Dir. SERVE's mission is to promote and support the continuous improvement of educational opportunities for all learners in the Southeast. This federally funded education laboratory is a coalition of business leaders, governors, policy makers, and educators who are seeking systemic, lasting improvement in education in Alabama, Florida, Georgia, Mississippi, North Carolina, and South Carolina. It has six offices, one each in Alabama, Florida, Mississippi, and South Carolina, as well as the North Carolina office listed here. Products and services offered by SERVE include SERVE-LINE, a computerized communication system; a free information and retrieval service; Sharing Success, a program to identify successful programs in the area; free and low-cost publications and videotapes designed to give educators practical information and the latest research on common issues and problems; field services and technical assistance; conferences and teleconferences; research and development project on practical issues related to school-based educational improvement; policy analysis and improvement; and toll-free numbers to call for information and assistance. *Meetings:* For dates and topics of Conferences and Workshops, contact Jan Crotts, (910) 334-3211. *Publications: Reengineering High Schools for Student Success*; *Schools for the 21st Century: New Roles for Teachers and Principals* (rev. ed.); *Designing Teacher Evaluation Systems That Promote Professional Growth*; *Learning by Serving: 2,000 Ideas for Service-Learning Projects*; *Sharing Success: Promising Service-Learning Programs*; *Future Plans* (videotape, discussion guide, and pamphlet); *Future Plans Planning Guides*; *Reducing Baby Bottle Tooth Decay: A SERVE Research Brief.*

Southwest Educational Development Laboratory (SEDL). 211 East Seventh St., Austin, TX 78701. (512) 476-6861. Fax (512) 476-2286. E-mail jpollard@sedl.org. Preston C. Kronkosky, Exec. Dir.; Joyce Pollard, Dir. Institutional Communications & Policy Services. One of ten Office of Educational Research and Improvement (OERI) regional educational laboratories designed to help educators and policymakers solve educational problems in their schools. Using the best available information and the experience and expertise of professionals, SEDL seeks to identify solutions to education problems, tries new approaches, furnishes research results, and provides training to teachers and administrators. SEDL serves Arkansas, Louisiana, New Mexico, Oklahoma, and Texas. *Publications:* SEDL publishes *SEDLETTER* for general distribution and a range of topic-specific publications related to educational change, policy, mathematics, and science. It also maintains a gopher and a MOSAIC interface to the Internet.

*Speech Communication Association (SCA). 5105 Backlick Rd., Bldg. E, Annandale, VA 22003. (703) 750-0533. James L. Gaudino, Exec. Dir. A voluntary society organized to promote study, criticism, research, teaching, and application of principles of communication, particularly of speech communication. *Membership:* 7,000. *Dues:* $75. *Publications: Spectra Newsletter* (mo.); *Quarterly Journal of Speech*; *Communication Monographs*; *Communication Education*; *Critical Studies in Mass Communication*; *Journal of Applied Communication Research*; *Text and Performance Quarterly*; *Speech Communication Teacher*; *Index to Journals in Communication Studies through 1990*; *Speech Communication Directory of SCA and the Regional Speech Communication Organizations* (CSSA, ECA, SSCA, WSCA). For additional publications, request brochure.

*Theater Library Association (TLA). 111 Amsterdam Ave., Rm. 513, New York, NY 10023. (212) 870-1670. Richard M. Buck, Secy./Treas. Seeks to further the interests of collecting, preserving, and using theater, cinema, and performing arts materials in libraries, museums, and private collections. *Membership:* 500. *Dues:* $20 individual, $25 institutional. *Publications: Broadside* (q.); *Performing Arts Resources* (membership annual).

*Training Media Association. 198 Thomas Johnson Dr., Suite 206, Frederick, MD 21702. (301) 662-4268. Robert A. Gehrke, Exec. Dir. An organization dedicated to the protection of film and videotape copyright and copyright education. *Membership:* 85 voting members and associate members. *Dues:* Based on number of employees. *Meetings:* Senior Management Seminar, February 25-26, 1995, Scottsdale, AZ; Annual Membership Meeting, June 4, 1995, Dallas, TX. *Publication: Previews* (newsletter).

USA Toy Library Association (USA-TLA). 2530 Crawford Ave., Suite 111, Evanston, IL 60201. (847) 864-3330. Fax (847) 864-3331. E-mail foliog@aol.com. Judith Q. Iacuzzi, Exec. Dir. The mission of the USA-TLA is to provide a networking system answering to all those interested in play and play materials to provide a national resource to toy libraries, family centers, resource and referrals, public libraries, schools, institutions serving families of special needs, and other groups and individuals involved with children; to support and expand the number of toy libraries; and to advocate for children and the importance of their play in healthy development. *Membership:* 60 insts.; 150 inds. *Dues:* $150 insts.; $50 inds.; $15 students. *Publications: Child's Play* (q. newsletter); *How to Start and Operate a Toy Library*; *Play Is a Child's Work* (videotapes).

WestEd. 730 Harrison St., San Francisco, CA 94107-1242. (415) 565-3000. Fax (415) 565-3012. E-mail tross@wested.org. Dr. Dean Nafziger, CEO. WestEd is a public agency established December 1, 1995, uniting Far West Laboratory for Educational Research and Development and Southwest Regional Laboratory to serve the education communities in Arizona, California, Nevada, and Utah. The new organization combines the strengths of the two institutions to help improve teaching and learning and create greater educational opportunity for children and adults. WestEd helps practitioners and policy makers apply the best available knowledge from research and practice. Funded in part by the U.S. Department of Education, WestEd addresses a broad range of educational priorities, including issues of early childhood, curriculum, assessment, educational technology, career/technical preparation, teacher and administrator professional development, and science and mathematics education. A publications catalog is available.

World Future Society (WFS). 7910 Woodmont Ave., Suite 450, Bethesda, MD 20814. (301) 656-8274. Edward Cornish, Pres. Organization of individuals interested in the study of future trends and possibilities. *Membership:* 30,000. *Dues:* $35/yr., general; $95 professional; call Society for details on all membership levels and benefits. *Meeting:* 1996, General Assembly, July 14-18, Washington, DC, "FutureVision: Ideas, Insights, and Strategies." *Publications: The Futurist: A Journal of Forecasts, Trends and Ideas About the Future*; *Futures Research Quarterly*; *Future Survey*. The society's bookstore offers audio- and videotapes, books, and other items.

Canada

This section includes information on eight Canadian organizations whose principal interests lie in the general fields of education, educational media, instructional technology, and library and information science. Organizations listed in the 1995-1996 *EMTY* were contacted for updated information and changes have been made accordingly.

ACCESS NETWORK. 3720 - 76 Ave., Edmonton, AB T6B 2N9, Canada. (403) 440-7777. Fax (403) 440-8899. E-mail promo@ccinet.ab.ca. Dr. Ronald Keast, Pres.; Kate Hildebrandt, Communications Mgr. The ACCESS Network (Alberta Educational Communications Corporation) was purchased by Learning and Skills Television of Alberta in 1995. In acquiring ACCESS, LTA has taken over the responsibility for educational television in the province, and has moved to provide an enhanced schedule of formal curriculum-related programming for students at all levels and both formal and informal educational programming for adults. The newly privatized network will work with Alberta's educators to provide all Albertans with a progressive and diverse television-based educational and training resource to support their learning and skills development needs using cost-effective methods and innovative techniques, and to introduce a new private sector model for financing and efficient operation of educational television in the province.

Association for Media and Technology in Education in Canada (AMTEC). 3-1750 The Queensway, Suite 1818, Etobicoke, ON M9C 5H5, Canada. Gary Karlsen, Pres.; Mary Anne Epp, Sec./Treas. AMTEC is Canada's national association for eductional media and technology professionals. The organization provides national leadership through annual conferences, publications, workshops, media festivals, and awards. It responds to media and technology issues at the international, national, provincial, and local levels, and maintains linkages with other organizations with similar interests. *Membership:* 350. *Dues:* $80.25 Canadian regular, U.S. members add $20 U.S. for shipping and handling; $32.10 student and retiree. *Meeting:*

1996, Annual Conference, AMTEC '96, June 2-6, Vancouver, B.C., "Riding the Wave"; 1997, June, Saskatoon, SK. *Publications: Canadian Journal of Educational Communication* (q.); *Media News* (q.); *Membership Directory* (with membership).

Canadian Broadcasting Corporation (CBC)/Société Radio-Canada (SRC). 1500 Bronson Ave., P.O. Box 8478, Ottawa, ON K1G 3J5, Canada. (613) 738-6784. Fax (613) 738-6742. Perrin Beatty, Pres. and CEO; Paula Sanders, Communications Officer. The CBC is a publicly owned corporation established in 1936 by an Act of the Canadian Parliament to provide a national broadcasting service in Canada in the two official languages. CBC services include English and French television networks; English and French AM Mono and FM Stereo radio networks virtually free of commercial advertising; CBC North, which serves Canada's North by providing radio and television programs in English, French, and eight native languages; Newsworld and its French counterpart, Le Réseau de l'information (RDI), 24-hour national satellites to cable English-language and French-language news and information service respectively, both funded entirely by cable subscription and commercial advertising revenues; and Radio Canada International, a shortwave radio service that broadcasts in seven languages and is managed by CBC and financed by External Affairs. The CBC is financed mainly by public funds voted annually by Parliament.

*Canadian Education Association/Association canadienne d'éducation (CEA). 252 Bloor St. W., Suite 8-200, Toronto, ON M5S 1V5, Canada. (416) 924-7721. Fax (416) 924-3188. Robert E. Blair, Exec. Dir.; Suzanne Tanguay, Communications Officer. The Canadian equivalent of the U.S. National Education Association. *Membership:* 400 individual, 43 associate, 100 school board. *Dues:* $90 individual, $380 associate, 10 cents per pupil for school board. *Meetings:* September 19-22, 1995, Winnepeg, Man. *Publications: CEA Handbook*; *Education Canada* (q.); *CEA Newsletter* (9/yr.); *Violence in the Schools*; *Criteria for Admission to Faculties of Education in Canada: What You Need to Know*; *First Nations and Schools: Triumphs and Struggles*; *The Canadian Education Association: The First 100 Years 1891-1991*; *The Multi-Grade Classroom: Myth and Reality*; *French Immersion Today*; *Heritage Language Programs in Canadian School Boards.*

Canadian Library Association. 200 Elgin St., Suite 602, Ottawa, ON K2P IL5, Canada. (613) 232-9625. Fax (613) 563-9895. E-mail ai281@freenet.carleton.ca. Karen Adams, Exec. Dir. The mission of the Canadian Library Association is to provide leadership in the promotion, development, and support of library and information services in Canada for the benefit of Association members, the profession, and Canadian society. In the spirit of this mission, CLA aims to engage the active, creative participation of library staff, trustees, and governing bodies in the development and management of high quality Canadian library service; to assert and support the right of all Canadians to the freedom to read and to free universal access to a wide variety of library materials and services; to promote librarianship and to enlighten all levels of government as to the significant role that libraries play in educating and socializing the Canadian people; and to link libraries, librarians, trustees, and others across the country for the purpose of providing a unified nationwide voice in matters of critical concern. *Membership:* 2,300 personal, 700 institutional, 100 Associates and Trustees. *Dues:* Range from $50 to $1,600. *Meetings:* 1996, Annual Conference, June 6-9, Halifax, NS, "Sail into Our Future." *Publication: Feliciter* (membership magazine, 10/yr.).

Canadian Museums Association/Association des musées canadiens (CMA/AMC). 280 Metcalfe St., Suite 400, Ottawa, ON K2P 1R7, Canada. (613) 567-0099. Fax (613) 233-5438. John G. McAvity, Exec. Dir. The Canadian Museums Association is a nonprofit corporation and registered charity dedicated to advancing public museums and museum works in Canada, promoting the welfare and better administration of museums, and fostering a continuing improvement in the qualifications and practices of museum professionals. *Membership:* 2,000. *Meeting:* 1996, CMA Annual Conference, June 15-18, Vancouver, BC. *Publications: Museogramme* (bi-mo. newsletter); *Muse* (q. journal). Canada's only national, bilingual, scholarly magazine devoted to museums, it contains museum-based photography, feature articles, commentary, and practical information; *The Official Directory of Canadian Museums and*

Related Institutions (1993-94 edition) lists all museums in Canada plus information on government departments, agencies, and provincial and regional museum associations.

National Film Board of Canada (NFBC). 1251 Avenue of the Americas, 16th Floor, New York, NY 10020. (212) 596-1770. Fax (212) 595-1779. E-mail gsem78a@prodigy.com. John Sirabella, U.S. Marketing Mgr./Nontheatrical Rep. Established in 1939, the NFBC's main objective is to produce and distribute high-quality audiovisual materials for educational, cultural, and social purposes.

Ontario Film Association, Inc. (also known as the Association for the Advancement of Visual Media/L'association pour l'avancement des médias visuels). 3-1750 The Queensway, Suite 1341, Etobicoke, ON M9C 5H5, Canada. (416) 761-6056. Fax (905) 820-7397. Margaret Nix., Exec. Dir. A volunteer organization of buyers and users of media whose objectives are to promote the sharing of ideas and information about media; to showcase media; to publish *Visual Media*; to do advocacy; and to present workshops. Sponsors the Grierson Documentary Seminar on film and video and the Annual Showcase of video, a marketplace for buyers. *Membership:* 144. *Dues:* $120 regular and commercial, $180 extended. *Meeting:* 1996, OFA Media Showcase, April 15-18, Toronto, ON. *Publication: Visual Media/Médias Visuels* (5/yr.).

Part Seven
Graduate Programs

Doctoral Programs in Instructional Technology

This directory presents information on 37 doctoral (Ph.D. and Ed.D.) programs in instructional technology, educational communications/technology, media services, and closely allied programs in 21 states. Notification of one new program is also included. Information in this section for 24 of the programs was obtained from, and updated by, the institutional deans, chairs, or their representatives, in response to an inquiry questionnaire mailed to them during the fall of 1995. Updated information was requested with the proviso that, if no reply was received, information provided for the 1995-1996 edition would be used; programs for which no information has been received since 1994 or before would be dropped. Ten programs for which we received updated information for the 1995-1996 edition but no response for this edition are indicated by an asterisk (*); 12 program listings have been dropped for lack of recent information.

Entries provide as much of the following information as was provided by respondents: (1) name and address of the institution; (2) chairperson or other individual in charge of the doctoral program; (3) types of degrees offered and specializations, including information on positions for which candidates are prepared; (4) special features of the degree program; (5) admission requirements, including minimal grade point average; (6) number of full-time and part-time faculty; (7) number of full-time and part-time students; (8) types of financial assistance available; and (9) the number of doctoral degrees awarded in 1995.

Directors of advanced professional programs for instructional technology/media specialists should find this information useful as a means of comparing their own offerings and requirements with those of institutions offering comparable programs. This listing should also assist individuals seeking a school at which to pursue advanced graduate studies in locating institutions that best suit their interests and requirements.

Additional information on the programs listed, including instructions on applying for admission, may be obtained by contacting individual program coordinators. General or graduate catalogs usually are furnished for a minimal charge; specific program information normally is sent at no charge.

In endeavoring to provide complete listings, we are greatly indebted to those individuals who responded to our requests for information. Although considerable effort has been expended to ensure completeness of the listings, there may be institutions within the United States or its territories that now have programs or that have been omitted. Readers are encouraged to furnish new information to the publisher who, in turn, will follow up for the next edition of *EMTY*.

Institutions in this section are listed alphabetically by state.

ARIZONA

Arizona State University. Division of Psychology in Education, Box 870611, Tempe, AZ 85287-0611. (602) 965-3384. Fax (602) 965-0300. E-mail icnla@asuvm.inre.asu.edu. James D. Klein, Assoc. Prof., Learning and Instructional Technology; Nancy Archer, Admissions Secy. *Specializations:* Ph.D. in Learning and Instructional Technology. *Features:* Research and publication prior to candidacy. *Admission Requirements:* Undergraduate GPA of 3.0; GRE score of 1200. *Degree Requirements:* 84 semester hours beyond bachelor's degree, comprehensive examination, research/publication, and dissertation. *Faculty:* 5 full-time. *Doctoral*

Students: 18 full-time; 6 part-time. *Financial Assistance:* Assistantships and student loans. *Doctoral Degrees Awarded in 1995:* 5.

Arizona State University. Educational Media and Computers, Box 870111, Tempe, AZ 85287-0111. (602) 965-7192. Fax (602) 965-7058. E-mail bitter@asu.edu. Dr. Gary G. Bitter, Coord., Educational Media and Computers. *Specializations:* Ph.D. and M.A. in Educational Media and Computers. *Admission Requirements:* Bachelor's degree; TOEFL, 550 min. score; GRE, 500 min.; Miller Analogy Test, 45 min. *Minimum Degree Requirements:* 33 semester hours, (24 hours in educational media and computers, 6 hours education, 3 hours outside education). *Faculty:* 6 full-time; 1 part-time. *Students:* 18 full-time; 11 part-time. *Financial Assistance:* Assistantships, grants, student loans. *Doctoral Degrees Awarded 1995:* 1.

CALIFORNIA

*United States International University. School of Education, 10455 Pomerado Rd., San Diego, CA 92131-1799. (619) 635-4715. Fax (619) 635-4714. E-mail feifer@sanac.usiu.edu. Richard Feifer, contact person. *Specializations:* Ed.D. in Technology and Learning offers three specializations: Designing Technology for Learning, Planning Technology for Learning, and Technology Leadership for Learning. Completely revamped program begun in fall of 1994. *Features:* Interactive multimedia, cognitive approach to integrating technology and learning. *Admission Requirements:* Master's degree, English proficiency, interview, GPA greater than 3.0 and GRE score of at least 1900 or GPA greater than 2.0 and MAT score of at least 115. *Minimum Degree Requirements:* 88 graduate quarter units, dissertation. *Faculty:* 2 full-time; 4 part-time. *Students:* Master's, 32 full-time; 12 part-time; Doctoral, 6 full-time; 1 part-time. *Financial Assistance:* graduate assistantships, grants, student loans, scholarships. *Degrees Awarded 1994:* Ed.D., 1; Master's, 42.

University of Southern California. 702C W.P.H., School of Education, Los Angeles, CA 90089-0031. (213) 740-3288. Fax (213) 746-8142. E-mail kazlausk@mizor.usc.edu. Dr. Richard Clark, Prof., Doctoral programs; Dr. Edward J. Kazlauskas, Prof., Prog. Chair, Master's programs in Instructional Technology. *Specializations:* M.A., Ph.D., Ed.D. to prepare individuals to teach instructional technology; manage educational media/training programs in business or industry, research and development organizations, and higher educational institutions; perform research in instructional technology and media; and deal with computer-driven technology. Satellite Ed.D. program in Silicon Valley in northern California. A new Ed.D. program in Human Performance Technology was scheduled to be implemented in 1996. *Features:* Special emphasis upon instructional design, systems analysis, and computer-based training. *Admission Requirements:* A bachelor's degree and satisfactory performance (combined score of 1,000) on the GRE aptitude test. *Faculty:* 5 full-time; 1 part-time. *Students:* 5 full-time; 41 part-time. *Financial Assistance:* Part-time work available (instructional technology-related) in the Los Angeles area and on the university campus. *Doctorates Awarded 1995:* Data not reported.

COLORADO

University of Colorado-Denver. School of Education, Campus Box 106, P.O. Box 173364, Denver, CO 80217-3364. (303) 556-6022. Fax (303) 556-4479. E-mail bwilson@carbon. cudenver.edu. R. Scott Grabinger, Prog. Chair, Formation and Learning Technologies, Division of Technology and Special Services. *Specializations:* Ph.D. in instructional technology, in instructional development, and/or instructional computing for use in business/industry and higher education. *Features:* Courses in management and consulting, emphasizing instructional development, multimedia technologies, evaluation, and internship opportunities in a variety of agencies. *Admission Requirements:* Satisfactory GPA, GRE, writing/publication background, letters of recommendation, transcripts, and application form. *Faculty:* 5 full-time; 3 part-time. *Students:* 2 full-time; 20 part-time. *Financial Assistance:* Assistantships. *Doctorates Awarded 1995:* 5.

University of Northern Colorado. College of Education, Greeley, CO 80639. (970) 351-2687. Fax (970) 351-1622. E-mail caffarel@edtech.univnorthco.edu. Edward P. Caffarella, Prof., Chair, Educational Technology, Division of Educational Psychology, Statistics, and Technology. *Specializations:* Ph.D. in Educational Technology with emphasis areas in distance education, instructional development/design, interactive technology, and technology integration. *Features:* Graduates are prepared for careers as instructional technologists, course designers, trainers, instructional developers, media specialists, and human resource managers. *Admission Requirements:* GPA of 3.2, three letters of recommendation, congruency between applicant's statement of career goals and program goals, GRE combined test score of 1,650, and interview with faculty. *Faculty:* 5 full-time; 2 part-time. *Students:* 14 full-time; 10 part-time. *Financial Assistance:* Assistantships, grants, student loans, scholarships. *Doctorates Awarded 1995:* 1.

FLORIDA

Florida State University. Instructional Systems Program, Department of Educational Research, College of Education, 305 Stone Bldg., Tallahassee, FL 32306. (904) 644-4592. Fax (904) 644-8776. Marcy P. Driscoll, Prof. *Specializations:* Ph.D. degree in instructional systems with specializations for persons planning to work in academia, business, industry, government, or military; Specialist Degree. *Features:* Core courses include systems and materials development, analysis of media, project management, psychological foundations, current trends in instructional design, and research and statistics. Internships are recommended. *Admission Requirements:* Total score of 1,000 on the verbal and quantitative sections of the GRE, or a GPA of 3.3; international students, TOEFL score of 550. *Faculty:* 5 full-time; 5 part-time. *Students:* 45. *Financial Assistance:* Some graduate research assistantships on faculty grants and contracts; university fellowships. *Doctorates Awarded 1995:* 15.

Nova Southeastern University. Fischler Center for the Advancement of Education, 3301 College Ave., Fort Lauderdale, FL 33314. (954) 475-7440. (800) 986-3223, ext. 7440. Fax (954) 423-1224. E-mail pet@fcae.nova.edu. Abbey Manbury, Ed.D. program in Instructional Technology and Distance Education; Johanne Peck, Ph.D., M.S. and Ed.S. programs in Educational Media and in Computer Science Education. *Specializations:* Ed.S. and M.S. programs in Instructional Technology and Distance Education; Master's and Educational Specialist programs in Educational Media and in Computer Science Education. A 4-year combination M.S./Ed.D. program is also available. *Features:* ITDE program is delivered online via Internet worldwide with a few extended weekend meetings on campus. *Admission Requirements:* B.A. or B.S. for master's and educational specialist programs; M.A. or M.S. plus experience working in the field of education or training for doctoral programs. *Minimum Degree Requirements:* M.S., 36 semester hours including a practicum (1 to 1.5 years); Ed.S. 62 semester hours including a practicum (3 years). *Faculty:* 4 full-time; 10 part-time. *Students:* 50. *Financial Assistance:* one assistantship, student loans. *Doctorates Awarded 1995:* New degree.

GEORGIA

University of Georgia. College of Education, 607 Aderhold Hall, Athens, GA 30602-7144. (706) 542-3810. Fax (706) 542-4032. E-mail kgustafs@moe.coe.uga.edu. Kent L. Gustafson, Prof. and Chair, Dept. of Instructional Technology. *Specializations:* M.Ed, Ed.S., Ed.D, and Ph.D. for leadership positions as specialists in instructional design and development. The program offers advanced study for individuals with previous preparation in instructional media and technology, as well as a preparation for personnel in other professional fields requiring a specialty in instructional systems/instructional technology. Representative career fields for graduates include designing/developing/evaluating new courses, tutorial programs, and instructional materials in a number of different settings; military/industrial training; medical/dental/nursing professional schools; allied health agencies; teacher education/staff development centers; state/local school systems; higher education/teaching/research; and publishers/producers of instructional products (textbooks, workbooks, films, etc.). *Features:* Minor areas of study available in a variety of other departments. Personalized programs are planned around a common core of courses; practica, internships, and/or clinical experiences. Research activities include special assignments, applied projects, and task forces, as well as thesis and dissertation studies. *Admission Requirements:* Application to graduate school, satisfactory GRE score, other criteria as outlined in Graduate School Bulletin. *Faculty:* 10 full-time; 3 part-time. *Students:* 25 full-time; 10 part-time. *Financial Assistance:* Graduate assistantships available. *Doctorates Awarded 1995:* 5.

ILLINOIS

Northern Illinois University. College of Education, DeKalb, IL 60115. (815) 753-0464. Fax (815) 753-9371. Dr. Gary L. McConeghy, Chair, Instructional Technology, College of Education—LEPS. *Specializations:* Ed.D. in Instructional Technology, emphasizing instructional design and development, computer education, media administration, production, and preparation for careers in business, industry, and higher education. *Features:* Considerable flexibility in course selection, including advanced seminars, internships, individual study, and research. Program is highly individualized. A total of 60 courses offered by several departments, including Library Science, Radio/Television/Film, Art, Journalism, Educational Psychology, and Research and Evaluation. *Admission Requirements:* 2.75 undergraduate GPA, 3.5 M.S. GPA; combined score of 1,000 on GRE; a writing sample; and three references. *Faculty:* 8 full-time; 3 part-time. *Students:* 88 part-time. *Financial Assistance:* Assistantships available at times in various departments. *Doctorates Awarded 1995:* 5.

*Northwestern University. Institute for Learning Sciences, 1890 Maple Ave., Evanston, IL 60201. (708) 467-1332. Fax (708) 491-5258. E-mail tina@ils.nwu.edu. Roy D. Pea, Chair, Learning Sciences Ph.D. Program. Tina Turnbull, Grad. Prog. Coord., contact person. *Specializations:* Ph.D. in the Learning Sciences with three flexible tracks: teaching-learning environments; cognitive aspects of learning; and the design and development of effective computational and multimedia architectures for learning and teaching. *Features:* An integrated body of coursework and apprenticing activities is designed for all students, regardless of specialization, to develop their facility with theory and methods through laboratory work, field experiences, studies in nonlaboratory settings, participation in ongoing research and development projects, and independent research guided by faculty mentors. *Admission Requirements:* Data not reported. *Degree Requirements:* seven quarter core courses in the learning sciences; three or more methods courses; three advanced topic courses; participation in a variety of research laboratories and activities; a written preliminary examination; publication-quality predissertation paper reporting research conducted under the supervision of a faculty member; an oral qualifying examination; and a dissertation demonstrating original and significant research. *Faculty:* 22. *Students:* Data not reported. *Financial Assistance:* Students are eligible for competitively awarded multiyear funding. *Doctorates Awarded 1994:* Data not reported.

Southern Illinois University at Carbondale. Department of Curriculum and Instruction, Carbondale, IL 62901-4610. (618) 536-2441. Fax (618) 453-4244. E-mail sashrock@siu.edu. Sharon Shrock, Coord., Instructional Technology/Development. *Specializations:* Ph.D. in education including specialization in instructional technology. *Features:* All specializations are oriented to multiple education settings. *Admission Requirements:* 3.25 GPA or better; Miller Analogies Test or GRE score; letters of recommendation; and a writing sample. *Faculty:* 6 full-time; 2 part-time. *Students:* 25. *Financial Assistance:* Assistantships, scholarships. *Doctorates Awarded 1995:* 2.

University of Illinois at Urbana-Champaign. Department of Educational Psychology, 210 Education Bldg., 1310 S. 6th St., Champaign, IL 61820. (217) 333-2245. Fax (217) 244-7620. E-mail c-west@uiuc.edu. Charles K. West, Prof., Div. of Learning and Instruction, Dept. of Educational Psychology. *Specializations:* Ph.D. in educational psychology with emphasis in instructional psychology, instructional design, and educational computing. *Features:* Individually tailored program. Strongly research-oriented with emphasis on applications of cognitive science to instruction. *Admission Requirements:* Excellent academic record, high GRE scores, and strong letters of recommendation. *Faculty:* 14. *Students:* 36. *Financial Assistance:* Scholarships, research assistantships, and teaching assistantships available. *Doctorates Awarded 1995:* 5.

INDIANA

*Indiana University. School of Education, W. W. Wright Education Bldg., Bloomington, IN 47405-1006. (812) 855-1791. Fax (812) 855-3044. Thomas Schwen, Chair, Dept. of Instructional Systems Technology. *Specializations:* Offers Ph.D. and Ed.D. degrees with four program focus areas: Foundations; Instructional Analysis, Design, and Development; Instructional Development and Production; and Implementation and Management. *Features:* Requires computer skills as a prerequisite and makes technology utilization an integral part of the curriculum; eliminates the separation of the various media formats; and establishes a series of courses of increasing complexity integrating production and development. The latest in technical capabilities have been incorporated in the new Center for Excellence in Education, including teaching, photographic, computer, and science laboratories, a 14-station multimedia laboratory, and television studios. *Admission Requirements:* Data not reported. *Degree Requirements:* Ed.D., 60 post-bachelor's degree credit hours including nine credit hours in inquiry; portfolio examination; and dissertation (may be project based). Ph.D., 90 post-bachelor's degree credit hours of which 27 hours of credit must be in inquiry; publication; portfolio examination; participation in a research colloquium; and research-based dissertation. *Faculty:* 6 full-time; 3 part-time. *Students:* Data not reported. *Financial Assistance:* Data not reported. *Doctorates Awarded 1994:* Data not reported.

Purdue University. School of Education, W. Lafayette, IN 47907-1442. (317) 494-5673. Fax (317) 494-1622. Dr. James D. Russell, Prof. of Educational Computing and Instructional Development, Dept. of Curriculum and Instruction. *Specializations:* Ph.D. programs in instructional research and development or educational computing. *Admission Requirements:* GPA of 3.0 or better, three recommendations, scores totaling 1,000 or more on the GRE, statement of personal goals. *Faculty:* 6 full-time. *Students:* 8 full-time; 16 part-time. *Financial Assistance:* Assistantships and fellowships. *Doctorates Awarded 1995:* 6.

IOWA

Iowa State University. College of Education, Ames, IA 50011. (515) 294-6840. Fax (515) 294-9284. E-mail mrs@iastate.edu. Michael Simonson, Prof., Curriculum and Instruction Dept., College of Education. *Specializations:* Ph.D. in education with emphasis in instructional computing, instructional design, and technology research. *Features:* Practicum experiences related to professional objectives, supervised study and research projects tied to long-term studies within the program, development and implementation of new techniques, teaching strategies, and operational procedures in instructional resources centers and computer labs. *Admission Requirements:* Top half of undergraduate class, autobiography, three letters of recommendation, GRE general test scores. *Faculty:* 8 part-time. *Students:* 30 full-time; 30 part-time. *Financial Assistance:* 10 assistantships. *Doctorates Awarded 1995:* 6.

University of Iowa. College of Education, Iowa City, IA 52242. (319) 335-5519. Fax (319) 335-5386. Stephen Alessi, 361 Lindquist Center, Iowa City, IA 52242. *Specializations:* Ed.D. and M.A. with specializations in Classroom Instruction, Computer Applications, Instructional Development, Media Design and Production, and Training and Human Resource Development. *Features:* Flexibility in planning to fit individual needs, backgrounds, and career goals. The program is interdisciplinary, involving courses within divisions of the College of Education, as well as in the schools of Business, Library Science, Radio and Television, Linguistics, and Psychology. *Admission Requirements:* A composite score of at least 1,000 on GRE (verbal and quantitative) and a 3.2 GPA on all previous graduate work for regular admission. (Conditional admission may be granted.) Teaching or relevant experience may be helpful. *Minimum Degree Requirements:* 90 semester hours. *Faculty:* 3 full-time; 2 part-time. *Students:* 15 full-time; 10 part-time. *Financial Assistance:* Assistantships, grants, student loans, and scholarships. *Doctorates Awarded 1995:* 3.

KANSAS

*Emporia State University. School of Library and Information Management, 1200 Commercial, P.O. Box 4025, Emporia, KS 66801. (316) 341-5203. Fax (316) 341-5233. E-mail vowell@esuvm.bitnet. Faye N. Vowell, Dean, School of Library and Information Management. *Specializations:* Ph.D. in Library and Information Management; Master's of Library Science (ALA accredited program). *Features:* The MLS program is also available in Colorado, Oregon, North Dakota, and New Mexico. Video courses are being developed. *Admission Requirements:* Selective admissions process for M.L.S. and Ph.D. based on a combination of admission criteria, including (but not limited to): minimum GRE or TOEFL score; personal interview; GPA; statement of goals and references. Please request admission packet for specific criteria. *Minimum Degree Requirements:* Total of 83-97 semester hours depending on the number of hours received for an M.L.S. *Faculty:* 12 full-time; 35 part-time. *Students:* 100 full-time; 500 part-time in all sites. *Financial Assistance:* Assistantships, grants, student loans, scholarships. *Doctoral Degrees Awarded in 1994:* Data not reported.

Kansas State University. Educational Computing, Design, and Telecommunications, 363 Bluemont Hall, Manhattan, KS 66506. (913) 532-7686. Fax (913) 532-7304. E-mail dmcgrath@coe.educ.ksu.edu. Dr. Diane McGrath, contact person. *Specializations:* Ph.D. and Ed.D. in Curriculum & Instruction with an emphasis in Educational Computing, Design, and Telecommunications. *Admissions Requirements:* Ph.D./Ed.D.: B average in undergraduate and graduate work; one programming language; GRE or MAT; three letters of recommendation; experience or course in educational computing. *Minimum Degree Requirements:* Ph.D.: 90 semester hours (minimum of 21 hours in Educational Computing, Design, and Telecommunications or related area approved by committee; 30 hours for dissertation research); thesis required; internship or practicum not required but available. Ed.D.: 94 semester hours (minimum of 18 hours in Educational Computing or related area approved by committee; 16 hours for dissertation research; 12 hours of internship); thesis required. *Faculty:* 2 full-time; 1 part-time. *Students:* 12 full-time; 19 part-time. *Financial Assistance:* Five assistantships; other assistantships sometimes available in other departments depending on skills and funds available. *Doctorates Awarded 1995:* 2.

MARYLAND

*University of Maryland. College of Library and Information Services, College Park, MD 20742-4345. (301) 405-2038. Fax (301) 314-9145. Ann Prentice, Dean and Prog. Chair, College of Library and Information Services. *Specializations:* Ph.D. in Library Science and Educational Technology/Instructional Communication. *Features:* Program is broadly conceived and interdisciplinary in nature, using the resources of the entire campus. The student and the advisor design a program of study and research to fit the student's background, interests, and professional objectives. Students prepare for careers in teaching and research in information science and librarianship and elect concentrations including educational technology/instructional communication. *Admission Requirements:* Baccalaureate degree (the majority enter with master's degrees in library science, educational technology, or other relevant disciplines), GRE general tests, three letters of recommendation, and a statement of purpose. Interviews required when feasible. *Faculty:* 15 full-time; 8 part-time. *Students:* 9 full-time; 8 part-time. *Financial Assistance:* Assistantships, grants, student loans, scholarships. *Doctorates Awarded in 1994:* 2.

MASSACHUSETTS

Boston University. School of Education, 605 Commonwealth Ave., Boston, MA 02215-1605. (617) 353-3181. Fax (617) 353-3924. E-mail whittier@bu.edu. David B. Whittier, Acting Dir., Program in Educational Media and Technology. *Specializations:* Ed.D. specializing in instructional design/development for developing and teaching academic programs in instructional technology in community colleges and universities; or specialization in such application areas as business and industrial training, biomedical communication, or international development projects. Program specializations in instructional development, media production and design, and multimedia design and development for education and training. Students participate in mandatory research sequence and may elect courses in other university schools and colleges. *Features:* Doctoral students have a great deal of flexibility in program planning and are encouraged to plan programs that build on prior education and experience that lead to specific career goals; there is strong faculty participation in this process. *Admission Requirements:* Three letters of recommendation, Miller Analogies Test or GRE test score(s), undergraduate and graduate transcripts, completed application form with statement of goals. Minimum GPA is 2.7 with Miller Analogies Test score of 50. *Degree Requirements:* 60 credit hours, comprehensive exam, dissertation. *Faculty:* 1 full-time; 10 part-time. *Students:* 5 full-time; 15 part-time. *Financial Assistance:* Assistantships, grants, student loans, scholarships. *Doctorates Awarded 1995:* 11.

MICHIGAN

Wayne State University. 395 Education, Detroit, MI 48202. (313) 577-1728. Fax (313) 577-1693. E-mail rrichey@cms.cc.wayne.edu. Rita C. Richey, Prof., Program Coord., Instructional Technology Programs, Div. of Administrative and Organizational Studies, College of Education. *Specializations:* Ed.D. and Ph.D. programs to prepare individuals for leadership in business, industry, health care, and the K-12 school setting as instructional design and development specialists; media or learning resources managers or consultants; specialists in instructional video; and computer-assisted instruction and multimedia specialists. *Features:* Guided experiences in instructional design and development activities in business and industry are available. *Admission Requirements:* Master's, GPA of 3.5, GRE, and Miller Analogies Test, strong professional recommendations, and an interview. *Faculty:* 4 full-time; 5 part-time. *Students:* 125 at the doctoral level, most of them part-time. *Financial Assistance:* Student loans, scholarships, and paid internships. *Doctorates Awarded 1995:* 16.

MISSOURI

University of Missouri-Columbia. College of Education, 212 Townsend Hall, Columbia, MO 65211. (314) 882-3832. Fax (314) 884-5455. E-mail wedmanjf@showme.missouri.edu. John F. Wedman, Assoc. Prof., Educational Technology Program, Curriculum and Instruction Dept., College of Education. *Specializations:* Ph.D. in Instructional Theory and Practice. The program emphasizes learning and instructional design, electronic performance support systems (including multimedia development), and change processes. *Features:* Program includes a major in Instructional Theory and Practice with two support areas (i.e., Educational Psychology and Computer Science), research tools, and R&D apprenticeship experiences. The program is rapidly expanding, providing the cornerstone for improving mathematics, science, and technical education. These areas have been identified for enhancement and supported with an annual R&D budget of over $300,000. *Admission Requirements:* Graduate GPA above 3.2 and a combined score of 1,500 or better on the GRE; letters of recommendation; and a statement of purpose. *Faculty:* 5 full-time; 4 part-time, plus selected faculty in related fields. *Students:* 20 full-time; 12 part-time. *Financial Assistance:* Graduate assistantships with tuition waivers; numerous academic scholarships ranging from $200 to $10,000. *Doctorates Awarded 1995:* 5.

NEW JERSEY

Rutgers-The State University of New Jersey. The Graduate School, New Brunswick, NJ 08903. (908) 932-7447. Fax (908) 932-6916. Lea P. Stewart, Prof., Dir., Ph.D. Program in Communication, Information, and Library Studies, The Graduate School. *Specializations:* Ph.D. programs in communication; information systems, structures, and users; information and communication policy and technology; and library and information services. *Features:* Program provides doctoral-level coursework for students seeking theoretical and research skills for scholarly and professional leadership in the information and communication fields. *Admission Requirements:* Typically, students should have completed a master's degree in information studies, communication, library science, or related field. The undergraduate GPA should be 3.0 or better. The GRE is required; TOEFL is also required for foreign applicants whose native language is not English. *Faculty:* 43 full- and part-time. *Students:* 104 full- and part-time. *Financial Assistance:* Assistantships and Title II-B fellowships. *Doctorates Awarded 1995:* 8.

NEW YORK

New York University. School of Education, New York, NY 10003. (212) 998-5520. Fax (212) 995-4041. Francine Shuchat Shaw, Assoc. Prof., Dir., Educational Communication and Technology Program; Donald T. Payne, Assoc. Prof., Doctoral Advisor, Educational Communication and Technology Program, 239 Greene St., Suite 300, School of Education. *Specializations:* Ph.D., Ed.D. in education for the preparation of individuals to perform as instructional media designers, developers, producers, and researchers in education, business and industry, health and medicine, community services, government, museums, and other cultural institutions; and to teach in educational communications and instructional technology programs in higher education, including instructional television, microcomputers, multimedia, and telecommunications. *Features:* Emphasizes theoretical foundations, in particular a cognitive perspective of learning and instruction and their implications for designing media-based learning environments—all efforts focus on multimedia, instructional television, and telecommunications; participation in special research and production projects and field internships. *Admission Requirements:* Combined score of 1,000 minimum on GRE, responses to essay questions and interview related to academic and/or professional preparation and career goals. *Degree Requirements:* 54 semester hours including specialization, foundations, research, content seminar, and elective coursework; candidacy papers; dissertation; and English Essay Examination. *Faculty:* 2 full-time; 10 part-time. *Students:* 14 full-time; 30 part-time. *Financial Assistance:* Graduate and research assistantships, student loans, scholarships, and work-study programs. *Doctorates Awarded 1995:* 2.

State University of New York at Albany. School of Education, 1400 Washington Ave., Albany, NY 12222. (518) 442-5032. Fax (518) 442-5008. E-mail swan@cnsunix.albany.edu. Karen Swan (ED114A), contact person. *Specialization:* Ph.D. and M.Ed. in Curriculum and Instruction with specializations in Instructional Technology, Design, and Theory. *Minimum Degree Requirements:* 78 semester hours, internship, thesis, portfolio certification. *Faculty:* 13 full-time; 7 part-time. *Students:* 20 full-time; 50 part-time. *Financial Assistance:* Fellowships. *Doctoral Degrees Awarded 1995:* Data not reported.

*State University of New York at Buffalo. Graduate School of Education, Buffalo, NY 14214. (716) 636-3164. Fax (716) 645-2481. Taher A. Razik, Prof. of Education, Dept. of Educational Organization, Administration and Policy, 480 Baldy Hall. *Specializations:* Ph.D., Ed.D., and Ed.M. in instructional design systems and management. Emphasis is on the systems approach, communication, and computer-assisted instruction and model building, with a specific focus on the efficient implementation of media in instruction. *Features:* The program is geared to instructional development, systems analysis, systems design and management in educational and noneducational organizations; research is oriented to the analysis of communication and information theory. Laboratories are available to facilitate student and faculty research projects in educational and/or training settings. Specifically, the knowledge and skills are categorized as follows: planning and designing; delivery systems and managing; and evaluating. *Admission Requirements:* Satisfactory scores on the Miller Analogies Test and/or GRE, minimum 3.0 GPA, sample of student writing, and personal interview. *Faculty:* 3 full-time; 3 part-time. *Students:* 18 full- and part-time. *Financial Assistance:* Some graduate assistantships and various fellowships (apply by March 10). *Doctorates Awarded 1993-94:* 5.

Syracuse University. School of Education, 330 Huntington Hall, Syracuse, NY 13244-2340. (315) 443-3703. Fax (315) 443-5732. Philip L. Doughty, Prof., Chair, Instructional Design, Development, and Evaluation Program, School of Education. *Specializations:* Ph.D. and Ed.D. degree programs for instructional design of programs and materials, educational evaluation, human issues in instructional development, media production (including computers and videodisc), and educational research and theory (learning theory, application of theory, and educational and media research). Graduates are prepared to serve as curriculum developers, instructional developers, program and product evaluators, researchers, resource center administrators, communications coordinators, trainers in human resource development, and higher education instructors. *Features:* Field work and internships, special topics and special issues seminar, student- and faculty-initiated minicourses, seminars and guest lecturers, faculty-student formulation of department policies, and multiple international perspectives. *Admission Requirements:* A master's degree from an accredited institution and GRE (V, Q & A) scores. *Faculty:* 5 full-time; 4 part-time. *Students:* 44 full-time; 29 part-time. *Financial Assistance:* Some fellowships, scholarships, and graduate assistantships entailing either research or administrative duties in instructional technology. *Doctorates Awarded 1995:* 9.

OHIO

The Ohio State University. College of the Arts, Dept. of Art Education, 340 Hopkins Hall, 128 North Oval Mall, Columbus, OH 43210. (614) 292-0235; (614) 292-7183. Fax (614) 292-1674. E-mail carol@cgrg.ohio-state.edu. Dr. Carol Gigliotti, contact person. *Specializations:* Ph.D. and M.A. in Art Education with specializations in the teaching and learning of computer graphics and computer-mediated art; multimedia production and its curricular applications; telecommunications in the arts; and ethical, aesthetic, and cultural aspects of interactive technologies. *Features:* Specialization at the Advanced Computer Center for the Arts and Design (ACCAD). *Faculty:* 1 full-time; 1 part-time in specialty. *Students:* 15 full-time; 3 part-time in specialty. *Financial Assistance:* Assistantships, grants, student loans, and scholarships. *Doctorates Awarded 1995:* Data not reported.

PENNSYLVANIA

Pennsylvania State University. 270 Chambers Bldg., University Park, PA 16802. (814) 865-0473. Fax (814) 865-0128. E-mail jonassen@psu.edu. D. Jonassen, Prof. in Charge. *Specializations:* Ph.D. and D.Ed. in Instructional Systems. Current teaching emphases are on corporate training, emerging technologies, and educational systems design. Research interests include hypermedia/multimedia, visual learning, educational reform, emerging technologies, and constructivist learning. *Features:* A common thread throughout all programs is that candidates have basic competencies in the understanding of human learning; instructional design, development, and evaluation; and research procedures. Practical experience is available in mediated independent learning, research, instructional development, computer-based education, and dissemination projects. *Admission Requirements:* GRE, TOEFL, transcript, three letters of recommendation, writing sample, vita/resume, and letter of application detailing reasoning. *Degree Requirements:* Candidacy exam, courses, residency, comprehensives, dissertation. *Faculty:* 9 full-time. *Students:* 25 full-time; 20 part-time at the doctoral level. *Financial Assistance:* Two assistantships and internships and assistantships on grants, contracts, and projects. *Doctorates Awarded 1995:* 6.

*University of Pittsburgh. School of Education, Pittsburgh, PA 15260. (412) 612-7254. Fax (412) 648-7081. E-mail bseels+@pitt.edu. Barbara Seels, Assoc. Prof., Prog. Coord., Program in Instructional Design and Technology, Dept. of Instruction and Learning, School of Education. *Specializations:* Ed.D. and M.Ed. programs for the preparation of instructional technologists with skills in designing, developing, using, evaluating, and managing processes and resources for learning. Certification option for instructional technologists available. *Features:* Program prepares people for positions in which they can effect educational change through instructional technology. Program includes three competency areas: instructional design, technological delivery systems, and communications research. *Admissions Requirements:* Submission of written statement of applicant's professional goals, three letters of recommendation, demonstration of English proficiency, satisfactory GPA, sample of professional writing, GRE, and personal interviews. *Faculty:* 3 full-time. *Students:* 39 at the doctoral level. *Financial Assistance:* Tuition scholarships and assistantships may be available. *Doctorates Awarded 1994:* 6.

TENNESSEE

*University of Tennessee Knoxville. College of Education, Education in Sciences, Mathematics, Research, and Technology Unit, 319 Claxton Addition, Knoxville, TN 37996-3400. (615) 974-4222 or (615) 974-3103. Dr. Al Grant, Coord., Instructional Media and Technology Program. *Specializations:* M.S. in Ed., Ed.D., and Ed.S. under Education in Sciences, Mathematics, Research, and Technology; Ph.D. under the College of Education, concentration in Instructional Media and Technology, Ed.D. in Curriculum and Instruction, concentration in Instructional Media and Technology. *Features:* Coursework in media management, advanced software production, utilization, research, theory, psychology, instructional computing, television, and instructional development. Coursework will also meet the requirements for state certification as Instructional Materials Supervisor in the public schools of Tennessee. *Admission Requirements:* Send for the Graduate Catalog, The University of Tennessee. *Media Faculty:* 1 full-time, with additional assistance from Curriculum and Instruction and university faculty. *Students:* 2 part-time at the doctoral level. *Doctorates Awarded 1994:* 1.

TEXAS

Texas A&M University. College of Education, College Station, TX 77843. (409) 845-7276. Fax (409) 845-9663. Ronald D. Zellner, Assoc. Prof., Coord. Educational Technology Program, Dept. of Curriculum & Instruction. *Specializations:* EDCI Ph.D. program with specializations in educational technology and in distance education; Ph.D. in Educational Psychology Foundations: Learning & Technology; M.Ed. in Educational Technology. The purpose of the Educational Technology Program is to prepare educators with the competencies required to improve the quality and effectiveness of instructional programs at all levels. A major emphasis is placed on multimedia instructional materials development and techniques for effective distance education and communication. The program goal is to prepare graduates with a wide range of skills to work as professionals and leaders in a variety of settings, including education, business, industry, and the military. *Features:* Program facilities include laboratories for teaching, resource development, and production. Computer, video, and multimedia development are supported in a number of facilities. The college and university also maintain facilities for distance education materials development and fully equipped classrooms for course delivery to nearby collaborative school districts and sites throughout the state. *Admission Requirements:* GPA 3.0, GRE 800. *Degree Requirements:* 40 hours. *Faculty:* 5 full-time; 1 part-time. *Students:* 3 full-time. *Financial Assistance:* Several graduate assistantships. *Doctorates Awarded 1995:* 1.

The University of Texas. College of Education, Austin, TX 78712. (512) 471-5211. Fax (512) 471-4607. DeLayne Hudspeth, Assoc. Prof., Area Coord., Instructional Technology, Dept. of Curriculum and Instruction, College of Education. *Specializations:* Ph.D. program emphasizes research, design, and development of instructional systems and communications technology.

Features: The program is interdisciplinary in nature, although certain competencies are required of all students. Programs of study and dissertation research are based on individual needs and career goals. Learning resources include a model LRC, computer labs and class-rooms, a color television studio, interactive multimedia lab, and access to a photo and graphics lab. *Admission Requirements:* Minimum 3.25 GPA and a score of at least 1200 on the GRE. *Faculty:* 4 full-time; 2 part-time. Many courses are offered cooperatively by other departments, including Radio-TV Film, Computer Science, and Educational Psychology. *Students:* 31. *Financial Assistance:* Assistantships may be available to develop instructional materials, teach undergraduate computer literacy, and assist with research projects. There are also some paid internships. *Doctorates Awarded 1995:* 9.

UTAH

Brigham Young University. Department of Instructional Science, 201 MCKB, BYU, Provo, UT 84602. (801) 378-5097. Fax (801) 378-8672. E-mail paul_merrill@byu.edu; http://www.byu. edu/homepage.htal. Paul F. Merrill, Prof., Chair. *Specializations:* Ph.D. degrees in instructional design, research and evaluation, instructional psychology, literacy education, and second language acquisition. *Features:* Course offerings include principles of learning, instructional design, assessing learning outcomes, evaluation in education, empirical inquiry in education, project management, quantitative reasoning, microcomputer materials production, multimedia production, naturalistic inquiry, and more. Students are required to participate in internships and projects related to development, evaluation, measurement, and research. *Admission Requirements:* Transcript, 3 letters of recommendation, letter of intent, and GRE examination. Apply by February 1. Students agree to live by the BYU Honor Code. *Faculty:* 9 full-time, 2 half-time. *Students:* 47 full-time, 3 part-time. *Financial Assistance:* Internships, tuition waivers, loans, and travel to present papers. *Doctorates Awarded 1995:* 4.

Utah State University. College of Education, Logan, UT 84322-2830. (801) 797-2694. Fax (801) 797-2693. E-mail dsmellie@ce.usu.edu. Don C. Smellie, Prof., Chair, Dept. of Instructional Technology, College of Education. *Specializations:* Ph.D. in Instructional Technology. Offered for individuals seeking to become professionally involved in instructional development in corporate education, public schools, community colleges, and universities. Teaching and research in higher education is another career avenue for graduates of the program. A six-year program is available. *Features:* The doctoral program is built on a strong master's and specialist's program in instructional technology. All doctoral students complete a core with the remainder of the course selection individualized, based upon career goals. *Admission Requirements:* 3.0 GPA, successful teaching experience or its equivalent, a verbal and quantitative score at the 40th percentile on the GRE, and three written recommendations. *Faculty:* 9 full-time; 7 part-time. *Students:* Ph.D., 12 full-time; 14 part-time; Ed.S., 8 full-time; 10 part-time. *Financial Assistance:* Approximately 18 to 26 assistantships (apply by June 1). *Doctorates Awarded 1995:* 3; Ed.S., 1.

VIRGINIA

University of Virginia. Curry School of Education, Ruffner Hall, Charlottesville, VA 22903. (804) 924-7471. Fax (804) 924-7987. John B. Bunch, Assoc. Prof., Coord. Instructional Technology Program, Dept. of Leadership, Foundations and Policy Studies. *Specializations:* Ed.D. or Ph.D. degrees offered with focal areas in media production, interactive multimedia, and K-12 educational technologies. For specific degree requirements, write to the address above or refer to the UVA *Graduate Record. Faculty:* 3 full-time; 2 part-time. *Students:* 10 full-time; 4 part-time. *Doctorates Awarded 1995:* Data not reported.

*Virginia Polytechnic Institute and State University. College of Education, Blacksburg, VA 24061-0313. (540) 231-5598. Fax (540) 231-9075. Terry M. Wildman, Prog. Area Leader, Instructional Systems Development, Curriculum and Instruction. *Specializations:* Ed.D. and Ph.D. in Instructional Technology. Preparation for education, business, and industry. *Features:*

Areas of emphasis are instructional design, educational computing, evaluation, and media management. Facilities include 70 computer lab microcomputers (IBM, Macintosh), interactive video, speech synthesis, and telecommunications. *Admission Requirements:* 3.3 GPA for master's degree, interview, three letters of recommendation, transcripts of previous academic work. *Faculty:* 8 full-time; 5 part-time. *Students:* 30 full-time; 8 part-time at the doctoral level. *Financial Assistance:* 10 assistantships, tuition scholarships, and contracts with other agencies. *Doctorates Awarded 1994:* Data not reported.

WASHINGTON

University of Washington. College of Education, Seattle, WA 98195. (206) 543-1847. Fax (206) 543-8439. E-mail stkerr@u.washington.edu. Stephen T. Kerr, Prof. of Education, College of Education. *Specializations:* Ph.D. and Ed.D. for individuals in business, industry, higher education, public schools, and organizations concerned with education or communication (broadly defined). *Features:* Emphasis on instructional design as a process of making decisions about the shape of instruction; additional focus on research and development in such areas as message design (especially graphics and diagrams); electronic information systems; interactive instruction via videodisc, videotex, and computers. *Admission Requirements:* GRE scores, letters of reference, transcripts, personal statement, master's degree or equivalent in field appropriate to the specialization, 3.5 GPA in master's program, two years of successful professional experience and/or experience related to program goals. *Faculty:* 2 full-time; 3 part-time. *Students:* 12 full-time; 32 part-time. *Financial Assistance:* Assistantships awarded competitively and on basis of program needs; other assistantships available depending on grant activity in any given year. *Doctorates Awarded 1995:* 3.

Master's Degree and Six-Year Programs in Instructional Technology

During the fall semester of 1995, an inquiry-questionnaire was sent to the program chairs or their representatives for the 146 programs in 38 states and the District of Columbia that are listed in the 1995-1996 yearbook. Responses were received from 76 of the programs. Information that was updated in 1995-1996 is also included in this edition for 34 additional programs, which are indicated by an asterisk (*) before the name of the institution. We would like to express our appreciation for the many responses that were received. Thirty-six programs have been dropped from this listing for lack of current/recent information.

Each entry in the directory contains as much of the following information as was available to us: (1) name and mailing address of the institution; (2) name, academic rank, and title of program head or the name of a contact person; (3) name of the administrative unit offering the program; (4) minimum degree requirements; (5) number of full-time and part-time faculty; and (6) number of students who graduated with master's degrees from the program in 1995 or during the one-year period between 1 July 1994 and 30 June 1995. The availability of six-year specialist/certificate programs in instructional technology and related media is indicated where appropriate following the description of the master's program.

Several institutions appear in both this list and the list of graduate programs in educational computing, either because their computer technology programs are offered separately from the educational/instructional technology programs, or because they are separate components of the overall educational technology program.

To ensure completeness of this directory, considerable effort has been expended. However, readers who know of either new programs or omissions are encouraged to provide information to the publisher who, in turn, will follow up on them for the next edition of *EMTY*. Information on any programs that have been discontinued would also be most welcome.

Individuals who are interested in any of these graduate programs are encouraged to make direct contact with the head of the program to obtain the most recent information available.

Institutions in this section are arranged alphabetically by state.

ALABAMA

Auburn University. Educational Foundations, Leadership, and Technology, 4036 Haley Center, Auburn, AL 36849-5221. (334) 844-4291. Fax (334) 844-5785. E-mail bannosh@mail.auburn.edu. Susan H. Bannon, Coord., Educational Media and Technology. *Specializations:* M.Ed. and Ed.S. for library media certification; M.Ed. (non-thesis) or M.S. (with thesis) for instructional design specialists who want to work in business, industry, the military, etc. *Features:* Both programs have concentrations in educational computing and interactive technologies. *Admission Requirements:* Recent GRE Basic test score; 3 letters of recommendation; graduate of accredited college/university; teacher certification (for library media program only). *Degree Requirements:* Library Media Master's: 56 quarter hours, 40 in media/technology, 300 clock hour internship required. Library Media Six-year: 40 quarter hours, 32 in media/technology, thesis required; Instructional Design: 48 qtr. hrs., 36 in media/technology. *Faculty:* 5 full-time; 3 part-time. *Students:* 8 full-time; 20 part-time. *Financial Assistance:* Graduate assistantships. *Master's Degrees Awarded 1995:* 5.

Jacksonville State University. Instructional Media Division, Jacksonville, AL 36265. (205) 782-5011. Martha Merrill, Coord., Dept. of Educational Resources, Instructional Media Div. *Specializations:* M.S. in Education with emphasis on instructional media. *Minimum Degree Requirements:* 36 semester hours including 24 in library media. *Faculty:* 2 full- and part-time. *Students:* 30 full- and part-time. *Master's Degrees Awarded 1995:* Data not reported.

ARIZONA

Arizona State University. Educational Media and Computers, Box 870111, Tempe, AZ 85287-0111. (602) 965-7192. Fax (602) 965-7058. E-mail bitter@asu.edu. Dr. Gary G. Bitter, Coord., Educational Media and Computers. *Specializations:* M.A. and Ph.D. in Educational Media and Computers. *Admission Requirements:* Bachelor's degree; TOEFL, 550 min. score; GRE, 500 min.; Miller Analogy Test, 45 min. *Minimum Degree Requirements:* 33 semester hours (24 hours in educational media and computers, 6 hours education, 3 hours outside education). *Faculty:* 6 full-time; 1 part-time. *Students:* 59 full-time; 73 part-time. *Financial Assistance:* Assistantships, grants, student loans. *Master's Degrees Awarded 1995:* 21.

Arizona State University. Learning and Instructional Technology, Box 870611, ASU, Tempe, AZ 85287-0611. (602) 965-3384. Fax (602) 965-0300. E-mail incla@asuvm.inre.asu.edu. Nancy Archer, Admissions Sec., contact person. *Specializations:* Master's in Learning and Instructional Technology. *Minimum Degree Requirements:* 30 semester hours; comprehensive exam required; M.A. requires thesis. *Faculty:* 5 full-time. *Students:* 20 full-time; 10 part-time. *Financial Assistance:* Graduate assistantships available for qualified applicants. *Master's Degrees Awarded 1995:* 12.

ARKANSAS

University of Central Arkansas. Educational Media/Library Science Department, Campus Box 4918, Conway, AR 72035. (501) 450-5463. Fax (501) 450-5480. E-mail selvinr@cc1.uca.edu. Selvin W. Royal, Prof., Chair, Applied Academic Technologies. *Specializations:* M.S. Educational Media/Library Science and Information Science. Track 1 School Library Media, Track 2 Public Information Agencies, Track 3 Media Information Studies. *Admission Requirements:* File a departmental application form; provide transcripts of previous work and GRE general test scores; 2 letters of recommendation; a personal interview; and a written rationale for entering the profession. *Minimum Degree Requirements:* 36 semester hours, optional thesis, practicum (for Track 1), professional research paper. *Faculty:* 5 full-time; 2 part-time. *Students:* 9 full-time; 23 part-time. *Financial Assistance:* 3 to 4 graduate assistantships each year; 6 grants; Federal Grant (annually). *Master's Degrees Awarded 1995:* 13.

CALIFORNIA

California State University-San Bernardino. 5500 University Parkway, San Bernardino, CA 92407. (909) 880-5677. (909) 880-7011. Fax (909) 880-7010. E-mail rsantiag@wiley.csusb.edu. Dr. Rowena Santiago, Prog. Coord. *Specializations:* M.A. The program has two emphases: video production and computer application. These emphases allow students to choose courses related to the design and creation of video products or courses involving lab and network operation of advanced microcomputer applications. The program does not require teaching credential certification. *Admission Requirements:* Bachelor's degree, appropriate work experience, GPA of 3.0 or higher, completion of introductory computer course and expository writing course. *Minimum Degree Requirements:* 48 units including a master's project (33 units completed in residence); GPA of 3.0 (B), grades of "C" (2) or better in all courses. *Faculty:* 4 full-time; 4 part-time. *Students:* 106 full- and part-time, 78 of which have been classified. *Financial Assistance:* Contact Office of Graduate Studies. *Master's Degrees Awarded 1995:* Data not reported. Advanced certificate programs in Educational Computing and Educational Technology are available.

San Diego State University. Educational Technology, San Diego, CA 92182-0311. (619) 594-6718. Fax (619) 594-6376. E-mail patrick.harrison@sasu.edu; http://edweb.sdsu.edu. Dr. Patrick Harrison, Prof., Chair, Dept. of Educational Technology. *Specialization:* Master's degree in Educational Technology with specializations in Computers in Education, Workforce Education and Lifelong Learning. *Minimum Degree Requirements:* 36 semester hours including 6 prerequisite hours, GRE combined total 950 Verbal and Quantitative scores. *Faculty:* 7 full-time; 4 part-time. *Students:* 110. *Financial Assistance:* Graduate Assistantships. *Master's Degrees Awarded 1995:* Data not reported. The Educational Technology Department participates in a College of Education joint doctoral program with The Claremont Graduate School.

San Francisco State University. College of Education, Department of Instructional Technology, 1600 Holloway Ave., San Francisco, CA 94132. (415) 338-1509. Fax (415) 338-0510. E-mail michaels@sfsu.edu. Dr. Eugene Michaels, Chair; Mimi Kasner, Office Coord. *Specializations:* Master's degree with emphasis on Instructional Multimedia Design, Training and Designing Development, Instructional Computing, and Instructional Video Production. *Features:* This program emphasizes the instructional systems approach, cognitivist principles of learning design, practical design experience, and project-based courses. *Admission Requirements:* Bachelor's degree, appropriate work experience, GPA of 2.5 or higher, interview with the department chair. *Minimum Degree Requirements:* 30 semester hours, field study thesis or project required. *Faculty:* 3 full-time; 11 part-time. *Students:* 250-300. *Financial Assistance:* Contact Office of Financial Aid. *Master's Degrees Awarded 1995:* 50. The school also offers an 18-unit Graduate Certificate in Training Systems Development, which can be incorporated into the master's degree.

*United States International University. School of Education, 10455 Pomerado Rd., San Diego, CA 92131-1799. (619) 635-4715. Fax (619) 635-4714. E-mail feifer@sanac.usiu.edu. Richard Feifer, School of Education. *Specialization:* Master's in Designing Technology for Learning, Planning Technology for Learning, Technology Leadership for Learning. *Features:* Interactive multimedia, cognitive approach to integrating technology and learning. Completely revamped program begun in the fall of 1994; for additional information, see the listing for the doctoral program. *Faculty:* 2 full-time; 4 part-time. *Students:* (at the master's level) 32 full-time; 12 part-time. *Financial Aid:* Internships, grants, scholarships, student loans. *Master's Degrees Awarded 1994:* 42.

*University of Southern California. Instructional Technology, Division of Curriculum and Instruction, Los Angeles, CA 90007-0031. (213) 740-3476. Fax (213) 746-8142. Ed Kazlauskas, Prof., Chair, Dept. of Curriculum and Teaching, School of Education. *Specialization:* Master's degree. *Minimum Degree Requirements:* 31 semester hours, thesis optional. *Faculty:* 5 full-time; 1 part-time. *Students:* 1 full-time; 9 part-time. *Master's Degrees Awarded 1994:* 29.

COLORADO

University of Colorado-Denver. School of Education, Denver, CO 80217-3364. (303) 556-6022. Fax (303) 556-4479. E-mail bwilson@carbon.cudenver.edu. R. Scott Grabinger, Program Chair, Information and Learning Technologies, Division of Technology and Special Services. Master's degree. *Minimum Degree Requirements:* For several tracks, including instructional computing, corporate training and development, library/media and instructional technology, 36 semester hours including comprehensive; project or internship required. *Faculty:* 5 full-time; 3 part-time. *Students:* 4 full-time; 200 part-time. *Financial Assistance:* Assistantships. *Master's Degrees Awarded 1995:* 30.

University of Northern Colorado. Division of Educational Psychology, Statistics, and Technology, Greeley, CO 80639. (970) 351-2687. Fax (970) 351-1622. E-mail caffarel@ edtech.univnorthco.edu. Edward F. Caffarella, Prof., College of Education. *Specializations:* M.A. in Educational Technology; M.A. in Educational Media. *Minimum Admission Requirements:* Bachelor's degree; undergraduate GPA of at least 3.0; GRE minimum score 1500 combined. *Minimum Degree Requirements:* 36 semester hours; comprehensive exam. *Faculty:* 5 full-time; 2 part-time. *Students:* Educational Technology—6 full-time; 29 part-time; Educational Media—1 full-time; 27 part-time. *Financial Assistance:* Graduate assistantships, grants, scholarships, and student loans. *Master's Degrees Awarded 1995:* M.A. in Educational Media, 24; M.A. in Educational Technology, 16.

CONNECTICUT

Central Connecticut State University. 1615 Stanley St., New Britain, CT 06050. (860) 832-2130. Fax (860) 832-2109. E-mail abedf@ccsu.ctstateu.edu. Farough Abed, Coord., Educational Technology Program. *Specializations:* M.S. in Educational Technology. Curriculum emphases include media management, materials production, librarianship, and computer technologies. *Admission Requirements:* Bachelor's degree; undergraduate GPA of at least 2.7. *Degree Requirements:* 33 semester hours; optional thesis or master's final project (3 credits). *Faculty:* 2 full-time; 4 part-time. *Students:* Data not reported. *Financial Assistance:* Graduate assistant position. *Master's Degrees Awarded 1995:* 10.

Fairfield University. Media Center, N. Benson Road, Fairfield, CT 06430. (203) 254-4000. Fax (203) 254-4087. E-mail imhefzalla@fair1.fairfield.edu. Dr. Ibrahim M. Hefzallah, Prof., Co-Dir. of Media/Educational Technology Program; Dr. John Schurdak, Assoc. Prof., Co-Dir., Computers in Education/Educational Technology Program. *Specializations:* M.A. in Media/Educational Technology with emphasis on theory, practice, and new instructional developments in computers in education, multimedia, and satellite communications. *Admission Requirements:* Bachelor's degree from an accredited institution with a minimum 2.67 GPA. *Degree Requirements:* 33 credits. *Faculty:* 2 full-time; 6 part-time. *Students:* 6 full-time; 54 part-time. *Financial Assistance:* Assistantships, student loans. *Master's Degrees Awarded 1995:* 14. A Certificate of Advanced Studies in Media/Educational Technology is available, which includes instructional development, television production, and media management; customized course of study also available.

Southern Connecticut State University. Department of Library Science and Instructional Technology, 501 Crescent St., New Haven, CT 06515. (203) 392-5781. Fax (203) 392-5780. E-mail libscienceit@csu.ctstateu.edu. Nancy Disbrow, Chair, Library Science/Instructional

Technology. *Specializations:* M.S. in Instructional Technology; Sixth-Year Professional Diploma Library-Information Studies (student may select area of specialization in instructional technology). *Minimum Degree Requirements:* For instructional technology only, 30 semester hours including 21 in media with comprehensive examination; 36 hours without examination. For sixth year: 30 credit hours with 6 credit hours of core requirements, 9-15 credit hours in specialization. *Faculty:* 1 full-time. *Students:* 30 full- and part-time in M.S./IT program. *Financial Assistance:* Graduate assistantship: salary $1,800 per semester; assistants pay tuition and a general university fee sufficient to defray cost of student accident insurance. *Master's Degrees Awarded 1995:* 6. The school also offers a Professional Diploma in Library Information Studies; students may select instructional technology as area of specialization.

DISTRICT OF COLUMBIA

*Gallaudet University. School of Education, 800 Florida Ave. NE, Washington, DC 20002-3625. (202) 651-5535 (voice or TDD). Fax (202) 651-5710. E-mail renomeland@gallua.bitnet. Ronald E. Nomeland, Prof., Chair, Dept. of Educational Technology. *Specializations:* M.S. in Special Education/Deafness with specialization in Educational Computing, Instructional Design, and Media Product Development. *Features:* Combines educational technology skills with study in special education and deafness to prepare graduates for positions in programs serving deaf and other disabled learners as well as in regular education programs, or in government and industry. *Minimum Degree Requirements:* 36 semester hours, including 26 in educational media and a comprehensive exam; optional practicum. *Faculty:* 3 full-time; 1 part-time. *Students:* 15. *Financial Assistance:* Partial tuition waiver; graduate assistantships. *Master's Degrees Awarded 1994:* 8.

*George Washington University. School of Education and Human Development, Washington, DC 20052. Dr. William Lynch, Educational Technology Leadership Program. Program is offered through Mind Extension University, ME/U Education Center. Contact Student Advisors at (800) 777-MIND. *Specialization:* M.A. in Education and Human Development with a major in Educational Technology Leadership. *Features:* The 36-hour degree program is available via cable television, satellite, and/or videotape to students across North America and in other locations. The degree is awarded by George Washington University (GWU). Students may work directly with ME/U or GWU to enroll. Student advisors at ME/U handle inquiries about the program, send out enrollment forms and applications, process book orders, and set up students on an electronic bulletin board system. *Minimum Degree Requirements:* 36 credit hours, of which 24 hours are required 3-hour courses. Required courses include Managing Computer Applications, Applying Educational Media and Technology, Design and Implementation of Educational Software, Policy-Making for Public Education, and Quantitative Research Methods. *Faculty:* Courses are taught by faculty at GWU. *Students:* Data not reported. *Financial Assistance:* For information, contact the Office of Student Financial Assistance, George Washington University, Washington, DC 20052. Some cable systems that carry ME/U offer local scholarships. *Master's Degrees Awarded 1994:* New program.

FLORIDA

Florida State University. Instructional Systems Program, Dept. of Educational Research, College of Education, 305 Stone Bldg., Tallahassee, FL 32306. (904) 644-4592. Fax (904) 644-8776. E-mail driscoll@cet.fsu.edu. Marcy P. Driscoll, Prof. and Prog. Leader, Instructional Systems Prog. *Specializations:* M.S. in Instructional Systems and Specialist Degree. *Admission Requirements:* GPA 3.0 in last two years of undergraduate program; TOEFL (for international applicants) 550. *Minimum Degree Requirements:* 36 semester hours; 2 to 4-hour internship required; written comprehensive exam. *Faculty:* 5 full-time; 5 part-time. *Students:* 51 (at the master's level). *Financial Assistance:* Some graduate research assistantships on faculty grants and contracts; university fellowships for high GRE students. *Master's Degrees Awarded 1995:* 29. A specialist degree program is now being offered for students with or without the M.S. in Instructional Systems.

Jacksonville University. Division of Education, 2800 University Boulevard North, Jacksonville, FL 32211. (904) 744-3950, ext. 7130. Fax (904) 745-7126. E-mail tvicker@junix.ju.edu. Dr. Tom Russ Vickery, Dir., MAT and Teacher Education Programs. *Specializations:* Master's degrees in Computer Education and in Educational Technology and Integrated Learning. *Features:* The Master's in Educational Technology and Integrated Learning is a program for certified teachers who wish to learn to use multimedia in their own instruction and to advance the incorporation of emerging technologies throughout the school. *Minimum Degree Requirements:* Computer Education: 36 hours, including 21 in computer science and 15 in education; comprehensive examination required. Educational Technology and Integrated Learning: 39 hours, including 6 in computer science and 33 in education; comprehensive examination to be done as a multimedia project. *Financial Assistance:* Student loans and discounts to area teachers as well as to evening students. *Master's Degrees Awarded 1995:* 15.

Nova Southeastern University. Fischler Center for the Advancement of Education, 3301 College Ave., Fort Lauderdale, FL 33314. (954) 475-7440. (800) 986-3223 ext. 7440. Fax (954) 423-1224. E-mail pet@fcae.nova.edu. Johanne Peck, M.S. and Ed.D. Programs for Teachers. *Specializations:* M.S., Ed.S., and Education Specialist in Educational Media and in Computer Science Education; Doctorate and Master's in Instructional Technology and Distance Education (ITDE). ITDE is delivered online via Internet to students worldwide, who also spend a few extended weekends on campus. *Admission Requirements:* Bachelor's degree and experience working in the field of education, training, etc. *Minimum Degree Requirements:* 36 semester hours, including a practicum (1 to 1.5 years). *Faculty:* 4 full-time; 10 part-time. *Students:* (Master's) 50 full-time. *Financial Assistance:* Student loans. *Master's Degrees Awarded 1995:* 2.

*University of Central Florida. College of Education, ED Room 318, UCF, Orlando, FL 32816. (407) 823-2153. Fax (407) 823-5135. Richard Cornell/Gary Orwig, Instructional Systems; Judy Lee, Educational Media; Donna Baumbach, Educational Technology. *Specializations:* M.A. Instructional Technology/Instructional Systems, 39-42 semester hours; M.Ed. Instructional Technology/Educational Media, 39-45 semester hours; M.A. Instructional Technology/Educational Technology, 39-45 semester hours; practicum required in all three programs; thesis, research project, or substitute additional coursework. *Students:* 99 Instructional Systems; 37 Educational Media; 10 full-time; 126 part-time. *Faculty:* 3 full-time; 5 part-time. *Financial Assistance:* Graduate assistantships in department and college awarded competitively; numerous paid internships; limited number of doctoral fellowships. *Master's Degrees Awarded 1994:* 25. A doctorate in C&I with an emphasis on Instructional Technology is offered. Board of Regents permission granted to conduct feasibility study for new free-standing Ph.D. in Instructional Technology.

University of South Florida. School of Library and Information Science, Tampa, FL 33620. (813) 974-3520. Fax (813) 974-6840. Kathleen de la Peña McCook, Prof., Dir., School of Library and Information Science. *Specialization:* Master's degree. *Minimum Degree Requirements:* 36 semester hours, thesis optional. *Faculty:* 7 full-time; 5 part-time. *Master's Degrees Awarded 1994-95:* 120.

GEORGIA

*Georgia State University. Middle-Secondary Education and Instructional Technology, Atlanta, GA 30303-3083. (404) 651-2510. Fax (404) 651-2546. E-mail mstfda@gsusgi2.gsu.edu. Dr. Francis D. Atkinson. *Specialization:* Master of Library Science. *Admission Requirements:* Bachelor's degree; undergraduate GPA of at least 2.5; Miller Analogy Test score 44 or GRE minimum score 800; TOEFL Exam minimum score 550. *Degree Requirements:* 60 quarter hours. *Faculty:* 4 full-time. *Students:* Data not reported. *Financial Assistance:* Data not reported. *Master's Degrees Awarded 1994:* Data not reported.

Georgia Southern University. College of Education, Statesboro, GA 30460. (912) 681-5307. Fax (912) 681-5093. Jack A. Bennett, Prof., Dept. of Educational Leadership, Technology, and Research. *Specialization:* M.Ed. *Features:* Strong emphasis on technology. *Minimum Degree Requirements:* 60 quarter credit hours, including a varying number of hours of media for individual students. *Financial Assistance:* See graduate catalog for general financial aid information. *Faculty:* 4 full-time. *Master's Degrees Awarded 1992-93:* Data not reported. The school also offers a six-year specialist degree program, and an Instructional Technology strand is available in the Ed.D. program in Curriculum Studies.

University of Georgia. College of Education, 607 Aderhold Hall, Athens, GA 30602-7144. (706) 542-3810. Fax (706) 542-4032. E-mail kgustafs@moe.coe.uga.edu. Kent L. Gustafson, Prof. and Chair, Dept. of Instructional Technology, College of Education. *Specializations:* Master's degree in Instructional Technology; master's degree in Computer-Based Education. *Minimum Degree Requirements:* 60 or more quarter hours in each master's degree; both have an oral examination and/or portfolio presentation. *Faculty:* 10 full-time; 3 part-time. *Students:* 10 full-time; 40 part-time. *Financial Assistance:* Limited assistance. *Master's Degrees Awarded 1995:* 15. The school also offers a 45-hour, six-year specialist degree program in instructional technology and a doctoral program.

*Valdosta State University. School of Education, 1500 N. Patterson St., Valdosta, GA 31698. (912) 333-5927. Fax (912) 333-7167. E-mail cprice@grits.valdosta.peachnet.edu. Catherine B. Price, Assoc. Prof., Dept. of Instructional Technology. *Specializations:* Master's degree with two tracks: Library/Media or Technology Applications. The program has a strong emphasis on technology. *Minimum Degree Requirements:* 65 quarter credits. *Faculty:* 4 full-time; 2 part-time. *Students:* 14 full-time; 70 part-time. *Financial Assistance:* Variety, including graduate assistantships. *Master's Degrees Awarded 1994:* 15. A six-year program is pending approval.

West Georgia College. Department of Media Education, Education Center, Carrollton, GA 30118. (404) 836-6558. Fax (404) 836-6729. E-mail bmckenzi@sun.cc.westga.edu. Dr. Barbara K. McKenzie, Assoc. Prof., Dir., Center for Technological Development and Implementation. *Specializations:* M.Ed. with specializations in Media and Instructional Technology and add-on certification for students with master's degrees in other disciplines. The program strongly emphasizes technology in the schools. *Admission Requirements:* For M.Ed.: 800 GRE; minimum 550 NTE Core Exam; undergraduate GPA of 2.5 is necessary. For Ed.S.: 900 GRE or minimum of 575 on NTE and graduate GPA of 3.25. *Minimum Degree Requirements:* 60 quarter hours minimum. *Faculty:* 4 full-time; 1 part-time. *Students:* 8 full-time; 110 part-time. *Financial Assistance:* One graduate assistantship for the department. *Master's Degrees Awarded 1995:* Data not reported. The school also offers a six-year Ed.S. program in media and a six-year program in Instructional Technology is pending.

IDAHO

*Boise State University. Division of Continuing Education-IPT, 1910 University Drive, Boise, ID 83725. (208) 385-4457; (800) 824-7017 ext. 4457. Fax (208) 385-3346. E-mail aitfenne@idbsu.idbsu.edu. Dr. David Cox, IPT Program Dir.; Jo Ann Fenner, IPT Program Developer and distance program contact person; Linda Burnett, IPT Office Coordinator and on-campus contact person. *Specialization:* M.S. in Instructional & Performance Technology available in a traditional campus setting or via computer conferencing to students located anywhere on the North American continent. The program is fully accredited by the Northwest Association of Schools and Colleges and is the recipient of an NUCEA award for Outstanding Credit Program offered by distance education methods. *Special Features:* Leading experts in learning styles, evaluation, and leadership principles serve as adjunct faculty in the program via computer and modem from their various remote locations. *Admission Requirements:* An undergraduate degree, a minimum GPA of 2.75, a minimum score of 50 on the Miller Analogy Text, a one-to-two page essay describing why you want to pursue this program and how it will contribute to your personal and professional development, and a resume of personal qualifications and work experience. *Minimum Degree Requirements:* 33 semester hours in instructional and performance technology and related coursework; project/thesis available for on-campus program and an oral comprehensive exam required for distance program (included in 33 credit hours). *Faculty:* 2 full-time; 5 part-time. *Students:* Approx. 125. *Financial Assistance:* DANTES provides funding to some military personnel; low-interest student loans are available to those who are eligible; and graduate assistantships for on-campus enrollees. *Master's Degrees Awarded 1994:* 30. (A total of 61 degrees have been awarded since the program's first graduates in 1989.)

ILLINOIS

Chicago State University. Department of Library Science and Communications Media, Chicago, IL 60628. (312) 995-2278; (312) 995-2503. Fax (312) 995-2473. Janice Bolt, Prof., Chair, Dept. of Library Science and Communications Media. *Specialization:* Master's degree in School Media. Program has been approved by NCATE: AECT/AASL through accreditation of University College of Education; State of Illinois Entitlement Program. *Minimum Admission Requirements:* Teacher's certification or a Bachelor's in Education; any B.A. or B.S. *Minimum Degree Requirements:* 36 semester hours; thesis optional. *Faculty:* 2 full-time; 3 part-time. *Students:* approx. 50 part-time. *Financial Assistance:* Assistantships. *Master's Degrees Awarded 1995:* 12.

*Eastern Illinois University. Rm. 213 Buzzard Bldg., Charleston, IL 61920. (213) 581-5931. Dr. John T. North, Dept. of Information Services and Technology. *Specialization:* M.S. in Information Service and Technology. *Admission Requirements:* Bachelor's degree; undergraduate GPA of at least 2.5; Miller Analogy Test score 50; GRE minimum score 1000; TOEFL Exam score 550. *Minimum Degree Requirements:* 32 semester credits; optional thesis worth 3 credits. *Faculty:* 3 full-time; 1 part-time. *Students:* Data not reported. *Financial Assistance:* Data not reported. *Master's Degrees Awarded 1994:* Data not reported.

Governors State University. College of Arts and Sciences, University Park, IL 60466. (708) 534-4082. Fax (708) 534-7895. Michael Stelnicki, Prof., Human Performance and Training, College of Arts and Sciences. *Specializations:* M.A. in Communication with HP&T major. *Features:* Emphasizes three professional areas—Instructional Design, Performance Analysis, and Design Logistics. *Minimum Degree Requirements:* 36 credit hours (trimester), all in instructional and performance technology; internship/master's project required. Metropolitan Chicago area based. *Faculty:* 2 full-time. *Students:* 40 part-time. *Master's Degrees Awarded 1995:* 10.

Northern Illinois University. Instructional Technology Faculty, LEPS Department, DeKalb, IL 60115. (815) 753-0464. Fax (815) 753-9371. Dr. Gary L. McConeghy, Chair, Instructional Technology. *Specializations:* M.S.Ed. in Instructional Technology with specializations in Instructional Design, Microcomputers, or Media Administration. *Minimum Degree Requirements:* 39 semester hours, practicum and internship highly recommended. *Faculty:* 8 full-time; 3 part-time. *Students:* 95 part-time. *Financial Assistance:* Assistantships available at times in various departments. *Master's Degrees Awarded 1995:* 27.

*Rosary College. Graduate School of Library and Information Science, River Forest, IL 60305. (708) 524-6850. Fax (708) 524-6657. Michael E. D. Koenig, Dean. *Specialization:* Master of Library and Information Science. *Minimum Degree Requirements:* 36 semester hours. A particularly relevant area of concentration is the School Library Media Program which, upon completion of the degree and with required education courses and supervised internships, meets the requirements for an Illinois Media Specialist (K-12) Certificate. *Faculty:* 11 full-time; 22 part-time. *Students:* 474 (217 FTE). *Financial Assistance:* Yes. *Master's Degrees Awarded 1 July 1993-30 June 1994:* 150. The school also offers post-master's certificate programs in Law Librarianship, Library Administration, and Technical Services, and several joint-degree programs.

Southern Illinois University at Carbondale. Dept. of Curriculum and Instruction, College of Education, Carbondale, IL 62901-4610. (618) 536-2441. Fax (618) 453-1646. E-mail sashrock@siu.edu. Sharon Shrock, Coord., Instructional Technology/Development. *Specializations:* M.S. in Education; specializations in Instructional Development and Computer-Based Instruction. *Features:* The ID program emphasizes nonschool (primarily corporate) learning environments. *Minimum Degree Requirements:* 32 semester hours plus thesis or 36 credit hours without thesis. *Faculty:* 6 full-time; 2 part-time. *Students:* 56 full- and part-time. *Financial Assistance:* Some graduate assistantships and scholarships available to qualified students. *Master's Degrees Awarded 1995:* 12.

Southern Illinois University at Edwardsville. Instructional Technology Program, School of Education, Edwardsville, IL 62026-1125. (618) 692-3277. Fax (618) 692-3359. E-mail cnelson@siue.edu. Dr. Charles E. Nelson, Dir., Dept. of Educational Leadership. *Specialization:* M.S. in Education with concentrations in Library/Media Specialist or Instructional Systems Design Specialist. *Features:* Evening classes only. *Minimum Degree Requirements:* 36 semester hours; thesis optional. *Faculty:* 6 part-time. *Students:* 86 full- and part-time. *Master's Degrees Awarded 1995:* 15.

University of Illinois at Urbana-Champaign. College of Education, 1310 S. Sixth St., Champaign, IL 61820-6925. (217) 333-0964. Fax (217) 333-5847. E-mail j-leach@uiuc.edu. James A. Leach, Assoc. Dean. *Specializations:* M.Sc., M.A., or M.Ed. *Minimum Degree Requirements:* 32 semester hours with emphasis on Theory and Design of Interactive Instructional Systems, Educational Psychology, and Educational Policy Studies. *Faculty:* 15. *Students:* 20. *Financial Assistance:* Fellowships for very highly academically talented; assistantships for about 10-15 percent; some tuition waivers. *Master's Degrees Awarded 1995:* Data not reported. The school also offers a six-year specialist degree program in Instructional Technology.

University of Illinois at Urbana-Champaign. Department of Educational Psychology, 210 Education Bldg., 1310 S. Sixth St., Champaign, IL 61820. (217) 333-2245. Fax (217) 244-7620. E-mail c-west@uiuc.edu. Charles K. West, Prof., Div. of Learning and Instruction, Dept. of Educational Psychology. *Specializations:* M.A., M.S., and Ed.M. with emphasis in instructional psychology, instructional design, and educational computing. *Minimum Degree Requirements:* 8 units for Ed.M., 6 units and thesis for M.A. or M.S. *Faculty:* 14. *Students:* 36. *Financial Assistance:* Scholarships, research assistantships, and teaching assistantships available. *Master's Degrees Awarded 1995:* Data not reported.

Western Illinois University. Media and Educational Technology, 37 Horrabin Hall, Macomb, IL 61455. (309) 298-1952. Fax (309) 298-2222. E-mail bo-barker@bgu.edu. Bruce O. Barker, Chair, Dept. of Media and Educational Technology. *Specialization:* Master's degree in Instructional Technology & Telecommunication. New program is now offered with emphasis in distance education, telecommunications, and instructional technology. *Minimum Degree Requirements:* 32 semester hours, thesis or practicum. *Faculty:* 6. *Students:* 20. *Financial Assistance:* Graduate and research assistantships, internships, residence hall assistants, veterans' benefits, loans, and part-time employment. *Master's Degrees Awarded 1995:* 1 (second year of program operation).

INDIANA

Indiana State University. Media Technology, Terre Haute, IN 47809. (812) 237-2937. Fax (812) 237-4348. Dr. James E. Thompson, Prog. Coord., Dept. of Curriculum, Instruction, and Media Technology. *Specializations:* Master's degree; six-year Specialist Degree program in Instructional Technology. *Minimum Degree Requirements:* 32 semester hours, including 18 in media; thesis optional. *Faculty:* 5 full-time. *Students:* 15 full-time; 8 part-time. *Financial Assistance:* Assistantships, fellowships. *Master's Degrees Awarded 1995:* 9. A six-year program is available.

*Indiana University. School of Education, W. W. Wright Education Bldg., Bloomington, IN 47405-1006. (812) 855-1791. Fax (812) 855-3044. Thomas Schwen, Chair, Dept. of Instructional Systems Technology. *Specializations:* Offers M.S. degree designed for individuals seeking to be practitioners in the field of instructional technology. *Features:* Requires computer skills as a prerequisite and makes technology utilization an integral part of the curriculum; eliminates the separation of the various media formats; and establishes a series of courses of increasing complexity integrating production and development. The latest in technical capabilities have been incorporated in the new Center for Excellence in Education, including teaching, photographic, computer, and science laboratories, a 14-station multimedia laboratory, and television studios. *Admission Requirements:* Bachelor's degree from an accredited institution. *Degree Requirements:* 40 credit-hour (minimum) including 16 credits in required courses; colloquia; an instructional product or master's thesis; and 12 credits in outside electives. *Faculty:* 6 full-time; 3 part-time. *Students:* Data not reported. *Financial Assistance:* Data not reported. *Masters Degrees Awarded 1994:* Data not reported. For information on the Ed.D. and Ph.D. programs, see the Doctoral listing.

Purdue University. School of Education, W. Lafayette, IN 47907-1442. (317) 494-5673. Fax (317) 496-1622. James Russell, Prof., Educational Computing and Instructional Development, Dept. of Curriculum and Instruction. *Specializations:* Master's degree, Educational Specialist, and Ph.D. in Educational Computing and Instructional Development. Master's program started in 1982 and specialist and doctoral in 1985. *Admission Requirements:* GPA of 3.0 or better; 3 letters of recommendation; statement of personal goals; total score of 1,000 or more on GRE for Ph.D. admission. *Minimum Degree Requirements:* Master's: 36 semester hours (15 in computer or instructional development, 9 in education, 12 unspecified); thesis optional. Specialist: 60-65 semester hours (15-18 in computer or instructional development, 30-35 in education; thesis, internship, and practicum required). *Faculty:* 6 full-time. *Students:* 6 full-time; 15 part-time. *Financial Assistance:* Assistantships and fellowships. *Master's Degrees Awarded 1995:* 12.

IOWA

Iowa State University. College of Education, Ames, IA 50011. (515) 294-6840. Fax (515) 294-9284. E-mail mrs@iastate.edu. Michael Simonson, Prof. and Coord., Curriculum and Instructional Technology (including media and computers). *Specialization:* M.S. in Curriculum and Instructional Technology. *Minimum Degree Requirements:* 30 semester hours; thesis required. *Faculty:* 6 full-time; 6 part-time. *Students:* 30 full-time; 30 part-time. *Financial Assistance:* 10 assistantships available. *Master's Degrees Awarded 1995:* 12.

University of Iowa. College of Education, Iowa City, IA 52242. (319) 335-5519. Fax (319) 335-5386. Stephen Alessi, contact person, Instructional Design and Technology Program. *Specializations:* Master's with concentrations in Instructional Development, Computer Applications, Classroom Instruction, Media Design and Production, and Training and Human Resource Development. *Minimum Degree Requirements:* 35 semester hours. *Faculty:* 7. *Students:* 40 full-time; 30 part-time. *Financial Assistance:* Assistantships, grants, student loans, scholarships. *Master's Degrees Awarded 1995:* 8. A six-year program is available.

*University of Northern Iowa. Educational Technology Program, Cedar Falls, IA 50614-0606. (319) 273-3250. Fax (319) 273-6997. E-mail smaldinos@uni.edu. Sharon Smaldino, contact person. *Specialization:* M.A. in Education. *Admission Requirements:* Bachelor's degree; undergraduate GPA of at least 3.0 of 4; TOEFL Exam minimum score 500. *Minimum Degree Requirements:* 38 semester credits; optional thesis worth 6 credits or alternate research paper of project; comprehensive exam. *Faculty:* 2 full-time; 6 part-time. *Students:* Data not reported. *Financial Assistance:* Data not reported. *Master's Degrees Awarded 1994:* Data not reported.

KANSAS

*Emporia State University. School of Library and Information Management, 1200 Commercial, P.O. Box 4025, Emporia, KS 66801. (316) 341-5203. Fax (316) 341-5233. E-mail vowell@esuvm.bitnet. Faye N. Vowell, Dean, School of Library and Information Management. *Specialization:* Ph.D. in Library and Information Management; Master's of Library Science (ALA accredited program). *Features:* The MLS program is also available in Colorado, Oregon, North Dakota, and New Mexico. Video courses are being developed. *Admission Requirements:* Selective admissions process for M.L.S. and Ph.D. based on a combination of admission criteria, including (but not limited to): minimum GRE or TOEFL score; personal interview; GPA; statement of goals and references. Please request admission packet for specific criteria. *Minimum Degree Requirements:* 42 semester hours, comprehensive examination. *Faculty:* 12 full-time; 35 part-time. *Students:* 100 full-time; 500 part-time in all sites. *Financial Assistance:* Assistantships, grants, student loans, scholarships. *Master's Degrees Awarded 1994:* 169. The school also offers a School Library Certification program, which includes 27 hours of the MLS program.

KENTUCKY

University of Louisville. School of Education, Louisville, KY 40292. (502) 852-0609/6437. Fax (502) 852-1417. E-mail crrude01@ulkyvm.louisville.edu. Carolyn Rude-Parkins, Dir., Education Resource & Technology Center. *Specialization:* M.Ed., Occupational Education with Instructional Technology focus. *Features:* Technology courses are appropriate for business or school audiences. *Minimum Degree Requirements:* 30 semester hours; thesis optional. *Faculty:* 2 full-time; 1 part-time. *Students:* 3 full-time; 17 part-time. *Financial Assistance:* Graduate assistantships. *Master's Degrees Awarded 1995:* Data not reported.

LOUISIANA

Louisiana State University. School of Library and Information Science, Baton Rouge, LA 70803. (504) 388-3158. Fax (504) 388-4581. Bert R. Boyce, Dean, Prof., School of Library and Information Science. *Specializations:* M.L.I.S., C.L.I.S. (post-master's certificate), Louisiana School Library Certification. *Minimum Degree Requirements:* M.L.I.S., 37 hours; comprehensive examination; one semester full-time residence; completion of degree program in five years. *Faculty:* 10 full-time. *Students:* 72 full-time; 74 part-time. *Financial Assistance:* A large number of graduate assistantships are available to qualified students. *Master's Degrees Awarded 1995:* 75. An advanced certificate program is available.

*McNeese State University. Burton College of Education, Dept. of Administration, Supervision, and Educational Technology, P.O. Box 91815, Lake Charles, LA 70609-1815. (318) 475-5421. Fax (318) 475-5467. E-mail vdronet@mcneese.edu. Dr. Virgie M. Dronet. *Specialization:* M.Ed. in Educational Technology with concentrations in educational technology, computer education, and instructional technology. *Minimum Degree Requirements:* 30 semester hours for educational technology or instructional technology, 36 hours for computer education. *Faculty:* 2 full-time; 5 part-time. *Students:* 24. *Financial Assistance:* 4 graduate assistantships per year (teaching and lab). *Master's Degrees Awarded 1994:* Data not reported. Advanced certificate programs are offered in Computer Literacy and Computer Education.

MARYLAND

The Johns Hopkins University. 2500 E. Northern Parkway, Baltimore, MD 21214. (410) 254-8466. Fax (410) 254-8266. E-mail sjm@jhunix.hcf.jhu.edu. Dr. Jacqueline A. Nunn, Dir., Center for Technology in Education; Dr. Sarah McPherson, Prog. Coord. *Specialization:* M.S. in Education with a concentration in Instructional Technology, Assistive Technology, or School-Based Technology Leadership. *Features:* Focuses on the integration of technology with effective instructional programs for all students preschool through grade 12. *Admission Requirements:* Bachelor's degree with strong background in teaching, curriculum and instruction, special education, or a related service field. *Minimum Degree Requirements:* 36 semester hours, 7 required courses in technology-related courses, with remaining courses being electives with the Technology for Educators program areas. *Faculty:* 3 full-time; 15 adjunct. *Students:* 150 part-time. *Financial Assistance:* Grants, student loans, scholarships. *Master's Degrees Awarded 1995:* 25.

*University of Maryland. College of Library and Information Services, 4105 Hornbake Library Bldg., South Wing, College Park, MD 20742-4345. (301) 405-2033. Fax (301) 314-9145. Ann E. Prentice, Dean and Prog. Chair. *Specialization:* Master's of Library Science, including specialization in school library media; Doctorate in Library and Information Services. *Minimum Degree Requirements:* 36 semester hours for MLS; thesis option. *Faculty:* 15 full-time; 8 part-time. *Students:* 110 full-time, 130 part-time, M.L.S. *Master's Degrees Awarded 1994:* 120.

University of Maryland, Baltimore County (UMBC). Department of Education, 5401 Wilkens Ave., Baltimore, MD 21228. (410) 455-2310. Fax (410) 455-3986. Dr. William R. Johnson, Dir., Grad. Progs. in Education. *Specializations:* Master's degrees in School Instructional Systems, Post-Baccalaureate Teacher Certification, English as a Second Language, Training in Business and Industry. *Admissions Requirements:* 3.0 or higher GPA in undergraduate degree; GRE. *Minimum Degree Requirements:* 36 semester hours, including 18 in systems development for each program; an internship is required. *Faculty:* 15 full-time; 25 part-time. *Students:* 63 full-time; 274 part-time. *Financial Assistance:* Assistantships, scholarships. *Master's Degrees Awarded 1995:* 64.

Western Maryland College. Department of Education, Main St., Westminster, MD 21157. (410) 857-2507. Fax (410) 857-2515. Dr. Ramona N. Kerby, Coord., School Library Media Program, Dept. of Education. *Specializations:* M.S. in School Library Media. *Minimum Degree Requirements:* 33 credit hours, including 19 in media and 6 in education; comprehensive examination. *Faculty:* 1 full-time; 7 part-time. *Students:* 120 full- and part-time. *Master's Degrees Awarded 1995:* Data not reported.

MASSACHUSETTS

Boston University. School of Education, 605 Commonwealth Ave., Boston, MA 02215. (617) 353-3181. Fax (617) 353-3924. E-mail whittier@bu.edu. David Whittier, Acting Dir., Program in Educational Media and Technology. *Specialization:* Master's degree. *Features:* A generalized master's program with emphases on instructional design and development of computer-based multimedia and instructional video resources; research and evaluation of these materials in the settings in which they are used. *Admission Requirements:* Bachelor's degree (transcript); MAT or GRE scores; application with a personal statement. *Minimum Degree Requirements:* 36 semester credits which must include one research course; one instructional video course, instructional design; at least two computer-based authoring languages. *Faculty:* 1 full-time; 10 part-time. *Students:* 8 full-time; 25 part-time. *Financial Assistance:* Assistantships, grants, student loans, scholarships. *Master's Degrees Awarded 1995:* 11.

Simmons College. Graduate School of Library and Information Science, 300 The Fenway, Boston, MA 02115-5898. (617) 521-2800. Fax (617) 521-3192. E-mail jmatarazzo@vmsvax-simmons.edu. Dr. James M. Matarazzo, Dean. *Specializations:* M.S. *Features:* The program prepares individuals for a variety of careers, technology/media emphasis being only one. There are special programs for Unified Media Specialist and Archives Management with strengths in information science/systems, media management, etc. *Admission Requirements:* B.A. or B.S. degree with a GPA of 3.0 or better; application; statement; three letters of reference. *Minimum Degree Requirements:* 36 semester hours. *Faculty:* 14 full-time. *Students:* 89 full-time; 381 part-time. *Financial Assistance:* Assistantships, grants, student loans, scholarships. *Master's Degrees Awarded 1995:* 185. A Doctor of Arts in Administration is also offered.

*University of Massachusetts-Boston. Graduate College of Education, 100 Morrissey Blvd., Boston, MA 02125. (617) 287-7622 or 287-5980. Fax (617) 265-7173. Canice H. McGarry, Instructional Design Prog. *Specialization:* M.Ed. in Instructional Design; Graduate Certificate in Educational Technology (Fall 1995). *Minimum Degree Requirements:* 36 semester hours; thesis or project required. *Faculty:* 1 full-time; 9 part-time. *Students:* 8 full-time; 80 part-time. *Financial Assistance:* Graduate assistantships providing tuition plus stipend. *Master's Degrees Awarded 1994:* 24.

MICHIGAN

*Eastern Michigan University. 234 Boone Hall, Ypsilanti, MI 48197. (313) 487-3260. Fax (313) 484-6471. Bert Greene, Prof., Coord. Dept. of Teacher Education. *Specialization:* M.A. in Educational Psychology with concentration in Educational Technology. *Admission Requirements:* Bachelor's degree; undergraduate GPA of at least 2.75 or Miller Analogy Test score; TOEFL Exam minimum score 500. *Minimum Degree Requirements:* 30 semester hour credits; optional thesis worth 6 credits. *Faculty:* 8 full-time. *Students:* Data not reported. *Financial Assistance:* Data not reported. *Master's Degrees Awarded 1994:* Data not reported.

*Michigan State University. School of Education, 346 Erickson, East Lansing, MI 48824. (517) 353-9272. Fax (517) 349-8852. E-mail normbell@msu.edu. Dr. Norman T. Bell, Counseling, Educational Psychology, and Special Education. *Specialization:* M.A. in Educational Communications and Technology. *Admission Requirements:* Bachelor's degree; TOEFL Exam minimum score 80. *Minimum Degree Requirements:* 45 quarter credits; optional thesis worth 10 credits. *Faculty:* 10 full-time. *Students:* Data not reported. *Financial Assistance:* Data not reported. *Master's Degrees Awarded 1994:* Data not reported.

Wayne State University. College of Education, Detroit, MI 48202. (313) 577-1728. Fax (313) 577-1693. E-mail rrichey@cms.cc.wayne.edu. Rita C. Richey, Prof. and Prog. Coord., Instructional Technology Prog., Div. of Administrative and Organizational Studies. *Specialization:* Master's degrees in Business and Human Services Training, K-12 Educational Technology, Interactive Technologies, and Research and Theory. *Minimum Degree Requirements:* 36 semester hours, including required project; internship recommended. *Faculty:* 4 full-time; 5 part-time. *Students:* 400 full- and part-time. *Financial Assistance:* Student loans, scholarships, and paid internships. *Master's Degrees Awarded 1995:* 60. The school also offers a six-year specialist degree program in Instructional Technology.

MINNESOTA

*Mankato State University. MSU Box 20, P.O. Box 8400, Mankato, MN 56001-8400. (507) 389-1965. Fax (507) 389-5751. E-mail pengelly@vax1.mankato.msus.edu. Kenneth C. Pengelly, Assoc. Prof., Dept. of Library Media Education. *Specialization:* M.S. in Technology in Education. *Admission Requirements:* Bachelor's degree; undergraduate GPA of at least 3.0; GRE minimum score 1350; TOEFL Exam score 500. *Minimum Degree Requirements:* 51 quarter credits; comprehensive exam. *Faculty:* 4 full-time. *Students:* Data not reported. *Financial Assistance:* Data not reported. *Master's Degrees Awarded 1994:* Data not reported.

St. Cloud State University. College of Education, St. Cloud, MN 56301-4498. (612) 255-2022. Fax (612) 255-4778. E-mail jberling@tigger.stcloud.msus.edu. John G. Berling, Prof., Dir., Center for Information Media. *Specializations:* Master's degrees in Information Technologies, Educational Media, and Human Resources Development/Training. *Minimum Degree Requirements:* 51 quarter hours with thesis; 54 quarter hours, Plan B; 57 quarter hours, portfolio; 200-hour practicum is required for media generalist licensure; coursework applies to Educational Media master's program. *Faculty:* 7 full-time. *Students:* 10 full-time; 150 part-time. *Financial Assistance:* Assistantships, scholarships. *Master's Degrees Awarded 1995:* 10.

MISSOURI

University of Missouri-Columbia. 212 Townsend Hall, University of Missouri-Columbia, Columbia, MO 65201. (314) 882-3828. Fax (314) 884-5455. E-mail wedmanjf@showme. missouri.edu. John Wedman, Assoc. Prof., Coord., Educational Technology Prog., Curriculum and Instruction Dept., College of Education. *Specialization:* Master's degree emphasizing instructional development, performance support systems, multimedia design, production, and application. *Features:* Project-based learning experiences. *Admission Requirements:* Bachelor's degree; Miller Analogy Test score. *Minimum Degree Requirements:* 32 semester hours including 16 hours of upper-level graduate work. *Faculty:* 5 full-time; 4 part-time. *Students:* 20 full-time; 10 part-time. *Financial Assistance:* Assistantships; grants; student loans; scholarships. *Master's Degrees Awarded 1995:* 15. An Education Specialist degree program is also available.

*Webster University. Instructional Technology, St. Louis, MO 63119. Fax (314) 968-7118. Paul Steinmann, Assoc. Dean and Dir., Graduate Studies and Instructional Technology. *Specialization:* Master's degree. *Minimum Degree Requirements:* 33 semester hours, including 24 in media; internship required. State Certification in Media Technology is a program option; six-year program not available. *Faculty:* 4. *Students:* 6 full-time; 18 part-time. *Financial Assistance:* Partial scholarships, government loans, and limited state aid. *Master's Degrees Awarded 1994:* 7.

MONTANA

University of Montana. School of Education, Missoula, MT 59812. (406) 243-5785. Fax (406) 243-4908. E-mail cjlott@selway.umt.edu. Dr. Carolyn Lott, Asst. Prof. of Library/Media. *Specializations:* Master's degree; K-12 School Library Media specialization. *Admission Requirements:* Letters of recommendation, application, 2.5 GPA cum. *Minimum Degree Requirements:* 37 semester credit hours, 28 in library media; thesis optional. *Faculty:* 2 full-time. *Students:* 10 full-time; 10 part-time. *Financial Assistance:* Assistantships; contact the University of Montana Financial Aid Office. *Master's Degrees Awarded 1995:* 10 (all emphases). The school has a School Library Media Certification endorsement program at the undergraduate/graduate levels.

NEBRASKA

University of Nebraska at Kearney. Kearney, NE 68849. (308) 865-8833. Fax (308) 865-8097. E-mail fredrickson@platte.unk.edu. Dr. Scott Fredrickson, Dir. of Instructional Technology. *Specializations:* M.S. in Instructional Technology, M.S. in Educational Media/ Specialist in Educational Media. *Minimum Degree Requirements:* Information not reported. *Faculty:* 4 full-time; 9 part-time. *Students:* 55 full-time. *Financial Assistance:* Assistantships; grants; student loans. *Master's Degrees Awarded 1995:* 20.

University of Nebraska-Omaha. Department of Teacher Education, College of Education, Kayser Hall 208D, Omaha, NE 68182. (402) 554-2211. Fax (402) 554-3491. E-mail hasel@cwis.unomaha.edu. Verne Haselwood, Prof., Educational Media Prog. in Teacher Education. *Specializations:* M.S. in Education, M.A. in Education, both with Educational Media concentration. *Minimum Degree Requirements:* 36 semester hours, including 24 in media; practicum required; thesis optional. *Faculty:* 2 full-time; 4 part-time. *Students:* 10 full-time; 62 part-time. *Financial Assistance:* Contact Financial Aid Office. *Master's Degrees Awarded 1995:* 5. The school also offers an advanced certificate program in Educational Administration and Supervision.

NEVADA

*University of Nevada. College of Education, Reno, NV 89557. (702) 784-4961. Fax (702) 784-4526. Dr. LaMont Johnson, Chair, Dept. of Curriculum and Instruction. *Specializations:* M.A. or M.Ed. *Admission Requirements:* Bachelor's degree; undergraduate GPA of at least 2.75; GRE minimum score 750. *Minimum Degree Requirements:* 36 semester credits; optional thesis worth 6 credits; comprehensive exam. *Faculty:* 2 full-time. *Students:* Data not reported. *Financial Assistance:* Data not reported. *Master's Degrees Awarded 1994:* Data not reported.

NEW JERSEY

*Montclair State College. Department of Reading and Educational Media, Upper Montclair, NJ 07043. Robert R. Ruezinsky, Dir. of Media and Technology. *Specializations:* No degree program exists. Two certification programs, A.M.S. and E.M.S, exist on the graduate level. *Minimum Degree Requirements:* 18-21 semester hours of media and technology are required for the A.M.S. program and 30-33 hours for the E.M.S. program. *Faculty:* Includes 5 administrators and 1 adjunct, teaching on an overload basis. *Students:* Data not reported. *Certificates Awarded 1994:* Data not reported.

Rutgers-The State University of New Jersey. School of Communication, Information and Library Studies, New Brunswick, NJ 08903. (908) 932-9717. Fax (908) 932-6916. Dr. David Carr, Chair, Dept. of Library and Information Studies. *Specializations:* M.L.S. degree with specializations in Information Retrieval, Technical and Automated Services, Reference, School Media Services, Youth Services, Management and Policy Issues, Generalist Studies. A course on Multimedia Structure, Organization, Access, and Production is being offered. *Minimum Degree Requirements:* 36 semester hours, in which the hours for media vary for individual students; practicum of 150 hours. *Faculty:* 17 full-time; 10 adjuncts. *Students:* 86 full-time; 237 part-time. *Financial Assistance:* Scholarships, fellowships, and graduate assistantships available. *Master's Degrees Awarded 1995:* 155. The school also offers a six-year specialist certificate program.

William Paterson College. School of Education, 300 Pompton Rd., Wayne, NJ 07470. (201) 595-2140. Fax (201) 595-2585. Dr. Amy G. Job, Librarian, Assoc. Prof., Coord., Prog. in Library/Media, Curriculum and Instruction Dept. *Specializations:* M.Ed. for Educational Media Specialist, Associate Media Specialist. *Minimum Degree Requirements:* 33 semester hours, including research projects and practicum. *Faculty:* 6 full-time; 2 part-time. *Students:* 30 part-time. *Financial Assistance:* Limited. *Master's Degrees Awarded 1995:* 5.

NEW YORK

*Columbia University-Teachers College. Teachers College, Box 8, 525 W. 120th St., New York, NY 10027. (212) 678-3773. Fax (212) 678-4048. E-mail hb50@columbia.edu. Howard Budin, Coord., Dept. of Communications, Computing and Technology. *Specializations:* M.A. or M.Ed. *Admission Requirements:* Bachelor's degree; TOEFL Exam score. *Minimum Degree Requirements:* 32 credits (semester) for M.A., 60 credits for M.Ed.; master's project; comprehensive exam. *Faculty:* 4 full-time. *Students:* Data not reported. *Financial Assistance:* Data not reported. *Master's Degrees Awarded 1994:* Data not reported.

Ithaca College. School of Communications, Ithaca, NY 14850. (607) 274-1025. Fax (607) 274-1664. E-mail herndon@ithaca.edu. Sandra L. Herndon, Prof., Chair, Graduate Corporate Communications; Roy H. Park, School of Communications. *Specialization:* M.S. in Corporate Communications. *Minimum Degree Requirements:* 36 semester hours; required seminar. *Faculty:* 8 full-time. *Students:* Approx. 25 full-time; 15 part-time. *Financial Assistance:* Full- and part-time research/lab assistantships. *Master's Degrees Awarded 1993:* 25.

New York Institute of Technology. School of Education-Instructional Technology, Wheatley Rd., Old Westbury, NY 11568. (Also 1855 Broadway, New York, NY 10023, and Carlton Ave., Central Islip, NY 11722.) (516) 686-7777. Fax (212) 626-7206. Helen Greene, Dean, School of Education. (516) 686-7936. Davenport Plumer, Chair, Depts. of Instructional Technology and Elementary Education. (Courses are offered at three campuses and several off-campus sites in Metropolitan New York.) *Specializations:* Master's degree in Instructional Technology for Teachers; Master's Degree in Instructional Technology for Trainers; Computers in Education Certificate (18-credits); Distance Learning Certificate (18-credits). *Features:* Technology integration in virtually all courses; instruction delivered via computer with teleconferencing and interactive two-way audio/two-way video. *Admission Requirements:* Bachelor's degree from accredited college with 2.85 cumulative average; candidates for the Master's Degree in Instructional Technology must be provisionally certified. *Minimum Degree Requirements:* 36 credits with 3.0 GPA for master's degree; 18 credits with 3.0 GPA for certificates. *Faculty:* 9 full-time; 15 part-time. *Students:* 11 full-time; 438 part-time. *Financial Assistance:* Graduate assistantships, institutional and alumni scholarships, student loans. *Master's Degrees Awarded 1995:* Data not reported.

New York University. School of Education, 239 Greene St., Suite 300, New York, NY 10003. (212) 998-5520. Fax (212) 995-4041. Francine Shuchat Shaw, Assoc. Prof. and Dir., Prog. in Educational Communication and Technology. *Specialization:* M.A. in Education with program emphasis on design and production, application and evaluation of materials and environments for all instructional technologies. *Admission Requirements:* School application, minimum 3.0 undergraduate GPA, essay, and reference letters. *Minimum Degree Requirements:* 36 semester hours including final master's project and English Essay Examination. *Faculty:* 2 full-time; 10 part-time. *Students:* 15 full-time; 35 part-time. *Financial Assistance:* Graduate and research assistantships, student loans, scholarships, and work-study programs. *Master's Degrees Awarded 1995:* 15. The school also offers the Ph.D., the Ed.D., and a post-M.A. 30-point Certificate of Advanced Study in Education.

St. John's University. Division of Library and Information Science, 8000 Utopia Parkway, Jamaica, NY 11439. (718) 990-6200. Fax (718) 380-0353. E-mail libis@sjmusic.stjohns.edu. James Benson, Dir., Div. of Library and Information Science. *Specializations:* M.L.S. with specializations in School Media, Public, Academic, Law, Health/Medicine, Business, Archives. Double degree programs: Pharmacy and M.L.S., Government and Politics and M.L.S. *Admission Requirements:* 3.0 cum. GPA; 2 letters of reference; statement of professional goals. *Minimum Degree Requirements:* 36 semester hours; comprehensive; practicum (for a school media specialization). *Faculty:* 6 full-time; 15 part-time. *Students:* 21 full-time; 132 part-time. *Financial Assistance:* 15 assistantships and four fellowships. *Master's Degrees Awarded 1995:* 52. The school also offers a 24-credit Advanced Certificate program.

State University College of Arts and Science. School of Education, 204 Satterlee Hall, Potsdam, NY 13676. (315) 267-2527. Fax (315) 267-2771. E-mail lichtnc@potsdam.edu. Norman Licht, Coord., Instructional Technology and Media Management; Dr. Charles Mlynarczyk, Chair, Education Department. *Specializations:* Master of Science in Education with concentration in Instructional Technology and Media Management. *Minimum Degree Requirements:* 30 semester hours. *Faculty:* 7 full-time; 2 part-time. *Students:* 102 full-time; 34 part-time. *Financial Assistance:* Assistantships, student loans. *Master's Degrees Awarded 1995:* 42.

State University of New York at Albany. School of Education, 1400 Washington Ave., Albany, NY 12222. (518) 442-5032. Fax (518) 442-5008. E-mail swan@cnsunix.albany.edu. Karen Swan (ED114A), contact person. *Specialization:* M.Ed. and Ph.D. in Curriculum and Instruction with specializations in Instructional Technology, Design, and Theory. *Minimum Degree Requirements:* 30 semester hours with 15-18 credits in specialization. *Faculty:* 13 full-time; 7 part-time. *Students:* 100 full-time; 350 part-time. *Financial Assistance:* Fellowships. *Master's Degrees Awarded 1995:* Data not reported.

*State University of New York at Buffalo. Graduate School of Education, 480 Baldy Hall, Amherst, NY 14260. (716) 645-3164. Fax (716) 645-4281. Taher A. Razik, Prof., Instructional Design and Management, Dept. of Educational Organization, Administration, and Policy. *Specialization:* M.Ed. in Instructional Design and Management. *Minimum Degree Requirements:* 32 semester hours, including 21 hours in Instructional Design and Management; thesis or project required. *Faculty:* 3. *Students:* 10. *Financial Assistance:* Some graduate assistantships are available. *Master's Degrees Awarded 1994:* Data not reported.

Syracuse University. School of Education, Syracuse, NY 13244-2340. (315) 443-3703. Fax (315) 443-5732. Philip Doughty, Prof., Chair, Instructional Design, Development and Evaluation Prog. *Specializations:* M.S. degree programs for Instructional Design of programs and materials, Educational Evaluation, human issues in Instructional Development, Media Production (including computers and videodisc), and Educational Research and Theory (learning theory, application of theory, and educational and media research). Graduates are prepared to serve as curriculum developers, instructional developers, program and product evaluators, researchers, resource center administrators, communications coordinators, trainers in human resource development, and higher education instructors. *Features:* Field work and internships, special topics and special issues seminar, student- and faculty-initiated minicourses, seminars and guest lecturers, faculty-student formulation of department policies, and multiple international perspectives. *Minimum Degree Requirements:* 36 semester hours; comprehensive and intensive examination or portfolio required. *Faculty:* 5 full-time; 4 part-time. *Students:* 32 full-time; 42 part-time. *Financial Assistance:* Some fellowships, scholarships, and graduate assistantships entailing either research or administrative duties in instructional technology. *Master's Degrees Awarded 1995:* 25. The school also offers an advanced certificate program.

NORTH CAROLINA

Appalachian State University. Department of Library Science and Educational Foundations, Boone, NC 28608. (704) 262-2243. E-mail tashnerjh@alf.appstate.edu. John H. Tashner, Prof., Coord., Dept. of Library Science and Educational Foundations, College of Education. *Specialization:* M.A. in Educational Media and Technology with three areas of concentration: computers, telecommunications, and media production. *Features:* IMPACT NC (business/university/public school) partnership offers unusual opportunities. *Minimum Degree Requirements:* 36 semester hours, including 15 in Computer Education; thesis optional. *Faculty:* 2 full-time; 1 part-time. *Students:* 6 full-time; 25 part-time. *Financial Assistance:* Assistantships, grants, student loans. *Master's Degrees Awarded 1995:* 6.

East Carolina University. Department of Library Studies and Educational Technology, Greenville, NC 27858-4353. (919) 328-6621. Fax (919) 328-4368. E-mail lsauld@ecuvm. cis.ecu.edu. Lawrence Auld, Assoc. Prof., Chair. *Specializations*: Master of Library Science; Certificate of Advanced Study (Library Science); Master of Arts in Education (Instructional Technology Computers). *Features:* M.L.S. graduates are eligible for North Carolina School Media Coordinator certification; C.A.S. graduates are eligible for North Carolina School Media Supervisor certification; M.A.Ed. graduates are eligible for North Carolina Instructional Technology-Computers certification. *Admission Requirements:* M.L.S. and M.A.Ed., bachelor's degree; C.A.S., M.L.S. or equivalent degree. *Minimum Degree Requirements:* M.L.S., 38 semester hours; M.A.Ed., 36 semester hours; C.A.S., 30 semester hours. *Faculty:* 9 full-time. *Students:* 5 full-time; 70 part-time. *Financial Assistance:* Assistantships. *Master's Degrees Awarded 1995:* Data not reported.

North Carolina Central University. School of Education, 1801 Fayetteville St., Durham, NC 27707. (919) 560-6218. Fax (919) 560-5366. Dr. Marvin E. Duncan, Prof., Dir., Graduate Prog. in Educational Technology. *Specialization:* M.A. with special emphasis on Instructional Development/Design. *Features:* Graduates are prepared to serve as information and communication technologists in a variety of professional ventures, among which are institutions of higher education (college resource centers), business, industry, and professional schools such as medicine, law, dentistry, and nursing. *Admission Requirements:* Undergraduate degree in any area, but with at least 6 hours in education. *Minimum Degree Requirements:* 33 semester hours including project or thesis. *Faculty:* 2 full-time; 1 part-time. *Students:* 25 full-time; 30 part-time. *Financial Assistance:* Assistantships, grants, student loans, and scholarships. *Master's Degrees Awarded 1995:* 12.

*University of North Carolina. School of Education (CB#3500), Chapel Hill, NC 27599. (919) 962-5372. Fax (919) 962-1538. Ralph E. Wileman, Prof., Chair, Educational Media and Instructional Design. *Specialization:* M.Ed. in Educational Media and Instructional Design. *Features:* Skills based program; at least one practicum for each candidate; good placement record. *Admission Requirements:* 1000 minimum on Verbal/Quantitative GRE; 3.0 undergraduate GPA; 3 letters of recommendation. *Minimum Degree Requirements:* 36 semester hours; comprehensive examination. *Faculty:* 2 full-time; 1 part-time. *Students:* 16 full-time; 1 part-time. *Financial Assistance:* Assistantships; student loans. *Master's Degrees Awarded 1994:* 10.

OHIO

Kent State University. 405 White Hall, Kent, OH 44242. (330) 672-2294. Fax (330) 672-2512. E-mail tchandler@emerald.edu.kent.edu. Dr. Theodore Chandlet, Coord., Instructional Technology Program. *Specializations:* M.Ed. or M.A. in Instructional Technology and Instructional Computing. *Admission Requirements:* Bachelor's degree with undergraduate GPA of at least 2.75. *Minimum Degree Requirements:* 34 semester hours; thesis required for M.A. *Faculty:* 4 full-time; 6 part-time. *Students:* Data not reported. *Financial Assistance:* 8 assistantships; John Mitchell and Marie McMahan Awards. *Master's Degrees Awarded 1995:* Data not reported.

*Miami University. Room 301, McGuffey Hall, Oxford, OH 45056. (513) 529-6443. Fax (513) 529-4931. Dr. Robert Shearer, Coord., Dept. of Teacher Education. *Specialization:* M.Ed. Arts. *Admission Requirements:* Bachelor's degree in education; undergraduate GPA of at least 2.75; TOEFL Exam score. *Minimum Degree Requirements:* 30 credits (semester); optional thesis worth 6-12 credits. *Faculty:* 4 full-time; 1 part-time. *Students:* Data not reported. *Financial Assistance:* Data not reported. *Master's Degrees Awarded 1994:* Data not reported.

The Ohio State University. College of the Arts, Department of Art Education, 340 Hopkins Hall, 128 North Oval Mall, Columbus, OH 43210. (614) 292-0235; (614) 292-7183. Fax (614) 292-1674. E-mail carol+@cgrg.ohio-state.edu. Dr. Carol Gigliotti, Prog. Coord. *Specializations:* Ph.D. and M.A. in Art Education with specializations in the teaching and learning of computer graphics and computer-mediated art; multimedia production and its curricular implications; electronic networking in the arts; multicultural aspects of computing; hypermedia applications for teaching and art education research; the application of computing to arts administration, galleries, and museums; telecommunications in the arts; and ethical, aesthetic, and cultural aspects of interactive technologies. *Features:* Specialization at the Advanced Computing Center for the Arts and Design (ACCAD). The program is offered in an interdisciplinary environment. *Faculty:* 1 full-time; 1 part-time in specialty. *Students:* 15 full-time; 3 part-time in specialty. *Financial Assistance:* Assistantships, grants, student loans, and scholarships. *Master's Degrees Awarded 1995:* 8.

*University of Cincinnati. College of Education, 401 Teachers College, ML002, Cincinnati, OH 45221-0002. (513) 556-3577. Randall Nichols and Janet Bohren, Div. of Teacher Education. *Specialization:* M.A. or Ed.D. in Curriculum and Instruction with an emphasis on instructional design and technology. *Minimum Degree Requirements:* 54 quarter hours; written examination; thesis or research project. *Faculty:* 2 full-time. *Students:* 20 full-time. *Financial Assistance:* Scholarships, assistantships, grants. *Master's Degrees Awarded 1994:* 8.

Wright State University. College of Education and Human Services, Dept. of Educational Leadership, 244 Millett Hall, Dayton, OH 45435. (513) 873-2509 or (513) 873-2182. Fax (513) 873-4485. E-mail bmathies@desire.wright.edu or bonniekwsu@aol.com. Dr. Bonnie K. Mathies, Asst. Dean, Communication and Technology. *Specializations:* M.Ed. in Educational Media or Computer Education, or for Media Supervisor or Computer Coordinator; M.A. in Educational Media or Computer Education. Two specialist degrees are also available as of Winter 1996: Curriculum and Instruction: Focus on Educational Technology; and Higher Education: Focus on Educational Technology. *Minimum Degree Requirements:* M.Ed. requires a comprehensive examination that, for this department, is the completion of a portfolio and videotaped presentation to the faculty; the M.A. incorporates a 9-hour thesis; students are eligible for Supervisor's Certificate after completion of C&S; Computer Coordinator or C&S; Media Supervision programs. *Faculty:* 2 full-time; 12 part-time, including other university full-time faculty and staff. *Students:* Approx. 75 full- and part-time. *Financial Assistance:* 3 graduate assistantships in the College's Educational Resource Center; limited number of small graduate scholarships. *Master's Degrees Awarded 1995:* 12.

OKLAHOMA

*Southwestern Oklahoma State University. School of Education, 100 Campus Drive, Weatherford, OK 73096. (405) 772-6611. Fax (405) 772-5447. Lessley Price, Assoc. Prof., Coord. of Library/Media Prog. *Specialization:* M.Ed. in Library/Media Education. *Admission Requirements:* GPA of at least 2.5 on 4.0 scale; copy of GRE or GMAT scores; letter of recommendation; GPA x 150 + GRE = 1100. *Minimum Degree Requirements:* 32 semester hours, including 24 in library/media. *Faculty:* 1 full-time; 4 part-time. *Students:* Data not reported. *Master's Degrees Awarded 1994:* 16.

OREGON

Western Oregon State College. Ed. 202L, Monmouth, OR 97361. (503) 838-8471. Fax (503) 838-8228. E-mail forcier@fsa.wosc.osshe.edu. Richard C. Forcier, Prof., Dept. of Secondary Education. *Specialization:* M.S. in Educational/Information Technology. *Features:* Offers advanced courses in Library Management, Media Production, Instructional Systems, Instructional Development, and Computer Technology. Some specialization in distance delivery of instruction and computer-interactive video instruction. *Minimum Degree Requirements:* 45 quarter hours, including 36 in media; thesis optional. *Faculty:* 3 full-time; 6 part-time. *Students:* 5 full-time; 161 part-time. *Financial Assistance:* Assistantships, grants, student loans, scholarship, work study. *Master's Degrees Awarded 1995:* 13.

PENNSYLVANIA

Bloomsburg University. Institute for Interactive Technologies, 1210 McCormick Bldg., Bloomsburg, PA 17815. (717) 389-4506. Fax (717) 389-4943. E-mail bail@husky.bloomu.edu. Dr. Harold J. Bailey, contact person. *Specialization:* M.S. in Instructional Technology with emphasis placed on preparing for careers as interactive media specialists. The program is closely associated with the Institute for Interactive Technologies. *Admission Requirements:* Bachelor's degree. *Features:* Instructional design, authoring languages/systems, media integration, managing multimedia projects. *Admission Requirements:* Bachelor's degree. *Minimum Degree Requirements:* 33 semester credits—27 credits plus 6 credit thesis, or 30 credits plus three credit internship. *Faculty:* 3 full-time; 1 part-time. *Students:* 36 full-time; 16 part-time. *Financial Assistance:* Assistantships, some grants, student loans. *Master's Degrees Awarded 1995:* 55.

*Clarion University of Pennsylvania. Becker Hall, Clarion, PA 16214. (814) 226-2328. Fax (814) 226-2444. Carmen S. Felicetti, Chair, Dept. of Communications. *Specialization:* M.S. in Communication. *Admission Requirements:* Bachelor's degree; undergraduate GPA of at least 2.75; Miller Analogy Test score. *Minimum Degree Requirements:* 36 semester credit with minimum GPA of 3.0; optional thesis worth 6 credits. *Faculty:* 9 full-time. *Students:* Data not reported. *Financial Assistance:* Data not reported. *Master's Degrees Awarded 1994:* Data not reported.

Pennsylvania State University. Program in Instructional Systems, 270 Chambers Bldg., University Park, PA 16802. (814) 865-0473. Fax (814) 865-0128. D. D. H. Jonassen, Prof. in Charge, Instructional Systems Prog. *Specializations:* M.Ed., M.S. in Instructional Systems. *Minimum Degree Requirements:* 33 semester hours, including either a thesis or project paper. *Faculty:* 9 full-time; 2 affiliate; 2 part-time. *Students:* Approx. 160. *Financial Assistance:* Some assistantships, graduate fellowships, student aid loans. *Master's Degrees Awarded 1995:* 20.

Rosemont College. Graduate Studies in Education, 1400 Montgomery Ave., Rosemont, PA 19010-1699. (610) 526-2982; (800) 531-9431 outside 610 area code. Fax (610) 526-2964. E-mail rosteched@hslc.org. Dr. Robert J. Siegfried, Dir. *Specializations:* M.Ed. in Technology in Education, M.Ed. in Educational Studies, Certificate in Professional Study in Technology in Education, Certificate in Advanced Graduate Study in Education. *Minimum Degree Requirements:* Completion of 12 units (36 credits) and comprehensive exam. *Faculty:* 2 full-time; 5 part-time. *Students:* 110 full- and part-time. *Financial Assistance:* Graduate student grants, assistantships, internships, Federal Stafford Loan Program. *Master's Degrees Awarded 1995:* 23.

*****Shippensburg University**. Dept. of Communications and Journalism, 1871 Old Main Drive, Shippensburg, PA 17257-2292. (717) 532-1521. Fax (717) 532-1273. Dr. C. Lynne Nash, Dept. Chair. *Specialization:* Master's degree with specializations in public relations, radio/television, communication theory, press and public affairs. *Admission Requirements:* 2.5 GPA. *Minimum Degree Requirements:* Completion of between 30 and 33 credits plus a thesis or a professional project or a comprehensive examination. *Faculty:* 9 full-time; 1 half-time; 3 adjunct. *Students:* 15 full-time; 15 part-time. *Financial Assistance:* Assistantships, grants, student loans, scholarships. *Master's Degrees Awarded 1994:* 5.

*****University of Pittsburgh**. Instructional Design and Technology, School of Education, Pittsburgh, PA 15260. (412) 612-7254. Fax (412) 648-7081. E-mail bseels+@pitt.edu. Barbara Seels, Assoc. Prof., Coord., Program in Instructional Design and Technology, Dept. of Instruction and Learning. *Specialization:* Ed.D. and M.Ed. programs for the preparation of instructional technologists with skills in designing, developing, using, evaluating, and managing processes and resources for learning. Certificate option for instructional technologists available. *Features:* Program prepares people for positions in which they can effect educational change through instructional technology. Program includes three competency areas: instructional design, technological delivery systems, and communications research. *Minimum Degree Requirements:* 36 trimester hours, including 18 in instructional technology, 9 in core courses, and 9 in electives; comprehensive examination. *Faculty:* 3 full-time. *Students:* 72 master's, 33 doctoral. *Financial Assistance:* Assistantships and grants are available. *Master's Degrees Awarded 1994:* 9. The school also offers a 39-credit specialist certification program.

RHODE ISLAND

The University of Rhode Island. Graduate School of Library and Information Studies, Rodman Hall, Kingston, RI 02881-0815. (401) 792-2947. Fax (401) 792-4395. Jonathan S. Tryon, Prof. and Dir. *Specializations:* M.L.I.S. degree. Offers accredited master's degree with specialties in Archives, Law, Health Sciences, Rare Books, and Youth Services Librarianship. *Minimum Degree Requirements:* 42 semester-credit program offered in Rhode Island and regionally in Boston and Amherst, MA, and Durham, NH. *Faculty:* 6 full-time; 24 part-time. *Students:* 28 full-time; 211 part-time. *Financial Assistance:* Graduate assistantships, some scholarship aid, student loans. *Master's Degrees Awarded 1995:* 80.

TENNESSEE

East Tennessee State University. College of Education, Box 70684, Johnson City, TN 37614-0684. (615) 929-5848. Fax (615) 929-5746. E-mail millerr@eduserv.east_tenn_st.edu. Dr. Rudy Miller, Prof., Dir. Media Services, Dept. of Curriculum and Instruction. *Specializations:* M.Ed. in Instructional Media (Library), M.Ed. in Instructional Technology. *Minimum Degree Requirements:* 39 semester hours, including 18 hours in instructional technology. *Faculty:* 4 full-time; 2 part-time. *Students:* 2 full-time; 43 part-time. *Financial Assistance:* Scholarships, aid for handicapped. *Master's Degrees Awarded 1995:* 15. A six-year program is under development.

Middle Tennessee State University. Department of Educational Leadership, Murfreesboro, TN 37132. (615) 898-2855. Fax (615) 898-2859. Dr. Nancy Keese, Prof. and Chair, Dept. of Educational Leadership. *Specialization:* Master's degree. *Minimum Degree Requirements:* 33 semester hours, including 15 in media; no thesis required. *Faculty:* 1 full-time; 4 part-time. *Students:* 3 full-time; 30 part-time. *Financial Assistance:* Assistantships. *Master's Degrees Awarded 1995:* 6.

*University of Tennessee-Knoxville. College of Education, Knoxville, TN 37996-3400. (615) 974-4222 or (615) 974-3103. Dr. Alfred D. Grant, Coord., Graduate Media Prog., Dept. of Education in Science, Mathematics, Research, and Technology. *Specialization:* M.S. in Education, concentration in Instructional Media and Technology. *Minimum Degree Requirements:* 33 semester hours, thesis optional. *Faculty:* 1. *Students:* 1 full-time; 2 part-time at the master's level. *Master's Degrees Awarded 1994:* 2. The Department of Curriculum and Instruction also offers a six-year specialist degree program in Curriculum and Instruction with a concentration in Instructional Media and Technology.

TEXAS

*East Texas State University. Department of Secondary and Higher Education, East Texas Station, Commerce, TX 75429-3011. (903) 886-5607. Fax (903) 886-5603. E-mail mundayb@tenet.edu. Dr. Robert S. Munday, Prof., Head, Dept. of Secondary and Higher Education. *Specialization:* Master's degree in Learning Technology and Information Systems with emphasis on Educational Micro Computing, Educational Media and Technology, and Library and Information Science. *Admission Requirements:* 700 GRE. *Minimum Degree Requirements:* 30 semester hours with thesis, 36 without thesis. M.Ed. (Educational Computing), 30 hours in ed. tech.; M.S. (Educational Media and Technology), 21 hours in ed. tech.; M.S. (Library and Information Science), 15 hours in library/information science, 12 hours in ed. tech. *Faculty:* 3 full-time; 5 part-time. *Students:* 30 full-time; 150 part-time. *Financial Assistance:* Graduate assistantships in teaching, graduate assistantships in research, scholarships, federal aid program. *Master's Degrees Awarded 1994:* 20. A six-year program is available.

Texas A&M University. Dept. of Curriculum & Instruction, College Station, TX 77843-4232. (409) 845-7276. Fax (409) 845-9663. E-mail zellner@tamu.edu. Ronald D. Zellner, Coord., Dept. of Curriculum & Instruction. *Specialization:* M.Ed. in Educational Technology. *Admission Requirements:* Bachelor's degree; GRE minimum score 800; TOEFL Exam minimum score 550. *Minimum Degree Requirements:* 40 semester credits; oral exam. *Faculty:* 5 full-time; 1 part-time. *Students:* 15 full-time; 5 part-time. *Financial Assistance:* Teaching assistantships available. *Master's Degrees Awarded 1995:* 6.

*University of Texas-Austin. College of Education, Austin, TX 78712. (512) 471-5211. DeLayne Hudspeth, Assoc. Prof., Coord., Area of Instructional Technology, Dept. of Curriculum and Instruction, College of Education. *Specialization:* Master's degree. *Admission Requirements:* 3.25 GPA and a score of at least 1,200 on the GRE. *Minimum Degree Requirements:* 30-36 semester hours minimum depending on selection of program; 18 in Instructional Technology plus research course; thesis optional. A 6-hour minor is required outside the department. *Faculty:* 4 full-time; 2 part-time. *Master's Degrees Awarded 1994:* 18.

UTAH

Brigham Young University. Department of Instructional Science, 201 MCKB, Provo, UT 84602. (801) 378-5097. Fax (801) 378-8672. E-mail paul_merrill@byu.edu; http://www.byu. edu/homepage.html. Paul F. Merrill, Prof., Chair. *Specializations:* M.S. degrees are offered in instructional design, research and evaluation, and multimedia production. *Features:* Course offerings include principles of learning, instructional design, assessing learning outcomes, evaluation in education, empirical inquiry in education, project management, statistics, micro-computer materials production, multimedia production, naturalistic inquiry, and more. Students are required to participate in an internship and complete a Master's project. *Admission Requirements:* Transcript, 3 letters of recommendation, letter of intent, and GRE examination. Apply by February 1. Students agree to live by the BYU Honor Code. *Faculty:* 9 full-time; 2 half-time. *Students:* 25 full-time; 2 part-time. *Financial Assistance:* Internships, tuition waivers, loans, and travel to present papers. *Master's Degrees Awarded 1995:* 3.

Utah State University. Department of Instructional Technology, Logan, UT 84322-2830. (801) 797-2694. Fax (801) 797-2693.E-mail smellie@pc.usu.edu. Dr. Don C. Smellie, Prof., Head, Dept. of Instructional Technology. *Specializations:* M.S. and Ed.S. with concentrations in the areas of Instructional Development, Interactive Learning, Educational Technology, and Information Technology/School Library Media Administration. *Features:* Programs in Information Technology/School Library Media Administration and Educational Technology are also delivered via an electronic distance education system. *Admission Requirements:* 3.0 GPA, successful teaching experience or its equivalent, a verbal and quantitative score at the 43rd percentile on the GRE, three written recommendations. *Minimum Degree Requirements:* M.S.: 60 quarter hours, including 45 in media; thesis or project option. Ed.S.: 45 quarter hours if M.S. is in the field, 60 hours if it is not. *Faculty:* 9 full-time; 7 part-time. *Students:* 68 full-time; 65 part-time (in graduate program). *Financial Assistance:* Fellowships and assistantships. *Master's Degrees Awarded 1995:* 33. A six-year program is available.

VIRGINIA

Radford University. Educational Studies Department, College of Education, P.O. Box 6959, Radford, VA 24142. (540) 831-5302. Fax (540) 831-6053. E-mail ljwilson@ruet.edu. Dr. Linda J. Wilson, Human Services Dept. *Specialization:* M.S. in Education with Educational Media emphasis. *Features:* School library media specialist licensure. *Admission Requirements:* Bachelor's degree. *Minimum Degree Requirements:* 33 semester hours; thesis optional; practicum required. *Faculty:* 2 full-time; 3 part-time. *Students:* 3 full-time; 21 part-time. *Financial Assistance:* Assistantships, grants, student loans, scholarships. *Master's Degrees Awarded 1995:* 2.

University of Virginia. Curry School of Education, Ruffner Hall, Charlottesville, VA 22903. (804) 924-0834. Fax (804) 924-7987. E-mail jbb2s@curry.edschool.virginia.edu. Dr. John D. Bunch, Assoc. Prof., Coord., Instructional Technology Prog., Dept. of Leadership, Foundations and Policy Studies. *Specializations:* M.Ed., Ed.S. (Educational Specialist), Ph.D. and Ed.D. degrees offered, with focal areas in Media Production, Interactive Multimedia, and K-12 Educational Technologies. *Minimum Degree Requirements:* For specific degree requirements, write to the address above or refer to the UVA *Graduate Record. Faculty:* 3 full-time; 2 part-time. *Students:* 22 full-time; 11 part-time. *Master's Degrees Awarded 1995:* Data not reported.

*Virginia Polytechnic Institute and State University (Virginia Tech). College of Education, Blacksburg, VA 24061-0313. (540) 231-5598. Fax (540) 231-9075. Terry M. Wildman, Prof., Prog. Area Leader, Instructional Systems Development, Curriculum and Instruction. *Specializations:* M.S. in Instructional Technology, with emphases on Training and Development, Educational Computing, Evaluation, and Media Management. *Features:* Facilities include 70-computer laboratory (IBM, Macintosh), interactive video, speech synthesis, telecommunications. *Minimum Degree Requirements:* 30 semester hours, including 15 in

Instructional Technology; thesis optional. *Faculty:* 8 full-time; 5 part-time. *Students:* 8 full-time; 15 part-time. *Financial Assistance:* Assistantships are sometimes available, as well as opportunities with other agencies. *Master's Degrees Awarded 1994:* Data not reported. An advanced certificate program is available.

*Virginia State University. School of Liberal Arts & Education, Petersburg, VA 23806. (804) 524-5937. Vykuntapathi Thota, Acting Chair and Prog. Dir., Dept. of Educational Leadership. *Specializations:* M.S., M.Ed. in Educational Media and Technology. *Features:* Video Conferencing Center and PLATO Laboratory, internship in ABC and NBC channels. *Minimum Degree Requirements:* 30 semester hours plus thesis for M.S.; 33 semester hours plus project for M.Ed.; comprehensive examination. *Faculty:* 1 full-time; 2 part-time. *Students:* 5 full-time; 41 part-time. *Financial Assistance:* Scholarships through the School of Graduate Studies. *Master's Degrees Awarded 1994:* 5.

WASHINGTON

University of Washington. Department of Education, Seattle, WA 98195. (206) 543-1847. Fax (206) 543-8439. E-mail stkerr@u.washington.edu. Stephen T. Kerr, Prof. of Education, Prog. in Educational Communication and Technology, School of Education. *Specialization:* Master's degree. *Minimum Degree Requirements:* 45 quarter hours, including 24 in media; thesis optional. *Faculty:* 2 full-time. *Master's Degrees Awarded 1995:* 11.

Western Washington University. Woodring College of Education, Bellingham, WA 98225-9087. (360) 650-3090. Fax (360) 650-6526. E-mail lblack@wce.wwu.edu. Dr. Les Blackwell, Prof., Program Chair, Instructional Technology. *Specializations:* M.Ed. for Curriculum and Instruction, with emphases in Instructional Technology, elementary and secondary programs; Adult Education; Master's Degree with emphasis on Instructional Design and Multimedia Development for education and industry persons; and Learning Resources (Library Science) for K-12 school librarians only. *Admission Requirements:* 3.0 GPA in last 45 quarter credit hours; GRE examination, 3 letters of recommendation, and, in some cases, 3 years of teaching experience. *Minimum Degree Requirements:* 48-52 quarter hours (24-28 hours in instructional technology); 24 hours in education-related courses, thesis or field project required; internship and practicum possible. *Faculty:* 4 full-time; 8 part-time. *Students:* 5 full-time; 12 part-time. *Financial Assistance:* Assistantships, student loans. *Master's Degrees Awarded 1995:* 4.

WISCONSIN

University of Wisconsin-La Crosse. Educational Media Program, Rm. 109, Morris Hall, La Crosse, WI 54601. (608) 785-8121. Fax (608) 785-8119. Dr. Russell Phillips, Dir., Educational Media Prog., School of Education. *Specializations:* M.S. in Professional Development with specializations in Initial Instructional Library Specialist, License 901; Instructional Library Media Specialist, License 902 (39 credits). *Minimum Degree Requirements:* 30 semester hours, including 15 in media; no thesis. *Faculty:* 2 full-time; 4 part-time. *Students:* 21. *Financial Assistance:* Guaranteed student loans, graduate assistantships. *Master's Degrees Awarded 1995:* 7.

WYOMING

*University of Wyoming. Div. of Life Long Learning and Instruction, College of Education, Box 3374, Laramie, WY 82071-3374. (307) 766-3608. Fax (307) 766-6668. E-mail johncoc@uwyo.edu. Dr. John Cochenour, Head, Dept. of Instructional Technology. *Specialization:* M.S. in Instructional Technology. *Admission Requirements:* Bachelor's degree; undergraduate GPA of at least 3.0; GRE minimum score 900; TOEFL Exam score 25. *Minimum Degree Requirements:* 36 semester credits; required thesis or project paper worth 4 credits. *Faculty:* 3 full-time; 1 part-time. *Students:* Data not reported. *Financial Assistance:* Data not reported. *Master's Degrees Awarded 1994:* Data not reported.

Graduate Programs in Educational Computing

When the directory of graduate programs in educational computing first appeared in the *1986 EMTY*, there were 50 programs. This year's listing consists of 29 such programs in 20 states, down from the 1995-1996 total of 43 programs in 23 states. The information in this section has been revised and updates the information assembled in *EMTY 1995-1996*. Individuals who are considering graduate study in educational computing should contact the institution of their choice for current information. It should be noted that some programs that appear in this listing also appear in the listings of master's and six-year programs and doctoral programs.

Copies of the entries from the 1995-1996 *EMTY* were sent to the programs with a request for updated information and/or corrections, with the proviso that, if no response was received this year or in 1995-1996, the entry would be dropped. Programs from which a response was received for 1995-1996 but not for 1997 are indicated with an asterisk (*). It should be noted that not all of the information in these descriptions is necessarily correct for the current year.

We would like to express our appreciation to the 22 program administrators who complied with our request for the 1997 edition. Of the remaining programs, 7 had been updated in the 1995-1996 edition; 16 have been dropped for lack of response since 1995 or before. Our special thanks go to those who notified us of the status of programs that have been discontinued.

Data in this section include as much of the following information as was provided to us: the name of the institution and the program, telephone and fax numbers, e-mail addresses, a contact person, the degree(s) offered, admission requirements, minimum requirements for each degree, the number of faculty, the number of students currently enrolled, information on financial assistance, and the number of degrees awarded in 1995.

This section is arranged alphabetically by state and name of institution.

ARIZONA

*Arizona State University. Educational Media and Computers, Box 870111, Tempe, AZ 85287-0111. Dr. Gary Bitter, Coord., Educational Media and Computers. (602) 965-7192. Fax (602) 965-7058. E-mail aogbb@asuvm.inre.asu.edu. *Specializations:* M.A. and Ph.D. in Educational Media and Computers. *Features:* A three semester hour course in Instructional Media Design is offered via CD-ROM/Internet (Internet access is through Home Page). *Minimum Degree Requirements:* Master's: 33 semester hours (21 hours in educational media and computers, 9 hours in education, 3 hours outside education); thesis not required; internship, comprehensive exam, and practicum required. Doctorate: 93 semester hours (24 hours in educational media and computers, 57 hours in education, 12 hours outside education); thesis, internship, and practicum required. *Admission Requirements:* MAT/TOEFL. *Faculty:* 7 full-time; 6 part-time. *Students:* M.A., 121 full-time; 32 part-time. Ph.D., 17 full-time; 8 part-time. *Financial Assistance:* Graduate assistantships, grants, student loans. *Degrees Awarded 1994:* M.A., 46; Ph.D., 3.

CALIFORNIA

*California State University-Dominguez Hills. 1000 E. Victoria St., Carson, CA 90747. (310) 516-3524. Fax (310) 516-3518. E-mail pdesberg@dhva20.csudh.edu. Peter Desberg, Prof., Coord., Computer-Based Education Program. *Specializations:* M.A. and Certificate in Computer-Based Education. *Admission Requirements:* 2.75 GPA. *Minimum Degree Requirements:* 30 semester hours including a master's project; 15 hours for the certificate. *Faculty:* 2 full-time; 2 part-time. *Students:* 50 full-time; 40 part-time. *Degrees Awarded 1994:* M.A., 20. An advanced certificate program is available.

CONNECTICUT

Fairfield University. Graduate School of Education and Allied Professions, Fairfield, CT 06430. (203) 254-4000, ext. 2697. Fax (203) 254-4087. Dr. Ibrahim Hefzallah, Prof. of Educational Technology; Dr. John J. Schurdak, Assoc. Prof., Co-Directors, Computers in Education/Educational Technology Program. *Specializations:* M.A. in two tracks: (1) Computers in Education, or (2) Media/Educational Technology (for school media specialists, see listing of Master's Programs). *Features:* Emphasis on theory, practice, and new instructional developments in computers in education, multimedia, and satellite communications. *Admission Requirements:* Bachelor's degree from an accredited institution, minimum 2.67 GPA. *Minimum Degree Requirements:* 33 semester credits, average B grade. *Faculty:* 2 full-time; 6 part-time. *Students:* 6 full-time; 54 part-time. *Financial Assistance:* Graduate assistantships, scholarships, student loans. *Degrees Awarded 1995:* 14.

FLORIDA

Barry University. School of Education, 11300 N.E. Second Ave., Miami Shores, FL 33161. (305) 899-3608. Fax (305) 899-3718. E-mail jlevine@bu4090.barry.edu. Joel S. Levine, Dir. of Educational Computing and Technology Dept. *Specializations:* Master's and Education Specialist, Ph.D. degree in Educational Technology Leadership. *Features:* Majority of the courses (30/36) in M.S. and Ed.S. programs are in the field of Educational Technology. *Admission Requirements:* GRE score; letters of recommendation; previous GPA; interview; and achievements. *Degree Requirements:* Master's or Ed. Specialist degrees: 37 semester credit hours. Ph.D. degree: 54 credits beyond the master's including dissertation credits. *Faculty:* 6 full-time; 10 part-time. *Students:* M.S.: 59 full-time, 181 part-time; Ed.S.: 5 full-time, 44 part-time; Ph.D.: 10 part-time. *Financial Assistance:* Assistantships, student loans. *Degrees Awarded 1995:* M.S., 42; Ed.S., 8.

GEORGIA

University of Georgia. College of Education, Athens, GA 30602-7144. (706) 542-3810. Fax (706) 542-4072. E-mail kgustafs@moe.coe.uga.edu. Dr. Kent L.Gustafson, Prof. and Chair, Dept. of Instructional Technology. *Specialization:* M.Ed. in Computer-Based Education. *Minimum Degree Requirements:* 60 quarter credit hours (25 hours in computers, 10 hours in education, 25 hours not specified [55 hours with applied project]); thesis not required; internship and practicum optional. *Faculty:* 10 full-time; 3 part-time. *Students:* 18 full-time; 7 part-time. *Degrees Awarded 1995:* 6.

ILLINOIS

Concordia University. 7400 Augusta St., River Forest, IL 60305-1499. (708) 209-3088. Fax (708) 209-3176. E-mail boosmb@crf.cuis.edu. Dr. Manfred Boos, Chair, Mathematics/Computer Science Education Dept. *Specialization:* M.A. in Mathematics Education; M.A. in Computer Science Education. *Admission Requirements:* GPA 2.85 or above, 2.25 to 2.85 provisional status; bachelor's degree from regionally accredited institution; two letters of recommendation. *Minimum Degree Requirements:* 48 quarter hours of course work. *Faculty:* 7 full-time; 5 part-time. *Students:* 2 full-time; 20 part-time. *Financial Assistance:* A number of graduate assistantships, Stafford student loans, and supplement loan for students. *Degrees Awarded 1995:* 5.

Northern Illinois University. Instructional Technology Faculty, LEPS Department, DeKalb, IL 60115. (815) 753-0464. Fax (815) 753-9371. Dr. Gary L. McConeghy, Chair, Instructional Technology Faculty. *Specialization:* M.S.Ed. in Instructional Technology with a concentration in Microcomputers in School-Based Settings. Master's program started in 1968. *Admission Requirements:* GPA 2.75; GRE 800 combined scores; two references. *Minimum Degree Requirements:* 39 hours (30 hours in instructional technology, 9 hours in education, 0 hours outside education); no thesis, internship, or practicum is required. *Faculty:* 8 full-time; 3 part-time. *Students:* 106 part-time. *Financial Assistance:* Some assistantships available at various departments on campus. *Degrees Awarded 1995:* 29. See also the listing in Master's Programs.

INDIANA

Purdue University. School of Education, Department of Curriculum and Instruction, West Lafayette, IN 47907-1442. (317) 494-5673. Fax (317) 496-1622. Dr. James Russell, Prof., Educational Computing and Instructional Development. *Specializations:* M.S., Ed.S., and Ph.D. in Educational Computing and Instructional Development. *Admission Requirements:* GPA of 3.0 or better; three letters of recommendation; statement of personal goals; total score of 1,000 or more on GRE for Ph.D. admission. *Minimum Degree Requirements:* Master's: 36 semester hours (15 in computer or instructional development, 9 in education, 12 unspecified); thesis optional. Specialist: 60-65 semester hours (15-18 in computer or instructional development, 30-35 in education); thesis, internship, and practicum required. Doctorate: 90 semester hours (15-18 in computer or instructional development, 42-45 in education); thesis, internship, and practicum required. *Faculty:* 6 full-time. *Students:* M.S./Ed.S., 6 full-time; 15 part-time; Ph.D., 8 full-time; 16 part-time. *Financial Assistance:* Assistantships and fellowships. *Degrees Awarded 1995:* Ph.D., 6; Master's, 12. See also listings in Doctoral and Master's Programs.

IOWA

*Dubuque Tri-College Department of Education (a consortium of Clarke College, The University of Dubuque, and Loras College). Graduate Studies, 1550 Clarke Drive, Dubuque, IA 52001. (319) 588-6331. Fax (319) 588-6789. Robert Adams, Clarke College, (319) 588-6416. *Specializations:* M.A. in Technology and Education. *Admission Requirements:* Minimum GPA 2.5 on 4.0 scale; GRE (verbal and quantitative) or Miller Analogies Test; application form and $25 application fee; and two letters of recommendation. *Minimum Degree Requirements:* 25 semester hours in computer courses, 12 hours in education. *Faculty:* 1 full-time; 1-2 part-time. *Students:* master's, 11 part-time. *Financial Assistance:* Scholarships, student loans. *Degrees Awarded 1994:* Master's, 0 (newly revised program).

Iowa State University. College of Education, Ames, IA 50011. (515) 294-6840. E-mail mrs@iastate.edu. Dr. Michael R. Simonson, Prof. *Specializations:* M.S., M.Ed., and Ph.D. in Curriculum and Instructional Technology with specializations in Instructional Computing, Instructional Design, and Distance Education. Participates in Iowa Distance Education Alliance: Iowa Star Schools Project. *Admission Requirements:* M.S. and M.Ed., three letters; top half of undergraduate class; autobiography. Ph.D., the same plus GRE. *Minimum Degree Requirements:* Master's: 30 semester hours; thesis required; no internship or practicum is required. Doctorate: 78 semester hours, thesis required; no internship or practicum is required. *Faculty:* 3 full time; 6 part-time. *Students:* Master's: 30 full-time; 30 part-time; Ph.D.: 30 full-time; 20 part-time. *Degrees Awarded 1995:* Master's, 12; Doctorate, 6.

KANSAS

Kansas State University. Educational Computing, Design, and Telecommunications, 363 Bluemont Hall, Manhattan, KS 66506. (913) 532-7686. Fax (913) 532-7304. E-mail dmcgrath@coe.edu.ksu.edu. Dr. Diane McGrath, contact person. *Specializations:* M.S. in Secondary Education with an emphasis in Educational Computing; Ph.D. and Ed.D. in Curriculum & Instruction with an emphasis in Educational Computing, Design, and Telecommunications. Master's program started in 1982; doctoral in 1987. *Admission Requirements:* M.S.B average in undergraduate work; one programming language; TOEFL score of 590 or above. Ph.D./Ed.D.B average in undergraduate and graduate work; one programming language, GRE or MAT; experience or course in educational computing; three letters of recommendation. *Minimum Degree Requirements:* M.S.: 30 semester hours (minimum of 12 in Educational Computing); thesis, internship, or practicum not required, but all three are possible. Ph.D.: 90 semester hours (minimum of 21 hours in Educational Computing, Design, and Telecommunications or related area approved by committee; 30 hours for dissertation research); thesis required; internship and practicum not required but available. Ed.D.: 94 semester hours (minimum of 18 hours in Educational Computing or related area approved by committee; 16 hours for dissertation research; 12 hours of internship); thesis required. *Faculty:* 2 full-time; 1 part-time. *Students:* M.S.: 4 full-time; 25 part-time; Ph.D.: 12 full-time; 19 part-time. *Financial Assistance:* Five assistantships, other assistantships sometimes available in other departments depending on skills and funds available. *Degrees Awarded 1995:* M.S., 5; Ph.D., 2.

MARYLAND

The Johns Hopkins University. School for Continuing Studies, Division of Education, Center for Technology in Education, 2500 E. Northern Parkway, Baltimore, MD 21214. (410) 254-8466. Fax (410) 254-8266. E-mail sjm@jhunix.hcf.jhu.edu. Dr. Jacqueline A. Nunn, Prog. Dir.; Dr. Sarah McPherson, Prog. Coord. *Specialization:* M.S. in Education with a concentration in Instructional Technology, Assistive Technology, or School-Based Technology Leadership. *Features:* Focuses on the integration of technology with effective instructional programs for all students preschool through grade 12. *Admission Requirements:* Bachelor's degree with strong background in teaching, curriculum and instruction, special education, or a related service field. *Minimum Degree Requirements:* 36 semester hours, 7 required courses in technology-related courses, with remaining courses being electives in the Technology for Educators program areas. *Faculty:* 3 full-time; 15 adjunct. *Students:* 150 part-time. *Financial Assistance:* Grants, student loans, scholarships. *Degrees Awarded 1995:* 25.

MASSACHUSETTS

Lesley College. 29 Everett St., Cambridge, MA 02138-2790. (617) 349-8419. Fax (617) 349-8169. E-mail nroberts@mail.lesley.edu. Dr. Nancy Roberts, Prof. of Education. *Specializations:* M.A. in Computers in Education; C.A.G.S. in Computers in Education; Ph.D in Education with a Computers in Education major. *Features:* Master's degree program is offered off-campus at 33 sites in 12 states; contact Professional Outreach Associates [(800) 843-4808] for information. *Minimum Degree Requirements:* Master's 33 semester hours in computers (number of hours in education and outside education not specified); integrative final project in lieu of thesis; no internship or practicum is required. Specialist: 36 semester hours (hours in computers, education, and outside education not specified); thesis, internship, practicum not specified. Ph.D. requirements available on request. *Faculty:* 5 full-time; 90 part-time on the master's and specialist levels. *Students:* 760. *Degrees Awarded 1995:* 360.

NEW YORK

Buffalo State College. 1300 Elmwood Ave., Buffalo, NY 14222-1095. (716) 878-4923. Fax (716) 878-6677. E-mail nowakoaj@snybufaa.cs.snybuf.edu. Dr. Anthony J. Nowakowski, Prog. Coord. *Specializations:* M.S. in Education in Educational Computing. *Admission Requirements:* Baccalaureate degree from accredited college or university; 3.0 GPA in last 60 hours; 3 letters of recommendation. *Minimum Degree Requirements:* 33 semester hours (15 hours in computers, 12-15 hours in education, 3-6 in electives); thesis or project required. *Faculty:* 8 part-time. *Students:* 2 full-time; 50 part-time. *Degrees Awarded 1995:* M.S., 16.

Pace University. Department of Educational Administration, Bedford Road, Pleasantville, NY 10570. (914) 773-3876; (914) 422-4199. Fax (914) 773-3521; (914) 422-4311. Dr. Lawrence Roder, Dir., Educational Administration Programs. *Specialization:* M.S.E. in Curriculum and Instruction with a concentration in Computers and Education. *Admission Requirements:* GPA

3.0; interview; application. *Minimum Degree Requirements:* 33-34 semester hours (15 in computers, 18 in educational administration). *Faculty:* 2 full-time; 12 part-time. *Students:* 60-70 part-time. *Financial Assistance:* Assistantships, scholarships. *Degrees Awarded 1995:* M.S.E., 25.

State University College of Arts and Science at Potsdam. 204 Satterlee Hall, Potsdam, NY 13676. (315) 267-2527. Fax (315) 267-2771. E-mail lichtnc@potsdam.edu. Dr. Norman Licht, Prof. of Education. *Specializations:* M.S. in Education, Instructional Technology, and Media Management with Educational Computing concentration. *Minimum Degree Requirements:* 30 semester hours (15 hours in computers, 18 hours in education, 0 hours outside education); thesis not required; internship or practicum required. *Faculty:* 7 full-time; 2 part-time. *Students:* 102 full-time; 34 part-time. *Financial Assistance:* Assistantships, student loans. *Degrees Awarded 1995:* M.S., 42.

NORTH CAROLINA

Appalachian State University. Department of Library Science and Educational Foundations, Boone, NC 28608. (704) 262-2243. E-mail tashnerjh@alf.appstate.edu. Dr. John H. Tashner. *Specialization:* M.A. in Educational Media and Technology with three areas of concentration: computers, telecommunications, and media production. *Features:* IMPACT NC (Business/University/Public School) Partnership offers unusual opportunities. *Minimum Degree Requirements:* 36 semester hours; thesis optional; internship required. *Admission Requirements:* Selective. *Faculty:* 2 full-time; 1 part-time. *Students:* M.A., 6 full-time; 25 part-time. *Financial Assistance:* Assistantships, grants, student loans. *Degrees Awarded 1995:* M.A., 6.

North Carolina State University. Department of Curriculum and Instruction, P.O. Box 7801, Raleigh, NC 27695-7801. (919) 515-1779. Fax (919) 515-6978. E-mail esvasu@unity.ncsu.edu. Dr. Ellen Vasu, Assoc. Prof., Dept. of Curriculum and Instruction. *Specializations:* Ph.D. in Curriculum and Instruction with focus on Instructional Technology as well as other areas; M.Ed. and M.S. in Instructional Technology-Computers (program track within one Master's in Curriculum and Instruction). *Minimum Degree Requirements:* Ph.D., 60 hours beyond Master's, minimum 33 in Curriculum and Instruction core, 27 in Research, other information available upon request; Master's, 36 semester hours; thesis optional; practicum required. *Faculty:* 3 full-time. *Students:* Master's, 13 part-time; Doctoral, 7 part-time. *Financial Assistance:* Data not reported. *Degrees Awarded 1995:* Master's, 3.

NORTH DAKOTA

Minot State University. 500 University Ave. W., Minot, ND 58707. (701) 858-3817. Fax (701) 839-6933. Dr. David Williams, Dir., Graduate School. *Specializations:* Master's in Education (including work in educational computing); M.S. in Management; M.S. in Math and Computer Science; M.S. in Early Childhood Special Education; M.S. in Severe Multiple-Handicaps. *Features:* All programs include involvement in computer applications appropriate to the area of study, including assistive technologies for handicapped persons. Computer laboratories for student use have been set up in the library and the Department of Education, and a computer course is worked into all graduate programs. Some courses will be offered through the North Dakota Wide Area Network, which currently has four sites for students. A special laboratory with assistive devices for use by hearing- and visually impaired students and a program in audiology are planned for the future. *Admission Requirements:* Application with $25 fee, three letters of recommendation, 300-word autobiography, transcripts. *Minimum Degree Requirements:* 30 semester hours (hours in computers, education, and outside education vary according to program); written comprehensive exams; oral exams, thesis, or project. *Faculty:* 14 full-time. *Students:* 61 full-time; 63 part-time. *Financial Assistance:* Loans, assistantships, scholarships. *Degrees Awarded 1995:* M.S., 66.

OHIO

Ohio University. School of Curriculum and Instruction, 248 McCracken Hall, Athens, OH 45701-2979. (614) 593-4457. Fax (614) 593-0177. John McCutcheon, contact person. *Specialization:* M.Ed. in Computer Education and Technology. *Admission Requirements:* Bachelor's degree; undergraduate GPA of at least 2.5; Miller Analogy Test score 35; GRE minimum test score 420 verbal, 400 quant.; TOEFL Exam minimum score 550; three letters of recommendation. *Minimum Degree Requirements:* 54 quarter credits; optional thesis worth 2-10 credits or alternative seminar and paper. Students may earn two graduate degrees simultaneously in education and in any other field. *Faculty:* 1 full-time; 4 part-time. *Students:* 24 full-time; 5 part-time. *Financial Assistance:* Assistantships. *Degrees Awarded 1995:* Master's, 24.

Wright State University. College of Education and Human Services, 244 Millett Hall, Dayton, OH 45435. (513) 873-2509 or (513) 873-2182. Fax (513) 873-4485. E-mail bmathies@desire.wright.edu. Dr. Bonnie K. Mathies, Chair, Dept. of Educational Leadership. *Specializations:* M.Ed. in Computer Education; M.Ed. for Computer Coordinator; M.A. in Computer Education. Two new Educational Specialist programs available as of winter 1996: Curriculum and Instruction Track, Technology Strand; Higher Education Track, Technology Strand. *Admission Requirements:* 2.7 GPA for regular admission; GRE or Miller Analogies Test. *Minimum Degree Requirements:* 48 quarter hours (hours in computers, education, and outside education not specified); thesis required for M.A. degree only; comprehensive examination in the form of the completion of a portfolio and a videotaped presentation to the faculty for M.Ed.; eligible for Supervisor's Certificate after completion of C&S; Computer Coordinator program. *Faculty:* 2 full-time; 12 part-time adjuncts and other university full-time faculty and staff. *Students:* Approx. 75 full- and part-time. *Financial Assistance:* Assistantships, limited number of small graduate scholarships. *Degrees Awarded 1995:* M.A. and M.Ed., 12.

OKLAHOMA

The University of Oklahoma. Department of Educational Psychology, 820 Van Vleet Oval, Norman, OK 73019. (405) 325-1521. Fax (405) 325-6655. E-mail tragan@uoknor.edu. Dr. Tillman J. Ragan, Prof. *Specialization:* M.Ed. in Educational Technology with Computer Applications emphasis. For additional options in Educational Technology, see the listing for Master's Programs. *Admission Requirements:* 3.0 GPA over last 60 hours of undergraduate work or at least 12 credit hours of graduate work with a 3.0 GPA from an accredited college or university. *Minimum Degree Requirements:* 32 semester hours (12 hours in computers, 21 hours in instructional technology [including computers 12]); internship required. *Faculty:* 10 full-time; 2 part-time. *Students:* 3 full-time; 14 part-time. *Financial Assistance:* Assistantships, out-of-state fee waivers, graduate scholarships (both general and targeted minorities). *Degrees Awarded 1995:* M.Ed., 6.

TEXAS

*East Texas State University. Department of Secondary and Higher Education, East Texas Station, Commerce, TX 75429-3011. (903) 886-5607. Fax (903) 886-5603. E-mail mundayb@ tenet.edu. Dr. Robert S. Munday, Prof., Head, Dept. of Secondary and Higher Education. *Specialization:* Master's degree in Learning Technology and Information Systems with emphasis on Educational Micro Computing, Educational Media and Technology, and Library and Information Science. *Admission Requirements:* 700 GRE. *Minimum Degree Requirements:* 30 semester hours with thesis, 36 without thesis. M.Ed. (Educational Computing), 30 hours in ed. tech.; M.S. (Educational Media and Technology), 21 hours in ed. tech.; M.S. (Library and Information Science), 15 hours in library/information science, 12 hours in ed. tech. *Faculty:* 3 full-time; 5 part-time. *Students:* 30 full-time; 150 part-time. *Financial Assistance:* Graduate assistantships in teaching, graduate assistantships in research, scholarships, federal aid program. *Degrees Awarded 1994:* Master's, 20. A six-year program is available.

Texas Tech University. College of Education, Box 41071, TTU, Lubbock, TX 79409. (806) 742-2362. Fax (806) 742-2179. Dr. Robert Price, Dir., Instructional Technology. *Specializations:* M.Ed. in Instructional Technology (Educational Computing emphasis); Ed.D. in Instructional Technology. *Features:* Program is NCATE accredited and follows ISTE and AECT guidelines. *Admission Requirements:* M.Ed., GRE score of 850 and GPA of 3.0 on last 30 hours of undergraduate program; Ed.D., GRE score of 1050; GPA of 3.0 on last 30 hours. *Minimum Degree Requirements:* Master's: 39 hours (24 hours in computing, 15 hours in education or outside education); practicum required. Doctorate: 87 hours (45 hours in educational technology, 18 hours in education, 15 hours in resource area or minor); practicum required. *Faculty:* 3 full-time; 2 part-time. *Students:* M.Ed., 5 full-time, 25 part-time; Ed.D., 8 full-time, 10 part-time. *Financial Assistance:* Teaching and research assistantships available ($7,800/9 months); small scholarships. *Degrees Awarded 1995:* Ed.D., 2; M.Ed., 8.

VIRGINIA

*Hampton University. School of Liberal Arts and Education, 301 A Phenix Hall, Hampton, VA 23668. (804) 727-5751. Fax (804) 727-5084. Dr. JoAnn W. Haysbert, Prof. and Coord. of Graduate Programs in Education. This program was phased out in 1996.

*Virginia Polytechnic Institute and State University. Instructional Systems Development, College of Education, War Memorial Hall, Blacksburg, VA 24061-0313. (540) 231-5598. Fax (540) 231-9075. Terry M. Wildman, Prof., Prog. Area Leader, Instructional Systems Development, Curriculum and Instruction. *Specializations:* Ed.D. and Ph.D. programs in Instructional Technology. *Features:* Areas of emphasis are Instructional Design, Educational Computing, Evaluation, Media Management, Speech Synthesis, and Telecommunications. *Admission Requirements:* 3.3 GPA for master's degree; three letters of recommendation; transcripts of previous academic work. *Faculty:* 8 full-time; 5 part-time. *Students:* 6 full-time; 6 part-time. *Financial Assistance:* 10 assistantships; tuition scholarships; contracts with other agencies. *Degrees Awarded 1994:* Data not reported.

WASHINGTON

Eastern Washington University. Department Computer Science, Cheney, WA 99004-2495. (509) 359-7092. Fax (509) 359-2215. Internet dhorner@ewu.edu. Dr. Donald R. Horner, Prof. of Computer Science. *Specializations:* M.Ed. in Computer Education (elementary); M.Ed. in Computer Education (secondary); M.S. in Computer Education (Interdisciplinary). Master's program started in 1983. *Admission Requirements:* GRE, at least 3.0 GPA for last 90 quarter credits (60 semester credits). *Minimum Degree Requirements:* M.S.: 52 quarter hours (30 hours in computers, 0 hours in education, 15 hours outside educationnot specifically computer science; the hours do not total to 52 because of freedom to choose where Methods of Research is taken, where 12 credits of supporting courses are taken, and where additional electives are taken); thesis not required (a research project with formal report is required, although it need not be a thesis in format); internship and/or practicum not required. M.S.: 52 quarter hours divided between computer science and another science or mathematics; one area is primary and includes a research project; the second area generally requires fewer hours than the primary. M.Ed.: 48 quarter hours minimum (24 hours in computer science, 16 hours in education, 8 hours outside education). Most projects involve the use of high-level authoring systems to develop educational products. *Faculty:* 3 full-time. *Students:* About 35. *Financial Assistance:* Some research and teaching fellowships; financial assistance. *Degrees Awarded 1995:* M.S. and M.Ed., 3.

Western Washington University. Woodring College of Education, Bellingham, WA 98225-9087. (360) 650-3090. Fax (360) 650-6526. E-mail lblack@wce.wwu.edu. Dr. Les Blackwell, Prof. of Education. *Specializations:* M.Ed. in Instructional Technology with Elementary, Secondary, Administrative, or Adult Education emphasis. *Features:* Emphasis on interactive multimedia development. *Admission Requirements:* Graduate Record Examination; 3.0 GPA on last 45 credits; transcript of all college work; letters of recommendation. *Minimum Degree Requirements:* 48-52 quarter hours (24-48 hours in instructional technology, 24 hours in education); field project or thesis required. *Faculty:* 4 full-time; 8 part-time. *Students:* 5 full-time; 16 part-time. *Financial Assistance:* Assistantships, student loans. *Degrees Awarded 1995:* M.Ed., 4.

WISCONSIN

*Edgewood College. Department of Education, 855 Woodrow St., Madison, WI 53711-1997. (608) 257-4861, ext. 2293. Fax (608) 257-1455. Internet schmied@edgewood.edu. Dr. Joseph E. Schmiedicke, Chair, Dept. of Education. *Specializations:* M.A. in Education with emphasis on Educational Computing and Educational Technology. Master's program started in 1987. *Features:* Classes conducted in laboratory setting with emphasis on applications and software. *Admission Requirements:* 2.75/4.0 GPA. *Minimum Degree Requirements:* 36 semester hours. *Faculty:* 2 full-time; 3 part-time. *Students:* 2 full-time; 130 part-time. *Financial Assistance:* Grants, student loans. *Degrees Awarded 1994:* M.A., 12.

Scholarships, Fellowships, and Awards

In the instructional technology/media-related fields, various scholarships, fellowships, and awards have been established. Many of these are available to those who either are or will be pursuing advanced degrees at the master's, six-year specialist, or doctoral levels.

Because various colleges, universities, professional organizations, and governmental agencies offer scholarships, fellowships, and awards and may wish to have them included in this section, it would be greatly appreciated if those aware of such financial awards would contact either the editors or the publisher for inclusion of such entries in the next edition of *EMTY*.

We are greatly indebted to the staff members of the Association for Educational Communications and Technology (AECT) for assisting with this section.

Information is furnished in the following sequence:

- Overview of AECT and ECT Foundation Awards
- AECT Awards
- ECT Foundation Awards

AECT AND ECT FOUNDATION AWARDS

The Association for Educational Communications and Technology recognizes and rewards the outstanding achievement of its members and associates through a program that provides for three major annual awards—Achievement, Special Service, and Distinguished Service—and through the ECT Foundation, which provides awards in the areas of leadership, scholarship, and research.

AECT encourages members and associates to apply for these awards, and to disseminate information about the awards to professional colleagues. Specific information about each award is available from the AECT national office. The annual deadline for submitting most award applications is October 15.

All ECT Foundation and AECT awards are presented during the AECT National Convention and InCITE Exposition.

For additional information on all awards, please contact:

AECT Awards Program
1025 Vermont Ave. NW
Suite 820
Washington, DC 20005
(202) 347-7834
Fax: (202) 347-7839
E-mail: aect@aect.org

AECT Service Awards

The Association for Educational Communications and Technology (AECT) provides for three annual awards:

Special Service Award: Granted to a person who has shown notable service to AECT as a whole or to one of its programs or divisions. The nominee must have been a member of AECT for at least 10 years and must not be currently serving as an elected officer of AECT, a member of the Board of Directors, or a member of the AECT Awards Committee.

Distinguished Service Award: Granted to a person who has shown outstanding leadership in advancing the theory and/or practice of educational communications and technology over a substantial period of time. The nominee need not be an AECT member, but must not have received this award previously, or be currently serving as a member of the AECT Awards Committee.

Annual Achievement Award: Honors the individual or group who during the past year has made the most significant contribution to the advancement of educational communications and technology. The contribution being honored should be publicly visible—a specific thing or event—and it must have taken place approximately within the past year. The nominee need not be a member of AECT, and the award can be given to the same person more than once.

ECT Foundation Awards

The ECT Foundation, a nonprofit organization that carries out the purposes of AECT which are charitable and educational in nature, coordinates the following awards:

AECT National Convention Internship Program: Provides complimentary registration and housing at the annual conference plus a cash award for five full-time graduate students (applicants must be a member of AECT and enrolled in a recognized program in educational communications and technology).

Richard B. Lewis Memorial Award: $750 is awarded to the outstanding school district media utilization program (awarded to either a public or private school having media utilization programs in place).

AECT Leadership Development Grant: One grant of $2,000 will support innovative leadership development activities undertaken by affiliates, divisions, or regions. (Special consideration will be given to proposals that demonstrate a commitment to leadership development, that propose programs unique to the applicant's organization, and that include activities of potential benefit to other AECT programs.)

AECT Memorial Scholarships: Donations given in memory of specific past leaders of the field provide a scholarship fund for grants to AECT members enrolled in educational technology graduate studies. Two scholarships of $1,000 each will be awarded to graduate students enrolled in a master's or specialist's program to fund graduate study or research.

Dean and Sybil McClusky Research Award: Two $500 awards are available to defray research expenses for the year's outstanding doctoral dissertation proposal that has been approved by the student's university.

Robert deKieffer International Fellowship Award: Recognizes a professional in educational communications and technology, at any level, from a foreign country who has demonstrated leadership in the field with a $200 cash prize and a plaque. The recipient must be a member of AECT who normally resides outside of the United States.

James W. Brown Publication Award: Recognizes the outstanding publication in the field of educational technology in any media format during the past year with a $500 cash award (excluded from consideration are doctoral, master's, or other types of dissertations prepared in fulfillment of degree program requirements).

ECT Qualitative Research Award: Provides $2,500 for the best original, unpublished qualitative research investigation in the field of educational communications and technology by an individual. Qualitative theories and methods may be applied from areas such as cultural anthropology, history, social psychology, and sociology. In addition, the winner will receive the opportunity to present the paper at the AECT National Convention.

ETR&D Young Scholar Award: Recognizes an unpublished paper that could guide research in educational technology by an individual who does not hold a doctoral degree or who has received the degree within the past five years. The winner receives a $250 cash award. In addition, the winning paper will be published in *Educational Technology Research and Development (ETR&D).*

Robert M. Gagné Award: Provides recognition and financial assistance for outstanding research done by a graduate student in the field of instructional development. The work must have been completed after December 31, 1992, while the candidate was enrolled as a graduate student. The award of $500 cash will be presented to the recipient during the AECT National Convention.

McJulien Minority Scholarship Award: Recognizes a minority graduate student enrolled in an educational communications and technology program at the master's or doctoral level by providing a $500 cash grant plus a plaque. The recipient must be an AECT member.

Carl F. & Viola V. Mahnke Multimedia Award: Honors excellence in message design with a $200 cash award for film, video, CD-ROM, or diskette product created by undergraduate or graduate students who are AECT members. Products must have been completed within a two-year period prior to the competition.

ECT Mentor Endowment Scholarship: One scholarship of $3,000 will be awarded to a graduate student in educational communications and technology for continued studies in the field. The scholarship may be used to assist the recipient to further his or her education in a summer session or academic year of graduate study at any accredited college or university in the United States or Canada. Programs may be at the master's or doctoral level. Recipient must be a member of AECT and accepted in or enrolled in a graduate-level program. The scholarship will be awarded during the ECT Gala at the AECT National Convention.

ECT Mentor Endowment Professional Development Grant: Two professional development grants of $2,000. One grant is given in honor of the past presidents of AECT. The grants are intended for use by professionals in the field of educational communications and technology for the purpose of enhancing professional growth and leadership in a manner other than formal graduate study at a college or university. Applicants must be members of AECT and employed in some area of the field of educational communications and technology. The scholarship will be awarded during the ECT Gala at the AECT National Convention.

AECT Special Service Award

Qualifications

- Award is granted to a person who has shown notable service to AECT. This service may be to the organization as a whole, one of its programs, or one of its divisions.
- Nominee currently must be a member of AECT and have at least 10 years of service to AECT.

Disqualifications

- Recipient may not now be serving as an elected officer of AECT nor as a member of the board of directors.
- Nominee must not be currently serving as a member of the AECT Awards Committee.

Nomination

Nominations are judged and selected on the basis of an outstanding contribution to a division, committee, commission, or program of AECT but not to an affiliate organization. Please provide as much information as you can.

- What year did nominee join AECT?
- The letter of nomination should be accompanied by three letters of support and the nominee's vita (5 pages maximum).

AECT Distinguished Service Award

Qualifications

- Award is granted to a person who has shown outstanding leadership in advancing the theory and/or practice of educational communications and technology over a substantial period of time.
- The nominee need not be a member of AECT.
- Award may be given posthumously.

Disqualifications

- Nominee must not have received this award previously.
- Nominee must not be currently serving as a member of the AECT Awards Committee.

Nomination

Nominations are judged primarily on the distinction or magnitude of the nominee's leadership in advancing the field rather than the association.

Categories

The following categories suggest areas in which the nominee may have rendered distinguished service to the field. The nominee may not be represented in these areas. Use those that apply or add others.

> • Leadership • Research/Theory • Development/Production • Publication
>
> • Major Contribution to Education Outside the United States

- The letter of nomination should be accompanied by three letters of support and the nominee's vita (5 pages maximum).

AECT Annual Achievement Award

Qualifications

- Recipient may be an individual or a group.
- The AAA honors the individual who during the past year has made the most significant contribution to the advancement of educational communications and technology.
- The nominee need not be a member of AECT.
- The contribution being honored should be publicly visible—a specific thing or event.
- It must be timely—taking place within approximately the past year.
- Award can be given to the same person more than once.

Nomination

The nature of this award precludes the use of a single checklist or set of categories for nomination. The nomination and selection are inherently subjective. You are asked simply to present a succinct argument in favor of your nominee. Your statement ought to answer the following questions:

- What is the specific achievement being honored?
- What impact has this achievement had, or is likely to have, on the field?
- How is the nominee connected with the achievement?
- The letter of nomination should be accompanied by three letters of support and the nominee's vita (5 pages maximum).

ECT Foundation
1997 AECT National Convention
Internship Program

Awards: Five students will be chosen as convention interns. Four winners will be designated Cochran interns and will receive complimentary convention registration, complimentary housing, and a $200 cash award. There will also be a limited number of division interns. The interns will be expected to arrive at the convention on the day before the convention and to stay until the close of the convention. (Applicants are encouraged to request financial support for transportation and on-site expenses from their institutions or state affiliate organizations.)

Program
Activities:
Each intern will be expected to participate fully in a coordinated program of activities. These activities include attending private seminars with selected association and professional leaders in the field, observing the AECT governance and program committees, and getting behind-the-scenes views of the convention itself, including helping with the actual convention set-up. Each intern will also be responsible for specific convention-related assignments, which will require approximately 15 hours of time during the convention. A former intern, who is now a member of the AECT Leadership Development Committee, will serve as the program coordinator.

Eligibility:
To qualify for consideration, an applicant must be a full-time student throughout the current academic year in a recognized graduate program in educational communications and technology, and must be a member of AECT. (Applicant may join AECT when applying for the award.)

Application
Process:
To apply for the internship program, qualified graduate students must complete and return an application form and must submit two letters of recommendation.

ECT Foundation
1997 Richard B. Lewis Memorial Award

Award:
$750, provided by the Richard B. Lewis Memorial Fund for "Outstanding School District Media Utilization," is awarded to the winner.

Selection
Process:
The winner will be selected by a unified committee appointed from the divisions of Educational Media Management (DEMM) and School Media Specialists (DSMS) of the Association for Educational Communications and Technology, and the National Association of Regional Media Centers (NARMC).

- Evidence of strong media utilization as gathered from:
  1. special utilization studies conducted by or for the school district;
  2. specific instances of good utilization as described in writing by school district or other personnel.

- Evidence of having provided in the school district budget means of implementing good utilization programs in its schools and of the degree to which AECT/ALA media standards are met for services, equipment, and personnel.

- Assessment of applicant's statements as to how the $750 (if awarded) would be spent, such as for:
  1. attending national, regional, or state conferences or workshops related to media utilization;
  2. selecting media specialist(s) to attend advanced training programs;
  3. buying software or hardware needed to improve media utilization programs;
  4. other purposes (indicating especially creative approaches).

- Recognition by an AECT state, regional, or national affiliate organization or representative, or from a National Association of Regional Media Centers state or regional representative:
  1. through prior recognition or awards;
  2. through a recommendation.

Eligibility: All school districts, public and private, having media utilization programs in place, and conforming to the preceding criteria, are eligible.

Other: The winning district will receive a plaque as part of this award.

ECT Foundation
1997 AECT Leadership Development Grant

Grants: One grant of up to $2,000 is provided by the ECT Foundation and administered by the AECT Leadership Development Committee. The grant is awarded to assist an AECT affiliate, an AECT division, or an AECT regional organization to undertake leadership development activities that will improve the participant's skills as a leader in the professional organization or in educational technology.

Selection: The grant award will be recommended by the Leadership Committee's Subcommittee on Leadership Development Grants.

Selection Criteria: All AECT state and national affiliates, divisions, and regional organizations are eligible for these competitive grants. An application from a previous grant recipient will not be considered unless a summary report has been submitted to the Leadership Development Committee and the AECT national office. Organizations that have not received a grant in the past are particularly invited to apply. Funds must be intended for some unique aspect or function not previously undertaken. Proposals that demonstrate a commitment to leadership development, that propose programs which are unique to the applicant's organization, and which include activities or products of potential benefit to other AECT programs will be given special consideration.

Awards: The awards will be presented during the AECT National Convention and InCITE Exposition.

ECT Foundation
1997 AECT Memorial Scholarships

Awards: Two scholarships of $1,000 each, funded by the ECT Foundation, will be awarded to graduate students or public school teachers in educational communications and technology to fund graduate study or research and development projects in the field. The scholarships may be used to assist the recipients to further their education in a summer session or academic year of graduate study at any accredited college or university in the United States or Canada. It is also available to public school teachers to attend summer sessions as well as seminars and training sessions to improve the teacher/learning process in their school district. Programs of study may be at the master's or educational specialist level or for public educators who are looking for funds to supplement their educational training through the use of educational communications and technology.

Eligibility: All recipients must be members of AECT.

Selection   Selections will be based on the following:
Criteria:

1. Scholarship;

2. Experience related to the field of educational media, communications, or technology, such as employment, field experience, course work, assistantships, publications, practical application in schools, innovative programs in public education, effective utilization of technology in systemic change in education, etc.;

3. Service to the field through association activities and membership in AECT or AECT state affiliates in related professional organizations;

4. Three letters of recommendation from persons familiar with the candidate's professional qualifications and leadership potential; and

5. The candidate's own knowledge of key issues and opportunities facing the educational communications/technology field today, with respect to the candidate's own goals.

ECT Foundation
1997 Dean and Sybil McClusky Research Award

Awards: Two $500 awards are available to honor outstanding doctoral research proposals in educational technology, as selected by a jury of researchers from AECT's Research and Theory Division. Each winner will be awarded $500.

Guidelines for
Preparing and   Submitted proposals may follow acceptable formats of individual schools
Submitting   but must include at least:
Papers:

1. The definition of the problem, including a statement of significance;

2. A review of pertinent literature;

3. Research hypothesis to be examined;

4. Research design and procedures, including statistical techniques.

Applicants are encouraged to review pages 157-61 of Stephen Isaac and William B. Michaels, *Handbook in Research and Evaluation*, Robert R. Knapp, San Diego, CA, 1971.

Eligibility: Applicants must be presently enrolled in a doctoral program in educational technology and have obtained committee acceptance of their proposal. The winner will be expected to sign a statement that the proposed doctoral study will be completed in accordance with the sponsoring university's graduate school policies (including any time limitations) or be required to return the funds received.

ECT Foundation
1997 Robert deKieffer
International Fellowship Award

Purpose: To recognize, annually, a professional in educational communications and technology at any level from a foreign country who has demonstrated leadership in the field.

Award: $200 and a plaque will be presented to the recipient at the AECT National Convention.

Selection: The Awards Committee of the International Division of the Association for Educational Communications and Technology (AECT) is responsible for the selection of the recipient of this award.

Selection Criteria: The following criteria will be used in the selection process:

1. The recipient will be a professional in educational communications and technology at any level.
2. The recipient will be a member of AECT.
3. The recipient normally resides outside of the United States.
4. The recipient will meet at least one of the following criteria:

    (a) has conducted a major project or been involved in the advancement of educational communication and technology outside of the United States;
    (b) is recognized as a leader in the field based on his/her teaching, research, or service records;
    (c) has been active and is instrumental in forging a professional tie in educational communications and technology between the United States and one or more foreign countries.

ECT Foundation
1997 James W. Brown Publication Award

Award: $500 cash award will be given to the author or authors of an outstanding publication in the field of educational technology.

Eligibility: Nominated items are not restricted to books or print; they may be in any media format (film, video, broadcast program, book, etc.). Any nonperiodic publication in the field of educational technology is eligible if it bears a publication date of 1995 or 1996.

Guidelines for Nominations: Nominations are solicited from all possible sources: AECT members, media-related publishers and producers, authors themselves, AECT nonperiodic publications committee members, and others.

Criteria: Nominated publications shall be judged on the basis of:

1. Significance of the item's content for the field of media/instructional technology, as defined in the *Definition of Educational Technology*, published by AECT in 1977, or in any subset of the publication.

2. Professional quality of the item.

3. Potential impact of the item's content on the field of media/instructional technology, as defined in the *Definition of Educational Technology*.

4. Technical quality of the item.

ECT Foundation
1997 Qualitative Research Award

Award: The ECT Foundation announces the creation of an annual award for the best qualitative research in educational communications and technology. This award is open to qualitative studies of all instructional areas including training. In addition to the $1,000 prize, the winner will receive a certificate of achievement and the opportunity to present a paper at the AECT National Convention. Qualitative theories and research methods may be applied from disciplines including, but not limited to, anthropology, art criticism, communication arts, cultural studies, history, literary criticism, philosophy, and sociology. This award supports the independent thinking of independent scholars or groups. Upon notice from the review committee, the Chair of the Award has the authority to split the annual prize fund and make more than one award.

Applications: Applications must include:

1. Cover letter: Indicate whether applicant requests ECT *sponsorship* for a planned project or a project under way, or *recognition* of a completed project.

2. Brief vita, one or two pages indicating:
   • Education: Degrees awarded, dates, and institutions
   • Employment history
   • Representative publications and/or productions
   • Achievements
   • Membership in professional societies

3. Abstract: Outline of a qualitative project in one page or less of double-spaced text.

4. Project narrative: Describe the qualitative project. It may be a *plan* for work to be completed, an *interim* report of work in progress, a *final* report, or a *synopsis* of a final report. This description may range from 15 to 20 pages of double-spaced text, including references. It should be prepared in accordance with a current style manual such as *Chicago* or those published by the APA or MLA.

- Identify clearly the *qualitative foundations* of the project by describing the theoretical base, the research issue, research strategy, and the results (if any at this time). Emphasize the importance of the project in developing understanding of educational communications and technology in a social or cultural context. It is to the applicant's advantage to show that the project has been approved by another agency, recently published, or accepted for publication.
- Justify *sponsorship* by ECT Foundation for *planned projects* and *projects under way*. Include a plan of action, assessment of its feasibility, time line, and budget if resources are needed.
- Justify *recognition* by ECT Foundation of *completed projects* by giving evidence of completion, a description of the project, and interpretation of the findings.

5. Scholars who have received other AECT awards are not eligible for this award.

ECT Foundation
1997 ETR&D Young Scholar Award

Award: $250 will be presented to the winner during the AECT National Convention. Additionally, the winning paper will be published in *Educational Technology Research and Development (ETR&D)*, the referred scholarly research journal published by the Association for Educational Communications and Technology (AECT).

For: The best paper discussing a theoretical construct that could guide research and/or development in educational technology.

Eligibility: An individual who does not hold a doctoral degree or who received a doctorate not more than five years prior to November 1, 1996.

Guidelines for
Preparing and
Submitting   The paper must be an original unpublished work dealing with research and
Papers: theory in educational technology. It must deal with a theoretical construct, analyses of related research, and original recommendations for future research and/or development. The paper may not be a report of a specific research study or development project. It must be 20-30 pages long, excluding references, and must conform to the *American Psychological Association Style Manual*, 3rd ed.

Selection   The selection of the winning paper will be the responsibility of the editor and
of Winner: editorial board of *ETR&D*. Only the best paper judged worthy of the award will win. (There may not be a recipient of this award every year.)

ECT Foundation
1997 Robert M. Gagné Award

Purpose: To provide recognition and financial assistance for outstanding research by a graduate student in the field of instructional development.

Award: $500 is awarded for the most significant contribution to the body of knowledge upon which instructional development is based. The Gagné Award competition is sponsored by the Association for Educational Communications and Technology (AECT) and its Division of Instructional Development. A jury of scholars will select the winning contribution. The award will be presented to the recipient during the AECT National Convention.

Eligibility: The work must have been completed after December 31, 1992, while the award candidate was enrolled as a graduate student.

Nomination
Procedure: You may nominate any individual (including yourself) for the Gagné Award.

ECT Foundation
1997 McJulien Minority
Graduate Scholarship Award

Award: The Wes McJulien Minority Graduate Scholarship Award has been established in memory of his son, Patrick D. McJulien. The award shall consist of $500 plus a plaque for the selected minority student, to be presented at the AECT National Convention.

Purpose: To recognize, annually, a minority graduate student in educational communications and technology.

Selection: Minorities in Media (MIM), an AECT national affiliate, shall be responsible for the selection of the award recipient.

Selection
Criteria: The following criteria will be used in the selection process:

1. The recipient must be a full-time graduate student enrolled in a degree-granting program in educational technology at the master's, educational specialist, or doctoral level.

2. The recipient must have a "B" average or better to apply for this award.

3. The recipient must be an AECT member.

4. The recipient must obtain three letters of reference.

ECT Foundation
1997 Carl F. and Viola V. Mahnke
Film Production Award

Award: $200 will be awarded to honor a film or video product that demonstrates excellence in message design and production for educational purposes. In addition, certificates of merit will be awarded to entries with outstanding qualities worthy of recognition. In the event that no entry demonstrates excellence, in the opinion of the judges, no award will be given.

Eligibility: Eligibility is limited to film, video, or video programs incorporated into multimedia products. The program must have a predominant educational objective in the judges' opinion. The submission must be produced by undergraduate or graduate students. Faculty and professional mentoring is acceptable; however, **all** production work must be done by the person(s) submitting the program. The winners must be members of AECT. Only entries completed within a two-year period prior to the competition will qualify.

Formats: All entries must be either on film, videotape, CD-ROM, or diskette. Film entries are limited to 16mm. Video entries can either be ½-inch VHS or ¾-inch U-matic. CD-ROM entries must work on the following platform:

- CPU: Intel 486SX/33 MHZ minimum (66 MHZ recommended)
- RAM: 4 MB minimum (8 MB recommended)
- Operating System: Windows 3.1
- CD-ROM Drive: Double spin (triple spin recommended)
- Monitor: VGA 640 X 480, 256 colors
- Sound Card: 8-BIT Sound Blaster or compatible (16-BIT recommended)
- Speakers: Amplified (shielded) speakers
- User Input: Keyboard and mouse

Video programs submitted on diskette must meet the following guidelines:

- Run on either Macintosh or PC platform
- Be a "runtime" or executable file to enable judges to view the video program without the application
- Created in multimedia authoring package (for example, Authorware, HyperCard, HyperStudio, MacroMind Director, and others)

Judging: All entries will be judged by a panel of judges from the AECT Media Design and Production Division during the AECT National Convention.

Entry Fee: Entrants must include an entry fee of $10 per program, made payable to MDPD-AECT. For programs consisting of more than one film, videocassette, CD-ROM, or diskette, each must be submitted separately. An entry form must be completed for each entry. The entry form may be duplicated if necessary.

ECT Foundation
1997 ECT Mentor Endowment Scholarship

Award: One scholarship of $3,000.

Purpose: This scholarship is intended for use by a graduate student in educational communications and technology to pursue studies in this field. The scholarship may be used to assist the recipient in enrolling in graduate study during an academic year or a summer session in any accredited college or university in the United States or Canada. Graduate study must be at the doctoral level.

Eligibility: Applicants must be members of AECT and accepted in or enrolled in a graduate-level program as outlined above.

Selection
Criteria: Selections will be based upon:

- Scholarship;
- Leadership potential;
- Experience related to the field of educational communications and technology, such as employment, field experience, course work, assistantships, presentations, publications;
- Three letters of recommendation from persons familiar with the candidate's professional qualifications and leadership potential.

ECT Foundation
1997 Mentor Endowment Professional
Development Grants

Award: Two professional development grants of $2,000. One grant is given in honor of the past presidents of AECT.

Purpose: These grants are intended for use by professionals in the field of educational communications and technology for the purpose of enhancing professional growth and leadership in a manner other than formal graduate study at a college or university. Appropriate uses of these grants may include, but are not limited to, participation in a workshop or conference, development of a new skill, involvement in a special project, or acquisition of materials, hardware, publications, or other resources.

Eligibility: Applicants must be members of AECT and employed in some area of the field of educational communications and technology.

Selection
Criteria: Selection of the ECT Mentor Endowment Professional Development Grants will be based on the following:

1. The quality of the Professional Development Plan proposed in the application and the appropriateness of that plan to the goals of the Mentor Grant Program.
2. Leadership potential.
3. Experience in the field of educational communications and technology such as employment, field experience, and professional involvement.
4. Three letters of recommendation from persons familiar with the candidate's professional qualifications and leadership potential.

Part Eight
Mediagraphy
Print and Nonprint Resources

Introduction

CONTENTS

This resource list includes media-related journals, books, ERIC documents and journal articles, and nonprint media resources of interest to practitioners, researchers, students, and others concerned with educational technology and educational media. Emphasis in this section is on *currency*; the vast majority of books cited here were published in 1995 or 1996. ERIC documents and journal articles were all *announced* in the ERIC database in 1996, but many of them were issued in the latter half of the previous year and bear a 1994 publication date. Media-related journals include those listed in past issues of *EMTY* and new entries in the field. The computer software, CD-ROMs, online resources, and videos listed are also recent products.

SELECTION

Items were selected for the Mediagraphy in several ways. The ERIC (Educational Resources Information Center) Database was the source for ERIC document and journal article citations. Most of these entries are from a subset of the database selected by the directors of the ERIC Clearinghouse on Information & Technology as being the year's most important database entries for this field. Media-related journals were either retained on the list or added to the list when they met one or more of the following criteria: were from a reputable publisher; had a broad circulation; were covered by indexing services; were peer reviewed; and filled a gap in the literature. Journal data were verified using *Ulrich's International Periodicals Directory 1996* on CD-ROM. In keeping with the title and original purpose of this section, we have included listings for a sampling of the wealth of current nonbook media products that are now becoming available. They include CD-ROMs, computer software, courseware, online products and resources, and videotapes. Currency is still a major factor–for example, online services not only provide additional ways of accessing information already available in standard printed formats, they also provide information that has been updated since the publication of the most recent printed version. All of the materials listed are produced by organizations that are well established in the field. Finally, the complete contents of the Mediagraphy were reviewed by the editors of *EMTY 1997*.

OBTAINING RESOURCES

Media-Related Periodicals and Books. Publisher, price, and ordering/subscription address are listed wherever available.

ERIC Documents. ERIC documents can be read in microfiche at any library holding an ERIC microfiche collection. The identification number beginning with ED (for example, ED 332 677) is used to find the document in the collection. Copies of most ERIC documents can also be ordered from the ERIC Document Reproduction Service. Prices charged depend upon format chosen (microfiche or paper copy), length of the document, and method of shipping. Online orders, fax orders, and expedited delivery are available.

To find the closest library with an ERIC microfiche collection, contact:

ACCESS ERIC
1600 Research Blvd.
Rockville, MD 20850-3172
1-800-LET-ERIC (538-3742)
E-mail: acceric@inet.ed.gov

To order ERIC documents, contact:

ERIC Document Reproduction Service (EDRS)
7420 Fullerton Rd., Suite 110
Springfield, VA 22153-2852
voice: 1-800-443-ERIC (443-3742), 703-440-1400
fax: 703-440-1408
E-mail: edrs@inet.ed.gov

Journal Articles. Photocopies of journal articles can be obtained in one of the following ways: (1) from a library subscribing to the title; (2) through interlibrary loan; (3) through the purchase of a back issue from the journal publisher; or (4) from an article reprint service. Articles noted as being available from the UMI (University Microfilms International) reprint service can be ordered using their ERIC identification numbers (numbers beginning with EJ, such as EJ 421 772).

UMI Information Store
500 Sansome Street, Suite 400
San Francisco, CA 94111
1-800-248-0360 (toll-free in U.S. and Canada)
(415) 433-5500 (outside U.S. and Canada)
E-mail: orders@infostore.com

Journal articles can also be obtained through the Institute for Scientific Information (ISI).

Genuine Article Service
3501 Market Street
Philadelphia, PA 19104
1-800-523-1850 ext. 1536
(215) 386-1011 ext. 1536
E-mail: tga@isinet.com

ARRANGEMENT

Mediagraphy entries are classified according to major subject emphasis under the following headings:

- Artificial Intelligence and Robotics
- CD-ROM
- Computer-Assisted Instruction
- Databases and Online Searching
- Distance Education
- Educational Research
- Educational Technology

- Electronic Publishing
- Information Science and Technology
- Instructional Design and Training
- Libraries and Media Centers
- Media Technologies
- Simulation and Virtual Reality
- Telecommunications and Networking

Mediagraphy

ARTIFICIAL INTELLIGENCE AND ROBOTICS

Media-Related Periodicals

Intelligent Tutoring Media. Information Today, Inc. (formerly Learned Information), 143 Old Marlton Pike, Medford, NJ 08055. q.; $125. Concerned with the packaging and communication of knowledge using advanced information technologies. Studies the impact of artificial intelligence, hypertext, interactive video, mass storage devices, and telecommunications networks.

International Journal of Robotics Research. MIT Press, Journals, 55 Hayward St., Cambridge, MA 02142. bi-mo.; $80 indiv. (foreign $102); $185 inst. (foreign $199); $50 students and retired (foreign $72). Interdisciplinary approach to the study of robotics for researchers, scientists, and students.

Journal of Artificial Intelligence in Education. Association for Advancement of Computing in Education, Box 2966, Charlottesville, VA 22902-2966. q.; $65 indiv. (for., $80), $93 inst., and $113 libraries. International journal publishes articles on how intelligent computer technologies can be used in education to enhance learning and teaching. Reports on research and developments, integration, and applications of artificial intelligence in education.

Knowledge-Based Systems. Elsevier Science Inc., P.O. Box 882, Madison Square Station, New York, NY 10159-0882. q.; $552. Interdisciplinary and applications-oriented journal on fifth-generation computing, expert systems, and knowledge-based methods in system design.

Minds and Machines. Kluwer Academic Publishers, Box 358, Accord Station, Hingham, MA 02018-0358. q.; $351 inst., U.S. Discusses issues concerning machines and mentality, artificial intelligence, epistemology, simulation, and modeling.

Journal Articles

Ray, Roger D., and others. (1995, Summer). Adaptive computerized instruction. **Journal of Instruction Delivery Systems, 9**(3), 28-31. EJ 510 391. Describes an artificially intelligent multimedia computerized instruction system capable of developing a conceptual image of what a student is learning while the student is learning it.

CD-ROM

Media-Related Periodicals

CD-ROM Databases. Worldwide Videotex, Box 3273, Boynton Beach, FL 33424-3273. mo.; $150 U.S., $190 elsewhere. Descriptive listing of all databases being marketed on CD-ROM with vendor and system information.

CD-ROM Professional. Online, Inc., 462 Danbury Rd., Wilton, CT 06897. bi-mo.; $55 indiv. and school libraries, U.S. (foreign $90); $98 inst. (foreign $148). Assists publishers, librarians, and other information professionals in the selection, evaluation, purchase, and operation of CD-ROM systems and titles.

CD-ROM World (formerly **CD-ROM Librarian**). PC World Communication Inc., 501 Second St., Suite 600, San Francisco, CA 94107. 10/yr.; $29. Articles and reviews for CD-ROM users.

Journal Articles

Clements, Jim, and Nicholls, Paul. (1995, September). A comparative survey of multimedia CD-ROM encyclopedias. **Computers in Libraries, 15**(8), 53-59. EJ 512 256. (Available UMI.) Provides historical background information on multimedia CD-ROM encyclopedias and evaluates 11 recent releases. A sidebar provides a 10-year chronology of CD-ROM encyclopedias.

DiMartino, Diane, and others. (1995, January). CD-ROM search techniques of novice end-users: Is the English-as-a-second-language student at a disadvantage? **College and Research Libraries, 56**(1), 49-59. EJ 510 306. (Available UMI.) Compares the CD-ROM search techniques of 42 undergraduate native speakers of English with those of 34 undergraduate English-as-a-second-language (ESL) speakers.

Graf, Nancy. (1995, October). Planning for CD-ROM purchases. **Technology Connection, 2**(6), 25-27. EJ 512 206. Provides guidelines for purchasing and installing CD-ROM technology in school libraries.

Parker, Dana J. (1995, March). Standard terminology: A lexicon of CD-ROM jargon. **CD-ROM Professional, 8**(3), 76-78. EJ 510 316. (Available UMI.) Discusses CD-ROM development, including common production terms, the roles of project team members, and the differences between CD-ROM hybrid disc standards.

Powers, Joan C. (1995). CD-ROM in schools: A survey of public secondary schools in Berkshire County, Massachusetts. **Reference Librarian, 49-50**(335-46). EJ 508 713. This survey report highlights library use of CD-ROMs, particular products, funding for these products, teacher and student interest, and future involvement with CD-ROM technology.

Singer, Linda A. (1995, September-October). Choosing multimedia CD-ROM encyclopedias. **MultiMedia Schools, 2**(4), 16-18,20-26. EJ 510 441. (Available UMI.) Discusses reasons why K-12 school libraries should purchase multimedia CD-ROMS and reviews four interactive CD-ROM encyclopedias.

Sylvia, Margaret. (1995, June). Upgrading a CD-ROM network for multimedia applications. **Computers in Libraries, 15**(6), 72-74. EJ 508 682. (Available UMI.) Addresses issues to consider when upgrading library CD-ROM networks for multimedia applications, including security, workstation requirements, local area network configurations, server performance bottlenecks, CD-ROM drives, and connection to the Internet.

Vane-Tempest, Stewart. (1995, March.) Choosing an optical disc system: A guide for users and resellers. **Information Management and Technology, 28**(2), 67-71. EJ 501 787. This guide for selecting an optical disc system highlights storage hierarchy; standards; data life cycles; security; optical jukebox systems; performance; quality and reliability; software; cost of online versus near-line; and growing opportunities.

Videos

Introduction to CD-ROM. (1995). RMI Media Productions, 1365 North Winchester St., Olathe, KS 66061. 30 min. $67.95. Describes various types of compact discs for use in the K-12 classroom and demonstrates the use of compact disc audios for music, sound, and the spoken word.

Ryba, Rich. (1995/96). **Power teaching: How to develop creative teaching techniques using CD-ROM technology to supercharge your classroom.** Educational Reform Group, 527 Sheffield Plain, Sheffield, MA 01257. 1 videotape; 25 min. $89 for home viewing; $179 allowing public performance rights for groups of more than 6. This tape presents the basics of

CD-ROM technology; features of CDs that can be used for more effective, creative teaching; samples of CD-ROM materials currently available; and various uses of CD-ROM as a tool and a source of resource material.

COMPUTER-ASSISTED INSTRUCTION

Media-Related Periodicals

Apple Library Users Group Newsletter. Library Users Group, Infinite Way, MS3042A, Cupertino, CA 95014. 4/yr.; free. For people interested in using Apple and Macintosh computers in libraries and information centers.

BYTE. Box 550, Hightstown, NJ 08520-9886. mo.; $29.95 ($34.95 Canada and Mexico; $50 elsewhere). Current articles on microcomputers provide technical information as well as information on applications and products for business and professional users.

CALICO Journal. Computer Assisted Language and Instruction Consortium, 014 Language Center, Box 90264, Duke University, Durham, NC 27708-0267. q.; $35 indiv. (Canada and Mexico $45, elsewhere $60); $65 inst. (Canada and Mexico $85, elsewhere $90); $125 corporations (Canada and Mexico $140, elsewhere $150). Provides information on the applications of technology in teaching and learning languages.

Computer Book Review. 735 Ekekela Place, Honolulu, HI 96817. 6/yr.; $30. Provides critical reviews of books on computers and computer-related subjects.

Computers and Education. Elsevier Science, 660 White Plains Rd., Tarrytown, NY 10591-5153. 8/yr.; $768. Presents technical papers covering a broad range of subjects for users of analog, digital, and hybrid computers in all aspects of higher education.

Computers and the Humanities. Kluwer Academic Publishers Group, P.O. Box 358, Accord Station, Hingham, MA 02018-0358. bi-mo.; $85.50 indiv., $180 inst., members $49. Contains papers on computer-aided studies, applications, automation, and computer-assisted instruction.

Computers in Human Behavior. Pergamon Press, 660 White Plains Rd., Tarrytown, NY 10591-5153. q.; $388. Addresses the psychological impact of computer use on individuals, groups, and society.

Computers in the Schools. Haworth Press, 10 Alice St., Binghamton, NY 13904. q.; $36 indiv., $75 inst., $115 libraries. Features articles that combine theory and practical applications of small computers in schools for educators and school administrators.

Dr. Dobb's Journal. Miller Freeman Inc., 600 Harrison St., San Francisco, CA 94107. mo.; $29.97 U.S.; $45 Mexico and Canada; $70 elsewhere. Articles on the latest in operating systems, programming languages, algorithms, hardware design and architecture, data structures, and telecommunications; in-depth hardware and software reviews.

Education Technology News. Business Publishers, Inc., 951 Pershing Dr., Silver Spring, MD 20910-4464. bi-w.; $286. For teachers and those interested in educational uses of computers in the classroom. Features articles on applications and educational software.

Electronic Learning. Scholastic Inc., 555 Broadway, New York, NY 10012-3999. 8/yr.; $19.95. Features articles on applications and advances of technology in education for K-12 and college educators and administrators.

Home Office Computing. Box 51344, Boulder, CO 80321-1344. mo.; $19.97 (foreign $27.97). For professionals who use computers and do business at home.

InfoWorld. InfoWorld Publishing, 155 Bovet Rd., Suite 800, San Mateo, CA 94402. w.; $130. News and reviews of PC hardware, software, peripherals, and networking.

Interpersonal Computing and Technology: An Electronic Journal for the 21st Century. Center for Teaching and Technology, Academic Computer Center, Georgetown University, Washington, DC 20057, with support from the Center for Academic Computing, The Pennsylvania State University, University Park, PA 16802. q. (electronic journal). Articles may be retrieved from gopher: guvm.ccf.georgetown.edu:70/11/listserv/ipct.

Journal of Computer Assisted Learning. Blackwell Scientific Publications, Journal Subscription Dept., Marstan Book Services, Box 87, Oxford OX2 0DT, England. q.; $48 indiv. U.S. and Canada; $197 inst. Articles and research on the use of computer-assisted learning.

Journal of Educational Computing Research. Baywood Publishing Co., 26 Austin Ave., P.O. Box 337, Amityville, NY 11701. 8/yr. (2 vols., 4 each); $95 indiv. (per vol.), $182 inst. (per vol.). Presents original research papers, critical analyses, reports on research in progress, design and development studies, article reviews, and grant award listings.

Journal of Research on Computing in Education. International Society for Technology in Education, University of Oregon, 1787 Agate St., Eugene, OR 97403-1923. q.; $74 U.S. nonmembers (foreign $84), $35 members (foreign $45). Provides reports on original research and detailed system and project evaluations.

Learning and Leading with Technology. The ISTE Journal of Educational Technology Practice and Policy (formerly **Computing Teacher**). International Society for Technology in Education, University of Oregon, 1787 Agate St., Eugene, OR 97403-1923. 8/yr.; $61 nonmembers (Canada $75.97, internatl. $71, internatl. air $91); $35 members (Canada $47.45, internatl. $45, internatl. air $51). Articles and columns on language arts, Logo, science, mathematics, telecommunications, equity, and international connections for K-12 teachers.

MacWorld. MacWorld Communications, Box 54529, Boulder, CO 80322-4529. mo.; $24. Describes hardware, software, tutorials, and applications for users of the Macintosh microcomputer.

Microcomputer Abstracts. (formerly **Microcomputer Index**). Information Today, Inc. (formerly Learned Information, Inc.), 143 Old Marlton Pike, Medford, NJ 08055-8750. bi-mo.; $159. Abstracts of literature on the use of microcomputers in business, education, and the home.

Microcomputer Industry Update. Industry Market Reports, Inc., Box 681, Los Altos, CA 94023. mo.; $355. Abstracts of product announcements and reviews of interest appearing in weekly trade press.

PC Magazine: The Independent Guide to IBM-Standard Personal Computing. Ziff-Davis Publishing Co., Box 54093, Boulder, CO 80322. bi-w.; $49.97. Comparative reviews of computer hardware and general business software programs.

PC Week. Ziff-Davis Publishing Co., 10 Presidents Landing, Medford, MA 02155-5146. w.; $195 (Canada and Mexico $250), free to qualified personnel. Provides current information on the IBM PC, including hardware, software, industry news, business strategies, and reviews of hardware and software.

PC World. PC World Communications, Inc., Box 55029, Boulder, CO 80322-5029. mo.; $29.90 U.S., $53.39 Canada, $49.90 Mexico, $75.90 elsewhere. Presents articles on applications and columns containing news, systems information, product announcements, and hardware updates.

Social Science Computer Review. Sage Publications Inc., 2455 Teller Rd., Thousand Oaks, CA 91320. q.; $52 indiv. ($67 foreign); $105 inst. ($117 foreign). Features include software reviews, new product announcements, and tutorials for beginners.

Software Digest Ratings Report. National Software Testing Laboratories Inc., Plymouth Corporate Center, Box 1000, Plymouth Meeting, PA 19462. mo.; $450. For IBM personal computer users. Each issue reports the ratings for one category of IBM PC software, based on multiple-user tests.

Software Magazine. Sentry Publishing Co., Inc., 1 Research Dr., Suite 400B, Westborough, MA 01581-3907. mo.; $65 U.S., $75 Canada, $125 elsewhere (free to qualified personnel). Provides information on software and industry developments for business and professional users, and announces new software packages.

Software Reviews on File. Facts on File, 460 Park Ave. S., New York, NY 10016. mo.; $210. Condensed software reviews from more than 150 publications. Features software for all major microcomputer systems and programming languages for library, school, home, and business use.

Books

Geisert, Paul G., and Futrell, Mynga K. (1995). **Teachers, computers, and curriculum: Microcomputers in the classroom, 2d ed.** Longwood Division, Allyn & Bacon, P.O. Box 10695, Des Moines, IA 50336-0695. 384pp. $43.95. Provides practical help for incorporating computers in teaching with emphasis on computer applications rather than hardware and software.

Hirschbuhl, John, and Bishop, Dwight, eds. (1996). **Computer studies: Computers in education, 7th ed.** Dushkin Publishing Group/Brown & Benchmark Publishers, 25 Kessel Court, Madison, WI 53711. 256pp. $16.89. This Annual Editions Publication presents 44 articles under eight topic headings: Introduction (overview of the current state of computers and their impact on education), Curriculum and Instructional Design, Classroom Applications and Software Evaluations, Teacher Training, Multimedia, Special Issues, The Internet and Computer Networks, and Distance Learning. Related CourseKits are also available.

Merrill, Paul F., Hammonds, Kathy, Vincent, Bret R., Reynolds, Peter L., Christensen, Larry, and Tolman, Marvin N. (1996). **Computers in education, 3d ed.** Longwood Division, Allyn & Bacon, P.O. Box 10695, Des Moines, IA 50336-0695. 384pp. $41.95. This comprehensive, research-based guide to possible educational applications of computers provides specific guidance on how given applications may be integrated into the classroom curriculum. Examples provided include multimedia and hypermedia applications and classroom applications of CD-ROM, videodisks, networks, and telecommunications.

Moursund, David. (1996). **Increasing your expertise as a problem solver—some roles of computers, 2d ed.** International Society for Technology in Education, 1787 Agate St., Eugene, OR 97403-1923. 150pp. $16.95 (members $15.25). Presents the use of computers in education to teach both teachers and students to be good problem solvers. For grades 11-adult.

Perkins, David N., Schwartz, Judah L., West, Mary Maxwell, and Wiske, Martha Stone, eds. (1995). **Software goes to school: Training for understanding with new technology.** 304pp. $45. This in-depth examination of how computer technology can support students' understanding of difficult concepts focuses on three broad themes: the nature of understanding, the potential of technology in the classroom, and the transformation of educational theory into practice.

Schellenberg, Kathryn, ed. (1995). **Computer studies: Computers in society, 6th ed.** Dushkin Publishing Group/Brown & Benchmark Publishers, 25 Kessel Court, Madison, WI 53711. 256pp. $16.89. This Annual Editions Publication presents 46 articles (41 of them new) that address eight different facets of the topic: the economy; computerized work and workplaces; computers, people, and social interaction; ethical and legal issues; privacy; technological risks; international perspectives and issues; and philosophical frontiers. CourseKits are also available.

Shade, Daniel D., and Haugland, Susan W. (1996). **Young children and computers: A world of discovery.** Longwood Division, Allyn & Bacon, P.O. Box 10695, Des Moines, IA 50336-0695. 304pp. $27.95. Discusses the issues involved in using technology with preschool, kindergarten and primary age children, and provides more than 700 evaluations of the developmental appropriateness of currently available software across all platforms.

ERIC Documents

Armel, Donald. (1995). **Something new about notetaking: A computer-based instructional experiment.** Paper given to the Association of Small Computer Users in Education (ASCUE), North Myrtle Beach, SC, June 18-22, 1995. 9pp. ED 387 091. The strategy for this study of the effect of computer-based notetaking on both achievement and instructional completion time added forced and optional notetaking to computer-based instruction.

Hope, Warren C. (1995). **Microcomputer technology: Its impact on teachers in an elementary school.** Ed.D. dissertation, Florida State University, Tallahassee. 219pp. ED 384 336. This study examined the initiation and implementation of microcomputer technology in the educational environment of a Florida elementary school and assessed its impact on teachers.

Liu, Lewis Guodo. (1995). **Computer education in developing countries: Analysis and an annotated bibliography.** Unpublished paper, University of Illinois at Urbana-Champaign. 42pp. ED 378 939. This overview of computer education in developing nations indicates that, although it has been proceeding quietly and on a limited scale, it has been progressing. A 93-item annotated bibliography on computer education as it relates to a developing country's social, economic, and political development is provided.

Quade, Ann M. (1995). **A comparison of online and traditional paper and pencil notetaking methods during computer-delivered instruction.** Paper presented to the Association for Educational Communications and Technology, Research and Theory Division, Anaheim, CA, February 16-20, 1995. 9pp. ED 383 330. This study of the notetaking strategies and behaviors of university students found that taking notes from computer-based instruction (CBI) using an online notepad promotes greater achievement than pencil and paper methods; is preferred by learners who report higher confidence ratings towards new technologies; and promotes minimal recording of the learner's own thoughts.

White, Daniel C. (1993). **Improving the student's use of computers within the middle school curriculum through a multi-faceted approach of increased computer accessibility and varied teaching/learning strategies.** Doctoral practicum report, Nova University. 99p. ED 377 822. Designed to encourage middle school students to connect what they learn in computer classes to other subject areas, this practicum provided for training in basic computer skills for teachers, improved computer accessibility, and the availability of more appropriate software in the school's computer laboratory.

Journal Articles

Azevedo, Roger, and Bernard, Robert. (1995, January). Assessing the effects of feedback in computer-assisted learning. **British Journal of Educational Technology, 26**(1), 57-58. EJ 499 780. (Available UMI.) A meta-analysis was conducted to determine the importance of feedback in computer-based learning based on 59 studies selected on the basis of design, sample size, and availability of appropriate statistics.

Barron, Daniel D. (1995, January). Bringing the world and information together: Geographic information systems for education. **School Library Media Activities Monthly, 11**(5) 49-50. EJ 496 539. Discusses geographic information systems (GIS) and their use in elementary and secondary education, including databases and a graphics package for maps.

Campbell, J. Olin, and others. (1995, Summer). Using computer and video technologies to develop interpersonal skills. **Computers in Human Behavior, 11**(2), 223-39. EJ 505 430. (Available UMI.) Two studies investigated ways in which computer and video technology can support expert human coaches in order to reduce instructor time and increase learner-centered environments; the goal was to train undergraduate students to facilitate others' interpersonal problem solving.

Christopher, Doris A. (1995, March). Designing a computerized presentation center. **T.H.E. Journal, 22**(8), 56-59. EJ 499 815. (Available UMI.) The Office Systems and Business Education Department at California State University (Los Angeles) developed a computerized presentation center, with multimedia classrooms and a multipurpose room, where students learn computerized presentation design skills, faculty can develop materials for class, and local business can do videoconferencing and distance training.

Cross, Linda. (1995, October). Preparing students for the future with project presentations. **Learning and Leading with Technology, 23**(2), 24-26. EJ 512 270. Describes an eighth grade computer literacy course in which students used spreadsheet programs to illustrate statistics for classroom presentations.

Davis, Elizabeth A., and others. (1995). Students' off-line and on-line experiences. **Journal of Educational Computing Research, 12**(2), 109-34. EJ 503 529. (Available UMI.) Examines the knowledge construction processes of novice programmers using parentheses and quotes in hypermedia and identifies characteristics of successful and unsuccessful students working off- and online.

Dyrli, Odvard Egil, and Kinnaman, Daniel E. (1995, January). What every teacher needs to know about technology. Part I: Technology in education: Getting the upper hand. **Technology and Learning, 15**(4), 37-43. EJ 497 873. (Available UMI.) This is the first in a five-part series of articles that form the basis for a professional development course on the impact of technology on classroom curriculum. It focuses on obstacles faced by teachers in bringing technology into the classroom and strategies to overcome them.

Evans-Andris, Melissa. (1995). An examination of computing styles among teachers in elementary schools. **Educational Technology, Research and Development, 43**(2), 15-31. EJ 508 657. (Available UMI.) Examines ways in which elementary school teachers organize their workplace behaviors as they respond to computers in their schools.

Gayeski, Diane M., Ed. (1995, May-June). DesignStation 2000: Imagining future realities in learning systems design. **Educational Technology, 35**(3), 43-47. EJ 503 494. (Available UMI.) Describes a software and hardware workbench for laptop computers for the design of learning systems that includes capabilities for needs analysis; client presentation and proposal generation; rapid prototyping of interactive media projects; collaboration and project tracking; assessment of results; and adding to a research database.

Gilmore, Alison M. (1995, Spring). Turning teachers on to computers: Evaluation of a teacher development program. **Journal of Research on Computing in Education, 27**(3), 251-69. EJ 510 356. (Available UMI.) Evaluates a program in New Zealand designed to introduce educational uses of computers to teachers and to facilitate their integration into classroom activities.

Hannafin, Robert D., and Freeman, Donald J. (1995, January-February). An exploratory study of teachers' views of knowledge acquisition. **Educational Technology, 35**(1), 49-56. EJ 496 586. (Available UMI.) This exploratory investigation examined relations between teachers' views of knowledge acquisition and their use of computers in the classroom.

Kenny, Richard F. (1995). The generative effects of instructional organizers with computer-based interactive video. **Journal of Educational Computing Research, 12**(3), 275-96. EJ 507 054. Sixty-one nursing students and faculty were studied to compare the use of participatory graphic organizers to final form and advance organizers as instructional aids for computer-based interactive video.

Knight, Bruce Allen, and Knight, Cecily. (1995, May). Cognitive theory and the use of computers in the primary classroom. **British Journal of Educational Technology, 26**(2), 141-48. EJ 507 051. (Available UMI.) Presents research as an attempt to provide scientifically supportable reasons why computers are effective in the primary classroom and examines the educational application of cognitive theory to classroom instruction.

Looking ahead: A report on the latest survey results. (1995, January). **Technology and Learning, 15**(4), 20-25. EJ 497 872. (Available UMI.) Reports on the results of a survey of software publishers and market researchers for educators that was conducted to determine development, purchasing, and upgrading plans for educational computer technology.

McDougall, Anne, and Squires, David. (1995). A critical examination of the checklist approach in software selection. **Journal of Educational Computing Research, 12**(3), 263-74. EJ 507 053. Surveys existing checklists and investigates the extent to which they enable the expression of useful assessments for software selection.

Pratt, D. (1995, September). Young children's active and passive graphing. **Journal of Computer Assisted Learning, 11**(3), 157-69. EJ 510 401. (Available UMI.) Reports on the graphing work of eight- and nine-year-old children who have access to portable computers across the curriculum.

Puntambekar, Sadhana. (1995, May). Helping students learn "how to learn" from texts: Towards an ITS for developing metacognition. **Instructional Science, 23**(1-3), 163-82. EJ 510 300. (Available UMI.) Defines metacognition and examines metacognitive differences in learners; reviews past and current developments in intelligent tutoring systems; and introduces a computer-based system to help learners develop metacognition in studying from texts.

Rieseberg, Rhonda L. (1995, Spring). Home learning, technology, and tomorrow's workplace. **TECHNOS, 4**(1), 12-17. EJ 499 868. Discussion of the characteristics and trends of home schools and workplaces argues that the use of computers and computer applications in home schooling provides a compatible environment for future home-based businesses and telecommuting trends.

Saar, Charles L. (1995, Winter). Individualized instruction as a result of learner analysis. **Journal of Educational Media & Library Sciences, 32**(2), 130-55. EJ 514 981. Examines instructional designers' use of learner analysis when designing and developing computer assisted instructional materials by surveying 14 instructional system designers.

Smith, Richard A. (1995, March). How computers can be used in schools: A parent's guide. **Computing Teacher, 22**(6), 8-11. EJ 499 807. (Available UMI.) Describes ways in which computers can be used in schools and lists 20 questions for parents to ask when evaluating a school's instructional computing program.

Snelbecker, Glenn E., and others. (1995, Spring). Elementary versus secondary school teachers retraining to teach computer science. **Journal of Research on Computing in Education, 27**(3), 336-47. EJ 510 361. (Available UMI.) Reports on a study that examined the extent to which selected computer-related attitudes, aptitudes, and interests have similar predictive value for the retraining of elementary versus secondary school teachers.

DATABASES AND ONLINE SEARCHING

Media-Related Periodicals

CompuServe Magazine. CompuServe, Inc., 5000 Arlington Centre Blvd., Columbus, OH 43220. mo.; $30 ($40 foreign). Gives current information on fundamentals of micro-based communications, computer and information industry news, coverage of CompuServe services, commentary, and computer product reviews.

Data Sources. Ziff-Davis Publishing Co., One Park Ave., New York, NY 10016. 2/yr.; $440. Comprehensive guide to the information-processing industry. Covers equipment, software, services, and systems, and includes profiles of 10,000 companies.

Database. Online, Inc. 462 Danbury Rd., Wilton, CT 06897. bi-mo.; $110 U.S. and Canada, $132 Mexico, $145 foreign airmail. Features articles on topics of interest to online database users; includes database search aids.

Gale Directory of Databases (in 2 vols: Vol. 1, **Online Databases**; Vol 2, **CD-ROM, Diskette, Magnetic Tape Batch Access, and Handheld Database Products**). Gale Research Inc., 835 Penobscot Building, Detroit, MI 48226. ann. plus semi-ann. update; set $280; vol. 1, $199; vol. 2, $119. Contains information on database selection and database descriptions, including producers and their addresses.

Information Today. Information Today, Inc. (formerly Learned Information, Inc.), 143 Old Marlton Pike, Medford, NJ 08055. 11/yr.; $39.95. Newspaper for users and producers of electronic information services. Articles and news about the industry, calendar of events, and product information.

Journal of Database Management (formerly **Journal of Database Administration**). Idea Group Publishing, 4811 Jonestown Rd., Suite 230, Harrisburg, PA 17109-1751. q.; $65 indiv., $110 inst. Provides state-of-the-art research to those who design, develop, and administer DBMS-based information systems.

Link-Up. Information Today, Inc. (formerly Learned Information, Inc.), 143 Old Marlton Pike, Medford, NJ 08055. bi-mo.; $25 U.S., $48 elsewhere. Newsmagazine for individuals interested in small computer communications covers hardware, software, communications services, and search methods.

Online. Online, Inc., 462 Danbury Rd., Wilton, CT 06897. 6/yr.; $110 U.S. and Canada, $132 Mexico, $145 foreign airmail. For online information system users. Articles cover a variety of online applications for general and business use.

Online and CD-ROM Review (formerly **Online Review**). Information Today, Inc. (formerly Learned Information, Inc.), 143 Old Marlton Pike, Medford, NJ 08055-8750. bi-mo.; $115; Canada and Mexico, $125. An international journal of online information systems featuring articles on using and managing online and optical information systems, training and educating online users, developing search aids, creating and marketing databases, policy affecting the continued development of systems and networks, and the development of new professional standards.

Resource Sharing and Information Networks. Haworth Press, 10 Alice St., Binghamton, NY 13904. semi-ann.; $42 indiv., $115 inst. and libraries. A forum for ideas on the basic theoretical and practical problems faced by planners, practitioners, and users of network services.

ERIC Documents

Smith, Marilyn E. (1995, April). **Access points to ERIC: Update 1995. ERIC Digest.** Syracuse, NY: ERIC Clearinghouse on Information and Technology. 3pp. ED 381 178. Access points to the database described in this digest include CD-ROM, online access through commercial services, locally-mounted systems and Internet access, print access, AskERIC, ERIC digests and other ERIC publications, and ACCESS ERIC.

Wehmeyer, Lillian Biermann. (1995). **Computer archives and the literature search.** Paper presented to the American Educational Research Association, San Francisco, CA, April 18-22, 1995. 26pp. ED 385 233. (Available in microfiche only.) Outlines the use of computer resources to conduct a search of textual information that is available online, including files offered on the Internet.

Journal Articles

Garland, Kathleen. (1995, January). The information search process: A study of elements associated with meaningful research tasks. **School Libraries Worldwide, 1**(1), 41-53. EJ 503

407. Describes a study at a Michigan high school that investigated elements which contributed to a meaningful library research task.

Hirsh, Sandra G., and Borgman, Christine L. (1995). Comparing children's use of browsing and keyword searching on the Science Library Catalog. **Proceedings of the ASIS Annual Meeting, 32**, 19-26 (58th, Chicago, IL, October 9-12, 1995). EJ 513 850. Describes a study that investigated fifth-grade children's search behavior using an automated library catalog designed for children called the Science Library Catalog.

Makulowich, John S., and Bates, Mary Ellen. (1995, July-August). Ten tips on managing your Internet searching. **Online, 19**(4), 32-37. EJ 507 078. (Available UMI.) Highlights area and level of expertise, request forms, lay terms for casual users, realistic times for retrieving results, a systematic approach, the operating platform and tools, a file of servers' and patrons' addresses, bookmarks and home pages, shortcuts, and the Internet Hunt.

Mokros, Hartmut B., and others. (1995, Summer). Practice and personhood in professional interaction: Social identities and information needs. **Library & Information Science Research, 17**(3), 237-57. EJ 513 753. Explores the human aspect of information retrieval by examining the behavior and pronoun use of librarians in the course of communicating with patrons during online computer search interactions.

Neuman, Delia. (1995, May). High school students' use of databases: Results of a national Delphi study. **Journal of the American Society for Information Science, 46**(4), 284-98. EJ 501 811. (Available UMI.) Discusses results of a Delphi study of secondary school library media specialists that identified difficulties students experienced in using online and CD-ROM databases, suggested design elements and curricular and instructional strategies to make them more valuable as learning resources, and determined policy issues relating to electronic information resources in schools.

Pappas, Marjorie L. (1995, April). Information skills for electronic resources. **School Library Media Activities Monthly, 11**(8), 39-40. EJ 499 875. Discusses the importance of developing strong skills in electronic searching and stresses the importance of teaching these skills across the curriculum. Several skill models are suggested and components of search strategies are briefly outlined.

Richards, Trevor. (1995, April). A comparative evaluation of four leading CD-ROM retrieval software packages. **Computers in Libraries, 15**(4), 70-75. EJ 503 480. (Available UMI.) Compares four CD-ROM retrieval software packages—i.e., CD Answer, SPIRS, KAware2, and ROMware—using the Revised Richards-Brown CD-ROM Software Evaluation Model.

Sheffield, P. W. (1995, Summer). The British Education Index, International ERIC and CD-ROM: Experience and impact of new technological media. **Education Libraries Journal, 38**(2), 5-11. EJ 513 761. (Available UMI.) Describes the release of the British Education Index on CD-ROM, summarizing the deliberations leading to the conjunction of the Australian, British, and Canadian education index databases on the International ERIC CD-ROM.

Stonehill, Robert M., and Smarte, Lynn. (1995, Winter). ERIC in cyberspace: Expanding access and services. **Education Libraries, 18**(3), 12-18. EJ 507 083. (Available UMI.) Describes the products and services offered by the Educational Resources Information Center (ERIC), and how users can access this information. It also lists resources for librarians who do training sessions on ERIC and sketches ERIC's future direction.

Valenza, Joyce. (1995, June). Steps to simplifying student searches. **Technology Connection, 2**(4), 21-22. EJ 505 411. Available Linworth Publishing, Inc., 480 East Wilson Bridge Rd., Ste. L, Worthington, OH 43085-2372. Presents six steps for simplifying students' online information searches and provides a search strategy worksheet.

Watt, Michael G. (1995, Winter). Information services in an age of education reform: A review of developments in four countries. **School Library Media Quarterly, 23**(2), 115-22. EJ 497 918. (Available UMI.) Discussion of the design of information systems for exchanging educational research-based information focuses on the development of the Educational Resources Information Center (ERIC), British Education Index (BEI), Canadian Education Index (CEI), and Australian Education Index (AEI) and examines how they meet the challenges of educational reform efforts.

Watt, Michael G. (1995, Summer). Systems for exchanging information on instructional resources: A review of recent services in four countries. **School Library Media Quarterly, 23**(4), 239-47. EJ 510 342. (Available UMI.) Traces the development of five information systems for exchanging information on instructional materials within the educational communities of the United States, United Kingdom, Canada, and Australia.

Wildemuth, Barbara M., and others. (1995, September). Medical students' personal knowledge, searching proficiency, and database use in problem solving. (1995, September). **Journal of the American Society for Information Science, 46**(8), 590-607. EJ 510 447. (Available UMI.) Discusses the relationship between personal knowledge in a domain and online searching proficiency in that domain, and the relationship between searching proficiency and database-assisted problem-solving performance based on a study of medical students.

Woodard, Mary. (1995, September). Singing the praises of media retrieval systems. **Technology Connection, 2**(5), 26-27. EJ 510 395. Discusses the uses and benefits of a centralized, computer operated media retrieval system for school audiovisual equipment and collections.

DISTANCE EDUCATION

Media-Related Periodicals

American Journal of Distance Education. Pennsylvania State University, School of Education, 403 S. Allen St., Suite 206, University Park, PA 16801-5202. 3/yr.; $30 indiv. ($36 Canada and Mexico, $45 elsewhere); $55 inst. (Canada and Mexico $61, $70 elsewhere). Focuses on the professional trainer, adult educator, college teacher, and others interested in the latest developments in methods and systems for delivering education to adults.

Appropriate Technology. Intermediate Technology Publications, Ltd., 103-105 Southampton Row, London, WC1B 4HH, England. q.; $28 indiv., $37 inst. Articles on less technologically advanced, but more environmentally sustainable, solutions to problems in developing countries.

Development Communication Report. Clearinghouse on Development Communication, 1815 N. Ft. Myer Dr., Suite 600, Arlington, VA 22209. q.; $10 (free to readers in developing countries). Applications of communications technology to international development problems such as agriculture, health, and nutrition.

Distance Education. University College of Southern Queensland Publications, Darling Heights, Toowoomba, Queensland 4350, Australia. semi-ann.; $A48 in Australia; $67 airmail overseas. Papers on the history, politics, and administration of distance education.

Journal of Distance Education. Canadian Association for Distance Education, Secretariat, One Stewart St., Suite 205, Ottawa, ON K1N 6H7, Canada. (Text in English, French) 2/yr.; $40; add $5 outside Canada. Aims to promote and encourage scholarly work of empirical and theoretical nature relating to distance education in Canada and throughout the world.

Open Learning. Pearson Professional, Subscriptions Dept., P.O. Box 77, Harlow, Essex CM19 5BQ, England. 3/yr.; £59 (U.K.), £60 Europe, $76 U.S. Academic, scholarly publication on any aspects of open and distance learning anywhere in the world. Includes issues for debate and research notes.

Open Praxis (formerly **International Council for Distance Education Bulletin**). International Council for Distance Education, National Extension College, 18 Brooklands Ave., Cambridge CB2 2HN, England. 2/yr.; $65 individual membership; $50 libraries. Reports on activities and programs of the ICDE.

ERIC Documents

Donnan, Peter, Ed.; McDonald, Anne, Ed. (1995, May). **Occasional papers in distance learning, Number 17.** Wagga Wagga, Australia: Charles Sturt University-Riverina, Open Learning Institute. 51pp. ED 385 222. Four papers on open learning and distance education focus on bridging courses, issues for researchers in evaluating interactive multimedia, designing study materials to address the special needs of distance students, and faculty attitudes concerning technology.

Holmberg, Borje. (1995, September). **The sphere of distance-education theory revisited. ZIFF Papiere 98.** Hagen, Germany: Fern University, Institute for Research into Distance Education. 21pp. ED 386 578. Proposes an eight-part general theory of distance education and discusses phenomena and concerns that are internal to its practice and external conditions influencing it or being influenced by it.

Holt, Gill. (1995, June). **SOCRATES. EPIC Europe Eurofocus 6.** Slough (England): National Foundation for Educational Research. 9pp. ED 385 219. Designed to encourage open and distance education, the European Community's new education program for its member states has three components: ERASMUS, the higher education component; COMENIUS, the school education section; and the Horizontal Measures initiatives.

Main, Robert G., and Riise, Eric. (1995, March). **A study of interaction in distance learning. Interim technical report for the period June-August 1994.** Chico, CA: California State University-Chico, College of Communication. 25pp. ED 383 282. (Available only as microfiche). This study attempts to qualify the concept of interaction in distance learning by applying various dimensions such as amount, timeliness, method, spontaneity, and quality.

Maxwell, Leigh, and others. (1995). **Graduate distance education: A review and synthesis of the research literature.** Paper presented to the International Communication Association, Instructional and Development Communication Division (45th, Albuquerque, NM, May 1995). 23pp. ED 387 118. Discusses the critical components of post-baccalaureate education, the most common media chosen to support the functions of graduate distance education, and the most pressing issues currently surrounding this area.

Olesinski, Raymond L., and others. (1995). **The operating technician's role in video distance learning.** Paper presented to the Instructional Technology SIG, American Educational Research Association (San Francisco, CA, April 18, 1995). 10pp. ED 383 282. Describes the non-technical activities of operating technicians in video, or televised, distance learning programs during the pre-instructional, instructional, and post-instructional phases of the video distance learning process, and their potential influence on the learning process.

Rogers, Patricia L. (1995). **Girls like colors, boys like action? Imagery preferences and gender.** Paper presented to the Association for Educational Communications and Technology, Anaheim, CA, February 9, 1995. 21pp. ED 378 956. Reviews characteristics of gender-based imagery preferences of children that have been identified in the literature; relates these characteristics to a taxonomy of aesthetic-developmental stages; and presents research guidelines and considerations for selecting images based on imagery preferences and gender-based influences with respect to aesthetic awareness and art experience.

Schrum, Lynne. (1995). **Online courses: What have we learned?** Paper presented to the World Conference on Computers in Education, Birmingham, UK, July 1995. 11pp. ED 385 245. This research looks at online education courses, identifies significant issues in the development of these courses, and determines characteristics of learners enrolled in them.

Tushnet, Naida C., and Fleming-McCormick, Treseen. (1995). **Equity issues in the Star Schools Distance Learning Program.** Paper presented to the American Educational Research Association, San Francisco, CA, April 18-22, 1995. 15pp. ED 385 225. The Office of Educational Research and Improvement of the Department of Education has provided funding for four cycles of 2-year Star Schools distance learning projects. This report is based on the second-year findings of a congressionally-mandated evaluation of the Star Schools program, which focuses on elementary and secondary school students and targets underserved populations through distance learning. The equity issue is approached by describing the characteristics of students at schools served in the 714 Star Schools.

Journal Articles

Anzalone, Stephen, and others. (1995, June). Multi-channel learning: A note on work in progress. **ED, Education at a Distance, 9**(6), J3-J7. EJ 513 763. Examines multi-channel learning—using learning channels such as teachers—to connect learners to knowledge, skills, and information found in the immediate learning environment and the community or delivered from a distance.

Biner, Paul M., and others. (1995). Personality characteristics differentiating and predicting the achievement of televised-course students and traditional-course students. **American Journal of Distance Education, 9**(2), 46-60. EJ 512 280. Describes a study conducted to determine whether the personality traits of students in televised college-level courses differ from those of students in traditional courses, and to identify the specific traits predictive of successful performance in televised classes.

Brenzel, Jeff. (1995, April). The false premise in teleteaching. **ED, Education at a Distance, 9**(4), J11-J12. EJ 510 493. Examines the negative aspects of teleteaching and distance education, and makes recommendations for teachers to follow to improve both classroom lecturing and distance education teleconferencing.

Campbell, J. Olin. (1995, Summer). Interactive distance learning: Issues and current work. **Journal of Instruction Delivery Systems, 9**(3), 32-35. EJ 510 392. Discussion of the changing economic environment and the resulting restructuring of society focuses on changes in education needs.

Dalziel, Chris. (1995, October). Fair use guidelines for distance education. **TechTrends, 40**(5) 6-8. EJ 512 299. (Available UMI.) Discusses fair use guidelines based on the Copyright Act of 1976 and their applications to distance education issues.

Dean, Raymond, and others. (1995, April). Distance education effectiveness: A systems approach to assessing the effectiveness of distance education. **ED, Education at a Distance, 9**(4), J17-J20. EJ 510 495. Reviews problems with research in determining the effectiveness of distance education, and presents a systems model to be used as a framework upon which researchers can build.

Drucker, Susan J., and Gumpert, Gary. (1995, Spring). Distance learning and education as place. **Telematics and Informatics, 12**(2), 69-73. EJ 512 320. Discusses distance learning and examines the role of the educational environment as a place with unique characteristics.

Figueroa, Maria Luisa. (1992, Fall). Understanding students' approaches to learning in university traditional and distance education courses. **Journal of Distance Education, 7**(3), 15-26. EJ 510 293. Presents steps taken in planning, implementing, and evaluating a descriptive study that compares student approaches to learning in a traditional university class with face-to-face instruction and a distance education course.

Frew, Elspeth A., and Weber, Karin. (1995, June). Towards a higher retention rate among distance learners. (Available UMI.) **Open Learning, 10**(2), 58-61. EJ 507 045. Presents results from questionnaires sent to past and present graduate tourism students from the Gippsland School of Business at Monash University (Australia) to determine factors that influenced student decisions to withdraw from a distance education tourism course.

Gilbert, Larry. (1995, March). Computer-based audiographics for distance education: An inexpensive, interactive and high-quality alternative. **Educational Media International, 32**(1), 32-35. EJ 507 018. (Available UMI.) Discussion of the higher education system in Nevada identifies characteristics of an ideal distance education delivery system.

Hardy, Darcy Walsh, and Olcott, Donald, Jr. (1995). Audio teleconferencing and the adult learner: Strategies for effective practice. **American Journal of Distance Education, 9**(1), 44-68. EJ 503 484. Discusses administrative and instructional issues; equipment needs and preliminary tests; the importance of the audio component in distance learning; and management and delivery strategies.

Hausafus, Cheryl O., Torrie, Margaret. (1995, October). Scanning to the beep: A teacher-tested computer-based observational assessment tool for the distance education classroom. **TechTrends, 40**(5), 26-27. EJ 512 305. (Available UMI.) Discusses the results of a study that examined preservice and inservice teachers' use of hand-held Computer-Based Observational Assessment Tools (CBOATs) in a distance education environment using the Iowa Communications Network.

Holmberg, Borje. (1995, June). The evolution of the character and practice of distance education. **Open Learning, 10**(2), 47-53. EJ 507 043. (Available UMI.) Examines the evolution of the character and practice of distance education through an historical explanation of early distance education and a review of its pioneers.

Holt, Dale M., and Thompson, Diane J. (1995). Responding to the technological imperative: The experience of an open and distance education institution. **Distance Education, 16**(1), 43-64. EJ 510 463. (Available UMI.) Examines the impact of technology on work outside and inside tertiary institutions and presents a case study of Deakin University (Australia), an open and distance education organization.

Johnson, Henry C. (1995, June). Distance education in Latin America: The challenge to create a technology of hope. **ED, Education at a Distance, 9**(6), J7-J10. EJ 513 764. Examines changes in Latin America that affect distance education, presents five directions for Latin American distance education, and discusses economic, cultural, and social problems of technologically mediated education.

Jonassen, David, and others. (1995). Constructivism and computer-mediated communication in distance education. **American Journal of Distance Education, 9**(2), 7-26. EJ 512 278. Describes the assumptions of a constructivist epistemology, contrasts them with objectivist assumptions, and describes instructional systems that can support constructive learning at a distance.

McMahen, Chris, and Dawson, A. J. (1995, Spring). The design and implementation of environmental computer-mediated communication (CMC) projects. **Journal of Research on Computing in Education, 27**(3), 318-35. EJ 510 360. (Available UMI.) Examines attempts by environmental educators to adopt computer-mediated communication (CMC), primarily computer conferencing, to enhance instruction.

Mena, Marta. (1992, Fall). New pedagogical approaches to improve production of materials in distance education. **Journal of Distance Education, 7**(3) 131-40. EJ 510 297. Analyzes problems involved in the production of instructional materials for distance education and suggests new pedagogical approaches to improve production of materials for distance education.

Menmuir, Joan. (1995, February). Quality assurance in the off-campus delivery of professional development opportunities. **Open Learning, 10**(1), 43-46. EJ 499 744. (Available UMI.) Explores the educational quality of the Postgraduate Awards Scheme in the Faculty of Strathclyde University (Scotland), which facilitates programs of continuous professional development through a flexible structure of credit accumulation leading to a postgraduate certificate, a diploma, and ultimately, a master's degree.

Moore, Michael G. (1995). The 1995 Distance Education Research Symposium: A research agenda. **American Journal of Distance Education, 9**(2), 1-6. EJ 512 277. Presents an overview of the 1995 Distance Education Research Symposium at Pennsylvania State University.

Moskowitz, Robert. (1995, October). Wired U. **Internet World, 6**(10), 60-61. EJ 510 433. Features four organizations that offer elementary, secondary, and postsecondary distance education courses. Topics include contracting with schools to convert their courses to an interactive environment; interactive courseware; testing; electronic discussion groups; and professional training.

Penaranda, Elizabeth A. (1995, Spring). Teletraining: From the mailbox to cyberspace. **Journal of Instruction Delivery Systems, 9**(2), 11-16. EJ 508 675. Examines various teletraining methods as cost effective, high quality alternatives in distance education.

Perrin, Elizabeth. (1995, March). The virtual university and other life forms. **ED, Education at a Distance, 9**(3), J6-J9. EJ 506 957. Briefly outlines the early history of distance education programs in the 1960s with emphasis on the success of the Open University in the United Kingdom.

Poole, Howard, and Schma, Geraldine. (1995, April). Statewide distance education networks in Michigan: One institution's perspective. **ED, Education at a Distance, 9**(4), J3-J9. EJ 510 492. Reviews the contributions made by four Michigan communication networks to further statewide distance education, examines the telecommunication services made available by each network, and reviews each network's benefits and limitations.

Portier, S. J., and Wagemans, L. J. J. M. (1995). The assessment of prior knowledge profiles: A support for independent learning? **Distance Education, 16**(1), 65-87. EJ 510 464. (Available UMI.) Analyzes prior knowledge based on the idea of knowledge structure and argues that the relevance of using knowledge profiles is important in independent, distance learning.

Redding, Richard E. (1995). Cognitive task analysis for instructional design: Applications in distance education. **Distance Education, 16**(1), 88-106. EJ 510 465. (Available UMI.) Provides an overview of cognitive task analysis-based instructional design (CTA-BID) and its applications in the design of instructional and testing materials for distance education.

Sand, Mary, and Chandler, Nick. (1995, Winter). Economic delivery of video teletraining. **Journal of Instruction Delivery Systems, 9**(1), 23-25. EJ 499 747. Discusses video teletraining as an alternative to traditional classroom education in terms of cost and program effectiveness; understanding the technology; support required to develop and deliver quality instruction; and the instructional design.

Thach, Elizabeth C., and Murphy, Karen L. (1995). Competencies for distance education professionals. **Educational Technology Research and Development, 43**(1), 57-79. EJ 501 723. (Available UMI.) Describes a study of the roles and competencies of distance education professionals within the United States and Canada based on a survey of approximately 100 distance educators.

Wagner, Ellen D., and McCombs, Barbara L. (1995, March-April). Learner Centered Psychological Principles in practice: Designs for distance education. **Educational Technology, 35**(2), 32-35. EJ 499 826. (Available UMI.) Discusses the use of Learner Centered Psychological Principles in instruction and training in terms of traditional versus learner centered instructional approaches, the challenge of designing such instruction, and learner centered designs for distance education.

Whitaker, George W. (1995, August). First-hand observations on tele-course teaching. **T.H.E. Journal, 23**(1), 65-68. EJ 510 406. (Available UMI.) Describes development of college English courses offered as distance education for industrial firms via communication technologies.

Videos

Distance learning series. (1996). RMI Media Productions, 1365 North Winchester St., Olathe, KS 66061. Series of 4 videotapes, each 30 min. $79.95 each. This introduction to the principles of teaching and learning at a distance provides real world examples of educators at colleges and universities to help explain the material. Individual titles are *MST-11: An introduction to distance education; MST-12: Methods and mediums; MST-13: Interactive learning environments;* and *MST-14: Telecourse techniques.*

The Iowa distance education series. (1995). Produced by the Iowa Distance Education Alliance. Order from the Association for Educational Communications and Technology, 1025 Vermont Ave. NW, Suite 820, Washington, DC 20005. Series of 9 videotapes, 11 to 15 min. running time. $350; $50 each; $225 or $40 each for AECT members. An introductory video, *A room with a view*, is followed by four videos on the foundations of distance education (*Definition and background; Theory and research; Technologies and terminology printer;* and *The classroom*), and four on applications (*The teacher; The student; The curriculum;* and *Iowa Communications Network*).

EDUCATIONAL RESEARCH

Media-Related Periodicals

American Educational Research Journal. American Educational Research Association, 1230 17th St., NW, Washington, DC 20036-3078. q.; $39 indiv., $51 inst. Reports on original research, both empirical and theoretical, and brief synopses of research.

Current Index to Journals in Education (CIJE). Oryx Press, 4041 N. Central at Indian School Rd., Phoenix, AZ 85012-3397. mo.; $245 ($280 outside North America); semi-ann. cumulations $250 ($285 foreign); combination $475. A guide to articles published in some 830 education and education-related journals. Includes complete bibliographic information, annotations, and indexes. Semiannual cumulations available. Contents are produced by the ERIC (Educational Resources Information Center) system, Office of Educational Research and Improvement, U.S. Department of Education.

Education Index. H. W. Wilson, 950 University Ave., Bronx, NY 10452. mo. (except July and August); variable costs. Author-subject index to educational publications in the English language. Cumulated quarterly and annually.

Educational Research. Routledge, 11 Fetter Ln., London EC4P 4EE, England. 3/yr.; £30 indiv. ($55 U.S. and Canada, £33 elsewhere); £68 inst. (£72 foreign). Reports on current educational research, evaluation, and applications.

Educational Researcher. American Educational Research Association, 1230 17th St., NW, Washington, DC 20036-3078. 9/yr.; $39 indiv., $51 inst. Contains news and features of general significance in educational research.

Research in Science & Technological Education. Carfax Publishing Co., 875-81 Massachusetts Ave., Cambridge, MA 02139. 2/yr.; £48 indiv., £178 inst. Publication of original research in the science and technological fields. Includes articles on psychological, sociological, economic, and organizational aspects.

Resources in Education (RIE). Superintendent of Documents, U.S. Government Printing Office, P.O. Box 371954, Pittsburgh, PA 15250-7954. mo.; $77 U.S, $96.25 elsewhere. (Semi-annual cumulations have been discontinued since 1994.) Announcement of research reports and other documents in education, including abstracts and indexes by subject, author, and institution. Contents produced by the ERIC (Educational Resources Information Center) system, Office of Educational Research and Improvement, U.S. Department of Education.

Books

Thompson, Ann D., Simonson, Michael R., and Hargrave, Constance P. (1996). **Educational technology: A review of the research, 2d ed.** Association for Educational Communications and Technology, 1025 Vermont Ave. NW, Suite 820, Washington, DC 20005. 96pp. $22; $15 for AECT members. This overview of the theories and research that support technology in teaching and learning covers audio, still pictures, films, television, computer-based learning, and hypermedia. It provides more than 200 references.

ERIC Documents

Arch, Elizabeth C. (1995). **The Baldwin Effect: A basis for sex differences in attitudes toward technology and science.** Paper presented to the American Educational Research Association, San Francisco, CA, April 18-22, 1995. 24pp. ED 387 121. Explores alternative explanations for the persistence of differences between girls and boys in their attitudes toward technology and science, and describes a project designed to introduce high school students in a science course to multimedia technology in a manner that would be conducive to encouraging girls as well as boys to become competent and interested.

Arnone, Marilyn P., and Small, Ruth V. (1995). **Arousing and sustaining curiosity: Lessons from the ARCS Model.** Paper presented to the Association for Educational Communications and Technology, Research and Theory Division, Anaheim, CA, February 16-20, 1995. 17pp. ED 383 285. Explores the construct of curiosity as an intrinsic motivator and examines its relationship to all of the components of the ARCS model, i.e., Attention, Relevance, Confidence, and Satisfaction.

Huang, James Chin-yun. (1995). **Digitized speech as feedback on cognitive aspects of psychomotor performance during computer-based instruction.** Paper presented to the Association for Educational Communications and Technology, Research and Theory Division, Anaheim, CA, February 16-20, 1995. 10pp. ED 383 301. This investigation of the effects of digitized feedback and student ability on the achievement of 68 Chung Cheng University (Taiwan) students during computer-based instruction compared the achievement of high and low-prior knowledge students among different feedback treatments.

Lebow, David G. (1995). **Constructivist values and emerging technologies: Transforming classrooms into learning environments.** Paper presented to the Association for Educational Communications and Technology, Research and Theory Division, Anaheim, CA, February 16-20, 1995. 8pp. ED 383 318. Lists and briefly defines values that summarize the constructivist framework reflected in student-centered learning approaches.

Molenda, Michael, and Olive, J. Fred, III. (1995). **The educational media and technology profession: An agenda for research and assessment of the knowledge base.** Paper presented to the Association for Educational Communications and Technology, Research and Theory Division, Anaheim, CA, February 16-20, 1995. 11pp. ED 383 329. This report is the first effort to stake out the territory to be included in research on the profession of educational media and technology (em/t) and to explore the existing knowledge base within that territory.

Reeves, Thomas C. (1995). **Questioning the questions of instructional technology research.** Paper presented to the Association for Educational Communications and Technology, Research and Theory Division, Anaheim, CA, February 16-20, 1995. 13pp. ED 383 331. Examines the current status of instructional technology research using a modification of Dick and Dick's (1989) research article classification scheme in an effort to distinguish between the goals and the methods of research.

Rezabek, Randy. (1995). **The relationships among measures of intrinsic motivation, instructional design, and learning in computer-based instruction.** Paper presented to the Association for Educational Communications and Technology, Research and Theory Division, Anaheim, CA, February 16-20, 1995. 13pp. ED 383 332. Designed to determine whether the design of instruction could positively affect learners' levels of intrinsic motivation toward the subject matter, this exploration of the intrinsic aspects of motivation addressed four questions using three computer-assisted instructional programs. Measures of intrinsic motivation were gathered from 121 subjects.

Richey, Rita C. (1995). **Expanding instructional technology's foundation of conceptual theory.** Paper presented to the Association for Educational Communications and Technology, Anaheim, CA, February 8, 1995. 10pp. ED 378 954. Argues that sound practice requires sound theory, and if instructional technology is to mature either as a field or a profession, theory that not only speaks to those problems unique to the field, but is also conceptually sound, is required.

Scholdt, Greg P., and others. (1995). **Sharing across disciplines—Interaction strategies in distance education. Part 1: Asking and answering questions.** Paper presented to the Association for Educational Communications and Technology, Research and Theory Division, Anaheim, CA, February 16-20, 1995. 6pp. ED 383 337. Investigates learner perceptions of the ease of asking and answering questions in the television classroom, and how these perceptions are affected by the location of the individual sending the message, the location of the individual receiving the message, and the type of message being sent.

Seels, Barbara. (1995). **Classification theory, taxonomic issues, and the 1994 definition of instructional technology.** Paper presented to the Association for Educational Communications and Technology, Anaheim, CA, February 8, 1995. 37pp. ED 378 948. Explores the implications of the 1994 Seels and Richey domain structure for instructional technology (IT) conceptual theory and classification systems for theory construction.

Sherry, Annette C., and Burke, William F. (1995). **Applying an interactive evaluation model to interactive television.** Paper presented to the Association for Educational Communications and Technology, Research and Theory Division, Anaheim, CA, February 16-20, 1995. 15pp. ED 383 336. Describes a study of the effectiveness of the Small Group Instructional Diagnosis (SGID) process for evaluating interactive television courses which used a structured, open-ended questioning format to obtain the perceptions of distance education graduate students.

Small, Ruth V., and Venkatesh, Murali. (1995). **The impact of closure on satisfaction with group decision-making.** Paper presented to the Association for Educational Communications and Technology, Research and Theory Division, Anaheim, CA, February 16-20, 1995. 17pp. ED 383 338. Investigates the impact of "need for closure" on information processing and decision confidence and the subsequent relationship between confidence and satisfaction with the outcomes of a group decision-making task.

Sugar, William A., and Boling, Elizabeth. (1995). **User-centered innovation: A model for "early usability testing."** Paper presented to the Association for Educational Communications and Technology, Research and Theory Division, Anaheim, CA, February 16-20, 1995. 9pp. ED 383 340. Describes the use of some concepts and techniques from disciplines outside Instructional Systems Development (ISD) in the earliest stages of the design of the Indiana University Center for Excellence in Education's (CEE) Virtual Textbook.

Journal Articles

Carr, Clay, and Totzke, Larry. (1995, March). The long and winding path (from instructional design to performance technology). **Performance and Instruction, 34**(3), 9-13. EJ 499 895. (Available UMI.) Presents a case study based on experiences at Amway Corporation that explains how the Human Resources Development Department progressed from providing training to providing a broader range of human performance technology interventions.

Hultman, Glenn, and Horberg, Cristina. (1995, March). Teachers' informal rationality: Understanding how teachers utilize knowledge. **Science Communication, 16**(3), 341-54. EJ 499 791. Discusses knowledge utilization processes, from general studies on utilization of research to a focus on those specific to educational settings. Factors that can facilitate the use of knowledge in school are examined.

Mayer, Richard E., and others. (1995). A generative theory of textbook design: Using annotated illustrations to foster meaningful learning of science text. **Educational Technology Research and Development, 43**(1), 31-43. EJ 501 721. (Available UMI.) Explains a generative theory of textbook design and describes three experiments that compared college students' solutions on transfer problems after reading science texts with illustrations adjacent to corresponding text and including annotations, and illustrations separated from text without annotations.

Newby, Timothy J., and others. (1995). Instructional analogies and the learning of concepts. **Educational Technology Research and Development, 43**(1), 5-18. EJ 501 719. (Available UMI.) Discusses instructional analogies and describes two studies that were designed to examine the effects of instructional analogy training on college students' ability to identify the application of advanced physiological concepts.

Rieber, Lloyd P. (1995). A historical review of visualization in human cognition. **Educational Technology Research and Development, 43**(1), 45-56. EJ 501 722. (Available UMI.) Presents a historical overview of visualization as a cognitive strategy in human creativity, discovery, and problem-solving and discusses implications for its use in multimedia learning environments, instructional design, and virtual reality.

Rosen, Larry D., and Weil, Michelle M. (1995, Spring). Computer anxiety: A cross-cultural comparison of university students in ten countries. **Computers in Human Behavior, 11**(1), 45-64. EJ 496 620. (Available UMI.) Based on a larger study of technophobia and technological sophistication, this study assessed computer anxiety among undergraduates in 10 countries and compared the factor structure found in the United States to that found in 9 other countries.

Wiedenbeck, Susan, and Scholtz, Jean. (1995, January). Introducing undergraduates to research: A case study from the field of human-computer interaction. **Computers and Education, 24**(1), 37-49. EJ 501 713. (Available UMI.) Reports on the design and implementation of an experimental summer program aimed at introducing undergraduates to research in computer science.

EDUCATIONAL TECHNOLOGY

Media-Related Periodicals

British Journal of Educational Technology. National Council for Educational Technology, Millburn Hill Rd., Science Park, Coventry CV4 7JJ, England. 3/yr.; £60 inst. U.K., £70 overseas airmail; personal subscriptions £32 U.K., £42 overseas. Published by the National Council for Educational Technology, this journal includes articles on education and training, especially theory, applications, and development of educational technology and communications.

Canadian Journal of Educational Communication. Association for Media and Technology in Education in Canada, AMTEC-CJEC Subscription, 3-1750 The Queensway, Suite 1318, Etobicoke, ON, M9C 5H5, Canada. 3/yr.; $45. Articles, research reports, and literature reviews on all areas of educational communication and technology.

Educational Technology. Educational Technology Publications, Inc., 700 Palisade Ave., Englewood Cliffs, NJ 07632-0564. bi-mo.; $119 U.S., $139 elsewhere, $25 single copy. Covers telecommunications, computer-aided instruction, information retrieval, educational television, and electronic media in the classroom.

Educational Technology Abstracts. Carfax Publishing Co., 875-81 Massachusetts Ave., Cambridge, MA 02139. 6/yr.; £79 indiv., £268 inst. An international publication of abstracts of recently published material in the field of educational and training technology.

Educational Technology Research and Development. Association for Educational Communications and Technology, 1025 Vermont Ave., NW, Suite 820, Washington, DC 20005-3516. q.; $55 U.S. ($63 foreign). Focuses on research and instructional development in the field of educational technology.

Innovations in Education and Training International (formerly *Educational and Training Technology International*). Kogan Page, FREEPOST 1, 120 Pentonville Road, London N1 9JN. q. £56 ($102 U.S.). The international journal of the Association for Educational and Training Technology emphasizes developing trends in educational technology and its efficient use. It is now extending its interest to include the field of staff and educational development.

Journal of Instruction Delivery Systems. Learning Technology Institute, 50 Culpeper St., Warrenton, VA 22186. q.; $60 indiv., $75 inst., add $15 postage for countries outside North America. Devoted to the issues and applications of technology to enhance productivity in education, training, and job performance.

Journal of Technology and Teacher Education. Association for the Advancement of Computing in Education (AACE), P.O. Box 2966, Charlottesville, VA 22901-2966. q.; $65 indiv. U.S. ($80 foreign), $83 inst. U.S. ($103 foreign). Serves as an international forum to report research and applications of technology in preservice, inservice, and graduate teacher education.

Science Communication (formerly **Knowledge: Creation, Diffusion, Utilization**). Sage Publications, Inc., 2455 Teller Rd., Thousand Oaks, CA 91320. q.; $58 indiv., $172 inst. (In California, add 7.25%.) An international, interdisciplinary journal examining the nature of expertise and the translation of knowledge into practice and policy.

Technology and Learning. Peter Li Education Group, P.O. Box 49727, Dayton, OH 45449-0727. 8/yr.; $24 ($32 foreign). Publishes features, reviews, news, and announcements of educational activities and opportunities in programming, software development, and hardware configurations.

TECHNOS. Agency for Instructional Technology, Box A, 1111 W. 17th St., Bloomington, IN 47402-0120. q.; $20 indiv., $16 libr. ($24 foreign). A forum for discussion of ideas about the use of technology in education, with a focus on reform.

TechTrends. Association for Educational Communications and Technology, 1025 Vermont Ave., NW, Suite 820, Washington, DC 20005-3516. 6/yr.; $40 U.S., $44 elsewhere, $6 single copy. Features authoritative, practical articles about technology and its integration into the learning environment.

T.H.E. Journal (Technological Horizons in Education). T.H.E., 150 El Camino Real, Suite 112, Tustin, CA 92680-3670. 11/yr.; $29 U.S. and Canada (free to qualified educators). For educators of all levels. Focuses on a specific topic for each issue, as well as technological innovations as they apply to education.

Books

Downs, Sylvia. (1995). **Learning at work: Effective strategies for making learning happen.** London: Kogan Page. Order from Taylor & Francis, Inc., 1900 Frost Rd., Suite 101, Bristol, PA 19007. 128pp. £9.99. Designed to help managers, trainers, and workplace learners to understand and practice the concepts and methods that help people learn, this clear and concise guide exposes pitfalls that inhibit learning and prescribes tried and tested learning methods.

Ely, Donald P., and Minor, Barbara B., eds. (1996). **Educational media and technology yearbook, 1995-1996. Volume 21.** Libraries Unlimited, Inc., P.O. Box 6633, Englewood, CO 80155-6633. 409pp. $60. Provides media and instructional technology professionals with an up-to-date, single-source overview and assessment of the field of educational technology. Covers trends, issues, and current developments, and provides leadership profiles and annotated listings of the organizations, agencies, and colleges and universities that serve the field.

Ely, Donald P., and Plomp Tjeerd, eds. (1995). **Classic writings on instructional technology.** Libraries Unlimited, P.O. Box 6633, Englewood, CO 80155-6633. 225pp. $54. This collection provides 32 seminal works in the field of educational technology that have contributed to the conceptual underpinnings of the field and are often used in educational technology courses.

Farmer, Lesley S. J. (1995). **Workshops for teachers: Becoming partners for information literacy.** Linworth Publishing, Inc., 480 E. Wilson Bridge Rd., Suite L, Worthington, OH 43085-2372. 142pp. $19.95. This guide illustrates how to conduct inservice training for teachers to equip them with the information skills they need to partner with librarians.

Grabe, Mark, and Grabe, Cindy. (1996). **Integrating technology for meaningful learning.** Houghton Mifflin, 181 Ballardvale St., Wilmington, MA 01887-7050. 384pp. $36.87. Written for future teachers in K-12 classrooms, this text presents technology as a valuable tool for enhancing the classroom learning experience rather than replacing it.

Guidelines for the accreditation of programs in educational communications and technology, 3d ed. (1996). Association for Educational Communications and Technology, 1025 Vermont Ave. NW, Suite 820, Washington, DC 20005. 74pp. $23.95; $16.95 for AECT members. Presents the officially approved standards for programs seeking accreditation by the National Council for Accreditation of Teacher Education (NCATE).

Hackbarth, Steven. (1996). **The educational technology handbook.** Educational Technology Publications, 700 Palisade Ave., Englewood Cliffs, NJ 07632-0564. 350pp. $37.95. Designed to help K-12 teachers make sense of the advanced technology available to them, this guidebook examines research on the use of technology in the classroom and provides guidelines for selecting technology.

Land, Ray, and Percival, Fred, eds. (1995). **Aspects of educational training and technology, vol. 28.** London: Kogan Page. Order from Taylor & Francis, Inc., 1900 Frost Rd., Suite 101, Bristol, PA 19007. 320pp. £35. Leading practitioners in the field from the 1994 Association of Educational and Training Technology's international conference discuss multimedia and hypermedia, computer-assisted learning, open and distance learning, course and academic management, and how to cut costs and increase flexibility through the use of information technology.

McGill, Ian, and Beaty, Liz. (1995). **Action learning. A practitioner's guide, 2d ed.** London: Kogan Page. Order from Taylor & Francis, Inc., 1900 Frost Rd., Suite 101, Bristol, PA 19007. 237pp. £19.95. New edition features an expanded section on the use of action learning in management, training, and the professions.

Reynolds, Karen E., and Barba, Roberta H. (1996). **Technology for science teaching and learning.** 256pp. $24.95. Addresses the needs of systemic reform, multicultural concerns, National Council for Accreditation of Teacher Education (NCATE) standards for teacher competency in technology, and National Science Teachers Association (NSTA) standards for science education. Practical examples and activities for teachers and children in grades K-8 are included.

Ross, Tweed, and Bailey, Gerald. (1995.) **Technology-based learning: A handbook for principals and technology leaders.** Scholastic Inc., 555 Broadway, New York, NY 10012. 192pp. $29.95. Presents material on five technology implementation models and provides a flowchart and other planning materials to help implement the model selected as being appropriate for a specific building or district.

Saunders, Danny, ed. (1995). **The simulation and gaming yearbook, vol. 3: Games and simulations for business.** 228pp. £35. Offers practical ideas, new theories, and examples of best practice in using gaming for sales, management training, accounting, and business process re-engineering.

Simonson, Michael, ed. (1995). **Research proceedings: 1995 AECT national convention.** Association for Educational Communications and Technology, 1025 Vermont Ave., NW, Suite 820, Washington, DC 20005-3547. Approx. 1,100pp. $45 AECT members; $60 nonmembers. The collection of research papers from AECT's 17th annual convention includes research on multimedia instruction, embedded training environments, compressed video, intelligent tutoring, and effects of various technologies on learning.

Willis, Jerry, Stephens, Elizabeth C., and Matthew, Kathryn I. (1996). **Technology, reading, and language arts.** 256pp. $27.95. Material about how to use technology is organized around the major approaches to teaching reading: constructivist, out-of-context direct instruction, and "in-context" or authentic direct instruction.

Wujcik, Anne, Bailey, Gerald, Lumley, Dan, and Ward, Anne. (1995). **Plans and policies for technology in education: A compendium.** National School Boards Association, Distribution Center, 1680 Duke St., Alexandria, VA 22314-3493. 250pp. $35. Technology plans and policies from real districts are provided together with guidelines to assist educators in conceiving, wording, formatting, and refining their own statements about technology in their schools.

ERIC Documents

Betrus, Anthony K. (1995). **Individualized instruction: A history of the critiques.** Paper presented to the Association for Educational Communications and Technology, Research and Theory Division, Anaheim, CA, February 16-20, 1995. 9pp. ED 383 308. Discusses critiques of three types of individualized instruction: audio-tutorial, personalized system of instruction, and computer assisted instruction.

Ely, Donald P. (1995, September). **The field of educational technology: Update 1995—A dozen frequently asked questions. ERIC Digest.** Syracuse, NY: ERIC Clearinghouse on Information and Technology. 4pp. ED 387 117. This digest provides background information and sources that help in understanding the concept of educational technology. Specific answers to 12 questions are provided.

Future plans: Making the most of technology in the classroom. Planning guides. (1993). Tallahassee, FL: SouthEastern Regional Vision for Education (SERVE); Atlanta, GA: Bell-South Foundation, Inc. [and] Southern Regional Education Board. Presented as white papers at the "BellSouth TechKNOWLEDGEy '93: Pathways to Progress" conference (August 5-6, 1993). 88pp. ED 384 348. A related videotape recording is also available from NEFEC/SERVE, Rte. 1, Box 8500, 3841 Reid St., Palatka, FL 32177 ($25 for tape and related publications plus $2 shipping). Three papers discuss the process of educational technology planning from the viewpoints of teachers, principals, technology facilitators, superintendents, and lay members of a site-based management team; district technology planning using a metaphorical approach; and state planning issues, concerns, and processes.

Graham, Charles D. (1995, April). **Layers of learning communities: Orchestrating a districtwide technology implementation. The Central Office Internal Facilitator's role in implementation of an integrated learning system.** Paper presented to the American Educational Research Association, San Francisco, CA, April 18-22, 1995. 11pp. ED 385 237. Describes the implementation of an integrated learning system (ILS) by the Colonial School District of Plymouth Meeting, Pennsylvania.

Hill, Janette R., and Hannafin, Michael J. (1995). **Technology for teachers: A case study in problem-centered activity-based learning.** Paper presented to the Association for Educational Communications and Technology, Research and Theory Division, Anaheim, CA, February 16-20, 1995. 10pp. ED 383 301. Discusses the implications of using a problem-centered, activity-based approach to teaching technology that addresses everyday teaching and learning problems for both teachers and learners.

Joining forces: Spreading successful strategies. Proceedings of the Invitational Conference on Systemic Reform (Washington, DC, February 23-25, 1995). Washington, DC: National Science Foundation; U.S. Department of Education. 100pp. ED 381 135. Outlines program activities and presents a set of briefing papers that provide a background for the conference. Sections previewing each of the 21 issue and theme conference sessions and outlines of the 47 workshops offered are included.

Jost, Karen Lee. (1995). **Creating a learning environment for teachers.** Paper presented to the Association for Educational Communications and Technology, Research and Theory Division, Anaheim, CA, February 16-20, 1995. 6pp. ED 383 313. Presents the theoretical framework for a new course for teacher education that is consistent with a constructivist view of learning, new educational goals, and a view of the role of technology as a tool that can support the attainment of educational goals and increased student learning.

Means, Barbara, and Olson, Kerry. (1995). **Technology's role within constructivist classrooms.** Menlo Park, CA: SRI International. Presented at a symposium, "Teachers, Technology, and Authentic Tasks: Lessons from Within and Across Classrooms," at the American Educational Research Association, San Francisco, CA, April 1995. 17p. ED 383 183. As part of a national study of the role of technology in supporting education reform, especially constructivist, student-centered teaching methods and instructional uses of computers and other technologies, this report discusses various factors involved based on case studies of nine sites that have been using technology in ways that enhance a restructuring of the classroom around students' needs and project-based activities.

1995 Education technology survey. (1995, July). Denver, CO: Quality Education Data, Inc. 2pp. ED 387 124. In-depth telephone interviews were conducted among elementary and secondary school educators in spring 1995 to determine usage, attitudes, and barriers to usage for five electronic in-school services: Cable in the Classroom; computers, laserdisc or CD-ROM; Internet; online computer services such as America Online and Prodigy; and Channel One.

Hiatt, Harriette. (1995, February). **North Carolina instructional technology plan and technological recommendations and standards.** North Carolina School Technology Commission. 101pp. ED 386 141. This long-range state technology plan is the culmination of a series of research and planning efforts on improving student performance and enhancing the teaching/learning process through the effective use of technology.

Simonson, Michael R., and Anderson, Mary Lagomarcino, eds. (1995). **Proceedings of selected research and development presentations at the 1995 National Convention of the Association for Educational Communications and Technology sponsored by the Research and Theory Division (17th, Anaheim, CA, 1995).** Washington, DC: Association for Educational Communications and Technology. 727pp. ED 383 284. Individual papers have been analyzed separately as ED 378 955, ED 380 121-123, and ED 383 285-347. This collection of conference presentations includes research on cognitive task analysis, instructional design, learning environments, hypermedia training, distance education, and effects of various technologies on learning at different education levels. Selected papers from the Division for Instructional Development are included.

Teachers and technology: Making the connection. OTA report summary. (1995, April). Washington, DC: Congress of the United States, Office of Technology Assessment. 9pp. ED 386 154. This report seeks to underscore the connection between teachers and the implementation of technology in schools. Key findings of a national survey are presented in this summary of the full report, and policy options and the governmental role are discussed. For the full report, see ED 386 155 (312pp.).

Technology: America's schools not designed or equipped for 21st century. Statement of Linda G. Morra, Director, Education and Employment Issues, Health, Education and Human Services Division. Testimony before the subcommittee on Labor, Health and Human Services, Education and Related Agencies, Committee on Appropriations, United States Senate. (1995, April 4). Washington, DC: General Accounting Office. 26pp. ED 381 153. (Available from the U.S. General Accounting Office, P.O. Box 6015, Gaithersburg, MD 20884-6015 as GAO/T-HEWS-95-127. First copy, free. Additional copies, $2 each). This statement reports the findings of a national survey of 10,000 schools which was conducted to determine whether America's schools have appropriate technologies, such as computers, and the facility infrastructure to support these technologies.

Winn, William. (1995). **Advantages of a theory-based curriculum in instructional technology.** Paper presented to the Association for Educational Communications and Technology, Anaheim, CA, February 8, 1995. 18pp. ED 381 126. Argues that students should master perceptual and human factors theory, cognitive theories of learning, and theories of how knowledge guides the way people interact with their environment, and that application of these theories as the graduate develops professional skill and status will improve the success of the profession.

Journal Articles

Anderson, Larry S. (1995, November-December). Making dreams come true! How to write a technology plan. **MultiMedia Schools, 2**(5), 14-19. EJ 513 826. (Available UMI.) Describes the steps involved in writing a school technology plan and recommends the National Center for Technology Planning as a helpful resource.

Banathy, Bela H. (1995, May-June). Developing a systems view of education. **Educational Technology, 35**(3), 53-57. EJ 503 496. (Available UMI.) Discussion of societal and technological changes in the 20th century and the resulting paradigm shift focuses on the need to develop a systems view of education. The genesis of the systems view is explained; an example of a possible systems model is presented; and applications in education are considered.

Connolly, Frank W. (1995, April). Intellectual honesty in the era of computing. **T.H.E. Journal, 22**(9), 86-88. EJ 501 735. (Available UMI.) Discussion of the need for intellectual honesty in using technology covers intellectual property laws; ethics; indirect results of copying software and images; the need for institutional policy; and the provision of facilities and resources that encourage respect for policy.

Cornell, Richard A., and Farkas, Peter R. (1995, March). Professional associations: What value? **Educational Media International, 32**(1), 44-46. EJ 507 021. (Available UMI.) Discusses the benefits of professional associations, including networking, technological advancements, sharing of knowledge, cost-effectiveness, and career opportunities; identifies the elements of a successful association; and describes procedures for setting up an association.

Davidson, George, and Maurer, Matthew M. (1995, April-May). Leadership in instructional technology. **TechTrends, 40**(3), 23-26. EJ 501 799. (Available UMI.) Explains the design of a pilot course for school principals that focused on the use of technology for instruction.

DeSieno, Robert. (1995, July-August). The faculty and digital technology. **Educom Review, 30**(4), 46-48. EJ 508 758. (Available UMI.) Discusses interactive instruction and student responsibility for learning, cost effectiveness, the potential for enriching curriculum, helping students reason and learn, applying instructional design more effectively, and connecting departments and other colleges.

Hancock, Vicki E. (1995, September). Information literacy, brain-based learning, and the technological revolution: Implications for education. **School Library Media Activities Monthly, 12**(1), 31-34. EJ 510 372. Presents 12 principles for "brain-based" learning that can serve as guidelines for defining and selecting instructional programs and methodologies.

Hayes, Jeanne, Bybee, Dennis L. (1995, October). Defining the greatest need for educational technology. **Learning and Leading with Technology, 23**(2), 48-50. EJ 512 274. Twelve-year student-per-computer trends in K-12 public schools are compared to identify the states with the greatest need for educational technology.

Johnson, Jenny K. (1995, September). The third degree: Survey of degree programs in educational communications and technology. **TechTrends, 40**(4), 27-29. EJ 512 191. (Available UMI.) Presents results of a survey of undergraduate, master's, and doctoral degree programs in educational communications and technology.

Jonassen, David H. (1995, July-August). Supporting communities of learners with technology: A vision for integrating technology with learning in schools. **Educational Technology, 35**(4), 60-63. EJ 507 039. (Available UMI.) Considers the goal of creating communities of learners and discusses ways to integrate technology with learning.

Khan, Badrul H. (1995, March-April). Obstacles encountered during stages of the educational change process. EJ 499 829. **Educational Technology, 35**(2), 43-46. (Available UMI.) Describes the stages of the change process when redesigning an education system, and analyzes common obstacles encountered during the change process based on a survey of 60 schools nationwide.

Lienard, Brian. (1995, June). Pre-course IT skills of teacher trainees: A longitudinal study. **Journal of Computer Assisted Learning, 11**(2), 110-20. EJ 505 420. (Available UMI.) Describes a longitudinal study conducted at the University of London (England) that investigated the prior instructional technology (IT) experience of Post Graduate Certificate in Education students.

Lund, Teri B., and Barksdale, Susan B. (1995, February). Strategic planning for education and training: A report from the field. **Performance and Instruction, 34**(2), 30-33. EJ 499 713. (Available UMI.) Reports on the state of strategic planning for education and training in service industries, manufacturing, retailing, and entertainment organizations.

Rhodes, Lewis A. (1995, November). Technology-driven systemic change. **Learning and Leading with Technology, 23**(3), 35-37. EJ 515 027. Argues that, for technology to become an integrated aspect of education, the focus must not be on technology itself, but on the information it enables students, teachers and administrators to access and process.

Rice, Marion. (1995). Issues surrounding the integration of technology into the K-12 classroom: Notes from the field. **Interpersonal Computing and Technology Journal, 3**(1), 67-81. EJ 499 802. [To retrieve this article, send the following e-mail message to LISTSERV@ GUVM.GEORGETOWN.EDU: GET RICE IPCTV3N1.] Discusses issues relating to the integration of information technology into K-12 curricula, focusing on the need for structured inservice programs for teachers to develop competency with technology and curricular applications. Also examines the issue of gender equity in education and the inclusion of inservice strategies to address the problem.

Rutherford, LeAne H., and Grana, Sheryl J. (1995, September). Retrofitting academe: Adapting faculty attitudes and practices to technology. **T.H.E. Journal, 23**(2), 82-86. EJ 510 474. (Available UMI.) Discusses factors that prevent faculty from adapting to the use of technology; suggests ways to learn about and use technology; and provides an example of a training workshop for using interactive television.

Spotts, Thomas H., and Bowman, Mary Ann. (1995, March-April). Faculty use of instructional technologies in higher education. **Educational Technology, 35**(2), 56-64. EJ 499 832. (Available UMI.) Reports on a survey that investigated the instructional technology knowledge and experience of the faculty of a midwestern university.

Yin, L. Roger, and Krentz, Roger F. (1995, November). Birth of a proactive instructional technology center: A case of system change. **T.H.E. Journal, 23**(4), 86-88. EJ 513 883. (Available UMI.) Discusses factors involved in the merger of two departments to create the Instructional Technology Center at the University of Wisconsin.

Computer Software

Desberg, Peter, and Fisher, Farah. (1995). **Teaching with technology.** 4 Macintosh disks. $39.95. Longwood Division, Allyn & Bacon, P.O. Box 10695, Des Moines, IA 50336-0695. This guide-on-disk enables the user to learn by doing and participating rather than by reading passive descriptions. Built-in pedagogical aids include electronic notebooks, the electronic "Find" command, online help, online glossaries, and online demonstrations.

Online Products/Resources

EdNet. A listserv that serves as a forum for educators on education and technology topics of their choice. To subscribe, send a message to listproc@lists.umass.edu and on the top line of the body of the message type: subscribe EdNet your name. Don't include anything else unless the mailer requires something in the subject field; then type in a single letter.

Infomart magazine. Covers technology trends and companies at http://www.loc.gov.

SyllabusWeb. From the publishers of *Syllabus* magazine. It features news, case studies, product reviews and announcements of interest to technology users in high schools and higher education at http://www.syllabus.com.

ELECTRONIC PUBLISHING

Media-Related Periodicals

Desktop Communications. International Desktop Communications, Ltd., 342 Madison Ave., Suite 622, New York, NY 10173-0002. bi-mo.; $24. Helps small business, corporate, and individual computer users to design and implement innovative and effective newsletters, reports, presentations, and other business communications.

Electronic Publishing: Origination, Dissemination, and Design. John Wiley, Inc., 605 Third Ave., New York, NY 10158. q.; $375. Covers structured editors, authoring tools, hypermedia, document bases, electronic documents over networks, and text integration.

Publish! Integrated Media, Inc., Publish!, Box 51967, Boulder, CO 80322-5415. mo.; $23.95. A how-to magazine for desktop publishing.

ERIC Documents

Riggsby, Dutchie, and others. (1995). **Electronic portfolio: Assessment, resume, or marketing tool?** Paper given to the Association of Small Computer Users in Education (ASCUE), North Myrtle Beach, SC, June 18-22, 1995. 7pp. ED 387 115. Presents the benefits of using an electronic portfolio as opposed to the more traditional type for the professional resume are presented.

Journal Articles

Gasaway, Laura N. (1995, Spring). Scholarly publication and copyright in networked electronic publishing. **Library Trends, 43**(4), 679-700. EJ 506 440. (Available UMI.) Argues that new models of copyright ownership and management can be developed for electronic publishing of scholarly works and research results that will provide greater control to the faculty author, ease the distribution and permissions process for use of copyrighted works in teaching and research, and reduce the costs to universities.

Lancaster, F. W. (1995, Spring). The evolution of electronic publishing. **Library Trends, 43**(4), 518-27. EJ 505 431. (Available UMI.) Discusses the evolution of electronic publishing from the early 1960s when computers were used merely to produce conventional printed products to the present move toward networked scholarly publishing.

Royalties, fair use & copyright in the electronic age. (1995, November-December). **Educom Review, 30**(6), 30-35. EJ 513 767. (Available UMI.) Bruce A. Lehman, chair of the Working Group on Intellectual Property Rights, discusses three issues related to the Copyright Act that will affect Internet transmissions: whether transmissions are performances or deliveries of copies; the scope of fair use; and whether there should be a copyright system in the electronic age.

van Brakel, Pieter A. (1995, August). Electronic journals: Publishing via Internet's World Wide Web. **Electronic Library, 13**(4), 389-96. EJ 512 229. (Available UMI.) Provides hints for setting up and maintaining a multimedia scholarly journal. Details include limitations of paper and electronic journals, and requirements for publishing successful electronic journals.

INFORMATION SCIENCE AND TECHNOLOGY

Media-Related Periodicals

Bulletin of the American Society for Information Science. ASIS, 8720 Georgia Ave., Suite 501, Silver Spring, MD 20910-3602. bi-mo.; $60 North America, $70 elsewhere, $10 single copy. Newsmagazine concentrating on issues affecting the information field; management reports; opinion; and news of people and events in ASIS and the information community.

Canadian Journal of Information and Library Science/Revue canadienne des sciences de l'information et de bibliothèconomie. CAIS, University of Toronto Press, Journals Dept., 5201 Dufferin St., Downsview, ON M3H 5T8, Canada. q.; nonmembers $95 Canada, $110 elsewhere. Published by the Canadian Association for Information Science to contribute to the advancement of library and information science in Canada.

Datamation. Cahners Publishing Co., 8773 S. Ridgeline Blvd., Highlands Ranch, CO 80126. 24/yr.; $75; $110 Canada, Mexico; $195 Japan, Australia, New Zealand; $165 elsewhere (free to qualified personnel). Covers semi-technical news and views on hardware, software, and databases, for data- and information-processing professionals.

Information Processing and Management. Pergamon Journals, Inc., 660 White Plains Rd., Tarrytown, NY 10591-5153. bi-mo. $152 indiv. (whose inst. subscribes); $559 inst. An international journal covering data processing, database building, and retrieval.

Information Retrieval and Library Automation. Lomond Publications, Inc., Box 88, Mt. Airy, MD 21771. mo.; $66 U.S. (foreign $79.50). News, articles, and announcements on new techniques, equipment, and software in information services.

Information Services and Use. I.O.S. Press, Box 10558, Burke, VA 22009-0558. 4/yr.; $220. An international journal for those in the information management field. Includes online and offline systems, library automation, micrographics, videotex, and telecommunications.

The Information Society. Taylor and Francis, 1900 Frost Rd., Suite 101, Bristol, PA 19007-1598. q.; $110. Provides a forum for discussion of the world of information, including transborder data flow, regulatory issues, and the impact of the information industry.

Information Technology and Libraries. American Library Association, Library and Information Technology Association, 50 E. Huron St., Chicago, IL 60611-2795. q.; $50 U.S. nonmembers, $55 Canada, Mexico, and Spain; $60 elsewhere. Articles on library automation, communication technology, cable systems, computerized information processing, and video technologies.

Journal of the American Society for Information Science. Subscription Department, 605 3rd Ave., New York, NY 10158-0012. 10/yr.; $550 U.S. nonmembers, $650 Canada and Mexico, $687.50 elsewhere. Publishes research articles in the area of information science.

Journal of Documentation. Aslib (Association for Information Management). Subsc. U.S., Learned Information, 143 Old Marlton Pike, Medford, NJ 08055-8750. £60 members, £90 ($200) nonmembers. Describes how technical, scientific, and other specialized knowledge is recorded, organized, and disseminated.

Books

Williams, Martha E., ed. (1995). **Annual review of information and science technology, vol. 30, 1995 (ARIST).** Information Today, Inc. (formerly Learned Information, Inc.), 143 Old Marlton Pike, Medford, NJ 08055-8750. $76 for members of the American Society for Information Science, $95 for nonmembers. A literary source of ideas, trends, and references that offers a comprehensive view of information science technology. The eight chapters in this edition fit into the fundamental structure of planning information systems and services, basic techniques and technologies, applications, and the profession.

ERIC Documents

Craig, Annemieke, and others. (1995, August). **Confronting issues of gender in information technology in Australia.** Unpublished report, Victoria University of Technology, Melbourne, Australia. 22pp. ED 385 298. Provides a synopsis of major projects and initiatives undertaken at eight Australian universities to encourage females to develop the necessary skills to enroll in computing courses and decrease female attrition.

Information literacy: Lifelong learning in the Middle States region. A summary of two symposia. (1995). Report on regional symposia held in Philadelphia, PA, March 27, 1995, and Rochester, NY, May 1, 1995. 28pp. ED 386 157. Provides a summary of two symposia that brought together institutions of the Middle States region which have made progress toward institutionalizing information literacy to enable them to share their expertise and enhance their varied approaches to information literacy initiatives.

Pollack, Thomas A. (1995). **Information technology curricula: Business and interdisciplinary perspectives.** Paper given to the Association of Small Computer Users in Education (ASCUE), North Myrtle Beach, SC, June 18-22, 1995. 8pp. ED 387 105. Presents a newly-revised information technology curriculum and an interdisciplinary curriculum that couples information systems (IS) and computer science. The MIS/Computer Science program at Duquesne University (Pittsburgh) entails receiving dual degrees from the School of Business and College of Liberal Arts.

Journal Articles

Heterick, Robert C., Jr., and Gehl, John. (1995, January-February). Information technology and the year 2020. **Educom Review, 30**(1), 22-25. EJ 496 603. (Available UMI.) Predicts technological changes that will occur over the next 25 years and their impact on higher education.

Jansen, Barbara A. (1995, October). Self evaluation: The forgotten step to achievement. **School Library Media Activities Monthly, 12**(2), 24-27. EJ 510 469. Discusses the need for elementary students to evaluate their own information problem-solving styles and presents self-evaluation techniques to be used before, during, and after the information problem-solving process.

Johnson, J. David, and others. (1995, March). A comprehensive model of information seeking: Tests focusing on a technical organization. **Science Communication, 16**(3), 274-303. EJ 499 789. Testing of a comprehensive model of information seeking which contained antecedents, information carrier factors, and information-seeking actions revealed that the most important variables were those related to an individual's existing information base.

Mahmood, Mo Adam, and Hirt, Shirley A. (1995, Summer). Reasons schools are not efficiently using information technology: A case study. **Journal of End User Computing, 7**(3), 22-28. EJ 507 066. Explores how a Texas public school district progressed with a state mandate to integrate information technology into the curriculum.

Rader, Hannelore B. (1995, Fall). Information literacy and the undergraduate curriculum. **Library Trends, 44**(2), 270-78. EJ 513 796. (Available UMI.) Discusses the integration of information and technological skills into the undergraduate curriculum and presents examples of successful curriculum integration programs at Earlham College, the University of Wisconsin-Parkside, and Cleveland State University.

Savolainen, Reijo. (1995, Summer). Everyday life information seeking: Approaching information seeking in the context of "way of life." **Library & Information Science Research, 17**(3), 259-94. EJ 513 754. Discussion of everyday life information seeking (ELIS) offers a framework for studying ELIS, and presents results of testing the framework via interviews with teachers and workers as seekers of information using electronic and printed media.

INSTRUCTIONAL DESIGN AND TRAINING

Media-Related Periodicals

Human-Computer Interaction. Lawrence Erlbaum Associates, 365 Broadway, Hillsdale, NJ 07642. q.; $39 indiv. U.S. and Canada, $69 elsewhere, $215 inst., $245 elsewhere. A journal of theoretical, empirical, and methodological issues of user science and of system design.

Instructional Science. Kluwer Academic Publishers, P.O. Box 358 Accord Station, Hingham, MA 02018-0358. bi-mo.; $345 inst. U.S. Aimed to promote a deeper understanding of the nature, theory, and practice of the instructional process and the learning resulting from this process.

Journal of Educational Multimedia and Hypermedia. Association for the Advancement of Computing in Education, Box 2966, Charlottesville, VA 22902-2966. q.; $65 indiv. $80 foreign); $83 inst.($103 foreign). A multidisciplinary information source presenting research and applications on multimedia and hypermedia tools that allow the integration of images, sounds, text, and data in learning and teaching.

Journal of Educational Technology Systems. Baywood Publishing Co., 26 Austin Ave., Box 337, Amityville, NY 11701. q.; $127 inst. plus $5.50 postage U.S. and Canada, $11.25 postage elsewhere. In-depth articles on completed and ongoing research in all phases of educational technology and its application and future within the teaching profession.

Journal of Interactive Instruction Development. Learning Technology Institute, Society for Applied Learning Technology, 50 Culpeper St., Warrenton, VA 22186. q.; $60 indiv., $75 inst.; add $15 postage outside North America. A showcase of successful programs that will give awareness of innovative, creative, and effective approaches to courseware development for interactive technology.

Journal of Technical Writing and Communication. Baywood Publishing Co., 26 Austin Ave., Box 337, Amityville, NY 11701. q.; $121 inst. Essays on oral and written communication, for purposes ranging from pure research to needs of business and industry.

Journal of Visual Literacy. International Visual Literacy Association, c/o John C. Belland, 122 Ramseyer Hall, 29 West Woodruff Ave., Ohio State University, Columbus, OH 43210. semi-ann.; $12 indiv., $18 libraries. Interdisciplinary forum on all aspects of visual/verbal languaging.

Performance and Instruction. International Society for Performance Improvement, 1300 L St. NW, Suite 1250, Washington, DC 20005. 10/yr.; $69 nonmembers. Journal of ISPI, intended to promote the advantage of performance science and technology. Contains articles, research, and case studies relating to improving human performance.

Performance Improvement Quarterly. International Society for Performance Improvement, 1300 L St. NW, Suite 1250, Washington, DC 20005. q.; $20 nonmembers. Represents the cutting edge in research and theory in performance technology.

Training. Lakewood Publications, Inc., 50 S. Ninth, Minneapolis, MN 55402. mo.; $68 U.S., $78 Canada, $89 elsewhere. Covers all aspects of training, management, and organizational development, motivation, and performance improvement.

Training Research Journal: The Science and Practice of Training. annual. Educational Technology Publications, 700 Palisade Ave., Englewood Cliffs, NJ 07632. annual. $60/yr. A new international, peer-reviewed publication that will provide a high-quality forum for theoretical and empirical work relevant to training. It will include empirical studies, theoretical reviews, meta-analyses, and articles of a conceptual nature that contribute to an understanding of the theory, research, and practice of the training of adult learners.

Books

Wilson, Brent G., ed. (1996). **Constructivist learning environments: Case studies in instructional design.** Educational Technology Publications, 700 Palisade Ave., Englewood Cliffs, NJ 07632-0564. 252pp. $43.95. This comprehensive look at tools and information that can be used in instruction and problem-solving activities offers an in-depth study of computer microworlds; classroom-based learning environments; open, virtual environments; and general issues of design and assessment.

ERIC Documents

Azevedo, Roger, and Bernard, Robert. (1995). **The effects of computer-presented feedback on learning from computer-based instruction: Meta-analysis.** Paper presented to the American Educational Research Association, San Francisco, CA, April 18-22, 1995. 24pp. ED 385 235. Reports the findings of a quantitative research synthesis (meta-analysis) of the literature concerning the effects of feedback on learning from computer-based instruction (CBI), an area in which empirical support for particular types of feedback information has been inconsistent and contradictory.

Cennamo, Katherine S., and others. (1995). **A "layers of negotiation" model for designing constructivist learning materials.** Paper presented to the Association for Educational Communications and Technology, Research and Theory Division, Anaheim, CA, February 16-20, 1995. 12pp. ED 383 288. Describes the process of designing a series of case-based interactive videodiscs to be used within a constructivist learning environment. The cases present two elementary teachers and their students as they progress through science lessons based on the conceptual change model of science teaching.

Dehoney, Joanne. (1995). **Cognitive task analysis: Implications for the theory and practice of instructional design.** Paper presented to the Association for Educational Communications and Technology, Research and Theory Division, Anaheim, CA, February 16-20, 1995. 13pp. ED 383 294. Considers two general models of cognitive task analysis, examines the procedures and results of analyses in three domains, and concludes that cognitive task analysis can and should be integrated into systematic instructional design.

Ellsworth, James B. (1995). **Planning for success: Considerations for managing dissemination of training technology.** Paper presented to the Association for Educational Communications and Technology, Research and Theory Division, Anaheim, CA, February 16-20, 1995. 12pp. ED 383 296. Summarizes the results of a study which examined the implementation of a computer-based trainer in a U.S. Army Advanced Individual Training center.

Fansler, A. Gigi, and others. (1995). **Using computers to write comprehensive examinations: A study of doctoral level examinations in educational administration departments.** Paper presented to the American Educational Research Association, San Francisco, CA, April 18-22, 1995. 12pp. ED 385 227. This preliminary study surveyed chairs of departments of educational administration from universities across the United States to learn how computers and models of alternative assessment are changing the face of comprehensive examinations.

Gatlin, Rebecca, and others. (1995). **Word processing competencies.** Conway, AR: University of Central Arkansas. 20. ED 383 182. Reports the findings of a survey of human resource managers in five Mid-South cities which indicate the extent of word processing use by businesses, the competencies required by those businesses, and how those competencies were being learned in this geographical area.

Humbert, Roxann A., and Kefferstan, Robert D. (1995). **Training: Reaching the haves and have nots.** Unpublished paper, Association for Information and Image Management. 7pp. ED 385 218. Focuses on methods for training the "haves"—those who have had computer technology training in a previous era—and the "have nots"—those who have Internet access but no prior computer or technology training.

Professional development. (1995, Winter). Rockville, MD: ACCESS ERIC. Rockville, MD. 37pp. ED 381 136. This issue of the *ERIC Review* announces research results, publications, and new programs relevant to the changing face of K-12 professional development for both preservice and inservice teachers.

Surry, Daniel W., and Farquhar, John D. (1995). **Adoption analysis and user-oriented instructional development.** Paper presented to the Association for Educational Communications and Technology, Research and Theory Division, Anaheim, CA, February 16-20, 1995. 12pp. ED 383 343. Argues that traditional instructional product development models are inadequate because they ignore social context, and presents two emerging theories, Adoption Analysis and User-Oriented Instructional Development, as tools that instructional developers can employ in order to increase the adoption of their products.

Wilson, Brent G. (1995). **Situated instructional design: Blurring the distinctions between theory and practice, design and implementation, curriculum and instruction.** Paper presented to the Association for Educational Communications and Technology, Research and Theory Division, Anaheim, CA, February 16-20, 1995. 14pp. ED 383 346. Presents a view of situated instructional development (ID) which incorporates a constructivist, situated view of learning and expertise, while at the same time viewing the ID process itself in situated terms, and makes a number of specific recommendations for practicing ID from a situated/constructivist perspective.

Journal Articles

Antonioni, David. (1995, Summer). Problems associated with implementation of an effective upward appraisal feedback process: An experimental field study. **Human Resource Development Quarterly, 6**(2), 157-71. EJ 507 024. Reports on an investigation of the effects of written upward appraisal reports (feedback) and performance reviews on the supervisory behavior of 96 managers.

Barker, Philip, and Banerji, Ashok. (1995, February). Designing electronic performance support systems. **Innovations in Education and Training International, 32**(1), 4-12. EJ 501 748. (Available UMI.) Outlines the basic nature of performance support and describes a generic model that can be used to facilitate electronic performance support system (EPSS) development.

Becker, Richard D. (1995, May-June). Task analysis without trauma. **Performance and Instruction, 34**(5), 4-7. EJ 508 637. (Available UMI.) Defines and discusses task analysis and presents a method by which goals can be achieved with the integration of task analysis and design.

Carr, Clay, and Totzke, Larry. (1995, April). The long and winding path (from instructional design to performance technology). Installment III: Four requirements for success in HPT. **Performance and Instruction, 34**(4), 7-10. EJ 501 827. (Available UMI.) This third part in a series of six articles on human performance technology (HPT) highlights four characteristics that are needed for managers to successfully advance from practicing training to practicing HPT.

Carr, Clay, and Totzke, Larry. (1995, May-June). The long and winding path (from instructional design to performance technology). Installment IV: Two basic tools of human performance technology. **Performance and Instruction, 34**(5), 12-16. EJ 508 638. (Available UMI.) Discusses two tools necessary for the successful practice of human performance technology: gathering data and interpreting data.

Collis, Betty, and Verwijs, Carla. (1995, February). Evaluating electronic performance support systems: A methodology focused on future use-in-practice. **Innovations in Education and Training International, 32**(1), 23-30. EJ 501 750. (Available UMI.) Discussion of evaluation methodology for computer software focuses on the evaluation of electronic performance support systems.

Collis, Betty A., and Verwijs, Carla. (1995, January-February). A human approach to electronic performance and learning support systems: Hybrid EPSSs. **Educational Technology, 35**(1), 5-21. EJ 496 582. (Available UMI.) Examination of new types of educational software focuses on electronic performance support systems (EPSSs).

Conlon, Tom, and Bowman, Norman. (1995, May). Expert systems, shells, and schools: Present practice, future prospects. **Instructional Science, 23**(1-3), 111-31. EJ 510 298. (Available UMI.) Examines present and future uses of expert system shells in schools, assesses three expert system shells, and proposes criteria for future learning by knowledge-based models.

Cyboran, Vince. (1995, May-June). Designing feedback for computer-based training. **Performance and Instruction, 34**(5), 18-23. EJ 508 639. (Available UMI.) Argues that purposeful design of feedback during computer-based training development projects is necessary for an instructionally sound product and examines various aspects of feedback.

Davis, David. (1995, February). Electronic performance support systems in elementary and secondary schools. **Innovations in Education and Training International, 32**(1), 31-34. EJ 501 751. (Available UMI.) Discusses the emergence of electronic performance support systems and describes some of the ways in which electronic performance support is now influencing learning strategies in elementary and secondary schools.

Dick, Walter. (1995, July-August). Instructional design and creativity: A response to the critics. **Educational Technology, 35**(4), 5-11. EJ 507 033. (Available UMI.) Discusses creativity and instructional system design (ISD) in light of situated cognition, constructivism, and anchored instruction.

Dick, Walter, and Wager, Walter. (1995). Preparing performance technologists: The role of a university. **Performance Improvement Quarterly, 8**(4), 34-42. EJ 512 310. Describes how the instructional systems program at Florida State University has responded to the changes that are required to expand its orientation from instructional technology to performance technology.

Haag, Brenda Bannan, and Grabowski, Barbara L. (1995, March-April). The design of CD-I: Incorporating instructional design principles. **Educational Technology, 35**(2), 36-39. EJ 499 827. (Available UMI.) Examines the characteristics of Compact Disc Interactive (CD-I) in terms of current learning theory and instructional design principles.

Harless, Joe H. (1995). Performance technology skills in business: Implications for preparation. **Performance Improvement Quarterly, 8**(4), 75-88. EJ 512 313. Reports the results of a survey of 23 business organizations regarding the current effectiveness of performance technologists and current preparation of people for the role.

Kerres, Micheal. (1995, June). Integrating CAL into the organisational context as an instructional design task. **Journal of Computer Assisted Learning, 11**(2), 79-89. EJ 505 418. (Available UMI.) Discusses instructional design and the integration of computer-assisted learning (CAL) into corporate training.

Larson, Timothy R. (1995, Winter). Making an interactive calculus textbook. **Journal of Interactive Instruction Development, 7**(3), 20-24. EJ 499 759. Presents a case study of the design and production of *Interactive Calculus,* an interactive multimedia textbook.

Lin, Xiaodong, and others. (1995, September-October). Instructional design and development of learning communities: An invitation to a dialogue. **Educational Technology, 35**(5), 53-63. EJ 512 186. (Available UMI.) Discusses insights from both the instructional design community and members of research groups seeking to transform typical classrooms into "learning communities," and encourages discussion among members of these two communities.

Loosmore, Judy. Color in instructional communication. **Performance and Instruction, 33**(10), 36-38. EJ 495 219. (Available UMI.) Presents guidelines for using color effectively in instructional communication.

McFarland, Ronald D. (1995, February). Ten design points for the human interface to instructional multimedia. **T.H.E. Journal, 22**(7), 67-69. EJ 499 716. (Available UMI.) Explains 10 factors to be considered in designing an effective human-computer interface, including appropriate screen presentations; the relationship of packaging and message; effectiveness of visuals and text; use of color, illustrations, and icons; redundancy; and culturally sensitive presentations.

Madhumita, and Kumar, K. L. (1995, May-June). Twenty-one guidelines for effective instructional design. **Educational Technology, 35**(3), 58-61. EJ 503 497. (Available UMI.) Discusses theories of learning; reviews previous generalizations for instructional design; and presents 21 guidelines for effective instructional design that are related to planning, preparation, implementation, and evaluation.

Mann, Bruce. (1995, January). Enhancing educational software with audio: Assigning structural and functional attributes from the SSF model. **British Journal of Educational Technology, 26**(1), 16-29. EJ 499 778. (Available UMI.) The Structured Sound Function (SSF) Model is proposed as a method for adding audio to educational computer programs.

Medsker, Karen, and others. (1995). HPT in academic curricula: Survey results. **Performance Improvement Quarterly, 8**(4), 6-21. EJ 512 308. Describes a survey that determined the extent to which human performance technology (HPT) is being taught in 82 academic programs that traditionally emphasized training.

Moersch, Christopher. (1995, November). Levels of Technology Implementation (LoTi): A framework for measuring classroom technology use. **Learning and Leading with Technology 23**(3), 40-42. EJ 515 029. Describes the Levels of Technology Implementation (LoTi) framework, which is designed to help school districts restructure staff development curricula to include concept/process based instruction, authentic uses of technology, and qualitative assessment.

Sammons, Martha C. (1995, May). Students assess computer-aided classroom presentations. **T.H.E. Journal, 22**(10), 66-69. EJ 503 458. (Available UMI.) Describes results of a pilot program conducted at Wright State University in which students judged instructors on their use of computer-aided classroom presentations.

Savery, John R. and Duffy, Thomas M. (1995, September-October). Problem based learning: An instructional model and its constructivist framework. **Educational Technology, 35**(5), 31-38. EJ 512 183. (Available UMI.) Discusses the link between the theoretical principles of constructivism, the practice of instructional design, and the practice of teaching.

Schuster, James M. (1995, May-June). Learning to improve learning: A case study. **Educational Technology, 35**(3), 23-25. EJ 503 490. (Available UMI.) Describes an improvement program based on total quality management concepts that was developed at an IBM facility for use in training employees.

Solomon, Gwen, and Solomon, Stan. (1995, November). Technology and professional development—10 tips to make it better. **Learning and Leading with Technology, 23**(3), 38-39,71. EJ 515 028. Offers 10 suggestions for improving professional development courses so that they encourage teachers to use technology in the classroom.

Stape, Christopher J. (1995, March). Techniques for developing higher-level objective test questions. **Performance and Instruction, 34**(3), 31-34. EJ 499 897. (Available UMI.) Discusses taxonomies that define learning outcomes and provides examples of various types of tests.

Thoms, Karen J., and Kellerman, Debra K. (1995, April). Ask a silly question, get a silly answer: Designing effective questionnaires for needs assessment instruments. **Performance and Instruction, 34**(4), 4-6. EJ 501 826. (Available UMI.) Provides eight guidelines for the effective design of questionnaires to be used in the assessment of training needs.

Wilson, Brent G. (1995, September-October). Metaphors for instruction: Why we talk about learning environments. **Educational Technology, 35**(5), 25-30. EJ 512 182. (Available UMI.) Defines constructivist learning environments and explains why the idea is worthy of study.

Yelon, Stephen. (1995, May-June). Active learning: A taxonomy of trainee activities. **Performance and Instruction, 34**(5), 38-41. EJ 508 640. (Available UMI.) Provides a comprehensive view of active learning based on the premise that learning to do a task via instruction is a cumulative process.

Zeitz, Leigh E. (1995, April). Developing a technology workshop series for your faculty and staff. **Computing Teacher, 22**(7), 62-64. EJ 499 917. Describes the development of 13 technology workshops for school personnel based on a needs assessment questionnaire.

Computer Software

Authorware Academic [and] Director Academic. Prentice Hall, Technical Reference Division, Box 11073, Des Moines, IA 50381-1073. (800) 811-0912. Fax (515) 284-2607. $150 per program. Two software programs for creating multimedia instructional materials have been developed by Macromedia and Prentice Hall for use by instructors. Both are available in versions for Macintosh (CD-ROM) and for Windows (CD-ROM). Authorware Academic enables educators who don't have years of instructional design experience to build multimedia lessons right from the start, while Director Academic provides for the integration of a variety of media types to build real world learning materials.

Online Products

Training Media Database. (1996). National Information Center for Educational Media (NICEM), P.O. Box 8640, Albuquerque, NM 87198-8640. (505) 265-3591; (800) 926-8328. Fax (505) 256-1080. E-mail: nicem@nicem.com. The portion of the NICEM database that deals with human resource issues is now being offered by the Human Resource Information Network Corporation (HRIN). It comprises approximately 100,000 records describing nonprint media materials appropriate for corporate and industrial training, staff development, and personnel management. For additional information, contact HRIN Corp., 7200 Wisconsin Ave., Suite 601, Bethesda, MD 20814. (800) 638-8094; (301) 961-6749. Fax (301) 961-6720.

LIBRARIES AND MEDIA CENTERS

Media-Related Periodicals

Book Report. Linworth Publishing, 480 E. Wilson Bridge Rd., Suite L, Worthington, OH 43085-2372. 5/school yr.; $39 U.S., $47 Canada, $9 single copy. Journal for junior and senior high school librarians provides articles, tips, and ideas for day-to-day school library management, as well as reviews of audiovisuals and software, all written by school librarians.

Collection Building. M.C.B. University Press Ltd., 60-62 Toller Ln., Bradford, W. Yorks. BD8 9BY, England. q.; $89. Focuses on all aspects of collection building, ranging from microcomputers to business collections to popular topics and censorship.

College and Research Libraries. Association of College and Research Libraries, 50 E. Huron St., Chicago, IL 60611. bi-mo.; $50 U.S. nonmembers, $55 Canada and Spain, $60 elsewhere, $14 single copy. Publishes articles of interest to college and research librarians.

Computers in Libraries. Information Today, Inc. (formerly Learned Information, Inc.), 143 Old Marlton Pike, Medford, NJ 08055-8750. 10/yr.; $87.95 U.S.; $97.95 Canada, Mexico; £68 Europe; $105.95 outside Europe. Covers practical applications of microcomputers to library situations and recent news items.

Electronic Library. Learned Information Europe Ltd., Woodside, Hinksey Hill, Oxford OX1 5BE, UK. 6/yr.; £95; $106 North America only. For librarians and information center managers interested in microcomputer and library automation. Features industry news and product announcements.

Emergency Librarian. Box 34069, Dept. 284, Seattle, WA 98124-1069. bi-mo. (except July-August); $49. Articles, review columns, and critical analyses of management and programming issues for children's and young adult librarians.

Government Information Quarterly. JAI Press, 55 Old Post Rd., No. 2, P.O. Box 1678, Greenwich, CT 06836-1678. q.; $70 indiv., $90 foreign; $145 inst., $165 foreign. International journal of resources, services, policies, and practices.

Information Services and Use. Elsevier Science Publishers, Box 10558, Burke, VA 22009-0558. 4/yr.; $220. Contains data on international developments in information management and its applications. Articles cover online systems, library automation, word processing, micrographics, videotex, and telecommunications.

Journal of Academic Librarianship. JAI Press, 55 Old Post Rd., No. 2, Box 1678, Greenwich, CT 06836-1678. bi-mo.; $50 indiv., $80 foreign; $145 inst., $165 foreign. Results of significant research, issues and problems facing academic libraries, book reviews, and innovations in academic libraries.

Journal of Government Information (formerly **Government Publications Review**). Elsevier Science Ltd., Journals Division, 660 White Plains Rd., Tarrytown, NY 10591-5153. bi-mo.; £251, $400 U.S. An international journal covering production, distribution, bibliographic control, accessibility, and use of government information in all formats and at all levels.

Journal of Librarianship and Information Science. Worldwide Subscription Service Ltd., Unit 4, Gibbs Reed Farm, Ticehurst, E. Sussex TN5 7HE, England. q.; $125. Deals with all aspects of library and information work in the United Kingdom and reviews literature from international sources.

Journal of Library Administration. Haworth Press, 10 Alice St., Binghamton, NY 13904-1580. q.; $36 indiv., $94.50 inst. Provides information on all aspects of effective library management, with emphasis on practical applications.

Library Hi Tech. Pierian Press, Box 1808, Ann Arbor, MI 48106. q.; $45 indiv.; $75 inst. Concentrates on reporting on the selection, installation, maintenance, and integration of systems and hardware.

Library and Information Science Research. Ablex Publishing Corp., 355 Chestnut St., Norwood, NJ 07648. q.; $45 indiv., $95 inst. Research articles, dissertation reviews, and book reviews on issues concerning information resources management.

Library Journal. Box 59690, Boulder, CO 80322-9690. 20/yr.; $94.50 U.S., $116 Canada, $159 elsewhere. A professional periodical for librarians, with current issues and news, professional reading, lengthy book review section, and classifieds.

Library Quarterly. University of Chicago Press, Journals Division, Box 37005, Chicago, IL 60637. q.; $32 indiv., $37.24 Canada, $35 elsewhere; $58 inst., $65.06 Canada, $61 elsewhere; $25 students, $29.71 Canada, $28 elsewhere. Scholarly articles of interest to librarians.

Library Resources and Technical Services. Association for Library Collections and Technical Services, 50 E. Huron St., Chicago, IL 60611-2795. q.; $55 nonmembers U.S., Canada, and Mexico; $65 elsewhere. Scholarly papers on bibliographic access and control, preservation, conservation, and reproduction of library materials.

Library Software Review. Sage Publications, Inc., 2455 Teller Rd., Thousand Oaks, CA 91320. q.; $49 indiv., $152 U.S. inst.; foreign add $8. Emphasizes practical aspects of library computing for libraries of all types, including reviews of automated systems ranging from large-scale mainframe-based systems to microcomputer-based systems, and both library-specific and general-purpose software used in libraries.

Library Trends. University of Illinois Press, Journals Dept., 1325 S. Oak St., Champaign, IL 61820. q.; $50 indiv. U.S.; $75 inst. U.S.; add $7 for overseas. Each issue is concerned with one aspect of library and information science, analyzing current thought and practice and examining ideas that hold the greatest potential for the field.

LISA: Library and Information Science Abstracts. Bowker-Saur Ltd., Maypole House, Maypole Rd., E. Grinsted, W. Sussex, RH19 1HH, England. mo.; $675 U.S.; £380 elsewhere. More than 500 abstracts per issue from more than 500 periodicals, reports, books, and conference proceedings.

Microcomputers for Information Management. Ablex Publishing, 355 Chestnut St., Norwood, NJ 07648. q.; $40 indiv., $120 inst. Focuses on new developments with microcomputer technology in libraries and in information science in the United States and abroad.

The Public-Access Computer Systems Review. An electronic journal published on an irregular basis by the University Libraries, University of Houston, Houston, TX 77204-2091. Free to libraries. E-mail: LThompson@uh.edu. Contains articles about all types of computer systems that libraries make available to their patrons and technologies to implement these systems.

Public Libraries. Public Library Association, American Library Association, 50 E. Huron St., Chicago, IL 60611-2795. bi-mo.; $50 U.S. nonmembers, $60 elsewhere, $10 single copy. News and articles of interest to public librarians.

Public Library Quarterly. Haworth Press, 10 Alice St., Binghamton, NY 13904. q.; $40 indiv., $90 inst. Addresses the major administrative challenges and opportunities that face the nation's public libraries.

Reference Librarian. Haworth Press, 10 Alice St., Binghamton, NY 13904-9981. 2 vols./yr.; $60 indiv., $120 inst. per vol.; 2 issues per vol. Each issue focuses on a topic of current concern, interest, or practical value to reference librarians.

RQ. Reference and Adult Services Division, American Library Association, 50 E. Huron St., Chicago, IL 60611-2795. q.; $42 nonmembers North America, $52 elsewhere, $12 single copy. Covers all aspects of library service to adults, and reference service and collection development at every level and for all types of libraries.

School Library Journal. Box 57599, Boulder, CO 80322-7559. mo.; $79.50 U.S., $105 Canada, $125 elsewhere. For school and youth service librarians. Contains about 2,500 critical book reviews annually.

School Library Media Activities Monthly. LMS Associates, 17 E. Henrietta St., Baltimore, MD 21230. 10/yr.; $49 U.S., $54 elsewhere. A vehicle for distributing ideas for teaching library media skills and for the development and implementation of library media skills programs.

School Library Media Quarterly. American Association of School Librarians, American Library Association, 50 E. Huron St., Chicago, IL 60611-2795. q.; $40 nonmembers U.S., $50 elsewhere, $12 single copy. For library media specialists, district supervisors, and others concerned with the selection and purchase of print and nonprint media and with the development of programs and services for preschool through high school libraries.

Special Libraries. Special Libraries Association, 1700 18th St., NW, Washington, DC 20009-2508. q.; $60 nonmembers (foreign $65), $10 single copy. Discusses administration, organization, and operations. Includes reports on research, technology, and professional standards.

The Unabashed Librarian. Box 2631, New York, NY 10116. q.; $30 U.S., $36 elsewhere. Down-to-earth library items: procedures, forms, programs, cataloging, booklists, software reviews.

Voice of Youth Advocates. Scarecrow Press, 52 Liberty St., Box 4167, Metuchen, NJ 08840. bi-mo.; $38.50 U.S., $43.50 elsewhere. Contains articles, bibliographies, and media reviews of materials for or about adolescents.

Wilson Library Bulletin. H. W. Wilson Co., 950 University Ave., Bronx, NY 10452. 10/yr.; $52 U.S., $58 elsewhere. Print edition ceased June 1995. Now available URL:http://www. hwwilson.com/default.html. Also available in microform from UMI, PMC. Significant articles on librarianship, news, and reviews of films, books, and professional literature.

Books

Bruwelheide, Janis H. (1995). **The copyright primer for librarians and educators. 2d ed.** Book Order Fulfillment, American Library Association, 155 North Wacker Drive, Chicago, IL 60606-1719. 133pp. ALA Members: $19.80; Others: $22; or NEA Professional Library, P.O. Box 509, West Haven, CT 06516. This guide provides a concise overview of current copyright law and its interpretations that are of particular interest to classroom educators, librarians, school media specialists, and their constituents.

Information for a new age: Redefining the librarian. A Library Instruction Round Table (LIRT) 15th anniversary publication. (1995). Libraries Unlimited, P.O. Box 6633, Englewood, CO 80155-6633. 192pp. $26.50. The 14 papers and essays in this volume describe approaches to proactive interaction with library users with the single goal of achieving an information literate society.

Simpson, Carol Mann. (1995). **Internet for school library media specialists.** Linworth Publishing, Inc., Ordering Dept., 480 E. Wilson Bridge Rd., Worthington, OH 43085. 144pp. $23.95. Provides easy step-by-step instructions that guide the user from getting online to helping students and administrators understand how to use the Internet.

Valauskas, Edward J., and John, Nancy R. (1995). **The Internet initiative: Libraries providing Internet services and how they plan, pay, and manage.** American Library Association, Book Order Fulfillment, 155 N. Wacker Dr., Chicago, IL 60606. 240pp. $25. The 18 reports in this sourcebook detail the organization, governance, and use of Internet services in all types and sizes of libraries and library agencies.

ERIC Documents

Crannell, Philip A. (1995). **Multimedia centers: Concepts for the future.** Paper presented to the Florida Library Association, Fort Lauderdale, FL, May 9-12, 1995. 89pp. ED 385 250. Created to support librarians in the planning and rethinking of new multimedia libraries, this guide provides an illustration of important issues involved in ensuring multimedia service and flexibility.

Journal Articles

Adams, Judith A., and Bonk, Sharon C. (1995, March). Electronic information technologies and resources: Use by university faculty and faculty preferences for related library services. EJ 499 854. **College and Research Libraries, 56**(2), 119-31. (Available UMI.) A survey conducted by the SUNY University Center Libraries to assess faculty use of electronic information technologies and resources at Albany, Binghamton, Buffalo, and Stony Brook revealed inequities in access to electronic information among disciplines, and a lack of knowledge about resources.

Balas, Janet L. (1995, September). Of mice and keyboards: Ergonomic information online. **Computers in Libraries, 15**(8), 30,32-33. EJ 512 255. (Available UMI.) Discusses online resources on ergonomics for librarians seeking to improve working environments or planning for staff and public work areas.

Barron, Daniel D. (1995, October). Converging and complementary technologies, techniques, and professions. **School Library Media Activities Monthly, 12**(2), 48-50. EJ 510 472. Discussion of the effects of technology on elementary and secondary education focuses on the interrelationship of technologies, teaching techniques, school librarians, and computer service professionals.

Bartlett, Virginia. (1995, Fall). Technostress and librarians. **Library Administration and Management, 9**(4), 226-30. EJ 513 748. (Available UMI.) Presents causes and symptoms of "technostress," which is caused by rapidly changing technology in the workplace, together with solutions for dealing with the problem.

Blodgett, Teresa, and Repman, Judi. (1995, January-February). The electronic school library resource center: Facilities planning for the new information technologies. **Emergency Librarian, 22**(3), 26-30. EJ 497 898. (Available UMI.) Addresses the necessity of incorporating new computer technologies into school library resource centers and notes some administrative challenges.

Catenazzi, Nadia, and Sommaruga, Lorenzo. (1995, September). Hyper-lib: A formal model for an electronic library based on hyper-books. **Journal of Documentation, 51**(3), 244-70. EJ 513 758. Presents hyper-lib, a model for an electronic library, and defines the model in terms of structural and functional components.

Eaton, Gale, and McCarthy, Cheryl. (1995, September-October). The art of the possible: Integrating information skills and literature into the curriculum. **Emergency Librarian, 23**(1), 24-28,30. EJ 512 292. (Available UMI.) Describes a case study that investigated how a part-time elementary school teacher-librarian was working toward fulfilling the goals of AASL's *Information Power.*

Eisenberg, Michael B., and Berkowitz, Robert E. (1995, August). The six study habits of highly effective students: Using the Big Six to link parents, students, and homework. **School Library Journal, 41**(8), 22-25. EJ 510 346. (Available UMI.) Presents the Big Six and its problem solving strategies for students in all grade levels and subject areas.

Glogoff, Stuart. (1995). Library instruction in the electronic library: The University of Arizona's Electronic Library Education Centers. **RSR: Reference Services Review, 23**(2), 7-12,39. EJ 501 768. (Available UMI.) Discusses two Electronic Library Education Centers (ELECs) created at the University of Arizona to improve library instruction in the use of online resources.

Grover, Robert, and Carabell, Janet. (1995, January). Diagnosing information needs in a school library media center. **School Library Media Activities Monthly, 11**(5), 32-36,48. EJ 496 537. Discussion of the role of the school library media specialist focuses on how to diagnose information needs.

Haycock, Ken. (1995, Summer). Research in teacher-librarianship and the institutionalization of change. **School Library Media Quarterly, 23**(4), 227-33. EJ 510 340. (Available UMI.) Reviews research in school librarianship and the implementation of change, highlighting the characteristics of effective programs that affect student achievement and have the support of school administrators.

Krashen, Stephen D. (1995, Summer). School libraries, public libraries, and the NAEP reading scores. **School Library Media Quarterly, 23**(4), 235-37. EJ 510 341. (Available UMI.) Discussion of the relationship between reading ability and library quality and use focuses on results of a multiple regression analysis of data that examined fourth-grade scores on the 1992 NAEP Reading Comprehension test.

Jansen, Barbara A. (1995, December). Authentic products: The motivating factor in library research projects. **School Library Media Activities Monthly, 12**(4), 26-27. EJ 515 153. Provides guidelines for designing an "authentic project" that is the result of an information search based on a problem-driven task.

Kuhlthau, Carol Collier. (1995, January). The process of learning from information. **School Libraries Worldwide, 1**(1), 1-12. EJ 503 404. Describes the Information Search Process Approach as a model for developing information skills fundamental to information literacy, and discusses process learning.

McGregor, Joy H. (1995, January). Process or product: Constructing or reproducing knowledge. **School Libraries Worldwide, 1**(1), 28-40. EJ 503 406. Discusses how one-on-one interaction between teacher-librarians and students can turn library research projects into positive experiences in which students use a process of constructing knowledge for themselves rather than reproducing knowledge they find in information sources.

Marson, Barbara Miller, and others, eds. (1995, Fall). Resource sharing. Acting locally: Resource sharing through a community network [and] A new vision for resource sharing: TRLN Document Delivery Project [and] The Internet comes to school [and] Vision becomes reality [and] Just say no?: Special collections and interlibrary loan [and] The birth and growth of library resource sharing in Wayne County; [and] *North Carolina Libraries*: The ultimate resource sharing [and] Resource sharing: A webliography. **North Carolina Libraries, 53**(3), 97-123. EJ 513 814. (Available UMI.) Eight articles discuss resource sharing in a variety of settings.

Neuman, Delia, and others, eds. (1995, Fall). Current research. Restructuring elementary schools to help at-risk students become effective readers: Present strategies and future directions of "success for all" [and] Notes from ERIC. **School Library Media Quarterly, 24**(1), 35-43. EJ 513 780. (Available UMI.) The first of two articles discusses the features and structure of the "Success for All" (SFA) reading program and presents findings from an evaluation of SFA sites in four cities. The second summarizes eight documents and five articles about SFA that are abstracted in the ERIC database.

Rotman, Laurie, and others. (1995, March-April). The Draper Gopher: A team approach to building a virtual library. **Online, 19**(2), 21-24, 26, 28. EJ 499 836. (Available UMI.) Describes the creation of the Draper Laboratory Library, which resulted in user focused reference services; increased interlibrary loan services; replacement of the public catalog; and increased library credibility and recognition.

Stripling, Barbara K. (1995, Spring). Learning-centered libraries: Implications from research. **School Library Media Quarterly, 23**(3), 163-70. EJ 503 400. (Available UMI.) Implications from research suggest that library programs must be based around learning, that students' prior learning or mental models affect new learning, and that no significant learning occurs unless students are supported in their content and process learning.

Todd, Ross J. (1995, January). Information literacy: Philosophy, principles, and practice. **School Libraries Worldwide, 1**(1), 54-68. EJ 503 408. Provides a philosophical framework for the development of information literacy programs integrated into school curriculums; reports on research in Australia that examines the impact of integrated information literacy programs on secondary school student learning and attitudes; and explores general principles for information literacy instructional design.

Wallio, Wendy. (1995, May). Special children and the library media center. **School Library Media Activities Monthly, 11**(9), 31,34,38. EJ 501 802. Discusses how a school library media specialist can serve the needs of physically and mentally disabled K-6 students.

Walter, Virginia A. (1995). Kids count: Using output measures to monitor children's use of reference services. **Reference Librarian,** (49-50), 165-78. EJ 508 703. Examines three publications as guides for evaluating library reference services, and the potential of one for the development of children's services.

Wikel, Nancy. (1995, January-February). A community connection: The public library and home schoolers. **Emergency Librarian, 22**(3), 13-15. EJ 497 896. (Available UMI.) Describes two main groups of home schoolers, "ideological" and "pedagogical," and suggests 12 ways in which libraries can serve home schoolers' information needs.

Online/Electronic Resources

ICONnect. American Association of School Librarians (AASL), American Library Association (ALA), 50 East Huron St., Chicago, IL 60611. Gopher address: ericir.syr.edu 7070. Gopher URL: gopher://ericir.syr.edu:7070/. Home page address: http://ericir.syr.edu/ICONN/ihome.html. A technology initiative of AASL and ALA, ICONnect is designed to get students, library media specialists, and teachers connected to learning using the Internet. Its resources are designed to help students develop information and visual literacy skills, and to train teachers and library media specialists to navigate the Internet effectively and to develop and use meaningful curriculum connections.

MEDIA TECHNOLOGIES

Media-Related Periodicals

Broadcasting and Cable (formerly **Broadcasting**). Box 6399, Torrence, CA 90504. w.; $117 U.S., $320 elsewhere. All-inclusive newsweekly for radio, television, cable, and allied business.

CableVision. Cablevision Magazine, Box 7698, Riverton, NJ 08077-7698. 26/yr.; $55 U.S., $85 Canada, $165 elsewhere. A newsmagazine for the cable television industry. Covers programming, marketing, advertising, business, and other topics.

Communication Abstracts. Sage Publications, Inc., 2455 Teller Rd., Thousand Oaks, CA 91320. bi-mo.; $147 indiv., $474 inst. Abstracts communication-related articles, reports, and books. Cumulated annually.

Communication Booknotes. Center for Advanced Study in Telecommunications (CAST), Ohio State University, 210 E. Baker Systems, 1971 Neil Ave., Columbus, OH 43210-1971. bi-mo.; $45 indiv., $95 inst. (add $5 for foreign). Newsletter that reviews books and periodicals about mass media, telecommunications, and information policy.

Communications News. Nelson Publishing Co., 2504 N. Tamiami Trail, Nokomis, FL 34275. mo.; $50 (free to qualified personnel). Up-to-date information from around the world regarding voice, video, and data communications.

Document and Image Automation (formerly **Optical Information Systems Magazine**). Meckler Publishing Corp., 11 Ferry Lane W., Westport, CT 06880-5808. bi-mo.; $125. Features articles on the applications of videodisc, optical disc, and teletext systems; future implications; system and software compatibilities; and cost comparisons. Also tracks videodisc projects and covers world news.

Document and Image Automation Update (formerly **Optical Information Systems Update**). Meckler Publishing Corp., 11 Ferry Lane W., Westport, CT 06880-5808. 12/yr.; $297. News and facts about technology, software, courseware developments, calendar, conference reports, and job listings.

Educational Media International. Turpin Distribution Services Ltd., Blackhorse Road, Letchworth, Herts. SG6 1HN, England. q.; £45; $85 U.S. The official journal of the International Council for Educational Media.

Federal Communications Commission Reports. Superintendent of Documents, Government Printing Office, Box 371954, Pittsburgh, PA 15250-7954. irreg.; price varies. Decisions, public notices, and other documents pertaining to FCC activities.

Historical Journal of Film, Radio, and Television. Carfax Publishing Co., 875-81 Massachusetts Ave., Cambridge, MA 02139. q.; £60 indiv., £208 inst. Articles by international experts in the field, news and notices, and book reviews.

International Journal of Instructional Media. Westwood Press, Inc., 23 E. 22nd St., 4th floor, New York, NY 10010. q.; $105 per vol. Articles discuss specific applications and techniques for bringing the advantages of a particular instructional medium to bear on a complete curriculum system or program.

Journal of Broadcasting and Electronic Media. Broadcast Education Association, 1771 N St., NW, Washington, DC 20036. q.; $75 U.S., $90 elsewhere. Includes articles, book reviews, research reports, and analyses. Provides a forum for research relating to telecommunications and related fields.

Journal of Educational Television. Carfax Publishing Co., 875-81 Massachusetts Ave., Cambridge, MA 02139. 3/yr.; $128 indiv., $352 inst. This journal of the Educational Television Association serves as an international forum for discussions and reports on developments in the field of television and related media in teaching, learning, and training.

Journal of Popular Film and Television. Heldref Publications, 1319 Eighteenth St., NW, Washington, DC 20036-1802. q.; $34 indiv., $66 inst. Articles on film and television, book reviews, and theory.

Media International. Oakfield House, Perrymount Rd., Haywoods Heath, W. Sussex RH16 3BR, England. mo.; £42 to Europe; £76 elsewhere. Contains features on the major media developments and regional news reports from the international media scene.

Multimedia Monitor (formerly **Multimedia and Videodisc Monitor**). Future Systems, Inc., Box 26, Falls Church, VA 22040. mo.; $395 indiv., $150 educational inst. Describes current events in the videodisc marketplace and in training and development.

MultiMedia Schools. Online, Inc., Subscription Dept., 462 Danbury Rd., Wilton, CT 06897-2126. 5/yr.; $38 U.S. and Canada, $51 Mexico, $60 elsewhere. Reviews new titles, evaluates hardware and software, offers technical advice and troubleshooting tips, and profiles high-tech installations.

Technology Connection. Linworth Publishing, Inc., 480 E. Wilson Bridge Rd., Suite L, Worthington, OH 43085-9918. 10/yr.; $39. A forum for K-12 educators who use technology as an educational resource, this journal includes information on what works and what does not, new product reviews, tips and pointers, and emerging technology training.

Telematics and Informatics. Elsevier Science, Journals Division, 660 White Plains Rd., Tarrytown, NY 10591-5153. q.; £395. Contains information on applied telecommunications and information technology, and policy and legislation resource management; examines socioeconomic implications.

Video Systems. Intertec Publishing Corp., 9800 Metcalf, Overland Park, KS 66212-2215. mo.; $45 (free to qualified professionals). For video professionals. Contains state-of-the-art audio and video technology reports.

Videography. Miller Freeman, PSN Publications, 2 Park Ave., 18th floor, New York, NY 10016. mo.; $30. For the video professional; covers techniques, applications, equipment, technology, and video art.

Books

Abrams, Arnie H. (1996). **Multimedia magic: Exploring the power of multimedia production.** Longwood Division, Allyn & Bacon, P.O. Box 10695, Des Moines, IA 50336-0695. 320pp. with Macintosh CD-ROM. $29.95. Presents the knowledge and skills needed to develop multimedia activities using two multimedia programs—Adobe Photoshop and Adobe Premiere—and an authoring package called Digital Chisel.

Agnew, Palmer W., Kellerman, Anne S., and Mayer, Jeanine. (1996). **Multimedia in the classroom.** Longwood Division, Allyn & Bacon, P.O. Box 10695, Des Moines, IA 50336-0695. 308pp. $33.95. Presents a process for planning and coaching multimedia projects that focuses on active, authentic learning experiences, and considers the theory and practice of selecting and modifying projects and assessing students' results. Six projects are featured.

Barron, Ann E., and Orwig, Gary W. (1995). **New technologies for education: A beginner's guide, 2nd ed.** Libraries Unlimited, P.O. Box 6633, Englewood, CO 80155-6633. 250pp. $39. Designed for all educators interested in instructional applications of technology, this book provides an overview of compact disc technologies, videodiscs, digital audio, digitized video, telecommunications, and hypermedia.

Culp, George H., and Watkins, G. Morgan. (1995). **The educator's guide to HyperCard and HyperTalk, rev. ed. HyperCard 2.2 and color tools.** Longwood Division, Allyn & Bacon, P.O. Box 10695, Des Moines, IA 50336-0695. 256pp. with 3 diskettes. $35.95. Designed to enable teachers to design and develop instructional computing materials suited to their individual needs, this guide provides step-by-step instructions for creating applications, art, documents, and databases with emphasis on scripting and color.

Handler, Marianne G., Dana, Ann S., and Moore, Jane Peters. (1995). **Hypermedia as a student tool: A guide for teachers.** Libraries Unlimited, P.O. Box 6633, Englewood, CO, 80155-6633. 272pp. $33.50. This comprehensive guide and activity book is designed to help students build hypermedia skills as they learn in language arts, mathematics, science, social studies, and foreign language.

Knapp, Linda Roehrig, and Glenn, Allen D. (1996). **Restructuring schools with technology.** Longwood Division, Allyn & Bacon, P.O. Box 10695, Des Moines, IA 50336-0695. 208pp. $33.95. Presents arguments for restructuring traditional education that point toward an approach advocating interactive learning through exploration, critical analysis, problem solving, and communication in multiple media.

Valmont, William J. **Creating videos for school use.** (1995). Longwood Division, Allyn & Bacon, P.O. Box 10695, Des Moines, IA 50336-0695. 225pp. $25.95. This non-technical, machine-independent guide is designed to enable teachers to create their own classroom videos and help students create videos as projects.

Yoder, Sharon, and Moursund, David. (1996). **Introduction to MicroWorlds: A logo-based hypermedia environment, 2nd ed.** International Association for Technology in Education, 1787 Agate St., Eugene, OR 97403-1923. 210pp. $27.95 (members $25.15). This updated and revised edition, which covers *MicroWorlds* for the Macintosh and MS-DOS, features the use of *MicroWorlds* objects such as turtles, buttons, text boxes, and sliders, to integrate graphics, color, sound, music, and text into computer-generated projects.

Yoder, Sharon, and Smith, Irene. (1996). **HyperTalk 2.3 for educators—an introduction.** International Association for Technology in Education, 1787 Agate St., Eugene, OR 97403-1923. 424pp. $34.95 (members $31.45). Explains how to create sophisticated HyperCard applications starting with simple, accessible examples and moving on to major concepts.

ERIC Documents

Brumbaugh, Ken. (1995). **K-12 planning guide for videodisc usage for teachers and administrators.** Denton, TX: Texas Center for Educational Technology; and St. Paul, MN: Emerging Technology Consultants, Inc. 56pp. ED 380 124. Presents information on how to integrate videodisc materials into existing K-12 curricula and how to review, evaluate, and select software and hardware.

Bruwelheide, Janis H. (1995, April). **Copyright issues for the electronic age. ERIC Digest.** Syracuse, NY: ERIC Clearinghouse on Information and Technology. 4pp. ED 381 777. Focuses on a variety of issues confronting copyright law in the digital age.

Franchi, Jorge. (1995, June). **Virtual reality: An overview. ERIC Digest.** Syracuse, NY: ERIC Clearinghouse on Information and Technology, Syracuse. 4pp. ED 386 178. Defines

Virtual Reality (VR), describes how it works, and discusses its applications in surgery, scientific exploration, and education and training.

Gibbs, William J. (1995). **Multimedia and computer-based instructional software: Evaluation methods.** Paper given to the Association of Small Computer Users in Education (ASCUE), North Myrtle Beach, SC, June 18-22, 1995. 9pp. ED 387 096. Computerized tracking systems, videotape recording techniques, and verbal protocol analysis are presented as means by which to conduct more direct comprehensive evaluations of multimedia and hypermedia learning environments, as well as for observing learners' information processing.

Winn, William, and others. (1995, April 22). **Semiotics and the design of objects, actions and interactions in virtual environments.** Paper presented to the American Educational Research Association, San Francisco, April 18-22, 1995. 21pp. ED 385 236. Discusses work in the design and construction of virtual environments (VEs) from the standpoint of semiotic theory and describes the use of a constructivist learning paradigm with 120 seventh and eighth graders who undertook the construction of VE worlds through a process based on semiotic-centered practices.

Journal Articles

Ackermann, Frank. (1995, March). Groupware: A useful tool or a salesman's paradise? **Information Management and Technology, 28** (2), 72-75. EJ 501 788. Explores reasons for organizations' use of groups and the need for groupware systems.

Aiken, Milam W., and Hawley, Delvin D. (1995, September). Designing an electronic classroom for large college courses. **T.H.E. Journal, 23**(2), 76-77. EJ 510 473. (Available UMI.) Describes a state-of-the-art electronic classroom at the University of Mississippi School of Business designed for use by large numbers of students and regularly scheduled classes.

Botterbusch, Hope R. (1995, April-May). Copyright activities at InCITE'95. **TechTrends, 40**(3), 8-9. EJ 530 566. (Available UMI.) Reviews copyright issues that were addressed at the InCITE 1995 workshop, including copyright law, fair use guidelines, multimedia issues, copyright policy statements by national professional organizations, legal activities related to the Internet, and multimedia guidelines.

Considine, David M. (1995, July-August). Are we there yet? An update on the media literacy movement. **Educational Technology, 35**(4), 32-43. EJ 507 036. (Available UMI.) Discussion of the media literacy movement addresses topics ranging from "infotainment" and "tabloid-ism" to school restructuring and Goals 2000.

Enser, Peter. (1995, Spring). Image databases for multimedia projects. **Microform Review, 24**(2), 64-68. EJ 508 672. (Available UMI.) Provides an overview of European multimedia imaging projects based in museums, libraries, and other organizations, that are supported by the European Commission (EC) and the British Library Research and Development Department (BLRDD).

Harrigan, Kevin. (1995, Spring). The SPECIAL System: Self-Paced Education with Compressed Interactive Audio Learning. **Journal of Research on Computing in Education, 27**(3), 361-70. EJ 510 363. (Available UMI.) Describes a computer system (SPECIAL) that allows for the capture and playback of audio and slides from a lecture.

Jacobson, Michael J., and Spiro, Rand J. (1995). Hypertext learning environments, cognitive flexibility, and the transfer of complex knowledge: An empirical investigation. **Journal of Educational Computing Research, 12**(4), 301-33. EJ 510 379. Investigated a theory-based learning environment that provided instruction in a complex and ill-structured domain.

Jacques, Richard, and others. (1995, Spring). Engagement as a design concept for multimedia. **Canadian Journal of Educational Communication, 24**(1), 49-59. EJ 510 377. Describes how an understanding of "engagement" can be applied to multimedia systems design and support learning goals and motivation.

Johnson, Doug. (1995, November-December). Lean mean times: Budgeting for school media technology. **MultiMedia Schools, 2**(5), 32-34,36-37. EJ 513 829. (Available UMI.) Discusses budgeting strategies for school media technology programs.

Kearsley, Greg, and Heller, Rachelle S. (1995). Multimedia in public access settings: Evaluation issues. **Journal of Educational Multimedia and Hypermedia, 4**(1), 3-24. EJ 501 782. Examines studies that evaluate public access systems spanning experiments, field tests, and prototypes, and discusses quality control, cost-effectiveness, and issues for future research.

Large, Andrew, and others. (1995, June). Multimedia and comprehension: The relationship among text, animation, and captions. **Journal of the American Society for Information Science, 46**(5), 340-47. EJ 505 389. (Available UMI.) Reports on the second phase of a cognitive study of multimedia and its effects on sixth graders' learning that focused on the relationship among text, animation, and captions.

Litchfield, Brenda. (1995, April). Helping your students plan computer projects. **Computing Teacher, 22**(7), 37-41, 43. EJ 499 916. Discusses a process developed at Moss Point High School (Mississippi) to help students plan their hypermedia projects and help teachers evaluate student efforts and products.

Lookatch, Richard P. (1995, Summer), The strange but true story of multimedia and the Type I Error. **TECHNOS, 4**(2), 10-13. EJ 506 947. Examines the Type I Error in research on multimedia's impact on learning.

Milone, Michael N., Jr. (1995, October). Electronic portfolios: Who's doing them and how? **Technology & Learning, 16**(2), 28-29,32,34,36. EJ 513 735. (Available UMI.) Describes three schools that are successfully developing digital multimedia portfolios for use by students and teachers.

Misanchuk, Earl R., and Schwier, Richard A. (1995, Spring). The mythology of color in multimedia screen design: Art, science, and connoisseurship. **Canadian Journal of Educational Communication, 24**(1), 3-26. EJ 510 375. Summarizes the results of literature on color use in multimedia screen design for instructional purposes; discusses problems and the lack of guidance for instructional designers; and suggests renewed research and the development of a connoisseurial approach to screen design that values the contributions of both research and aesthetic experience.

Moersch, Christopher, and Fisher, Louis M., III. (1995, October). Electronic portfolios: Some pivotal questions. **Learning and Leading with Technology, 23**(2), 10-14. EJ 512 269. Discusses some technical and nontechnical aspects of using electronic portfolios in the classroom with examples from Learning Quest's software for the Macintosh computer.

Peterson, Norman K., and Orde, Barbara J. (1995, February). Implementing multimedia in the middle school curriculum: Pros, cons and lessons learned. **T.H.E. Journal, 22**(7), 70-75. EJ 499 717. (Available UMI.) Describes a study conducted by the University of Wyoming at its laboratory school on the use of multimedia in education.

Tsalgatidou, Aphrodite, and others. (1995, January-February). A Multimedia Title Development Environment (MTDE). **Information Processing and Management, 31**(1), 101-12. EJ 496 660. (Available UMI.) Presents a Multimedia Title Development Environment (MTDE) which integrates multimedia information, tools used to produce it, and their formats and storage media as objects in an Asset Repository for use by cooperative design teams.

Tuttle, Harry Grover. (1995, November-December). The multimedia report: Dos and don'ts of multimedia presentations. **MultiMedia Schools, 2**(5), 28-31. EJ 513 828. (Available UMI.) Presents guidelines for helping students produce effective multimedia presentations.

Weiss, Andrew M. (1995, September-October). What's in the walls: Copper, fiber, or coaxial wiring? **MultiMedia Schools, 2**(4), 34-36,38-39. EJ 510 442. (Available UMI.) Presents planning guidelines for wiring specifications for K-12 schools by reviewing advantages and disadvantages of using copper, fiber-optic, and coaxial wire.

Weiss, Jiri. (1995, September). Digital copyright: Who owns what? **NewMedia, 5**(9), 38-43. EJ 510 397. Examines digital copyright issues for developers and users of CD-ROMS and online information systems.

CD-ROMS

Multimedia University. (1996). Integrated Media Group, 10 Davis Drive, Belmont, CA 94002-3098. 3 CD-ROMs (Macintosh and PC versions). This new CD-ROM-based series presents the principles and practices of multimedia interactively using the tools of multimedia— text, graphics, sound, animation, and motion video. Developed in conjunction with San Francisco State University, the series provides students with hands-on experience and practice in developing multimedia materials. The first three CD-ROMS were issued in 1996: *Introduction to multimedia* ($64.25 each version); *Designing multimedia* (Macintosh $64.25; PC $60.50); and *Producing multimedia* ($64.25 each version).

Online Products

A-V ONLINE. Knight-Ridder Information (formerly Dialog), 2440 El Camino Real, Mountain View, CA 94040. (DIALOG File 46; CompuServe KI046. For information on a tape lease agreement, contact Access Innovations, Inc., P.O. Box 40130, Albuquerque, NM 87196.) Updated quarterly, this NICEM database provides information on nonprint media covering all levels of education and instruction. Nonprint formats covered are 16mm films, videos, audiocassettes, CD-ROMs, software, laserdisc, filmstrips, slides, transparencies, motion cartridges, kits, models, and realia. Entries date from 1964 to the present, with approximately 420,000 records as of January 1995.

NICEM (National Information Center for Educational Media) EZ. NICEM, P.O. Box 8640, Albuquerque, NM 87198-8640. (505) 265-3591; (800) 926-8328. Fax (505) 256-1080. E-mail nicem@nicem.com. For more than 25 years, NICEM has been serving the education and research communities with quality indexes to educational media. NICEM now offers a custom search service—NICEM EZ—to help those without access to the existing NICEM products tap the resources of this specialized database. Fees are $50 per hour search time plus $.20 for each unit identified.

NICEM (National Information Center for Educational Media) Masterfile. NICEM, P.O. Box 8640, Albuquerque, NM 87198-8640. (505) 265-3591; (800) 926-8328. Fax (505) 256-1080. E-mail nicem@nicem.com. NlightN (a division of The Library Corporation). (800) 654-4486; (703) 904-1010. E-mail info@nlightn.com. Web site: http://www.nlightn.com. NlightN, an Internet online service, widens the accessibility of information in the NICEM database to users of the Internet. The NICEM masterfile provides information on nonprint media for all levels of education and instruction in all academic areas.

SIMULATION AND VIRTUAL REALITY

Media-Related Periodicals

Aspects of Educational and Training Technology Series. Kogan Page Ltd., 120 Pentonville Rd., London N1 9JN, England. ann. £35. Covers the proceedings of the annual conference of the Association of Educational and Training Technology.

Simulation and Gaming. Sage Publications, Inc., 2455 Teller Rd., Thousand Oaks, CA 91359. q.; $59 indiv., $200 inst. An international journal of theory, design, and research published by the Association for Business Simulation and Experiential Learning.

Virtual Reality Report. Cobb Group, Inc., 9420 Bunsen Pkwy., Suite 300, Louisville, KY 40220. 12/yr.; $327. Covers developments in the field of virtual reality and cyberspace.

Journal Articles

Dede, Chris. (1995, September-October). The evolution of constructivist learning environments: Immersion in distributed, virtual worlds. **Educational Technology, 35**(5), 46-52. EJ 512 185. (Available UMI.) Discusses the evolution of constructivist learning environments and examines the collaboration of simulated software models, virtual environments, and evolving mental models via immersion in artificial realities.

Goodman, Frederick L. (1995, June). Practice in theory. **Simulation and Gaming, 26**(2), 178-90. EJ 505 425. (Available UMI.) Discussion of games and game-like exercises developed by the author focuses on the relationship between theory and practice in education.

Milheim, William D. (1995). Virtual reality and its potential application in education and training. **Machine-Mediated Learning, 5**(1), 43-55. EJ 506 987. Provides an overview of current trends in virtual reality research and development, and explores the implications for education and training.

Uretsky, Michael. (1995, June). Simulation and gaming: Directions, issues, ponderables. **Simulation and Gaming, 26**(2), 219-24. EJ 505 427. (Available UMI.) Discusses the current use of simulation and gaming in a variety of settings, describes advances in technology that facilitate the use of simulation and gaming, and considers their future use.

TELECOMMUNICATIONS AND NETWORKING

Media-Related Periodicals

Canadian Journal of Educational Communication. Association for Media and Technology in Education in Canada, 3-1750 The Queensway, Suite 1318, Etobicoke, ON M9C 5H5, Canada. 3/yr.; $45 Canada, $45 U.S. elsewhere. Concerned with all aspects of educational systems and technology.

Classroom Connect: Your Practical Monthly Guide to Using the Internet and Commercial Online Services. Wentworth Worldwide Media, P.O. Box 10488, Lancaster, PA 17605-0488. 9/yr.; $39. Provides pointers to sources of lesson plans for K-12 educators as well as descriptions of new World Wide Web sites, addresses for online "keypals," Internet basics for new users, classroom management tips for using the Internet, and online global projects. Each 20-page issue offers Internet adventures for every grade and subject.

Computer Communications. Elsevier Science, Inc., P.O. Box 882, Madison Square Station, New York, NY 10159-0882. 14/yr.; $835. Focuses on networking and distributed computing techniques, communications hardware and software, and standardization.

Data Communications. Box 473, Hightstown, NJ 08520. mo.; $125 U.S., $130 Canada. Provides users with news and analysis of changing technology for the networking of computers.

EDUCOM Review. EDUCOM, 1112 Sixteenth St., NW, Suite 600, Washington, DC 20036-4823. bi-mo.; $18 U.S., $24 Canada, $43 elsewhere. Features articles on current issues and applications of computing and communications technology in higher education. Reports of EDUCOM consortium activities.

EMMS (Electronic Mail & Micro Systems). Telecommunications Reports, 1333 H Street NW, 11th Floor-W., Washington, DC 20005. semi-mo.; $595 U.S., $655 elsewhere. Covers technology, user, product, and legislative trends in graphic, record, and microcomputer applications.

Internet Research (previously **Electronic Networking: Research, Applications, and Policy**). MCB University Press Ltd., 60-62 Toller Ln., Bradford, W. Yorks. BD8 9BY, England. q.; $239. A cross-disciplinary journal presenting research findings related to electronic networks, analyses of policy issues related to networking, and descriptions of current and potential applications of electronic networking for communication, computation, and provision of information services.

Internet World (formerly **Research and Education Networking**). Mecklermedia Corporation. Orders for North and South America, Internet World, P.O. Box 713, Mt. Morris, IL 61054; elsewhere, Mecklermedia Ltd., Artillery House, Artillery Row, London SW1P 1RT, UK. m.; $29 U.S, $44 Canada, Central and South America, £36 elsewhere. Analyzes development with National Research and Education Network, Internet, electronic networking, publishing, and scholarly communication, as well as other network issues of interest to a wide range of network users.

Telecommunications. (North American Edition.) Horizon House Publications, Inc., 685 Canton St., Norwood, MA 02062. mo.; $75 U.S., $135 elsewhere (free to qualified individuals). Feature articles and news for the field of telecommunications.

T.I.E. News (Telecommunications in Education). International Society for Technology in Education, 1787 Agate St., Eugene, OR 97403-1923. q.; $20 members, $29 nonmembers U.S.; $31.40 members, $41.33 nonmembers Canada; $30 members, $29 nonmembers elsewhere. Contains articles on all aspects of educational telecommunications.

Books

Ackermann, Ernest. (1995). **Learning to use the Internet: An introduction with examples and exercises.** Franklin, Beedle and Assocs., 8536 SW St. Helens Dr., Suite D, Wilsonville, OR 97070. 368pp. $17. This hands-on book covers the development of the Internet, proper etiquette, and social and ethical issues, as well as all of the Internet staples and how to use Web browsers such as Mosaic, Lynx, and Netscape.

Ackermann, Ernest. (1996). **Learning to use the World Wide Web: An introduction with examples and exercises.** Franklin, Beedle and Assocs., 8536 SW St. Helens Dr., Suite D, Wilsonville, OR 97070. 404pp. $14.40. This introduction to the Internet through the World Wide Web uses an example-driven approach to show students how to browse the Web using Netscape Navigator. The book is also available with specially packaged Internet software.

Barron, Ann E.,and Ivers, Karen S. (1996). **The Internet and instruction.** Libraries Unlimited, P.O. Box 6633, Englewood, CO 80155-6633. 150pp. $26.50. Intended for educators and students, this guide to telecommunications and the Internet provides exemplary activities that span the curriculum for grades 4-12.

Crossroads on the Information Highway: Convergence and diversity in communications technologies. (1995). The Aspen Institute, P.O. Box 222, 2010 Carmichael Road, Queenstown, MD 21658. 166pp. $10. Each of the seven articles in this volume provides a perspective on either the forces that are influencing the convergence of the telecommunications, computer, and cable television industries or on the impact that this convergence is having on the rest of the world.

Educator's Internet funding guide. (1996). Classroom Connect, 1866 Colonial Village Lane, P.O. Box 10488, Lancaster, PA 17605-0488. 385pp. and diskette. $44.95. Comprehensive reference guide covers how to apply successfully for government, corporate, and foundation grants; develop a groundroots fundraising campaign; prepare a grant; and assess funding needs.

Groves, Dawn. (1996). **The Web page workbook.** Franklin, Beedle and Assocs., 8536 SW St. Helens Dr., Suite D, Wilsonville, OR 97070. 170pp. $15.96. A six-hour, hands-on course in which only rudimentary word processing skills are required enables students to create their own web page on the PC while learning about web-page design techniques, home pages, HTML, and the practical use of web pages. Free copies of *SPRY Mosaic* and *HotDog Web Editor,* and a quick reference HTML card are included.

Leshin, Cynthia. (1995). **Internet adventures: Step-by-step guide for finding and using educational resources.** XPLORA Publishing, 3104 East Camelback Rd., Suite 424, Phoenix, AZ 85016-4595. 321pp. $29.95. The tutorial design of this book for educators and students is intended to have them quickly using Internet tools and integrating resources into the curriculum.

Leshin, Cynthia. (1995). **Netscape adventures: A step-by-step guide to Netscape Navigator and the World Wide Web.** (1995). XPLORA Publishing, 3104 East Camelback Rd., Suite 424, Phoenix, AZ 85016-4595. 149pp. $27.95. A practical guide with hands-on, step-by-step instructions for navigating the Internet using the browser Netscape Navigator to access the World Wide Web, Gopher, FTP, and Usenet newsgroups.

Proceedings of ISTE's Tel-Ed '95 Conference. (1995). [SouthEastern Regional Vision for Education] International Society for Technology in Education, 1787 Agate St., Eugene, OR 97403-1923. 267pp. $20, members $18. Contains papers and detailed abstracts for the sessions at ISTE's International Conference on Telecommunications and Education. Topics covered include distance education and telecommunications projects in all subject areas.

ERIC Documents

Anderson, Susan E., and Harris, Judith B. (1995). **Educators' use of electronic networks: An e-mail survey of account-holders on a statewide telecomputing system.** Paper given to the American Educational Research Association, San Francisco, CA, April 18-22, 1995. 31pp. ED 385 229. This investigation of educators' use of TENET, a statewide educational telecomputing network in Texas, also documented the development and testing of a lengthy theory-based questionnaire and verified the efficacy of a method for administering surveys via electronic mail.

Community Update: Goals 2000. April 1994 to March 1995. (1995). Washington, DC: Department of Education. 54pp. ED 381 151. [**Community Update,** (12-22).] This document comprises 11 issues of a newsletter which provides information to help schools and communities reach the National Education Goals.

Fast, Michael Graham. (1995). **Interaction in technology—Mediated, multisite, foreign language instruction.** Paper presented to the American Educational Research Association, San Francisco, CA, April 18-21, 1995. 36pp. ED 385 231. Designed to provide some evidence to counter the claim that distance learning fails to create the conditions necessary for achieving the goals of widely accepted foreign or second language (L2) communicative curriculum, this study analyzed the discourse generated in Russian L2 classes in two geographically remote high schools linked on the fiber-optic network in the state of Iowa.

Gonzalez, Emilio. (1995, June). **Connecting the nation: Classrooms, libraries, and health care organizations in the information age. Update 1995.** Washington, DC: National Telecommunications and Information Administration [and] Office of Telecommunications (DOC). 41pp. ED 386 184. Connecting every classroom, library, hospital, and clinic in the United States to the National Information Infrastructure (NII) is a priority for the Clinton Administration; this status report on the initiative is based on current data on Internet connectivity, a benchmark for NII access.

Hauck, Rita M. (1995). **Training in the use of the Internet.** Paper presented to the Association of Educational Communications and Technology, Anaheim, CA, February 11, 1995. 17pp. ED 378 953. This outline of ways to teach an introductory workshop about the Internet includes field-tested instruction and materials, training session agendas, exercises, materials for use with or without hands-on computer work, a pre-workshop needs assessment form, an instructor evaluation form, and Internet navigation exercises.

Heaviside, Sheila, and others. (1995, February). **Advanced telecommunications in U.S. public schools, K-12.** Rockville, MD: Westat, Inc. 61pp. ED 378 959. Presents the findings of a survey which gathered data from a nationally representative sample of 1,380 schools regarding the types and location of advanced telecommunications equipment; services currently available; access to the Internet and selected Internet capabilities; plans to implement or upgrade wide area networks; sources of such plans and of the school's budgetary decisions for telecommunications technology; and the various barriers that limit acquisition or use of advanced telecommunications.

Hoadley, Christopher M., and others. (1995). **Networked multimedia for communication and collaboration.** Berkeley, CA: University of California-Berkeley, Graduate Group in Science and Mathematics Education. 21pp. ED 382 181. Describes networked multimedia as a tool for collaborative learning; outlines the background and application of collaborative learning; and examines several dimensions of media that influence the evolution of its use.

Hunter, Barbara, and Bagley, Carole A. (1995). **Global telecommunications projects: Reading and writing with the world.** Stillwater, MN: The Technology Group. 13pp. ED 387 081. This discussion of the potential of telecommunications in education proposes that classrooms begin telecomputing by communicating with electronic pen pals, where students write for a distant audience and learn about different cultures through interaction on the computer, and examines the use of telecommunications in the development of reading, writing, and collaborative research and problem-solving skills.

King, Lisabeth, and others, comps. (1995, May). **Directory of electronic journals, newsletters and academic discussion lists.** Washington, DC: Association of Research Libraries, Office of Scientific and Academic Publishing. Available from the Association of Research Libraries, Office of Scientific and Academic Publishing, 21 Dupont Circle, Suite 800, Washington, DC 20036 (ARL Members: $41; others: $62; plus $5 shipping and handling). 760pp. ED 383 351. This directory is a compilation of entries for nearly 2,500 scholarly discussion lists and 675 electronic journals, newsletters, and related titles such as newsletter-digests, that are available on the Internet. Instructions are provided for accessing each publication.

Knapp, Wallace C. (1995). **Designing and integrating a fiber optic network with an existing copper network.** Paper given to the Association of Small Computer Users in Education (ASCUE), North Myrtle Beach, SC, June 18-22, 1995. 15pp. ED 387 101. Outlines the process that Catonsville Community College (Maryland) went through in moving from a copper to a fiber network, from obtaining management support and writing the request for proposal (RFP) through the implementation of the initial system and the identification of problems with that system.

Langan, John, and Flynn, Richard. (1995, July 30). **Nebraska K-12 Internet evaluation progress report and executive summary—18 months.** Unpublished report, University of Nebraska, Omaha. 102pp. ED 385 246. Fifteen Educational Service Unit (ESU) servers, located across Nebraska, provide access to the Internet for almost all public K-12 schools. An evaluation team from the University of Nebraska at Omaha, in cooperation with the ESUs, is currently investigating the impact of the statewide effort to connect schools and teachers to the Internet.

Ormerod, Dana E. (1995). **Computers across the curriculum: Teaching a computer literacy course for multi-disciplinary use in a network environment—Content and pedagogy.** Paper presented to the Association of Small Computer Users in Education, North Myrtle Beach, SC, June 18-22, 1995. 9pp. ED 387 104. Responses to a survey of applied business associate degree graduates of Kent State University (Ohio) Regional Campuses indicated a need for computer literacy appropriate to the employment situation.

Pereira, Francis, and others. (1995, April). **Building the National Information Infrastructure in K-12 education: A comprehensive survey of attitudes towards linking both sides of the desk.** Los Angeles, CA: University of Southern California, Center for Telecommunications Management Research Report Series. 191pp. ED 387 080. This report of the Global Telecommunications Infrastructure Research Project documents the findings of a survey of 3,145 members of professional education organizations that was designed to elicit their perceptions on four issues concerning the NII (National Information Infrastructure), and to test whether these visions of the NII were shared by educators.

Ruberg, Laurie F., and Taylor, C. David. (1995). **Student responses to network resources: Formative evaluation of two classes.** Paper presented to the American Educational Research Association, San Francisco, CA, April 18-22, 1995. 5pp. ED 385 221. Provides detailed descriptions, analyses, and interpretations of student interactions and participation that occurred in computer-mediated interactive writing activities in two different college classroom network situations.

United States education and instruction through telecommunications: Distance learning for all learners. (1995). Washington, DC: Council of Chief State School Officers; Department of Commerce; [and] National Telecommunications and Information Administration. 92pp. ED 384 343. Available from ERIC only on microfiche; or from the Council of Chief State School Officers, One Massachusetts Ave., N.W., Suite 700, Washington, DC 20001-1431 ($20). Presents the findings and recommendations of the United States Education and Instruction Through Telecommunications (USE IT) project, which assessed the relationship of distance learning to the nation's educational needs at all levels, especially its role in achieving the National Education Goals.

Williams, Arthur E. (1995). **Distance and distance research: The need for Internet proficiency in the shadow of shrinking resources.** Paper given to the Association of Small Computer Users in Education (ASCUE), North Myrtle Beach, SC, June 18-22, 1995. 7pp. ED 387 113. Discusses the need for students and faculty at small, under-funded academic libraries in rural areas to have Internet proficiency so they can access more sources of information.

Yowell, Brenda. (1995). **The world at our fingertips.** Unpublished paper, Burleson Independent School District, TX. 22pp. ED 378 957. This telecommunications project involved teachers sending a message to the listserv KIDLINK, which asked other countries to participate in a "key-pals" program. Groups of students selected one of the 13 participating countries, composed messages off-line, and then uploaded their messages to their foreign computer friends using the Texas Education Network (TENET).

Journal Articles

Barron, Ann E., and Orwig, Gary W. (1995, Summer). Digital video and the Internet: A powerful combination. **Journal of Instruction Delivery Systems, 9**(3), 10-12. EJ 510 389. Provides an overview of digital video and outlines hardware and software necessary for interactive training on the world wide web and for videoconferences via the Internet.

Beck, Susan Gilbert. (1995). A galaxy of rustling stars: Places on the WEB and other library and information paths for the deaf. **Library Hi Tech, 13**(4), 93-100. EJ 513 840. Reviews technological advances of computer and non-computer services for the deaf community, describes world wide web sites and library services that provide information paths for the deaf, and reviews the progress of institutions devoted to deaf education.

Bender, Robert M. (1995, May). Creating communities on the Internet: Electronic discussion lists in the classroom. **Computers in Libraries, 15**(5), 38-43. EJ 506 954. (Available UMI.) This case study offers insights into the process, pitfalls, and advantages of utilizing an Internet electronic discussion list to form a communication community in an undergraduate course that discussed gender differences.

Black, Libby, and others. (1995, May). Observations from the Boulder Valley Internet Project. **T.H.E. Journal, 22**(10), 75-80. EJ 503 460. (Available UMI.) Since the summer of 1991, the Boulder Valley Internet Project has been providing network links between the district's K-12 schools and the community. This article focuses on the project's planning, training, and support issues.

Buchanan, Madeline. (1995, June). Can the Internet be used with K-5 students? The answer is elementary! **Technology Connection, 2**(4), 20,22. EJ 505 410. Available Linworth Publishing, Inc., 480 East Wilson Bridge Rd., Ste. L, Worthington, OH 43085-2372. Description of Internet use for electronic mail projects in elementary education discusses typing directly versus composing offline, and the effect of electronic letter-writing activities on improving grammar, spelling, social studies, science, and mathematics skills.

Carlitz, Robert D., and others. (1995, April). Standards for school networking. **T.H.E. Journal, 22**(9), 71-74. EJ 501 732. (Available UMI.) Discusses standards for the design and implementation of the electronic data networks developed for, and adopted by, the Pittsburgh Public Schools as district policy.

Clayman, Stuart, and others. (1995). The interworking of Internet and ISDN networks for multimedia conferencing. **Information Services and Use, 15**(2), 75-101. EJ 503 533. Examines the interworking between Internet- and ISDN-based conferences, and shows how Internet and ISDN multimedia conferencing environments can be connected.

Doty, Robert. (1995, March). Teacher's aid. **Internet World, 6**(3), 75-77. EJ 499 753. Discusses ways teachers can get free Internet access. A sidebar lists state-supported Internet sites.

Eurich-Fulcer, Rebecca, and Schofield, Janet Ward. (1995, April). Wide-area networking in K-12 education: Issues shaping implementation and use. **Computers and Education, 24**(3), 211-20. EJ 500 646. (Available UMI.) Identifies issues involved in the use of computer networks in K-12, business, and university environments, and reviews elements that play a major role in shaping wide-area networking use in elementary and secondary education.

Evans, V. Tessa Perry. (1995, September 15). Blackout: Preventing racial discrimination on the Net. **Library Journal, 120**(15), 44-46. EJ 510 488. (Available UMI.) Presents issues relating to equity of access to information technology and the Internet for the African American community, and suggests measures that black information professionals can take to ensure universal access to information and affirmative entrepreneurial opportunities.

Fowell, S., and Levy, P. (1995, September). Developing a new professional practice: A model for networked learner support in higher education. **Journal of Documentation, 51**(3), 271-80. EJ 513 759. Examines a new professional practice in higher education that supports learning through computer-mediated communication and offers a preliminary model for its development.

Fowler, Thomas B. (1995, October). How telecommunications improves efficiency and reduces costs. **Telecommunications, 29**(10), 45-46,48,51,53. EJ 512 284. (Available UMI.) Analyzes the effects of information systems and telecommunications on worker productivity.

Free speech and copyright in cyberspace: Legal issues surrounding the Internet. (1995, March). **Online Libraries and Microcomputers 13**(39), p1-4. EJ 499 880. Characterizations of major legal and political issues surrounding the Internet provide a framework for the future development of the Internet and cyberspace: free speech (libel), intellectual property rights (copyright), jurisdictional questions, and privacy.

Freedman, Joan. (1995, November). Using the world wide web to deliver educational software. **Multimedia Monitor, 13**(11), 19-22. EJ 513 80771. Addresses the advantages and disadvantages of using the world wide web (WWW) as an electronic medium to transfer educational materials to students and teachers, reviews educational WWW projects created at the Johns Hopkins School of Medicine, and discusses future trends of educational computing.

Goldberg, Bruce, and Richards, John. (1995, September-October). Leveraging technology for reform: Changing schools and communities into learning organizations. **Educational Technology, 35** (5), 5-16. EJ 512 179. (Available UMI.) Describes the creation and design of Co-NECT, a computer and networking project created by Bolt Beranek and Newman Educational Technologies to help improve teaching and learning in K-12 schools.

Harris, Judi. (1995, March). Educational telecomputing projects: Interpersonal exchanges. **Computing Teacher, 22**(6), 60-64. EJ 499 811. (Available UMI.) Presents six different types of interpersonal exchanges, or educational telecomputing activities, that incorporate the use of interpersonal skills: "keypals," global classrooms, electronic "appearances," electronic monitoring, question-and-answer services, and impersonations.

James, Michael L., and others. (1995, Winter). An exploratory study of the perceived benefits of electronic bulletin board use and their impact on other communication activities. **Journal of Broadcasting and Electronic Media, 39**(1), 30-50. EJ 508 714. (Available UMI.) A random sample of bulletin board users was selected from two online services, and they were interviewed using electronic mail.

Johnson, Doug. (1995, March-April). Captured by the web: K-12 schools and the world-wide web. **Multimedia Schools, 2**(2), 24-30. EJ 499 841. (Available UMI.) Discusses the world wide web, a system used to display and distribute information on the Internet through hypertext links. Topics include browsing software called Mosaic; web resources for elementary and secondary education students and teachers; online educational resources; web server sites; and creating a home page.

Johnson, Doug. (1995, January-February). Student access to Internet: Librarians and teachers working together to teach higher level survival skills. **Emergency Librarian, 22**(3), 8-12. EJ 497 895. (Available UMI.) Discusses issues involving physical and intellectual access to the Internet.

Lomarcan, Diana L. (1995, March). Networks: The basics. **Computers in Libraries, 15**(3), 19-24. EJ 499 912. (Available UMI.) Introduces the information superhighway (the Internet), and presents a guide to navigating it.

McMurdo, George. (1995). Netiquettes for networkers. **Journal of Information Science, 21**(4), 305-18. EJ 510 410. Presents 20 guidelines for networking etiquette taken from electronic and print sources.

Mazur, Joan M., and others. (1995, Summer). Forum: Censorship and electronic communication in the K-12 environment. Right-of-way on the information superhighway: Access and policy issues for schools [and] Censorship and electronic environments in schools [and] The Internet may be the safest haven [and] A delicate balance: Keeping children out of the gutters along the information highway. **TECHNOS, 4**(2), 14-25. EJ 506 948. Four essays discussing Internet use in schools focus on censorship of online information.

Pask, Judith M., and Snow, Carl E. (1995, Fall). Undergraduate instruction and the Internet. **Library Trends, 44**(2), 306-17. EJ 513 798. (Available UMI.) Describes several projects that integrate the Internet and specific Internet resources into undergraduate teaching and learning.

Richardson, Eric C. (1995, October). Internet cum laude. **Internet World, 6**(10), 38-41. EJ 510 429. Discusses Internet's role in colleges and universities.

Rothstein, Russell I., and McKnight, Lee. (1995, October). Architecture and costs of connecting schools to the NII. **T.H.E. Journal, 23**(3), 91-96. EJ 512 286. (Available UMI.) Discusses connecting K-12 schools to the National Information Infrastructure; presents four technology models and the estimated costs for each; and examines programs that could help reduce hardware, training, support, and retrofitting costs, and estimates potential savings.

Silva, Marcos, and Cartwright, Glenn F. (1993, June). The design and implementation of Internet seminars for library users and staff at McGill University. **Education for Information, 11**(2), 137-46. EJ 495 151. Describes seminars developed at McGill University library to teach faculty, students, and staff about the Internet.

Tiene, Drew, and Whitmore, Evonne. (1995, May-June). Beyond "Channel One": How schools are using their schoolwide television networks. **Educational Technology, 35**(3), 38-42. EJ 503 493. (Available UMI.) Examines the use of television equipment in schools that subscribe to Channel One based on a survey of secondary schools in the Midwest.

Tuttle, Harry Grover. (1995, March-April). From productivity to collaboration. Part I: School networks deliver innovative education. **Multimedia Schools, 2**(2), 31-35. EJ 499 842. (Available UMI.) Examines the use of various networks in schools for productivity and collaboration.

Vacca, John R. (1995, October). CU on the Net. **Internet World, 6**(10), 80-82. EJ 510 436. The Global Schoolhouse, a K-12 Internet project, connects schools nationally and internationally, and demonstrates how the Internet can be used as a tool for research and as a medium for interactive and collaborative learning.

Multimedia Kits

Educator's Essential Internet Training System. (1996). Classroom Connect, 1866 Colonial Village Lane, P.O. Box 10488, Lancaster, PA 17605-0488. Two loose leaf binders, two VHS videos, four Mac/Win diskettes, Trainer's Guide, blackline masters, workbooks, 20 Seminar Participant Paks. $199. Provides everything needed to conduct a complete Internet workshop for staff members.

Educator's Internet Companion. (1996). Classroom Connect, 1866 Colonial Village Lane, P.O. Box 10488, Lancaster, PA 17605-0488. Book/diskette/videotape kit. $39.95. Provides a guided tour to educational resources for both Internet veterans and first-time users.

Educator's World Wide Web TourGuide. (1996). Classroom Connect, 1866 Colonial Village Lane, P.O. Box 10488, Lancaster, PA 17605-0488. Book/diskette/videotape kit. Book/CD-ROM package. $39.95. All grades and major subject areas are covered in this visual tour of more than 200 educational Web sites.

Online/Electronic Resources

Clearinghouse for Subject-Oriented Internet Resource Guides. Jointly sponsored by the University of Michigan's University Library and School of Information and Library Studies. It can be accessed by: anonymous FTP (host: una.hh.lib.umich.edu, path:/inetdirsstacks); Gopher (gopher.lib.umich.edu, under the menus Other Gophers/University of Michigan); and World Wide Web/Mosaic (URL:http://www.lib.umich.edu/chhome.html). WAIS indexing allows full-text searching of the guides. This clearinghouse serves as a central location for a collection of subject-oriented Internet resource guides compiled by individuals throughout the Internet. Volunteers publicize and market the service, process newly submitted guides, obtain updated versions of existing guides, create and label menu items for new guides, answer users' questions, and reindex the collection for full-text searching.

ICONnect. American Association of School Librarians (AASL), American Library Association (ALA), 50 East Huron St., Chicago, IL 60611. Gopher address: ericir.syr.edu 7070. Gopher URL: gopher://ericir.syr.edu:7070/. Home page address: http://ericir.syr.edu/ICONN/ihome.html. *See* description under *Libraries and Media Centers.*

Johnson, Peggy, with English, Lee. (1995). **Roadmaps for the information superhighway: The searchable Internet bibliography: An on-disk annotated guide to timely materials about Internet.** American Library Association, Book Order Fulfillment, 155 N. Wacker Dr., Chicago, IL 60606. Dos diskettes. $35. This electronic bibliography offers some 1,000 recent, annotated sources arranged in a database for quick and easy searching.

NICEM (National Information Center for Educational Media) Web Page. NICEM, P.O. Box 8640, Albuquerque, NM 87198-8640. (505) 265-3591; (800) 926-8328. Fax (505) 256-1080. E-mail nicem@nicem.com. The NICEM database, which now contains more than 420,000 bibliographic citations to audiovisual materials, covers all media formats: 16mm film, video, audiocassette/CD, CD-ROM, software, laserdisc, filmstrip, slide, transparency, kit, model, and realia. All levels of education are covered from the pre-school to the post-graduate, adult, and professional levels, teacher education, and industrial training and education. Eventually NICEM plans to offer the capability to search the database via its web page on the Internet: http://www.nicem.com. Information is currently available from the data from several vendors in print, CD-ROM, and online.

Videos

Drake, Chuck. (1995/96). **Internet: Your lesson in navigating the information superhigh-way: A how-to guide to mining its treasures.** Educational Reform Group, 527 Sheffield Plain, Sheffield, MA 01257. 1 videotape; 60 min. $89 for home viewing; $179 allowing public performance for groups of more than 6. One of four videotapes on Internet-related topics, this tape provides an introduction to the Internet including a step-by-step lesson in connecting to the Net and a tutorial on how to navigate it. Other titles are *Create your own Web pages: A guide to the basics* (Rich Enderton, 1995/96, 70 min.); *Netscape—The easiest way to surf the Internet: Your guide to downloading, searching and browsing* (Chuck Drake, 1995/96, 70 min.); and *Teaching and the World Wide Web: Global online projects for science, math, language, literature, arts, and foreign language teachers* (Rich Enderton, 1995/96, 70 min.).

Educator's Guide to the Internet. 1995. RMI Media Productions, 1365 North Winchester St., Olathe, KS 66061. Set of 4 videotapes, 20 min. each. $239 or $69.95 each. *Cruisin' the information highway: Findin' on-ramps and gettin' up to speed* is designed to get new users up to speed on hardware, software, terminology, and e-mail basics, including listservs and newsgroups. The other three videotapes are entitled *Gophers, armadillos, and other Internet critters: Getting started with Internet tools*; *Surfin' the Internet: Practical ideas for k-12*; and *Spinnin' the Web and beyond: Expanding your Internet skills.*

The Internet revealed. Classroom Connect, 1866 Colonial Village Lane, P.O. Box 10488, Lancaster, PA 17605-0488. Four videotapes: $39 each tape; $125 complete set. This set provides a visual guide to the educational Internet for students and teachers. Individual videotapes cover *The amazing Internet* (introduction to Internet communication, research, and navigation tools and the World Wide Web, 20 min.); *Internet e-mail* (30 min.); *Searching the Internet* (30 min.); and *Discovering the World Wide Web* (55 min.).

Index

This index lists names of associations and organizations, authors, titles, and subjects (indicated by bold entries). In addition, acronyms for all organizations and associations are cross-referenced to the full name. Please note that a classified list of U.S. organizations and associations appears on pages 183-87.

Que's Computer User's Dictionary (Pfaffenberger), 109-10
"Questioning the questions of instructional technology research," 306
Quinlan, L., 116, 124-26
"Quit blaming teachers" (Salpeter), 123, 124

Rader, Hannelore B., 317
Radford University, 265
Random House Personal Computer Dictionary (Margolis), 110
RASD. See Reference and Adult Services Division (RASD)
Ray, Roger D., 290
RBS. See Research for Better Schools, Inc. (RBS)
RC. See ERIC Clearinghouse on Rural Education and Small Schools (RC)
"Reaching a 'critical mass': Survey shows record number of professors use computer in the classroom" (DeLoughry), 10-11
"Ready to be a cybernaut?" (Powell), 116
"Reasons schools are not efficiently using information technology: A case study," 317
The Reciprocal Nature of Universal Grammar and Language Learning Strategies in Computer Assisted Language Learning (Wright), 70, 73-74, 73 table
Redding, Richard E., 304
Reengineering the Corporation: A Manifesto for Business Revolution (Hammer and Champy), 24
Reeves, Thomas C., 306
Reference and Adult Services Division (RASD), 191
Reference Librarian, 325
"A reflection on 12 studies of education reform" (Shanker), 119
The Reflective Practitioner: How Professionals Think in Action (Schon), 38
The Regional Laboratory for Educational Improvement of the Northeast and Islands, 227
Reigeluth, C. M.; R. J. Garfinkle, 135
Reigeluth, Charles M., 25-26, 32, 133-35. See also Leshin, C. B.; Molenda, M.; Roma, C. M.
Reinhardt, Andy, 104, 105
Reinventing Government: How the Entrepreneurial Spirit Is Transforming the Public Sector (Osborne and Gaebler), 24
Reiser, R. A.; W. Dick, 118
Reiser, R. A.; D. F. Salisbury, 132
"The relationships among measures of intrinsic motivation, instructional design, and learning in computer-based instruction," 306
Repman, Judi, 327

Research and Theory Division (RTD), 196
Research for Better Schools, Inc. (RBS), 227
Research in Science & Technological Education, 305
"Research in teacher-librarianship and the institutionalization of change," 327
"Research on CALL" (Pederson), 74-75, 76, 78
Research proceedings: 1995 AECT national convention, 310
"Research trends in computer-assisted language learning" (Chapelle and Jamieson), 74, 76, 77
Researching on the Internet: The Complete Guide to Finding, Evaluating, and Organizing Information Effectively (Rowland and Kinnaman), 123
"Resource Sharing," 328
Resource Sharing and Information Networks, 298
Resources in Education (RIE), 305
"Responding to the technological imperative: The experience of an open and distance education institution," 303
Restructuring Education Through Technology (Frick), 135
Restructuring schools with technology, 331
"Retrofitting academe: Adapting faculty attitudes and practices to technology," 314
Review of the book Instructional Technology: Past, Present, and Future, 2nd ed. (Yeaman), 47
"A review of the research for use of computer-related technologies for instruction: An agenda for research" (Williams and Brown), 75, 76, 77, 78
Revolution and Evolution in the Twentieth Century (Boggs and Boggs), 44
Reynolds, Karen E., 310
Reynolds, Peter L., 294
Rezabek, Randy, 306
Rhode Island
  graduate programs in instructional technology, 263
Rhodes, Lewis A., 314
Rice, Marion, 314
Richards, John, 340
Richards, Trevor, 299
Richardson, Eric C., 341
Richey, Rita C., 41, 42, 306
Richter, Randy L. See Munson, Janet R.
Rieber, Lloyd P., 308
Rieseberg, Rhonda L., 297
Riggsby, Dutchie, 315
Riise, Eric, 301
"The rite of right or the right of rite: Moving toward an ethics of technological empowerment" (Anderson), 39-40
Ritzer, G., 50
The Road Ahead (Gates), 90